CORPORATE POLICY
A CASEBOOK

CORPORATE POLICY
A CASEBOOK

JULES J. SCHWARTZ

School of Management
Boston University

PRENTICE-HALL, INC., *Englewood Cliffs, New Jersey 07632*

Library of Congress Cataloging in Publication Data

SCHWARTZ, JULES J. (date)
  Corporate policy.

  1. Industrial management—Case studies.
2. Business—Case studies I. Title.
HD31.S342   658.4   78-8679
ISBN   0-13-174813-0

Printed in the United States of America

10 9 8 7 6 5 4 3 2 1

Prentice-Hall International, Inc., *London*
Prentice-Hall of Australia Pty. Limited, *Sydney*
Prentice-Hall of Canada, Ltd., *Toronto*
Prentice-Hall of India Private Limited, *New Delhi*
Prentice-Hall of Japan, Inc., *Tokyo*
Prentice-Hall of Southeast Asia Pte. Ltd., *Singapore*
Whitehall Books Limited, *Wellington, New Zealand*

Contents

Preface   vii

CHAPTER **1**
Introduction   1

CHAPTER **2**
Formulating Business Strategy   3

THE COLONIAL BEEF COMPANY   17
ZWICKEL GYMNASTIC TAILORS, INC.   30
SAFEGUARD INDUSTRIES, INC.   43
THE COLONIAL PIPELINE CO.   73
FLAGSTAFF CORPORATION   86
SEMICONDUCTOR STRATEGIES   96

CHAPTER **3**
**Managing Decisions in
Business Organizations**   105

TOWN ENTERPRISES, INC.   110
MINICOMPUTER, INCORPORATED   130
WOMAN'S MEDICAL COLLEGE
      OF PENNSYLVANIA (A)   143
WOMAN'S MEDICAL COLLEGE
      OF PENNSYLVANIA (B)   154

SUN VENTURES, INC.   156
NELSON LABORATORIES   168
ARCAIR, INC.   177
A.H. ROBINS CO.   191
ARCO CHEMICAL COMPANY   202
LAVENTHOL, KREKSTEIN,
      HORWATH & HORWATH   216

CHAPTER **4**
Implementing Decisions   229

STRATEGY AND FINANCIAL STATEMENTS   235
CORNELL BUILDING SERVICES, INC.   239
THE TASTY BAKING COMPANY   247
CLEVEPAK CORPORATION   265
JOHNSON CONTROL, INC.   276
BURNS AND ROE, INC.   293
BELMONT CHEMICAL COMPANY, INC.   311
STAHL CORPORATION   326
MUNICIPAL PUBLICATIONS, INC.   339
CHILTON COMPANY   353
PRESQUE MAGNUM   364

CHAPTER **5**
The Integrative Role
of Corporate Policy   375

FEDERAL EXPRESS CORPORATION   412
REINHARDT'S BAKERY   424
H&R BLOCK, INC.   438

LUCE LABORATORIES   376
PHILADELPHIA ELECTRIC COMPANY   386

Preface

Writing a casebook in a place like the Wharton School, an institution that is committed to an eclectic approach to teaching and research, is a special challenge—but a particularly worthwhile one. It may be of special interest to other teachers of policy in similar institutions that many of these cases were originally researched and drafted by undergraduate and graduate students at the Wharton School as part of their business policy course. And all the cases have been used successfully with students who are not particularly experienced in the "method."

Traditionally, the purpose of a preface is to acknowledge all the help and encouragement one has received in preparing a manuscript and to exonerate everyone named from responsibility for the contents. Although I'm concerned that I shall inadvertently omit someone, it's a special pleasure to try to assign the credit for what is good here to the following people: Dean Donald C. Carroll and Professor Edward B. Shils, who encouraged me to develop a case method, business policy course—a new idea for the Wharton School; Associate Dean John F. Lubin, who provided some of the logistic support for the effort; my colleagues, Professors Adrian McDonough and

Ernest Dale, who thought this project was a good idea and often said so.

I would also like to extend special thanks to Professer James E. Walter, who wrote the Presque Magnum case and gave me permission to include it here; Mr. James Coyne, who helped supervise the Belmont Chemicals case; Professors John M. Dutton, Associate Dean of the Graduate School of Business Administration at New York University, Walter H. Klein, Chairman of the Department of Administrative Sciences at Boston College, and Charles Kuehl of the School of Business Administration at the University of Missouri —St. Louis, who all reviewed the manuscript and made helpful suggestions; and all the students who worked so hard on the cases.

I am indebted to innumerable people at the Harvard Business School, who shaped my ideas regarding business policy and how it should be taught, including Professors Kenneth R. Andrews, Joseph L. Bower, Raymond A. Bauer, Malcolm S. Salter, Norman A. Berg, Bruce R. Scott, and C. Roland Christensen.

My good friend, Judge Murray M. Schwartz, kept me so busy on other assignments that meeting the completion deadline for this book seemed like a special accomplishment.

Dr. Jordon J. Baruch, Assistant Secretary of Commerce, who has opened many doors for me, has been a mentor since my doctoral program days.

My mother, Marion Schwartz, always takes an optimistic view of my undertakings.

Many people at Wharton contributed to the secretarial and editorial effort including Joanne Cohen, Cindi Kee, Evelyn Mayo, Susan Shaw, Chris Smith, and Diana Krigelman.

And my wife, Sandy, who tried hard—very hard—to convince me that I would one day finish, in the meantime remained my best friend.

CHAPTER I

Introduction

This book is about *business policy*; that is, it deals with general managers and the decisions general managers make. Throughout the text and cases that follow we shall concern ourselves with the problems general managers confront and the way that they solve them. Our viewpoint will be that of the practitioner; our goal will be the best *possible* solution, not necessarily the theoretically optimum solution. We shall look to the considerable body of descriptive theory only when it seems relevant to helping managers to make better decisions.

WHO ARE GENERAL MANAGERS?

General managers are the executives in any business organization who are responsible for profit and loss. Notice that this definition can include managers at many levels in the firm, not just the chief executive officer. In our study we shall examine the role of general managers in formulating strategy, in influencing the decisionmaking process in their organizations and in implementing decisions that bear upon the present and future profitability of their companies, divisions, product lines or project groups. These executives usually have the responsibility for defining organizational purpose, mobilizing essential resources and assigning and supervising the tasks to be performed.

WHY STUDY THE GENERAL MANAGER?

Many of the cases you will be called upon to analyze involve jobs you might expect to hold within a few years after completing this course. Others will deal with decisions faced by people in large organizations whom you may be called upon to advise.

What other reasons do we have for studying business policy? Such studies provide a framework with which we can integrate the various functional disciplines, including finance, accounting, personnel, marketing, engineering, and production. Further, dealing with these decisions helps one to develop skills in working with multidimensional problems, skills in making assumptions and estimating, in recognizing the great variety of business tradeoffs, and in contending at the same time with both a surplus and a deficiency of data. Those who plan to be specialists will gain a further appreciation of the generalist approach and come to realize that the successful senior specialist is one who understands the language and perspective of the general manager, for many functional decisions can only be understood intelligently in the context of a policy approach.

The cases have been drawn from a great variety of real situations in different industries. In studying these problems and formulating your conclusions you will have the opportunity to identify competitive strategies in these industries. You will no doubt find the concepts you learn applicable to other situations. Consider the advantage in understanding a firm's strategy if you are a sales representative selling to it, a securities analyst recommending its shares, a bank lending officer approving its loans, or a purchasing agent choosing its products.

THE PLAN OF STUDY

This study of policy is divided into three major sections that describe the key tasks of general management:

1. Formulating strategic options;
2. Making decisions regarding the options; and
3. Implementing these decisions.

The organization is simply one of convenience. As it makes little sense to choose a strategic option without a plan for implementing it, this division should not lead you to think that a manager's activities can be neatly compartmentalized.

THE CASE METHOD

Later sections will suggest some of the questions you may want to ask as you deal with the general manager's problems. Here we will consider a few that are applicable in every case.

How and at what organizational level did the manager's problem arise and who will be affected by his decision? The answer to this should help you to decide if the problem really requires a decision, how promptly it must be made, who should be consulted, and what kinds of solutions will be most acceptable.

Is the right question being asked? As Elting Morison put it, "It is much harder to ask the right question than to find the right answer . . . the right answer to the wrong question isn't worth much." Seek to diagnose before you prescribe.

Who has the authority and who should make the decision? Young managers err as often in making too many decisions as in failing to decide.

Specifically how does one succeed in this business? Understanding the "name of the game" is as essential to a business practitioner as anatomy is to a surgeon.

How is this organization doing relative to its stated and implied goals and relative to its competitors? The answer to this question will help to define the options actually available to the manager. Both resources and discretion normally accrue to managers who have been doing well.

What necessary data seem to be missing? Is it possible to estimate these data? If not, do a range of reasonable assumptions result in any change in your conclusions? Such a "sensitivity analysis" may lead you to reassess the need for information.

As you may have concluded, case analysis is an art, not a science; but then, so is management.

CHAPTER 2

Formulating Business Strategy

Strategy involves a choice of goals and the methods for achieving them. It is the result of an assessment of opportunities and threats in the environment, an analysis of the capabilities and limitations of the organization and a continuing negotiation to satisfy the preferences of the organization's constituencies. The outcome of these efforts depends first on understanding the existing situation and developing creative options, and then on the preferences of the people who are influential in choosing between the options.

Results can vary considerably from industry to industry and year to year, as is illustrated in Figure 2-1, which shows years of highest and lowest performance.

Even within an industry, performance varies significantly between companies. For example, Table 2-1 lists the range of post-tax return on equity for the four largest firms in a number of industries in the first quarter of 1976.

This chapter will point up important questions concerning the strategies of both indus-

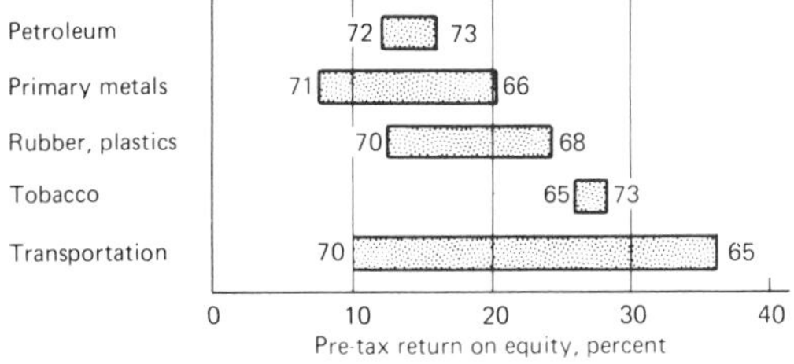

Source: *New York Times*, August 4, 1974.

FIGURE 2-1 Pretax Return on Equity, Percentage

TABLE 2-1
Range of Return on Equity

Industry	Lowest–Highest %
Autos	9–16
Banks	8–18
Business Machines	14–20
Chemicals	11–19
Drugs	16–27
Petroleum	8–16
Rubber	4–10
Steels	4–10

tries and individual companies within them; significant trends, and typical tradeoffs and strategic options available to general managers.

In analyzing corporate strategy it is vital that you gain an understanding of the industry involved. Recognizing the danger of a "cookbook" approach, you will probably want to avoid checklists. It may be useful, however, to enumerate some of the data and ideas you will want to investigate in order to get a feel for any business. These include: 1) the technology of the product and its applications; 2) the nature of competition; 3) marketing and distribution channels; 4) production technology and scale; and 5) financing. We shall examine each of these and suggest some of the questions you might ask.

PRODUCT

- What are the essential economic characteristics of the product? How and where is it used?
- Is its demand derived from another product or process?
- Is it a necessity? Are there substitutes?
- Is it expensive or an important part of the user's budget?
- Does its cost or quality, the age of the technology, or the availability of raw materials suggest that someone should be developing an alternative?

Technological innovation has become a major form of product competition. It is well to understand the nature of technical changes occurring in a product. Has it become faster, lighter, stronger, or more versatile or reliable? What design factors are contributing to the changes? Examples have been the introduction of jet engines into aircraft, transistors into electronic gear and synthetic fabrics into textile products.

There are interesting data that indicate that the rate of substitution of new technology, once it begins, is reasonably predictable. Figures 2–2, 2–3, and 2–4 illustrate some conclusions reached in a paper by R. H. Pry of

General Electric.[1] He describes a substitution factor:

$$F = \frac{\text{Usage of substitute product}}{\text{Total usage, including substitute}}$$

Plotting the function, $\log (F/1-F)$ against years for many substitutions, he and others have found a striking similarity between many replacement phenomena.

The slope of each of these substitution functions somewhat represents the rate at which replacement occurs. The rate for a given new product or process appears to be about the same in different countries, no matter when the process begins. Of note, if one plots the value of the substitution factor F against time, in each case, the result approximates the S-growth curve one would expect.

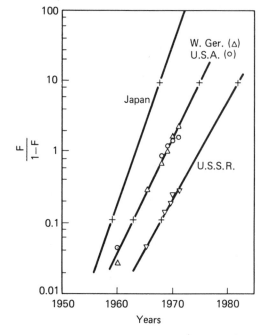

FIGURE 2–2 Substitution Plot of BOF for Open Hearth and Bessemer Steel Production in Japan, U.S.S.R., West Germany, and U.S.A. Since 1960

[1] *Forecasting the Diffusion of Technology,* R. H. Pry, General Electric Company Report No. 73CRD220, July 1973.

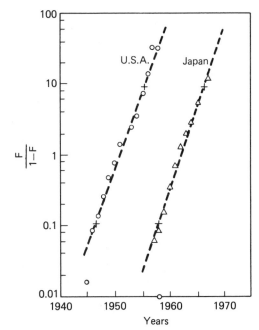

FIGURE 2-3 Substitution Plot of Synthetic Detergents for Soap in U.S.A. and Japan

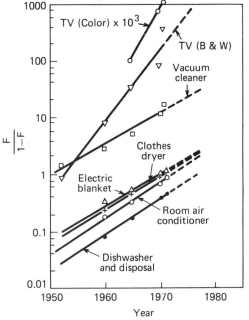

FIGURE 2-4 Substitution Plots for "Fraction of Households that Have" Various Consumer Appliances

COMPETITION

~~Who are the competitors and what market~~ share does each command? There is some empirical evidence that in the long run, competition tends to stabilize if product market shares are distributed among three major firms in somewhat the following manner:

TABLE 2-2

Competitor	Relative Market Share
A	57%
B	38
C	15

This relationship applies to autos, baby foods, airplanes, and soft drinks, among others. It seems to be based on the ability of the two smaller competitors to respond effectively to price cutting or product innovation by the largest firm. If Firm C had a smaller market share, it might not be able to realize necessary economies of scale and might have insufficient production experience to remain in competition.

Work done by the Marketing Science Institute in its 1970–1973 PIMS (Profit Impact of Market Strategy) Study confirms that profitability correlates closely with relative market share as shown in Figure 2-5.

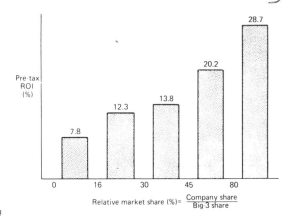

FIGURE 2-5 Relationship Between Pre-Tax Return on Investment and Relative Market Share

This seems to be particularly true in the middle stage of the product life cycle, after the design becomes stable and the market has ceased to grow.

With any product or geographic market, competition may take several forms. The obvious ones are price and quality. In recent years service has also become a significant factor.

What is the competitive advantage of each firm contending for market share? Among other things, an advantage may be based on the technological superiority of its product or manufacturing processes, extensive vertical integration that reduces acquisition and distribution costs, geographic location that affords lower transportation costs, buying power that reduces the cost of production factors, lower capital costs, lower labor costs, an established customer franchise, or a portfolio of products

that spreads and reduces unit administrative and selling costs. Less evident may be a better organization or management.

MARKETING

The critical questions here are: Who are the customers? How is the product sold? How is it distributed? The size of customers relative to their suppliers can have great impact on profit margins, unless the supplier has a monopoly. The ability of a customer to integrate backward toward its supplier is an effective threat that limits profit margins.

Marketing costs vary greatly for both consumer and nonconsumer products. Figures 2–6 and 2–7 show both selling and total marketing costs for a number of products of both classes, based on 1971 data assembled by The Conference Board.

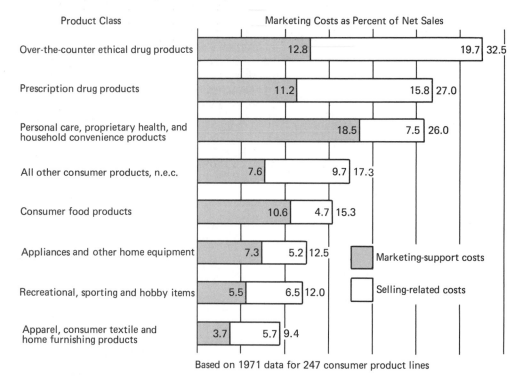

Note: Due to rounding, details do not always add up to totals.
Source: The Conference Board.

FIGURE 2-6   Average Marketing-Cost Ratios for Consumer Product Classes

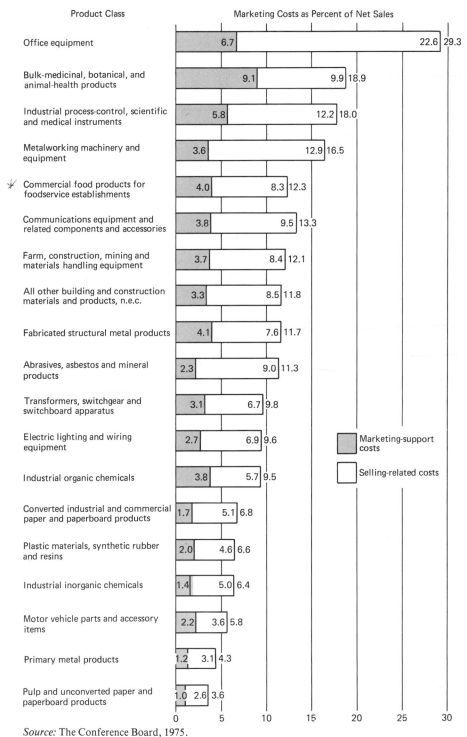

Product Class | Marketing Costs as Percent of Net Sales

Product Class	Marketing-support costs	Selling-related costs	Total
Office equipment	6.7	22.6	29.3
Bulk-medicinal, botanical, and animal-health products	9.1	9.9	18.9
Industrial process-control, scientific and medical instruments	5.8	12.2	18.0
Metalworking machinery and equipment	3.6	12.9	16.5
Commercial food products for foodservice establishments	4.0	8.3	12.3
Communications equipment and related components and accessories	3.8	9.5	13.3
Farm, construction, mining and materials handling equipment	3.7	8.4	12.1
All other building and construction materials and products, n.e.c.	3.3	8.5	11.8
Fabricated structural metal products	4.1	7.6	11.7
Abrasives, asbestos and mineral products	2.3	9.0	11.3
Transformers, switchgear and switchboard apparatus	3.1	6.7	9.8
Electric lighting and wiring equipment	2.7	6.9	9.6
Industrial organic chemicals	3.8	5.7	9.5
Converted industrial and commercial paper and paperboard products	1.7	5.1	6.8
Plastic materials, synthetic rubber and resins	2.0	4.6	6.6
Industrial inorganic chemicals	1.4	5.0	6.4
Motor vehicle parts and accessory items	2.2	3.6	5.8
Primary metal products	1.2	3.1	4.3
Pulp and unconverted paper and paperboard products	1.0	2.6	3.6

Source: The Conference Board, 1975.

FIGURE 2-7 Average Marketing-Cost Ratios for Nonconsumer Product Classes

PRODUCTION

In many industries production processes and facilities can be a more important factor in competition than the product itself. This is most evident where the product is a standardized one, such as a commodity, and cost competition prevails. It may also be the case where the process produces a superior product. Within the limits of its resources, every firm seeks to realize economies of scale in its production facilities by using specialized labor and equipment and by trying to spread management and overhead costs over more output. The tradeoff is that larger scale operations require a firm to reach out farther to assemble the necessary factors of production and to ship its product farther to cater to the larger markets that the larger plant must serve. Ultimately, then, the increased transportation costs for inputs and outflows are a constraint on scale economies.

The relative scale of an operation can usually be measured by the number of workers per establishment. Remember that economies of scale most often attach to the plant, not to the firm. A company with two or more appropriately scaled plants rarely has any scale advantages compared to a company with a single well-scaled plant, except that its purchasing, sales, and corporate overhead costs can be spread over more output. Table 2-3 lists the average number of workers per plant for a number of different businesses.

To understand the significance of transportation costs, you must know something about the production process. For example, the fact that pig-iron production requires the assembly of some three and one-half tons of low-value raw materials, such as coke, limestone, and ore, in addition to substantial quantities of water, to produce just one ton of low-valued product suggests that plant locations must be selected to minimize transportation costs.

It is also useful to know the bulk value of the final product, as this factor may influence the form in which it will be shipped and how far. For example, tin cans, once assembled, occupy a great deal of space relative to their value. This suggests that can making should be accomplished near the customer's plant.

TABLE 2-3

Average Number of Workers per Establishment

SMALL-SCALE INDUSTRIES	
Beverages	50
Meat packing	60
Childrens' outerwear	60
Bakeries	65

MEDIUM-SCALE INDUSTRIES	
Industrial chemicals	120
Pulp mills	250
Petroleum refining	270
Flat glass	360

LARGE-SCALE INDUSTRIES	
Primary aluminum	1100
Cigarettes	2200
Aircraft	3400
Tires and inner tubes	4700

Table 2-4 illustrates the great variance in the bulk value of materials; value per cubic foot may be the better indicator. Analyses of transportation costs are further complicated by the wide range of tariffs set by the Interstate Commerce Commission for commodity shipments.

It is well established that competitive firms learn to reduce their costs as they produce more product. The relationship between average unit cost and cumulative production has been charted for a great number of products. The result is known as an "experience" or "learning" curve. This logarithmic function was first noted in the 1930s and seems to hold for most standardized products. An example for electric power is shown in Figure 2-8.

Note that the average unit cost declines by a constant percentage, in this case 20 percent, each time the total number of units produced to date doubles. Boston Consulting Group has suggested that a knowledge of the learning

TABLE 2-4
Bulk Value of Commodities[a]

Product	$ Per Pound	$ Per Cubic Foot
Lumber	0.04	2
Bituminous coal	0.07	6
Scrap newspaper	0.01	8
Corn	0.22	10
Wheat	0.23	11
Soybean oil	0.21	12
Fuel oil	0.28	15
Gasoline	0.38	17
Scrap steel	0.04	19
Leather	0.38	22
Cotton	0.74	35
Beef	0.64	38
Rubber	0.40	38
Wool	1.90	78
Aluminum	0.48	79
Zinc	0.37	164
Lead	0.25	178
Copper	0.65	361
Gold	1630.00	1,960,000

[a]Spot prices, December 1976.

curve can be used strategically, as a firm can cut its prices to seize market share in anticipation of cost savings to be realized with additional production experience. The slope of the learning curve is viewed by some as a measure of the technology-intensiveness of a production process.

You will also want to develop a feel for the relative costs of the factors that go into producing any product: raw materials, energy, labor, and capital. Where the raw material costs are a large proportion of final cost and profit margins are low, the value added, defined approximately as

Value added = Revenues − Purchased goods

will be low. Perhaps the best measure of capital intensiveness is the ratio of depreciation charges to value added; some authorities use the ratio of gross plant and equipment to sales. Similarly labor intensiveness is described by the ratio of labor cost to value added. Where the financial statements of a firm do not isolate labor cost, you may be able to approximate it by multiplying the number of employees in the firm by your estimate of their annual wages.

The ratio of value added to sales provides a measure of the degree of vertical integration of a firm relative to other companies in the same industry. The PIMS Study cited earlier found evidence that in mature industries more vertically-integrated firms tended to achieve higher return on investment. Not surprisingly,

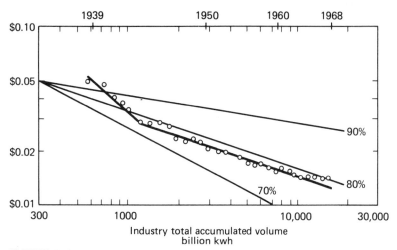

FIGURE 2-8 Learning Curve for U.S. Electric Power

the opposite seemed true for younger, high-growth industries, where production technologies had not yet stabilized. Figure 2-9 summarizes these conclusions.

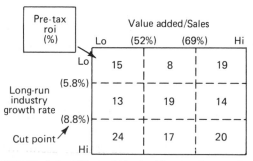

FIGURE 2-9 Effect of Vertical Integration on Return on Investment

The ratio of sales to employees offers a measure of relative productivity within any industry. The PIMS Study concluded that productivity seems to influence return on investment most in high-growth industries, as shown in Figure 2-10.

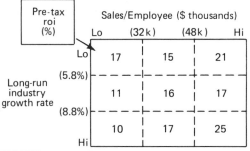

FIGURE 2-10 Effect of Productivity on Return on Investment

Energy has become a major cost in many products since the OPEC nations raised oil prices. Table 2-5 shows the relative energy cost of a number of products.

Still another consideration in designing a production facility is the tradeoff between fixed and variable costs. Where management chooses to replace labor, a variable cost, with equipment, a fixed (depreciation) expense, the result is an increase in *operational leverage*.

TABLE 2-5

How Industries Depend on Energy

Industry	Cost of Fuel as Percent of Gross Product
Primary metals	17.1%
Stone, clay & glass	15.3
Paper & allied products	8.7
Chemicals & allied products	7.8
Petroleum	6.8[a]
Textiles	4.4
Fabricated metal products	3.4
Rubber	3.2
Lumber	3.0
Food	2.9
Transport equipment	2.9
Nonelectrical machinery	2.2
Electrical machinery	2.0
Instruments	1.8
Furniture	1.8
Leather & shoes	1.6
Apparel	1.2
Printing & publishing	1.2
Tobacco	0.4

[a]Not including price of crude oil
Source: Data Resources, Inc., Energy Group

That is, profits become more sensitive to volume changes. This is most easily illustrated in the familiar formula for pre-tax profits:

$$\text{Pre-tax profit} = \text{Volume} \times (\text{Unit price} - \text{Unit variable cost}) - \text{Fixed cost}$$

Where borrowed money is used to finance the asset investment, still more fixed costs are added in the form of interest payments. The increased sensitivity of profits to volume is termed *financial leverage*. If you are not already familiar with this concept, you may wish to test this relationship. For example, try the following data:

$$\text{Volume} = 10,000 \text{ Units}$$
$$\text{Unit price} = \$10/\text{Unit}$$
$$\text{Unit variable cost} = \$6/\text{Unit}$$
$$\text{Fixed cost} = \$20,000$$

First calculate pre-tax profit (equal to $20,000 in this case), then increase volume 10 percent to 11,000 units and recalculate the profit. This volume change produces a 20 percent profit increment. If there had been no fixed cost, the percentage profit change would have been the same as the percentage volume change. As the effect is similar on the down side, it should be clear that firms with high fixed costs (and related operational and financial leverage) resulting from capital intensiveness will strive to maintain volume, often cutting unit price to get orders. They benefit as long as the price still exceeds unit variable cost and so makes a contribution to fixed costs.

These calculations are based on the assumption that output can be increased without further capital investment, except, perhaps, in working capital. It is important, then, to know if a plant is operating at capacity and what investment might be required to increase production. The PIMS Study concluded that capacity utilization was of particular importance when market share was low. Figure 2–11 shows the pre-tax return on investment achieved by some 600 firms, for different relative market shares.

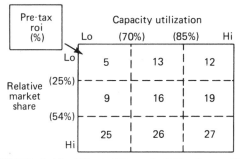

FIGURE 2–11 Effect of Capacity Utilization on Return on Investment for Varying Levels of Market Share

As one would expect, the return realized by these companies, as shown in Figure 2–12, was much more dependent on capacity utilization when fixed capital intensity was high. (Fixed capital intensity is defined as the ratio of gross book value of plant and equipment to sales.)

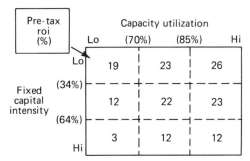

FIGURE 2-12 Effect of Capacity Utilization on Return on Investment for Varying Levels of Fixed Capital Intensity

You will probably find it most useful to accumulate information from the cases regarding the costs of finished products and efficiently scaled processes. Table 2–6 lists a few of these. Almost every industry has such rules of thumb.

TABLE 2-6
Costs of Some Typical Products and Processes

Item	Cost
Jumbo oil tanker	$150/ton
Machined steel parts	$1.25/pound
Aircraft	$10/pound
Nuclear fuel	$20/pound
New construction, including average land value	$40/square foot
Computation cost	$.01/bit per second
Nuclear power station, 1000 megawatt	$1.3 billion
Oil refinery, 200 thousand barrels per day	$2,000–3,000/barrel per day
Styrene plant, world scale, 150 thousand tons per year	$350/ton per year
Ammonia plant, 500 thousand tons per year	$45/ton per year
Paper mill, 600 tons per day	$1,000/ton per year

A useful scaling rule that applies to many plant facilities uses the *Lang Factor*. Plant designers have found that plants usually scale according to the following formula:

Cost of new plant = Cost of existing plant ×

$$\left(\frac{\text{Capacity of new plant}}{\text{Capacity of existing plant}} \right)^L$$

where L, the *Lang Factor,* is normally about 0.7.

This means that the cost of a production facility will not increase as fast as output capacity.

FINANCE

The basic question in financing any enterprise is: where will the money come from to pay for the necessary assets? As the balance sheet suggests, there are four normal sources: suppliers, creditors, and preferred and common shareholders. In recent years off-balance sheet financing, in the form of long-term leases, has also become an important means of providing resources. Strategic financial decisions involve the choices of financing and the implications of these choices to the level and stability of the firm's return on investment.

Some of the questions you will want to ask in examining a company's financial statement are:

1. Where are its funds invested?
2. Where did the funds come from and what did they cost?
3. What is the firm achieving with its investments?
4. What are the requirements and sources for additional funds to pay for asset replacements or additions, reduction of indebtedness, or payment of dividends?

We shall discuss each of these questions in turn.

The two essential investments in most businesses are in certain current assets and in plant and equipment. Necessary current assets include: *cash,* to meet payrolls and pay claims as they come due; *accounts receivable,* to finance customers' purchases; and *inventories,* for input to the production process and for timely deliveries to customers. Of these items, accounts receivable are particularly dependent on customers' activities. A customer's operating cycle (days of inventory plus days of receivables) determines how soon he can turn what he purchases back into cash and so influences his demand for trade credit.

The form and duration of financing must logically be related to the assets to be acquired. Trade financing, for example, is credit advanced by suppliers in the form of deferred payment for products purchased and added to inventories. The cost, if any, is the loss of discounts for prompt payment. Debt financing will usually have a maturity tied to the life of the assets to be purchased. Long-term mortgages, for example, are normally used to finance plant and equipment; short-term borrowing may be used to provide funds for such short-lived items as inventories and receivables.

An important consideration in choosing between sources of funds is the federal corporate tax law. Interest paid on borrowed money is a tax deductible expense, and with corporate tax rates at about 50 percent, the after-tax cost of interest is only half of the actual rate paid. Dividends paid on preferred and common shares, on the other hand, come out of after-tax earnings.

If the after-tax cost of any new debt is less than ROA (the after-tax return that can be earned on the assets the borrowed funds will buy), the additional profit goes to the common shareholders and ROE (return on equity) is improved. The cost in electing debt over equity financing is increased financial leverage and reduced flexibility. As we saw earlier the earnings of a firm that has debt in its financial structure will fluctuate more with cyclical or other volume changes than those of a debt-free concern. This means improved ROE may be gained at the price of less stable earnings. The willingness of the market to extend credit to a firm and the interest rate it will demand is, in part, influenced by earnings stability, so the capacity of the firm to assume additional debt is further constrained by the earnings instability debt engenders. The other problem with debt financing is the requirement that the obligation be repaid. This is rarely a concern for successful firms, since they can usually simply borrow new funds to pay off their bonds as they mature, a practice called *rolling over* their debt. This option may not be available to less successful companies.

The cost of preferred stock is simply the ratio of the preferred dividends to the market price of the shares. The cost of funds realized from the sale of common equity must be regarded as equal to ROE achieved on the present equity, since dilution of ROE will occur if similar results cannot be achieved with the new funds.

The management of a corporation can be evaluated in terms of the return it achieves on the resources made available to it. Average return on assets, then, is a measure of the chief executive officer's competence as an operating manager. Unfortunately this single measure is not a sufficient one because it does not take into account the chief executive officer's ability as a financial manager. Here, average return on equity may be the better yardstick.

Some firms apply ROA as a measure to subordinate general managers in their organizations. ROE is less often used for these managers because they don't decide financial structure. In some firms the asset base used in calculating ROA includes the gross, rather than the depreciated, value of plant and equipment, so that a junior manager's performance doesn't improve simply because his asset base is getting older.

For most purposes cash flow, the sum of post-tax profits and depreciation, serves as a good measure of the normal discretion available to management in repositioning its resources. Sale of existing assets, additional borrowing, and sale of more equity provide extraordinary opportunities to reposture a firm. Without additional financing, however, the growth of a company is further limited by its need to pay dividends and the inflation rate, which increases the cost of adding to or replacing assets. Without the supplementary funds, growth rate of a firm is constrained by the following formula:

Internal growth rate =

$$\frac{\text{Profit after tax} - \text{Dividends}}{\text{Total assets}} - \text{Inflation rate}$$

Notice that depreciation has been omitted, as it must be used simply to maintain the size and quality of the existing asset base.

We have been dealing so far with the firm as an entity. Most companies choose to have a portfolio of businesses for the sake of diversity or synergism. Each of these businesses will have different requirements for cash. The decision to allocate limited funds between them is a strategic one. It is essential that you recognize the different demands made by the various activities of a company.

An idea suggested in *Strategy and Organization*[2] provides another helpful way to think about the investment requirements of a business:

$$\text{Asset requirements per dollar of sales} = \frac{\text{Operating assets} - \text{Current liabilities}}{\text{Sales}}$$

In some cases a more stable business, in a non-growing field, will generate surplus cash that can be used to underwrite the growth of another endeavor. Boston Consulting Group summarizes this concept well in the matrix shown in Figure 2-13. Their assumption is that high market-share products are likely to generate more cash, which is shown to be true in Figure 2-5.

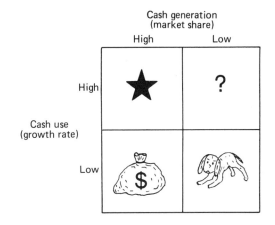

FIGURE 2-13   Growth Share Matrix

[2] Uyterhoeven, *et al.*, Irwin, 1973.

The conclusion is that funds should be "milked from the cash cow" in the lower, left-hand quadrant of the matrix to support any "star" business that has achieved a high market share in a growth industry. Businesses with low growth rates and poor market share should be eliminated and businesses with low market share that generate substantial cash demands are gambles that should be examined carefully.

Still another test you may wish to apply to a business is to determine the age of its plant and equipment. Old equipment may portend obsolescence or an early need for substantial capital investment. The ratio of accumulated depreciation to *gross* plant and equipment will give you a rough measure of fixed asset age to compare to the competition. Remember, though, that there is no necessary relationship between the rate at which a firm takes depreciation and the loss in economic value of its assets. Technological innovation can make a new plant obsolete long before it wears out or is fully depreciated.

BUSINESS TRENDS

Built into your analysis of business strategy must always be a test for consistency, not only with today's situation, but also with your

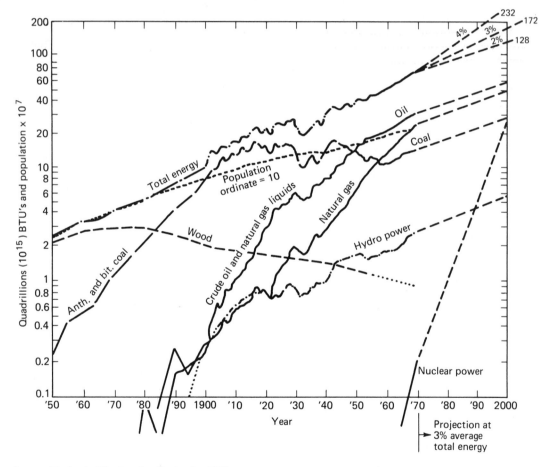

Source: Mechanical Engineering, September 1973.
FIGURE 2-14   U.S. Energy Consumption by Fuels Since 1850

understanding of the way the environment is changing. Simply for illustration, we shall list here some trends for the seventies and eighties pointed up by R. B. Huff, vice president of Bell and Howell Corporation:

1. Increased worldwide competition for raw materials;
2. Increased pressure for social reform;
3. More environmental protection legislation;
4. Comparatively decreased productivity;
5. Vast new non-U.S. labor markets;
6. Increased international competition;
7. More countrywide specialization in a freer world economy; and
8. Tighter federal controls over domestic economic issues.

The competition for raw materials must also include energy. Growth in energy consumption has been inexorable in this country, resulting in part from seeming abundance, underpricing of resources discovered abroad and profligate waste. Nonetheless, the results have been remarkable. It is no accident that

productivity and GNP growth rate correlate well with growth in energy consumption. Figure 2–14 shows trends in United States energy consumption since 1850.

Mr. Huff's pessimism regarding productivity may reflect such things as the trend to more service occupations and more investment in pollution and safety controls, but a recent survey took a more sanguine view.

Fortune magazine reported in its February 1972 issue that productivity of United States industries has been increasing more or less continuously since 1890 at an average rate in excess of 2 percent annually. Most importantly, the improvement appears to be accelerating, as shown in Figure 2–15.

GENERAL MANAGEMENT TRADEOFFS

Included in all the previous discussion has been a series of strategic tradeoffs that confront general managers. In Table 2–7 we shall summarize them and add a few more.

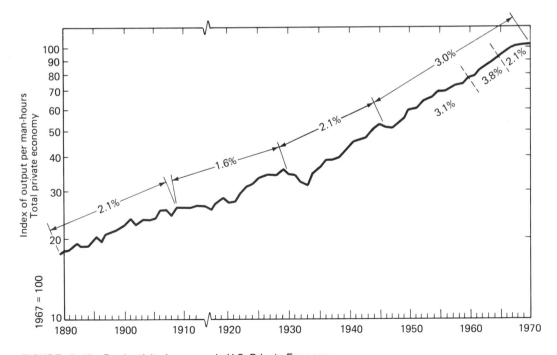

FIGURE 2-15 Productivity Increases in U.S. Private Economy

TABLE 2-7

Tradeoff	Comment
1. Long- or short-run profits	What is the discounted value of future earnings?
2. Debt or equity	Return versus stability
3. Capital for labor	Operational leverage, threat of obsolescence, labor problems
4. Growth or dividends	More need for external financing
5. Profit margin or turnover	Object is to maximize the product of these factors
6. Profit margin or market share	Slope of learning curve?
7. Liquidity (flexibility) or return on investment	Investments in receivables, inventory and cash usually don't earn the return of those in fixed assets
8. Risk versus return	Management preference

STRATEGIC OPTIONS

With all the choices and tradeoffs we've cited it may be helpful to label the usual kinds of options available to a general manager and the necessary tests each must pass.

He can seek a special niche in the market, either by product or geographic sector. The product niche can be defined by a combination of price, quality, and services. Will customers recognize such a differentiation and if so, can competitors copy it quickly?

He can devote resources and seek to seize market share by appropriate pricing and service policies. Success here depends on competitive response.

He can seek to diversify or broaden his product line horizontally or geographically. Does he have adequate management competence and structure to accomplish this?

He can integrate vertically forward toward the market. The risk here is that customers will see his firm as a competitor. Or, he can integrate backward toward raw material supplies to increase value added, decrease costs, and increase overall profit margin on final sales. The risk here is an increased asset com-

mitment to a process or product that may become obsolete.

Any option must pass at least four tests to be a viable strategy.

1. Is it consistent with your understanding of the firm's present and future operating environment?
2. Is it consistent with your assessment of the firm's capabilities and limitations?
3. Does it take advantage of any comparative advantage the firm may have relative to its competition?
4. Is there an adequate plan for implementing the option?

Beyond these questions there remains still the most basic one. Does the option fit the personal preferences and style of the people making the decision, their concept of the mission and social responsibilities of the firm, and their view of an acceptable level of risk.

On this note, we shall end this chapter as we did the first one. The questions we are left with as basic to strategic choice don't lend themselves to simple payoff quantification, probability assessment, and decision-tree analysis. We're dealing with an art, not a science.

THE COLONIAL BEEF COMPANY

In July 1974 Louis Waxman, president of the Colonial Beef Company was debating the future of his company.

Waxman bought full control of Colonial in 1946, at a time when the company was near bankruptcy. Since then, sales had grown from $2 million to over $20 million and earnings had increased in proportion. The company, which enjoyed a national reputation in its market, sold portion control meat to the institutional sector of the food industry.

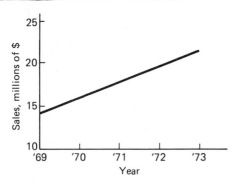

At the age of sixty-two Waxman was not yet thinking of retiring. In fact he still felt himself on top of all the company's problems and had more fun running the business than going on vacation. However, he was aware that by the time he would be ready to retire, both of his partners would have left the business, creating a problem of management continuity. With no obvious successors, Waxman was beginning to consider his options for the future.

This case was prepared by P. Jeremy Bard and Fred Mertens under the supervision of Professor Jules J. Schwartz as the basis for class discussion rather than to illustrate either effective or ineffective handling of an administrative action.

THE MEAT PACKING INDUSTRY

The meat business can trace its roots back further than practically any other American industry, yet it was not until the coming of the railroads that the industry began to take on its modern form. In order to provide the population centers with meat, the major problems to be overcome were: 1) how to limit weight loss during shipment of live animals, and 2) how to minimize shipping costs associated with fat, bone, and offal, which make up 50 percent of the weight of a live animal but which are of only marginal commercial use.

The opening up of the western rangelands and the midwestern corn belt combined with the development of the refrigerated railroad car to cause livestock breeding to move west.

An oligopolistic industry structure developed around the turn of the century and is still in existence. The twelve major meat packers, led by Esmark (formerly Swift) and Armour, handle two-thirds of the 34 billion pounds of red meat consumed annually in the United States.

In recent years, with the advent of superhighways and refrigerated trucks, small meat packers have sprung up to service local territories. They are able to provide quicker and more flexible service and their plants are often newly constructed with modern cost-saving equipment, which enables them to operate with low overhead.

The meat business can be viewed as an industry of byproducts. One animal becomes a very large number of different products ranging from various cuts of meat to leather and pharmaceuticals. There is a great disparity in prices for the different products, all of which have their own price elasticity of demand. This has reinforced the meat packer in his desire to specialize in specific cuts of meat, so that he does not have to worry about the full range of products. In addition buying precut meat such as sirloin and chuck instead of a whole side of beef has helped to reduce shipping costs.

Approximately 2.5 percent of per capita disposable income is spent on beef, which has always been the mainstay of the American diet. Over the years this proportion has been fairly stable, ·but recently poultry and hog consumption have increased at the expense of beef, reflecting price movements.

Meat consumption can conveniently be split into two major segments: the retail and the institutional markets. In 1973 the latter accounted for 17 percent of meat product sales and comprised establishments involving mass catering such as schools, hospitals, restaurants, and hotels. *Quick Frozen Foods* (April 1973) estimated that 30 percent of all meals are consumed away from home and there is strong evidence that this market segment is growing steadily over time.

PORTION CONTROL

In the 1950s a new concept of selling to the institutional meat markets gained some support. This idea was known as portion control and it involved selling the butchering as well as the meat. Meat was to be sold after it had been cut into individual portions of the desired size, trimmed, and tenderized. This would permit the buyer to serve his customer a uniform product that could be relied on for weight, quality, size, and taste.

Other benefits that would accrue from portion control were knowledge of the exact cost of each portion, which would facilitate accurate menu pricing and better inventory control, as it would be a simple matter to determine the quantity of each cut in inventory. In addition it was thought that selling meat in this way would eliminate poor cutting practices in institutional kitchens and provide a saving in labor costs. Time and labor required to receive, weigh, store, and portion primal cuts and also to salvage trimmings, would no longer be necessary.

Taken together these arguments provided a powerful justification for institutions to buy portion control meats in sizeable quantities despite the higher price charged. However, the sale of portion control meat means the sale of frozen as opposed to fresh meat. The frozen food industry has been fighting a battle to persuade the consumer of the advantages of its products. However, consumer reluctance to accept the new technology, especially in the case of frozen meats, has made this a long uphill struggle over the last twenty-five years.

COMPANY HISTORY

The history of the Colonial Beef Company goes back to 1889 but it was not until Waxman was firmly in control of the company after World War II that Colonial became one of the leading spokesmen for portion control meats. Waxman became convinced that he would be able to develop a large market in the institutional food sector by offering good quality meats cut into individual portions and frozen when the meat was in prime condition. He challenged the industry maxim "sell the best, freeze the rest."

He made many speeches to trade associations and wrote articles for meat industry journals. Even though Colonial's sales were only $2,400,000 in 1950, Waxman was already a well-known spokesman.

Waxman, a Wharton School alumnus, was a professional accountant. He had become involved in auditing meat packing companies in the Philadelphia area. With this basic knowledge of costing and the overall economics of the industry, he developed an underlying policy to support his bid to develop a market for portion control meats:

- Price at what the market will bear for good quality products.
- Control costs by reorganization and innovation.
- Keep a very close personal control over all major elements of the business.
- Be wary of expansion into either allied or unrelated activities.

In 1946 Waxman purchased all the equity of Colonial. In 1974 he held 65 percent, with members of his family owning the balance. There was one subsidiary company that operated as a distributor in the New Jersey area in which Colonial held a 75 percent interest. The manager of the company held the remaining 25 percent of the common stock.

Colonial, operating from a modern plant in Philadelphia, sold its production on a nationwide basis and also had a number of export customers. Its largest sales area was on the Atlantic seaboard. Fifteen percent of sales were in the export market and two-thirds of these were sales to U.S. military bases. Recently the firm had been negotiating with a number of European companies with a view to closer cooperation and possible joint ventures.

In the past Colonial had generated a number of new ventures. These ranged from a truck franchise system selling portion control meat nationwide, to carrying frozen seafood to widen its product line. Despite the fact that these ventures showed profit potential, Waxman decided not to pursue them for two reasons: First, he felt that he could not devote sufficient time to them, and second, he found that he was not able to use his expertise in the portion control meat business in these areas.

In 1973, 85 percent of Colonial's sales were made under the company's brand names, Minuteman and Redicut. These differentiated between top quality meat and medium grade categories. The balance of sales were made up of sourced production for other companies.

Exhibits 1 and 2 show two-year balance sheets and five-year earnings statements of the company. Exhibits 3 and 4 show comparative industry data.

MARKETING

Market

Colonial's market was the $40 billion institutional food service industry. The meat market in this industry represented $6 billion and was one of the battlefields of the big meat packers. Colonial's rifle, however, was pointed toward the quality end of the meat portion control market ($150 million) in which it was a leader with a 14 percent market share. According to Waxman this market had a potential of $500 million within three to five years. He believed two chief factors would cause this growth. First, people were becoming more aware that newly developed freezing procedures could only help retain the quality. "In too many instances toughness and poor flavor have been suggested as being the results of freezing, when in truth the meat was of poor quality before it was frozen. If you put something away that is not in top condition, it is going to come out worse." Second, buyers of institutional foods were becoming more aware of the advantages of portion control and in particular, labor savings.

In 1973 Colonial sold 95 percent of its products to the institutional market with the balance to the retail market. It had been the company's policy to avoid being dependent on large customers. "The larger your customer, the more pressure he can put on you."

Product

Colonial's product policy was that a satisfactory meat product, on which a profit can be realized, had to be made available for use in food service operations where high, moderate, or low priced menus were offered. Precut and packaged frozen portion control meats constituted approximately 90 percent of the volume. Beef (75 percent), veal, lamb, and pork were handled.

To fill the individual requirements of each food service operator, Colonial offered a full product line in three dimensions: type of meat, quality, and portion size. This three-dimensional approach resulted in 230 products offered to distributors and customers.

Competition in the portion control market was mostly on the basis of price, but Waxman had never believed in this sort of competition and had fought the concept. In a 1960 speech before the National Association of Hotel and Restaurant Meat Purveyors, he commented:

> Just as the giving of trading stamps gave some supermarkets a temporary advantage, an advantage that was only short-lived and left

them with a headache, so also, are there many temporary advantages in our operations that ultimately operate as a boomerang and hurt us too. Advantages such as those gained by improper pricing, improper cutting of the product, misrepresentation, unnecessary discounts, foolish overextension of credit and reciprocal arrangements with buyers, are something that will put the out-of-business sign on the doors of many operations in our industry.

Colonial's product philosophy could best be described as a shift away from thinking in tonnage and volume toward marketing product, matching 1) eye appeal ("If the eye is sold, half the selling job is done.") with 2) consistent quality, 3) integrity, and 4) convenience. Waxman had positioned his company as "the Cadillac of the industry."

Because of the nature of the product itself, its lack of both sophistication and patent protection, as well as the low investment involved in new product launching, the portion control market was very "open door" minded. Although Colonial's completely new product ideas were generated without a specific plan, there was a kind of systematic search to upgrade existing industry products where possible. Packaging was considered as an integral part of the product and there was a continuous effort to improve the quality and appearance of the package.

Price

Mark-ups on products were determined as a function of the product's uniqueness and competition. For example, the margin on the specialized beef-kabob was much higher than for the beef patties. Price sensitivity was tested regularly. Colonial tried to maintain stable quarterly prices, which it published in a distributor price list. A wholesale price list was also made up for the use of the distributors, whose margins were constructed in such a way that they shared in Colonial's mark-up pattern. Margins varied from 15 to 25 percent of the wholesale price; the distributor was allowed to discount or raise the prices at his own discretion.

Colonial's prices were the same all over the country and were higher than its competitors' prices. The firm backed all its products with an unconditional and unique guarantee for the industry. "Money cheerfully refunded if the customer is not completely satisfied."

Distribution

Most of the volume was sold through distributors, and only 20 percent went directly to the food service operators on condition that no conflict would arise with the distributors. Even when an operator who had been originally a customer of one of the distributors bought directly from Colonial, the distributor got a part of his normal profit in the form of a moderate commission.

Waxman commented:

When a distributor is "long" on a product, we will take it back in exchange for other products. Even when it is slightly deteriorated due to prolonged storage, he will get a salvage value, but never in cash. In most cases we are able to rework it. A good working relationship with the distributors is of extreme importance, because they sell Colonial's products, carry inventory and accounts receivable, and pay salesmen's salaries and expenses, as well as maintain a good relationship with the ultimate users of our products, the food service operators.

Colonial supported its distributors through advertising, sales aids (catalogs and other illustrations), assistance in organizing shows and training of their sales personnel.

To supply its local customers the firm used its own trucks, but for all other shipping it relied on freight companies. In the past Colonial had done some of this shipping, but backhauling and freight licenses had caused such problems that the company had decided to drop the practice. "Shipping is not our business. We are in the meat business."

For more than a year Colonial had been exploring the possibility of selling eight of its top products through the home delivery service of Abbotts Retailers under the slogan "Enjoy in your home the very same top-quality meats served in America's finest restaurants, now delivered to your door by your Abbotts' milkman." Although Waxman realized that home delivery dairies were a declining business, he believed that Abbotts would maintain its position because "the American housewife loves the milkman." He saw the potential to entice one out of every five Abbotts' 100,000 customers with the convenience of the arrangement and sell him around $10 worth of meat each week. "What's nice in this business is that I use somebody else's equipment, trucks, and labor to sell my products in a completely new market."

Promotion

Colonial advertised regularly in the principal trade journals. It had also designed a special four-page, full-color illustrated brochure representing its different product categories and some plant operations. It gave a great deal of promotional material, such as catalogs, "School-Pak" products information, easy-references cooking charts, product streamers, table tents, and menu clip-ons, to the distributors and food service operators. The firm also had a slide show (made in Hollywood) of its products and operations with accompanying text for sales presentations.

Years ago Colonial took part in national and trade shows, but, Waxman found that the costs involved exceeded by far the benefits, and dropped that participation. However, the firm always participated and assisted in the organization of distributors' shows. Once, it helped a Pittsburgh distributor to set up a very successful boat trip show on the river. "Your customers, whether they want to or not, have to listen to you because they can't run away."

Perhaps the best promotional tools had been Waxman's many speeches before trade associations. He had worked himself into "the clique" of the regularly invited guest speakers and spoken on topics ranging from the meat industry in general to control systems for administrative efficiency. On nearly every occasion he found the opportunity to connect the topic to some Colonial examples and to do some missionary work in the portion control field.

The company favored a hard selling approach, because "the main purpose of business is to sell merchandise." Waxman commented on his policy toward salesmen:

> We know that every buyer has certain items he likes to buy cheaply and we don't restrain our salesmen from making sales of this nature. We leave it up to their judgment and good sense and try to average out on other items further down the list; we don't insist that every sale must stand on its own. If the salesman sells twelve items and loses money on one or two of them, we go along as long as the overall sale makes money.
>
> At the end of the week we supply them with an adding machine tape, showing their weekly tonnage and dollar sales, as well as pertinent information on their customers' deliveries. In addition we present them with an expense analysis. The purpose of this sheet is primarily to show them what it cost us to handle their business. This sheet shows the salesman's name, gross sales, returns and allowances, and net sales. It also shows every expense incurred by and on behalf of the salesman, such as: salary, automobile depreciation and travel, entertainment, and telephone expenses. In addition, packaging and delivery charges are included, the reasoning being that neither of these last two expenses would have been incurred were it not for the sales involved. When these cost figures are added and the sales figure divided into them, we ascertain the salesman's cost to us percentagewise per dollar sale and cost per pound, two figures which the salesmen vie with each other to reduce.
>
> We have discarded all sales schemes. We pay every one of them a flat salary that we know is higher than the average prevailing in the business. No percentages nor bonuses; none of the things that would get us into wrangles. We want our people selling, not worrying why they did not get a commission on some item they had sold that doesn't make a profit. We give them a generous expense account: they are not subjected to a third degree for expenditures made by them as long as they are in proportion to their production. We don't care how much they spend as long as they

make us more than they have spent. This is something that is left almost entirely to their discretion. They have common sense and we like them to use it.

PRODUCTION, COST CONTROL, AND LABOR RELATIONS

The production process involves five distinct phases:

1. Storage of raw meat;
2. Cutting, trimming, and tenderizing the various products;
3. Freezing and packing;
4. Internal quality control and U.S. government inspection; and
5. Holding finished goods in refrigerated inventory.

reduced inv ?

Colonial used to carry a large raw material inventory because it aged its meat, but it found out that no aging was required if the animal had "youth." This, combined with a technological breakthrough whereby aging could be done in a vacuum pack (Cry-O-Vac), reduced the quantity of raw meat inventory that needed to be held for processing.

Another major development had been the purchase of meat in cuts instead of carcasses. This had several advantages. First, carcass butchering could be done in the West and Midwest where labor costs were cheaper and transport costs could be saved by not having to ship fat and bones. Second, carcass shrinkage during storage, which was 0.5 percent of the weight, could be cut. Third, the required storage space could be reduced. Fourth, it gave the company much greater scope to design its product mix as it detected changes in customer demand. (For example, a carcass has only two filets and two sirloin strips.)

new plant

A modern plant went a long way towards streamlining Colonial's production process. The latest machines and mechanical aids were installed to ensure uniform products and to cut down on increasingly expensive labor cost. Because meat was purchased in cuts rather than carcasses and modern machines did much of the cutting, packers could take over most of the butcher's work. (Packers made $3 to $5 per hour less than butchers.) Over a

period of years the company succeeded in cutting its labor force and specifically its butchers. Exhibit 5 shows the evolution over the last five years of both the annual production and the number of shop employees.

Regarding maximum plant capacity, Waxman felt that by increasing his labor force and using three shifts instead of one shift, he would be able to process 25,000,000 pounds of meat per year.

From the beginning Waxman had been convinced that an effective work control system would constitute a big competitive advantage because manufacturing costs had always caused problems in the meat industry. A cost control schedule was set up for each piece of meat entering production. It detailed the breakdown of how much meat went into each of the final products and the type of labor spent on the various operations. It also gave an analysis of how much was lost in fat and trimming. Variable overhead was allocated on a predetermined basis and fixed overhead was considered as a period cost. This enabled the company to estimate fairly accurately the cost of each finished product, and hence its profitability.

Colonial used to be on a two-year labor contract but successfully achieved a three-year contract in 1971 after weathering a strike. Although the strike lasted for three-and-a half weeks, the financial loss incurred was minimal. Waxman stated:

> We notify customers that we are entering into labor negotiations and advise them to increase their inventory of our products in the event of a strike. We also increase our inventories in public cold storage companies so that our products can be shipped to customers even if our plant is closed because of a strike. These steps put us in a strong position to negotiate. (Exhibit 6.)

When Colonial moved into its new plant Waxman installed a closed circuit television system. As expected, the union demanded an explanation for this change of policy. Waxman explained, "In any factory there are always two or three dishonest employees and the television system has been put in in order to protect all the other employees from suspicion of guilt.''

Throughout the plant, storage room, and office area, ''easy listening'' music was broadcast, and when special events such as the World Series were taking place, they were played over the system.

FINANCE

Although Colonial was not a publicly owned company, Waxman had always been very conscious of the need to have the best looking financial statements possible. This was not only a practical matter in terms of borrowing money from the banks, but also a matter of professional pride going back to his days as an auditor. For example, when he needed to make a large investment in machinery and equipment in the early 1960s, Waxman decided to borrow money personally and lease the machinery to Colonial through a wholly-owned leasing company that he set up for this purpose. He was able to use the lease agreement as collateral for his bank loan and in this way limit his own liability while protecting Colonial's balance sheet.

In recent years Colonial had not paid dividends on its common stock, mainly for tax reasons, and, as a result, the company was able to considerably reduce its current and long-term debt.

The company operated from a 54,000 square-foot plant, which was custom built for its needs in 1965 by the City of Philadelphia in the Food Distribution Center. Under the lease agreement, the costs would be $70,000 per annum until 1989 and then would drop to one-third of this amount until the remaining options expire in 2009. It was estimated that the current annual rent of refrigerated industrial buildings in Philadelphia was $4 per square foot. One of the reasons Waxman had been able to obtain such a beneficial lease was a scheme he used that struck a sensitive nerve. Colonial had purchased seven acres of land in New Jersey. A press release to the newspapers produced the following headline: ''Philadelphia employer moving to New Jersey.'' This had been sufficient pressure to persuade the City of Philadelphia to agree on the lease.

Life insurance policies valued at $1,350,000 were carried on the lives of the company's management, including $1,000,000 on the life of Waxman.

THE FUTURE

Waxman felt that there were three main options for the future: 1) go public; 2) seek a merger with another company; or 3) sell the business but keep the lease.

For a number of years the accounts of Colonial had been audited by an internationally recognized accounting firm in order to keep open the option of going public. Waxman felt that the company would be well received by the market, but was anxious that the timing of a possible issue be right.

Twice in the previous five years Colonial been approached by other companies with possible merger proposals. The first proposal ran into antitrust problems for the other company. The second failed because Waxman was apprehensive that his decisionmaking power in this new company might be limited. Waxman had been keeping in touch with a New York investment banking firm to be prepared if a suitable situation arose.

In order to get much fuller utilization from his plant and equipment, Waxman was planning to increase sales significantly, measured in both dollar and weight terms over the next three years. His labor force was on a new contract and there was nothing holding him back. He was aware that he might have to relax his personal control over the company's operation; however, despite his sixty-two years, he felt that this objective could be achieved with the present management structure.

Whatever option was decided upon, Waxman stated: ''It has always been my philosophy to try to put the company in better shape at the end of the day than it was at the beginning, and when I leave, I want it to be in perfect working order.''

EXHIBIT 1

COLONIAL BEEF COMPANY
Consolidated Balance Sheets, 1972 and 1973

ASSETS

	December 29, 1973	December 30, 1972
Current Assets		
Cash	$ 489,450	$ 914,633
Marketable securities—at cost		
(market value $600—1973; $17,500—1972)	600	12,000
Accounts receivable:		
Trade, less allowance for doubtful accounts of $140,543 and $134,080	1,516,183	1,865,833
Employees and others	24,187	23,249
Officer-stockholder	39,500	
Inventories		
Meats	1,880,137	1,705,750
Supplies	149,016	125,560
Prepaid expenses	79,320	83,164
Prepaid taxes		68,450
Total Current Assets	4,178,393	4,798,639
Other Assets		
Security deposit—Food Distribution Center	51,180	51,180
Cash surrender value of life insurance		
(net of loans of $50,596—1973; $49,800—1972)	17,143	13,651
Mortgage loan receivable	15,000	6,267
	83,323	71,098
Property, Plant, and Equipment—at cost		
Land	7,547	7,547
Building and improvements	291,962	291,962
Machinery and equipment	924,219	908,563
Furniture and fixtures	113,971	115,654
Transportation equipment	198,042	188,606
Deposit on equipment		9,000
	1,535,741	1,521,332
Less accumulated depreciation and amortization	769,901	688,417
	765,840	832,915
	$5,027,556	$5,702,652

EXHIBIT 1 (cont.)

COLONIAL BEEF COMPANY
Consolidated Balance Sheets, 1972 and 1973

LIABILITIES AND STOCKHOLDERS' EQUITY

	December 29, 1973	December 30, 1972
Current Liabilities	*current!?*	
Notes payable to bank	$1,750,000	$2,600,000
Accounts payable and accrued expenses	370,625	527,480
Accrued payroll and related taxes	29,371	43,385
Taxes on income	122,425	7,805
Current installments of long-term debt	94,946	94,669
Due to officer	50,000	50,000
Total Current Liabilities	2,417,367	3,323,339
Long-Term Debt, less current installments	234,029	328,975
Deferred Income Taxes	67,000	61,000
Minority Interest in Subsidiary	68,431	52,875
Stockholders' Equity		
Capital stock:		
Class A 7% preferred stock, par value $100 a share:		
Authorized 1,500 shares		
Issued and outstanding 500 shares—1972		50,000
Class B 5% preferred stock, par value $100 a share:		
Authorized 2,500 shares		
Issued and outstanding 1,500 shares	150,000	150,000
Common stock, no par value:		
Authorized 3,500 shares		
Issued and outstanding 2,000 shares stated at	200,000	200,000
Additional capital	61,000	61,000
Retained earnings	1,829,729	1,475,463
	2,240,729	1,936,463
	$5,027,556	$5,702,652

[handwritten annotation:] understated because of lease obligations

EXHIBIT 2

COLONIAL BEEF COMPANY
Consolidated Income Statements
1969–1973 Inclusive

	1973	1972	1971	1970	1969[a]
Net Sales	$21,065,087	$19,334,580	$17,582,199	$15,771,750	$14,675,718
Cost of Product Sold					
Purchases	15,231,159	13,531,580	12,433,476	10,818,059	10,291,432
Packaging	394,275	301,552	268,969	275,401	261,137
Freight In.	8,562	4,672	8,209	10,025	12,025
Production payroll	1,171,718	1,388,826	1,494,759	1,359,975	1,160,137
Manufacturing costs	738,783	684,232	576,086	501,021	434,193
	17,544,497	15,910,862	14,781,499	12,964,481	12,158,924
Merchandise inventory					
Beginning	1,705,751	1,713,553	1,189,639	1,039,835	897,518
Total Merchandise available	19,250,248	17,624,415	15,971,138	14,004,316	13,056,442
Ending	1,880,137	1,705,751	1,713,553	1,189,639	1,039,835
	17,370,111	15,918,664	14,257,585	12,814,677	12,016,607
Earnings before operating expenses	3,694,976	3,415,916	3,324,614	2,957,073	2,659,111
Operating Expenses					
Warehouse & delivery	881,073	895,962	824,278	796,458	778,874
Selling _HIGH_	√778,057	760,665	700,114	689,435	526,112
Administrative	522,531	496,545	453,605	417,513	380,765
Occupancy	116,749	117,192	119,399	109,732	106,920
Interest	257,087	191,661	186,324	213,858	178,851
Provision for bad debts	27,589	40,789	58,623	29,318	10,733
Officers' salaries	209,350	180,900	172,100	146,600	123,975
Profit sharing contribution	52,696	48,040			
Other				46,004	
	2,845,122	2,731,754	2,514,443	2,448,918	2,106,230
Earnings Before Taxes on Income	894,854	684,162	810,171	508,155	552,881
Provision for Taxes on Income	473,600	384,500	413,500	270,500	297,939
Net Earnings	$ 376,254	$ 299,662	$ 396,671	$ 237,655	$ 254,942

[a]Based on 53 weeks

EXHIBIT 3
COLONIAL BEEF COMPANY
Net Earnings as a Percentage of Sales
1969–1973

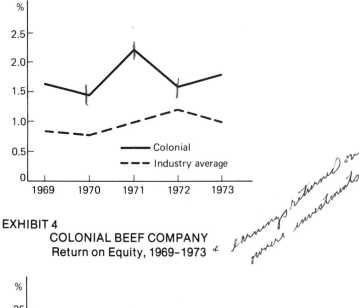

EXHIBIT 4
COLONIAL BEEF COMPANY
Return on Equity, 1969–1973 ← *earnings returned on owners investments*

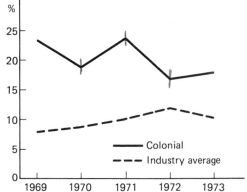

EXHIBIT 5
COLONIAL BEEF COMPANY

	Pounds of Meat Per Year	Number of Shop Employees
1969	10,801,176	188
1970	11,346,105	184
1971	11,478,406	162
1972	12,282,323	152
1973	11,007,284	130

EXHIBIT 6

COLONIAL BEEF COMPANY
A Precautionary Measure

Food Distribution Center • Philadelphia, Pa. 19148 • Phone HO 7-0900 • Cable: COLBECO

COLONIAL BEEF COMPANY

A PRECAUTIONARY MEASURE

WE ARE PRESENTLY IN THE MIDST OF NEGOTIATING A NEW LABOR CONTRACT; THE PRESENT ONE EXPIRES JUNE 30th. WHILE WE HOPE THERE WILL BE NO BUSINESS INTERRUPTION, NEVERTHELESS, THE POSSIBILITY EXISTS THAT THERE COULD BE.

AS A PRECAUTIONARY MEASURE, PLEASE INCREASE YOUR INVENTORY OF OUR PRODUCTS BY PLACING ORDERS LARGE ENOUGH TO CARRY YOU FOR AT LEAST FOUR WEEKS. INCIDENTALLY, HAVE NO FEAR OF ORDERING EIGHT TO TWELVE WEEKS SUPPLY AS ALL INDICATIONS POINT TO SUBSTANTIALLY HIGHER PRICE LEVELS BY MID-SUMMER ..... PROBABLY AS MUCH AS 20% HIGHER.

YOUR COOPERATION WILL BE APPRECIATED FOR OUR MUTUAL BENEFIT.

THANK YOU.

                    COLONIAL BEEF COMPANY
                       Louis E. Waxman
                          President

MAY, 1971

LEW/lcm

EXHIBIT 7

COLONIAL BEEF COMPANY

THE COMPANY BEHIND THE PRODUCT ☐ Serving the Food Service Industry since 1889 ☐ Pioneer in Portion Control meat products ☐ International network of Brokers and Distributors ☐ New ultramodern U.S.D.A. Inspected Plant ☐ Research and Product Development—Test Kitchens and qualified experienced consultants ☐ Highest quality control standards in the industry

Saw cutting line for portioning bone-in meat products

Custom boning, prior to fabricating into Portion Control cuts

Kabobs being assembled on stainless steel skewers

Vacuum packaging to minimize bacterial count, extend shelf life

Automatic packaging machine operation for consumer products

Mechanical forming operation for chopped meat products

Finished product passing metal detector for maximum protection

Orders being transferred to low temperature shipping area

COLONIAL BEEF COMPANY

Food Distribution Center • Philadelphia, Pennsylvania 19148, U.S.A. • Telephone: 215-467-0900 • Cable: **COLBECO**
Price List available upon request.

HR

ZWICKEL GYMNASTIC TAILORS, INC.

Zwickel Gymnastic Tailors, Inc., is a producer of stretch fabric athletic uniforms. Walter Zwickel formed the corporation in 1969 in Roslyn, Pennsylvania, an outgrowth of a business in gymnastic competition trousers he had operated from his North Philadelphia custom tailoring shop. On January 1, 1969, when the new business was formally separated from the custom tailoring shop, sales were $48,000. By the end of 1973 sales were $584,000, accounting for 80 percent of the gymnastics uniform market. (See Exhibit 1.) The company projected sales of $1,000,000 for 1974 and $2,000,000 for 1975.

Mr. Zwickel was an entrepreneur. He had previously developed two highly successful spin-off products while running his tailoring shop. The first product was a pre-tied parade scarf that he designed and produced at the request of his Army Reserve superior in 1950. The scarf displayed an unusual degree of uniformity and was subsequently ordered in large numbers by other Reserve units. By the end of a year he had sold 708,000 scarfs at a 300 percent mark-up. The product soon became standard Army equipment. When the Army required bids for later purchases, he was underbid by a large manufacturer, who was able to make the scarfs cheaper.

His second product was a tonneau cover for M. G. sportcars. One afternoon in 1958 Zwickel found the tonneau cover of his M. G. slashed. Learning that a replacement cover would cost $75, he decided to make it himself. Within a few months he was selling 400 to 500 tonneau covers a week at $12 a piece. M. G.

This case was prepared by Joseph E. Sabella under the supervision of Professor Jules J. Schwartz as the basis for class discussion rather than to illustrate either effective or ineffective handling of an administrative action.

then decided to make the covers standard equipment, and he was forced out of that business also.

HISTORY

Walter Zwickel had been in the tailoring business all his life. His father, Benjamin Zwickel, operated a custom tailoring shop in North Philadelphia, and from the time he was thirteen years old, Walter used to help out after school and on weekends. Before he finished high school he had become a journeyman tailor and could make all types of garments. In 1949 he received a degree in marketing and industrial management from Temple University. By that time he had also become manager of children's camp clothing at a local department store.

Since 1921 his father's firm had manufactured white wool gymnastic competition trousers for a local athletic club. Because the business was located on the first floor of the building that housed the club's headquarters and gymnasium, Zwickel developed many friends among the members. The company also produced black wool trousers for physical education majors and sold about a hundred pairs a year as a side line.

In 1960 Carl Patterson, the Temple University gymnastics coach who had been Zwickel's classmate at Temple and an old friend, brought in a pair of Swiss-made stretch pants that had recently been introduced in the United States. He encouraged Zwickel to develop a similar product.

Walt, you should figure out how to make these pants. Stretch is the thing for the gymnast because it makes movement easy. If you make something equal or better, the coaches around the country will drive you crazy. Right now we wait six months for delivery from Switzerland. Metric sizing makes it difficult to order correctly. ... And if we have any problems, we don't have anyone to talk to.

In gymnastics superior trousers will result in a better score. The gymnast is judged by the straightness of his legs, unless a bent knee is part of the move. If the stretch pants are made properly, they can help to hide a minor bend at the knee and so contribute to a higher score in the exercise.

Zwickel started experimenting in an eight by ten foot room in his shop. From 1960 to 1965 he made pants out of various fabrics in his spare time and tested them on Patterson's students. Some of the test models stretched and stayed stretched; some did not stretch enough; some shrunk or stretched after washing.

Another obstacle was the development of stretch fabric. In the early sixties stretch fabric was available only in socks, shirts, and woven fabrics. Zwickel described his approach to the problem in this way:

> I started out by doing a selling job on Du Pont to convince them that stretch fabric was the thing of the future. When I called one of their new product managers, he asked, "For what applications?" I couldn't say gymnastics, because he would say "What's that?" So I said, "Skiing is the coming thing. Millions of people will be skiing in no time now. We are all buying imports. Why don't you make the fabric here?" He said, "Yes, it makes sense." Well, it turned out that I was a prophet. They were probably thinking in that direction and that call was what they needed to go the rest of the way.

By 1965 Zwickel had developed a pair of pants that performed well, washed well, and held up well. (See Exhibit 2.) Also, under Patterson's guidance, he had developed a toe cup (Exhibit 3) that brings the pants down and encloses the toes. It makes the gymnast's toes appear to point properly even if he can't point well. The toe cup makes a bad point look like a good point made by a gymnast with a "fat" heel; and the judge cannot deduct for a heel

with a fat appearance because it is a physiological characteristic.

A year later the competition trouser was selling at a rate of 500 to 600 pairs a year, representing 10 to 15 percent of the American market. This was a significant increase from the 50 to 150 pairs the firm had been selling annually in the past. More significantly, this market share represented sales to the top coaches in the United States. Patterson was well known among these coaches and they all placed orders when he told them that high quality stretch competition trousers were available in the United States without a six-month wait. The word spread quickly because coaches met each other at meets around the country where they could spot the superior uniforms quite easily.

The new uniforms became very popular and the coaches started asking the Zwickel firm to supply knitted jerseys, shoes, warmups, and handguards. Although Zwickel was not in a position to make these products himself, he found a leotard manufacturer to make jerseys for him, a place to buy warmups, and a source in Switzerland where he could buy shoes and handguards. He still made the gymnastic trousers in the back room where the experiments had begun and continued to run three men's clothing stores with his mother and brother-in-law.

The Olympics

Then in the spring of 1968 Patterson said to him, "Walt, why don't you put in a pitch for the Olympics?" At that point Zwickel considered the gymnastics business a sideline and was still feeling his way along. He had no clear idea of what direction the business would take. At first he was reluctant. But after he learned that Patterson had just been named chairman of the Olympic committee that would select the uniforms for the team, he agreed to submit a proposal. He felt that he could not emphasize quality because he would be competing against foreign uniforms that were definitely superior at that time. His only argument was that an American team should go to the Olympics in American-made uniforms. He didn't know whether it was Patterson's influence, his own sales pitch, or his uniforms, but he won the contract. Shortly afterward, the word spread to coaches and competitors below the top level. Revenues for the year 1968 rose to $48,000.

With sales rising, Zwickel decided to turn his full attention to his gymnastic trousers interest. He was happy to leave the business in North Philadelphia where he had been plagued by crime, shoplifters, high insurance, his partners and many other problems. He opened his new business in January 1969 in Roslyn. When the new firm first started operations, he performed every task himself. He was a salesman, cutter, designer, tool and die maker, janitor, presser, and shipper. By the end of 1969 sales were up to $89,000; he had begun production of jerseys, leotards, and briefs, and was also selling shoes and handguards.

From the experience of the 1968 Olympics Zwickel learned to sell first to the top-level coaches. When he began selling other types of sporting goods, he continued the practice of starting with the top people first. He found out what type of uniform they wanted, made it to satisfy them, and promoted it first to the leading coaches. After he succeeded with the top coaches, demand developed quickly among the others.

Zwickel made it a policy to provide free uniforms to any American team that went overseas or competed for this country against a visiting foreign team. He reasoned that this gained him a lot of loyalty from the people who run the Olympic teams. In the past they always had had to be concerned about raising money for uniforms. The policy was advantageous for the firm too. As long as coaches got uniforms free, they were not likely to look at anyone else's. The firm could advertise that every American international gymnastic team wore its uniforms. Also, the company realized a tax deduction on the uniforms it gave away. Because of his contacts among the Olympic Committee, Zwickel became official supplier to the United States Gymnastics Federation and chief uniform consultant to the United States Gymnastic Committee.

MARKETING

The company sold its uniforms at all levels of the sport: college coaches, individual athletes, and sporting goods dealers and distributors. Its base price was called the "school price." The school price for highest quality competition pants varied between $21.95 and $25.95, depending on the specific style and options selected. A dealer who purchased fewer than six of a given item at one time got a 25 percent discount from school price. A distributor buying more than six of a given item in a single order was granted a 35 to 40 percent discount and distributors purchasing very large quantities, such as 200 units at a time, received a 50 percent discount. Profit margins had been maintained despite inflation because of increasing production efficiencies as the company grew.

Zwickel had campaigned hard to eliminate quality and efficiency problems in marketing. Athletic directors generally controlled the budget, so coaches had to clear their needs for new uniforms with them. After approval, the coaches' specifications, often based on Zwickel model and catalog numbers, went out to the school's bidder list. The bid request thus went to all the firms that normally did business with the school, including its builders, furniture suppliers, and others. Generally bids came only from the few dealers authorized to handle uniforms. But, some dealers bid on anything and worried about getting the uniforms after they got the contract. Zwickel's local dealer was often underbid and the school didn't realize what had happened. At the time of delivery an unscrupulous dealer might have claimed that Zwickel had failed to deliver and offered the coach a substitute brand.

In many guest appearances and in written articles for the suppliers group of the National Health and Physical Education Association, Zwickel recommended tighter specifications.

If the schools received unsatisfactory uniforms, the specifications stood as good evidence for a court suit.

He also recommended a change in the law to permit direct negotiation for items previously purchased under a bid system. This change provided that the final negotiated price be no more than the last bid price. He pushed for, and occasionally received agreement on unified purchasing directly from large school systems. There are significant savings to be realized in buying directly from a manufacturer. For example, an athletic suit could be provided to the New York City school system, with individual school colors and lettering, at a one-third price reduction.

Zwickel created a lot of goodwill with the coaches by his policy of immediately replacing a faulty uniform without charge and letting the coaches keep the original. He claimed that no one abused this policy and the company's sales had increased because his customers told their colleagues about it.

When Zwickel first started he was competing with eight importers who bought from such countries as Japan, Germany, Sweden, Switzerland, and Italy. No one in the United States was making gymnastic uniforms; only a few companies were making leotards for dance and physical fitness enthusiasts; and one company was making warmup suits of a rather inferior quality.

In 1968 Zwickel discovered that the competitors who called themselves shoe importers were really merchants who were importing 500 to 700 pairs of shoes at a time. He found it was possible to get an additional 25 percent discount by buying 2000 pairs and began to import large numbers of shoes himself. He then resold to the former importers.

Initially Zwickel's uniforms were not price competitive so he competed with service, faster delivery, free uniforms, styling, and color choice. He also offered unique technical features in his garments such as the shape of the pants and the toe cup.

In 1973, when the dollar deteriorated abroad, Zwickel began to have a price advantage because foreign uniforms became more expensive in the United States. Subsequently seven of the eight original competitors joined him as distributors and the eighth went bankrupt. Thus, no matter where the Olympic Committee went they would get Zwickel uniforms.

Zwickel recognized there was a possibility that someone might try to copy his designs, but he didn't view this as a serious threat. He stated:

> There is nothing stopping anyone else from getting into this; but the law does not say that I have to give lessons, I could describe our basic merchandising policies, but that applies to anything. However, I am not taking anyone into the cutting room and sewing shop to show how we produce the garments. That is the technical aspect of the business that even my staff does not completely know. The man who runs assembly knows nothing about cutting and design, and the man who runs cutting knows nothing about assembly. I intend to keep it that way.
>
> The uniform can be bought, disassembled, and traced. But, the hyperextension curve, that line of the pants leg that is the key to the men's uniform and warmup suit, is not based on the fact that the garment is cut and sewn. It is based on a differential tension in the stretch nylon. The two panels, the front panel and the back panel, are cut at different lengths. When these two panels are sewn, one is stretched to the other and the stretching is spaced over a given area. This is what gives them their hyperextension curve.
>
> If someone were to attempt to take our pants apart they would think that the parts would not go together again. If they did figure out that one has to be stretched to the other, they still would not know where that stretch belongs to give it the curve. Also, during the seaming the panels are trimmed as they are sewn, so that the disassembled pattern is not the same size as the originally cut pattern. There are a lot of these technical factors. The whole thing is working with stretching, the differential tension of the fabric, knowing where to put the tension. In certain areas it must stretch, and in others it must sag.

The company's market position was unique in the athletic uniform market. All the other manufacturers concentrated on items that could be produced in high volume for the lowest possible price. Zwickel took the opposite approach. He sought relatively small-scale production, at the highest quality. He met the most exacting standards and made the highest profits. In fact, one of the threats that he identified is the possibility that his products might become too popular, a mass consumer item. If Wilson were to come out with $5.95 gymnastic competition pants, they would probably succeed in invading his market. They could manufacture 10,000 pairs at a much lower cost than he could. But this market was not there for them; and so he had what there was all to himself.

By 1972 the popularity of warmups had reached the point where many firms had entered the market. Zwickel felt he still had an advantage because his competitors' products were designed just for appearance while his warmups contributed to performance. He cited the fact that he still could not keep up with demand and that wherever his warmups (Exhibit 4) were offered, competition disappeared.

Because of stringent foreign restrictions on imports of nylon goods, Zwickel's foreign sales were still small in 1973. After showing his uniforms to foreign coaches during the Olympic competitions, he concluded that if the controls were lifted, foreign gymnasts would prefer his uniforms. His company's policy was to give a uniform to any foreign national coach who asked for it. He thought it did much for American goodwill and the international brotherhood of gymnasts. Also, he realized that if the international political and economic picture were to change, he would have a ready market.

WRESTLING UNIFORMS

The line of wrestling uniforms was developed after Zwickel met Bill Farrel, an Olympic wrestling gold medalist and the American Athletic Union wrestling chairman in 1970. Farrel owned one of the largest wres-

tling supply stores in the country and had the best wrestling equipment lines from Japan, particularly shoes and protective gear, locked in on contract. At that time he was also selling some gymnastic wear. Zwickel was able to convince him to drop the Japanese gymnastic wear in favor of his line. When the first devaluation of the dollar occurred in 1972, Zwickel warmup suits also became competitive with Japan's, so Farrel switched.

In 1972 Farrel was named Olympic wrestling coach. Shortly after, Zwickel, anticipating another currency devaluation, developed a line of wrestling uniforms with Farrel's help. The wrestling uniforms were designed to satisfy the coach's technical specifications and were to be promoted by him.

Zwickel learned about the requirements of a wrestling uniform from several wrestling experts. The garment had to stretch enough to provide freedom of motion. For example, in an around-the-body hold, when the opponent tries to turn a man by twisting his body, the uniform should rotate around the man so that he will not be forced to move. A wide range of sizes are required and there has to be a certain tolerance and flexibility of fit to accommodate a wide range of shoulder, waist and hip measurements in any weight class.

In 1972 there were two American firms making wrestling uniforms; but they had neither Farrel's understanding of what the uniforms should do, nor Zwickel's technical skill to make it work. Farrel had never purchased from domestic sources because he had always been satisfied with Japanese products before the devaluation. Following the devaluation, which made Japanese wrestling uniforms more expensive relative to American ones, Zwickel became well entrenched with Farrel in uniforms and warmups. Farrel bought 2000 wrestling uniforms in 1972 and 9000 in 1973. He was expected to buy 20,000 in 1974. Thus, with the combination of Zwickel's production and Farrel's distribution, it was anticipated that the company would have 80 percent of the wrestling uniform market by the end of 1974 or 1975. Zwickel was confident that there was nothing to stop him from doing it. Competitors were reacting but with little success.

Zwickel had also started to develop a line of fencing uniforms with the help of his son-in-law, who was an Olympic-level fencer. Again, he found out what the uniform had to do, made it perform and picked off the top accounts in the country. He expected to have the bulk of this market by the end of 1975.

Plans for the future included football, track, and basketball. When asked about skiwear, Zwickel explained, "There are 10 million companies making skiwear and they are all cutting each other's throats."

He commented on his ability to develop quickly uniforms for other sports:

> The beautiful thing about starting in gymnastics is that it is the grandfather and grandmother of every sport or athletic endeavor. Every conceivable body motion has not only been done in gymnastics, but thoroughly analyzed. What I have learned about tailoring for gymnastics is applicable to any other sport. If I get the freedom of motion and the good fit, that is what they want. In other words, I have learned to make stretch fabric work for the body in motion. This is mostly what I know and I will teach it to my sons as they get older.
>
> I don't intend to give this knowledge away. We have been offered a lot of money for it already. E. R. Moore, which is a division of Beatrice Foods, was in at the old place, the hole in the wall, and offered us about $1.5 million for the designs. I said no, because according to their formula, this business was worth twice that much and it will be worth twice as much again by the end of 1974.

ORGANIZATIONAL STRUCTURE

The Zwickel organization consisted of five departments. Exhibit 5 shows that production, cutting, and the office reported directly to Zwickel. There was a shipping department that reported to warehousing, which in turn reported to the office. Zwickel's wife, assisted by three employees, ran the office. Four cutters, supervised by Harmon, cut the fabric into panels in preparation for assembly. Production was supervised by Ristagno; it combined thirteen sewing machine operators and an assistant. The assistant clipped, pressed, and folded the garments. He also set up piles of fabric panels for the operators so that the panels would unfold into orientations that placed the seams together prior to sewing.

Before becoming supervisor of the cutting department, Harmon had been a cutter. He learned his trade under the G.I. Bill after World War II and had subsequently spent fourteen years with a very large company that produced military uniforms. In 1958 he became a cutting foreman supervising 150 people. Later he began working for a firm that produced school band uniforms and became foreman in 1967, supervising sixty people. The work was similar to Zwickel's operation because band uniforms were produced with many color combinations and style specifications. Both companies were characterized by high quality, high priced products.

Harmon began working for Zwickel on a part-time basis in 1971, expecting to stay only three weeks. By September 1972 he was working full time and supervising three cutters. His additional responsibilities included the reordering of materials, working around an occasional incomplete cutting instruction, and sometimes assisting Zwickel on styling and design. He felt that the success of the business was tied to Zwickel's ingenuity and drive.

By the time Ristagno was twenty-eight years old, he had been in the tailoring business fifteen years. As a teenager he enjoyed tailoring so much, he used to cut school classes to work in tailoring shops around Philadelphia. He attended a school of clothing design, but learned most from working in the shops. Ristagno became accomplished at producing all types of garments and eventually managed a custom tailoring shop with 150 sewing machine operators.

Ristagno had been with the company since 1969. When he started, Zwickel cut and

Ristagno assembled the uniforms. Ristagno did not have any desire to work in the marketing and financial aspects of the business. Consequently he chose to take a bonus based on sales rather than the cut of the profits he had been offered.

EXPANSION

By August 1973 the business had outgrown its original space in Roslyn and had moved to Wyncote, Pennsylvania. The building Zwickel rented was among a complex that had a history of high turnover. He estimated he could produce about four times his present volume within the space he was currently renting, and ten times as much by eventually moving into the rest of the buildings as other tenants moved out. He had every step of his expansion planned in advance. One of the future options under consideration was the purchase of the building complex.

Zwickel was confident that the market was large enough to support ten times his 1973 volume. The volume he did through 1973 was achieved without really selling. His catalog went out on request only. His advertising consisted of a monthly ad in *Modern Gymnast* magazine, which he ran to help support the magazine. He had a waiting list of distributors and was not accepting new accounts. In fact, he thought if he gave contracts to the list of people who wanted to handle his uniforms and set up a few displays at some sporting goods shows, he could have ten times 1973 volume within a few weeks.

One of the limitations in increasing production was the training of personnel. The operation was not a typical assembly line. The machine operators had to be retrained no matter how skilled they were.

Another limiting factor was finance. By plowing back the previous years' profits Zwickel felt he could double production each year without having to obtain outside capital.

The company had little success in building inventory. Although there was usually a slow period between March and April when some inventory built up, it was depleted by early Fall.

As the business grew Zwickel delegated some responsibility to others in the organization. His wife, Leda Zwickel, handled money receipts and disbursements and others in the office took care of bookkeeping and order expediting. He did not feel it was necessary to constantly review his books because he usually had a good feel for receivables and payables.

Zwickel gave Harmon cutting tickets and priority lists every two days, and Harmon cut the fabric as he saw fit. Zwickel had worked with Harmon for over a year before giving him this much discretion.

When the business first started Zwickel cut and assembled the uniforms. Later, he cut and Ristagno assembled. After Harmon was trained, Zwickel relinquished both operations. From the time the cutting ticket was written and the priority assigned, he heard nothing about the garment until he saw the invoice for pricing or heard from the customer.

When a new item was introduced, Zwickel made the first unit. He showed Ristagno how he thought the garment should be assembled. Ristagno made the garment and offered recommendations that often resulted in pattern changes. After that Ristagno supervised the operators.

Zwickel still did many tasks himself in order to keep costs down. He paneled his office on Sundays, made work benches, and always filled in wherever needed. He also prepared the company catalog including all art work, photography, layout, and copy. Although he was planning to hire a sales manager within a few years, his desire to protect the secrets of his trade required that he continue to do all design work, patternmaking, and new product set up for the shop.

One solution to the expansion problem was to subcontract assembly. The firm could cut the fabric and send it out for subassembly provided he could find someone who would subassemble at a price that made it profitable.

The company had several incentive programs. The sewing machine operators earned about 30 percent more in take home pay and fringe benefits than they would have with a union pay scale. Because Zwickel got a high price for his product, he felt he could easily afford this pay rate. He always made it clear to his workers that mastery of their present job would lead to advancement, which he clearly defined in terms of the pay raises they would receive. He had plans for sending some employees to evening school to learn production management and control.

Harmon's base pay had been 30 percent higher than a typical cutter when he started. He now received incentive pay based on the number of units that went through the cutting room, generally amounting to an additional $100 a week. Quality control was maintained because poorly cut fabrics required rework time that sharply lowered efficiency. One damaged panel cost him 25 or 30 units.

Ristagno received his base pay plus an incentive based on sales. The incentive pay was computed as a percentage of the previous years sales, plus a larger percentage of the increase in current sales. As a returned garment counted as a negative sale, he had an incentive to maintain quality in the assembly operation.

Since opening the business with $3,500 in 1969, Zwickel had financed all expansion from internally generated funds. On January 1, 1974, receivables were $100,000 and payables were $9,800. Zwickel had no intention of going public or issuing long-term debt. He was quite determined to keep 100 percent control.

> One thing I do not want to do is give away any control. I know where the business is going and I would rather get there a couple of years later and keep 100 percent ownership. I do not want to get there tomorrow and have to give away 90 percent of it. We could go public tomorrow and I'd be a paper millionaire. But, I'd be only a paper millionaire with a board of directors, the stockholders, the S.E.C. and all the other headaches. This way it is all mine! If I want to lease a Cadillac, I lease a Cadillac. If I want to go to a convention and take my wife along, she goes because she is an officer of the company. You know, I don't have to answer to anybody, it's mine! I've had too many partners and too many aggravations to look at it any other way.

Zwickel viewed his personal finances and the finances of the company as one. For example, he drew no more than a $45,000 salary because, above that, the Federal personal income tax schedule went over 50 percent, which was the corporate tax rate. He was planning an employee profit-sharing plan that would require four years of employment to be eligible, with two-year vesting. The plan would also act as a personal tax shelter because there was a high turnover of sewing machine operators.

Because he was the highest paid employee, he expected to reap the most benefit from this scheme. All remaining cash was plowed back into the business unless limited manpower availability temporarily prevented expansion. This allowed continued growth and shielded still more funds from Federal income taxes.

Zwickel had two objectives for the future. First, he would like the organization to be running smoothly enough so that he could cut back from a seven-day week. Second, he wanted to increase the size of the business so that he would have the option in the future of either turning it over to his sons or selling it.

EXHIBIT 1
ZWICKEL GYMNASTIC TAILORS, INC.
Annual Sales

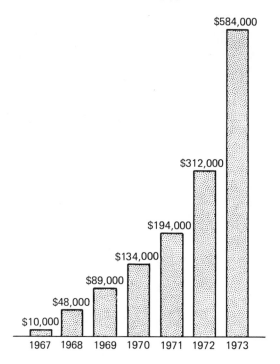

EXHIBIT 2

ZWICKEL GYMNASTIC TAILORS, INC.

Competition pants

World's largest line of quality
competition pants. More features, wider selection, exclusive designs. Made in the
U.S.A. and selected for every
U.S.A. International Gymnastic Team. Official tailors for
the United States Gymnastics
Federation.

EXHIBIT 3

TOE CUP

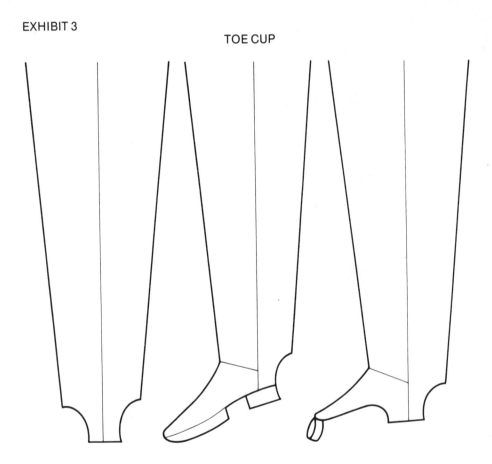

G-91: German Stirrup- Our Gymnastique Economy model. Made of the same fine fabric, but with frills eliminated. Features concealed waistband, stitched creases, and German Stirrup. White or off white.

G-92: Toe Cup- Featuring concealed waistband, improved Patterson toe cup, detailed side seams, sewn creases. Made of nylon Gymnastique in white or off white.

G-93: Toe Strap- Identical to model G-92 except for bottom. Made with improved Swiss Toe Strap. Off white.

EXHIBIT 4

ZWICKEL WARMUP SUITS

EXHIBIT 5
ZWICKEL GYMNASTIC TAILORS, INC.
Organization Chart

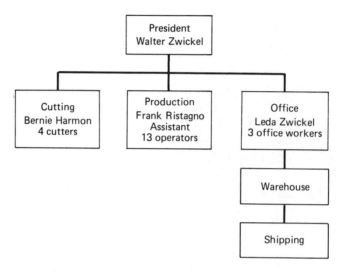

SAFEGUARD INDUSTRIES, INC.

In early September 1976, Warren V. Musser, Chairman of the Board of Safeguard Industries, Inc., along with a group of business students reviewed two of the options he felt might increase the market value of his firm. Although Safeguard's revenue from automotive parts and business forms subsidiaries had climbed from $7 million in 1967 to $107 million in 1976, its shares commanded a price-to-earnings ratio of only 5. He wondered whether paying a dividend would be appropriate. In addition, he discussed the advisability of divesting one of the company's two major business segments. Perhaps, if Safeguard shed its conglomerate image, investers would award it a higher earnings multiple.

CORPORATE HISTORY

Safeguard Industries was originally incorporated in 1953. An initial investment of $300,000 had been used to gain control of Safeguard Checkwriters Corporation, a firm that manufactured check protection machines.

To encourage the use and sale of both checks and other forms the company proceeded to introduce a special writing board on which several different recordkeeping forms and carbons were held. With the forms in perfect alignment, writing on the top form produced the same entries on the forms beneath. This efficiency concept, called simply the "one-write form system," helped to standardize

recording procedures and to increase accuracy in the posting process for hundreds of thousands of customers. (See Exhibit 1.) Results were excellent and revenues grew significantly. By 1965 sales were about $2 million, with a projection of $10 million by 1970. With this strong track record as a base and good prospects for investor acceptance, Safeguard Industries made its initial public stock offering. Within six months the price of the common had rocketed from $10 to $40 per share, a price-to-earnings ratio of 60 to 1. (See Exhibits 2 and 3.)

While management was understandably flattered by the market response, it was also concerned with "building some value into the stock so that it would not fall back down." In the context of the late 1960s, Safeguard saw acquisitions as the most desirable vehicle for developing an earnings potential to match the market's expectations. Between 1968 and 1972 Safeguard acquired over twenty companies in the varied businesses of automotive parts supply, advertising, emblem embroidery, business forms, and primary land development. (See Exhibit 4.) Reflecting on the mix of business, the chairman explained, "Expansion resulted from desire and imagination more than anything else." In the early stages the acquisition strategy seemed to pay off; by 1970 revenues approached $70 million and Safeguard was listed on the New York Stock Exchange.

In 1972, however, the situation had changed dramatically and Safeguard found itself in the midst of a general business downturn. It was hard pressed to exert sufficient managerial control over its acquisitions. These had previously been strongly managed by owner-entrepreneurs with significant operating

This case was prepared by Grant Behrman, William Blackham, J. Michael Kennedy, and Barry Michael under the supervision of Professor Jules J. Schwartz as the basis for class discussion rather than to illustrate either effective or ineffective handling of a managerial action.

expertise. At the same time Safeguard was adversely affected by changes in generally accepted accounting principles (GAAP). These involved the recognition of income on installment contracts for the sale of land and rulings on acquisition methods and procedures and consolidation principles for financial reporting. From the corporate viewpoint the conglomerate structure no longer seemed attractive.

Safeguard turned quickly to a divestiture strategy that its chairman described as "a creative, entrepreneurial weeding out process." The corporation believed that the small, entrepreneurial nature of the various businesses would allow them to be sold separately to individuals and run as smaller operations. (See Exhibit 4.) Accordingly, Safeguard's approach was to sell a business back to the former owner or to employees, while retaining some form of financial participation. This strategy not only freed Safeguard from servicing the debt and capital requirements of the companies but also provided it with an interest in the future growth of these firms. Sales in 1976 reached $107 million despite the divestiture of companies whose sales totalled $30 million. Safeguard had successfully completed its consolidation program and felt it was free to focus its efforts on the management of its core businesses—Safeguard Automotive Corporation and Safeguard Business Systems, Inc.

THE AUTO PARTS INDUSTRY

The auto parts industry falls into two market categories: *original equipment*—parts and accessories for a new car; and *replacement*—aftermarket parts and accessories. Many firms are active in both markets.

Original Equipment Manufacturers (OEMs). In 1975 there were approximately 2,000 American firms engaged primarily in manufacturing the myriad of parts that large automobile manufacturers put into motor vehicles. Most of these firms were small, with 1,100 employing fewer than twenty workers. In addition to these companies, there were many thousands of smaller firms that supplied parts to Detroit.

Most original equipment was manufactured under annual contracts covering the model year, although such agreements frequently were somewhat elastic with regard to price and aggregate volume. Contracts were usually renewed unless a design change eliminated the need for a product, another company offered an improved or lower-priced line, or the car builder decided to produce the item itself. A recent development had been the growing use of multiyear supply contracts. Under the longer-term contracts, parts companies could lower their unit costs through larger plant investment, greater research and development, and better capacity utilization. Periodic design changes, shifting integration policies concerning captive production, fluctuations in demand for new cars, and keen competition for business made the OEM market very challenging.

Replacement Part Manufacturers. This business had been wider-margined than OEM, and manufacturers had benefited from a 37 percent growth in the number of vehicles in operation in the decade that ended in 1975. In addition to the OEMs, oil companies, large retailers, and 25,000 auto dealers accounted for about half of all sales. Thousands of small firms were active in distributing parts, most specializing in just a few items. Some characteristics of the major firms and a composite of overall industry performance are included in Exhibits 5 and 6.

Prospects for strong future demand were good, based on the steadily rising number of new cars and trucks in use, growing complexity of the new vehicles, and broadening state auto safety inspection programs. Even in a downturn, this industry often did better then OEMs, as people tended to prolong the lives of their cars by spending more on maintenance rather than buying a new car.

While demand might remain healthy, there were several issues with which industry had to grapple. These included: 1) future government activity to regulate fuel consumption; 2) advances in technology, creating new and better diagnostic items and new electrical products; and 3) shifts in distribution. Of these, the shift in distribution would probably be most significant, highlighted by merger activity among major firms already in the industry, and the initiation of auto parts merchandising by major supermarket and retailing companies.

SAFEGUARD AUTOMOTIVE CORPORATION

Safeguard operated in both the automotive replacement parts and power transmission markets through a wholly-owned subsidiary, Safeguard Automotive Corporation. As the company's first acquisition, the automotive group represented a major challenge to top management. According to board chairman Musser, the firm had raised and put forward $50,000 in "good faith money" and had had to "hock everything in sight" to raise the remainder of the $2.7 million purchase price. The major attraction of the auto parts business was that it had offered a countercyclical cushion for Safeguard. Safeguard Automotive accounted for over half of the parent's revenues in 1975. It was composed of the Automotive Parts Group and the Power Transmission Group. (See Exhibit 7.)

The Parts Group supplied the automotive aftermarket with parts that had been recycled and rebuilt using modern production-line techniques. It also served the automobile aftermarket with new replacement parts. (See Exhibit 8.)

The Power Transmission Group provided Safeguard entree into the large agricultural and industrial equipment markets. Typical end-uses of the power transmission units included power takeoff devices for farm vehicles, irrigation units, construction equipment, and energy-related uses such as cooling towers for oil and gas field applications.

Safeguard Automotive operated in an extremely competitive environment where margins were characteristically very low. Costs had increased faster than prices. The subsidiary lost money in 1974 but earned an operating profit in 1975, after boosting sales and introducing strict cost controls. (See Exhibit 9.)

THE BUSINESS FORMS INDUSTRY

Prior to the 1950s business forms were used extensively by individuals with or without the help of typewriters, mechanical calculators, and other office machines. With the advent of the computer, new dimensions in information processing were added, and growth of business forms usage accelerated. As a result business forms shipments increased faster than the general economy and doubled between 1958 and 1968. Computer forms captured an increasing share of the market—41 percent in 1968 compared with 29 percent in 1958—and shipments grew to $1.3 billion.

As other nonpaper media such as magnetic tape gained acceptance, total forms usage had slowed somewhat, but computer forms still continued to capture an increasing share of the forms market. According to a study by Predicasts, Inc., these trends were to continue and computer forms shipments were expected to approach $3.3 billion by 1980, or almost two-and-one-half times 1970 levels. (See Exhibit 10.)

The computer forms and papers industry consisted primarily of firms specializing in the manufacture of a diverse line of forms and papers. Many forms companies also manufactured their own lines of business equipment and had then sought to develop or acquire their own EDP capabilities. Some examples included Moore Corporation, Uarco, Standard Register, Wallace Business Forms, and Ennis Business Forms.

More recently many business equipment manufacturers had sought to follow IBM's and NCR's lead and develop positions within the forms and papers industry. By developing these capabilities business equipment manufacturers were able to provide a complete service to their customers and fill their own captive requirements. Some equipment manufacturers who had important positions in the forms and papers industry were Addressograph-Multigraph, Control Data, Acme Visible

Records, Litton, SCM, Diebold, and Burroughs.

Merger and acquisition activity had been significant in recent years. Chiefly, business equipment manufacturers had acquired forms manufacturing capabilities. Total shipments of continuous and unit-set forms increased from $328 million in 1958 to $940 million in 1968, an average annual growth rate of 11 percent, compared to 7 percent for the GNP. (See Exhibit 11.)

Consumption of one-time carbon and carbonless papers in manifold forms was estimated at $90 million in 1968 compared to $30 million in 1958. Together these papers accounted for almost a fourth of the total cost of all raw materials consumed in the manifold forms industry and a tenth of the value of product shipments. By 1980 carbonless paper consumption was expected to surpass one-time carbon in market share. (See Exhibit 12.)

SAFEGUARD BUSINESS SYSTEMS, INC.

Safeguard Business Systems, Inc. (SBSI), a wholly-owned subsidiary of Safeguard Industries, was the vehicle through which the parent operated in the data collection and processing fields. SBSI had been a key factor in the parent's success. Compound earning growth for the previous ten years had exceeded 32 percent. Compound sales growth exceeded 25 percent for the same period. In 1976 SBSI contributed about 90 percent of corporate earnings and slightly less than half of annual revenues. (See Exhibit 13.) The subsidiary was organized into four business groups—Business Systems, Data Processing, Business Forms, and Business Products. (See Exhibit 14.)

The major strengths of the business were a strong, profit-oriented management team, a broad and diverse base of customers, a national distribution network, modern regional manufacturing facilities, and an established corporate image for quality products among accountants and other professional groups.

Through the manufacture and distribution of a variety of "one-write" systems and computerized financial reporting, the Business Systems Group accounted for fully one-third of total revenue. The principal product of the group continued to be the one-write record-keeping system—the method of collecting, organizing, standardizing, and processing essential business information in one writing.

The Data Processing Group operated service bureaus and produced revenues of about $5 million in 1976. Input was simplified by use of Safeguard forms, and the turnaround times were very short, 2 to 3 days. This relatively new area was having great success, especially with professional group practices. The Group had over 250,000 customers and approximately 400 distributors in the United States and in Canada.

Safeguard had acquired two forms manufacturers in the late 1960s and organized them into its Business Systems Group, which produced multiple-part forms, customized snap-a-part business forms, and continuous forms for a variety of business uses, including the computer market. Most of the sales were in the southeastern United States, from plants in Tennessee, Florida, and Alabama. Sales were about 20 percent of SBSI's revenues, but forms were a lower margin contributor than the other businesses.

SBSI recognized that its 290,000 customers and a potential market of some 4 million business people and professionals used a broad range of complementary office products. To serve this market, the firm, in 1976, organized its Business Products Group.

This Group offered standard business forms, envelopes, labels, and office organization equipment, using flyers and a catalog distributed by mail and by its distributor force.

Careful selection of high quality products, along with speedy order processing and fulfillment had been rewarded with rapid sales growth. The Business Products Group was optimistic about its ability to reach this vast market.

Safeguard's management viewed the production side of the business, with its strict quality control and ability to customize and expedite orders, as a very important asset.

Competition in this business was fragmented, but major competitors included

Reynolds and Reynolds, Shaw-Walker, the Royal McBee Division of Litton, and Controllofax, none of whom was dominant nationally. Banks were also offering more services to their customers and might present competition in the future.

An accountant, convinced of the advantages of standardization and accuracy derived from the use of Safeguard's one-write system and forms, would recommend specific Business Systems Group products to his clients. In targeting its distribution efforts, the company believed that the most likely prospects were end-users who wrote at least fifty checks each month.

In addition to appealing to the other local independent businessmen, the independent nature of the Safeguard distributors was often cited as a key factor in their drive, helping to set them apart from competitors' company-owned sales forces. The highly motivated distributor had been responsible for over 90 percent of all product improvements in one-write systems. Safeguard's management believed that in the final analysis the distributor, operating as an independent business, was the key to the systems market.

Distribution for the Business Forms Group, on the other hand, was through approximately 800 independent forms distributors who sold direct to the consumer. The combination of superior quality, fast and reliable delivery, and competitive prices had earned the Business Forms Group a strong reputation in the industry with sales increases far above the industry average.

PLANNING AND CONTROL

Safeguard Industries, Inc., was organized on a decentralized basis, with twenty-seven profit centers, geographically distributed in the continental United States. For a profile of Safeguard's sales see Exhibit 15.

The firm was committed to elaborate planning and control systems. At the beginning of each planning year a three-year strategic business plan was generated. This required coordination and planning among profit center, group management, and corporate staff. The plan was updated and reevaluated on an annual basis. This document was then used to generate the following year's budget and operational profit plan. (See Exhibit 16.) From the annual plan emanated specific action plans that were communicated to each level of management. (See Exhibit 17.) Periodic review of these action plans took place between superior and subordinate on an informal basis.

Management at Safeguard believed that the success of the company to date could in large measure be attributed to the identification of opportunities, risks, and rewards prevailing in the marketplace and to the well-directed, coordinated team effort of its employees toward the attainment of a common set of objectives. The planning process had formalized the relationships between the functional areas and enabled market opportunities to be translated into operational profits.

Compensation System

Like many companies Safeguard had sought to develop a compensation system geared to recruit, retain, and motivate its top and middle managers, some 120 people. It had developed a base-plus-incentive compensation program to identify and reward outstanding contributions. The challenge had been to structure a system consistent with the overall philosophy of decentralization that evaluated performance by measuring variables over which the manager had reasonable control.

To accomplish this, management had developed an incentive compensation program that mirrored team and individual performance in the twenty-seven separate profit centers, which ranged in size from $1 million to $15 million. Most profit centers included a team of managers, consisting of a general manager and managers for production, marketing, finance, and materials. An individual manager's incentive compensation was a function of three variables: his standard bonus rate, his profit center's performance, and his individual performance.

The standard bonus rate was an important part of the process of awarding incentive compensation. The company had established a companywide schedule of standard bonus rates, predicated on base salary. To earn bonus compensation the manager's profit center had to meet return-on-assets targets set during the previous planning cycle.

At the same time that the system tried to reward team performance, it also provided incentive compensation for individual performance. Only 75 percent of the total bonus pool available to a profit center was paid out as a result of overall team performance and scheduled bonus rates. The remaining quarter might be paid out, at the discretion of the profit center manager, to reward individual performance.

At the corporate level the annual budget and specific profit plan for each group formed the basis of the management control and information system. Since the key factors for success in each business were different, management was obliged to monitor a variety of variables. Some of these were:

Forms

- Average number of days required to process an order
- Customer service response rate
- The capacity at which the plant was currently operating

Business Systems/Data Processing

- Turnaround time of orders from receipt of order to delivery
- Backlog

Automotive Parts

A. *Power Transmission*
- Incoming order review
- Standard profit margins on incoming orders
- Extent and profitability of backlog
- Standard labor rates

- Variances of material cast
- Product mix and standard profit margins
- Efficiency measure in the plant
- All variable cost fluctuations

B. *Automotive Aftermarket*
- Percentage of orders placed that have been shipped
- Inventory control—re-order level and quantity

Corporate staff normally reviewed group operating results on a quarterly basis. At this time group management submitted a statistical report to corporate staff for analysis. (See Exhibit 18.) A sales report documenting actual versus planned sales was reviewed by management on a weekly basis.

CONCLUSION

The first downward movement in sales of the business forms industry was reported in 1975. Sales that year amounted to approximately $2 billion. The slackened demand was attributed to general economic conditions, reductions in high customer forms backlogs, and cutbacks in computer expenditures. Increasing capacity in the industry was triggering price competition, while direct labor and material cost increases also contributed to decreasing profit margins. Despite this, Safeguard had reported record sales and earnings in its forms business.

Chairman Musser was concerned about investor apathy and the low price-to-earnings ratio attributed the company. What action was appropriate? Could he spin off Safeguard Business Systems from the parent company? Doubts had been raised as to what effect it would have on the corporation as a whole. The last time Safeguard Industries, Inc., had paid a dividend had been in 1965. The stock was trading in the $4 range, close to its all-time low. (See Exhibits 19 through 22) for the company's financial data.)

EXHIBIT 1

SAFEGUARD INDUSTRIES, INC.
One-Write Form System

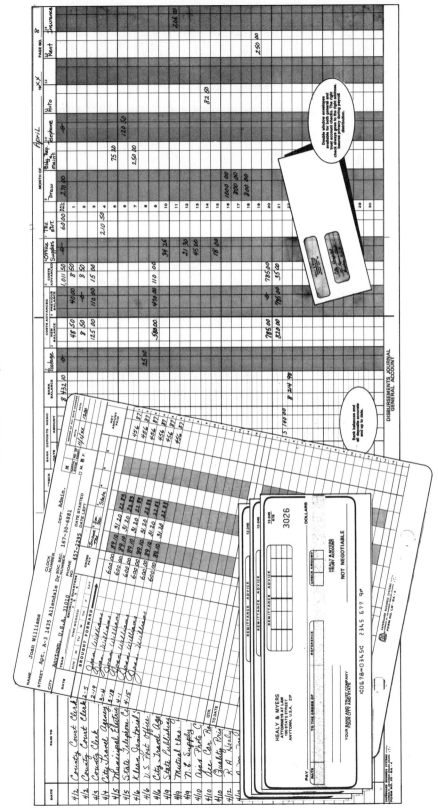

EXHIBIT 2

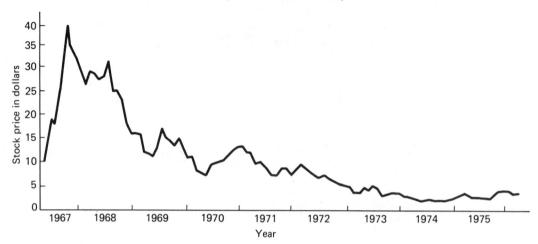

SAFEGUARD INDUSTRIES, INC.
Average Stock Price History

EXHIBIT 3

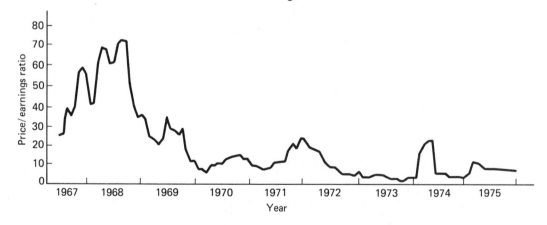

SAFEGUARD INDUSTRIES, INC.
Price/Earnings Ratio

EXHIBIT 4
SAFEGUARD INDUSTRIES, INC.

ACQUISITIONS

1969	Eveready Manifold Corp., Abey Works, Inc., Integrated Data Corp.
1969	Composing Room, Inc.
1969	Carr Automotive and five other firms
1969	Butler Industries
1969	Autographics Corp.
1969	Lion Brothers
1970	Kratky Automotive Products
1970	Inter-American Enterprises
1970	American International Development Co., Arizona Land Research, Australian Land Title, Ltd.
1970	Posner Printing, Apex Gear Co.
1972	Wholert New Oil Pump
1972	Partex Co.

DIVESTITURES

1971	Autographics Corp.
1972	Butler Industries
1972	Australian Land Title, Ltd.
1973	Arizona Land Research
1973	Lion Brothers
1973	Composing Room, Inc.

EXHIBIT 5
COMPOSITE STATISTICS OF THE REPLACEMENT AUTO PARTS INDUSTRY
(Figures are Represented as a Percentage of Sales)

Sales ($ millions)	12,900
Operating margin	13.2%
Depreciation	2.0%
Net income	5.0%
Income tax rate	48.0%
New income margin	4.9%
Working capital	27.0%
Long-term debt	9.0%
Net worth	36.0%
Average annual P/E ratio	13.5

Source: Value Line, 1977.

EXHIBIT 6

CHARACTERISTICS OF MAJOR FIRMS IN AUTOMOTIVE AFTERMARKET
(1975 data)

	Bearings, Inc.	Champion	Echlin	General Auto Parts	Genuine Parts	Globe Union	Maremont	Monroe	Purolator	Raybestos
Capital Expenditures										
$ millions	2.64	22.10	6.67	1.94	7.94	77.93	7.18	20.69	13.93	9.70
As percent of gross plant	18.3	11.4	20.3	10.5	13.8	12.8	8.2	26.0	18.70	9.10
Net Income										
1967 = Base of 100	312	190	388	384	378	600	195	81	200	209
As percent of sales	5.2	10.2	4.9	5.0	4.4	2.5	3.0	4.4	4.8	3.7
Sales										
1967 = Base of 100	256	224	548	279	318	278	150	259	305	179
Profit Margins										
Percent	11.4	23.0	14.5	10.2	10.0	9.9	9.1	12.3	12.6	11.1

Source: Standard & Poor's Composite Industry Data, 1977

EXHIBIT 7

SAFEGUARD AUTOMOTIVE CORPORATION

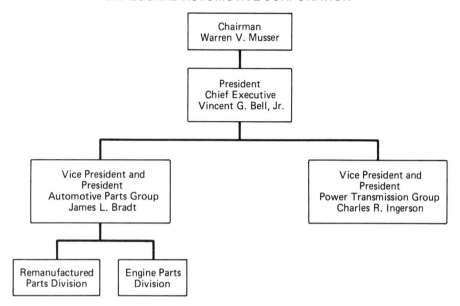

EXHIBIT 8

SAFEGUARD INDUSTRIES, INC., AND SUBSIDIARIES FACILITIES

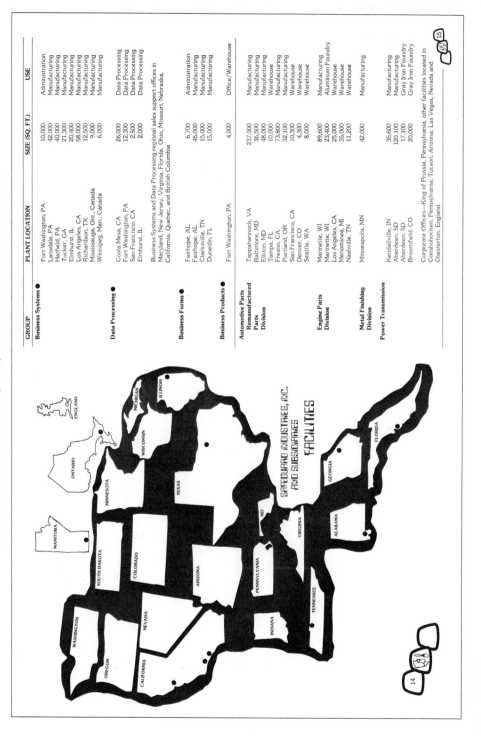

GROUP	PLANT LOCATION	SIZE (SQ. FT.)	USE
Business Systems ●	Fort Washington, PA	10,000	Administration
	Lansdale, PA	42,000	Manufacturing
	Hatfield, PA	40,000	Manufacturing
	Tucker, GA	21,300	Manufacturing
	Elmhurst, IL	20,400	Manufacturing
	Los Angeles, CA	58,000	Manufacturing
	Richardson, TX	12,500	Manufacturing
	Mississauga, Ont., Canada	9,000	Manufacturing
	Winnipeg, Man., Canada	6,000	Manufacturing
Data Processing ●	Costa Mesa, CA	26,000	Data Processing
	Fort Washington, PA	12,300	Data Processing
	San Francisco, CA	2,500	Data Processing
	Elmhurst, IL	2,000	Data Processing
	Business Systems and Data Processing regional sales support offices in Maryland, New Jersey, Virginia, Florida, Ohio, Missouri, Nebraska, California, Quebec, and British Columbia		
Business Forms ●	Fairhope, AL	6,700	Administration
	Fairhope, AL	46,000	Manufacturing
	Clarksville, TN	15,000	Manufacturing
	Dunedin, FL	15,000	Manufacturing
Business Products ●	Fort Washington, PA	4,000	Office/Warehouse
Automotive Parts			
Remanufactured Parts Division	Tappahannock, VA	237,000	Manufacturing
	Baltimore, MD	36,500	Manufacturing
	Elkton, MD	48,000	Manufacturing
	Tampa, FL	10,000	Warehouse
	Fresno, CA	73,800	Manufacturing
	Portland, OR	32,100	Manufacturing
	San Francisco, CA	10,300	Warehouse
	Denver, CO	4,300	Warehouse
	Seattle, WA	8,000	Warehouse
Engine Parts Division	Marinette, WI	89,600	Manufacturing
	Marinette, WI	23,400	Aluminum Foundry
	Los Angeles, CA	25,000	Warehouse
	Menominee, MI	35,000	Warehouse
	Nashville, TN	11,200	Warehouse
Metal Finishing Division	Minneapolis, MN	42,000	Manufacturing
Power Transmission	Kendallville, IN	35,600	Manufacturing
	Aberdeen, SD	120,100	Manufacturing
	Aberdeen, SD	17,100	Gray Iron Foundry
	Broomfield, CO	20,000	Gray Iron Foundry
	Corporate Offices—King of Prussia, Pennsylvania; other facilities located in Conshohocken, Pennsylvania; Tucson, Arizona; Las Vegas, Nevada and Chesterton, England.		

EXHIBIT 9
SAFEGUARD AUTOMOTIVE CORPORATION
Revenues and Pre-Tax Earnings from Operations

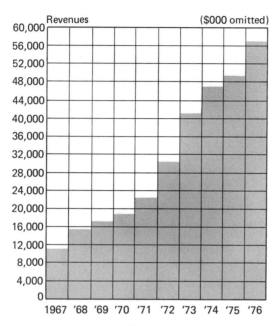

Revenues   ($000 omitted)

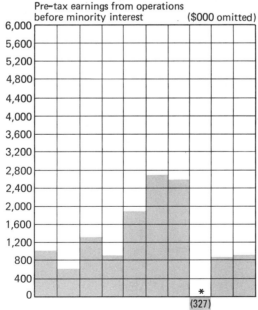

Pre–tax earnings from operations
before minority interest   ($000 omitted)

(327)

1967 '68 '69 '70 '71 '72 '73 '74 '75 '76

*Adoption of LIFO inventory method reduced
earnings by $1,445,000

EXHIBIT 10

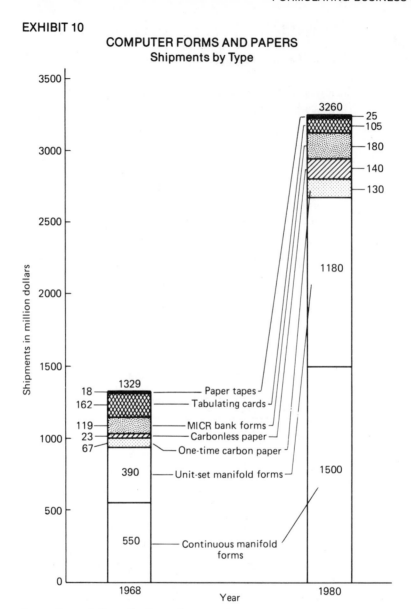

COMPUTER FORMS AND PAPERS
Shipments by Type

Source: Research Group Predicasts, Inc.

EXHIBIT 11

MANIFOLD FORMS SHIPMENTS
By Type

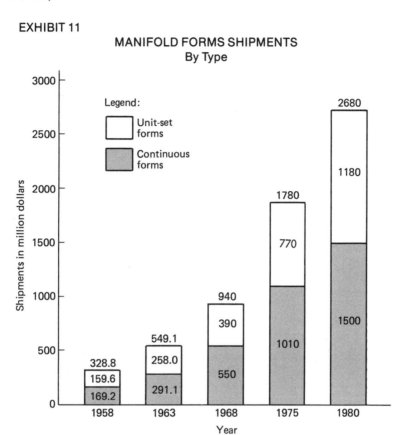

Source: Research Group Predicasts, Inc.

EXHIBIT 12

ONE-TIME CARBON AND CARBONLESS PAPER
CONSUMPTION IN MANIFOLD FORMS

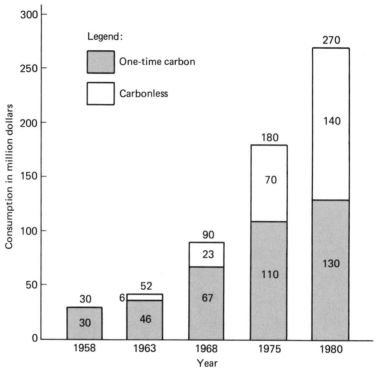

Source: Research Group Predicasts, Inc.

EXHIBIT 13
SAFEGUARD BUSINESS SYSTEMS, INC.
Revenues and Pre-Tax Earnings from Operations

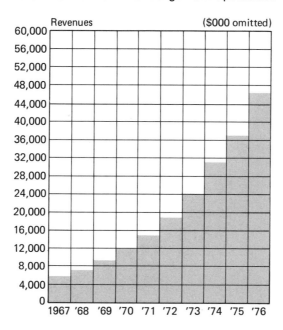

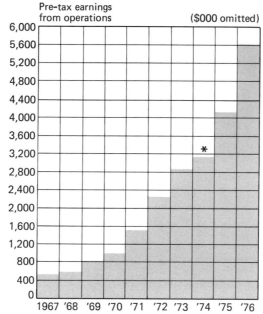

*Adoption of LIFO inventory method reduced
earnings by $490,000

EXHIBIT 14

SAFEGUARD BUSINESS SYSTEMS, INC.

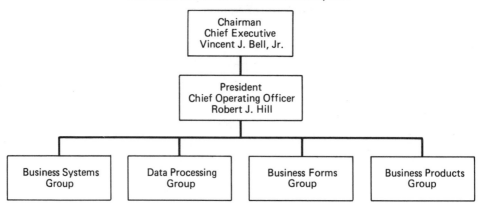

```
                    ┌─────────────────────────┐
                    │       Chairman          │
                    │   Chief Executive       │
                    │  Vincent J. Bell, Jr.   │
                    └─────────────────────────┘
                                │
                    ┌─────────────────────────┐
                    │      President          │
                    │ Chief Operating Officer │
                    │    Robert J. Hill       │
                    └─────────────────────────┘
```

| Business Systems Group | Data Processing Group | Business Forms Group | Business Products Group |

EXHIBIT 15
SAFEGUARD INDUSTRIES, INC.
Product Profile
(% sales)

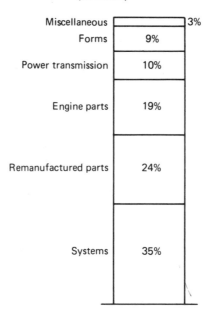

Miscellaneous	3%
Forms	9%
Power transmission	10%
Engine parts	19%
Remanufactured parts	24%
Systems	35%

EXHIBIT 16

SAFEGUARD INDUSTRIES, INC.
Profit Plan Summary

SCHEDULE A–2
($000 omitted)

COMPANY _____

PROFIT PLAN SUMMARY
(Safeguard Business Systems, Inc., companies *ONLY*)

	1976 4th Qtr Estimate	%	1977 Plan	%	1976 Actual/ Estimate	%	1975 Actual	%
Net Sales		100.0		100.0		100.0		100.0
Variable Costs								
Material								
Labor								
FRP processing costs								
Variable selling costs[a]								
Total								
Product Contribution								
Fixed Costs								
Manufacturing overhead								
Selling								
General & administrative								
Interest expense								
Other income								
Division expense								
Headquarters charge								
Total								
Pre-Tax Earnings								
Breakeven Point								
Percent of Increase from Prior Year:								
Net sales								
Pre-tax earnings								

[a]By analysis of total selling expense.

EXHIBIT 16 (cont.)

SAFEGUARD INDUSTRIES, INC.
Profit Plan Summary

SCHEDULE A-2
($000 omitted)

COMPANY _____

PROFIT PLAN SUMMARY
(Manufacturing Companies)

	1976 4th Qtr Estimate	%	1977 Plan	%	1976 Actual/ Estimate	%	1975 Actual	%
Net Sales		100.0		100.0		100.0		100.0
Direct Costs								
Material								
Labor								
Variable mfgr. exp.[b]								
Variable selling costs								
Total								
Standard Product Contrib.								
Nonstandard cost[b]								
Actual Product Contribution								
Fixed Costs								
Manufacturing overhead								
Selling								
General & administrative								
Interest expense								
Other income								
Headquarters charge								
Total								
Pre-Tax Earnings								
Operating Ratios								
Percent of Increase from Prior Year:								
Net sales								
Pre-tax earnings								

Breakeven Point

[b]SAC companies only.

EXHIBIT 17

ACTION PLAN

Safeguard ACTION PLAN

_____

DEPT._____   DATE _____

KEY RESULT EXPECTED:

NO.	ACTION STEPS	PERSON RESPONSIBLE	COMPLETION DATE

HOW TO MEASURE RESULTS?

WHAT COULD GO WRONG?   **HOW TO AVOID?**

EXHIBIT 18

TYPICAL STATISTICAL REPORT

COMPANY_____

STATISTICAL REPORT

	Trade Accts. Rec.		Inventory			Return on Assets			Number of Employees	Backlog (if applies)
	Dollars	Days Out-standing	Dollars	Turnover on Sales	Turnover on Cost of Sales	Asset Turnover	Return on Sales	Return on Assets		
December 1973										
December 1974										
1975 March										
June										
September										
December										
1976 March										
June										
September										
December (Est.)										
1977 March (Est.)										
June (Est.)										
September (Est.)										
December (Est.)										

This *Statistical Report Forecast* schedule indicates the Company's forecasted investment in accounts receivable and inventory during the forthcoming year, together with a mathematical calculation of the forecasted return on assets. This schedule should be prepared concurrently with the Balance Sheet and Cash Flow Forecast.

EXHIBIT 19

FIVE-YEAR FINANCIAL HIGHLIGHTS
($000 omitted)

	1976[a]	1975[a]	1974[a]	1973	1972
Revenues	$107,142	$90,660	$82,639	$73,106	$59,216
Earnings from					
continuing operations	2,790	1,506	385	1,995	1,769
Net earnings	2,790	999	385	1,981	2,387
Earnings per share					
Earnings from					
continuing operations	.66	.37	.09	.48	.42
Net earnings	.66	.24	.09	.48	.57
Long-term debt	18,616	19,502	22,177	20,936	22,637
Shareholders' equity	28,323	24,115	23,037	22,851	21,340
Shareholders' equity					
per common share	6.42	5.88	5.58	5.49	5.06

[a]In 1974, the Company adopted the last-in; first-out (LIFO) method of accounting for inventories. As a result, 1974 to 1976 financial results are not comparable with prior years.

EXHIBIT 20

FIVE-YEAR SUMMARY OF OPERATIONS
($000 omitted)

	%	1976[a]	1975[a]	1974[a]	1973	1972
Revenues						
Business systems						
Systems	35%	$ 37,298	$30,332	$24,114	$18,806	$14,659
Forms	9	9,618	7,222	7,118	5,380	4,509
	44	46,916	37,554	31,232	24,186	19,168
Automotive Parts						
Remanufactured Parts	24	26,160	23,142	19,282	19,607	12,521
Engine Parts	19	20,193	16,328	15,735	13,616	11,405
Power Transmission	10	10,800	10,094	11,946	7,879	6,243
	53	57,153	49,564	46,963	41,102	30,169
Other	3	3,073	3,542	4,444	7,818	9,879
	100%	107,142	90,660	82,639	73,106	59,216
Cost and Expenses						
Material, labor and other		63,361	54,223	50,537	43,003	34,379
Selling		22,334	18,749	16,246	13,322	10,642
General and administrative		12,146	9,731	9,370	8,446	7,416
Depreciation and amortization		1,941	1,825	1,730	1,470	1,241
Interest		1,750	2,115	2,561	1,965	1,069
(Income) loss on equity investments, net		(220)	150	173	131	295
Minority interest		20	179	(72)	611	627
Loss on investments		660	500	1,068		
		101,992	87,472	81,613	68,948	55,669
Earnings from Continuing Operations before Taxes		5,150	3,188	1,026	4,158	3,547
Taxes on income		2,360	1,682	641	2,163	1,778
Earnings from Continuing Operations		2,790	1,506	385	1,995	1,769
Earnings from discontinued operations						380
Earnings before Extraordinary Items		2,790	1,506	385	1,995	2,149
Extraordinary items			(507)		(14)	238
Net Earnings		$ 2,790	$ 999	$ 385	$ 1,981	$ 2,387

EXHIBIT 20 (cont.)

FIVE-YEAR SUMMARY OF OPERATIONS
($000 omitted)

	%	1976[a]	1975[a]	1974[a]	1973	1972
Earnings Per Share of Common Stock						
Earnings from continuing operations		$.66	$.37	$.09	$.48	$.42
Earnings before extraordinary items		$.66	$.37		$.48	$.51
Net earnings		$.66	$.24	$.09	$.48	$.57
Assuming full dilution:						
Earnings from continuing operations		$.63	$.35	$.09	$.46	$.41
Earnings before extraordinary items		$.63	$.35	$.09	$.46	$.50
Net earnings		$.63	$.23	$.09	$.46	$.55
Average Shares Outstanding—Primary		4051	4052	4076	4105	4156
—Fully Diluted		4337	4200	4224	4253	4304
Operating Income[b]						
Business Systems	94%	$ 5,658	$ 4,170	$ 3,160	$ 2,916	$ 2,246
Automotive Parts	15	885	647	(254)	2,010	2,065
Other	(9)	(513)	(285)	120	(66)	204
	100%	6,030	4,532	3,026	4,860	4,515
Deduct corporate expenses, net		440	694	759	571	673
(Income) loss on equity investments		(220)	150	173	131	295
Loss on investments		660	500	1,068		
		$ 5,150	$ 3,188	$ 1,026	$ 4,158	$ 3,547

[a]In 1974, the Company adopted the last-in; first-out (LIFO) method of accounting for inventories. As a result, 1974 to 1976 financial results are not comparable with prior years.
[b]Operating income represents pre-tax earnings after deducting minority interest but before earnings from discontinued operations and extraordinary items.

EXHIBIT 21

SAFEGUARD INDUSTRIES, INC., AND SUBSIDIARIES
Consolidated Balance Sheet

ASSETS

	December 31	
	1976	1975
Current Assets		
Cash, including certificates of deposit ($500,000—1976;		
$1,225,000—1975)	**$ 2,952,200**	$ 3,206,900
Receivables less allowances ($406,500—1976; $374,500—1975)	**15,425,800**	13,505,400
Inventories	**16,911,200**	15,376,400
Prepaid expenses	**1,655,900**	1,599,600
Total Current Assets	**36,945,100**	33,688,300
Other Assets		
Investments	**5,585,300**	6,170,500
Notes receivable	**1,927,900**	1,694,100
Land and land contracts receivable	**3,643,400**	5,616,200
Excess of cost over net assets of businesses acquired	**1,251,400**	2,001,700
Deferred costs	**206,800**	305,200
Miscellaneous	**1,060,900**	859,500
	13,675,700	16,647,200
Property, Plant, and Equipment		
Land	**538,600**	532,200
Buildings and improvements	**10,128,900**	8,655,000
Machinery and equipment	**17,524,500**	15,414,900
	28,192,000	24,602,100
Less accumulated depreciation and amortization	**10,959,100**	9,534,800
	17,232,900	15,067,300
	$67,853,700	$65,402,800

EXHIBIT 21 (cont.)
SAFEGUARD INDUSTRIES, INC., AND SUBSIDIARIES
Consolidated Balance Sheet

LIABILITIES AND SHAREHOLDERS' EQUITY

	December 31	
	1976	1975
Current Liabilities		
Notes payable	**$ 1,025,000**	$ 880,000
Accounts payable	**6,113,000**	4,180,200
Accrued expenses	**4,483,300**	4,191,300
Taxes on income	**1,575,800**	1,140,300
Current maturities of long-term debt	**1,232,000**	1,495,900
Total Current Liabilities	**14,429,100**	11,887,700
Long-Term Debt	**18,616,000**	19,501,600
Deferred Taxes on Income	**2,295,300**	2,667,600
Other Liabilities	**925,000**	925,000
Subordinated Convertible Notes	**3,265,000**	3,600,000
Minority Interest in Subsidiary		2,705,900
Commitments		
Shareholders' Equity		
Preferred stock, par value $10 a share		
Authorized 200,000 shares		
Series 7 and 8, stated value $100 a share		
Issued and outstanding—2,939 shares	**293,900**	293,900
Series 10, stated value $15 a share		
Issued and outstanding—134,882 shares	**1,786,400**	
Common stock, par value $.10 a share		
Authorized 12,000,000 shares		
Issued—4,206,519 shares	**420,600**	420,600
Additional paid-in capital	**7,189,200**	7,189,200
Retained earnings	**19,377,800**	16,953,700
Common stock in treasury, at cost		
1976—196,340 shares		
1975—196,160 shares	**(744,600)**	(742,400)
	28,323,300	24,115,000
	$67,853,700	$65,402,800

EXHIBIT 22

SAFEGUARD INDUSTRIES, INC., AND SUBSIDIARIES
Consolidated Statement of Changes in Financial Position

	Year Ended December 31	
	1976	1975
Working Capital Provided		
Operations		
Earnings before extraordinary charge	**$ 2,790,300**	$1,506,100
Items not affecting working capital		
Depreciation and amortization	**1,941,000**	1,825,100
(Income) loss on equity investments, net	**(220,400)**	149,800
Minority interest in income of subsidiary, net	**13,500**	108,800
Increase (decrease) in deferred income taxes	**(372,300)**	170,500
Decrease in land and long-term land contracts		
receivable, net	**1,972,800**	435,500
Loss on investment	**660,000**	300,000
Total from Operations	**6,784,900**	4,495,800
Extraordinary charge		(507,000)
Increase in other liabilities not requiring outlay of working		
capital		925,000
Total from Extraordinary Charge		418,000
Financing and other		
Refinancing of long-term debt	**6,500,000**	
Borrowing of long-term debt	**1,712,100**	244,000
Issuance of preferred stock	**1,779,600**	
Elimination of excess of cost over net assets of businesses		
acquired	**741,300**	
Disposals of property, plant and equipment	**404,900**	203,100
Total	**11,137,900**	447,100
Working Capital Provided	**17,922,800**	5,360,900

EXHIBIT 22 (cont.)
SAFEGUARD INDUSTRIES, INC., AND SUBSIDIARIES
Consolidated Statement of Changes in Financial Position

| | Year Ended December 31 | |
	1976	1975
Working Capital Used		
Reduction of long-term debt	9,097,700	2,919,500
Expenditures for property, plant and equipment	4,460,400	1,777,800
Acquisition of minority interest	2,692,200	
Retirement of subordinated notes	335,000	
Dividends paid	359,400	17,700
Other assets, net	262,700	196,100
Working Capital Used	17,207,400	4,911,100
Increase in Working Capital	$ 715,400	$ 449,800
Changes in Working Capital		
Current Assets increase (decrease)		
Cash	$ (254,700)	$ 469,200
Receivables	1,920,400	434,300
Recoverable income taxes		(1,216,100)
Inventories	1,534,800	(1,610,200)
Prepaid expenses	56,300	230,400
	3,256,800	(1,692,400)
Current Liabilities increase (decrease)		
Notes payable	145,000	(2,200,000)
Accounts payable	1,932,800	(477,200)
Accrued expenses	292,000	101,000
Taxes on income	435,500	1,140,300
Current maturities of long-term debt	(263,900)	(706,300)
	2,541,400	(2,142,200)
Increase in Working Capital	$ 715,400	$ 449,800

EXHIBIT 22 (cont.)

SAFEGUARD INDUSTRIES, INC., AND SUBSIDIARIES
Consolidated Statement of Earnings

| | Year Ended December 31 | |
	1976	1975
Revenues		
Net sales	$106,545,900	$90,212,700
Other income	596,100	447,500
	107,142,000	90,660,200
Cost and Expenses		
Material, labor, and other	63,360,800	54,223,200
Selling	22,334,200	18,748,900
General and administrative	12,146,000	9,730,700
Depreciation and amortization	1,941,000	1,825,100
Interest	1,750,100	2,115,400
(Income) loss on equity investments, net	(220,400)	149,800
Minority interest	20,000	179,000
Loss on investments	660,000	500,000
	101,991,700	84,472,100
Earnings before Taxes on Income	5,150,300	3,188,100
Taxes on income	2,360,000	1,682,000
Earnings before Extraordinary Charge	2,790,300	1,506,100
Extraordinary charge		507,000
Net Earnings	$ 2,790,300	$ 999,100
Earnings Per Share of Common Stock		
Earnings before extraordinary charge	$.66	$.37
Extraordinary charge		(.13)
Net earnings	$.66	$.24
Assuming full dilution:		
Earnings before extraordinary charge	$.63	$.35
Extraordinary charge		(.12)
Net earnings	$.63	$.23
Average common shares outstanding	4,051,000	4,052,000

THE COLONIAL PIPELINE CO.

Colonial Pipeline Co. was incorporated in 1962. The firm built a pipeline from Houston, Texas, to Linden, New Jersey, to serve two basic needs: 1) to supply the growing requirement for petroleum products in the Southeast and 2) to supply a through route for the surplus products of the Gulf Coast refining area to serve the increasing demand of the large metropolitan areas of the northeastern United States.

The pipeline provided an efficient, dependable and economical means of transportation for vast quantities of gasoline, kerosene, home heating oils, diesel fuels, turbine fuels, and other refined petroleum products to a number of cities in the southeastern part of the United States. In addition the line served such major areas along the eastern seaboard as Washington, Baltimore, Philadelphia, and the New York harbor. (See Exhibit 1.)

The company was a common carrier regulated by the Interstate Commerce Commission and its services were available to all shippers without discrimination. The initial system consisted of some 1540 miles of main line ranging from thirty to thirty-six inches in diameter, 1487 miles of lateral lines ranging from six to twenty-two inches in diameter, ten source points, and deliveries to approximately 194 marketing terminals and interconnections with five other carrier pipelines.

Construction of the original system was completed early in 1965 with a capacity of 732,000 barrels per day. Initial shipments

approximated 600,000 barrels per day. Less than a year later management realized that additional capacity would be needed. Early in 1966 a four-step expansion program was initiated, increasing the line's capacity to 1,152,000 barrels per day.

With many prospects for increased competition from new shippers, Colonial in 1971 invested $124 million in another program that increased main line mileage to 2000; lateral line mileage to 1600; tankage to approximately 24,000,000 barrels and capacity from 1,152,000 to 1,584,000 barrels per day, or double the original 1965 capacity. This second expansion was completed in May 1972.

The Colonial system was carefully designed and engineered to exceed the requirements of all industry codes and government safety regulations. During twelve years of operation it had transported 4.6 billion barrels of essential petroleum products without causing a single death or harming the environment. Colonial utilized the latest fail-safe devices and continued to improve its system as technology advanced.

HISTORY

The Colonial project did not emerge overnight. Such a pipeline had been under consideration for over twenty years, dating back to the early days of World War II when existing modes of fuel transportation were insufficient to meet this country's defense efforts. Two earlier attempts to build a line to the east coast, one by U.S. Pipe Line Co. in 1951 to 1952, and the other by American Pipeline Corp. in 1953 to 1954, failed for lack of financing, even after those firms had obtained steel alloca-

This case was prepared by June Brownstein, Gary Finger, Dale Kramer, and Richard Steingraber under the supervision of Professor Jules J. Schwartz, as the basis for class discussion rather than to illustrate either effective or ineffective handling of an administrative action.

73

tions from the Petroleum Administration for Defense (PAD) and accelerated tax write-off approvals.

A pipeline extending from the Gulf Coast to the New York harbor area could not have been built by any one oil company, for no single company could have provided the volume of products necessary to use a line of sufficient diameter to be economically feasible. A million-barrels-per-day line capable of competing with tankers could only be financed and built as a joint venture by a number of oil companies. The following companies own Colonial Pipeline:

	Stock ownership
Gulf Oil Corp.	16.78%
Amoco Pipe Line Co. (Standard Oil of Indiana)	14.32
Texaco, Inc.	14.27
Cities Service Co.	13.98
Mobil Pipe Line Co. (Mobil Oil)	11.49
B.P. Oil, Inc. (Standard Oil of Ohio)	8.96
Continental Pipe Line Co. (Continental Oil)	7.55
Phillips Petroleum International Investment Co.	7.10
Union Oil of California	3.97
Atlantic-Richfield	1.58
	100.00%

Petroleum pipelines in this country have traditionally been conceived and built by oil companies or their pipeline affiliates. Because the fixed-capital investment in a pipeline is substantial, an assured, continuous throughput at near capacity levels is required if the line is to operate successfully. An assured throughput sufficient to permit profitable operation of the line is a prerequisite in obtaining financing and is even more critical in the case of a pipeline than in other modes of transportation. One could not expect oil companies to enter into this kind of long-range financial commitment without having some part of the ownership and reward for assuming the risk.

Common carrier pipeline transportation differs from other forms of common carrier transportation because pipelines serve only one industry and move over fixed routes in one direction with fixed points of delivery. Other modes of transportation can handle several types of freight flowing in different directions for many different industries. Once a pipeline is installed it is dependent upon the oil industry it serves to provide liquid petroleum to move over these fixed routes. While it is true that in some instances a line reversal might be practicable, it would completely change the economics of the project. Colonial's required minimum throughput was estimated at about 650,000 barrels per day. The total volume available from the original nine owners of Colonial was required to maintain this minimum.

Colonial had historically financed its long-term capital needs through 10 percent equity and 90 percent long-term borrowings. (See Exhibit 2.) The security offered through the backing of its stockholders, in the form of the throughput agreement, qualified Colonial's debt issues for a ready market at favorable rates, with high ratings assigned to the bonds by the rating agencies. The ratings are the average of those of its stockholders. In other words the rating agencies looked to the throughput agreement and beyond that to the stockholders in assigning the rating to Colonial.

Without the throughput agreement or similar financial commitment by substantial companies, Colonial could not have borrowed enough money to meet its capital needs. This would have left the equity market as the only other means of furnishing permanent capital, and investors would have demanded a return commensurate with their higher risk.

If Colonial had raised capital wholly by equity in the public market, its cost of capital would probably have been much higher. Accordingly Colonial would have had to charge more for transportation services.

The uncertainties associated with a company such as Colonial would be considered well above an average risk by an investor if no throughput agreement from the owners existed. All these factors would have been taken into consideration in any future expansion program proposed by Colonial.

The total initial capital required by Colonial was approximately $378 million; since 1962 the firm's capital increased to $542 million. Economic necessity required that Colonial build a large diameter joint venture line. Pipelines need a high original investment and have a relatively low annual operating cost. Construction costs increase at a much slower rate than the diameter of the line.

Colonial's fixed costs for 1974 were approximately $80 million. In terms of risk this means that for every day the system is completely shut down for whatever reason, the company incurs a cost of approximately $219,000 with no operating revenue to apply against this cost. Fortunately for Colonial partial or complete shutdowns do not occur frequently. However, shutdowns are unpredictable, except for planned maintenance or construction, and there is no way to make up the loss in revenue.

Pipeline rates average about 20 percent of that of railroads and 3.6 percent of that of trucks and can usually compete favorably with all marine transportation except ocean going, long-haul, jumbo tankers. Moreover average pipeline rates increased only 1.03 percent during the twenty-five-year period from 1947 to 1972 in sharp contrast to rail and truck rates, which increased about 47 percent and 65 percent, respectively. In 1976 the cost of transporting petroleum products from Houston to metropolitan New York was less than one cent a gallon, one-eighth the price of mailing a post card.

Colonial headquarters in Atlanta, Georgia, maintained a staff of 130 employees. In addition there were 459 operating and maintenance employees in the field. They were based in an Atlanta suburb, Sandy Springs, and in Richmond, Virginia. In addition to the 589 full-time employees, varying numbers of maintenance personnel were hired under contractual arrangements. Colonial maintained an average

of approximately $1 million per employee invested in facilities, as compared with approximately $80,000 to $85,000 per employee in the oil industry, and about $50,000 per employee for industry in general. The high degree of automation made this possible; many locations were operated for periods of time on an unattended fail-safe basis.

In Exhibit 3 is a diagram of the firm's organizational chart. Colonial's board of directors, which met quarterly, consisted of one director from each of the stockholder companies. The president reported to the board of directors.

Three main functional areas were headed by the vice president and general counsel, the vice president of administration, and the vice president of operations. Reporting to the vice president of operations were the department managers for engineering, project management (right-of-way acquisition), products movement, and purchasing and materials, as well as the two regional managers (western and eastern). The regions were broken up into areas, each of which was headed up by an area manager. The vice president of administration had reporting to him the department managers of employee and community relations, information systems (including the computer department), treasury (including taxes), and the accounting department, planning and the chief pilot. The vice president and general counsel had the manager of right-of-way reporting to him.

Why was Colonial able to face and solve the many problems that had doomed similar proposals for a pipeline along the east coast?

One Colonial executive was able to answer this question. "I think the one basic reason it went so smoothly," he said, "was experienced personnel. The cream-of-the-crop were assigned to Colonial by the nine owner oil companies. You get the best brains in the business pooling their talents on a job like this, and there isn't anything they can't do. Colonial proves it. They did it."

The practice of using a great number of specialists temporarily was certainly an essential factor in Colonial's basic organization. From conception of the pipeline company through its construction stage, key experienced personnel, temporarily loaned to Colonial by the participating oil companies, served as field supervisors and inspectors, as specialists in design engineering, purchasing, transportation, and various other phases of company operations, and as decisionmakers in top-level management.

When their jobs were completed, and their talents were no longer needed by Colonial, these people returned to their positions with their respective oil companies. This "instant expertise" made available to Colonial a fortune in training and experience and knowledge at just the cost of salary.

COLONIAL'S SYSTEM

The most important asset that Colonial maintained was its complex, fully-automated pipeline system. Along the route of the main line there were thirteen tank farms strategically located to receive products from the main line for further distribution into shipper terminals at those same locations and also to supply the various spur pipelines. These tank farms ranged in size from five to seventy-one tanks. Because of the high rate of flow through the Colonial main line, delivery was made into this operating tankage for redelivery to shipper terminal tankage. The shippers' tankage could not handle the high rates of flow directly.

No tankage was provided by Colonial for storage, holding, or terminaling purposes. The system necessarily operated on a "full" basis with a barrel entering the system for every barrel delivered. There were 17 million barrels of liquid petroleum products in the system at any one time. Typical in-transit times were:

Houston to Atlanta	4.5 days
Houston to Greensboro	6.5 days
Houston to New York	11.0 days

At current pumping rates, speed of flow through the thirty-six-inch segment was 7.5 mph, 6.5 mph through the thirty-two-inch segment, and 7.0 mph through the thirty-inch segment.

Pump stations receiving the products into the system were located in Houston, Port Arthur, and Beaumont, Texas; Lake Charles and Baton Rouge, Louisiana; and Collins, Mississippi. Through these initiating locations products were received from twenty-three shippers with a total of 109 different grades of product. Seven of these products were handled on a fungible basis, that is, one might be replaced by another subject to the receiver's acceptance. The remainder of the products, including all gasoline products, were handled on a segregated basis.

To operate a pipeline system this extensive, Colonial had a supervisory system located at its control center in Atlanta. This control system provided high-speed data gathering and panel display, status and alarm display in the event of a changed condition, and remote station control. A distinctive feature of the control system was the central intelligence provided by two process-type computers that scanned the system between Houston and New York every ten seconds, updating the information.

When in normal operation the primary computer controlled the supervisory system. A second computer served as a backup to take over operations in the event of a malfunction in the primary system. All main line booster stations were remotely controlled from the Atlanta control center. Remotely operated pump stations were located on all other spur lines and were controlled by pump station personnel located at the initial point of the spur line rather than by the Atlanta control center. Pressure readings, flow rates, signals of units in operation, and other data were continuously transmitted to the Atlanta control center to provide the dispatcher with a full knowledge of station operation.

Shipments were received from shipper tank farms at refineries or other locations connected to the system. The products movement department accumulated shipper requirements, planned the flow of products through the system, coordinated operation details, and accounted for specific products on a daily basis.

Scheduling

The job of planning exactly how product batches would move, precisely when they should be extracted, how to keep each shipper's products separate from those of other shippers, and how to protect against contamination or undesirable degrading among similar products was complex. All these factors had to be coordinated in order to make a schedule that insured the efficient and smooth delivery of shipper products.

The key to Colonial's scheduling was the ten-day product cycle. This meant that each shipper's grades of products would be picked up and delivered at ten-day intervals. Each cycle was made up of a series of batches arranged in proper sequence. The sequence used aimed to control contamination and to protect and insure quality of product at destination points. Once scheduling details were worked out execution fell to the dispatchers, who coordinated the activities of operating personnel so the products would flow through the pipe as scheduled.

The dispatchers in the Atlanta control center had a three-pronged job, which involved keeping track of all batches in the line, operating remote facilities, and issuing operating instructions to field personnel. The dispatchers had to know exactly where each batch was located with respect to each delivery point or pumping station, the scheduling of the next batch, and the status of all current and succeeding deliveries.

Colonial believed it could not sustain its high level of line utilization without the supervisory control equipment, the function of which was to supply the dispatchers with operating information from all locations along the system and to permit the dispatchers to control pumping units. In operating thirty-two pump stations in series between Houston and Greensboro, the transfer of information had to be fast and accurate.

One of the most difficult problems in pipeline operation was the actual movement of a number of different products through the same pipeline. The receiving, handling, and delivering of a variety of products belonging to a number of different shippers was a complicated operation and required continuous coordination.

The various shippers compiled a listing of their product requirements for a thirty- to sixty-day period and requested the pipeline to transport the product from the lifting locations to their terminals at various points on the pipeline. The company then organized a sequence of requested products that would satisfy the delivery requirements of all shippers and permit economical operation of the pipeline. The pumping program was subject to frequent revisions, necessitated by fluctuating consumer demands.

One means of meeting fluctuating demands was to make batches as large as possible, within the constraints of customer requirements. A minimum batch size of 75,000 barrels had been established for the Colonial pipeline system to meet this need and keep the pumping schedule within reasonable quantities. Fluctuations of supply and demand were not within complete control of the shipper. The pipeline had therefore to allow the shipper to make revisions in his proposed shipping schedule. With many different products and a number of shippers, rescheduling usually became almost a continuous operation.

The dispatching department was responsible for the actual movement of product into and out of the pipeline system. Dispatchers had to issue the daily and hourly operating instructions to all stations. It was the dispatcher's responsibility to see that the batches went into the line on time and in the quantity scheduled, were kept on schedule throughout the trip and were delivered to the proper terminals with a minimum amount of contamination. To carry out this function properly, the dispatcher had to be allowed a certain amount of leeway to change planned operations and he had to be supplied with all data that would affect operations in any way over the entire system.

Quality

Colonial maintained product integrity throughout its system with the capability of handling as segregated batches 100 separate products out of a total of 109 different entry points. All costs of contamination occurring as a result of .handling these products was absorbed by Colonial. All shippers were guaranteed delivery on a 100 percent of barrels tendered basis.

The Colonial pipeline system provided, in addition to low cost, an efficient means of transportation with an unequalled safety record. The system was entirely underground and had little effect on surface use of land or aesthetic values. It was a very secure and dependable form of transportation because Colonial operated continuously and quietly, unaffected by surface conditions, such as storms, ice, fog, or accidents. The system did not require the return of empty containers to the starting point and did not pollute the atmosphere, block traffic, or clutter up the highways. It was the safest, most economical, and efficient means of transporting petroleum products.

THE INTERSTATE COMMERCE ACT

Interstate oil pipelines were made common carriers subject to regulation under Part 1 of the Interstate Commerce Act by the Hepburn Amendment of 1906. Under the Interstate Commerce Act, a common carrier pipeline's tariffs had to be just and reasonable and equally applicable to owners and nonowners, had to be filed with the Interstate Commerce Commission (ICC) before transportation of products began, and had to be applicable to all shippers on a nondiscriminatory basis. Reasonable facilities for delivery of products to connecting lines also had to be provided on a nondiscriminatory basis.

Violation of the Interstate Commerce Act could· subject the violator to a proceeding before the ICC, as welł as a federal court action, and was punishable by penalties that could include both fines and imprisonment. The ICC had broad remedial powers under the act, should the pipeline fail to conduct its operations in accordance with statutory and regulatory requirements.

Fred F. Steingraber, former president of the Colonial Pipeline Co., in his statement to the Subcommittee on Antitrust and Monopoly of the Senate Committee on the Judiciary, said:

> Such pervasive regulation by the ICC should and does ensure that pipelines will. be operated as common carriers in every sense of the word, and that their operations and practices will be fair and reasonable and will place no one at a competitive disadvantage, even though this ensurement is already dictated and made necessary by the forces of competition with tankers, barges, rail tank cars, trucks, and other pipelines.

A United States Senate committee had considered a modified version of Senator Haskell's amendment to the Alaska Pipeline Bill that would require divestiture of any ownership or interest in common carrier pipelines by companies that produced or refined crude oil to insure observation of the ICC's tariff guidelines. Passage of such a bill might create serious problems concerning the future ownership and construction of new pipeline facilities.

Exhibit 4 shows oil pipeline shipments in the United States for 1973, broken down by nonowner shippers and shipper owners as well as between independents and majors.

A prime example of the evidence that influenced the Haskell proposal was the testimony presented by a Colonial shipper, which implied that it had difficulty getting onto the system as a nonowner shipper. This company was invited to and attended a prospective shipper's meeting called by Colonial on May 7, 1963, attended by twenty-three prospective shippers (including nine Colonial owners). This meeting was held prior to the beginning of Colonial's operations and while the system was still under construction.

The company's first request to become a shipper on Colonial was on September 4, 1970.

On that date Colonial was advised on what the shipping firm's initial requirements would be in December 1970. On October 21, 1970, Colonial urged the firm to meet with it as soon as possible in order to schedule an allocation to meet both companies' time tables. The company actually began shipping on the Colonial system on January 1, 1971. Space was allocated in accordance to the company's forecast, reduced by the percentage of proration in effect at that time under Colonial's proration policy. (See Exhibit 5.) This policy had been in effect and applied uniformly to all shippers since July 1967, when the Colonial system first went on full-time proration.

Tariffs generally provided that when tendered shipments exceeded the capacity of the line, any transportation furnished by the line would be ratably apportioned among all shippers who are then tendering product. To protect shippers further against discrimination, a pipeline was prohibited from disclosing to others data concerning volumes shipped and their destinations.

Colonial felt that in this decision the request to become a shipper was processed into the schedule as quickly as possible, was consistent with the handling of all new shippers' requests, and conformed to the time table that shipper had set for itself.

Since 1969 approximately fifteen similar cases protesting the tariffs of one or more pipelines have been filed and considered by the ICC. These protests have raised and put in issue questions such as whether the line's valuation base, which determines rates, is excessive and thus permits the carrier to earn an unacceptably high rate of return; whether the line's rates or revenues per mile, when compared to those of other pipelines and other carriers, are excessive; whether new service, storage, loading, and unloading charges are excessive or discriminatory; and whether rates and charges are discriminatory because they grant an undue preference to other shippers, served by the same carrier, in different areas. These cases prove that shippers were willing to challenge pipeline rates and

practices when they felt it was in their interests to do so and that the ICC acted promptly on such challenges.

Two additional issues, the earnings and dividends of interstate oil pipelines, had been the subject of extensive litigation resulting in the Elkins Act Consent Decree. This decree limited pipeline annual dividend payments to shipper-owners to no more than 7 percent of its ICC valuation. This valuation included properties purchased with borrowed funds. Colonial operated within this decree, and reported annually on both earnings and dividends.

GROWTH AND EXPANSION

There had always been a tremendous logistic problem in the distribution of petroleum products in the United States. The seventeen eastern seaboard states consumed 39.8 percent of the nation's petroleum products, but produced only one-half of one percent of the crude oil. East coast refineries processed about one-fourth of the area's demand. This complex problem had been compounded by the present energy shortage, the uncertainty as to volumes, locations and kinds of imports, and ecological impediments.

Meanwhile the use of oil pipelines for transport had been increasing faster than the demands for petroleum products. Since the original Colonial system was built Colonial had doubled its capacity at a cost of approximately $200 million. This additional investment had been added to the original owner's commitment, while the nonowner shippers were able to utilize the availability of additional space without financial commitments of any kind, other than the tariff obligation.

Concurrent with such growth come two major factors that must be considered: acquisition of the rights of way, and safety. Before a pipeline can become a reality its builders must select the most feasible, practical route. In building its network Colonial made every effort to avoid densely-populated residential and industrial areas, while making allowance for its prime objective to serve key markets in congested metropolitan areas. Once the proposed route had been determined, action to acquire the necessary rights of way began.

Rights of Way

An oil pipeline right of way such as Colonial's is unusual in at least one respect. Unlike other rights of way, such as for a public highway or a railroad, the easements do not deprive the property owner of many normal uses of his land. The pipeline is buried in the ground at a minimum of thirty inches, so the land owner may grow grass above it or even farm above it, as long as he does not penetrate the earth too deeply.

The most important accomplishment of Colonial's right-of-way program, however, was that the pipeline went to all reasonable lengths in negotiating with the owners in order to reach an agreement without going to court to obtain easements through condemnation proceedings. The legal key here is the power of eminent domain. This law confers upon civil authorities and companies that operate in the public interest the right to obtain land at a fair price from property owners who impede completion of a project for one reason or another.

The right to eminent domain is conferred to pipelines by most states (excluding North Carolina, Alabama, and Maryland) in a similar pattern:

1. Pipelines must first negotiate with the land owner in an effort to work out a mutually satisfactory agreement.
2. Failing to agree, the company must file a petition with an appropriate court asking legal assistance to obtain use of the land at a fair price.
3. The court appoints a group to hold hearings to determine a settlement agreement fair to all parties concerned.

In acquiring the land for its 2,900 miles of pipeline Colonial has fared well. Some 17,000 individual easements were acquired, in addition to some 5000 permit acquisitions to accommodate crossings of highways, railways,

city streets, and rivers. Of this total Colonial authorized its legal department to file for condemnation in 668 individual cases. Of this number, however, only 122 have gone to hearings. Once the negotiations for the rights-of-way are completed, construction can proceed.

In the interest of safety and efficiency the entire Colonial system was built in accordance with rigid codes and engineering standards prescribed for the industry. Colonial spent millions of dollars on control equipment and safety features not required by industry codes. Steingraber commented, "We have never sacrificed quality or safety by buying inferior equipment. I do not believe that the question of safety, involving the possible loss of life or injury, should ever be reduced to a cold statistic in terms of dollars and cents. The most profitable pipelines are safe pipelines. If they are not safe, they cannot be profitable."

A New Project

In November 1975 Colonial approved the addition of an $88 million pipeline paralleling its existing thirty-six-inch system between Beaumont, Texas, and Baton Rouge, Louisiana. The project would consist primarily of 185 miles of forty-inch pipeline between the two cities. The new system of pipes, called "looping," would increase capacity about 12 percent for the entire operation, an increase to 180,000 total barrels handled per day.

A community relations official reported that Colonial expected to get this new expansion under way just as soon as it could get materials and labor on the site. Colonial had already placed orders for pipe and other equipment for the project and the new system was to be completed by December 1976.

The cost of pipelines had been rising sharply; each new project had to compete in the market for speculative money. Pipeline projects are now also finding it harder to take advantage of lower interest rates and long-term private financing made possible by the shipper-owners, high credit ratings, and financial commitments.

EXHIBIT 1

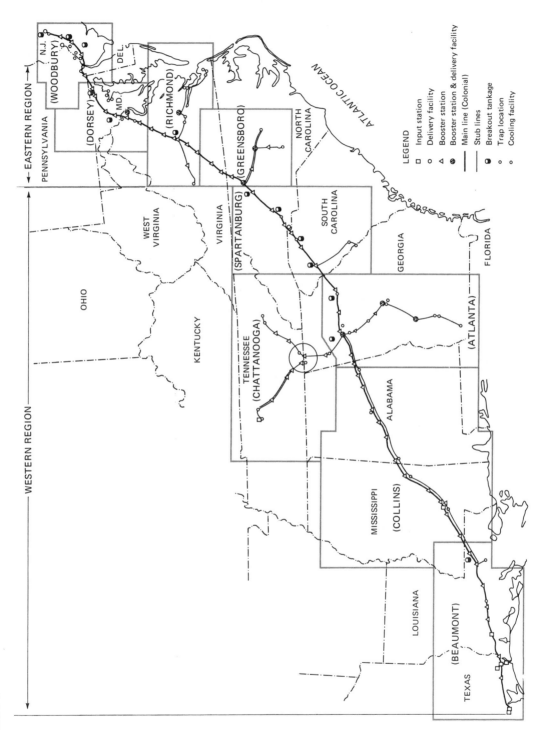

EXHIBIT 2

COLONIAL PIPELINE COMPANY
Balance Sheet at December 31, 1974
Whole Dollars (Final Unaudited)

ASSETS

Cash in Banks	419,325	
Short-Term Investments	20,219,005	20,638,330
Receivable from Affiliated Companies		11,889,307
Accounts Receivable		9,295,213
Interest Receivable		82,352
Material and Supplies		1,544,558
Prepayments		43,633
Other Current Assets		42,900
Investments in Affiliated Companies		227,052
Sinking and Other Funds		20,486
Property, Plant, and Equipment	538,818,056	
Accrued Depreciation	122,024,762–	416,793,294
Noncarrier Property, Plant, and Equipment	1,997,646	
Noncarrier Accrued Depreciation	81,506–	1,916,140
Organization Costs		38,629
Miscellaneous Other Assets		5,705
Other Deferred Charges		1,011,933
Total Assets		463,549,532

LIABILITIES AND CAPITAL

Payable to Affiliated Companies		197,951
Accounts Payable		6,756,893
Salaries and Wages Payable		937,579
Interest Payable		1,980,433
Dividends Payable		
Taxes Payable		8,969,274
Long-Term Debt Payable within 1 yr Series A, C, D, F and G		11,938,000
Other Current Liabilities		49,124
Long-Term Debt Payable after 1 Year		
Series A–4.829% Notes Due 6/1/90	167,751,000	
Series C–4.736% Notes Due 6/1/90	15,095,000	
Series D–5.464% Notes Due 6/1/90	20,376,000	
Series E–6.500% Notes Due 6/1/02	50,000,000	
Series F–8.500% Notes Due 6/1/02	72,450,000	
Series G–7.875% Notes Due 6/1/02	48,260,000	373,932,000
Other Noncurrent Liabilities		435,879
Acc. Deferred Income Tax Credits		9,573,000
Capital Stock		
Common Stock, $1,000 Par Value		
60,000 Shares Authorized		
36,000 Shares Issued		36,000,000
Additional Paid-In Capital		10,980,000
Unappropriated Retained Income		
Beginning Balance	5,233,010	
Current Year to Date Earnings	26,914,389	
Dividends Declared	30,348,000–	1,799,399
Total Liabilities and Capital		463,549,532

EXHIBIT 3

COLONIAL PIPELINE CO.
Organizational Chart

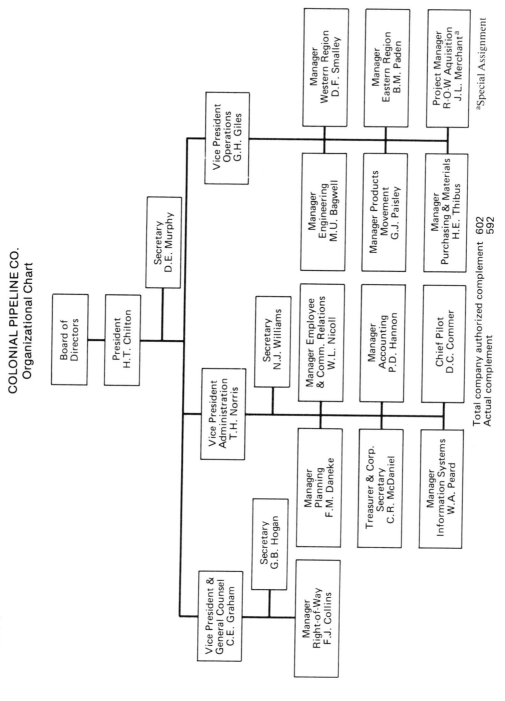

Board of Directors

President
H.T. Chilton

Secretary
D.E. Murphy

Vice President
Administration
T.H. Norris

Vice President
Operations
G.H. Giles

Vice President &
General Counsel
C.E. Graham

Secretary
G.B. Hogan

Manager
Right-of-Way
F.J. Collins

Secretary
N.J. Williams

Manager
Planning
F.M. Daneke

Manager Employee
& Comm. Relations
W.L. Nicoll

Treasurer & Corp.
Secretary
C.R. McDaniel

Manager
Accounting
P.D. Hannon

Manager
Information Systems
W.A. Peard

Chief Pilot
D.C. Commer

Manager
Engineering
M.U. Bagwell

Manager Products
Movement
G.J. Paisley

Manager
Purchasing & Materials
H.E. Thibus

Manager
Western Region
D.F. Smalley

Manager
Eastern Region
B.M. Paden

Project Manager
R-O-W Aquisition
J.L. Merchant[a]

Total company authorized complement 602
Actual complement   592

[a]Special Assignment

EXHIBIT 4
Oil Pipeline Shipments in the U.S., 1973

	Product pipelines	Crude trunk lines	Gathering systems
Total number of shippers	909	559	291
Nonowner shippers	806	491	252
Owner shippers	103	68	39

Breakdown of Nonowner Shippers and Owner
Shippers between Independent and Major[a] Companies

	Product pipelines	Crude trunk lines	Gathering systems
Nonowner shippers			
Independent	573	292	146
Majors[a]	233	199	106
Total	806	491	252
Owner shippers			
Independent	17	17	9
Majors[a]	86	51	30
Total	103	68	39

[a]Majors include Exxon, Gulf, Standard (Ind.), Texaco, Shell, ARCO, Mobil, Socal, Sun, Union, Phillips, Continental, Cities Service, Getty, Sohio, Hess, Skelly, and Marathon.

EXHIBIT 5

COLONIAL PIPELINE COMPANY
Proration Policy

Colonial's main line and some of its stub lines become completely full from time to time and are prorated among all shippers on an equitable basis. New shippers who are accepted during times of proration must realize that space allocations for all shippers may be less than nominations, depending upon the extent of proration in effect at the time. Proration is handled as follows.

Allocations to New Shippers

A "new shipper" is any shipper (as defined in Colonial's published tariff) who does not qualify as a regular shipper. The shipper will become a regular shipper at the end of thirteen months from the beginning of the first month in which the new shipper received deliveries.

A new shipper requesting space during periods of proration (and who has otherwise satisfied applicable requirements of the tariff rules) will be allocated space as follows: New shipper forecast volumes will be added to the aggregate of the regular shipper forecasts to determine the demand for pipeline space in each month. The forecast volumes of each new shipper will then be reduced proportionately by the extent that total forecast volumes exceed total line capacity. The total forecast volumes of regular shippers will also be reduced by the same percentage.

Allocations to Regular Shippers

Space (adjusted as described in paragraph 2.5.1) will be allocated to regular shippers on the historical percentage basis that the total barrels shipped by and delivered to each regular shipper bears to the total barrels shipped by and delivered to all regular shippers during the twelve-month period ending one month prior to the month of allocation.

General Requirements

Colonial will carefully examine forecasts using every means available to ensure that they are true and realistic and will challenge any forecasts that appear to be inflated. To maintain equitable allocation of space on the system, if a new shipper is unable to deliver products equal to the space allocated to it and such inability has not been caused by *force majeure* or other cause beyond control of such shipper, satisfactory to Colonial, its volumes for the following month will be reduced by the amount of allocated throughput not utilized during the preceding month.

In no event will any portion of an allocation granted to a new shipper be used in such manner that it will increase the allocation of another shipper beyond what it is entitled to under the proration policy. Colonial will require written assurances from responsible officials of shippers respecting use of allocated space stating that this requirement has not been violated. In the event any new shipper should, by any device, scheme or arrangement whatsoever, make available to another shipper, or in the event any shipper should receive and use any space from a new shipper through violation of this requirement, the allocated space for both shippers will be reduced to the extent of the excess space so made available or used in the shipping cycles next following discovery of the violation that are under proration.

Colonial reserves the right to adjust any shipper's allocation in the event of a substantial sale, transfer, or change affecting that shipper's throughput that served as the basis for the allocation.

If any shipper, new or regular, is unable to deliver products equal to the space allocated because of a strike, labor slowdown, or fire or other *force majeure,* Colonial may adjust the allocations to prevent the loss of that shipper's allocation percentage.

Source: Colonial Pipeline Company manual titled "Shipping Instructions."

FLAGSTAFF CORPORATION

Flagstaff Corporation is one of the nation's "Big Six" institutional food distributor chains and the largest distributor in the Northeast. Flagstaff attributed its last seven years of record sales to its acquisition program and its role as a pioneer in the food distribution business. Frozen foods had become pivotal in the entire Flagstaff operation. The company distributed a full line of products to its customers and prided itself on the individuality of its operations.

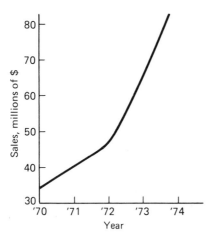

A major question before the Flagstaff directors in 1975 was the possibility of adding Coffee-Mat Corporation to its list of acquisitions. Coffee-Mat primarily designs, manufactures, and sells coin-operated hot beverage dispensing machines.

This case was prepared by Pauline J. Albert under the supervision of Professor Jules J. Schwartz as a basis for class discussion rather than to illustrate either effective or ineffective handling of an administrative action.

86

FLAGSTAFF HISTORY

A. Peltz and Sons, a small produce and bakery supplies distributor, was founded in New York in 1895 by Adolph Peltz, grandfather of the present Flagstaff managers. In the 1940s the firm went into the frozen foods business, buying and selling within the food service industry, principally for Snow Crop of New York. The firm began to branch out in 1969, with the formation of APS Food Systems. The company's main objective was to set up a distribution network in the Northeast. A further move in this direction occurred in the same year when APS acquired Miller Produce Company of Boston, a leading institutional frozen food distributor. In early 1970 APS purchased Philadelphia Portion Pak, another frozen food distributor. With the addition of Eichorn Food Products of Baltimore in 1971, APS covered almost the entire Northeast with its frozen food line.

In 1971, when APS merged on a pooling-of-interest basis with Flagstaff/Flink Corporation, a small public company, it was able to offer a full line of institutional food supplies. Flagstaff/Flink had been the result of a 1969 merger of B. Flink and Sons and Flagstaff Foods. Both carried frozen foods but their major strength was in groceries. Flagstaff also sold supplies and equipment. The new company changed its name to Flagstaff Corporation and made a public stock offering shortly after the merger. In 1972 Flagstaff acquired Irving Levitt Company and Nathan Kadish Corporation. Both were institutional meat processing and distribution operations located in Boston. In 1973 Trenton Frozen Foods, a frozen food distributor, was added to the list of acquisitions. Philadelphia Portion Pak was then integrated with the Trenton firm in a new Trenton distribution center as the Flagstaff Food Service Company, Delaware Valley Division. Flagstaff entered into dairy distribution in 1973 with the purchase of H. Wool and Sons, Inc., of New York.

The eight distribution centers operated by Flagstaff were located throughout the Northeast and served customers from Maine to Virginia. Flagstaff's rapid, yet carefully planned growth during the last five years was accomplished through the use of unsecured loans and the proceeds of its 1972 public offering. The objective of the acquisition program centered around the expansion of company activities into a full-line operation with a sales force marketing a complete line of products. The Peltz brothers saw the need for a large distributor that could provide over 90 percent of the products needed by institutional food operators. All food items, except for highly perishable produce, and many nonfood items, including equipment and dispenser products, could then be offered by one distributor. In addition a better working relationship would be established with customers. With the trend toward convenience food items, the need for a distributor such as Flagstaff became even more evident.

THE FOOD SERVICE INDUSTRY

With more wives working, more disposable income and more mobility, the food service industry had undergone explosive growth since World War II. In the last decade volume had more than doubled, reaching $65 billion in 1974. This represented about 40 percent of the American food dollar. The business involved many uncertainties however, because of its labor-intensive as well as food-intensive nature. Labor and food costs, which presently account for 50 to 60 percent of retail operating expenses, had risen at extraordinary rates.

The industry had undergone, and was continuing to experience, a great deal of change. Eating out had become routine for the average American. It had become so ingrained that it was no longer considered a luxury or even a special occasion.

The food service industry was a highly diffuse business, which only complicated the problem of soaring costs. Each segment of the market was different. Factories and offices were totally different from hospitals, and these contrasted with fast food chains and airlines. Each had a different purpose, different food, different hiring and training systems, and each fed different kinds of people. Soaring costs were only part of the problem faced by the institutional food service business. Schools, factories, hospitals, and other institutions dealt with a captive market that guaranteed a continuing group of customers. This also often meant feeding the same group on a daily basis and presented a constant problem of providing quality and variety while holding down costs. All these factors made institutional feeding very difficult.

Labor had become one of the most critical problems within many segments of the industry, resulting in a greater demand for frozen convenience foods to eliminate the need for highly trained labor. Some hospitals had done away with their big kitchens and were using a system of microwave ovens for cooking flash-frozen entrees. Trays of food were delivered daily and refrigerated until needed. Kitchens that formerly might have employed forty people were operating with four.

One chain of restaurants decided it wanted to beat the costs by kicking the convenience food habit. It learned an interesting lesson. Rather than buying frozen main dishes, it began cooking from scratch. The change required more skilled labor, and good cooks cost between $5 and $6 per hour. The net result was an 8 percent drop in product costs with a 12 to 15 percent rise in labor costs.

Standardization was becoming more widespread, even in higher-priced restaurants. Supplying restaurants were scores of frozen food companies. The negative image associated with the American T.V. dinner was being fought most effectively by these companies, though many eating establishments would not admit their use of frozen products, for fear of this stigma. The typical restaurant commercial freezers held all types of food —from sauces and shrimp to dishes like beef stew, lasagna, flounder, lobster newburg, and chicken in wine sauce. Many of these seasonal products were impossible to transport and store fresh. In any case if these dishes were not frozen, there might not be enough fine chefs to go around. There were nearly 100,000 "quality" restaurants in the United States, yet there were perhaps only one-tenth that number of gourmet chefs, according to industry sources. With frozen foods, lower-skilled labor could be used. This enabled owners to hold down costs while maintaining or increasing quality, as frozen foods were often produced under the direction of highly-trained chefs. An example of the changing trend was demonstrated when Flagstaff drew compliments from the Wine and Food Society of New York after serving them an all-frozen-food dinner at the renowned "21" Club, which had built a reputation on serving only fresh foods in season.

Good management had also become a critical issue. For public eating places, rising costs had changed many priorities. Average net margins were down to 3 to 5 percent; some restaurants averaged as little as 1 to 1.5 percent and others were losing money. Many fancy big city restaurants were closing their doors only to be replaced by fast food operations or limited menu restaurants.

The food service business had thus undergone a great deal of change and was likely to experience even more as Americans continued to increase their away-from-home food consumption. Predictions were that by 1980 half of the American food dollar would be spent away from home.

Flagstaff Corporation felt that this kind of growth potential was promising for the larger supplier who could provide the big food servers with consistent quality service and timely delivery at low prices.

FLAGSTAFF SERVICES AND PHILOSOPHIES

Flagstaff Corporation had grown rapidly in its services to the away-from-home food market. It had built its sales leadership in the last ten years with annual sales increasing from $4 million to $84 million. (See Exhibit 1.) Flagstaff offered a line of nearly 6000 food items and over 1000 nonfood items purchased from 1500 suppliers. Its products included all types of frozen and convenience foods and nonfood items such as kitchen equipment, janitorial and kitchen supplies, flatware, and china. Supplying the institutional market with a full line of products provided economies of scale, as well as convenience to customers who could deal with only one company. In its annual report Flagstaff listed the following among the services it furnished its customers:

- Cycle menu planning to meet consumer demand for greater variety.
- Control of portion sizes and costs to limit waste and boost margins.
- Pre-prepared food systems to counter rising labor costs and a national scarcity of skilled kitchen help.
- Use of private label products to guarantee product reliability throughout the trading area.

Flagstaff could become a large customer's primary source of supply for both food and nonfood items. Flagstaff's administration maintained that "only a single-source distributor, delivering items from its own inventory, is likely to offer a program of controlled portion costs and also limit the handling and inventory problems of his customers. Many uncertainties are eliminated for the customer."

The firm set out to distinguish itself by developing systems tailored to each customer. It felt that for the operator to realize the full benefits of purchasing items in convenience food form, the products had to be part of a total system. The system operated in the following fashion: A company representative called on a prospective customer asking for his menus and the average cost of his meals. Flagstaff would then develop menus using convenience frozen foods that would meet the objectives of the client. (See Exhibit 2.) In addition to menu development, Flagstaff also sought to design a line built around food themes with an ethnic or international flavor. (See Exhibit 3.)

Flagstaff tried to differentiate itself from other distributors in several other ways as well. Its acquisitions were made in areas adjoining already existing territories, creating a distributorship that covered much of the eastern seaboard. Flagstaff presented the image of an integrated operation offering a full-line of products to its customers. Its system of programmed selling found wide acceptance throughout the institutional market. The firm was very successful at maintaining sales growth throughout the 1974 recession, due mainly to its emphasis on the large institutional market. The restaurant business was badly hit in many parts of the United States that year. Distribution to restaurants represented 13 percent of Flagstaff's business, compared to an industry average of 45 percent. The company concentrated on large institutional users such as schools and colleges, hotels, medical centers, plants, government agencies, and other volume feeders. (See Exhibit 4.) These markets remained rather stable. Flagstaff supplied more than 15,000 customers. No one customer accounted for more than 2 percent of total sales.

THE FLAGSTAFF PRIVATE LABEL

More than 75 percent of Flagstaff's products were sold under its private labels, which included Flagstaff, Levitt, Sno Farms, and Sno Top. Convenience foods represented an increasing proportion of these items. The objective of developing the private labels was to accumulate the best from various sources. Using standard specifications, products were offered under a uniform label, affording the customer consistent quality and supply. Peter May, executive vice president at Flagstaff, explained that private label products were essential in the successful implementation of a convenience food program, which depended on the availability of the right product for a particular need at the right price. No single packer or manufacturer could even begin to meet the total needs of any institutional customer. It was also impossible physically and financially for any one distributor to carry the thousands of labels and products from each of the packers whose products had merit. Flagstaff was therefore able to provide its customers with the variety they needed as well as the convenience and quality associated with using a single distributor.

THE FLAGSTAFF ORGANIZATION

Nelson Peltz led Flagstaff's management team as president and chief executive with his brother, Robert Peltz, serving as chairman of the board and chief operating officer. Both had been officers of APS Food Systems, Inc., Flagstaff's predecessor. Peter May, executive vice president, directed all financial and administrative matters. Four senior vice presidents, who also served on the board of directors, completed Flagstaff's management team.

The company operated on a divisional profit center basis. Day-to-day operations were handled at the divisional level. Each of the divisions and all the 200 full-time salesmen marketed most of the items in Flagstaff's inventory. As Peter May explained, "The subsidiaries are allowed to do what they do best, selling and delivering." The corporate staff developed broad policy guidelines and assisted the divisions by eliminating duplication of effort and by maximizing economies of scale. The staff generally managed functions such as purchasing, financing and accounting, and inventory control. This enabled the smooth integration of acquisitions, as a subsidiary was allowed a certain degree of operating independence.

COFFEE-MAT CORPORATION

Since its founding in 1951 Coffee-Mat Corporation had been involved primarily in the design, manufacture, and sale of coin-operated dispensing machines. It concerned itself with all kinds of vending devices, though it specialized in coffee machines. It was the first manufacturer of fresh-brewed coffee machines. Its products were sold to vending service companies throughout the United States and Canada, Western Europe, and England. The vending machine manufacturing industry was considered highly competitive. Although Coffee-Mat was not the largest manufacturer in the business, it was the principal producer of single-cup, fresh-brewed coffee vending machines, maintaining 43 percent of that market.

Coffee-Mat was a fabricator, not merely an assembler. It designed and manufactured the majority of its component parts to its own specifications. Steel was the major raw material used in the manufacturing process.

The firm had a reputation as the producer of one of the best machines on the market. It was Coffee-Mat's reputation, in addition to its place as a leader in vending machines, that led Flagstaff to become interested in acquiring the firm. If consummated, this would be Flagstaff's first acquisition of a public company. Though Coffee-Mat suffered considerably during the 1974 recession (see Exhibit 5), Flagstaff felt its situation would stabilize. The 1975 decline in sales appeared to reflect customer cutbacks in vending facilities, as well as the postponement of the replacement of existing machines.

Flagstaff considered Coffee-Mat's business to be complementary to its own. Flagstaff maintained a small dispenser business under its Sno Farm label, offering dispensers of the type used in cafeterias. These ranged from coffee and tea dispensers to mashed potato dispensers. Coffee-Mat products would serve to supplement Flagstaff's line of labor-saving devices. The Flagstaff administration believed that the customers of both companies were also complementary. Further, Coffee-Mat distributed its products internationally, so the acquisition would also enlarge the geographical area covered by Flagstaff.

There also appeared to be secondary financial considerations in examining the possible acquisition of Coffee-Mat. The cash requirements in a business such as Flagstaff were very high. Most of the investment was in inventories. Coffee-Mat, on the other hand, was a very high cash flow business. Funds were not tied up in inventory to a very great extent because most of the machines were made to order. Coffee-Mat therefore seemed to offer Flagstaff very practical economic advantages.

THE FUTURE FLAGSTAFF CORPORATION

The food business is fast growing and presents many opportunities to a company with foresight and a good business sense. Flagstaff Corporation had thus far been a successful pioneer in the industry. It had to consider its future direction. In addition to the opportunities available through Coffee-Mat, Flagstaff was looking into the possibility of manufacturing some of its own private label products. The company was also eager to expand geographically, possibly to international scope.

EXHIBIT 1

FLAGSTAFF CORPORATION
Financial Data

			Fiscal Year Ended			
	April 27, 1974	April 28, 1973	April 29, 1972	April 30, 1971	May 1, 1970
Operating Statistics					
Net Sales	$84,058,000	$61,323,000	$44,796,000	$40,053,000	$34,740,000
Earnings before income taxes	$ 3,340,000	$ 2,971,000	$ 2,088,000	$ 1,647,000	$ 1,369,000
Net earnings	$ 1,682,000	$ 1,403,000	$ 1,056,000	$ 811,000	$ 635,000
Net earnings as a percentage of sales	2.0%	2.3%	2.4%	2.0%	1.8%
Net earnings per common share	$.66	$.61	$.50	$.39	$.33
Balance Sheet Statistics					
Working capital	$15,889,000	$ 9,136,000	$ 6,992,000	$ 5,368,000	
Current ratio	2.82:1	2.19:1	2.64:1	2.17:1	
Total assets	$32,158,000	$22,698,000	$15,373,000	$13,032,000	
Stockholders' equity	$13,759,000	$12,105,000	$ 7,732,000	$ 6,600,000	
Book value per common share	$5.40	$4.76	$3.66	$3.15	

EXHIBIT 2

TYPICAL DAILY MENU FOR 6000 PEOPLE

Item	Brand	Case Pack	Portions	Size	Cost	No. Cases Required	Equipment/Preparation
Breakfast							
Melon balls		6/8 lb. tins	192	4 oz.	.10	32	Thaw
Western omelet	Juno	120 3 ozs.	120	3 oz.	.33	50	Oven heat—need sheet pan or grill
Bacon, precooked		20 trays/25 ea.	125	4 strips each	.19	48	Oven heat on trays
Waffles w/syrup	Sno Top	8/12's to ctn.	32	3 each	.11	188	Oven heat—need sheet pans
Blueberry muffins	Flagstaff	100 indiv.	100	1 each	.05	(60)	
	Sno Top	4/18's	36	2 each	.30	167	Thaw
Lunch							
Stuffed clams on shell	Sno Top	36/2 oz. to ctn.	18	2 each	.33	334	Oven heat—need sheet pans
Beef braciola	Sno Top	40/4 oz. to ctn.	20	2 pcs.	.80	300	Oven heat—need deep pans
Boiled potatoes		6/10 tins	192	4 oz.	.07	32	Pot warm
Peas & carrots	Sno Top	12/2½ to ctn.	120	4 oz.	.09	50	Pot boil
Cocoanut layer cake	Sno Top	4/4.5 lb. 10 ctn.	48	1/12 cut	.29	125	Thaw/slice
Dinner							
Consomme	Flagstaff	6/5 lb. tins	384	5 oz.	.02	(2)	
Tenderloin steak (5 oz.)	Levitt	6/20/8 oz. (45 tins)	20	6 oz.	2.06	50	Grill
Tater tots w/cheese	Oreida	12/1 lb.	87	8 pcs. ea.	.04	69	Oven heat—need sheet pans
Broccoli spears	Sno Top	12/2 lb.	96	4 oz.	.10	63	Pot boil
Chocolate eclair	Rich's	4/12's	48	1 each	.21	125	Thaw

EXHIBIT 3

FOOD THEMES

EXHIBIT 4

CUSTOMER BREAKDOWN

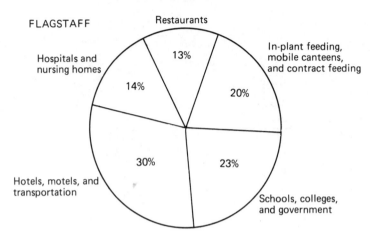

FLAGSTAFF

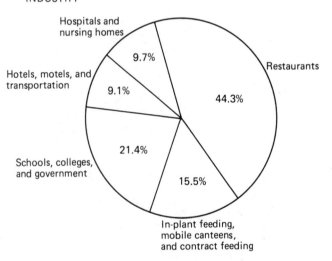

INDUSTRY

EXHIBIT 5

COFFEE-MAT FINANCING
Five-Year Summary of Operations and Other Financial Information

	Fiscal Years Ended March 31				
	1975	1974	1973	1972	1971
Net sales	$9,473,435	$13,040,610	$10,779,096	$8,436,443	$6,475,009
Cost of sales, selling & administrative	7,475,073	8,612,215	6,947,495	5,318,285	4,126,677
Other (income) expense, principally interest	201,412	114,953	(210,279)	(212,126)	(181,991)
Income before income taxes	1,796,950	4,313,442	4,041,880	3,330,284	2,530,323
Provision for income taxes	812,178	2,041,300	1,873,691	1,567,200	1,260,646
Income from continuing operations	984,772	2,272,142	2,168,189	1,763,084	1,269,677
Loss from discontinued operations	–	–	–	–	76,293
Extraordinary items—(net)	–	–	–	–	75,636
Net income	$ 984,772	$ 2,272,142	$ 2,168,189	$1,763,084	$1,117,748
Per share data:					
Income on continuing operations	$ .61	$ 1.36	$ 1.10	$ .89	$ .64
Loss on discontinued operations	–	–	–	–	(.04)
Extraordinary items—net	–	–	–	–	(.04)
Net income	$ .61	$ 1.36	$ 1.10	$ .89	$ .56
Cash dividends	$ .48	$ .54	$ .39	$ .36	$ .30
Stock dividends	2%	–	–	–	–
Working capital	$5,175,422	$ 5,444,980	$ 7,355,171	$7,290,409	$6,031,876
Stockholders' equity	$5,994,123	$ 5,787,565	$ 9,083,116	$9,006,335	$7,564,802
Average shares outstanding	1,621,579	1,672,876	1,976,385	1,984,670	1,988,320

SEMICONDUCTOR STRATEGIES

The competitive atmosphere within today's high technology industries has taken a unique and most interesting form. Competition through technological innovation has been directed at lowering cost, creating new products, and improving the quality of present products. The billion dollar semiconductor industry has grown tremendously in the last two decades, chiefly through this competition.

The challenges encountered by management within such a competitive atmosphere were often met by unique responses. Intel Corporation and National Semiconductor Corporation, based about a mile apart in Santa Clara, California, were both leaders in the semiconductor industry. The managements of both firms were faced with high-risk decisions in companies that dealt with rapidly changing technologies. However, their successes had been generated through completely different strategies and leadership styles.

Both Intel and National Semiconductor primarily designed, developed, and manufactured advanced semiconductor circuits known as "integrated circuits" (ICs). A semiconductor is a device that makes decisions and provides certain memory functions used in computers. It provides amplification for radio, TV, telephone, and other electronic instruments. It supplies receiving, transmitting, and computing capabilities used in missiles, spacecraft, and satellites. Exhibit 1 shows the distribution of IC sales.

This case was prepared by Pauline J. Albert under the supervision of Professor Jules J. Schwartz as the basis for class discussion rather than to illustrate either effective or ineffective handling of an administrative action.

THE SEMICONDUCTOR INDUSTRY

The semiconductor itself is an element, such as silicon, germanium, or gallium, that can be "doped" with minute quantities of other elements to change its electrical behavior. By the use of small biasing voltages, conductivity in the semiconductor can be altered, resulting in an amplifying or switching effect.

The IC is a particular kind of semiconductor device and is produced by two distinct processes, metal oxide semiconductor (MOS) technology and bipolar technology. Though MOS products accounted for only one percent of semiconductor sales in 1969, they constituted 20 percent of 1976 sales and were expected to reach 30 percent by 1980. MOS parts generally operate more slowly than other ICs, but MOS had outstripped the bipolar process because designers could squeeze more functions onto a silicon chip using fewer manufacturing steps. Integrated circuits are made in small flat packages and are at least fifty times smaller in size and weight than the circuits built from discrete components.

Exhibits 2 and 3 show the annual growth in United States production of semiconductor devices. Many of the savings normally experienced with such rapid growth had been passed on to customers. A particular firm's competitive advantage would generally be exhibited when it quickly and efficiently improved on present technologies and products. A semiconductor manufacturer who was first into the market with a new product could build up production rates faster than his competitors and advance down the "learning curve." The learning curve for ICs is illustrated in Exhibit 4.

An industry principle held that when production doubled, experience and higher yields on good parts would drop manufacturing costs by about 27 percent. Therefore a company that was first to deliver a new product in high volume could drop its prices faster and maintain the largest market share. Price cutting along the learning curve had thus become "the name of the game" for the semiconductor industry. Prices were dropped to seize market share when a firm familiarized itself with how to produce a product. Then the resulting profits were reinvested to reduce the manufacturing costs still further.

As manufacturing unit costs declined, circuit integration increased. ICs were classified according to the number of functions of each chip. The groups of chips are:

	Number of Functions
Small-scale integration (SSI)	Less than 15
Medium-scale integration (MSI)	15 to 200
Large-scale integration (LSI)	More than 200

Larger-scale integration had resulted in higher-speed devices. These products were cheaper and more reliable than the hard-wired circuits on printed circuit boards. They were also priced lower, with the cost-per-function declining as the number of functions per chip increased.

The total cost of package materials, labor, and testing was approximately the same no matter how many functions were included on a chip. Some reduction in net gain was possible, however, because adding additional functions increased the chance of producing a bad circuit. These factors, combined with an increase in operating speeds as technology developed, enabled producers to market bigger systems. For several years semiconductor designers doubled annually the number of electronic functions they could fit on a chip.

Exhibit 5 lists the leading producers of integrated circuits in 1975. Texas Instruments (TI), which manufactured a broad line of electronic equipment and components, was clearly the leader within the industry. Founded in 1930, it was among the first firms in the semiconductor business, entering the industry in 1952.

The semiconductor business, certainly one of the world's most important industries, was shaping the future of many other industries as well as creating whole new ones, including minicomputers, microcomputers, calculators, and digital watches. However, this rapid growth had been accompanied by some painful periods. Because of the nature of semiconductor competition, many firms did not survive or suffered badly from steep downturns in 1961 and again in the 1974 to 1975 period.

The 1975 recession was perhaps the worst in the industry's twenty-year history. In March of 1976 many plants were still operating at half capacity. Price cutting was a constant problem during 1975, running as much as 60 percent on some products. After 1974, when a production peak had been reached, over 50,000 people were furloughed from their jobs and over $750 million in production capacity was lost.

In 1973 sales soared and orders were coming in faster than they could be filled. Fear that they would not be able to buy enough parts to keep production moving caused purchasing agents to double-order, thus creating an artificially large backlog. A significant part of the 1974 downturn was attributed to inventory adjustments, but recognizing this did not make it easier for firms to weather the difficult storm. The firms that were able to anticipate the downturn and plan for it quickly suffered the least. Companies such as National and Texas Instruments scaled down operations, abandoned business plans, and stopped hiring.

A 1976 to 1977 sales surge was expected to be strong but would rest on a new generation of more complex circuits. Not all the industry leaders were prepared to respond to this switch in emphasis. For example, both Motorola and Fairchild had apparently had problems with new technologies. Both companies had experienced heavy losses and had suffered from management and manufacturing problems. The brighter futures would be enjoyed by firms who were adapting to new technologies and important new products.

INTEL CORPORATION

Robert N. Noyce was the forty-eight-year-old chairman and founder of Intel. A founder of Fairchild Camera and Instrument Corporation's original semiconductor operations in the late 1950s, he was credited with much of the work that led to the development of integrated circuits. Noyce left Fairchild in 1968 to start Intel, in an effort to seek undiscovered niches where new technological ideas could create new markets. He was considered a brilliant scientist-entrepreneur who had built his reputation on technological breakthroughs. He explained the Intel philosophy in a *Business Week* interview: "We've tried to identify markets early and then make them happen."

An example of this approach was Intel's creation of microprocessors and memories for computers. The microprocessor provided the solution to a problem that had long troubled the developers of large-scale integrated circuits (LSIs). When the complexity of the circuits increased, so did the number of chip designs and design costs became extravagant. Intel conceived the idea of developing a general purpose computer-on-a-chip that could be programmed for an infinite variety of tasks. This way the company could make a few devices well and inexpensively. Intel was the only company to enter this market early and whole-heartedly. The microcomputer had been considered by most industry analysts as the machine of the future. The microcomputer market had grown to $60 million in 1975, after five years of existence, a 50-percent growth rate in a recession year. Exhibit 6 illustrates the industry forecasts for growth in this market.

Intel had made these markets "happen" to the extent that they generated an estimated 60 percent of Intel's sales in 1975. Development

of these new products had naturally required large research and development budgets. Even in 1975 when the recession was having a heavy impact, research and development spending was raised from 7.9 percent to 10.6 percent of sales. Noyce explained, "We want to do one good job of engineering and sell it over and over again." These breakthroughs were also accompanied by highly efficient manufacturing operations.

Being first or near the top in microprocessors appeared to be the key to future success within the semiconductor industry. The new microprocessor squeezed onto one or two tiny chips all the arithmetic and logic functions of a programmable general purpose computer. This piece of new technology was expected to pave the way for the semiconductor industry's entry into high-volume consumer markets. Microprocessor brains were already used in microwave ovens. The auto and TV industries were beginning to use microprocessors. Keeping up with technology was becoming progressively harder because the new circuits had become more complex, making them more difficult to design and produce.

Intel came through the 1975 "semiconductor depression" exceptionally well. The firm increased its sales to $137 million in that year. While its profits dropped to $16.3 million, its profit margin of 12 percent was the highest in the industry, which averaged only 7 percent. A special effort was made in the final quarter, when Intel's sales were boosted 29 percent and profits rose 53 percent. Exhibit 7 presents an historical picture of Intel's earnings since its inception in 1968.

Intel had come a long way during its first eight years of operations. A great deal of its success was certainly due to the ingenuity and entrepreneurial genius of its founder. However, Noyce was also aware of the evolution that had to occur after the first phases of his company's development. Intel was placing more emphasis than before on manufacturing and marketing skills. "The entrepreneurial phase is not entirely over at Intel," Noyce said, "but the emphasis is shifting to control. When the company was small we could run it by personal contact; now it is more important to run it by the numbers."

NATIONAL SEMICONDUCTOR CORPORATION

Charles E. Sporck, president of National Semiconductor, might best be characterized as a "watchdog of manufacturing efficiency." He left Fairchild in 1967 to join National, which had sales of only $8 million that year and was losing money. Sporck's goal was to make National a superefficient manufacturer of high-volume products. To achieve his goal, Sporck ran a tight ship indeed, coupling efficient operations with an ability to adapt. His tactics had enabled National to increase 1975 sales to $235 million and earnings to $16 million despite the "semiconductor depression."

National was a small transistor manufacturer when Sporck joined the company. He had played a key role in its becoming the second largest manufacturing company for semiconductor and end-user electronics in the United States. National's earnings per share had soared at a compound rate of 55 percent from 1970 to 1975. (See Exhibit 8.) For the fiscal year ending May 1975, National's net increased 2.3 percent, while the income of the largest producer fell 30.9 percent.

National had been able to maintain a strong position because it had anticipated the downturn and literally turned itself around within a very short period of time. It abandoned a $400 million business plan and scaled down operations to handle reduced business requirements.

Another reason for the firm's good performance could be attributed to its broad line of semiconductor products, particularly within the fast-growing integrated circuit line. It also produced a number of end-user electronic products such as low-priced calculators, digital watches, and point-of-sale systems for supermarkets. National was able to offset the 1975 slump in component parts with an increase in calculator sales, a number of new calculator products, and a new independent point-of-sale system. In 1973 the firm entered the end-user market and made 90 percent of the components used in digital watches and electronic calculators.

While Noyce was moving Intel somewhat away from its entrepreneurial phase, Sporck was also changing National with the times. The emphasis on high-volume manufacturing had been so intense that researchers were not always able to get onto a production line for testing. National was now spending more money on development of its new lines. Engineers were working on microprocessors and memories. Sporck stayed in close touch with day-to-day manufacturing operations. Although he left most of the operating decisions to the managers who had profit and loss responsibility, he did not hesitate to step in when trouble arose. In 1975 he took control of consumer products when sales were dipping and profit margins were not being maintained. He continued to run that operation until the area stabilized.

By mid-1976 the worst part of the recession seemed to be over for the semiconductor industry, which had been hit so hard by 1975 economic conditions. A strong recovery was expected at National although the officers recognized that the volatile and cyclical nature of demand would most probably persist. The firm was broadening its product base and moving more into end-user products. Management thought that this would not only help to reduce the cyclical phenomena but could widen profit margins as well.

Though the managerial styles exhibited by Noyce and Sporck were clearly different, one could see some common characteristics in the two firms. Both men believed in "no frills," egalitarian approaches to management, which certainly attracted superior technical talent. Both firms encouraged employees to share their ideas and key employees of both firms benefited from the successful performances of their companies. A true "esprit de corps" existed within each firm.

Because the strategies of both firms converged, Noyce and Sporck found themselves competing for some of the same growth markets. These early confrontations were not too painful, as those markets were growing very rapidly. However, one must wonder what the future would bring for Intel and National Semiconductor. Should they try to compete with Texas Instruments? Within what niches of the industry should they operate?

EXHIBIT 1

DISTRIBUTION OF IC SALES
BY AREA OF APPLICATION, 1969–1975

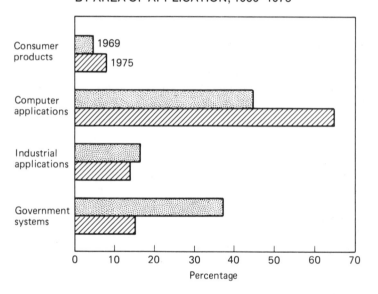

EXHIBIT 2

U.S. SHIPMENTS OF
SEMICONDUCTOR DEVICES
($1,000 value)

1963	$ 608.3
1964	$ 640.9
1965	$ 798.9
1966	$ 995.8
1967	$1,103.7
1968	$1,191.7
1969	$1,391.7
1970	$1,397.5
1971	$1,556.2
1972	$2,136.4
1973	$3,125.
1974	$3,249.5

EXHIBIT 3
U.S. FACTORY SALES OF SEMICONDUCTORS
($ billions)

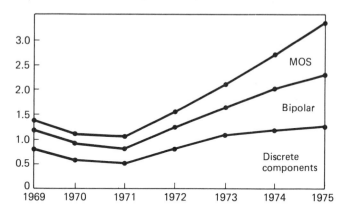

Source: Business Week, April 20, 1974

EXHIBIT 4

EXPERIENCE CURVE FOR
IC'S AND IC FUNCTIONS

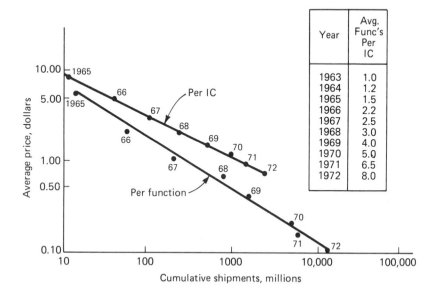

Year	Avg. Func's Per IC
1963	1.0
1964	1.2
1965	1.5
1966	2.2
1967	2.5
1968	3.0
1969	4.0
1970	5.0
1971	6.5
1972	8.0

EXHIBIT 5

TOP PRODUCERS OF
INTEGRATED CIRCUITS IN 1975

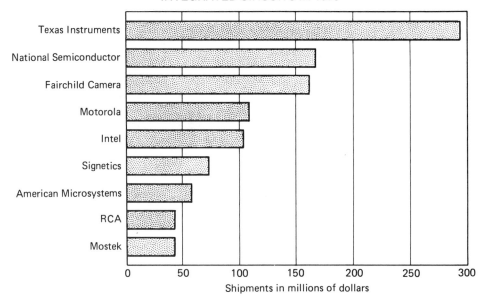

Shipments in millions of dollars

EXHIBIT 6
GROWTH OF THE MICROCOMPUTER

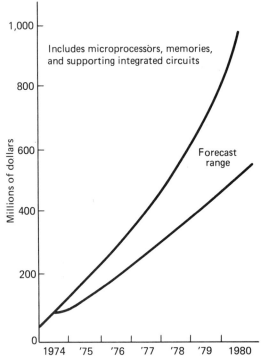

Includes microprocessors, memories, and supporting integrated circuits

Forecast range

Millions of dollars

Source: Business Week estimates, March 1, 1976

EXHIBIT 7

INTEL CORPORATION
Earnings-Dividend Record

Year Ended Dec. 31	Net Revenues (millions)	Earnings/Share	Share Price Range
1975	$136.79	$ 2.35	88–20¾
1974	134.46	2.96	84–15½
1973	66.17	1.41	63–18
1972	22.97	.49	24⅜–7⅜
1971	9.19[a]	.17	
1971	9.17	.07	10⅞–5¼
1970	3.93	(.46)	
1969	.37	(1.66)	
1968	NIL[b]	(.89)	

[a]Restated.
[b]From July 18, 1968, date of incorporation.
Source: O-T-C and Regional Exchange Stock Reports, Standard & Poor's Corp., Ephrata, PA., April 26, 1976

EXHIBIT 8

NATIONAL SEMICONDUCTOR
Earnings-Dividend Record

Year Ended May 31 of Next Year	Net Sales (millions)	Earnings/Share	Share Price Range
1974	$235.5	$1.34	25⅛–6¼
1973	213.4	1.33	36¼–7¾
1972	99.0	.32	13¼–6½
1971	59.8	.19	6⅞–3⅛
1970	38.1	.11	9⅜–1⅞
1969	41.8	.16	11⅜–7
1968	22.9	.06	8⅜–7
1967	11.0	.04	8⅛–1¼
1966	7.2	.10	1⅛–¾
1965	5.3	.04	

Source: Standard N.Y.S.E. Stock Reports, Standard & Poor's Corp., Ephrata, PA., April 12, 1976

CHAPTER 3

Managing Decisions in Business Organizations

There is a considerable body of both descriptive and prescriptive literature on the subject of decisionmaking. Unfortunately what is described is not what one would prescribe. To anyone who has had any experience in dealing with large organizations (including university administrations), a description of the *bureaucratic* model of decisionmaking strikes a familiar note and usually evokes a promise that any organization he might manage will certainly behave more rationally.

The problem of a manager is to resolve the essential conflict between the natural bureaucratic tendencies of his firm and the need to reach and implement *rational* decisions.

In Chapters 1 and 2 we pointed up a rational approach to developing strategic options, but we recognized that final choices would, in part, be based on the preferences of influential constituencies. Preferences are not necessarily rational. In this chapter we will describe the symptoms of bureaucratic behavior and suggest that general managers, who understand the problem, can do things to manage the decision process.

First let's take a look at how a bureaucracy appears to function. Cyert and March[1] describe

[1]Richard M. Cyert and James G. March, *Behavioral Theory of the Firm* (Englewood Cliffs, N. J., Prentice-Hall, Inc., 1963), pp. 1–129.

such an organization in which the subunits are functionally specialized. Each subunit has parochial priorities and perceptions based on its technical expertise. Each looks for decisions that contribute to satisfying its aspirations or alleviating its peculiar problems. Because power is fragmented, the solution to conflicting demands is found by sequential attention to goals. Thus, no group is ever fully satisfied. The process results only in meeting acceptable-level constraints.

Central coordination and control systems conflict with the interests of the specialists and so can attain only limited success. In such an organization each subunit performs according to standard operating procedures and standard repertoires. Though this approach affords quick response, it lacks the flexibility to react to new problems. When new problems do arise, a search is instituted aimed only at alleviating any undesirable symptoms.

The engine for this model is the cognitive process of problemsolving. But the subunits that seek to solve problems lack an overall organizational perspective to guide their search. An organization modeled in this manner can only respond to threats; it cannot search for opportunity. Change is slow unless crisis proves the process to be inadequate. Only when an outside authority demands change are standard operating procedures rewritten and responsibilities redefined.

These ideas build on Herbert Simon's analysis of how individuals make decisions when faced with uncertainty. He concluded that people factor problems, that is, they break them up and deal with only parts of them; they accept the first solution that is good enough rather than an optimum one—Simon called this *satisficing;* and they try to avoid uncertainty by using standard operating procedures that provide for standard corrections for any deviation from the norm, the way thermostats do.

If this model seems an unsatisfactory one for managing a business, you'll have to find a way to influence strategic decisions. For a manager, making a decision is a way of assuming risk. Too many managers forget, however, that no decision is also a decision. Managers simply cannot avoid risk.

ROUTINE DECISIONS

To understand how managers choose to assume risks and allocate scarce resources to implement their decisions, we should first review briefly what we know of more routine resource allocation decisions. Bower has shown that such routine decisions may really be viewed as two interrelated activities both of which can be influenced by management.[2]

The first of these activities is *definition,* in which a proposal gains its substantive content, the technical details that differentiate it from other alternatives. The second is *impetus,* in which the proposal gains advocacy and support within the organization and moves forward to approval.

Managers can influence both of these activities by setting *context,* that is, the way they articulate strategy, the way they organize the work of the firm, the resource allocation, control, information, and incentive systems they institute, and the personal style they

[2] J. L. Bower, *Managing the Resource Allocation Process,* Division of Research, Harvard Business School, 1970.

adopt. (Corporate context is discussed in more detail in Chapter 4.)

LEVELS OF ACTIVITY

It is helpful to divide the activities in the firm that contribute to definition, impetus, and context into the three organizational levels shown in Figure 3-1. At the lowest level, specialists and functional managers concern themselves with details of definition. These are the people who confront specific problems and possess the expert knowledge to solve them.

Activity / Level	Definition	Impetus	Context
Senior managers			X
Middle managers		X	
Functional managers & specialists	X		

FIGURE 3-1   Resource Allocation Decisions

At the second level, middle managers, who are generalists, seek to integrate the activities of the specialists who work for them. They give impetus in several ways: 1) they decide which proposals will go forward for approval; 2) they interpret between senior management and specialists, clarifying corporate purpose for the specialists and abstracting and translating technical detail for senior managers; and 3) they accept risk by staking their own reputation on proposals.

Senior managers are also generalists, but their chief influence on proposals usually takes the form of setting the *context* in which the other two activities take place.

While Bower and others have concluded that each level of management in the firm is a principal contributor to a specific activity, as indicated in Figure 3-1, it should be evident that each level can influence definition, impetus, and context. When a senior manager suggests that a new building be painted white, for example, he is contributing to the technical definition. He is also influencing impetus because implicit in his intervention is the notion that he will approve a proposal for a white building.

INNOVATIVE DECISIONS

Research on decisions concerning change shows that they differ from routine allocation decisions in two important ways, both involving tasks for middle managers. First, greater risks are perceived and must be dealt with. Second, more work must be done to reach a shared conception of the problem faced and the criteria on which to evaluate the proposed solutions.

RISK

Consider the problem of risk first. One problem, suggested by Jordon Baruch of the Harvard Business School and others, is the payoff facing advocates of change in less innovative firms. Figure 3-2 illustrates this idea as a simplified matrix. It shows the payoffs to a middle manager based on GO, NO-GO outcomes. If he rejects a proposal and it later proves to be a bad deal, he will receive some credit, tempered by the consideration that he has shown a "negative attitude." If he rejects an idea that someone else later succeeds with, he'll lose standing but the extent of his loss will be limited by the results of any alternative projects—if business is good, it won't matter. If he supports a proposal that turns out well, he'll do well but will have to share credit with others. But if he supports a

failure, he will probably receive much of the blame. The resultant matrix is not likely to encourage advocacy!

Interestingly, senior managers, because they have a larger, more diversified project portfolio, may be more risk prone than middle managers. If you have only one project, you can't afford a failure; if you have several projects, it's your average that counts.

Finally, innovative proposals involve more dimensions of risk than routine ones. When a new product is proposed, marketing and production problems are a factor. Simple additions to capacity entail fewer of these risks. Timing is also a key factor when the firm innovates, as the first firm entering a market has greater uncertainty but also an early advantage.

HANDLING THE RISKS

The middle manager integrates the activities of specialists. It is he who must bring market and production plans together with the technical proposal to assemble the necessary business plan, as individual specialists are rarely equipped to do this. We have found that most innovative proposals either take too long or fail to win approval because they lack a credible business plan. If they do finally gain approval on technical merit alone, they often fail in implementation because they lack such plans.

In successful firms the middle managers consciously enter the proposal phase early to develop essential business plans. In a product division of a successful electronics firm, for example, project teams, including marketing, production and technical people, worked to write these plans concurrently with the technical proposals. While there was some expensive repetition of effort when normal technical revisions were encountered, this was accepted as more desirable than the long delays that would have attended sequential efforts.

Too often a specialist approaches his boss with a grand plan calling for big cash contributions in return for a technical result, date

Manager's recommendation	The proposal later	
	Succeeds	Fails
Supports the proposal	+ 3	− 10!
Rejects the proposal	− 1?	+ 1

FIGURE 3-2 A Payoff Matrix for Innovation

unspecified. Early management involvement in the proposal phase may help to avoid this common problem in innovative efforts that results from failure to accurately assess schedule risks. Setting mileposts provides management with a way of judging a subordinate's capacity to implement his proposal and of controlling the activity if it is approved.

Requiring a specialist to factor, or break down, his proposal lets a manager make judgments concerning at least parts of the proposal, even when he isn't equipped to evaluate the entire scheme. The factored proposal also lends itself more easily to scheduling. The middle manager can influence the critical time definition of a proposal by trading his ability to give impetus in return for a negotiated schedule.

AGREEING ON THE PROBLEM

It is the responsibility of the chief executive to articulate strategy for his organization. Specialists, however, don't always understand the language and intent of senior management. An important role for middle-level generalists is to *translate* corporate strategy into terms specialists can understand and accept. Innovative firms devote much of their time to clarifying and sharing their conception of problems and criteria on which solutions will be judged.

INNOVATION STRATEGIES

The firm that can make innovative decisions fast has several strategic choices not open to its slower competitors. As the time needed to make a decision often exceeds that needed to prepare a proposal, the organization that can decide faster can allow its specialists a longer period to develop good options and still implement its choice in a timely manner.

The firm that elects not to pioneer can make up for its competitor's headstart if it can quickly make its decision to be second. This approach leaves the major initial risks to others and prepares the company to offer a rapid response.

In Chapter 2 we discussed the concept of the experience curve. Decisions and learning rates are related. Cost reductions along the experience curve result from a combination of economies of scale, where production rates are higher, and a series of incremental process and product innovations, often called learning. The firm that can decide about implementing these innovations more quickly than its competitors can learn faster and so entitle itself to still greater market share. Any competitor with less production experience is thus at a distinct cost disadvantage.

ORGANIZING FOR DECISION

We have seen that an innovative decision requires extra work within the organization and imposes special risks. How can a senior manager set a context that will encourage definition and advocacy for such proposals?

First, it's management's task to clearly articulate strategy. Employees must understand where the company wants to go.

The manager must get involved. A shirt-sleeve style demonstrates management's interest in innovation and its willingness to share the risk.

The manager should recognize the differences between himself and his subordinates in both the scale and horizon of their planning. Subunits will most often propose new projects that fit only the scale of their own operations. He must seek proposals that will be significant relative to the scale of the corporation.

The manager should also consider that horizons vary with each person's job tenure and position in the organization. As a subordinate nears the date when he believes he may be considered for promotion, he may become more risk averse. Why should he advocate proposals that impact negatively on his current financial picture and pay off later for someone else?

Finally, the manager must understand the politics of his organization. He should know what groups are interested in a decision, how interested they are and what value system they will apply to any options proposed. Successful politicians always make a point of studying these questions in order to steer their legislative proposals. This information is essential to the process of negotiation.

IMPLICATIONS FOR MANAGEMENT

A business organization is a dynamic thing; it flourishes by recognizing and exploiting opportunities and by responding quickly to competitive threats. Because the environment in which it operates is constantly changing, the firm must change too if it is to survive. Change, then, is a management responsibility; and decisions, particularly nonroutine ones, must be managed if they are to be timely.

Although universities analyze the political processes we've been describing in their political *science* departments, who doubts that it is an *art* we are discussing?

TOWN ENTERPRISES, INC.

In April of 1975 Town Enterprises (TEI), a consumer finance company, filed for bankruptcy in the Federal District Court in Delaware. Following prescribed procedures, a receiver was appointed by the court to manage the affairs of the debtor. As a result of an innovative plan of arrangement arrived at to recapitalize the company, Town Enterprises now has a variety of options other than liquidation of its assets. Fred Selah, chief operating officer, has been analyzing these other options.

THE CONSUMER FINANCE INDUSTRY

The history of financial institutions in the United States is closely associated with the changing character of the consumer marketplace in the past 250 years. Viewed in this perspective, the economic importance of this industry becomes evident.

There was little need for consumer finance companies when bartering was the common method of exchange. With the advent of a systematized monetary system, institutional credit became an important factor in the growth of the economy. By the 1870s the first finance institutions had evolved in response to the credit needs of the American people. Credit transactions in the United States have helped the economy develop its mass production/mass consumption structure. Through the resulting economies of scale, lower unit

costs for goods and services have become available to the consumer. Simply stated, finance companies have responded to the banks' inability to satisfy a variety of credit needs. Finance companies now fulfill many diverse needs of their customers, unlike earlier days when they provided credit only for specific purposes.

Today the consumer installment credit industry is defined by the National Consumer Finance Association (NCFA) to include those businesses whose primary purpose is to finance the consumer through either direct cash loans or the purchase of sales finance paper. Direct cash loans are made directly to individuals on either a secured or unsecured basis.

Because of increasing complexity in market requirements, there has been a proliferation of specialized consumer finance companies. Now they can be categorized into three groups: 1) captive and independent sales finance companies, 2) consumer finance, or small loan, companies, and 3) industrial banks. These groups accounted for $42.7 billion, or 24 percent of the total consumer installment credit outstanding at the end of 1975. This credit was extended by over 34,000 companies with over 26,000 offices throughout the United States. (See Exhibit 1.)

Finance companies compete with many other financial institutions that also finance consumer purchases of goods and services. The most important of these are commercial banks, savings and loan associations, mutual savings banks, and credit unions. A distinguishing characteristic of these competitors is the use of time or demand deposits as their source of loanable funds. While certain finance companies do accept deposit-like liabili-

This case was prepared by Lewis G. Furman, Robert M. Hellauer, Edward G. Preble, and Thomas A. Shively under the supervision of Professor Jules J. Schwartz as the basis for class discussion rather than to illustrate either effective or ineffective handling of an administrative action.

ties, these deposits are not the industry's primary source of funds.

Borrowers differ in their financial characteristics and are therefore forced to rely on different kinds of institutions to fulfill their credit needs. This helps to explain the variety of institutions detailed above. Sales finance companies limit their credit to consumer durables, while commercial banks lend most of their money to business and industry. Savings and loan associations tend to specialize in real estate mortgages. Credit unions, of course, lend only to their members.

It should be noted that consumer loans are classified both by the nature of their proposed use and by the type of lender making them. They are broken down into four broad categories: automobile paper, other consumer goods paper, repair and modernization loans, and personal loans. Although these categories would seem to imply use of different kinds of collateral, this is not always the case. Historically, collateral requirements have evolved from household goods, to wage assignments, to the present trend toward unsecured loans.

Of the $42.7 billion in consumer installment credit outstanding at the end of 1975, $17.2 billion, or 40 percent, were personal loans and $13.4 billion, or 31 percent, were based on retail automobile paper. Because states usually set maximum interest charges at a lower level for sales finance paper than for other types of loans, the sales finance business is generally a low margin activity requiring very high volume. Sales financing is offered primarily to attract new customers who can then be solicited for direct cash loans. In recent years commercial banks, credit unions, and manufacturers' subsidiaries, like General Motors Acceptance Corporation, have moved into this field, causing many independent companies to switch their emphasis to personal loans.

All four credit categories listed above have increased in volume as the industry developed. There was rapid growth from the industry's conception in 1870 to the beginning of World War II, when there was $2.3 billion in install-

ment credit outstanding. After a four-year slowdown during the war, the industry began to boom again and installment loans outstanding increased to $31.7 billion in 1970.

The development of the industry has not been a smooth one. As a result, legal interventions have been common. Today the finance industry is one of the most highly regulated, by both state and federal law, in the country.

As early as 1907 the need for legal safeguards had been recognized by leaders in the field. To help meet this challenge the Russell Sage Foundation sponsored the development of a small loan law. In 1917 the uniform Small Loan Law emerged as the first real model on which states could fashion their own legislation. Virtually all states passed strict laws governing the operations of finance companies.

Most states vest supervisory authority in their banking departments or commissions, which then issue administrative law to supplement the statutes. A state banking commissioner thus wields a great deal of power over the state's finance companies. Each state regulates the maximum amount that can be loaned and the maximum interest rate that can be charged on loans of different amounts and maturities. Each finance company must obtain a license from its state regulatory agency and submit an annual report of operations. Most states require at least one banking commission examination of each office every year. The scope of an examination can be quite broad, as almost all loan office activities are prescribed by law. Most states also provide for the collection of certain fees, such as delinquent fees and extension charges levied when a customer makes a late payment or wishes to defer a payment. In addition almost all states regulate the commissions loan companies can earn on the sale of credit life, health, and accident insurance. Such fees and commissions often form a significant part of the operating income of these firms.

The federal government also plays an important part in the regulatory process. This role has become more dominant, as it has in other industries, because of the changing nature and increased complexity of the American economic system.

As more diverse institutions, subject to different regulatory bodies, began to compete for the credit customer, there was an increasing recognition of the need for a more uniform regulatory system. As a result the National Conference of Commissioners on Uniform State Laws began a study in 1963 that culminated in the Uniform Consumer Credit Code (UCCC). This code has been adopted by several states to date, but has not yet received widespread acceptance. The UCCC provides a common rate structure, significant consumer protection provisions, and civil and criminal sanctions for violators.

All firms within the industry must comply with the following laws:

1. Federal Consumer Credit Protection Act, which provides for disclosure statements to borrowers and procedures for credit checks, and restricts advertising content;
2. Fair Credit Billing Act, which prescribes procedures for correction of billing errors;
3. Equal Credit Opportunity Act, which prohibits discrimination on sexual or marital grounds; and
4. Consumer Credit Protection Act ("Truth-in-Lending-Law"), which requires a uniform statement of the real annual interest rates charged on loans.

The primary source of income for finance companies is interest earned on outstanding receivables. As mentioned earlier, state law usually sets the maximum rate of interest that may be charged; it also specifies which of two basic methods may be used to compute the rate. The first method is simple interest computed on a monthly basis on the outstanding balance of the loan. The second method is commonly referred to as "discounting." Under this method interest is added on to the loan. For example, a borrower might receive $840 in cash and sign a note promising to repay $1000 in twenty-four monthly installments. This translates into an annual percentage rate (APR) of 17.33 percent. The $160 difference between the loan receivable and the cash advanced is recorded on the loan company's books as "unearned income" and amortized over the life of the loan. As almost all states allow this income to be recognized on the sum-of-the-months-digits basis, an accelerated method, there is an advantage for the firm to encourage its borrowers to pay off early or to refinance their loans before maturity. By offering a small cash advance to convince customers to refinance early, a consumer finance company can almost double the effective yield on a given receivable.

People who borrow from finance companies are often unable to obtain credit from commercial banks or other institutions that charge lower rates than those typically charged by a loan company. The risks inherent in lending to such marginally credit worthy customers justify higher interest charges. The industry bad-debt rate was 3.3 percent in 1975, when typical annual percentage rates were 20 to 25 percent. The average loan maturity is eighteen months, but maturities as long as sixty months are not uncommon. The National Consumer Finance Association (NCFA) 1974 annual survey depicted the average borrower as a male, skilled or semiskilled laborer who earned between $6,000 and $12,000 per year. He was usually married, under fifty years of age, and owned his own home. (See Exhibit 2.)

Finance companies find their sources of funds in many of the same places as other business organizations; capital and retained earnings, loans from commercial banks, commercial paper, and long-term subordinated and unsubordinated debentures. Two distinguishing characteristics exist. First, the industry is highly leveraged; debt-to-equity ratios, for the 1960 to 1975 period remained fairly constant, in the range of 5.1 to 5.7, compared to a ratio of 0.7 for all manufacturing firms in 1966. Second, the NCFA reported that in 1975 over 55 percent of all debt was either short-term or current. This capital structure is made possible by the supposedly liquid nature of the assets, mostly loan receivables, and the minimal investment in fixed assets. However, the term structures of assets and liabilities are usually imperfectly coordinated, and most companies are dependent on their ability to "roll over" their short-term liabilities by borrowing new funds to pay off debts as they mature. Interest charges on debt are significant; rates are frequently several points above prime, and often account for a third or more of operating expenses. In economic downturns consumer finance companies are often whipsawed between restrictive credit policies and sharply increasing interest rates imposed by their creditors and increasing deterioration of portfolios as layoffs occur, unemployment rises, and payments become delinquent. (See Exhibit 3.)

Consumer finance companies in 1974 had a return on equity of only 8.8 percent while manufacturing corporations in the United States experienced a return of 14.9 percent, as reported by the Federal Trade Commission.

TOWN ENTERPRISES

Russell C. Mansfield founded Town Enterprises, Inc., in Delaware in 1953. TEI is a holding company involved in the management and ownership of its consumer finance subsidiaries. The subsidiaries make loans on both a secured and unsecured basis, operating under appropriate state laws. In addition, they sell insurance on the borrower, when possible.

Mansfield has served as president and a director of TEI since its founding. He was a high-school drop-out and an admitted graduate of the school of "hard-knocks." Before organizing TEI he had worked for the Family Finance Corporation.

In 1963 the son of the founder began working for TEI at its Morris Plan Bank in Chelsea, Massachusetts. From 1959 to 1963 he had worked for the American Finance Corporation, where he had been responsible for collections on small loans. As assistant vice president of TEI's Chelsea subsidiary, he was primarily responsible for loan collections until his transfer to the home office in Dela-

ware in 1966. Between 1966 and 1970 he held the position of assistant treasurer, filling in for vacationing or short-handed subsidiary managers. In 1970 he was made vice president and slowly began to assume control of TEI's operations, until the point was reached where his father would only appear at the office a few mornings a week.

Operations in fiscal years 1971 and 1972 provided net earnings of $57,000 and $94,000 respectively. (See Exhibit 4.) Mansfield commented in the 1972 annual report that that year's results would have been a great deal more favorable were it not for an increase in operating expenses in the last half of the year. He went on to explain these costs as "an increase in personnel and related expenses that were not fully productive during the period, and in the interest on [borrowed funds]."

In 1973 TEI experienced a before-tax operating loss in excess of $6,000, despite an 11 percent increase in operating income. Operating expenses had increased 16 percent over 1972, mostly because of increased interest on borrowed money and a 10 percent increase in salaries.

Earnings in 1974 again dropped sharply, despite a slight rise in operating revenues. The drop was a result of a further 24 percent rise in interest costs and a substantial increase in the provision for losses on receivables.

It should be noted that TEI used the recency method, rather than the contractual method, for determining the delinquency of an office's loan portfolio. Effectively this meant that if any payment was made on a loan, regardless if earlier payments were missed, that loan was not classified as delinquent. The implication of such a policy was to show fewer bad loans than under the more widely used contractual method.

TEI used two major sources for funds to finance its lending activities. It had a $6 million bank line of credit with a sliding interest rate pegged at several points above prime and ostensibly collateralized by loan receivables. TEI and eight of its subsidiaries also sold investment certificates (ICs) and passbook accounts to individual investors. The ICs were similar to normal savings accounts, and interest was either paid or accumulated. At the time of the bankruptcy, these ICs accounted for about two-thirds of total capitalization. (See Exhibit 5.) TEI's management believed that its ICs were exempt from the registration requirements of the 1933 Securities Act, and the SEC did not challenge this position for over twenty years. In early 1975, however, the SEC undertook an investigation of TEI and its subsidiaries. In April 1975 the companies consented to a final judgement prohibiting TEI and five subsidiaries from continuing these sales unless the requirements of the 1933 Act were met.

Meanwhile ever increasing costs of borrowing and overhead expenses, coupled with an economic downturn and increasing delinquency in its portfolio, caused further losses. TEI's consolidated retained earnings plummeted from $540,000 in September of 1973 to a deficiency of over $3.5 million two years later. (See Exhibit 6.) As it could no longer issue ICs, TEI had insufficient working capital to meet its debts as they matured. Faced with insolvency and its growing deficiency in net worth, TEI filed a petition in April of 1975 in the Federal District Court in Delaware, seeking protection under Chapter XI of the Bankruptcy Act. Shortly thereafter five subsidiaries also filed; all proceedings were brought into the Federal Court in Delaware and a common receiver appointed.

Robert Davis, the current assistant treasurer and a thirteen-year employee of TEI, blamed the bankruptcy on fraudulent loans made by office managers, a poor management that lacked adequate controls, and the SEC action.

At the time of the bankruptcy TEI had twenty-six offices, most of which were run by natives of the office area. None of the managers had college degrees, but some had completed college courses. They ranged in age from twenty-six to sixty-two and received an average salary of $13,000 to $14,000.

Under the provisions of Chapter XI a debtor is protected by the court from the demands of its creditors. Management is permitted to continue to operate the business, free from the threat of creditor lawsuits, and is charged with developing an acceptable "Plan of Arrangement" to pay off its debts. A receiver is normally appointed by the court to oversee the assets and supervise the affairs of the debtor while the company remains under court supervision. In effect, the receiver assumes the position of the board of directors, while the debtor's management is given the opportunity to propose an arrangement, which must be approved by the court and agreed to by a majority of the affected creditors. If such an arrangement cannot be agreed upon by the interested parties, liquidation usually results.

If outsiders, such as the creditors or the SEC, file a successful petition with the court, the proceedings usually fall under Chapter X of the Bankruptcy Act. In these cases the court normally appoints a trustee who is charged with controlling the firm during the reorganization period and preparing a formal "Plan of Reorganization." Such a plan must be reviewed by the SEC for fairness to all parties and overall feasibility, in addition to receiving court and creditor approval. A corporate reorganization often offers creditors an equity interest in the debtor in satisfaction of at least part of their claims, while a Chapter XI arrangement typically restructures the debtor's liabilities without changing the ownership of the firm.

TEI's management, after substantial delay, was unable to put together an acceptable plan of arrangement. As the firm had expended considerable effort and money in meeting the procedural requirements of Chapter XI, a change to Chapter X was deemed too costly and time consuming. The creditor committees' attorneys and other parties of interest decided to petition the court to amend the receiver's orders to assign him the basic responsibilities of a Chapter X trustee, while remaining in Chapter XI. After a hearing at which no objections were raised, the court approved the petition.

At the time of bankruptcy, TEI and its debtor subsidiaries (those that also filed for bankruptcy) stopped selling ICs and making new loans, but continued to collect on and renew old loans. In November 1975 the Bankruptcy Court authorized the receiver to enter into an agreement with American Security and Trust Company (AS&T), the bank that had provided the original line of credit. Under this agreement AS&T would lend money at prime to TEI, upon the pledge of the loan paper. TEI's subsidiaries were thus able to resume operations. All debtor subsidiaries, with the exception of Allstate Industrial Loan Plan, again began to make new loans.

AS&T's claim was approximately $6.3 million, and was allegedly secured by the pledge of loan accounts receivable of certain TEI subsidiaries. However, the receiver disputed the validity of these pledges, since they may have constituted preferences or fraudulent transfers under the Bankruptcy Act. As part of the new agreement the receiver and AS&T entered into a stipulation under which the receiver paid the bank amounts collected on the disputed receivables. In return AS&T agreed to lend the additional money to TEI. The receiver also agreed to delay contesting the AS&T claim, while AS&T agreed to forgive interest on the unpaid balance between the date of bankruptcy and the date of the confirmation of the plan of arrangement.

During the bankruptcy, the receiver tried to retrench TEI's business by reducing overhead and increasing loans outstanding. A basic strategy was developed to sell the most unprofitable offices either for loan paper or for cash to be used to expand the remaining offices. This would result in fewer offices, but more loans per office, and thus bring each office closer to the breakeven point established by the receiver, some $1 million of loans outstanding per office. (See Exhibit 7.)

Three offices in Georgia were closed and offices in Tennessee and Delaware were consolidated. The receiver also entered into agreements with ITT Thorp Corporation to sell virtually all of the loan portfolios of TEI's unprofitable subsidiaries in Kentucky and Maryland. Some of the proceeds of these sales were used to purchase paper in the areas of the remaining offices. By these means, the number of offices was reduced to sixteen. The plan of arrangement contemplated retaining only the nine most potentially profitable offices. (See Exhibit 8.)

A major determinant of the value of an office's loan portfolio is its delinquency, or the number of loans in the portfolio that have one or more payments past due. Evaluation of a large portfolio can be quite time-consuming. Each loan is analyzed to determine the number of payments past due to estimate whether the customer will fulfill his obligation.

TEI typically realized between 60 and 80 percent of the net book value (gross amount of the notes minus unearned income) of the receivables it sold. In purchasing loan paper for its Philadelphia office, it paid a premium of 15 percent over net book value. This was the only loan paper that TEI found for sale in the areas of its remaining offices.

After long rounds of negotiations with the different creditor groups, a consolidated plan of arrangement was filed in April 1976, containing the following provisions:

1. Trade creditors, whose claims totaled about $10,000, would be paid in full.
2. Unsecured creditors with claims under $500 would be paid 75 percent of their claims. These claims totaled about $229,000. The plan had to be approved by a majority of these creditors.
3. Unsecured creditors with claims over $500 would be paid 10 percent in cash, with their remaining claim paid 40 percent in income bonds and 60 percent in preferred stock. Claims of these creditors totaled about $10.2 million. This class of creditors also had the right to approve the plan of arrangement by majority vote.
4. The income bonds would bear an interest rate of 6.5 percent. TEI would be required to retire 20

percent of these bonds each year from the fourth to the eighth year after confirmation. Interest on the bonds would be cumulative, but not compounded.

5. The preferred stock would have a par value of $0.10 and a liquidation value of $100 plus accumulated dividends. The dividend would be $6.50 and cumulative.

6. A new seven-member board of directors would be established. Five of the directors would be elected by the preferred shareholders. One of the remaining directors would be elected by the holders of Class A common stock, and the other by holders of Class B common stock.

7. TEI would issue another class of bonds to AS&T equal to the latter's claim, less money remitted to AS&T under the June 30, 1975, stipulation, plus any loans made to TEI in the interim. This amounted to about $4.4 million. The bonds would bear an interest rate of 6.5 percent and would mature from the sixth to the tenth years of the plan.

8. AS&T would also lend TEI an additional $600,000 between the confirmation date and the fourth year after confirmation. In the six years it would lend additional money so that the total, when added to the bonds held by AS&T, would equal no more than $7 million. Loans made under this provision would bear interest at AS&T's prime rate and would be secured by a pledge of loan accounts receivable.

9. The receiver would serve on the board of directors. (A pro forma condensed balance sheet giving effect to the plan of arrangement is presented in Exhibit 9.)

On July 19, 1976, some 90 percent of all creditors approved the proposal. The Bankruptcy Court confirmed the plan on September 9, after extensive testimony on feasibility by the receiver.

As the plan of arrangement was developed and its feasibility studied, it become increasingly apparent that the current information and internal control systems at TEI were painfully inadequate. A series of employee defalcations uncovered in Tennessee had clearly demonstrated the weakness of the existing system. A search uncovered only one commercially-available computer system specifically designed for finance companies that met the security criteria set by management. Development of a custom package was rejected because of the small size of the company and its lack of personnel experienced in EDP applications. Management estimated that the proposed system would be cost-effective even at relatively low levels of loan volume, and decided to install the system. It was expected to be operational in early 1977.

Fred Selah, the chief operating officer, had more than twenty-five years of consumer loan industry experience. Before coming to TEI in 1973 Selah had been vice president of another consumer loan company in Georgia, responsible for seventy offices. His experience and contacts in the loan industry were a valuable asset for TEI. Further, he was well liked and genuinely respected by TEI's employees.

Selah was optimistic about the future, based in part on the loyalty of the employees, many of whom stayed with TEI out of a desire to, in Selah's words, "see the company through." In addition, he was hopeful because plans were underway to sell the unprofitable Massachusetts subsidiaries, thus providing more cash and paper. Selah believed he had a good working relationship with the receiver, who had been elected chairman of the board. Further, TEI's net losses in 1974, 1975, and the first-half of 1976 had created a significant tax loss carry-forward, which would be available to offset any taxable income that TEI might generate in the next few years. Finally, while much of TEI's existing loan portfolio was delinquent, Selah believed that an adequate allowance for loan losses had been established, and that the loans currently being made were of premium quality.

On the other hand, even though all the remaining offices were slowly increasing their portfolios, Selah recognized that internal growth alone would not be sufficient to bring the smaller offices up to profitable levels within a reasonable time. As TEI did not deal in sales finance paper, it had to rely primarily on former borrowers, present customers, and individual recommendations to generate loan volume. Selah required each office manager to maintain contacts with reputable retailers in the area of the loan office. Small commissions were offered for acceptable referrals, where allowed by law. TEI used no paid advertising media, as Selah did not believe it to be cost-effective.

As a result of the plan of arrangement, TEI had currently available about $1.7 million in cash, marketable securities, and credit from AS&T. To service the debt under the plan of arrangement adequately, all TEI's assets had

to be as productive as possible. The firm expected to earn an annual percentage rate of 23 to 25 percent on its loans and hoped to bring bad debts down to the industry norm of 3 percent. Therefore Selah was considering alternative proposals to present to the board of directors. They included:

1. Diversify geographically;
2. Diversify the product line;
3. Buy paper for the existing offices; and
4. Sell the company.

EXHIBIT 1
THE CONSUMER FINANCE INDUSTRY

NUMBER OF FINANCE COMPANIES BY SIZE

	June 30			
	1960	1965	1970	1975
Companies having short-and intermediate-term credit outstanding of:				
Under $100,000	2,124	1,199	826	863
$100,000 and less than $500,000	2,770	1,771	1,065	1,204
$500,000 and less than $1,000,000	652	535	424	415
$1,000,000 and less than $5,000,000	631	498	399	500
$5,000,000 and less than $25,000,000	175	164	112	204
$25,000,000 and less than $100,000,000	45	82	77	102
$100,000,000 and over	27	44	58	88
Total	6,424	4,293	2,961	3,376

Source: Federal Reserve Board

EXHIBIT 1 (cont.)

THE CONSUMER FINANCE INDUSTRY

ASSETS OF FINANCE COMPANIES
(In millions of dollars)

	1960	1965	June 30 1970	1975
Consumer receivables	15,192	22,357	31,773	42,760
Personal cash loans	4,570	8,695	12,380	16,715
Retail automobile paper	7,559	8,822	9,250	9,933
Mobile homes and campers	n a	1,120	2,327	3,461
Revolving consumer installment credit	n a	n a	n a	5,752
All other[a]	3,064	3,720	7,816	6,895
Business receivables	8,489	12,931	22,999	39,286
Wholesale paper	n a	4,239	7,521	10,945
Retail paper	n a	4,033	6,563	11,067
Lease paper	n a	841	3,802	8,065
Other business credit	n a	3,818	5,113	9,208
Other receivables	n a	194	2,342	3,948
Total gross receivables	23,681	35,482	57,113	85,994
Less reserves for unearned income	2,001[b]	2,633	5,131	7,684
Subtotal	n a	32,849	51,982	78,310
Less reserves for losses	n a	637	1,123	1,623
Total net receivables	21,680	32,212	50,859	76,687
Cash and non-interest bearing deposits	1,440[c]	1,481[c]	1,920	2,667
Time deposits	n a	n a	102	202
Other loans and investments	1,025	1,917	6,041	6,745
All other assets	834	666	1,655	2,416
Total assets	24,978	36,275	60,577	88,716

Note: Parts may not add to totals due to rounding.
na: Not available.

[a]Includes mobile home and revolving credit if any in 1960, includes revolving credit in 1965 and 1970.
[b]Reserves for unearned income and reserves for losses were combined in the 1960 survey.
[c]Includes interest-bearing time deposits in 1960 and 1965.
Source: Federal Reserve Board

EXHIBIT 1 (cont.)
THE CONSUMER FINANCE INDUSTRY

LIABILITIES, CAPITAL, AND SURPLUS OF FINANCE COMPANIES
(In millions of dollars)

	1960	1965	June 30 1970	1975
Loans and notes payable to banks	5,649	5,559	7,550	8,617
Short-term	5,162	5,290	6,581	7,900
Long-term	487	269	969	718
Commercial paper	4,642	8,933	22,073	25,905
Directly placed	n a	7,677	19,247	23,686
Dealer placed	n a	1,256	2,826	2,218
Other short-term notes and loans payable[a]	n a	547	975	2,815
Deposit liabilities and thrift certificates[b]	n a	707	639	1,480
Other current liabilities	1,758	2,209	3,468	3,113
Long-term senior debt (other than subordinated)	6,076	9,159	11,154	23,404
Subordinated debentures	2,280	3,497	4,347	5,609
All other liabilities	506	220	424	3,823
Capital, surplus and undivided profits	4,066	5,443	9,947	13,951
Total	24,978	36,275	60,577	88,716
Summary				
Short-term borrowing	9,804	14,770	29,629	36,620
Long-term borrowing	8,843	12,925	16,470	29,731
Subtotal—borrowing	18,647	27,695	46,099	66,351
Deposit liabilities and thrift certificates[b]	n a	707	639	1,480
Subtotal	n a	28,402	46,738	67,831
Other liabilities	2,264	2,429	3,892	6,936
Subtotal—liabilities	20,911	30,831	50,630	74,767
Capital, surplus and undivided profits	4,066	5,443	9,947	13,951
Total	24,978	36,275	60,577	88,716

Note: Parts may not add to totals due to rounding.

[a]In 1960, included with commercial paper.
[b]In 1960, included with other current liabilities.
n a: Not available.
Source: Federal Reserve Board

EXHIBIT 2

BORROWER PROFILE AND INDUSTRY DATA

PERCENTAGE DISTRIBUTION OF LIABILITIES, CAPITAL, AND SURPLUS FOR CONSUMER FINANCE COMPANIES RESPONDING TO NCFA QUESTIONNAIRE

	December 31					
	1965	1970	1971	1972	1973	1974
Balance Sheet Item						
Notes payable to banks	17.2	14.3	13.3	11.9	11.1	10.9
Commercial paper and other short-term debt	9.9	19.7	19.5	16.8	18.0	18.8
Deposit liabilities and thrift certificates (short-term)	1.8	1.6	1.7	4.1	4.0	3.1
Long-term debt (excluding subordinated debentures)	35.5	31.3	30.6	32.7	34.1	34.2
Subordinated debentures and notes	9.0	7.9	8.4	8.1	7.9	7.5
Other liabilities	4.8	4.3	4.2	4.5	5.2	6.0
Capital and surplus	21.8	20.9	22.3	21.9	19.7	19.5
Total	100.0	100.0	100.0	100.0	100.0	100.0

Note: Parts may not add to totals due to rounding.
Source: National Consumer Finance Association

GROSS INCOME OF CONSUMER FINANCE COMPANIES—SOURCES AND USES

	(Percent of gross income)					
	1965	1970	1971	1972	1973	1974
Sources of Gross Income						
Accounts receivable	84.7	79.8	80.0	80.0	78.4	82.7
Other	15.3	20.2	20.0	20.0	21.6	17.3
Total	100.0	100.0	100.0	100.0	100.0	100.0
Uses of Gross Income						
Expenses other than cost of borrowed funds						
Wages and salaries	24.9	24.7	22.2	23.3	20.4	21.5
Advertising and publicity	3.1	2.3	1.9	2.2	2.4	1.9
Net losses and reserves	9.5	8.6	9.4	10.5	12.0	12.4
Other	19.5	19.4	22.6	18.8	22.7	19.0
Subtotal	57.0	55.0	56.1	54.8	57.5	54.8
Cost of borrowed funds	18.0	27.1	23.2	22.4	26.0	31.9
Federal income taxes	10.1	5.8	6.9	7.2	6.2	3.4
Net income	14.9	12.1	13.8	15.6	10.3	9.9
Total	100.0	100.0	100.0	100.0	100.0	100.0

Note: Parts may not add to totals due to rounding.
Source: National Consumer Finance Association

BORROWER PROFILE AND INDUSTRY DATA

PERCENTAGE DISTRIBUTION OF THE MONTHLY INCOME OF BORROWERS FROM CONSUMER FINANCE COMPANIES, SELECTED YEARS

| | Borrowers from Finance Companies Percent of: | | All Households Percent of: | |
	Number of loans	Amount of loans	Number of households	Amount household income[a]
By Annual Income				
Less than $3,500	3.8[b]	2.3[b]	16.0	2.7
$ 3,500 to $ 5,999	16.8[b]	12.8[b]	12.8	4.9
$ 6,000 to $ 8,999	30.3	26.2	14.3	8.6
$ 9,000 to $11,999	23.8	25.6	13.7	11.5
$12,000 and over	25.3	33.1	43.2	72.3
Total	100.0	100.0	100.0	100.0
By Age				
Less than 25 years	18.5	15.8	8.2	5.4
25 to 34 years	27.9	29.5	21.0	21.5
35 to 44 years	24.1	26.1	16.7	20.6
45 to 54 years	23.5	22.3	18.2	23.9
55 to 64 years	5.5	5.9	15.9	17.0
65 years and over	0.5	0.4	20.0	11.6
Total	100.0	100.0	100.0	100.0

Note: Parts may not add to totals due to rounding.
[a]Amount of income by income levels is NCFA estimate.
[b]$3,600 or less in income in the first group and $3,600 to $6,000 in the second group.
Source: NCFA Surveys and Bureau of the Census.

PERCENTAGE DISTRIBUTION OF THE MONTHLY INCOME OF BORROWERS FROM CONSUMER FINANCE COMPANIES, SELECTED YEARS

| | (Percent of Number of Loans Extended) | | | | | |
	1965	1970	1971	1972	1973	1974
Monthly income of borrowers						
$ 0.01 to 100.00	0.2	0.5	0.4	0.1	0.1	0.5
$ 100.01 to 200.00	2.2	1.2	1.0	1.0	0.8	0.9
$ 200.01 to 300.00	8.8	8.8	5.6	3.2	2.6	2.4
$ 300.01 to 400.00	16.3	12.7	12.0	8.9	7.6	7.1
$ 400.01 to 500.00	23.1	15.2	14.2	11.3	9.9	9.7
$ 500.01 to 750.00	33.5	32.7	36.0	37.1	33.7	30.3
$ 750.01 to 1,000.00	12.2	17.7	16.9	18.6	20.2	23.8
$1,000.00 and over	3.7	11.2	13.9	19.8	25.1	25.3
Total	100.0	100.0	100.0	100.0	100.0	100.0

Note: Parts may not add to totals due to rounding.
Source: National Consumer Finance Association survey data for years through 1965 as reported by companies which operated over 1,800 offices in 1965. For 1970 data as reported by companies that operated 4,857 offices, for 1971 companies that operated 4,813 offices, for 1972 companies that operated 2,620 offices, for 1973 companies that operated 3,372 offices, and for 1974 companies that operated 4,663 offices.

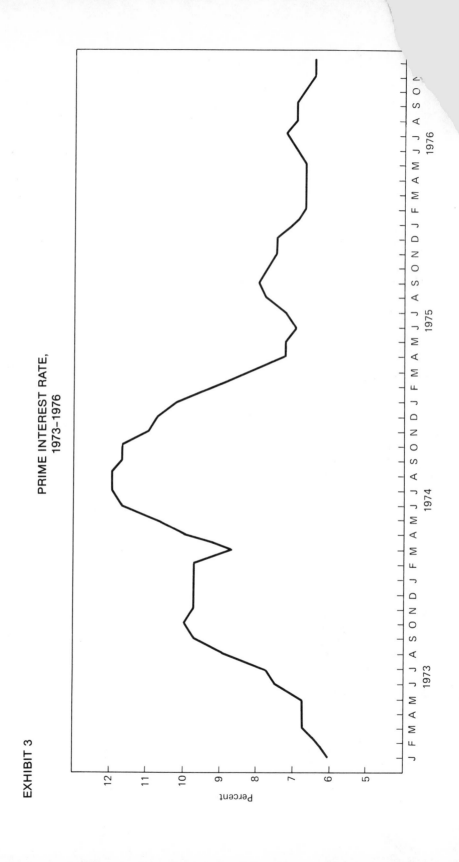

EXHIBIT 3

PRIME INTEREST RATE,
1973–1976

EXHIBIT 4

123

TOWN ENTERPRISES, INC., AND SUBSIDIARIES
Statement of Consolidated Income (Loss) and Retained Earnings (Deficit)
For the Six Months Ended March 31, 1976 and the Five Years Ended September 30, 1975
(Unaudited)

	Six Months Ended March 31, 1976	Years Ended September 30,				
		1975	1974	1973	1972	1971
Operating income						
Interest, discounts, fees, etc.	$1,314,697	$3,898,836	$5,637,823	$5,629,923	$5,069,788	$4,251,314
Operating expenses						
Salaries	418,754	1,184,998	1,444,831	1,416,699	1,299,904	1,190,619
Loan loss provision	634,951	1,444,710	1,396,252	697,465	708,564	472,972
Interest	227,193	1,516,700	2,296,928	1,857,330	1,533,379	1,335,241
Other operating expenses	427,130	1,377,068	1,697,283	1,664,872	1,331,666	1,119,684
	1,708,028	5,523,476	6,835,294	5,636,366	4,873,513	4,118,516
Income (loss) before other charges (credits), income taxes, extraordinary credit, and cumulative effect of accounting change	(393,331)	(1,624,640)	(1,197,471)	(6,443)	196,275	132,798
Other charges (credits)						
Receivership administration costs	900,000	—	—	—	—	—
Increase (decrease) in provision for additional estimated loan losses	(174,000)	900,000	—	—	—	—
Loss on write-off of goodwill, prepaid expenses, deferred charges and assets of doubtful value	—	227,838	—	—	—	—
Loss on sale of receivables and other assets	—	143,675	—	—	—	—
	726,000	1,271,513 •	—	—	—	—
Income (loss) before taxes, extraordinary credit and cumulative effect of accounting change	(1,119,331)	(2,896,153)	(1,197,471)	(6,443)	196,275	132,798
Provision (credit) for income taxes						
Current						
Federal	—	—	(20,000)	(3,000)	89,000	42,000
State	—	—	26,000	25,000	23,000	29,800
Deferred	—	—	7,000	(10,000)	(10,000)	4,400
	—	—	13,000	12,000	102,000	76,200

TOWN ENTERPRISES, INC., AND SUBSIDIARIES
Statement of Consolidated Income (Loss) and Retained Earnings (Deficit)
For the Six Months Ended March 31, 1976 and the Five Years Ended September 30, 1975
(Unaudited)

Income (loss) before extraordinary credit, and cumulative effect of accounting change	(1,119,331)	(2,896,153)	(1,210,471)	(18,443)	94,275	56,598
Net proceeds of life insurance on former president of purchased subsidiary				155,896		
Cumulative effect on prior years to September 30, 1972, of changing method of reporting finance income, less related taxes, $82,000				(76,000)		
Cumulative effect on prior years of changing method of reporting insurance commission income		(67,750)				
Net income (loss)	(1,119,331)	(2,963,903)	(1,210,471)	61,453	94,275	56,598
Retained earnings (deficit) at beginning of year	(3,632,167)	(688,264)	542,207	512,922	440,329	383,731
	(4,751,498)	(3,632,167)	(668,264)	574,375	534,604	440,329
Less cash dividends				32,168	21,682	
Retained earnings (deficit) at end of year	($4,751,498)	($3,632,167)	($668,264)	$542,207	$512,922	$440,329
Weighted average number of common shares outstanding	202,701	202,701	204,506	215,050	216,864	217,027
Net income (loss) per weighted average number of shares of Class A and Class B Common Stock outstanding:						
Income (loss) before extraordinary credit, and cumulative effect of accounting change	($5.52)	($14.29)	($5.92)	($.09)	$.43	$.26
Extraordinary credit				.73		
Cumulative effect of accounting change, less related taxes		(.33)		.35		
Net income (loss)	($5.52)	($14.62)	($5.92)	$.29	$.43	$.26
Cash dividends per share of common stock				$.15	$.10	

EXHIBIT 5

TOWN ENTERPRISES, INC. AND SUBSIDIARIES
Consolidated Balance Sheet
March 31, 1976 and September 30, 1975 and 1974
(Unaudited)

ASSETS	March 31, 1976	September 30, 1975	September 30, 1974
Cash, including time deposits, 1975, $318,582; 1974, $200,000	$ 1,169,094	$ 1,736,925	$ 1,185,600
Marketable securities at cost, plus accrued interest, market values, 1976, $4,442,656; 1975, $2,936,227; 1974, $1,069,286	$ 4,589,303	$ 3,150,983	$ 1,135,858
Receivables			
Installment notes and contracts	$14,648,376	$18,672,953	$29,796,846
Less unearned discount	1,462,187	1,939,558	3,631,049
	$13,186,189	$16,733,395	$26,165,797
Demand notes and accrued interest	369,492	380,526	549,405
Loans with repossessed collateral	591,046	688,117	609,381
Other accounts	397,555	409,445	142,071
	$14,544,282	$18,211,483	$27,466,654
Less allowance for estimated loan losses	2,073,539	2,403,704	1,441,161
	$12,470,743	$15,807,779	$26,025,493
Property and equipment, at cost	$ 595,152	$ 633,903	$ 747,563
Less accumulated depreciation and amortization	366,161	345,301	387,620
	$ 228,991	$ 288,602	$ 359,943
Other assets			
Prepaid expenses	$ 38,208	$ 54,295	$ 55,849
Deferred charges	—	—	210,487
Excess of cost of investment over acquired net assets of subsidiaries	—	—	43,956
	$ 38,208	$ 54,295	$ 310,292
	$18,496,339	$21,038,584	$29,017,186

EXHIBIT 5 (cont.)

TOWN ENTERPRISES, INC. AND SUBSIDIARIES
Consolidated Balance Sheet
March 31, 1976 and September 30, 1975 and 1974
(Unaudited)

LIABILITIES AND SHAREHOLDERS' EQUITY (DEFICIENCY)

Liabilities			
Investment certificates	$15,704,561	$16,403,082	$19,738,300
Notes payable			
Banks	3,529,548	5,139,610	6,630,000
Other	16,298	16,409	72,990
Accounts payable and accrued expenses	212,591	158,557	269,126
Receiver's administration costs payable	900,000	—	—
Accrued interest	203,194	251,647	322,597
Unearned insurance commission income	24,208	49,009	—
Subordinated debentures	1,583,450	1,583,450	1,583,450
Total liabilities	$22,178,850	$23,601,764	$28,616,463
Commitments and contingencies			
Shareholders' equity (deficiency)			
Capital stock, $2.50 par			
Class A common, authorized 200,000 shares; issued 178,267 shares	$ 445,668	$ 445,668	$ 445,668
Class B common, authorized, issued and outstanding 40,000 shares	100,000	100,000	100,000
Additional paid-in capital	569,210	569,210	569,210
Deficit	(4,751,498)	(3,632,167)	(668,264)
	($ 3,636,620)	($ 2,517,289)	$ 446,614
(Add) Deduct 15,566 Shares of Class A common stock held in treasury at cost	(45,891)	(45,891)	45,891
	($ 3,682,511)	($ 2,563,180)	$ 400,723
	$18,496,339	$21,038,584	$29,017,186

EXHIBIT 6

CONSOLIDATED STATEMENT OF INCOME (LOSS) AND
RETAINED EARNINGS (DEFICIT)
Seven Months Ended April 30, 1975
(Unaudited)
($000)

	Operating Income	Net Income (Loss)	Retained Earnings (Deficit)
Town Enterprises, Incorporated[a] (Delaware)	$587	($1,417)	($2,086)
Town Finance Corporation[a] (Delaware)	460	(20)	64
County Savings and Loan[a] (Tennessee)	598	255	(799)
County Thrift and Loan[a] (Maryland)	83	(31)	(60)
Town Finance Corporation[a] (Georgia)	306	(191)	(306)
Allstate Industrial Loan Plan[a] (Kentucky)	167	(113)	(108)
Town Finance Corporation (Pennsylvania)	1	(9)	(139)
Town Consumer Discount (Pennsylvania)	79	(42)	(80)
The New Bedford Morris Plan (Massachusetts)	292	28	610
Morris Plan Bank and Banking Company (Massachusetts)	368	(198)	164
Allstate Finance Corporation (Kentucky)	29	(9)	(242)
Family Savings and Loan (West Virginia)	101	(46)	(14)
Allstate Finance Corporation (West Virginia)	209	(57)	(327)
Allstate Credit Corporation (Ohio)	23	(29)	(69)
Allstate Industrial Mortgage Corp. (Ohio)	22	(7)	23
County Savings and Loan Company (Tennessee)	...	Inactive	(316)
Allstate Finance Company (Kentucky)	...	Inactive	(195)
Allstate Industrial Plan, Incorporated (Kentucky)	...	Inactive	(21)

[a]Filed for bankruptcy.

EXHIBIT 7

BUDGETED STATEMENT OF PROFIT AND LOSS
FOR A TYPICAL OFFICE WITH $1,000,000 LOANS OUTSTANDING
FY 1977

Gross Operating Revenue		$215,000
Occupancy expense	$15,000	
Personnel expense	45,000	
Provision for bad debts	35,000	
Home office overhead	20,000	
All other	25,000	
		140,000
Income before Interest Expense		$ 75,000

BUDGETED STATEMENT OF PROFIT AND LOSS
Wilmington, Delaware, Office
FY 1977

Gross Operating Revenue		$490,000
Occupancy expense	$15,000	
Personnel expense	90,000	
Provision for bad debts	55,000	
Home office overhead	50,000	
All other	30,000	
		240,000
Income before Interest Expense		$250,000

EXHIBIT 8

OFFICES RETAINED UNDER PLAN OF ARRANGEMENT

Office	Loans Outstanding	No. Loan Accounts	No. Employees
Wilmington, Delaware	$2,350,000	1550	9
Philadelphia, Pennsylvania	750,000	705	3
Rossville, Georgia	475,000	800	3
Chattanooga, Tennessee	1,200,000	540	4
Oak Ridge, Tennessee	1,120,000	460	3
Huntington, West Virginia	275,000	390	3
Madison, West Virginia	390,000	526	4
Marmet, West Virginia	390,000	625	4
Family S&L (Huntington, W. Va.)	750,000	350	4

EXHIBIT 9

TOWN ENTERPRISES, INC. AND SUBSIDIARIES
Pro Forma Condensed Balance Sheet—March 31, 1976
(Unaudited)
(In Rounded Thousands)

The following pro forma condensed balance sheet includes the unaudited March 31, 1976 consolidated balance sheet of Town Enterprises, Inc., and its subsidiaries, giving effect to the transactions described in the notes to the pro forma condensed balance sheet.

	Historical March 31, 1976 (Unaudited)	Pro Forma Adjustments	Pro Forma (Unaudited)
ASSETS			
Cash and marketable securities	$ 5,758	($ 3,220) (1)	$1,138
		870 (2)	
		(1,370) (3)	
		(900) (4)	
Receivables	$14,544	($ 4,555) (1)	$9,989
Less allowance for estimated loan losses	2,073	(270) (1)	1,803
	$12,471	($ 4,285)	$8,186
Other assets	$ 267	($ 131) (1)	$ 136
	$18,496	($ 9,036)	$9,460
LIABILITIES AND SHAREHOLDERS' EQUITY (DEFICIENCY)			
Liabilities			
Investment certificates	$15,705	($ 4,832) (1)	$ 568
		(10,305) (3)	
Note payable, bank	3,530	(3,530) (2)	—
Receivership administration costs payable	900	(900) (4)	—
Other liabilities	461	(103) (1)	233
		(125) (3)	
Subordinated debentures	1,583	(1,583) (1)	—
Bonds payable, bank		4,400 (2)	4,400
Income bonds		3,640 (3)	3,640
Total liabilities	$22,179	($13,338)	$8,841
Shareholders' Equity (Deficiency)			
Preferred stock	$	$ 6 (3)	$ 6
Common stock (Class A & B)	546	—	546
Additional paid-in capital	569	5,357 (3)	5,926
(Deficit)	(4,752)	(1,118) (1)	(5,813)
		57 (3)	
	($ 3,637)	$ 4,302	$ 665
Add (deduct) treasury stock	(46)	—	($ 46)
	($ 3,683)	$ 4,302	$ 619
	$18,496	($ 9,036)	$9,460

MINICOMPUTER, INCORPORATED

Minicomputer, Incorporated, (MI) is a major factor in the small electronic computer industry. It had experienced a spectacular growth of almost 3000 percent between 1962 and 1972. (Exhibit 1 summarizes MI's progress.)

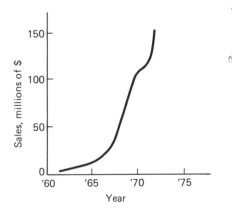

This case reviews the development of the MIX family, and particularly the MIX-5 computer, at MI and traces the events and decisions taken in bringing this major innovation to market. The program unfolds over a five-year period. Exhibit 2 will help the reader follow the chronology.

THE MIX-1 STUDY

In the second half of 1967 a team of MI engineers was assigned the task of developing the specifications for a new, 16-bit, MI computer. Designated the MIX-1, the design advanced the state of the art substantially and offered performance comparable to that finally achieved five years later by the MIX-5. Upon review, corporate managers killed the program; the machine was fast and powerful but too expensive. It was not regarded as a logical extension of the firm's minicomputer line, and no one on the project team would speak up to defend the system. The designers were unable to present a business plan that would place the proposed machine in a defined market. Manufacturing had also voiced concern over problems that might arise in implementing the design, because it required high-density circuits, multilayered printed circuit boards, and sophisticated testing.

THE MIX-2 STUDY

In March 1968 an MI mathematician led a group study of the EAM (electric adding machine), a smaller 16-bit machine. The team maintained tight security, reporting directly to MI president, Stanley Allen. The system that evolved in the following year bore little resemblance to the MIX-1. It was cheaper and perhaps slower.

When the concept surfaced, the engineering staff responded quickly. They asserted that the EAM was "a bad tool," wasn't general enough, and failed to satisfy their market specifications for easy programming and use.

Concern that MI was losing market shares to newer and cheaper 16-bit computers led to a design freeze in February 1969. Corporate management had directed that the EAM be developed as a low-priced, 16-bit machine positioned between existing computer systems, but it still wasn't off the drawing board.

In a hectic three-day session during the week prior to the design freeze the EAM was junked in favor of a new 16-bit MIX design. A corporate consultant undertook to convince MI management of the choice. In a memorandum to the operations committee dated February 1969 he argued that the EAM was not well thought out, that it would be difficult to program, and that its central processing (logic) unit was not big enough to allow it to fully exploit the system structure. What was needed was a general architecture that could be expanded into a line of compatible computers, using standard software and peripheral equipment. The plan for this architecture would give MI a sales tool on paper with which to resist market encroachments by Varian, Hewlett-Packard, and Data General. (The consultant wanted MI to build "machines his friends would buy.") The operations committee agreed with the memo. Allen publicly committed MI to the new system, now called the MIX-2, the first in a line of compatible MIX systems. The MIX, like IBM's 360 systems, was to be a large family.

THE MIX-3 AND MIX-4 STUDIES

Early in 1970 two new studies were started aimed at developing larger new systems. One project, called the MIX-4 study, reported to a vice president; another, the MIX-3, was headed by Roger Carr, who had previously worked on MIX-2. Carr reported to Andrew Morgan, product line manager for the MIX family. Exhibit 3 shows part of the MI organization at the time.

The MIX-4 manager was tied down on another project during the study, so technical direction fell to one of the consultant's students. The charter for this study was not clear. The young manager did not understand that it was just a study. He felt that his task was to develop a medium-scale computer for MI; accordingly, he undertook design of a new 18-bit machine.

Carr's effort was more directed. Morgan had instructed him to devote part-time effort to developing a cheaper, faster version of the new MIX-2, to be designated MIX-3. The

MIX-3 was targeted for a logic speed of 400 to 450 nanoseconds.[1]

Study budgets at MI were quite informal. A project account could be set up at the discretion of a product line manager without a specific dollar commitment and expensed against his operating results.

Before long MIX-3 team members began to criticize MIX-4's radical 18-bit architecture and sniping began between the two study groups. The issue was whether the MIX-4 should be compatible with the 16-bit MIX family.

In a series of confidential memos directed to the consultant, the MIX-4 group defended their design, pointing up its technical superiority and proposing a new family of 18-bit machines. In their memos the MIX-4 team argued that their 18-bit configuration was the only feasible choice and outlined all the shortcomings of the current MIX instruction (programming) set.

In March 1970 the MIX-4 group solicited comments on their design from the engineering committee. In a memo summarizing their position, they claimed:

1. The MIX-4 was superior to the proposed MIX-3 system.
2. Both systems would require new hardware and equivalent engineering costs.
3. The MIX-4 could use any combination of redesigned MIX peripherals.
4. Software was still 75 percent unwritten for both designs.
5. With a translator, the MIX-4 could also use standard MIX software.
6. The MIX-4 could be marketed no more than two months later than a MIX-3.
7. The MIX-4 market would be longer-lived.

The consultant replied in a long memo to the operations committee, dated April 1970. He supported the MIX-3 configuration and urged MI "to get on with it!" He refuted several of the technical claims made for the

[1]Central processor speeds are often expressed in cycle times. Speed is inversely related to cycle time, so shorter cycle times designate faster units.

MIX–4 and observed that the design did not reflect MI's market and profit objectives. He suggested that there were several ways to make the choice between the two designs:

1. Have an "emotional free-for-all;"
2. Evaluate the designs for conformity with MI's announced plans;
3. Perform a weighted quantitative evaluation of the relative technical merits of the two systems.

He concluded that enough information already existed to make a decision. MIX–3 was clearly more consistent with announced plans and also looked better technically. Debate about the MIX–4 should cease and MI should either kill it or fund it. Procrastination would just build tension.

THE MIX–5 EFFORT

In June 1970 the operations committee ordered work halted on the MIX–4 and instituted still another engineering study using MIX architecture. Ross Cotter, a young, successful product line manager of the MIC–11, was given a tight six-person budget. He gave up control of the $12–15 million business to undertake the new study, convinced that it would succeed and ultimately be a major enterprise at MI.

Charter

Cotter saw his assignment this way:

1. Develop a better "mousetrap."
2. Deliver maximum performance within a central processing unit (CPU) price limit of approximately $20,000.
3. Demonstrate performance of each part of the system before making a final commitment, budgeting about 10 percent of the development funds to this effort.
4. Reclaim "emotional leadership" from competitor Data General's SUPER NOVA.

Cotter conferred with Morgan and the MIX marketing manager. They agreed that market estimates for a high-speed machine were promising. Morgan had been developing marketing plans since the beginning of 1970, using inputs from industry statistics, field salesmen, consultants' reports, and customers. They were convinced that Carr's MIX–3 study should seek to compete in the medium-performance market, while Cotter should take on a projected high-performance computer. Cotter was to emphasize speed, not cost; his design could not be technically mediocre. Business was good at MI in early 1970 and Morgan submitted optimistic plans to the operations committee, which used the plans as the basis for budgeting decisions.

TRADEOFFS IN THE MIX FAMILY

Slowly a family of compatible computers was defined. Exhibit 4 shows the positioning of each machine relative to its MIX–2 progenitor. Typical costs, relative speed, relative speed/cost ratios, and order of introduction are presented along with the design criteria.

The optimization of a computer design was always a topic of heated debate at MI. If an engineer was asked the measure of merit for any system, he would invariably choose speed. If a senior executive was asked the same question, he would pick price, reflecting President Allen's often articulated strategy of positioning MI to offer the best values in its market. The product line manager's job was to trade cost and performance in order to develop and market systems that fall in the mini market and offer good speed-to-cost performance.[2] One contingent at MI believed that corporate growth required a five-fold increase in performance with any new computer family. Morgan and Cotter agreed that the MIX–5 project would seek to maximize this ratio by pushing speed over cost to achieve the result. Next the MIX–6 should be developed as the low-priced computer in the

---

[2]Optimization of the performance/cost parameter is only possible if a maximum cost is set, as it is almost always possible to add something to a system and achieve a disproportionate increase in performance for the added cost. This partially explains Allen's concern that his engineers tended to design increasingly expensive machines.

MIX family. Still later a MIX-3 would use the latest technology to outperform both the MIX-5 and MIX-6. (In general, true optimization is achieved by operating on both the speed and cost criteria to maximize the speed/cost ratio.) In undertaking development of the new logic or CPU, it was necessary to make projections of future cost, availability, and performance of components used in the machine, as each of these factors was interdependent and also time dependent. (In time, almost any specification might be met.)

Morgan explained his "visceral" feel for the uncertainty in forecasting performance with an illustration shown in Exhibit 5. Notice that at a later time, T_2, the uncertainty may be less for any required speed/cost ratio. He felt that the sharp knee in the curve could be identified by intelligent testing and evaluation. As Morgan saw it, the MIX-5 and MIX-6 were positioned to avoid the knee. RCA's mistake with the Spectra 70 Computer family had been to select design parameters above the knee and bet on a favorable shift in the curve during the development cycle. The shift hadn't occurred and RCA had had to "buy solutions." Short-term uncertainties, according to Morgan, could usually be dimensioned as time—more time to get the job done.

Cotter didn't exactly agree with Morgan about the initial position of the MIX-5 design, but conceded that the technical choices had turned out to be conservative. His efforts to resolve technological risks and optimize his design are discussed in a later section.

Both Cotter and Morgan agreed that engineers were unlikely to discover the knee of the uncertainty-performance curve because they tended to use the wrong performance criteria, usually speed, instead of speed/cost ratio.

MI product managers all seemed to agree that proposing the sophisticated concept of speed/cost optimization to both management and engineers was more difficult than selling the idea of either speed or cost alone.

Carr had experienced problems with his MIX-3 study in making these tradeoffs. He was faced with improving both cost and performance, but lacked the budget resources to do either.

The impact of a failure to achieve the performance/cost objectives on schedule was not entirely clear. If attempts were made to get back on schedule by spending money for such things as overtime or culling delivered parts to find acceptable ones, the loss to profits was obvious. Where a delay in reaching the market with a new computer was accepted in order to meet these objectives, people at MI had different opinions about the delay's effect on sales. These are illustrated in Exhibit 6, which graphs unit sales relative to time. Engineers often theorized that a loss in time in the market resulted in an irretrievable loss of sales (Area A of graph). Product line managers, like Cotter, held that, given more time to shake out its production line problems before introduction, MI could simply come on stream faster and make up the time lost (graph Area B). Senior managers seemed to believe that the market existed and was waiting for MI's entry, so a delay would simply shift the entire sales curve in time.

Though none of these explanations was likely to be exactly right, they did offer some additional insights into MI's strategy. President Allen had built a responsive manufacturing capability that allowed him to catch up with competition. MI's major position in its market probably did reserve some sales for it, as customers might hesitate to buy a competitor's offering until they saw how MI would respond.

THE EARLY MIX-5 STUDY

Cotter had inherited some problems with the new engineering study. Two engineers who joined this team were unhappy over the cancellation of the earlier MIX-4 effort and were still feuding. The recession had hit MI and the program would have to live within a tight budget.

Although the effort was designated as an engineering study by the operations committee and Cotter had accepted the assignment to get back into engineering from his previous marketing job, he was certain that the MIX–5 would need a big technical sales effort. He commented later:

> Marketing strategy sells toothpaste and surveys result in Edsels. You can't derive a good product definition in the technology area unless your engineers have empathy for the user. ... We don't control technical developments the way IBM or Texas Instruments do. We have to capitalize on timely application. The technology is inexorable.

Cotter saw his task at this point as defining alternatives. His tactic was to make his final commitments only after information was developed. He prepared a "wish list." The engineers were put to work evaluating the practical performance limits of available components and preparing tradeoffs of the benefits of added features against the technical complexity that might result. Target speed was 200 nanoseconds.[3]

It soon became clear that four technical decisions would influence the speed of the new design:

1. Microprogramming implementation. Rather than programming a CPU to do many standard operations, using its usual logic circuits, it is often possible to use microprogramming, building in hard-wired circuits specifically designed to perform these operations at very high speeds. Literally, hardware is substituted for software.
2. The speed of the memories employed.
3. The density of the circuit boards used. Crowded, high-density boards could shorten signal paths.
4. The switching time for the medium-scale integrated circuits that would perform the necessary logic functions. Medium scale ICs have from two to 100 gates per silicon chip.

Although microprogramming was new to MI, no problems were expected and design in this area went forward. The decision on memories came later. The high-density circuit

---

[3]Logic speeds are estimated by tracing signal paths and then summing the switch time for the components encountered and the transit time along the path. Speed can often be increased by driving with higher voltage but energy dissipation then becomes a problem.

boards were to lead to a major innovation at MI. The principal issue faced during the study was the choice of ICs for the logic functions. A detailed account of the work leading to this decision lends further understanding of the resolution of uncertainty at MI.

THE SCHOTTKY LOGIC DECISION

Engineering was responsible for the evaluation of the IC alternatives. In retrospect many people at MI felt that there really was only one choice possible; but Cotter reasoned: "One could be criticized for jumping without a study and an evaluation would keep the vendors honest." Three candidate medium-scale ICs were seriously considered, 1) transistor-transistor logic (TTL); 2) Schottky transistor-transistor logic (STTL), and 3) emitter-coupled logic (ECL).

MI had had a great deal of experience with TTL but these devices were relatively slow, and higher speeds could only be realized by buying large lots of the devices and culling to find those few that exhibited high speed switching characteristics. Essentially this meant using the ICs that happened to fall far out on the favorable tail of the statistical speed distribution curve. The rejected chips could be used in other applications, but the cost would be high because of the testing expense.

Schottky (STTL) logic was a major modification of TTL. It had been developed only six months earlier by Texas Instruments and samples were immediately introduced at MI.

Emitter-coupled logic (ECL) was just being introduced to the market by Motorola. MI had had no previous experience with such devices nor with Motorola as a supplier. Only limited samples were available at MI. The relative speeds of a CPU using various ICs are shown in Exhibit 7.

The close relationship between MI and its traditional supplier, Texas Instruments (TI), greatly influenced the evaluation. MI's purchasing director spoke highly of this firm, praising the open manner in which it provided information. A vice president of TI exchanged visits with MI representatives during the study. MI's engineers spent several months in Texas. The firm had met its previous commitments on TTL prices; it had promised a final price under $0.50 and had succeeded in bringing the actual price down from $2.50 to $0.25. At one time MI had accounted for a large percentage of all usage of these devices. A major question that had to be resolved was whether TI was accurately extrapolating the Schottky logic learning curve. The device, at projected cost, would represent perhaps 15 percent of purchased goods in the MIX–5 central processor.

The MI buyer was also impressed by TI's commitment. He quoted Allen's axiom: "We're-going-to-do-it is a better position than can-we." MI had asked for and received good samples. It appeared that other sources for STTL would soon be available. Cotter was also pleased with the communications, crediting purchasing with "good service" and TI with "keeping things cool and technical at all times."

Engineers accepted many of TI's test results but also developed a number of their own. The problem was a common one in engineering. Could they accept components built to TI's specifications and expect them to perform consistently in an MI application? If they could avoid writing additional delivery specifications, they would be able to use standard components, benefit from TI's production experience, and avoid substantial costs. Late in August 1970 the engineers had made their choice and supported it in a long memo to Cotter and the MI engineering committee. This memo can be summarized as follows:

REASONS FOR CHOOSING STTL OVER MECL–10K

1. More circuit choices will be available in STTL, so fewer ICs are needed to accomplish the logic functions. Texas Instruments has its own ECL but isn't pushing it.
2. STTL is already available on medium-scale integrated circuits. Motorola can only promise that ECL will be available on medium-scale chips.
3. Only STTL is fully compatible with the MIX–5 power supplies.
4. ECL performance degrades when a temperature gradient occurs between two connected chips.
5. STTL will be available from at least two other suppliers. Other firms produce ECL chips, but they're not compatible with Motorola's ECL.
6. ECL is faster on a gate-for-gate basis by 20 to 30 percent. This speed advantage will be lost, however, if a variety of circuit choices are not available, as longer signal paths will result from using several chips to accomplish what the appropriate chip can do.
7. Projections indicate that ECL will cost 30 percent more than STTL.
8. ECL will require multilayer printed circuit boards because of its power supplies. STTL won't.
9. STTL is pin-for-pin compatible with the older TTL, so it is possible to pursue CPU development with TTL until the full family of STTL chips is delivered or to use culled TTL if the particular STTL circuits are not ultimately made available.

No response was forthcoming from the engineering committee. The secretary of the committee recalled that it was never discussed. He felt that the decision was "obvious" and explained that the engineering committee normally "makes recommendations, points out oversights, or keeps quiet."

Engineers who had followed this work from their vantage point in the MIX–3 study, had "never agonized over the choice of ECL, as the choice of STTL was evident."

Cotter agreed that the choice was inevitable because MI was committed to compatible TTL devices throughout the rest of the MIX system. It had occurred to him that his company could buy out a substantial portion of TI's early production of STTL and thus deter competition from developing computers using the Schottky devices. He regarded point number nine of the memo as an important factor in the final choice because it offered a fall-back position.

THE MIX–5 DEVELOPMENT PROGRAM

As 1970 wore on the recession took its toll. The MIX–3 effort was postponed. The decision was made to take the MIX–5 forward with a new target speed of 300 nanoseconds, reflecting the limitations of STTL logic devices.

Budget

With the approval of his six-month budget, Cotter viewed the MIX–5 effort as a full-fledged development program. His sales plan projected a market for about 2000 of the new systems as illustrated in Exhibit 8. The MIX–5 would be sold: first, to knowledgeable users, who could program it themselves; next, to those users who would benefit from software developed by the early buyers; and finally, to people with specific programming problems that MI would help solve. This sales program was based on:

1. MIX–5 system sales only, although these would contribute to overall market leadership for the MIX family;
2. No new MI entry at this performance level during the period projected, although Cotter was already thinking about future modifications to the MIX–5 to expand its market;
3. Substantial expansion of the MIX software programs to solve customer problems;
4. No new competitive entry that was radically better than the MIX–5; and
5. The idea that being the first and biggest in a market has substantial advantages.

Cotter's original budget was "well thought out for twelve months and a guess for twenty-four months." It was to be revised quarterly or when errors were greater than 5 percent. As commercialization proceeded he expected the quality of his estimates to improve. Some $2 million to $3 million was to be committed in bringing the first MIX–5s to market and Cotter might ultimately manage a $40 million to $50 million per year business. No return on investment calculations were made; but, with typical paybacks of two years in the mini-computer markets, return "had to be great." Because the FY72 budget made the necessary provisions for going into production, there were no significant discussions about money; the costs to get there were simply incurred.

Organization

Initially Cotter kept the title of engineering manager himself to avoid the problem of choosing between two of his engineers who were still feuding over previous MIX–4 decisions. Exhibit 9 shows the applicable part of the MI organization at the time.

Engineering

Cotter was not without problems on his team. For about six weeks his engineers debated the CPU design, one talking theory and another arguing over which part of the "wish list" to implement. During this time Cotter was away part time at a management seminar at a nearby university. When he returned he resolved part of the problem by assigning each man specific project goals.

In one situation he sat the disputants down and demonstrated that "a common decision could be reached no matter what values were assigned to the branches of the decision tree." At another point Cotter asked a friend with a Ph.D. from his old group to help his engineers with a difficult hardware problem and get it back on schedule. Cotter felt that his friend was "better equipped to argue on the theoreticians' technical turf" than he was.

Later when Morgan was promoted to vice president with continued responsibility for the MIX family, Cotter continued as product line manager for the MIX–5 but relinquished the title of engineering manager.

Cotter still viewed the MIX–5 as a "risky" program. He cited several issues that were resolved only during development:

1. Could a satisfactory source for multilayered printed circuits be found?
2. Would the projected speeds for ICs be achieved on circuit boards?
3. Would the cost of ICs drop as planned and would the new vendors come on stream?
4. Could a second source be found for the Read-Only-Memory?

The MIX–5 engineers were faced with special problems in estimating the time required to complete their tasks. They had been "burned on previous schedules and were reluctant to commit themselves to new ones." Cotter taught them to focus on problems when discussing plans, to tell people when the information would be available to set a real schedule. Cotter spoke of confidence levels in achieving objectives. Goals were set where 50 percent assurance could be reached in three months, 80 percent in five months and 100 percent in seven months.

"Engineers may be too conservative in estimating design time but it's useless to push them too hard." Cotter conceded that product line managers tend to sympathize with their engineering team's problems. If the engineering "pad" is insufficient, time gets squeezed out of the manufacturing team's schedule because manufacturing can't hide or excuse its delays. Hardware, or the lack of it, is a more visible output.

Morgan was very aware of the debates in the MIX-5 group and was content. He commented later: "Our president prefers rubbing interfaces between competing guilds. He wants arguments that lead to consensus or cause issues to surface. If there's no argument, Allen will play devil's advocate to get some." Morgan believed that you have to reach a consensus to get the job done. "You need commitment and you get it by getting people involved."

RESULTS OF THE MIX-5 PROGRAM

The first MIX-5 was delivered at the end of May 1972. Twenty-eight units were delivered in June. Cotter regarded the program as a success. His measures were: 1) whether a job was completed on schedule and within budget, and 2) the nature of market acceptance. Though the MIX-5 was about four months late and the budget had been overrun by 75 percent, a six-month backlog of sales was soon booked.

Cotter attributed the overruns to design problems with the multilayered printed circuit boards, late design changes, and a switch in memory speeds for marketing purposes. He pointed out that early sales had called for more software support in the field than MI had planned for.

Though average system prices were lower than projected because early customers ordered fewer peripheral units than expected, sales in the first eight months were 50 percent higher than MI's forecast.

Cotter was somewhat dismayed that the sales had been misestimated, but he was pleased with the direction of the error. The additional sales represented substantial changes in the minicomputer user environment, more sophistication and new applications. The "flexibility and responsiveness that is MI's unique competence lets us cash in on such changes."

The contribution of the MIX-5 to profits was more difficult to assess, but, with typical aftertax margins, it was expected to contribute from $5 million to $10 million. Cotter conceded that he could not directly control profits because he had no authority in manufacturing. Engineering could, however, affect factory costs and cost of purchased goods, which together accounted for 70 to 85 percent of all costs. If factory or purchased goods costs were too high, engineering could contribute to reducing them by redesign or reconsideration of tolerances. Cotter remarked:

A product line manager must learn to be comfortable with responsibility for things he can't control. This place relies on open communication. My job is to make sure the people around here know my goals. We have to keep uncertainty in the open. ... The questions to be asked on STTL were evident; the answers weren't. I like risky, nontrivial jobs and I'll accept being measured after the fact—maybe because I've been lucky. The sanctions around here are against people who aren't open or who build empires. ... The advantage of working for a firm that's growing as fast as MI is that personal success doesn't have to be at anyone's expense.

When Cotter was hired, he told his first boss that his goal was to own his own company in the biochemical business and committed himself to just a year with MI. People remembered this as being "pretty brassy." His boss replied: "We hope to make your job interesting enough so that you won't want to leave for a long time." (A substantial stock option also helped to account for Cotter's stay.)

LATER DEVELOPMENTS IN THE MIX FAMILY

In 1972 MI introduced both the MIX–6 and the MIX–3. Both markets developed quickly and the systems appeared to be successful.

Morgan's prediction was confirmed; the MIX–3 would be the "breadwinner" of the MIX line. The machine was easy to make and "not at all risky." Cotter had a reservation, that the performance/cost parameters for the MIX–3 had been optimized with too much emphasis on performance, rather than on cost. But Cotter had other things on his mind, too. What should a new high-performance machine in the MIX family look like? "We're busy now but we'll get asked to do it. Mr. Allen will probably raise this issue over coffee in the next few months. He's concerned with what we're not doing, not what we are."

EXHIBIT 1

MINICOMPUTER, INCORPORATED
Financial Results, 1962–1972

Fiscal Year	Sales	$ Millions Net Income	Equity	Adjusted Per Share Earnings	Average Share Price	Market Value of All Shares ($ Billions)
1962	5.2	0.6	—	.055	Not Traded	—
1963	7.9	1.0	1.2	.08	Not Traded	—
1964	8.7	0.7	2.9	.06	Not Traded	—
1965	12.0	0.6	3.5	.05		—
1966	18.2	1.6	5.1	.12	4.50	.06
1967	31.1	3.6	12.6	.26	15.50	.22
1968	45.8	5.5	18.1	.39	22.50	.32
1969	73.0	7.5	36.3	.52	37.50	.53
1970	108.1	11.5	61.0	.76	43.00	.66
1971	117.4	8.5	100.7	.53	34.50	.55
1972	150.1	12.2	115.8	.75	42.50	.70
Compound annual growth rates	40%	34%	56%	30%	45%	49%

EXHIBIT 2

A CHRONOLOGY FOR THE MIX-5 SYSTEM DEVELOPMENT

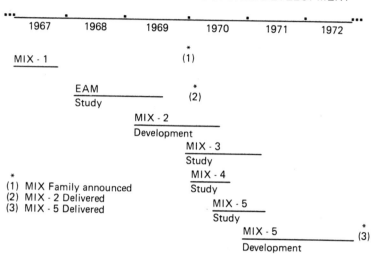

```
···_____·_____·_____·_____·_____·_____·___···
    1967      1968      1969      1970      1971      1972

     MIX - 1                       *
     _____                     (1)

               EAM                 *
               _____          (2)
               Study

                    MIX - 2
                    _____
                    Development
                              MIX - 3
                              _____
                              Study
     *                        MIX - 4
(1)  MIX Family announced     _____
(2)  MIX - 2 Delivered        Study
(3)  MIX - 5 Delivered            MIX - 5
                                  _____
                                  Study
                                       MIX - 5                *
                                       _____            (3)
                                       Development
```

EXHIBIT 3

PRODUCT LINE MANAGEMENT ORGANIZATION
(Early 1970)

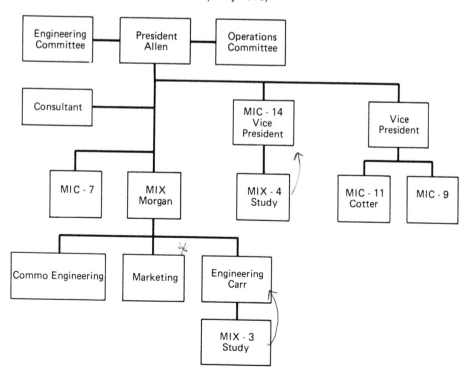

EXHIBIT 4

MIX SYSTEM BUSINESS PLAN

System:	MIX-6	MIX-2	MIX-3	MIX-5
Intent	Cheap	Progenitor	Breadwinner	Fast
Order of introduction	2	1	3	2
Order of development	3	1	4	2
CPU cost	$7000	$13,000	$13,000	$22,000
System cost	$5–20K	$10–35K	$13–45K	$25–150K
Relative speed	0.8	1.0	2.0	5.0
Relative speed/cost	1.22	1.0	2.0	1.3–2.0

EXHIBIT 5
UNCERTAINTY, PERFORMANCE, AND TIME

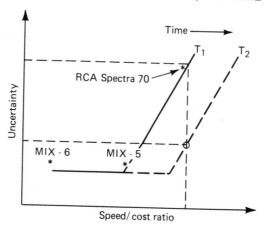

EXHIBIT 6

EFFECT OF DELAYED INTRODUCTION ON SALES

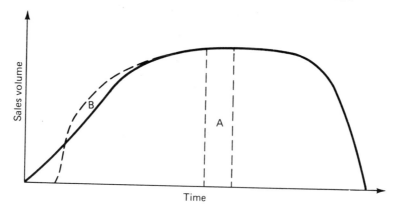

EXHIBIT 7

RELATIVE CPU SPEEDS WITH VARIOUS ICs

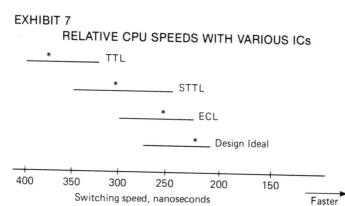

EXHIBIT 8

UNIT SALES FORECAST FOR MIX-5

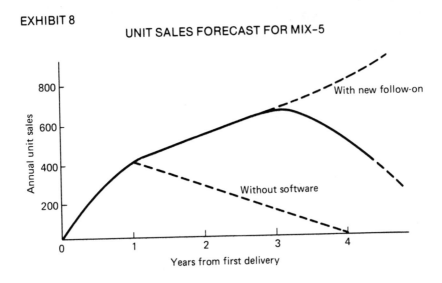

EXHIBIT 9
MIX-5 PRODUCT LINE MANAGEMENT

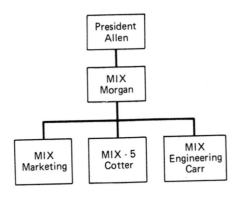

WOMAN'S MEDICAL COLLEGE OF PENNSYLVANIA (A)

The board of corporators of Woman's Medical College of Pennsylvania met in September 1969 to decide whether to admit male students. Disagreement had developed concerning the impact of any integration decision on the mission of the college, the quality of education offered, and future fund raising. There was also controversy regarding who should have what voice in making the decision.

The academic community debated whether reverse discrimination was possible or moral. Could an institution devote itself to serving a deprived minority exclusively without discriminating against the majority? Specifically, had Woman's Medical unfairly discriminated against men by excluding them?

In 1848 Geneva College awarded the degree of Doctor of Medicine to Elizabeth Blackwell who thus became the first woman so recognized in the Western Hemisphere. Encouraged by this event some Quaker physicians braved the disapproval of their colleagues to obtain a charter for the Female Medical College of Pennsylvania. On October 12, 1850, the first women's medical school was opened in Philadelphia. Two years later it graduated its first class of eight women. Its name was later changed to Woman's Medical College of Pennsylvania.

Nineteen similar schools were formed later. By 1895 all had disappeared; the last lost its identity through merger, leaving Woman's Med as the only all-female medical school in the country.

By 1968 Woman's Med had about 3000 graduates, half of them living. It also ran a nursing school, a 365-bed teaching hospital and small graduate radiology and medical lab technician programs. Space and facilities were regarded as inadequate for the number of students and patients. The college had never been successful in raising a significant endowment fund and so operated on a hand-to-mouth basis, sustained by federal and commonwealth grants, tuition, and alumnae and foundation gifts.

On October 4, 1968, on the recommendation of President G. E. Leymaster, M.D., the chairman of the board of corporators appointed a twelve-member committee on admission policies chaired by board member, Mrs. John T. Brugger. The Brugger Committee, as it came to be known, was charged with advising the board and the president "regarding procedures for further investigation of the desirability of the Woman's Medical College becoming co-educational."

The committee included representatives from among the board, the faculty, the alumnae, the administration, and the student body. Beginning in November 1968, monthly meetings were held. Mrs. Brugger appointed subcommittees on joint education, cost and facilities, fund raising, and trust funds. These groups were active in developing information regarding educational policy, estimates of cost, impact on funding, and legal implications on restricted trust funds.

The Brugger Committee was particularly concerned with whether the college was in violation of the spirit or letter of existing civil rights legislation in excluding men, and what effect admission of men would have on fundraising efforts. A basic issue was the loss of the unique character of the institution as the only women's medical school in the country.

Would the opportunities for women in medicine be reduced if limited seats in the college's program were assigned to men?

In December 1968 a letter announcing the formation of the committee was sent to state and accrediting agencies and to members of the faculty, staff, Nursing School, and all alumnae. The letter was regarded as a courtesy by the board of corporators anticipating public announcement; its intent was informational, but responses were invited.

In May of 1969 the committee submitted its report. It recommended that male students be accepted and that the name of the college be changed. As all students lived off campus, no additional operating costs were attributed to the decision to admit men in place of women. Those trust funds tied to continuing as an exclusively female school would probably be jeopardized, but their value was considered to be negligible.

The report recognized the importance of maintaining the continuity of the college in terms of purposes and standards, but stated that it was necessary to demonstrate a "capacity to adapt to rapidly changing circumstances." The report cited the college's primary purpose of excellence in education of physicians with special emphasis on the education of women and concluded that this mission could "best be achieved in conjunction with the education of men." It recommended that coeducation be achieved by the addition of male students rather than by the supplanting of women. To this end, it further recommended a substantial increase in the size of classes as soon as supporting funds could be obtained.

The committee was heavily influenced by Dr. Leymaster's opinions that faculty and house staff recruitment and morale would be favorably affected and that the attitude of medical educators and the profession toward the college would greatly improve.

The recommendations of the committee were not unanimously supported. A minority report (see Exhibit 1) was filed by (then) Alumnae President E. Cooper Bell, M.D., supported by student member Lourdes Corman.

Woman's Med had been founded to afford women the opportunity in medicine from which they had previously been barred. While it was generally agreed that women had been discriminated against in the past, it could not be demonstrated that medical schools favored male students. It was evident that only a small number of women were being admitted to medical schools, but national records revealed that the same proportion of men and women were chosen from among the applicants of each sex.

Marion Fay, PhD., had served as dean and president of Woman's Medical from 1946 to her retirement in 1963. She had previously been a faculty member for twenty-eight years. She continued to serve on the board of corporators and had served as acting president for the past two years after the resignation of Dr. Leymaster to accept another post. Discussing the issue of discrimination, she observed that "the prejudice against women in medical schools can be very subtle. Some schools have quotas; a few others take two women so one won't be lonesome." She also pointed out that the failure of income tax laws to allow child care deductions also discriminated against mothers in school and in practice.

Dr. Lourdes Corman had been an officer of the college's junior class and a student member of the Brugger Committee. At the time she was interviewed, she was interning at Woman's Med and planned to do her residency there in internal medicine, where her boss would be "a chauvinist, but a charming man, who wants the school to be just like other medical schools." She and others argued that the college was obligated to make a positive statement concerning the opportunities for women in medicine. "In a way, we need 'unequal opportunity.' The women applying for medical education are superior. They have to be because men are given more encouragement. I'm not saying I'm really being fair, but a student poll proved that a lot of girls who were qualified for medicine wouldn't be admitted if we didn't exist."

Recent civil rights legislation had raised the question whether the college's exclusion of male students was legal. At stake were the possible cancellation of the school's federal subsidies and research grants, which represented about one-third of the budget. Exhibit 2 provides background on a similar issue at the University of Michigan.

Although Woman's Med was a small school with limited resources, its students had placed twelfth overall in the examinations administered nationally to the students of most of the 102 medical schools in the United States. Despite this fact the accrediting committee had placed the college in the lowest quartile because of its inadequate teaching facilities.

Dr. Walter Rubin, a young member of the college's faculty, conceded that prejudice against women in medicine was real but argued, "A woman is only 60 percent of a man because she is less likely to practice. Further, she will probably have children and thus be prevented from taking a residency or going directly into practice. When she does get back to medicine, she's out of date." Records at Woman's Med showed the proportion of its graduates staying in medicine was higher than the national average for women doctors. Dr. Fay thought this was partly due to the fact they hadn't been coddled at the college.

Dr. Rubin went on to say, "We all want the institution to grow and improve. Segregation must limit the quality of the student body. Any limitation on applicants accepted on any basis but ability results in a second-rate student body. We certainly wouldn't compromise on faculty quality to get women; so why students?"

He also argued that women need association with medical men during training, to prepare them for the environment they would experience in practice. He felt that married women were happy at Woman's Med, but that single ones were not because of the limited social life.

Finally, he submitted that good men and women were less likely to apply for positions on the faculty of an all-women's school because it could not be the best school. Several departments, such as surgery, always suffered because of lack of participation in these specialties on the part of the women students.

It cost about $13,000 a year to educate a medical student in 1969. Operating on a $4 million annual budget, inevitably complicated by its intertwining with the larger hospital budget, Woman's Med was dependent on federal and commonwealth funds, tuition, and alumnae and foundation gifts. (The last portion of the small unrestricted endowment was cashed and spent to balance the 1970 budget.)

Vice President for Planning and Development Charles Glanville, a member of the Brugger Committee, filled in much of the background on the school. He commented on the difficulty in obtaining grants from foundations:

> They're not allocated to a monument; we're a relic. Money goes to innovative schools. The ideas developed with such funds must be exportable, useful to others; they won't be from a girl's school. Rather than debate the issue of advantages versus the disadvantages of coeducational medical education, foundation executives are more likely to make token contributions instead of generous grants.

The Commonwealth of Pennsylvania subsidized medical schools in the state in proportion to the number of students enrolled. The four other Philadelphia schools had 50 to 80 percent Pennsylvania students. Woman's Med couldn't fill its classes with women from within the state even if it had wanted to; so it had only 30 percent Pennsylvanians. The state was unwillingly subsidizing nonresidents. Dr. Fay noted that "several members of the board were concerned that the legislature would cut off this subsidy; it had been proposed but not considered seriously. The proposer died recently; a judgment perhaps."

Dr. Fay explained that fund raising was a special problem for women's schools. Even noted women's schools like Barnard, Wellesley, and Bryn Mawr had always had trouble getting funds. Women most often made gifts and bequests to their husbands' colleges. Alumnae gave to their undergraduate schools, where the happy memories were. She had wondered whether it was possible to use an offer to admit men to pry money from the people who had been critical of the exclusion policy in the past.

Several of the people interviewed commented on the way the board of corporators and the Brugger Committee had handled the integration issue.

Glanville said, "The battle of 1850 is over. Why beat a dead horse? We're having trouble recruiting board members. Our new governor, Milton Shapp, resigned from our board, probably because we move so slowly. The Brugger Committee was dominated by the establishment point of view. There was insufficient ventilation of the issues. Discussion was cut off and there weren't enough meetings. The report was not redrafted to get any consensus."

Dr. Fay felt that the board of corporators was divided on the problem of integration. The issue had been considered on many occasions in the past and had always stalled in committee. "I was on the fence. For years I heard the usual 'Why don't you girls get generous?' jokes. The Brugger Committee probably moved too fast. The alumnae were solicited by mail for advice—but doctors never read their mail."

Dr. Corman felt that she was chosen for the committee because she had originally openly favored integration. Only the year before had the student body finally been granted membership on such committees. Although the Brugger Committee had wanted opinions from the student body, they were unwilling to give any feedback. Dr. Corman had conducted a poll of the students, which is described in Exhibit 3. After much debate the results were released to the students. All committee meetings were closed to nonmembers.

On the decisionmaking process, Dr. Corman volunteered, "I think Dr. Leymaster was a terrible public relations man, terrible. At first I was convinced we should go coed; I was waiting for them to tell me why. The committee wasn't appointed to determine whether but rather, when and how we should integrate. The board was just soothing a few factions. The committee was very upset because things didn't go as smoothly as expected. They tried to suppress any minority report, pressing for a unanimous position. If the deliberations were emotional, it was mostly on my part. My ideas were ignored as being outside of the committee's charge. Their whys just didn't match mine. The results of the student poll changed my mind. Lisa, the other student member, and I polled the students with a questionnaire. We had tried hard to get a fair response. Many of our students are married (about 30 percent), with children; they expect understanding of their problems. They thought that they would be less likely to get it if we went coed."

Dr. Corman suggested that the integration issue called for open discussion. She thought that "they shouldn't have pretended to examine an issue when the decision had already been made."

EXHIBIT 1   WOMAN'S MEDICAL COLLEGE OF PENNSYLVANIA (A)

April 3, 1969

Board of Corporators
The Woman's Medical College of Pennsylvania
Philadelphia, Pennsylvania 19129

Dear Members:

As a member of the Committee on Admission Policies and as an alumna I respectfully submit the following opinion.

The *purpose* of the Woman's Medical College has been and should continue to be the training of women to become physicians.

The *challenge* facing this institution is to continue in excellence in its training.

The *challenge* facing our nation is to increase the number of physicians especially in the area of clinical medicine. To help meet this national need Woman's Medical College should increase its number of students. Womanpower in the United States is underutilized in the medical profession and I believe this institution can best serve the nation by increasing its student body with more women students. Please compare our percentage as shown in the following tabulation:

Percentage of Women Physicians to Total M.D.s in Selected Countries, 1965

Country	Percentage
Philippines	24.7
Finland	24.2
Israel	24.0
Thailand	23.8
Germany	20.0
Italy	18.8
Austria	17.4
Scotland	17.0
Denmark	16.4
South Korea	16.1
England and Wales	16.0
Sweden	15.4
Hong Kong	14.5
Switzerland	13.6
France	12.8
Australia	12.6
Netherlands	12.5
India	12.0
Norway	12.0
New Zealand	10.1
Republic of South Africa	10.0
Japan	9.3
Canada	7.6
Brazil	7.1
Republic of China	6.7
UNITED STATES	6.7
South Vietnam	6.1
Madagascar	4.6
Spain	2.5

EXHIBIT 1 (cont.)

WOMAN'S MEDICAL COLLEGE OF PENNSYLVANIA (A)

Replacement of women students by male students at Woman's Medical College will doubtless reduce the percentage of women physicians in the United States.

As evidence let me remind you that 93 (of 128 students who answered the questionnaire) of our current student body were accepted only by Woman's Medical College in spite of the fact that they made an average of 4.9 applications. In view of the fact that our institution accepts about 1 in 4 applicants I believe it should not be concluded that we have an inferior pool of applicants from which to choose. Moreover, our present freshman class is described as a superior group of students, so it must be conceded we are attracting good students.

Second, let me tell you that Dr. Marvin Dunn, in recent personal interviews with members of admissions committees of 25 medical schools, reported as follows:

Two encourage the acceptance of women; three claim absolute neutrality; nineteen prefer to take men to the extent that a woman must be clearly superior, not equal, for them to accept *any more* than they now take.

Third, Dr. Glen Leymaster has stated that, until more teaching facilities are available, the admission of male students would necessitate a reduction in the number of female students admitted.

Finally, the fate of women applicants to Woman's Medical College rests with the Student Admissions Committee. I note with regret that three members of our current Admissions Committee have written statements favoring coeducation at Woman's Medical College. None of these three are alumnae of this institution. In fairness I wish to add that one member said she favors "a policy of retaining our identity by the institution of *active* programs related to their special needs (institution of a day care center, part-time residency programs, etc.)." She further states that to retain this identification with women it will be necessary to impose a quota. She favors "a fifty-to-fifty quota as the optimum."

For the above reasons, if coeducation is adopted, I believe that the number of female students admitted in the immediate future to Woman's Medical College will be decreased, and since the admission policies of other medical schools have shown no recent change in the 7–10 percent enrollment of female students, the percentage if not actual number of female physicians will decrease in the United States.

One of the chief arguments offered for adopting coeducation at Woman's Medical College is the increase in money obtained from state and federal governments. However, I wish to remind you that Dr. Marion Fay has said that "Today there are some five of the older medical schools that are in financial difficulties." Obviously coeducation has not prevented the financial difficulties at these schools.

Second, Dr. Marvin Dunn has stated that to garner needed state financial support Woman's Medical College will have to provide the promise of more Pennsylvania students. He listed the following facts:

(1) Pennsylvania has more places for first-year students/population unit than all other states excepting California and New York.
(2) Pennsylvania ranks 15th in numbers of students graduating from college/population unit among the states (the number of medical school applicants parallels this quite closely).
(3) The absolute numbers of applicants (male and female considered separately also) from Pennsylvania is inadequate to justify and fill the number of first-year places available within the state.

EXHIBIT 1 (cont.)

WOMAN'S MEDICAL COLLEGE OF PENNSYLVANIA (A)

(4) The projected increases in Pennsylvania applicants for the next five years is less than the projected increases in plans for first-year students in the state.

Dr. Dunn concluded as follows: "To me this leads to a single conclusion: we would have one heck of a time trying to boost our present enrollment of 20 percent Pennsylvania residents even to the low of the other schools (60 percent at the University of Pennsylvania, not well received by the legislature) with no other changes being made than the admission of men."

The second major reasons given for adopting coeducation is the enlistment of better qualified teaching and resident staff. This is undoubtedly a valid reason at the present time. However, if the institution is sufficiently endowed financially, this argument will not hold. If salaries are sufficiently attractive the sex of the students will be of minor importance to the professors.

I have no objection to the admission of male students *per se,* but until other medical schools accept female students on the basis of *equal* qualifications I believe there is a need for an institution such as Woman's Medical College to protect and provide a place for women desiring a medical education.

Instead of coeducation I urge that this institution accept as its goal the conversion of the Woman's Medical College to a *National Institute* for the undergraduate education of women physicians and the postgraduate training of those women physicians who need it. With the present national shortage of physicians and the underutilization of women in medicine I believe a strong appeal to state and federal bureaus as well as private and industrial sources would be favorably received. As one alumna has noted, since we are now practicing *reverse* discrimination in both public and private areas it is reasonable to suppose that public and private agencies might be influenced to support women in medicine if the proper publicity and propaganda are forcefully utilized.

The men and women who founded Woman's Medical College recognized the need for educating women in medicine. They met the challenge! The unique institution founded by them has survived for 119 years. Are we less visionary or courageous than they?

There still is, in the opinion of many, a need for a special institution for the education of women physicians. Like the late Dr. Martin Luther King, "I have a dream!" I hope you, the members of the Board of Corporators, have the same dream—a National Institute for the education of women physicians at Woman's Medical College.

Sincerely yours,

E. Cooper Bell, M.D.

P.S. I hope you will read certain letters, such as those of Dr. Maria Kirber and Dr. Virginia Lautz, which list problems and possible solutions.

EXHIBIT 2

Sex Discrimination:
Campuses Face Contract Loss over HEW Demands

The women's liberation movement has a new ally: the Department of Health, Education, and Welfare. HEW is demanding that colleges and universities, under threat of losing all federal contracts, stop discriminating against women students and employees. Furthermore, HEW is demanding that female employees be compensated for financial loss suffered because of discrimination over the last 2 years. The government is currently withholding new contracts from the University of Michigan and at least three other campuses, pending compliance with HEW demands.

The HEW action, begun last spring (*Science,* 1 May 1970), is authorized by Executive Order 11246, which prohibits discrimination by federal contractors. The Order, amended by President Johnson in 1968 to include sex discrimination, requires contractors to survey their own labor practices and submit an affirmative action plan for correcting deficiencies. HEW is charged with regulating all federal contracts to educational institutions.

The sex discrimination provisions of the order have been largely ignored and still would be, but for the efforts of Bernice Sandler, a staff member for the House Education Committee, who founded Women's Equity Action League (WEAL). WEAL, a Washington-based group with a membership that includes several congresswomen, sent letters to women's groups at campuses across the country advising them of the potential power of Executive Order 11246. WEAL offered to assist the groups in filing complaints against their respective campus administrations. So far WEAL has presented HEW with over 200 complaints, including, according to Dr. Sandler, charges against the entire college and university systems of New York City, New York state, and California. Because of a shortage of staff, HEW is investigating the complaints a few at a time, but HEW officials insist that all the complaints will be thoroughly investigated. HEW's eagerness to clamp down on sex discrimination is partially explained by the political pressure that WEAL presented along with the demands; feminism is currently a popular cause with several members of Congress.

Ann Arbor FOCUS on Equal Employment for Women, a group of students and university employees, filed the specific complaint against the University of Michigan, charging, among other things, that the university has only a small percentage of women faculty members (5.3 percent excluding the School of Nursing), few female administrators, and quotas on the admission of female students. The complaint also charged that women employees with degrees were assigned as clerk-typists but were expected to perform administrative duties for which men are paid higher salaries.

HEW's demands of each institution differ, depending on the types of complaints and HEW's subsequent investigation; but the demands for Michigan (see box) illustrate the nature of the requirements for an affirmative action program. HEW officials expect some negotiation of the exact terms of the demands, and certain campuses, notably the University of Illinois, are quietly working toward an acceptable affirmative action plan, although none are yet complete. But, Michigan and certain other institutions not identified by HEW officials have chosen to resist. Calling the demands "totally unreasonable," Michigan officials circulated copies to several other university administrations in an attempt to gain support.

EXHIBIT 2 (cont.)

HEW's Demands for Michigan

The following are excerpts from HEW's nine requirements for an affirmative action plan for ending sex discrimination at the University of Michigan.

The university must:

1. Achieve salary equity in every job category in the university.
2. Compensate, through the payment of back wages, each female employee who has lost wages due to discriminatory treatment by the university. Payment must be retroactive to 13 October 1968 (the date President Johnson amended Executive Order 11246 to include sex discrimination).
3. Achieve a ratio of female employment in academic positions at least equivalent to availability as determined by the number of qualified female applicants.
4. Increase ratios of female admissions to all Ph.D. graduate programs.
5. Increase the participation of women in committees involving the selection and treatment of employees.
6. Develop a written policy on nepotism which will insure correct treatment of tandem teams.
7. Analyze past effects of nepotism and retroactively compensate (to 13 October 1968) any person who has suffered discrimination.
8. Assure that female applicants for nonacademic employment receive consideration commensurate with their qualifications.[a] The university must also ensure that the concept of male and female job classifications is eliminated through changes in recruitment procedures.
9. Assure that all present female employees occupying clerical or other nonacademic positions and who possess qualifications equal to or exceeding those of male employees occupying higher level positions be given primary consideration for promotion to higher level positions.

—R. J. B.

---

[a]"Sex Discrimination," Bazell, R. J., *Science,* Vol. 170, pp. 834–35, 20 November 1970. Copyright 1970 by the American Association for the Advancement of Science.

EXHIBIT 3

WOMAN'S MEDICAL COLLEGE OF PENNSYLVANIA
Philadelphia, Penna, 19129
Founded in 1850

February 10, 1969

To: Members of Committee on Admission Policies
From: Lisa Luwisch and Lourdes Corman
Re: Students' Response to Questionnaire on Admission Policies

Total response was 128 students (55 percent) of the student body. These students applied to an average of 5.8 schools and were accepted by an average of 1.4 schools. Ninety-three students applied to an average of 5.7 schools but were accepted only to WMC.

TABLE I

	% Response	Average No. of Applications Per Student	Average No. of Acceptances Per Student
Class of 1969	28%	4.90	1.68
Class of 1970	47	5.80	1.31
Class of 1971	57	6.15	1.40
Class of 1972	75	5.90	1.26
No class listed	6 students	5.10	1.30

For 47 students WMC was their first choice, while for 81 it was not. Seven students of the 47 who chose WMC did so because of its segregated nature, while for 36 of the 81 students who did not choose WMC, the reason was its segregated policy. Eighteen of the 47 students (39 percent) for whom WMC was their first choice attended an all-women undergraduate school. On the other hand, 23 of the 81 students for whom WMC was not their first choice (28 percent) attended an all-women undergraduate school.

TABLE II

	A		B	
	WMC Was 1st Choice	% Attended Segregated Colleges	Other School Was 1st Choice	% Who Attended Segregated Colleges
Class of 1969	7 students	28%	9 students	11%
Class of 1970	10	20	13	38
Class of 1971	12	33	22	45
Class of 1972	14	50	35	20
No class listed	4	75	2	0

EXHIBIT 3 (cont.)

WOMAN'S MEDICAL COLLEGE OF PENNSYLVANIA
Philadelphia, Penna, 19129
Founded in 1850

Thirty-nine percent of the students who answered felt that the environment of both segregated and nonsegregated schools were equally beneficial to their education. Twenty-two percent of the students answering felt a segregated environment such as WMC was *more* beneficial, while 31 percent felt that the *more* beneficial was a nonsegregated environment. Eight percent of the students answering did not reply to this question.

Forty-three percent (56 students) felt that women physicians have to "prove themselves" to male physicians. And of these, 57 percent felt that WMC was preparing them to do so.

Assuming equal standards of admission, students (57 percent) would like to see WMC accept men. However, of these students only 34 (47 percent) would favor admitting men without increasing the size of the entering class. For 50 percent of the students who answered the questionnaire, the acceptance of men would be acceptable only if the size of the entering class is increased.

Of these students (73) who would favor a change in admission policy, 47 (64 percent) believed that the number of male students should be limited by a quota and suggested quotas ranging from 10 to 50 percent, and including a percent equal to that by which the size of the entering class would be increased. Twenty-three students of the 47 favoring a quota (48 percent) suggested 50 percent.

Sixty-two students (or 49 percent of the total number who answered) chose to comment. The comments were varied in both content and length, and we were not able to decide on a method to include them in this report without introducing a bias. We are open to suggestions from the members of the committee.

WOMAN'S MEDICAL COLLEGE
OF PENNSYLVANIA (B)

The board of corporators of Woman's Medical College of Pennsylvania voted to admit men students in September 1969. The decision was made that at least sixty places would be reserved for women in each class and that at least 50 percent of every entering class would be women. The decision was to be reconsidered in two years.

Three men were enrolled in the 1969 Fall class. The men accepted had slightly higher grade-point averages and admission-test scores than the typical student. In 1969 there were six applicants for each place in the entering class; for the 1970 class there were eleven applicants per slot; preliminary estimates indicate twenty for 1971.

Paul Siegel, M.D., was appointed to chair a Mission Planning Council. The council affirmed the board's plans for the make-up of subsequent entering classes. The working draft of a "Statement of Mission" is attached as Exhibit 1.

Commenting on the council's deliberations, alumna Lourdes Corman, M.D., said: "If the council decides on a fifty-fifty ratio now, I think that things will change enough that there's no guarantee that in ten years this school won't be 90 percent male."

Dr. Siegel remarked,

> Our mission is "expanded" to also educate men; this meets all priority needs: national, ours, integration. With perhaps 1400 to 2000 women due to graduate nationally in future years, whether we admit sixty more women is irrelevant to the future of women in medicine. Our people should be evangelists to recruit women into medicine. Why do ten times as many men apply as women? Medicine is no more demanding than any other profession, if you're going to do it right. Another benefit of integration, we can now pick up men from foreign schools to fill third-year dropout slots. There's no future for a small school in medicine.

In February 1970 the board of corporators voted to change the name of the school to the Medical College of Pennsylvania (MCP) effective in July. Suggestions for the new name had been solicited in the alumnae magazine. Just prior to the effective date the alumnae president, Phyllis Marciano, wrote a letter to all alumnae urging they send telegrams to the school rejecting the name change, arguing the new name was poor, that no change was needed to appease the few male students and that the change was being made too fast and without consultation. The letter further suggested that future alumnae donations be placed in a trust fund and not administered by the school.

Dr. Marciano argued, in summary,

> I'm not a feminist and I'm not against coeducation. We gave up before we started. Our name identifies our past and our commitment. Harvard and Vassar didn't change theirs. Neither did Episcopal Hospital when it admitted Catholic interns. We need a place where women are more equally appraised on their qualifications. Why does the word "woman" make anyone feel intimidated? In Africa Woman's Med meant something; MCP means nothing. You can't be truly coed without discriminating against women. As I see it, every time you admit a man and turn away a qualified woman, you've discriminated against that woman.

In closing Acting President Marion Fay said,

It's too soon to see improvement in fund raising. Private funds were peculiarly tied to the female nature of the school in the past. What do we use now? There's not enough feedback from the alumnae to their representatives on our board. We received only a negative response on the name change. My phone rang for days. We should have waited and changed the name after the men's admission policy was assimilated, perhaps when the first men graduated. Our commitment to women may be further served by developing part-time internships and residencies and by tying our admissions ratio to the policies of other schools regarding women.

EXHIBIT 1
THE MEDICAL COLLEGE OF PENNSYLVANIA
Statement of Mission

The Mission of the Medical College of Pennsylvania is twofold:

— to teach those arts and sciences related to the preservation of human health and the prevention and treatment of disease, and to advance the body of knowledge in these areas; and
— to continue its commitment to the education of women physicians and to develop and maintain programs that will expand the opportunities for women in the medical professions.

MCP proposes to carry out its mission by:

1. Operating effective educational programs in medicine, in related sciences, and in allied health professions;
2. Providing high quality health services to individuals and to community groups, responsive to the changing needs of modern society;
3. Pursuing vigorous programs in basic and applied research;
4. Encouraging coordination of the educational, service, and research activities to obtain the maximum benefit from all three;
5. Committing substantial portions of its resources to all aspects of the education of women in medicine; and
6. Developing as rapidly as resources permit from a medical college with associated activities into a health sciences university with a comprehensive medical center.

SUN VENTURES, INC.

Sun Ventures, Inc., is a wholly-owned subsidiary of the Sun Oil Company. Established by Sun Oil in 1971, the policies of the venture group are still evolving. This case examines the role of a senior venture manager in implementing the group's acquisition strategy and describes a particular venture acquisition.

Sun Oil Company is one of the larger fully-integrated petroleum operations. It is engaged in oil and gas explorations and production, the transportation and refining of crude oil and its derivatives, and the marketing of a full range of refined petroleum products, including gasolines, distillate and residual fuel oils, motor oils, cleaning solvents, propane, and wax. The firm also produces a variety of petroleum-based chemical products.

Sun Oil's sales in 1972 were $1.9 billion, with net income of $155 million. This resulted in a return on revenues of roughly 8 percent, and a return on equity of about 8.9 percent (see Exhibit 1). Sun's rate of return had been in a declining trend in recent years, due to external factors.

> During 1972 ... scant change occurred in the climate that has contributed to a progressive economic deterioration of the petroleum industry. The average price of U.S. crude oil, measured in constant dollars, declined for the thirteenth time in the past 51 years, bringing the total drop since 1957 to more than one-third. In the final quarter there was a welcomed firming trend in gasoline prices, but on average over the year the price Sun was able to obtain for refined products remained virtually unchanged from 1971.[1]

[1] *Annual Report*, Sun Oil Company, 1972.

This case was prepared by John S. Chu and Richard S. Nason under the supervision of Professor Jules ·J. Schwartz as the basis for class discussion rather than to illustrate either effective or ineffective handling of administrative action.

Dr. W. E. Bonnet, president of Sun Ventures, summarized the problem:

> Everybody recognizes that the petroleum industry is very mature ... It's also highly regulated. We see a paradox down the road: a seller's market but moving toward a utility status. We see limitations on our profit margins; our ventures are intended basically as a supplement.[2]

ORGANIZATION AND STRATEGY

Sun Ventures was organized to generate alternative sources of income for its parent (see Exhibits 2 and 3). It had two principal arms for doing this: one, under Mr. Hauptfuhrer, made venture investments; the other, under Dr. Wynkoop, did internal research and development. The patent and license department was a corporate-wide service attached to Sun Ventures as a matter of convenience. The research department did petroleum-related work, but its principal purpose was the generation of technology that could serve as a basis for new ventures.

Dr. Bonnet was charged with developing several ventures that, within ten years, would contribute a total of $300 million to $500 million in sales. The guidelines for his selections were:

1. A potential venture should have long-term potential and could involve high risk.
2. A new venture should have less capital intensity than that exhibited by the petroleum industry.
3. A potential venture investment should have external environmental influences different from those of the petroleum industry.

[2] *Forbes*, October 15, 1973.

156

4. Acquisition of the new venture should allow Sun Oil to broaden or minimize risks inherent in other venture areas or in the mainstay of the company's business.
5. The venture should generate a return on equity higher than that of Sun's petroleum business—at least 10 percent.

Little direction had been given to the venture group beyond these guidelines. Bonnet reasoned that Sun wanted to gain experience in the venture area, so he would have to allow his people freedom to explore new areas. Sun budgeted $5 million annually for new acquisitions. With these funds Bonnet tried "to seek flexibility for the future." "So far," he commented, "we have had no product or technical failures. There have been people failures. Many entrepreneurs are good inventors but are not good managers." Bonnet looked for, but did not insist upon, entrepreneurs who had had some recent experience in large corporations.

Concerning the generality of the venture strategy, Bonnet felt that as experience was gained, more specific guidelines would be developed for his analysts. A list of potential business areas had been prepared by his subordinates and ranked by Sun Venture's management, as shown in Exhibit 4. The approach to management of a new venture, however, really depended on the individual case, according to Bonnet. "We'll supply whatever the venture needs."

Some banks expected Sun to guarantee loans for its ventures. Bonnet had concluded that majority control was necessary to justify this step. One tactic used to acquire control called for buying convertibles issued by the new venture. In the event of disaster, Sun could make the conversion and acquire a controlling position. Sun could then install its own management or make other necessary changes in the venture's operation.

R. P. Hauptfuhrer managed the nonpetroleum investments. In this position he had tried to acquire firms smaller than those on the Fortune 500 list. He considered it more likely that such ventures could expand into larger entities using Sun's capital. Hauptfuhrer reasoned that, to achieve long-range growth, Sun's management could not simply sit on a venture's board; it had to be actively involved in the venture's business. Investments should not be capital intensive; this way, cyclical economic trends in the petroleum industry could be counterbalanced. He looked for an entrepreneur who could integrate his activities into a larger organization and would be opportunistic in order to make his venture grow. For the long term Hauptfuhrer had concluded that petroleum would continue to be the major profit contributor. Sun Oil should not become conglomerate.

Sun Ventures had been very selective in its investment choices. Since its establishment it had screened about 250 proposals. Only nine ventures were chosen for acquisition and only six of these nine had actually been acquired.

Examples of Sun Ventures' early acquisitions and product specialties included:

1. Plastic Development Corporation, manufacturers of polyurethane furniture parts for sale to furniture manufacturers;
2. Analytics, consultants in electronic systems, including acoustics;
3. The Fourth Network, programmers for cable television;
4. Medetel, providers of computerized diagnostic aids for medical doctors;
5. Tennessee Nuclear, processors of nonradioactive byproducts from uranium enrichment for conversion into metallic uranium for use as a material of construction, among others; and
6. Residex Corporation, a heavy construction company, specializing in sewer and water systems.

New ventures were acquired and managed under the supervision of R. A. Franzoni, director of the venture investments group. Before taking his present position, he was director of operations research for Sun Oil.

The group's decision process is outlined in Exhibit 5. Proposals originated from banks, personal friends, contacts in the venture field, and lawyers or brokers. Franzoni's analysts did not actively seek new ventures.

After eliminating obviously undesirable choices, Sun conducted a financial audit of each potential acquisition and its management. While the firm was still in the proposal stage, the entrepreneur was subjected to a similar investigation. An independent firm conducted "an exceptional, even excessively thorough" audit, according to Franzoni. The audit served as a check on the financials in the venture manager's report.

In making his selection Franzoni viewed each potential venture deal as part of an investment portfolio. For purposes of analysis the assumption was made that a venture would be liquidated after approximately ten years.

Analysis proceeded by relating the cash flows generated by all the ventures, taking into account the risks involved. This analysis was done to "diversify away the risk." Diversifying risk, Franzoni explained, "implies that one assembles different investments such that an optimal balance between risk and return is achieved for the portfolio."

As a tool, risk and decision-tree analysis were used as tools (see Exhibit 6). The possible outcomes or payoffs of the venture acquisition decision were determined by Franzoni and his venture analysts, giving account to the business, the character of the entrepreneur and environmental conditions that might prevail in the future. "We do these assessments together," Franzoni told the case writer, "however, the probability for each outcome is assigned by me."

His venture managers agreed that while a business concept was important, the entrepreneur was even more important. Thus, it was their policy to meet with the prospective entrepreneur to become acquainted with both the new business and its manager. They also considered whether the venture was part of a growing industry and whether the venture conformed with Sun Ventures' requirements for business acquisitions.

Franzoni was very concerned about the entrepreneur. He reasoned that a successful venture required not only a good idea but a certain kind of person. Even if a venture was successful, some managers couldn't handle growth. Entrepreneurs could be divided according to their ability; most could effectively manage ventures up to $5 million in sales. Not all, however, could manage firms with higher sales.

If a decision was made to buy the idea, negotiations decided the amount and the vehicle (type of financial instrument) to be used to gain control. The bargaining parties included Franzoni, the entrepreneur, and any necessary financial institutions.

Sun Ventures had a staff of nine venture analysts. Five were engineers from Sun Oil's economic planning unit. Four analysts had quantitative backgrounds in finance or operations research. Some had graduate degrees in business administration.

As a senior venture manager, E. C. Larsen sat on the boards of three of the ventures. Larsen previously worked as a chemical engineer in Sun Oil's economic planning unit. He had a B.S. degree in chemical engineering and an M.B.A. from New York University.

Larsen pointed out that managers had the chance to guide a venture from start to finish, allowing great personal satisfaction. The opportunity to control the direction of a venture was unique. One manager resigned from Sun Ventures and Sun Oil to take a major position in one of the ventures.

Problems did arise in the venture process. For instance, creditors sometimes assumed that Sun would supply the credit standing for any outside capital. Sun also had had problems in supplying personnel to these unique ventures. But reflecting upon Sun's philosophy, Larsen concluded that Sun took an appropriate long-range interest in its ventures, while other venture groups often speculated, trying to get in, make their money fast and run.

FOURTH NETWORK

The Fourth Network was an example of Sun Venture's acquisition program. The firm's specialty and its sole product was programming material for cable television (CATV) operators.

The Fourth Network did no programming production but bought programs in video cassette tape form and distributed the tape to its customers. A typical customer received one fourteen-hour package of material each week. The package was broadcast from the CATV studio, using a standard one-inch video tape player. A diagram of the operation is shown below.

Programmed source material	(acquired externally)
Reprogrammed source material	(edited and converted standard 1-inch video cassette units)
CATV systems operator	(broadcast cable)

Fourth Network's promoter, D. C. Darling, had originally been referred to Sun Ventures by Sun Oil's director of research and development and also by a broker. Larsen regarded the venture as a start-up situation. Darling was looking for capital to implement an idea. Another investment, related to equipment manufacturing and sales, excited Sun's interest in both the CATV industry and Fourth Network. Larsen was convinced that the CATV industry had high growth potential.

Sun Ventures discovered Darling was dynamic, aggressive, and reputable. His former employer considered him an excellent salesman.

Initial discussions concerned the promoter's perception of a niche in the CATV market. The apparent niche arose when a 1969 Federal Communications Commission ruling provided that CATV operators could not simply reproduce broadcast network programming. The CATV operators were required to originate their own programming "to a significant extent."[3]

Darling had become convinced that compliance with this regulation was beyond the means of many CATV operators. There were

[3] First Order and Report, Docket 18397, October 27, 1969, pp. 4 and 19.

approximately 3000 of these operators in the country and more than half were located in small towns in rural areas (see Exhibit 7). Most CATV operators had neither the capital nor expertise to program. In addition, the broadcast networks could not, by law, own CATV stations or program for CATV. At the time Darling talked with Sun, no one provided this service.

Larsen felt that three factors had attracted Sun to Fourth Network. First, although relatively small, the CATV industry was growing at a rapid rate. Second, the industry had the potential for continued growth with the possibility of supplanting the present urban broadcast market. Finally, no one had filled the programming need. Larsen believed that Fourth Network had an opportunity to supply the small-to-medium size cable systems at reasonable prices.

Larsen had other reasons for selecting Fourth Network:

I felt comfortable with the venture. The risk was high, but there was low exposure. The total capital requirements were $255,000. [See following table.] The major risk lay in the marketing area. On the other hand, Fourth Network had potential for becoming a large cash generator.

Capital Requirements for First Year

Production equipment	$ 10,000
General equipment	10,000
Film & tape	40,000
Working capital (for first 6 months)	145,000
	$255,000

After Sun verified Darling's representations, the legal department and the Federal Communications Commission discussed the proposed venture in light of the FCC ruling. Larsen concluded that Fourth Network's product was an economical way for CATV operators to comply. From the operators' viewpoint, the ruling was both unreasonable and uneconomical, but Darling's product offered a solution.

In examining the business risk Larsen learned that, as an industry, CATV was vulnerable in the programming area. It was difficult to purchase large blocks of programmed material. Major broadcast producers could more profitably sell their material to UHF channels, which had a larger market, greater advertising revenue, and more capital.

Most of the potential customers did not have the subscriber count to purchase large blocks of programmed material. Quality programming only became feasible with a large subscriber count. "This subscribers' count game," Larsen commented, "is the key to this business in the production and marketing areas. If their subscriber count is sufficient, they can purchase directly from the large producers. At present, spot purchasing is the tactic."

At this point, Larsen looked at Darling's plans and found that weakness existed in the distribution and scheduling areas. A program was developed to correct these deficiencies.

Larsen and his superior (Franzoni's predecessor) had explained the proposal to Bonnet and received his approval. Larsen made his proposal to buy Fourth Network and his recommendation was approved by senior management.

The next step involved negotiating the deal. Darling proposed that Sun Ventures purchase a 30 percent interest at $5 per share. Eventually the price was reduced to $2.50 a share. Sun then bought 55 percent of the equity for $250,000. Sun had not set out to obtain a controlling interest. The usual tactic had been to obtain options so that control was possible if necessary, as Sun felt that it was to the benefit of both parties to have such options.

After the closing Sun hired an experienced manager to handle the finances and a partly-retired executive to handle the production and distribution for the new enterprise. Darling was to manage marketing and sales.

Since Sun Ventures acquired Fourth Network in September 1972, investment growth had been slower than expected. Exhibit 8 shows Larsen's preliminary projections.

According to Larsen Fourth Network had about achieved breakeven by Spring 1974. The service had been sold to some 200 cable systems. Present buyers evaluated Fourth Network's service on a business basis. The FCC, realizing that compliance would be difficult, had pursued a soft enforcement policy. Five years after the FCC ruling, no one knew precisely what compliance meant. The intent of the ruling was understood but how it would be implemented was still unclear.[4]

Larsen sat on the board of Fourth Network along with a Sun legal department attorney. Sun wanted a lawyer because contracting with suppliers and sellers would be a major activity. As senior venture manager, Larsen's capacity in Fourth Network's board was principally advisory. He assisted in projections, planning, and setting of goals and tried to keep the venture "pointed toward the long term."

Even if Fourth Network was very successful, Larsen expected to receive no unusually large reward. Sun had a policy that prohibited stock ownership in the investments by employees. On the other hand, if Fourth Network was unsuccessful, Larsen would not suffer unless he had a consistently bad record.

[4] *Cable Television: Opportunities and Problems in Local Program Origination* by N. E. Feldman, September 1970, Rand Corporation, Santa Monica, California 90406, R-570-FF.

EXHIBIT 1

FINANCIAL SUMMARY—CONSOLIDATED STATEMENT OF INCOME

	For the Years Ended December 31	
	1972	1971
	(thousands of dollars)	
Revenues		
Sales and Other Operating Revenues		
Refined products	$1,465,645	$1,392,303
Crude, condensate, and synthetic crude	81,939	86,339
Natural gas	114,540	108,870
Other related products and services	168,531	163,876
Shipbuilding and repair	87,322	70,655
	$1,917,977	$1,822,043
Other Income:	20,964	18,599
Total Revenues	$1,938,941	$1,840,642
Costs and Expenses		
Cost and operating expenses	$1,042,096	$ 990,801
Selling, general, and administrative expenses	302,467	284,710
Taxes, other than income taxes	112,893	103,424
Intangible development costs	52,145	50,564
Depreciation	114,070	106,911
Cost depletion	14,463	14,373
Amortization	22,267	23,111
Retirements	5,346	1,711
Interest and debt expense	38,895	28,967
Income Taxes:		
U.S. federal	30,999	41,081
Foreign and other	48,591	43,373
Total Costs and Expenses	$1,784,232	$1,689,026
Net Income	154,709	151,616
Net Income per Common Share:		
After provision for cash dividends on preferred stock	$3.21	$3.08
Stockholders' equity December 31 (thousands of $)	$1,760,132	$1,713,657
Return on average stockholders' equity (%)	8.9	9.0
Return on revenues (%)	8.0	8.2
Total number of employees, December 31	26,384	25,567

EXHIBIT 2

SUN OIL COMPANIES
Operating Organization Structure,
September 1, 1973

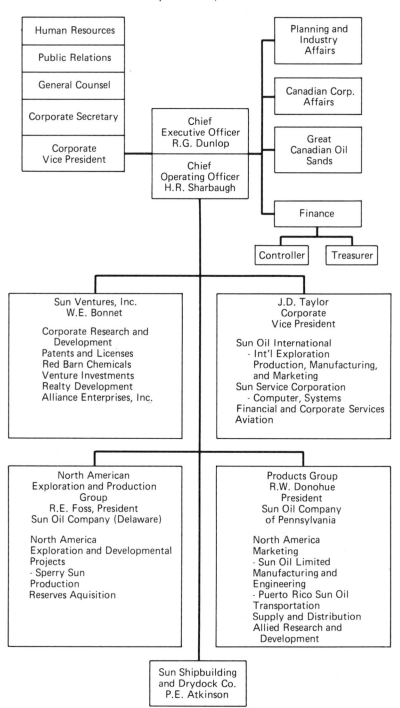

Human Resources
Public Relations
General Counsel
Corporate Secretary
Corporate Vice President

Chief Executive Officer
R.G. Dunlop

Chief Operating Officer
H.R. Sharbaugh

Planning and Industry Affairs

Canadian Corp. Affairs

Great Canadian Oil Sands

Finance

Controller

Treasurer

Sun Ventures, Inc.
W.E. Bonnet

Corporate Research and Development
Patents and Licenses
Red Barn Chemicals
Venture Investments
Realty Development
Alliance Enterprises, Inc.

J.D. Taylor
Corporate Vice President

Sun Oil International
- Int'l Exploration Production, Manufacturing, and Marketing
Sun Service Corporation
- Computer, Systems
Financial and Corporate Services
Aviation

North American Exploration and Production Group
R.E. Foss, President
Sun Oil Company (Delaware)

North America
Exploration and Developmental Projects
- Sperry Sun
Production
Reserves Aquisition

Products Group
R.W. Donohue President
Sun Oil Company of Pennsylvania

North America
Marketing
- Sun Oil Limited
Manufacturing and Engineering
- Puerto Rico Sun Oil
Transportation
Supply and Distribution
Allied Research and Development

Sun Shipbuilding and Drydock Co.
P.E. Atkinson

EXHIBIT 3

SUN VENTURES, INC.
Operational Organization

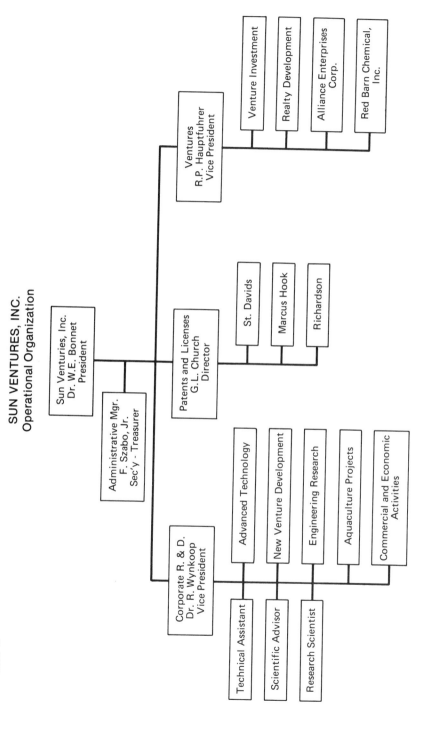

EXHIBIT 4

RANKING OF BUSINESS AVENUES

Examples

1. Positive interest: A valuable addition to an existing venture or an *a priori* decision to search for ventures in this area.	Replacement of natural resources Plastic fabrication and/or manufacture Petrochemicals (not existing commodities) Health care and medical services Alternative energy businesses Leisure & recreation Real estate (land, building, construction)
2. Not quite sure, but attracted to this business area. Willing to learn.	Building materials Food growing & processing (aquaculture, agriculture, cattle breeding & raising) Toys Government studies & contracts Pollution abatement & solid waste recycling Fire resistant materials
3. Interesting on the basis of higher return on investment potential only, i.e., a special situation.	Transportation Computer software Communication (TV, publishing, etc.) Analytical & management consulting Process equipment manufacture and machinery Services (repair, cleaning—probably industrial) Mining
4. No interest under present circum- stances.	Electronic component fabrication Insurance Mortgage Mail order Electrical equipment
5. No interest under any circum- stances.	Marginally illegal or unethical business such as pornography Liquor Gambling Professional sports Show business Fashion design

EXHIBIT 5

VENTURE INVESTMENTS—ACTIVITIES

   I. *Proposal Flow*
     A. Generation
     B. Monitoring
  II. *Screening Process*
 III. *Decision Process*
     A. Evaluation
     B. Verification
     C. Negotiation
     D. Closing process
  IV. *Venture Management and Testing of Business Concept*
     A. Directorship
     B. Performance measurement
     C. Financial support
     D. Direct management
   V. *Portfolio Management*
     A. Acquisition of going concerns
     B. Divestment
     C. Change in equity positions
     D. Portfolio additions
     E. Performance measurement
  VI. *Planning*
     A. Setting of objectives
     B. Identification & evaluation of diversification avenues
     C. Overall performance evaluation
 VII. *Pursuit of Subsidiary Building Strategy*
     A. Leverage financing
     B. Core acquisition
     C. Agglomeration
     D. Redeployment of assets

EXHIBIT 6

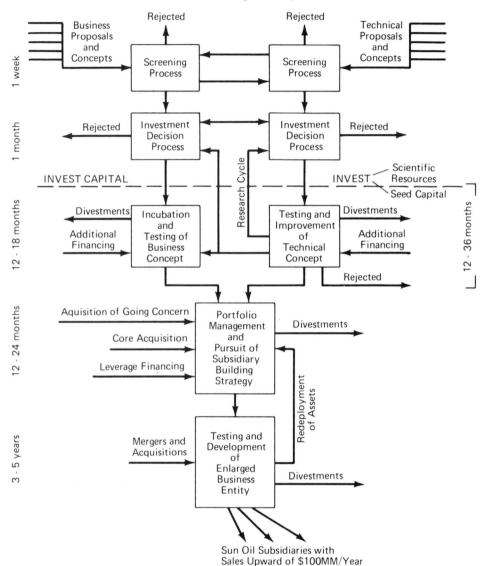

SUN VENTURES, INC.
Plan for Subsidiary Development

Sun Oil Subsidiaries with
Sales Upward of $100MM/Year

EXHIBIT 7

CABLE TV NETWORK, 1971

Number of Subscribers	Number of Systems
Under 50	34
50–500	731
500–1000	476
1000–2000	462
2000–3500	338
3500–5000	120
5000–10,000	176
10,000–20,000	60
Over 20,000	12
	2409

EXHIBIT 8

PROJECTED REVENUES

	After 6 Months	After 18 Months
Subscriber sales	$272,000	$1,000,000
Equipment rental income	60,000	60,000
Advertising	110,000	400,000
	$442,000	$1,460,000

NELSON LABORATORIES

In December 1975 Bill Prentice was sitting in his office in the Chicago headquarters of Marbrook, Inc., analyzing the problems he

This case was prepared by Bryant C. Brink, Helen M. Coyne, Norman W. Gorin, Glenn R. Haegele and Jane T. McCallister under the supervision of Professor Jules J. Schwartz as the basis for class discussion rather than to illustrate either effective or ineffective handling of an administrative action.

faced as president of Nelson Laboratories, one of Marbrook's subsidiaries. Chief among his concerns was that Nelson's sales and profit margin had not been growing as expected since the 1972 acquisition. Little formal profit planning had taken place at Nelson prior to June 1974, when Prentice succeeded Nelson's founder as president and supervised the company's move from Milwaukee to its present location. The move had resulted in immediate cost increases due to the new production facilities, upgraded quality control, and increased overhead charges from the parent company for management and staff services. Though Prentice felt that many of these problems were well on their way to being solved, budgeted profits were still below the level expected of Marbrook's new acquisitions.

THE PARENT COMPANY

Marbrook was the result of a 1957 merger of Marcus Laboratories, Inc., a drug manufacturer, and Brooks Chemical, a manufacturer of agricultural and industrial chemicals. Since that time sales increases had resulted primarily from growth in the existing product areas, and from entry into new markets through acquisitions. In 1970 Marcus acquired LaSalle, Inc., a producer of surgical instruments, disposable hospital products, and specialty hospital products. Sales revenues of LaSalle had grown at an annual rate of 25 percent for the past five years to over $20 million. In 1971 Marcus acquired Mediscope, which produced obstetrical equipment, and between 1967 and 1970 three overseas drug companies were purchased to provide greater access to the international market. In 1972 Marcus added dermatological products to its health care line with its acquisition of Nelson Laboratories.

As a result of these acquisitions and of the steady growth in existing product lines, Marbrook was a major competitor in industrial chemicals and in health care products, with reported sales of $169 million in 1974, the breakdown of which is shown below. (See Exhibits 1 and 2 for a more detailed financial picture.)

Product Line	% of Sales Revenue
Marcus Laboratories, Inc., Division	
Pharmaceuticals	
Analgesics	38%
Other pharmaceuticals	11
Hospital supplies &	

Product Line	% of Sales Revenue	
Hospital supplies & medical equipment	20	
Total health care products	69%	($117 million)
Brooks Chemical Division		
Industrial chemicals	18%	
Agricultural chemicals	13	
Total chemicals	31%	($ 52 million)
Total sales	100%	($169 million)

THE ETHICAL DRUG INDUSTRY

Marcus Laboratories was a manufacturer of ethical drugs. The ethical drug industry was differentiated from other segments of the drug industry in that it promoted its products exclusively to members of the medical profession. The other two major segments of the drug industry were manufacturers of proprietary drugs, those products promoted as well as sold to the general public, and manufacturers of medical, dental, and hospital equipment and supplies. The term "ethical drugs" encompassed both prescription and over-the-counter (OTC) products. Most of the leading ethical pharmaceutical manufacturers were active in more than one of these segments. They traditionally regarded the functions of the segments as dissimilar and treated them as separate businesses, at least in terms of marketing and research.

In 1974 the leading firms within the ethical drug industry were:

American Home Products	$2,049 million
Warner Lambert	$1,911 million
Pfizer, Inc.	$1,542 million
Merck & Co.	$1,330 million
Eli Lilly	$1,112 million
Squibb Corp.	$1,005 million

(These figures include total corporate sales of which ethical drug sales were only a part.) Total ethical drug sales alone in 1974 were estimated at $6.25 billion, up 14 percent from 1973. Eighteen companies had sales of over

$100 million (making up three-quarters of total industry sales). The largest firm had only 7.4 percent of the market.[1] Although entry was generally deemed to be difficult because of the expertise and relatively large expenditures required in research and marketing, competition was primarily along product group lines and small firms were thus able to succeed with a limited number of products. Overall capital requirements were not great, and as a consequence, many major firms had little or no long-term debt. Outlays for plant and equipment were relatively small. Although production costs generally took up the largest percentage of the sales dollar—and provided incentives for effective cost control—there were few economies of scale. By far the most competitive expenditures were on research and marketing.

Steady market growth was predicted in the ethical drug industry as:

1. Government involvement and spending in health care increased;
2. Research into previously unconquered diseases expanded the number and variety of remedies available;
3. The population continued to grow;
4. The emphasis on health and nutrition increased, encouraging more people to seek treatment; and
5. Rising per capita income enabled more people to afford medical care.

Although sales tended to be recession-resistant, adverse economic conditions were still important to the degree that they prompted consumers to delay visits to doctors and forced wholesalers to tighten up on inventories.

Increasingly, ethical pharmaceutical firms had been expanding their activities in foreign markets. Foreign operations have been growing at a rate of 10 to 12 percent a year, on the average, as opposed to 7 percent a year growth for domestic operations.[2] Low transportation costs, which permitted nationwide competition, also permitted American manufacturers to compete abroad economically. In addition factors such as the lower tax rate on earnings overseas, and some scattered benefits in materials and production costs, made foreign expansion increasingly attractive. Puerto Rican tax benefits had recently attracted many firms, and had become a major factor in reported profits.

Marketing

The nature of ethical pharmaceutical promotion created a unique marketing system that relied primarily on detail people, direct mail, sampling, and advertisements in trade journals to reach the targeted physician population. The immediate objective of promotional efforts was endorsement, not purchase; companies sought to persuade doctors, hospital staff personnel, or pharmacists, to recommend their products to the ultimate purchasers and users.

By far the most important element in successful market competition was the development of new and better products that could render the competitors' products obsolete or create new markets. To this end the ethical drug industry spent more on research as a percentage of sales than any other industry, approximately 12 percent of sales in 1974.[3]

The large number of new products generated made continued interaction with physicians imperative. Detail people visited in six-week cycles, trying to call upon 180 of the approximately 250 physicians in their territories each cycle. The costs of detailing were high. On the average $25,000 a year was spent to maintain each detail person in the field, including the cost of a car and expenses as well as salary, benefits, and commissions. Added to this was the expense of sampling, training programs, and other support activities. The result was that field promotion usually took up the largest percentage of the promotional dollar.

---

[1] *Standard and Poor's Industrial Survey: Health Care, Drug & Cosmetics—Basic Analysis,* July 10, 1975, p. H14.

[2] Ibid., p. H27.

[3] Ibid., p. H16.

Detail people generally had only five or ten minutes to spend with a physician on any one visit, during which time they could discuss at most, one or two products and perhaps leave behind samples of a third. Trade names were important, as doctors were more apt to prescribe products with easily remembered, or attractive names. Firms endeavored to build up brand loyalty among doctors, and sought a reputation either for quality products in general, or for superior performance within a given treatment area. It had been found that price was a secondary consideration; while price might have been important in certain segments, overall industry demand was fairly inelastic. The doctor paid primary attention to the product's effectiveness, possible side reactions, and the product's taste. Dosage form was another important criterion: whether the product was injectible, in tube, or in tablet form, for example, influenced the physician's decision. Dosage size was also a factor. Also, studies showed that the detail person's rapport with the physician played a role in the decision.

Profitability

Due to the high rate of change in the industry, progressive management skills such as planning, organization, and control became important. The ethical drug industry's return on sales was high; 10.3 percent in 1974, which put it second behind petroleum and coal producers for all manufacturing concerns.[4] Traditionally return had been generated primarily by high profit margins as opposed to high turnover. Manufacturers were generally able to pass on increased costs to the consumer. Price limitations seemed a possibility in the future, however, due to steadily increasing federal restrictions and increased consumer activism resulting in new regulations by federal and state agencies. A summary of important government regulations and proposed programs follows.

[4] Ibid., p. H26.

Department of Health, Education, and Welfare. In late 1975 HEW announced plans to limit drug prescription reimbursement under its health care programs to the "lowest cost at which the drug is generally available, unless there is a demonstrated difference in therapeutic effect." In essence, by establishing a policy of Maximum Allowable Cost, HEW would pay only the price of the generic version of a given drug. If the government increased its responsibility for the nation's health, an increase in generic price competition at the expense of brand-name drugs was a distinct possibility.

National Health Insurance Plan. This plan, proposed for implementation within the next five years, would funnel more drug sales into government institutional programs. The result would be a higher unit volume and a reduction in promotional expenses for the ethical drug industry. The industry predicted that savings in promotion expenses would be offset by increased price competition in the institutional markets.

Anti-substitution laws. Laws prohibiting pharmacists from supplying generic equivalents for physician prescribed, brand-name drugs were being modified in many states. The revision of these laws would also provide an increase in generic product competition.

Food and Drug Administration. New product development represented a substantial investment of time and research funds to the major drug producers. New drugs could not be sold, however, until the FDA approved a New Drug Application (NDA). Approval was based on "substantial evidence" of therapeutic efficacy and proof of safety. Therapeutic efficacy referred to the probability that a drug would have the medical curative results for which it was prescribed. The FDA also maintained requirements for label disclosure of possible side effects and other limitations in the use of the drug. The FDA was considering the institution of a bioequivalence rating system, which would relate drug efficacy to actual chemical composition. Drugs with the same chemical composition would receive equal ratings and one brand could not be promoted as being different or more effective than another brand with the same rating.

Federal Trade Commission. The FTC had charged that high ethical drug prices were partly due to the prescribing physician's ignorance of retail drug prices and to the consumer's inability to compare the various drug prices among pharmacies, and between brand-name drugs and generic equivalents. With FTC encouragement various states were repealing statutes prohibiting pharmacies from displaying prescription drug prices. Price competition would initially occur at the retail market level and later lead to the promotion of cheaper generic drugs by drug producers.

MARCUS LABS, HISTORY

Marcus Laboratories, Inc., was incorporated in 1935 as successor to a business begun in 1931 by Robert Fleming. The founder's son joined the company in 1941, when sales were $200 thousand. Marcus became publicly owned in 1950. Carl Cook joined the firm in 1964 as executive vice president and became its president in 1969.

The introduction of Dolarex, an ethical analgesic, and an expanded sales program in 1952, provided the first big step to growth of sales and profits. Sales increased from $750 thousand in 1952 to $40 million in 1967; net income rose from $50 thousand to $7 million in the same period.

In 1975 the Marcus Division produced twelve brand-name, ethical pharmaceuticals.

Growth at Marcus

Geoffrey Lyons, executive vice president of Marcus, viewed the corporate mission to be the field of health-care delivery systems. Within this framework Marcus' particular strengths were research, production, and marketing. Marcus specialized in products that were ready

for final consumer use. The main product line reflected the past specialization in pain relievers and tranquilizers. New product development was the responsibility of a forty-person research staff. Production facilities were modern and efficient, and quality control was rigorous.

In order to maintain the corporate goal of 15 percent annual growth in new profits, Marcus had become an active acquirer of companies with high growth potential. The maturity of its main product, Dolarex, with 40 percent market share and declining growth, had to be offset with high-growth products. Marcus executives believed that the following product areas presented the best opportunities and would fit well with corporate development plans:

Medical diagnostics
Proprietary pharmaceuticals
Cosmetic and beauty aids
Hospital and surgical instruments
Opthamological products
Dental supplies and instruments

The acquisition strategy was to purchase firms with quality products and self-supporting research and marketing expertise. Marcus would contribute production and distribution efficiency if necessary to complete the venture package. Potential subsidiaries had to demonstrate high sales growth and profitability, so earnings per share would not be diluted. The future acquisition had to have sales between $5 million and $20 million. Companies with sales of less than $5 million were considered simply too small; companies with sales exceeding $20 million would require special financing.

The acquisition of Nelson Labs was suggested by a finder who was aware of Marbrook's search for a dermatological product line to add to its health care business. Nelson offered a well known and competitively priced ethical product line with a quality image. Nelson's sales were below Marcus' acquisition standards, but continued rapid growth was expected, and Marcus could provide new production facilities and wider distribution.

NELSON LABORATORIES

Nelson Laboratories had been founded in the wake of World War II by R. Nelson Gould, a chemist. Gould's first commercial creation was a water-soluble steroid cream for the treatment of eczema. Gould's product, which he named Psorex, was a considerable advance in the field of eczema medication. Prior to Psorex's introduction sufferers of eczema had been required to apply medications that were, in fact, no different from ordinary calamine lotion.

In addition to having an effective product Gould had a talent for marketing. With ideas drawn from his own experience, Gould developed a very effective method of introducing his product. He promoted Psorex by literally handing it out free of charge to pharmacists and dermatologists. He built his business on the reorders he received when Psorex's high quality was recognized.

The success of Psorex was expanded with the introduction of Psorex lotion. A tireless worker, Gould continued to enlarge Nelson Lab's product line with the introduction of a series of skin medications. The distinctive feature of his contributions to the field of dermatology lay in the elegance of his products' formulations. With his chemical expertise Gould overcame a common problem among lotion manufacturers, chemical and oil separation. His compounding processes involved complicated procedures requiring a large number of steps under carefully prescribed conditions.

Gould established trademarks on his product names but never obtained patents either on his products or his processes. Rather than register his methods with the patent office, Gould protected his products through secrecy. His formulations were unknown to his competitors; indeed, he was the only one in his own company who knew every step of each process.

A flood that damaged his Madison, Wisconsin, plant, along with increased demand for his products, had forced Gould to move his organization to a larger facility in Milwaukee. It was in this new location that Gould refined his marketing strategy into the form that existed at the time of the company's acquisition by Marcus.

Nelson Labs maintained a complete line of nearly 100 dermatological products, which were priced approximately 25 percent below competitive items. The line was complete, even to the point of including special-purpose, low-volume items. Gould marketed his products solely on an ethical basis. Nelson's thirteen detail people sold to the nation's 4000 practicing dermatologists through numerous visits and extensive free sampling. Gould reinforced his promotions by personally attending and speaking at dermatological conventions and by advertising in trade publications. About 5 percent of Nelson's promotional dollars were invested in point-of-purchase displays. Ten to 15 percent went to convincing pharmacists to carry the line, and the lion's share went to cultivating the dermatologist relationship.

Nelson Labs experienced continuous sales growth and acquired a significant market share in the dermatological field. Under Gould's administration the firm successfully competed with the dermatological divisions of a number of very large pharmaceutical companies including the Dome Division of Miles Laboratories and Texas Pharmaceuticals Division of Warner-Lambert.

Acquisition of Nelson Labs by Marcus

Marcus acquired 100 percent control of Nelson Laboratories in 1972 through a $9 million exchange of stock. An integral part of the purchase agreement was the provision that Gould would remain as chief executive of Nelson Labs for at least five years, and longer if he desired. The basis for the five-year employment contract was the notion that it was essential to employ Gould's talents in Nelson

Labs' transition from an independent corporation to a subsidiary of Marcus.

From 1972 to 1974 Gould ran Nelson Labs much as he had for the previous twenty-five years. He was not comfortable with the larger company's call for formal planning, precise budgets, and other management controls, and as he did little to comply, the initial impact of new ownership on operating style was minimal. At the new Chicago headquarters of Marbrook, Inc., plans were made for further tightening of control over the new subsidiary. It was clear that certain changes would have to be effected to bring Nelson operations into line with Marbrook's standards. Discrepancies in production control, information reporting systems, and management practices would need to be eliminated. In addition it was evident that Nelson's growth rate would soon necessitate new plant facilities. This planning took on a sense of urgency as it became clear that Gould did not intend to renew his employment contract when it expired.

In early 1974 the decision was made to send a member of the Marcus organization to Milwaukee. His assignment would be to familiarize himself with the Nelson operation, to provide continuity of management when Gould left, and to arrange for the eventual expansion and move of Nelson Labs from Milwaukee to Chicago.

The task of easing the transition was given to William Prentice, a young manager respected within the ranks of Marbrook. Since joining the company in 1965 Prentice had worked his way up the executive ladder of Marcus through a variety of positions. His experiences within Marcus had provided him with a working knowledge of plant operations. He had managed the startup of another Marcus subsidiary, Greenwich Corporation, and had represented Marcus in the negotiation of its most recent labor contract.

Prentice was given the title of vice president of Nelson Labs on February 1, 1974. Prentice found himself in a difficult situation. Gould managed his company by executive fiat. He did not believe in delegation of authority; there

were no other titled executives. There were, however, six people who had some authority either because of their technical expertise or seniority within the firm. Nelson's workforce consisted of about 100 part-time workers. Quality control of the plant operations, though adequate, was not up to Marcus standards.

Once he had toured the Nelson operation, Prentice established three tasks for himself. Initially he wanted to familiarize himself with plant operations and acquaint himself with what each employee did. Next he sought to win the confidence of the employees and specifically of the managers and technicians who formed the loose management structure of Nelson. If at all possible, Prentice hoped to retain this talent through the transition and the move. Finally he tried to distinguish the essential components of the operation that would have to be moved from those that could be easily replaced in Chicago.

In July 1974 Gould was moved to the position of chairman of the board and Prentice was given the title of president of Nelson. In the next month Prentice strengthened his position by making several personal announcements to the employees. He started by relaxing some of the stringent working conditions, and as soon as the decision to move was made, he informed the employees that a significant portion of the operation would be closed. As trucks began traveling back and forth to Chicago, gradually moving machinery out of Milwaukee, Prentice assured the workers that every effort would be made to find them jobs.

When Nelson Labs officially shut down operations in Milwaukee at the end of 1974, few of the families had relocated, but Prentice had succeeded in persuading five of the six members of the management team to move. These people formed the nucleus upon which he built his operation in Chicago. Among them, Anthony Harris, who had managed the Nelson sales force since the mid 1950s, was made vice president of marketing, and Arnold Corson was appointed technical director.

The physical integration of production into the parent's facilities was not difficult.

Training of new personnel was minimal. The employees transferred from the old plant supervised this task. Problems emerged, however, because Nelson no longer had complete control over production and distribution of its products. Marcus supervisors seemed to view the new product line as a low priority and deadlines were repeatedly missed. In addition Nelson's relatively small shipments of orders would receive little attention on the shipment schedule while truckloads of Dolarex left the warehouse. Even in marketing and research and development, for which Nelson had complete responsibility, the parent company held the pursestrings. Prentice was caught in the middle, responsible for profitability and growth, yet lacking autonomous control of the important determinants.

As Prentice was trying to resolve some of the problems, the workers at the Chicago plant went on strike. For Nelson the move had already necessitated production lapses and the prospect of prolonged labor disputes further threatened sales.

Once operations in Chicago resumed Nelson's production costs rose considerably. No longer could Nelson take advantage of the relatively low wages paid to the part-time workers whom Gould had recruited for his operation in Wisconsin. Additional expenses also included management fees paid to both the Marcus Division and the holding company, Marbrook. The fee to Marcus covered production, shipping, accounting, finance, and warehouse services based on standard costs. No specific services were supplied for Marbrook's fee. Although other subsidiaries were assessed as well, Prentice felt that in light of Nelson's unique relationship with Marcus, these charges were unwarranted.

Though the foregoing problems were troublesome, Prentice considered long-term growth and the future of Nelson Labs to be a greater concern. Geoffrey Lyons, executive vice president of Marcus, and Prentice's immediate superior, differed with Prentice on how this growth should be accomplished. Nelson had retained its own sales force to promote to dermatologists and general practitioners who had a secondary specialty in dermatology. Prentice believed that growth could be accomplished through market expansion using the larger Marcus sales force to broaden exposure of his products to hospitals and to all the physicians visited by the Marcus detail people. Lyons believed that the Nelson products were not in sufficient demand among typical Marcus customers to cover the cost of including them in the presentation and sample bag. He recommended growth through new product development and expanded penetration of the present market, rather than expansion into broader markets.

Another approach to sales growth was the expansion of the target market to include the consumer who did not visit a dermatologist, but rather chose nonprescription medication for treatment of skin problems. Prentice believed this market was not only sizable, but tended to be less sensitive to economic recessions when a visit to a dermatologist might be considered a luxury. Penetration of this broad market would require direct advertising to the consumer of Nelson's over-the-counter products. Both Marcus and Nelson had historically been ethical drug firms, and neither had experience in the proprietary field.

Nelson had two research chemists who worked apart from the Marcus research staff. Since the move to Chicago no new products had been added to the dermatological line. Although the issue had not yet surfaced Prentice wondered about the possibility of a major high-volume dermatological product being developed by the Marcus research staff. Were this to happen he was unsure whether the product would automatically be given to Nelson to market, or whether it would be retained for the Marcus sales force. Prentice had doubts of this sort, but Lyons foresaw no such problem and even discussed the possibility of acquiring small companies specifically to extend Nelson's product line.

The issues concerning Nelson's future were discussed in a recent meeting of the Marcus executive committee, of which Prentice and Lyons were both members. The committee was concerned that profit growth had not met expectations for the acquisition, and that sales had essentially leveled off for the last three years. The committee recognized the problem of increased production costs and the effects of Marcus' marketing policy on the growth decisions of Nelson Labs. However, it maintained its original profit and growth goals. After some discussion Prentice accepted the goals as challenging, yet attainable. He was not happy, however, with the emphasis on high current profitability and cash generation and the implied tradeoff with sales growth and new product development. Prentice was also dissatisfied with the fit of Nelson into the Marbrook organization. Nelson, because of its location at the Marbrook headquarters, was not an autonomous subsidiary, but neither was it a fully integrated division. Considerable economies of administrative salaries could be achieved by entirely absorbing Nelson Labs into the Marcus operation and managing the line as a separate product group. On the other hand Lyons believed that the expected growth in the Nelson operation could best be achieved by a strong team effort. A complete management team would "build its own destiny" and "the growth of the subsidiary hinges on its people, their creativity, and their intelligence."

EXHIBIT 1

MARBROOK, INC.
Consolidated Income Statement
($ thousands)

	1974	1973
Revenue		
Net sales	169,011	145,443
Royalty income	3,538	2,938
	172,549	148,381
Costs and Expenses		
Cost of products sold	72,473	61,955
Selling, delivery, and administrative expenses	59,027	48,673
Research and development expenses	3,428	3,126
	134,928	113,754
Income		
Operating income	37,621	34,627
Interest expense	1,350	1,117
Interest and dividend income	2,912	2,660
Net income before taxes	39,183	36,170
Federal taxes	14,792	14,136
State and foreign taxes	4,643	3,824
Net income after taxes	19,748	18,210

Statement of Retained Earnings

	1974	1973
Retained earnings (beginning of year)	72,153	61,982
Net income	19,748	18,210
Dividends (per share: 1974—$1.00 1973— .92)	(8,738)	(8,039)
Retained earnings (end of year)	83,163	72,153
Earnings per share (shares outstanding = 8,738,000)	$2.26	$2.08

EXHIBIT 2

MARBROOK, INC.
Consolidated Balance Sheets
($ thousands)

	1974	1973
ASSETS		
Cash	9,211	8,164
Marketable securities @ cost	341	241
Accounts receivable (net of doubtful accounts)	34,372	26,258
Inventories	40,744	29,620
Other current assets	2,907	2,711
Total current assets	87,575	66,994
Property, plant and equipment (net)	37,755	31,815
Investment in foreign operations	2,467	5,354
Intangibles and other assets	9,887	7,850
Total assets	137,684	112,013
LIABILITIES		
Accounts payable	9,505	5,183
Notes payable to banks	7,905	273
Federal and other taxes (current)	4,631	4,174
Deferred income taxes (current)	5,232	5,061
Current portion long-term debt	1,421	1,490
Other current liabilities	7,195	5,245
Total current liabilities	35,889	21,426
Long-term debt	2,679	3,275
Deferred taxes	2,617	2,021
Other liabilities	1,224	720
Minority interest in foreign subsidiaries	410	318
Total liabilities	42,819	27,760
SHAREHOLDER'S EQUITY		
Common stock ($1.00 par 22,000,000 authorized)	8,738	8,738
Additional paid-in capital	4,549	4,549
Retained earnings	83,163	72,153
Less treasury stock @ cost	1,585	1,187
Total shareholders' equity	94,865	84,253
Total liabilities and shareholders' equity	137,684	112,013

ARCAIR, INC.

Sitting across the conference table from his boss, Gerald Frieling, Robert Roediger patted the report that lay in front of him as if calling upon its contents to corroborate the point he was making. As the general manager of Arcair, a wholly-owned subsidiary of the Metallurgical Systems Division (MSD) of Air Products and Chemicals, Inc. (APCI), Roediger had come to Air Product's Allentown headquarters to present a follow-up report on a proposed expansion of Arcair's Brazilian operations. This was the first time Arcair had sought corporate approval for international expansion. Roediger and William Khoury, Arcair's international manager, had flown in from Arcair's Lancaster, Ohio, headquarters to convince Frieling, the division president, that a prompt decision was needed.

After explaining the proposal Roediger again pointed to the report as he added: "the risk involved in this proposal is minimal because our capital investment is very small. Our biggest investment is our Brazilian manager. He's a good man. If we don't decide to expand, we'll lose him, and that's why we have to act *now!*"

HISTORY OF AIR PRODUCTS AND CHEMICALS (APCI)

The Early Years

Prior to World War II the traditional method of supplying industrial gases was to produce gas in a central plant and transport it to cus-

---

This case was prepared by Marcus V. Requeira, John M. Ruse, Susan R. Silver, Carl L. Snyder, and Gary L. Takacs under the supervision of Professor Jules J. Schwartz as the basis for class discussion rather than to illustrate either effective or ineffective handling of an administrative action.

tomers in cylinders, tube trailers, and railroad tank cars. Leonard Pool, the founder of Air Products, had a better idea. Pool, who had twelve years of experience as a salesman in the oxygen and industrial gas business, believed that industrial gases could be provided to customers at a reduced cost per cubic foot by locating gas manufacturing and generating facilities nearer the consumer:

> We had decided to build big plants and take revenues over time. At our own expense, we decided to build plants on or adjacent to the customer's property and supply oxygen via pipeline. The customer, in turn, agreed to purchase given quantities of oxygen during a contract period. Essentially we decided to sell the milk instead of the cow.

Though this approach was revolutionary Pool was convinced that if the high costs of transporting gas by traditional means could be eliminated, the demand for gases, and particularly oxygen, would increase. He and a young University of Michigan engineering student built their first oxygen generator in the spring of 1939.

During World War II Air Products devoted its efforts to supplying the government with oxygen generators that separated oxygen from air through fractional distillation. Prior to the war all gas production equipment in the United States had been made by Union Carbide. The rest was imported, primarily from Germany. The war generated a need for a domestic supply of this equipment, but other firms in the industry hesitated to enter the market. By the end of the war Air Products had produced 240 generators supplying nitrogen and oxygen to the military effort.

Pool's entrepreneurial skill heavily influenced the company during its crucial development period. The demands created by the war were important in the firm's early development, but without Pool's driving ambition and energy the concept of onsite gas production would never have become a reality. An associate cited Pool as being instrumental in demanding unusual performance:

> Leonard was always pushing us and forcing us to stretch. He even took an order for six generators to be used on ships, although we had never built them before. Our competitors thought the task was impossible. They thought oxygen generators had to remain level and that a rolling and pitching ship presented insurmountable problems.
>
> Leonard simply told the chief engineer that he had an order and needed designs within a week. Needless to say, the engineer came up with a solution after some bathtub experiments that made it possible to place oxygen generators on ships. Our generators were used throughout the war.

Postwar Years

At the end of the war military demand declined and Air Products was faced with a crisis. Although the company had gained a reputation for its skill and technology, its primary customer had been the government, and peacetime forced the firm to reckon with a basic problem: it lacked a commercial customer base.

It began to approach the private sector, seeking customers for its air separation process and service. It secured contracts with Wierton Steel in 1945 and with Ford Motor Company in 1947. The Wierton facilities became particularly important in 1947 when the company ordered a separation plant 100 times bigger than anything that Air Products had ever built and 50 times larger than any such facility in existence.

The success of this huge plant, which produced one-third of the total oxygen manufactured in the United States in 1947, was more than just a technological victory. It convinced potential customers that large-scale oxygen separation plants could be built on or near their facilities to reduce the cost of oxygen, and that Air Products was the premier supplier in the world in this market.

Company Growth Through Expansion and Acquisition

As its 1975 Annual Report put it, the company's growth and investment strategy was based on the "combination of high-technology, low-cost products sold at competitive prices, with continued emphasis on participation in markets with above-average growth potential." Since 1952 the firm's expansion and acquisition policy had continued, extending into new and related fields in high-technology products. In 1961 Air Products expanded into the chemical field with the purchase of Houdry, Inc.

Present Industry Position

By 1975 the organization comprised three major groups, including the parent company and sixteen domestic and foreign subsidiaries. Sales reached $699 million, compared to $333 million in 1969, ranking the company in a tie for seventh in the specialty-chemical industry. With industry sales at $11.4 billion in 1975, the company held a respectable 6 percent of a market in which the largest firm garnered 12 percent. The top four firms had 43 percent of the sales and the top eight firms had 70 percent. As the graphs in Exhibits 1 and 2 depict, the company achieved fifteen consecutive years of assets, sales, earnings, and net income growth. Capital spending during the same period showed comparable growth, as shown in Exhibit 3.

AIR PRODUCTS ORGANIZATIONAL STRUCTURE

Air Products and Chemicals, Inc., was organized into three groups: the catalytic group, the chemicals group, and the gases and equipment group (see Exhibit 4). Each of these was comprised of a number of divisions producing a wide variety of products and services.

The Catalytic Group

With sales of $20 million, this group accounted for roughly 3 percent of the company's total revenues in 1975. It offered a complete range of plant design, engineering, construction, maintenance, and management services to the power and process industries, both in the private and public sectors.

The Chemicals Group

This group had revenues of $260 million in 1975 and contributed 37 percent of total company sales. The group manufactured and sold proprietary chemicals and industrial catalysts that met the needs of a variety of industries. It also licensed process technology for petroleum refining and petrochemical industries.

The Gases and Equipment Group

Worldwide sales in this group were $418 million in 1975, representing 60 percent of company revenues. The gases and chemical group was organized into four divisions:

1. The Industrial Gas Division marketed and distributed the company's broad line of industrial gas products in cylinder and bulk quantities through a nationwide network of district and branch offices.
2. The Cryogenics Systems Division produced and marketed gas sold in large quantities, "tonnage" gas, for major industrial users and also produced a broad range of cryogenic equipment.
3. The Medical Products Division maintained its own product development program and manufacturing operations, producing highly technical products that were primarily used for inhalation therapy and anesthesiology.
4. The Metallurgical Systems Division (MSD) was formed in the early 1970s to take advantage of opportunities in the welding industry and related areas. In 1976 the division included Exomet, Metals Recovery, and Arcair.

ARCAIR

It had been Air Products' strategy to develop a welding business in specialty or proprietary areas. Arcair, which fit both categories, was acquired in 1969. Arcair had developed a specialized welding market that it dominated completely. It also had potential for further expansion.

History

William Khoury, International Division manager, called Arcair "one of the great American success stories."

The Arcair Company was founded in 1949 by a welding engineer in a shipbuilding yard. Working with two other men, he invented the Air Carbon Arc Process for removing metal in preparation for welding, repairing welds, or cutting off risers from castings.

During World War II chrome nickel electrodes were used to weld armor plates on naval ships. However, due to shortages of the metals, the composition of the electrodes was altered and cracks began to develop in the welds. Repairing the welds was a slow, tedious process of drilling adjacent holes and grinding out the area between them. The founder developed a process to remove these defective welds more efficiently, using an electric welder and compressed air.

The director of marketing for MSD described the early developments:

> The first attempt in 1943 was cumbersome, employing two men. One would reduce the weld to molten mass, while the other, following behind with an air hose, would blow away the molten metals.
>
> Several attempts were made to combine the carbon electrode and air jet. This combination torch, although clumsy, was finally produced in 1948.

The first torch was sold and the first distributor appointed in 1949. The company had grown every year since then, to a 1976 sales level of roughly $25 million per year. In 1953 Arcair recognized a better market for its process in the central United States where heavy metal work was concentrated; so the company moved from Seattle, Washington, to Lancaster, Ohio, where it is now based.

Air Products acquired Arcair in January 1969. In 1975 Air Products added its existing gas welding lines to the Arcair Company. The same year Arcair, in its expanded form, was merged with TekTran, another Air Products subsidiary.

TekTran was founded in 1970 as a joint venture between Rockwell and Air Products to transfer some of the technology from the Apollo Project—particularly nondestructive testing (NDT)—to commercial use. Robert Roediger, previously with Hobart Brothers, was appointed general manager of the company in August 1971. TekTran's main thrust was nondestructive testing, sophisticated welding techniques, and power supplies.

Between 1973 and 1974 Air Products bought out Rockwell's share in the company. On January 1, 1975, TekTran was moved thirty miles and combined with Arcair's expanded facilities in Lancaster, Ohio. Arcair's founder became chairman of the board of directors of the combined Arcair-TekTran Company, and Roediger was named president of the new organization, which he viewed as "the integration of a high-technology company (TekTran) with a specialty welding accessory company (Arcair)."

Products and Markets

In 1976 Arcair consisted of what management termed "four packages":

1. Oxy-acetylene cutting torches, tips, and gas regulators, manufactured by the gas and equipment group in Allentown, Pennsylvania.
2. Air carbon arc torch heads and gouging electrodes, used in the original "Arcair" process, manufactured or supplied through Lancaster, Ohio.
3. Electromechanical welding systems, power generators, and other related equipment, from the TekTran venture, manufactured in Lancaster.
4. Nondestructive testing systems, also from the TekTran venture, consisting of instrumentation and related systems enabling the user to look inside a material, find flaws, or determine properties—without destroying the piece being examined. These systems were also manufactured in Lancaster, Ohio.

Arcair Process

The equipment for the Arcair Process was made up of two parts. The nonexpendable torch head was the unique part of the process the founder developed and protected by patents. This part was manufactured by the Arcair Company. The gouging electrode, the metal rod that was consumed in the Arcair Process, was not manufactured by Arcair, but rather was purchased from others.

The Arcair Process was sold mainly to four industries—steel foundries, steel mills, shipbuilding, and heavy-metal working. These accounted for 85 percent of the product used. The process was also sold to four other industries—farm machinery, railroads, general maintenance, and construction.

In 1974 the basic patents for the Arcair Process expired. Though Arcair did have follow-on patents, for the first time in twenty years the firm faced competition, from Japan as well as several American companies. During the next two years Arcair continued to hold its leading market share position, but began to confront the challenge of maintaining market share despite competitive thrusts.

Roediger explained: "We intend to maintain leadership by developing new ways of applying technology." Through TekTran Arcair had access to sophisticated systems such as the power supplies that were developed jointly with Rockwell. By applying advanced power and control systems to the traditional welding procedures, Arcair sought to develop electromechanical welding systems as its future growth area.

Arcair International

The other way to maintain Arcair's leadership, in the face of losing the patent protection, was to improve Arcair's position internationally. Roediger said, "There is a need for new technology in the developing countries of the world, and we must be there to show leadership."

From Lancaster, Ohio, Arcair sold its products through 550 foreign distributors. Arcair International employed sixty people. William W. Khoury, International Division manager (see organizational chart in Exhibit 5), had complete profit and loss responsibility both for control of the three foreign subsidiaries and for all the export activities out of Lancaster. He was also responsible for all exploratory work necessary for the evaluation of new markets.

In the 1960s Arcair had instituted a program of international expansion of operations. It began to export, through independent distributors, to almost every industrialized country in the world. It successfully established three foreign subsidiaries: Arcair Europa in 1966, Arcair Canada in 1967, and Arcair de Mexico in 1968. Setting up an international subsidiary had traditionally been a four-stage program at Arcair:

1. Export into the country using the best local distributor to establish and quantify the market;
2. Establish an Arcair distributorship, manned by company personnel;
3. Establish a warehouse and/or a light assembly/manufacturing plant; and
4. Integrate into a full assembly/manufacturing operation.

Historically this had been a very successful procedure for Arcair. Arcair de Mexico was in the fourth stage, Arcair Europa was in the middle of the third stage, and Arcair Canada was in the beginning of the third stage.

History of the Proposal

In 1968, prior to being acquired by Air Products, Arcair had begun to export welding torches and electrodes to Brazil. Arcair chose S.A. White Martins and Oxigenio de Brasil as its distributors. Coincidentally both of these companies competed in the area of industrial gases against Arcair's parent, Air Products and Chemicals, Inc.

Khoury had informally appraised the Brazilian market. He concluded that, because of its rapid industrial growth, Brazil offered a potentially attractive opportunity for the Arcair Process. Moreover a Brazilian subsidiary could offer Arcair better access to the African market, providing a closer source of exports to the developing South African area.

In 1970 Arcair management determined that the system of independent distributors in Brazil was not working out. Sales had reached a peak of about $80,000 and then had begun to decline. The potential of the Brazilian market, on the other hand, was increasing steadily. It was clear that Japanese, French, and German firms were making inroads into the Brazilian arc gouging market.

Impetus for the expansion of operations in Brazil developed, at about the same time, at the corporate and divisional level. Frieling emphasized that "the decision to investigate Brazil seriously came about ... as a result of Air Products' strategic planning process." Air Products prepared two kinds of plans: a five-year strategic plan, which it updated annually, and a one-year operating plan. Through this process MSD had identified increased international expansion as a strategic goal. Arcair singled out Brazil as the country offering the best market potential for this expansion.

From the division's standpoint, it was decided to use Arcair as the "spearhead" for expansion into new foreign markets and to expand gradually Arcair's customer relationships to include other MSD products. Frieling believed that this tactic had worked in the past. In Europe, for example, clients initially served only by Arcair were later served by several MSD subsidiaries. At the corporate level Air Products was already involved in Brazil and had recently begun commercial operation of an industrial gas plant.

In early 1975 Khoury traveled to Brazil to collect data to corroborate Arcair management's proposal to expand its Brazilian operations beyond the export stage and to help decide what form the expansion should take. Because hard data was generally unavailable, Khoury relied on personal interviews with Brazilian businesspeople and government officials.

He and Roediger met with Frieling and reviewed the situation. The erosion of Arcair's sales in a growing market concerned them. Khoury pointed out that Brazil was one of the world's fastest developing countries. His study of the market convinced him that there was a solid industrial base that could use carbon arc torches. However, the current distributors were not developing this business fast enough, especially in the area of new applications.

Roediger's plan was to hire a Brazilian national as a sales manager and establish an in-country warehousing operation. The manager would develop a sales team to assist both distributors and end users. This arrangement would allow Arcair to respond quickly to orders from inventory on hand, and to develop new markets with its own sales force. Inventory could be replenished at planned intervals.

The project would need $50,000 to $100,000 for startup and working capital. Khoury thought the venture would recover these costs within a year after starting operations. Fixed investment would be limited to office furniture and equipment; warehousing would be leased. This plan had been followed in other countries with excellent results.

Frieling demurred on the warehousing decision, but agreed to hiring a sales manager. The person selected would assist Khoury in making a more detailed study of the Brazilian market. Frieling believed it was necessary to obtain a better understanding of the market requirements and the division's ability to satisfy these demands before he could arrive at a decision.

In March 1975 Khoury returned to Brazil and hired a Brazilian with extensive experience in the welding equipment industry. Together they compiled a report formatted as shown in Exhibit 6.

Most of the information was gathered in interviews with distributors and end users. Although a more detailed follow-up study would be necessary, Khoury was convinced that the report adequately justified the adoption of the warehousing strategy in the interim.

Khoury and Roediger met for the second time with Frieling to review the proposal. Frieling thought that excellent headway had been made, but he still required more information. In particular, he asked for cash flow forecasts, a study of competitors' probable reactions, and an analysis of risks associated with the selected product mix. Exhibit 7 summarizes the agreed upon format for this analysis.

Khoury again returned to Brazil to obtain the necessary information. In the meantime Arcair's Mexican facilities came on stream. It then became advantageous to ship electrodes from Mexico because of a tariff differential. As members of the Latin American Free Trade Association (LAFTA), Mexico and Brazil reciprocated in imposing much lower import tariffs. Goods shipped from the United States faced import duties set at approximately 50 percent of their value. Import duties for similar goods from a LAFTA country were being levied at only 8 to 10 percent of value. This enabled Arcair to be more price competitive, resulting in increased demand for its electrodes.

When Roediger and Khoury returned with the revised report, they were convinced it was in the company's best interest to act promptly. The Brazilian manager was a major investment whom they did not want to lose to a competitor. He had been waiting over a year and was eager to start operations. In addition current sales in Brazil exceeded the one year forecast by the end of the first quarter, and demand continued to look strong.

Khoury and Roediger discussed these factors and the rest of the report at length with Frieling. Frieling thought that, though a bit weak in the area of documentation of sources, the proposal was in good order. He appreciated their position and felt the company would act expeditiously on the proposal.

However, he admitted that he still had some questions about the risk involved in the marketing mix. Initially sales would be almost entirely in electrodes and hand-held torches, with a 90/10 split between electrodes and torches. Frieling felt that unless Arcair assured itself of the lowest cost electrode supply, it would be in a poor position in any competitive price war to gain market share.

Additionally there was an open question about the nature of the entity to be formed: Should Arcair operate for legal and tax reasons as a subsidiary of the Air Products operation in Brazil, or should it operate separately, reporting to Lancaster?

From a marketing point of view it was Arcair's opinion that its interests would be best served by operating as an independent entity. Arcair's current distributors competed directly with other divisions of Air Products in Brazil. On the other hand it appeared to be in Air Products' best financial interest to consolidate all Brazilian operations. As Frieling explained:

> This is an increasingly important consideration from the corporation's standpoint, but it is just a bother to someone like a Bill Khoury who wants to operate his own business.

A few weeks after meeting with Roediger and Khoury to receive their final report on the Brazilian proposal, Frieling took a moment to reflect on the history of the proposal. His deliberate manner contrasted sharply with the sense of urgency that Roediger had conveyed when, three weeks earlier, he argued for a prompt decision on the proposal. As Frieling put it:

> It must be remembered that Arcair has historically been an entrepreneurial company. The concept of operating with an analytical management system is different. Being in transition from an entrepreneurial company, the individuals who operated under both management styles can say, "Life was sure a lot less complicated in the old days than it is now. Why do we need this?"
>
> But I think one of our jobs is to make sure that they understand that we are looking for this kind of information so we can make a good decision and not think that we're embroiled in large company bureaucracy.

Frieling observed that a manager should ask "process" questions of his subordinates, rather than "content" questions. Then, recalling the initial report submitted by Roediger and Khoury, he continued: "You really ought to ask three questions: What factors did you consider in bringing this proposal forward? What alternatives were considered? and, what is the risk? The problem, he concluded, "is that they didn't present this type of analysis."

EXHIBIT 1

AIR PRODUCT AND CHEMICALS, INC.
Assets and Sales
($ millions)

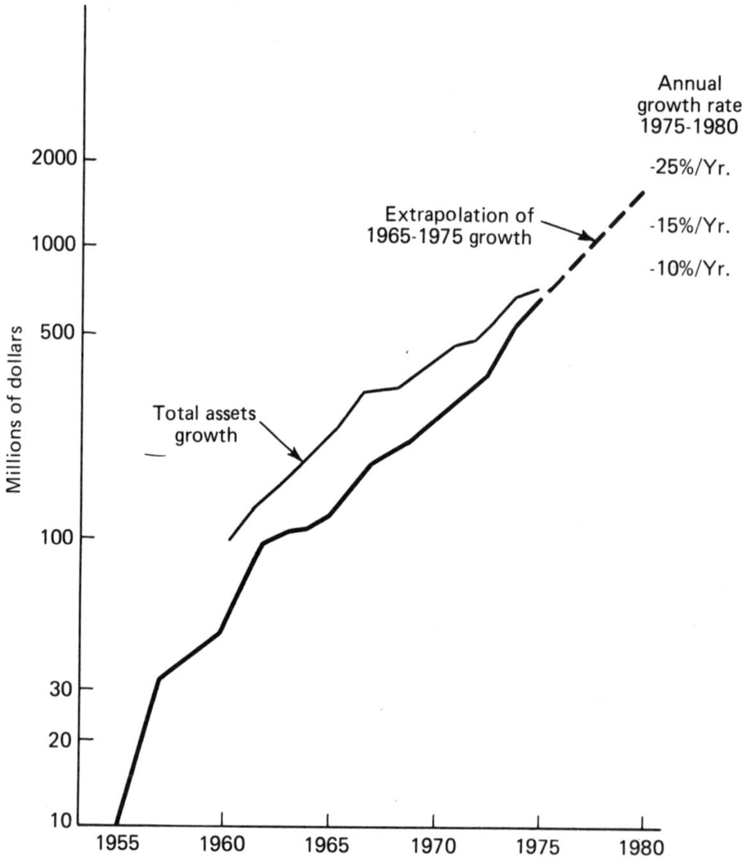
Annual
growth rate
1975-1980
-25%/Yr.
-15%/Yr.
-10%/Yr.
Extrapolation of
1965-1975 growth
Total assets
growth
Millions of dollars
2000
1000
500
100
30
20
10
1955
1960
1965
1970
1975
1980

EXHIBIT 2

AIR PRODUCTS AND CHEMICALS, INC.
Net Income ($ millions)

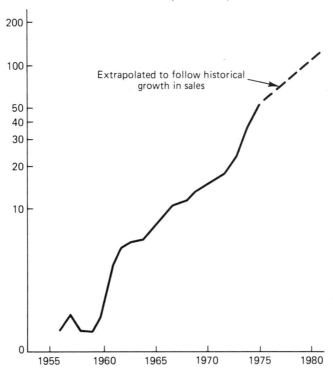

Extrapolated to follow historical growth in sales

EXHIBIT 3

AIR PRODUCTS AND CHEMICALS, INC.
Capital Spending ($ millions)

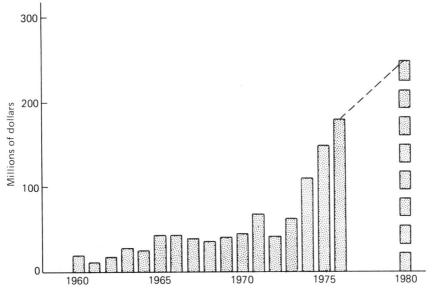

185

EXHIBIT 4

AIR PRODUCTS AND CHEMICALS, INC.
Organizational Structure

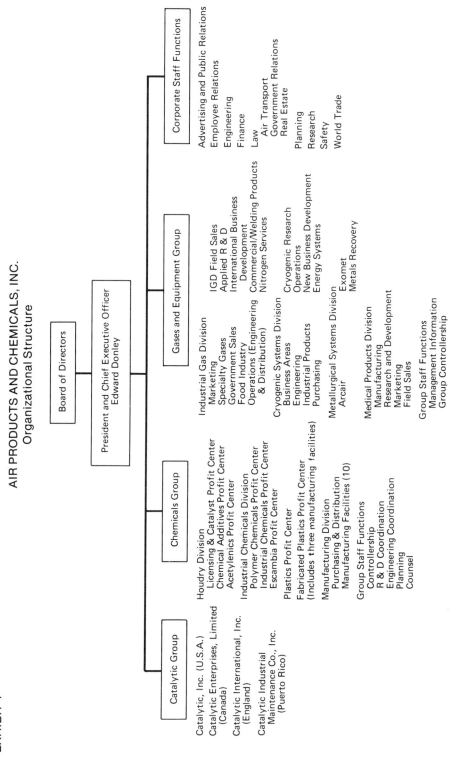

Board of Directors

President and Chief Executive Officer
Edward Donley

Catalytic Group

Catalytic, Inc. (U.S.A.)
Catalytic Enterprises, Limited (Canada)
Catalytic International, Inc. (England)
Catalytic Industrial Maintenance Co., Inc. (Puerto Rico)

Chemicals Group

Houdry Division
 Licensing & Catalyst Profit Center
 Chemical Additives Profit Center
 Acetylenics Profit Center
Industrial Chemicals Division
 Polymer Chemicals Profit Center
 Industrial Chemicals Profit Center
 Escambia Profit Center
Plastics Profit Center
Fabricated Plastics Profit Center
(Includes three manufacturing facilities)
Manufacturing Division
 Purchasing & Distribution
 Manufacturing Facilities (10)
Group Staff Functions
 Controllership
 R & D Coordination
 Engineering Coordination
 Planning
 Counsel

Gases and Equipment Group

Industrial Gas Division
 Marketing
 Specialty Gases
 Government Sales
 Food Industry
 Operations (Engineering & Distribution)
 IGD Field Sales
 Applied R & D
 International Business Development
 Commercial/Welding Products
 Nitrogen Services
Cryogenic Systems Division
 Business Areas
 Engineering
 Industrial Products
 Purchasing
 Cryogenic Research
 Operations
 New Business Development
 Energy Systems
Metallurgical Systems Division
 Arcair
 Exomet
 Metals Recovery
Medical Products Division
 Manufacturing
 Research and Development
 Marketing
 Field Sales
Group Staff Functions
 Management Information
 Group Controllership
Gases & Equipment Group - Europe

Corporate Staff Functions

Advertising and Public Relations
Employee Relations
Engineering
Finance
Law
Air Transport
Government Relations
Real Estate
Planning
Research
Safety
World Trade

EXHIBIT 5

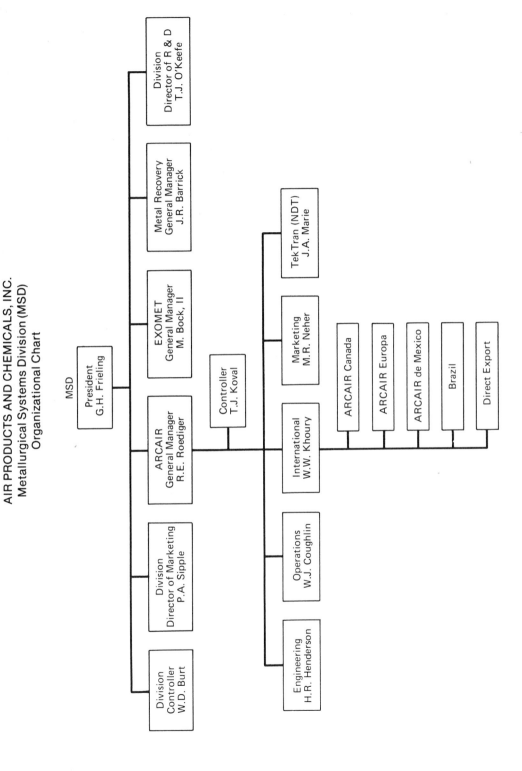

AIR PRODUCTS AND CHEMICALS, INC.
Metallurgical Systems Division (MSD)
Organizational Chart

EXHIBIT 6

FACTORS INCLUDED IN ARCAIR BRAZILIAN SUBSIDIARY ANALYSIS

1. Market environment
2. Engineering requirements
3. Distribution
4. APCI–MSD business plan
5. Import requirement and restrictions
6. Important potential customers for welding equipment
7. Principle magazines and newspapers
8. Main trade associations
9. Brazilian company law
10. Tax incentives in Brazil
11. Brazilian labor laws

The first report contained the above information. The first four sections are included in the following pages of Exhibit 6, including Tables 4 and 5, which complement the APCI–MSD business plan.

Market Environment

Arc welding comprises 65 percent of the welding equipment demand in Brazil. Oxy-fuel, butt welding, and resistance seam welding make up the other 35 percent of types of welding equipment used and manufactured in the country. Domestic producers are currently exporting to LAFTA countries, plus Canada, Portugal, and South America. The domestic production was estimated to be approximately 7000 machines per year, with the majority of these being arc welders. The market is a growth market, with semiautomatic gas shielded welding make up the other 35 percent of types of

Currently Brazil imports approximately $3,000,000 of welding equipment a year, which is an increase from approximately $800,000 in 1968. Most of the equipment is imported from the United States, with West Germany being the next largest supplier.

The major markets for welding equipment are:

Agricultural equipment
Automotive
Metal fabrication
Shipbuilding

Table 1 lists the most important potential customers for welding equipment in these industries. Within these industries, shipyards, metal structures, drums and pressure vessels, and oil and power station piping account for about 90 percent of the market. Boilermakers, electromechanical industries, and the automotive industry account for about 10 percent of the market. The total market is growing at a rate in excess of 10 percent per year.

The welding equipment most frequently purchased in Brazil is the following:

1. Semi-automatic gas shielded equipment;
2. DC generators;
3. AC/DC rectifiers; and
4. Oxy-fuel welding equipment.

Brazilian shipyards are pioneering in the use of multiple welding systems, which will have increased importance in the heavy construction industries. The major volume, however, still is in the smaller, portable welders.

Engineering Requirements

Brazil has adopted both the U.S. (NEMA) and German manufacturing standards. Regarding open circuit voltages, load voltage ratings and duty cycles, the Brazilian Standards Association (ABNT) is developing specific standards for Brazil, which are in publication. Normal voltage on electric machines in Brazil runs between 70 and 80 volts, with the maximum allowed as 100 volts.

There are no special codes or regulations for the design and manufacture of hand cutting and welding equipment, including oxygen regulators. The usual practice is to adhere to American standards. The main type of inlet connections used on gas regulators are right-hand thread, fourteen threads per inch, 21 mm internal diameter for inert gas and, for flammable gases, left-hand threads, fourteen per inch, 21 mm internal diameter.

Welding equipment manufactured in the United States is built according to United States standards. Currently there are no spe-

EXHIBIT 6 (cont.)
FACTORS INCLUDED IN ARCAIR BRAZILIAN SUBSIDIARY ANALYSIS

cial Brazilian regulations and American standards have been accepted.

Most equipment carries a six months to one year warranty against manufacturing defects. The equipment is usually installed at the buyer's expense. Maintenance and technical assistance on the equipment are provided at additional costs by the manufacturers and dealers after the six months or one year warranty has lapsed. Brazil does have some small firms specializing in maintenance and technical assistance for the equipment.

There are no legal labeling, technical, or other special requirements to be made. The metric system is becoming generalized for measurements, but currently the dual system of inches and millimeters is being used. New equipment should be made according to the metric system.

Electric power in some areas is still 50 cycle; however, the changeover to 60 cycle is expected to be completed throughout Brazil by 1975. In Sao Paulo, Brazil's main industrial region, the system is 60 cycle.

Distribution

Both manufacturers and importers of welding equipment wholesale directly to consumers and through dealers and wholesalers. As a general rule direct sales to consumers are made within the area of the main or branch offices of the company, principally in the large cities such as Rio de Janeiro and Sao Paulo. Dealer and wholesaler sales are made elsewhere in the country. Most of Brazil's national products are sold directly by the manufacturers to the end user. Most of the imported equipment is sold by or through representatives. Markups vary widely considering the type of equipment sold. They vary between 10 percent and 50 percent, with the usual markup in the 30 percent to 40 percent range from manufacturer to dealer.

Companies operating in Brazil use the following sales methods:

1. Direct sales calls by salesmen;
2. Product demonstrations;
3. Direct mailing;
4. Catalog distribution;
5. Magazine advertisements; and
6. Newspaper ads.

TABLE 4
MSD—Brazil, Market Survey

Product Lines	SAM[a] 1974 ($000)	1978 ($000)
Welding Equipment		
Oxy-fuel	3,000	5,500
MIG (incl. power supply)	4,000	9,100
TIG (incl. power supply)	250	800
Plasma (incl. power supply)	50	100
Cutting machines	500	1,100
Accessory Products		
Arcair torches	100	250
Arcair electrodes	250	600
Misc.	50	200
Annealing Equipment & Services		
Exoanneal & Exo-Lec	500	1,200
NDT Equipment		
Ultrasonic	300	750
Eddy current	250	400
Total	9,250	20,000

[a]Serviced available market.

APCI-MSD Business Plan

A market survey will be made to expand on and verify the information contained in Tables 4 and 5. This information is designed to determine the market size and competitive environment of selected products that the division is manufacturing domestically, and for which there appears to be a growing need in Brazil.

The basic business strategy will be to establish a marketing and warehousing facility in Brazil, initially distributing those products for which there is the greatest immediate need. After this marketing effort has become established, the operation will be expanded to include additional products and certain assembly work. The third phase will include distribution of the complete product line, plus local manufacturing.

The immediate study will attempt to make a judgment on the timing of each of these three phases and the selection of the products in which to begin the operation.

A complete business plan, including sales, profits, and investment, will be made at the completion of the current study.

TABLE 5
MSD—Brazil, Market Survey

Competitors	Mfg. or Import	Estimated Current Vol. ($000)
Welding Equipment		
White-Martin (Linde)	mfg./import	3500
AGA (ESAB)	mfg./import	1500
Oxigenio do Brazil (air liquide)	mfg./import	1500
Messer-Gresheim	import	100
Tanaka	import	150
Secheron	import	50
Hobart	import	150
Lincoln	import	300
B.O.C.	import	
Arcair Equipment		
Denver Co.	mfg.	40
Lincoln Electric	import	30
Ibigawa	import	50
White-Martin	import	100
Oxigenio do Brazil	import	100
Annealing Equipment		
Cooperheat	import	200
Kemwell	import	150
NDT Equipment		
Krautkramer-Branson	import	300
Forester	import	250

EXHIBIT 7

FACTORS INCLUDED IN ARCAIR BRAZILIAN SUBSIDIARY ANALYSIS

1. Statement of market need
   a. Market potential by product; and
   b. Segmentation of market by industry served.
2. Analysis of competitor position in the markets by product line.
3. Evaluation of other methods available to Arcair by which to serve the market.
4. Description of the proposed business approach
   a. Resource requirements;
   b. Brazilian law and regulations;
   c. Currency considerations; and
   d. Country of origin for torches and electrodes.
5. Economics—year by year forecast for five-year period of the following:
   a. Working capital, fixed assets, import deposits;
   b. Sales, cost of sales (by product lines);
   c. Operating expenses;
   d. Interest, taxes, exchange translation and other expenses; and
   e. Net income, return on investment, return on sales.

A.H. ROBINS CO.

On May 16, 1974, Robert G. Watts, senior vice president of A.H. Robins Company, sent a memo to the heads of the company's seven corporate divisions. The memo noted that President William L. Zimmer had requested that they give immediate attention to the feasibility of manufacturing certain selected chemicals. The memo announced the creation of a secret, high-level task force to be "responsible for providing recommendations for compounds to be considered, acquisition possibilities, site selection and facilities, as well as financial justification for any proposals."

The task force met June 1, 1974, and was broken down into two subgroups, one to study the purchase of a chemical plant, and the other to look into building one from scratch, the "build" or "buy" alternatives.

A.H. Robins was one of the major companies manufacturing and distributing ethical (prescription) pharmaceutical products in the United States. During 1974 the company ranked fifth among American firms, based on the number of prescriptions written. Pharmaceutical products accounted for 77 percent of total sales and 88 percent of total pretax profits; consumer products accounted for the balance of the sales and profits. (See Exhibits 2 through 5.)

The drug industry had historically been a growth industry, with gains in sales and earnings averaging 10 to 11 percent each year. Robins' total sales and profits increased at a compound rate of 14 percent and 15 percent respectively, from 1964 to 1973. The fastest growth had been in the international area,

This case was prepared by Rita Kollar under the supervision of Professor Jules J. Schwartz as the basis for class discussion rather than to illustrate either effective or ineffective handling of an administrative action.

which increased from 8.3 percent of total sales in 1963 to 28 percent in 1973.

ORGANIZATIONAL STRUCTURE

Robins had six major operating divisions. Production and marketing of ethical pharmaceutical products in the United States and Canada were handled by the Pharmaceutical Division. All those products were promoted directly to doctors, dentists, and pharmacists. The basic ingredients of all products Robins manufactured were purchased from outside sources.

The Research and Development Division was responsible for all new product development. It emphasized the development of new synthetic medicinal compounds and new formulations.

The International Division produced and marketed pharmaceuticals in ninety countries.

The responsibility of the Product Planning and Development Division was to oversee the use of the company's resources to maintain and supplement its pharmaceutical product line. The Product Planning and Development Division served largely as a resource to the pharmaceutical development committee, providing it with the information necessary for informed decisions and assuring development of approved products. Its staff drew on the specialized services of other units and departments to assure coordination of efforts. The committee was made up of the six senior officers charged with supervising Robins' efforts to develop further and to expand the line of pharmaceutical and health-care products. The committee was chaired by a senior vice president who reported to the president.

The committee's duties included immediate and long-range planning and coordination

of the research and development, pharmaceutical, and international divisions to assure
implementation of agreed upon goals in product planning and development. The committee
served as a staff adjunct to the president's
office in the area of new products. All new
product proposals had to be considered by it
before implementation. Its recommendations
were subject to review and approval by the
president and the chairman of the board.

The Consumer Products Division manufactured and marketed all the company's consumer products.

The corporate staff handled operations and
engineering services and personnel as well as
administrative and corporate planning.

THE MARKET

Robins competed in several specific market
segments and typically made its products
available in several strengths or dosage forms.
The company frequently marketed a family of
similar products within the same market
segment. Eleven of Robins' products were
among the 200 most widely prescribed drugs
in the United States. Exhibit 1 lists some of
the company's major markets.

In addition to these segments, Robins was a
lesser factor in several other markets, the most
significant being the antibiotic market.

Since late 1971 Robins had introduced
three branded-generic antibiotic products. A
branded-generic was a product that was marketed in direct competition with a well-
accepted brand name product on which the
patent had expired. Branded-generics were
differentiated on a price basis, marketed
under a brand name, and manufactured by
companies whose reputations for quality and
distribution were well established with physicians. These products, to be successful, had to
be promoted in order to be chosen by physicians.

In June 1973 Robins entered the nonam-
phetamine, antiobesity market. This market
had been growing faster than 12 percent a year
because physicians did not like to use amphe-
tamine products that had potential for abuse.

Because of this the company's promotional
effort for these products had been concentrated on direct selling or detailing, rather
than on nonpersonal journal advertising and
direct mail. The mode of activity of these
products had to be understood and anticipated by physicians and patients who were
familiar with other weight control products,
and who might equate the lack of stimulating
effects as a product failure.

Robins' antiobesity drug was one of only a
handful of products that were patent-protected. In 1972, 11 percent of net sales were
from pharmaceutical products that were
patent-protected. Patents on the company's
muscle relaxants, Robaxin and Robaxisal, had
expired in November 1973. In the past patent
protection had not played an important role in
the company's growth.

New Products

Since 1964 twenty-three new pharmaceutical products had been introduced by Robins
in the United States. Only one, a cough
product, ranked among the company's ten
top-selling pharmaceutical products in this
country. Three others, which were among
the company's twenty top pharmaceutical
products, representing 80 to 85 percent of its
drug sales, had first been marketed prior to
1964. Its third leading product had been marketed for forty years. For the past several
years Robins' ethical pharmaceutical sales in
the United States had increased at an average
of 7 to 8 percent a year, on a par with the
United States pharmaceutical market, despite
the age of the basic product line.

New product introductions had been one
source of growth for Robins during recent
years, but the company's most important
growth had come from older nonpatent-
protected products. The long-standing physician acceptance of Robins' major items,
in the face of the introduction of several competitive products, was one of the company's
greatest assets.

In 1962 Robins began to diversify away
from the ethical pharmaceutical business.

Most of the subsequent acquisitions had been in the consumer products field and ranged from pet products to snack and specialty food items.

THE INDUSTRY

Estimated sales of ethical drugs in the United States were approximately $6.75 billion for 1974, up 14 percent from the $5.91 billion in 1973. Ethical drug producers also had a large stake in international markets, with 1974 sales of approximately $4.54 billion, up 39 percent from $3.28 billion the previous year.

The cost of marketing to physicians on a national scale and of conducting research for new product development separated the major drug firms from the hundreds of smaller ones. Of the approximately 800 firms in the industry, some twenty-five to thirty dominated the private prescription market. The majority in the industry were small enterprises; it is estimated that at least 80 percent of the firms had fewer than twenty employees. The large companies traditionally emphasized brand name rather than price. The smaller firms typically sold their product by generic name to the retail trade or through wholesalers, or to governmental or nongovernmental institutions on the basis of competitive bidding.

Entry into the manufacture of generic drugs, was relatively easy. The technical expertise and ability to maintain the high quality necessary for drug manufacturing was well within the reach of small enterprises. Capital requirements for production were not a barrier. It was considerably more difficult and costly to market nationally and to become involved in new product development. Nevertheless there was still a high level of competition within the industry. The largest American ethical drug firm had only a 7.4 percent share of the total market. There were eighteen companies with annual sales in excess of $100 million; these accounted for nearly 75 percent of total sales.

The nature of demand for ethical drugs was very unusual; the end user did not make the buying decision. The decision was made for the consumer by his physician when the latter wrote out a prescription, generally by brand name. The pharmacist was obligated by law to fill the prescription exactly as it was written.

Patients, as well as doctors, were largely ignorant of the prices of prescription drugs. In forty-eight of the fifty states, pharmacists were forbidden by law to advertise prescription drug prices. Price is never mentioned in any of the promotional literature physicians receive from the major drug companies. It was argued that such knowledge might taint the physician's professional judgment.

The demand for prescription drugs with respect to price approached complete inelasticity. The patient visited a doctor for relief of symptoms. The doctor's prescription offered the hope that the symptoms would be cured. Unless he had absolutely no resources to pay for the prescription, the patient would usually have it filled regardless of price. Few people would shop around to have a prescription filled at the lowest price because it is a difficult task.

In the institutional (hospitals and governmental agencies) sector of the market, price could be a much more important factor in determining the choices made by purchasing authorities. There were upwards of 7000 ethical drugs, including single drugs and products with combinations of two or more active ingredients. It was estimated that 400 of these prescription products fulfill more than 99 percent of patients' drug requirements. Institutions can achieve economy through a provision that the hospital pharmacy may fill any prescription on a generic basis.

The sales approach for drugs was made to the doctor rather than to the patient. Thus the marketing of drugs required a highly trained sales force to sell doctors on the qualities of the products. The major drug producers had large detail forces that had long association with physicians, so new companies found it extremely difficult to develop the sales forces needed to enter the field. Large quantities of samples were the traditional types of promotion to physicians. Legislation was proposed to eliminate much of this promotion, however, as well as introduce more regulation for the training of detail people.

The pharmaceutical industry had a high ratio of privately-financed research to sales, higher than almost any other industry. Research and development were basic elements in the competitive strategy of the major companies. When research resulted in a product that could be patented, the patent could be exploited in many ways. The holder of the patent might create a monopoly for the firm or license the product to one or a few other manufacturers. Although the latter arrangement provided additional sellers in the market, it rarely led to price competition.

The patent system severely limited entry into the largest part of the prescription drug market. Because physicians were, to a great degree, insulated from price considerations, the major pharmaceutical companies could achieve and hold dominant positions in ethical drug markets solely through promotion of their brand names. A firm that had established itself as a leading seller of drugs could enjoy average revenues per unit of output that were two, three, or more times the revenues available to its generic competitors.

METHOCARBOMAL

In 1958 Robins' chemists first synthesized a white powdery chemical called methocarbomal, a muscle relaxant. After receiving government clearance methocarbomal was patented and sold in pill form under the name of Robaxin. Robins gave contracts to several chemical makers to supply raw methocarbomal, as the company made only finished pharmaceuticals.

Robaxin was very successful, and by 1967 the company believed it was buying enough methocarbomal, a glyceryl guaiacolate (GG) derivative, to consider making the chemical itself. The company was also purchasing large volumes of glyceryl guaiacolate for its Robitussin cough medicine. In 1974 President Zimmer circulated a memo proposing once again that Robins manufacture both petro-chemicals.

Earlier this idea had hit a snag when the Food and Drug Administration's Drug Efficacy Study, an industry-wide review of pharmaceuticals, gave methocarbomal a "questionable" rating in 1970. Although the FDA eventually cleared the chemical in 1974, that review had kept methocarbomal, along with Zimmer's idea of manufacturing it and GG, under a cloud for four years.

The idea was revived by the 1973–1974 oil crisis with resulting shortages of petroleum-based chemicals. "Skyrocketing chemical prices were cutting into our profit margins," said Zimmer, noting that the price of methocarbomal had shot up more than 40 percent in 1974 alone. At times methocarbomal and GG were unavailable at any price, causing costly production closedowns that "were cutting into the lifeblood of our business." Zimmer decided in April 1974 that Robins "would no longer be a pawn of the market."

THE TASK FORCES

The task force assigned to investigate the "build" alternative was headed by Robert G. Watts, a forty-one-year-old senior vice president who had been with the company fourteen years. Watts sought out six process-engineering firms for the initial groundwork and was eventually approached by dozens more. In early October 1974 the task force settled on Lockwood-Green Engineering Company of Atlanta.

In March 1975 Lockwood-Green delivered to Robins an inch-thick $16,000 volume that detailed design criteria, the chemical-making process, an equipment list, environmental impact statement, project schedule, drawings, and a preliminary cost estimate for a new plant. The engineering firm calculated that a plant making 200,000 pounds of GG and 500,000 pounds of methocarbomal annually, Robins' projected 1978 needs, would cost $6 million, plus 30 percent or minus 20 percent.

Robins' officers estimated that the same amounts of chemicals would cost $6,050,000 if purchased on the open market, but that they could be manufactured for only $3.5 million.

Based on a $6.2 million capital outlay ($6 million for the plant and $200,000 for the land), the pretax return on investment (compared with continued outside purchases) would exceed 40 percent, and the investment would pay for itself in less than three years.

Consultants for the "buy" task force identified over 100 existing plants that seemed to meet Robins' needs. Of these about twenty were actually contacted by the company and three strong candidates ultimately emerged. One was Hexagon Laboratories, Inc., of New York. Hexagon was up for sale and was already a big supplier of methocarbomal to Robins. Few plant modifications would have been necessary. "But Hexagon was then in New York City and there was no room for possible expansion," said Ernest Bender, Jr., senior vice president and member of the product development committee. Another senior officer noted the "Hexagon's plant was unionized and we've always tried to steer clear of unions." The buy group finally settled on a plant in Sheboygan, Wisconsin.

While investigation into the two alternatives progressed, "friendly" competition developed between the build and buy groups. As Robert Watts saw it, "the acquisitions people were pushing for something really big. They really wanted another feather in their cap." Architectural renderings of plants Watts had been responsible for in Puerto Rico and Richmond were prominently displayed in his office; one member of the acquisition team argued that Watts wanted to build a plant "so that he could have another picture hanging on his wall." Zimmer minimized the implications of such rivalry; he said that he had hoped for just such "creative tension."

Meanwhile serious doubts about whether Robins should get into the chemical business at all were being raised. Carl Lunsford, vice president in charge of chemical research, began to have reservations about the project. He suggested that the proposed plant be scaled down by half. He warned:

> You don't just go out and build a chemical plant. It takes technical expertise and know-

how. This is our first move into a new area, and I think it would be well to leave room for a third party to supply us. There's always the possibility of a plant going down because of fire or some other catastrophe.

Lunsford's hesitation came on the heels of a study commissioned by Robins at Chase Manhattan Bank. The Chase analysts argued that Robins should not go through with the project because of the cyclical nature of the chemical business: By prudent hedging operations—buying supplies when prices were low—Robins could assure itself of the necessary raw materials.

Zimmer, still vividly remembering the oil embargo, rejected the Chase argument out of hand. "Any savings we'd obtain would quickly be lost if supplies were interrupted," he said.

Planning for the project was coming to a head in the midst of a precipitous decline in the United States economy. One officer involved noted "that some of our meetings were pretty strained. Inflation was rushing along and the recession just kept getting worse. Some of us felt that we were just spinning our wheels, that the state of the economy—the sheer uncertainty of it all—would preclude a big commitment of capital."

The vice president and treasurer said that those who were worried about the recession were overruled because a company couldn't look at short-term fluctuations in determining capital spending policies. "This is long-term planning. A recession is a one-to-three-year thing. When you're talking about a new plant, you're talking ten to twenty years." Besides, Robins was able to minimize the recession's impact because its strong balance sheet would enable the company to finance the project internally rather than to compete for funds in the capital markets.

By March 1975 the management had studied its build and buy options for about ten months, and a decision was imminent. The proponents of purchasing the Sheboygan plant made a persuasive presentation. The next day the build task force presented an equally convincing proposal, aided by an artist's sketch, for a custom-built facility in Virginia. The costs were about equal. Zimmer was leaning in favor of the build option. "We really wanted that plant in Virginia. That way we could run down and touch it just to make sure it's there every once in a while."

A Third Option

A third possibility arose when Zimmer, in consultation with Chairman E. Clairborne Robins, was on the verge of making a final decision. In February 1975 Hexagon Laboratories, the New York concern previously considered as a potential purchase possibility, had been acquired by Boehringer Ingelheim, a large pharmaceutical and chemical company based in West Germany. Subsequently Hexagon officials had heard of Robins' plans for a captive source of methocarbomal and GG. Two Hexagon representatives were dispatched to Richmond in April to keep the Robins business. Hexagon offered to build a plant in Virginia and negotiate a long-term sales agreement with Robins. Robins, already well into its own plans, demurred. Hexagon offered an equity interest in the plant as a sweetener. Zimmer demanded 50 percent.

Pharma Investment Ltd., a holding company for the western hemisphere interests of Boehringer Ingelheim, had its own plans to construct a second chemical plant for use by Hexagon. Viktor Leyseiffer, executive vice president of Pharma, proposed a joint venture between Robins and Pharma. Both companies would participate as equal partners in the formation of a new company to build a chemical plant. The plant would be built primarily for the production of methocarbomal and GG and most of the output would be used by Robins.

A second plant, to be built by Pharma for Hexagon Labs, would adjoin the plant to be built by the joint venture company. The two plants would share a common service unit. The cost of the two plants with the common unit was estimated to be $10 million. The cost of a single plant and service unit for the joint venture company alone was estimated to be $6 million. Both plants would be multipurpose, that is, they would have the capability to produce more than one chemical.

Robins' goals were to gain the financial benefits of self-production of the chemicals it used in large volume. Ownership of chemical-manufacturing facilities could provide the additional possibility of producing other compounds that the company might develop or acquire in the future. Lastly, the company wanted to be assured of its supply of the needed chemicals. Zimmer wanted to make a decision very soon.

EXHIBIT 1

Market Segment	Total Market Est. Value 1973 ($millions)	Robins' Market Share (%)
Total ethical cough and cold	$220–240	10–16%
Prescription-oral decongestants[a]	70–80	20–22
Cough/cold combinations[a]	28–30	13–15
Cough products (over-the-counter)[a]	25–30	55–60
Antispasmodic-synthetic and belladonna	45–50	23–25
Oral muscle relaxants	30–40	24–26
Vitamin B complex with C	28–32	29–31
Narcotic-analgesics	50–55	13–15
Anti-diarrheals	28–34	9–11

[a]Specific market segments of ethical cough and cold market.
Source: Smith, Barney & Co. estimates

EXHIBIT 2

A. H. ROBINS COMPANY
Historical and Projected Sales, % Total, and % Change by Major Groups

	1974E	1973	1972	1971	1970	1969	1968	1967	Average Annual Growth Rate 1967-1973
Total Sales (000)	$208,500	$189,267	$166,700	$151,350	$132,552	$122,122	$115,428	$100,414	+11.2%
% change previous year	+10.2	+13.5	+10.1	+14.2	+8.5	+5.8	+15.0	+35.6	
International Sales	$59,500	$53,080	$43,509	$34,082	$24,769	$21,371	$20,496	$18,443	+19.8
% of total sales	28.5	28.0	26.1	22.5	18.7	17.5	17.8	18.4	
% increase previous year	+12.1	+22.0	+27.7	+37.6	+15.9	+4.3	+11.1	+66.0	
Domestic Sales (000)	$149,000	$136,249	$123,191	$117,268	$107,783	$100,757	$94,932	$81,971	+8.9
% of total sales	71.5	72.0	73.9	77.5	81.3	82.5	82.2	81.6	
% increase previous year	+9.4	+10.6	+5.1	+8.8	+7.0	+6.1	+15.8	+30.2	
Ethical Sales (000)	$160,500	$144,067	$121,524	$106,853	$91,461	$85,730	$81,223	$72,499	+12.2
% of total sales	77.0	76.1	72.9	70.6	69.0	70.2	70.4	72.2	
% increase previous year	+11.4	+18.6	+13.7	+16.8	+6.7	+5.5	+12.0	+15.1	
Consumer Products (000)	$48,000	$45,200	$45,176	$44,497	$41,091	$36,392	$34,205	$27,915	+8.6
% of total sales	23.0	23.9	27.1	29.4	31.0	29.8	29.6	27.8	
% increase previous year	+6.2	+0.1	+1.5	+8.3	+12.9	+6.4	+22.5	+152.3	

EXHIBIT 3

A. H. ROBINS COMPANY
Historical and Projected Sales by Major Products Group
(millions)

	1974E	1973	1972	1971	1970	1969	1968	1967
Total Ethical Sales	$160.5	$144.1	$121.5	$106.9	$91.5	$85.7	$81.2	$72.5
Cough & cold	53.0	48.5	41.7	36.3	33.2	31.8	28.9	23.1
Antispasmodics	18.4	17.0	15.0	15.1	14.6	14.7	13.9	14.1
Muscle relaxants	13.7	12.9	11.7	12.1	10.6	9.8	9.2	8.0
Dalkon shield (purchased 1970)	4.3	3.9	3.7	4.0	—	—	—	—
Scheurich (acquired 3/1/71)	10.4	8.6	7.8	5.8	—	—	—	—
Antibiotics	5.0	4.0	3.3	0.5	—	—	—	—
Brenner (acquired 1/1/72)	5.5	4.1	3.3	—	—	—	—	—
Viobin (acquired 2/73)	4.4	3.8	—	—	—	—	—	—
Pondimin (introduced 6/73)	7.5	2.5	—	—	—	—	—	—
Other	38.3	38.8	35.0	33.1	33.1	29.4	29.2	27.3
Total Brand Name Sales	$ 48.0	$ 45.2	$ 45.2	$ 44.5	$41.1	$36.4	$34.2	$27.9
Pet care	17.5	16.5	15.0	16.5	15.9	14.7	11.5	8.0
Chap stick								
Caron	30.5	28.7	30.2	27.8	25.2	21.7	22.7	19.9
Swinson								
Pretax Income								
Ethical	$ 52.4	$ 46.8	$ 39.3	$ 33.6	$27.7	$26.7	$25.0	$20.6
% Margin	32.6	32.5	32.3	31.3	30.3	31.3	30.9	28.4
Brand Name	$ 6.9	$ 6.5	$ 5.8	$ 5.5	$ 4.1	$ 5.5	$ 5.1	$ 4.3
% Margin	14.4	14.4	12.8	12.5	10.1	14.9	14.8	15.4

EXHIBIT 4

A. H. ROBINS AND SUBSIDIARIES
Consolidating Balance Sheet

	December 31 ($000)				
	1974	1973	1972	1971	1970
ASSETS					
Current Assets					
Cash	$ 5,004	$ 3,667	$ 6,606	$ 7,347	$ 5,367
Certificates of deposit and time deposits	10,346	18,033	14,768	16,465	5,216
Marketable securities (at cost which approximates market)	13,878	26,365	16,186		
Accounts receivable (less allowance for doubtful accts)[a]	33,011	32,844	28,105	25,801	23,413
Inventories	49,061	30,427	23,645	22,186	21,767
Prepaid expenses	4,101	2,917	2,573	2,699	3,100
Total current assets	$115,310	$114,253	$ 91,894	$ 74,499	$ 58,865
Property, plant, and equipment:					
Land	$ 2,285	$ 2,264	$ 2,336	$ 2,126	$ 2,062
Building and leasehold improvements	29,055	25,926	22,244	21,962	20,616
Machinery and equipment	21,717	18,375	15,247	13,206	10,682
	53,052	46,565	39,829	37,296	33,362
Less accumulated depreciation	22,634	19,581	10,381	14,057	11,437
	$ 30,418	$ 25,984	$ 23,447	$ 23,238	$ 21,924
Intangible and Other Assets					
Excess of cost over net assets of subsidiaries acquired	$ 36,315	$ 36,628	$ 38,174	$ 32,795	$ 25,253
Patents, trademarks, and goodwill	4,586	1,361	1,446	1,597	2,109
Deferred charges	2,696	1,713	2,237	2,044	938
Other assets	938	1,667	595	812	361
	44,535	41,369	42,452	37,249	28,662
	$190,263	$182,606	$157,799	$134,987	$109,452

EXHIBIT 4 (cont.)

A. H. ROBINS AND SUBSIDIARIES
Consolidating Balance Sheet

	December 31 ($ 000)				
	1974	1973	1972	1971	1970
LIABILITIES AND STOCKHOLDERS' EQUITY					
Current Liabilities					
Notes payable	$ 1,784	$ 1,864	$ 3,126	$ 4,847	$ 3,152
Accounts payable	12,096	8,849	6,476	5,959	5,081
Long-term debt payable within one year	750	4,750	7,750	4,100	4,119
Federal, foreign, and state income taxes	5,145	6,413	4,303	4,463	3,565
Accrued liabilities	6,076	5,279	4,693	3,564	2,415
Total current liabilities	$ 28,851	$ 27,155	$ 26,348	$ 22,934	$ 18,335
Long-term debt	$ 5,250	$ 16,750	18,000	$ 18,250	$ 11,600
Deferred income taxes	$ 341	—	—	—	—
Deferred foreign currency gains	$ 1,097	$ 1,097	—	—	—
Minority interest in foreign subsidiaries	29	94	95	198	241
Stockholders' Equity					
Capital stock					
Preferred $1 par authorized—10 million shares none issued					
Common $1 par authorized—40 million shares	26,127	26,124	12,792	12,725	12,712
Capital surplus	693	635	2,863	671	347
Retained earnings	130,875	110,751	97,693	80,207	66,216
	157,695	137,510	113,348	93,604	79,276
	190,263	183,606	157,796	134	109,452

ᵃAllowance is $626,000 for 1974, $554,000 for 1973, $456,320 for 1972.

EXHIBIT 5

A. H. ROBINS AND SUBSIDIARIES
Statement of Consolidated Earnings

	Year Ended December 31 ($000)				
	1974	1973	1972	1971	1970
Income					
Net sales	$210,713	189,216	166,700	151,350	132,552
Interest and other income	3,143	3,964	1,699	927	551
Total income	213,856	193,180	168,399	152,277	133,103
Costs and expenses					
Cost of sales	71,233	59,175	52,499	47,951	41,047
Research and development	9,568	8,050	6,583	6,003	5,881
Marketing, administrative, and general	79,015	70,209	62,365	57,237	52,663
Interest expense	1,134	2,488	1,810	1,937	1,752
Total costs and expenses	160,950	139,922	123,258	113,130	101,354
Earnings from continuing operations before income tax	52,906	53,258	45,141	39,147	31,758
Provision for income tax	25,989	26,738	22,341	19,393	16,030
Earnings from continuing operations	26,917	26,520	22,800	19,754	15,728
Discontinued operations and loss on disposal	—	(1,160)	—	(675)	—
Net earnings	$ 26,917	25,360	22,800	19,079	15,728
Earnings per common share					
Continuing operations	$1.03	$1.02	$.89	$.78	$.62
Discontinued operations and loss on disposal	—	(.05)	—	—	—
Net earnings	$1.03	$.97	$.89	$.78	$.62

ARCO CHEMICAL COMPANY

The ARCO Chemical Company, a division of Atlantic Richfield, had proposed the construction of a $500 million, world-scale olefins plant. Its function would be to provide the West Coast with a reliable domestic source of petrochemicals. This proposal had been developed to meet the rapidly increasing need of West Coast manufacturers for an adequate and stable supply of petrochemical raw materials. Company officials contended that if a stringent work schedule was met, the plant could come on stream as early as 1980.

ARCO Chemical was launched in early 1966 with the merger of Atlantic Refining and Richfield Oil. The expansion of the division had been enhanced substantially in 1969 by Atlantic Richfield's merger with Sinclair Oil, which made important contributions through its infusion of very competent people, excellent technology, and a position in basic aromatics, butadiene, and plastics. One unit, Sinclair-Koppers, had recently been reorganized as ARCO Polymers, a separate subsidiary of Atlantic Richfield.

In 1975 Atlantic Richfield was the eighth largest integrated oil company in the United States. With its many subsidiaries, Atlantic Richfield explored for, developed, produced, purchased, transported, and sold crude petroleum, natural gas, and petroleum products produced from crude oil, including petrochemicals. The firm conducted its operations principally in the United States, but it also obtained substantial quantities of crude petroleum from its interests in a number of foreign countries. This crude was either sold outside the United States or imported for use in Atlantic Richfield domestic refineries. Atlantic Richfield also sold certain refined products in Europe and elsewhere in world markets.

The company's production of crude oil, natural gas, and natural gas liquids was accomplished principally in the United States and in Canada, Venezuela, Iran, and Indonesia. In North America, as of December 1974, Atlantic Richfield was producing oil or gas or both from a total of 10,485 wells, and owned or had interests in seventy-six gas processing plants, of which it operated twenty-four. In 1974 Atlantic Richfield had sales of $7,166,933,000. Earnings per share of common stock came to $8.36. The financial summary in Exhibit 1 provides an appreciation of the size of the proposed investment in relation to the firm's overall operations.

ARCO Chemical was in the midst of an aggressive capital expenditure program. The largest part of the program involved the building of olefins plants—a mammoth undertaking. The total output of saleable products from the two plants being built in Channelview, Texas, would be greater than ARCO Chemical's total existing volume. Planned for completion in mid-1976 and mid-1977, these plants would annually take the raw materials (called feedstocks), gas oils, and napthas, and convert them into the following amounts of intermediate products:

2.6 billion pounds of ethylene
1.6 billion pounds of propylene
0.4 billion pounds of butadiene
0.004 billion barrels of aromatics

This case was prepared by James S. Blaszczyk, Kenneth W. Gerhart, Gary A. Grossman, Larry K. Miller, and Patrick J. O'Grady under the supervision of Professor Jules J. Schwartz as the basis for class discussion rather than to illustrate either effective or ineffective handling of an administrative action.

The products above are all examples of petrochemicals: chemical substances derived from petroleum or natural gas. The petrochemical industry was born in the 1920s and blossomed to maturity immediately following World War II. Growth since then has been phenomenal. By 1965 petrochemicals accounted for 37 percent of all chemical output in the United States. The industry spends more than one billion dollars each year on new plant and equipment. Expansion is expected to continue. Economists predict that by 1990 about 11 percent of all United States crude oil will go to make chemicals—more than double the 1976 share. The statistics for ARCO Chemical Division are also impressive. Employing over 6000 people in 1974, it produced over $700 million in sales.

The olefins project under consideration had been proposed by the Chemical Division of the Atlantic Richfield Company. The ARCO Chemical Division was divided into several departments, each concerned with its own particular aspect of the project. In charge of the project was Dr. Robert R. Chambers, vice president of nuclear operations and commercial development. Organization charts for both Atlantic Richfield Company and ARCO Chemical Division are provided in Exhibits 2 through 5. Division president, Robert D. Bent, also served as a senior vice president of the parent company.

To facilitate the handling of the olefins project, Dr. Chambers had split investigation of the proposal between two of his managers in Philadelphia. K. E. Cosslett's role was first to analyze the West Coast market for petrochemicals. This market had to be shown able to support an economically sized plant. After this evaluation had been made, Cosslett's job would become one of coordinating the transfer of sales activity to the marketing department. The other manager, I. E. Katz, was responsible for coordinating all other aspects of the project, which included evaluations, engineering, and environmental factors.

A third manager under Dr. Chambers was H.J. Kandal, based in California. Kandal was to keep on top of the engineering and environmental aspects of the project locally.

There were five full-time people working on the proposed project. In addition, a good deal of information was being submitted by the other departments of the Chemical Division. These included chemical operations, financial controls, and research and engineering.

According to Dr. Chambers, communications were extremely important both with his subordinates and his superiors in ARCO Chemical and the senior management of Atlantic Richfield. Every month Dr. Chambers briefed President Bent on the progress of the proposal. When all work was completed Bent and Chambers formally presented the proposal for an Official Authorization of Funds from Atlantic Richfield, where the final decision rested to build or not to build the plant.

ARCO Chemical Company maintained a highly specialized department for new ventures within its Research and Engineering Division. The purpose of this department was to explore and research investment opportunities, in this case, the olefins plant for the West Coast. In doing this the department had to examine a wide variety of external factors that were extremely important to the project.

The primary consideration that had been presented by the manager of the special projects department was location of the site. ARCO Chemical had purchased the option to buy a 3400 acre tract on the northern bank of the Sacramento River estuary that empties into the San Francisco Bay.

ARCO Chemical's plant was expected to cover only 20 percent of the 3400 acres. As much as possible of the remainder would be continued in agricultural use. The strategy that ARCO Chemical had devised was to solicit customers who could build plants on the ARCO Chemical site, enabling more economical centralized cryogenic storage. If ethylene products were shipped to diverse sites, cryogenic storage would be required at each site.

The planning and design of many individual projects made up the engineering and design work of a project the size of an olefins plant. In performing this task of organizing, many individual deadlines had to be met. Exhibit 6 depicts a schedule of individual tasks and projected completion dates.

The primary product of an olefins plant was ethylene. In the United States ethylene had been produced mainly from the so-called light feedstocks: ethane and propane. These were derived from natural gas. Ethane and propane had been readily available at low cost and had provided high ethylene yields with a minimum of the less valuable byproducts. Abroad, heavy feedstocks such as naphtha and gas oil were used to produce ethylene because many regions did not have significant natural gas supplies.

United States natural gas supplies were running short, but the shift to heavy feedstocks would be gradual, as most existing ethylene plants based on light feedstocks were not readily adaptable to process significant amounts of heavy feedstocks. Also, few petrochemical companies could effectively use or market the wide range or large quantities of byproducts associated with production from heavy feedstock.

The trend towards increased quantities of heavy feedstocks could bring a change in which greater proportions of United States ethylene would be produced by major integrated oil companies having a source of such feedstocks. Crude oil, naphtha, and natural gas were generally available to an oil company. Integrated refineries were also able to use the wide range of byproducts. By combining the oil refinery process with the ethylene production process, a synergism of the two processes could be attained. Atlantic Richfield would have the ability to efficiently handle all products and byproducts from a combined operation of this type.

Very little of the petrochemical industry's production went directly to the consumer. Most was sold instead to other industries, which used petrochemicals as a raw material.

Petrochemicals, then, were found in thousands of products the average person bought and used daily. Countless industries were heavily dependent on the petrochemical industry for their existence. Petrochemical derived products were used in textiles, medicines, agriculture, automotive products, construction, communications, and countless other applications.

As an intermediate product, the demand and production of petrochemicals was dependent on the demand for its derivatives. The increasing demand for these end products counted for the great growth of the petrochemical industry. The increases in petrochemical consumption were also tied to the development of successful methods to produce olefins in large industrial operations at low cost.

Exhibit 7 contains a chart of olefins products and some of their common uses and provides an outline of the types of products provided by a petrochemical plant.

The trend in ethylene prices from 1961 to 1973 had been steadily downward. Rising oil prices began to reverse this trend. Further reductions of conversion costs due to efficiency resulting from subdivision of labor and output of multiple products had not offset this rise. The value added was a smaller percentage of sales, while raw materials were an increasingly large proportion. Unless the prices of feedstock were to decline, the period of falling prices for ethylene and other petrochemicals would be over.

Location of the Plant

The location of a petrochemical complex was of vital importance. Two major tasks were involved in the decision for optimal location. The first was to determine which components of olefin production costs might be expected to vary regionally. These components include raw materials, fuel, electric power, labor, and transportation. Also, major cost differentials could be observed if the feasible size of production units differed regionally. Certain regions could reap the benefits of economies of scale that were denied smaller units in other regions. This was stressed by President Bent: "One inviolate criterion is the requirement that the project should be capable of supporting the largest scale, lowest unit cost, production facility possible at the time of commissioning."

The second major task in finding the best location was to compare regions. Does one locate at the raw material site, in the market area, or in neither? The decision here concerned transportation costs. With present-day technology ethylene could not be transported economically for more than 150 miles. However, the ethylene derivative, polyethylene, had a much greater transportation range.

Feasible locations for olefins plants were quite limited in the United States. Raw material locations were basically limited to the Gulf Coast and contiguous states. Market areas in the United States were mainly the East Coast, the Northeast, and the Midwest. Until this time California had been considered as a market area only on a smaller scale.

In 1969 what Bent termed the "lowest unit cost production facility" would not have been possible in California. This had changed, ARCO Chemical believed, primarily because of two developments. The first was the doubling of the size of the market since 1969 (see Exhibit 8). The second was the construction of oil production and transmission facilities between Prudhoe Bay and the port of Valdez in Alaska. Possibly by late 1977 great volumes of hydrocarbons from Alaska's North Slope might start flowing to the West Coast. Thus what has been called the most important potential deterrent to growth—feedstock shortage—could become minimal for a company owning a large share of the North Slope oil.

The competitive position of Atlantic Richfield was strengthened by the strategic location of its refineries on the West Coast. Atlantic Richfield planned to begin with its North Slope crude, refine it, break it into its various petrochemical components, including ethylene, and finally sell them to nearby clients. Ethylene, a basic chemical building block, could be sold to surrounding plants, which would in turn produce other products and materials. Dow Chemical Company was also investigating the possibility of a competitive petrochemical installation on the West Coast. However, Dow was considering the venture from the opposite end, based on its needs for ethylene.

Modern Olefins Plants

Great strides have been made in the design of newer and larger olefins plants. The result has been an increase in the yield of ethylene at the expense of the major byproducts of the production process, regardless of feedstock used.

The hydrocarbon feedstock, whether natural gas liquid or naphtha, plus recycled ethane and propane, enters the convection section of a furnace after some preheating by hot process steam. At a suitable point in the convection section dilution steam is added to the hydrocarbon feedstock in a weight ratio that varies depending on the composition of the feed.

After leaving the convection section the mixture of feedstock and steam is ready to enter the radiant section of the furnace, where transformation takes place. After leaving these furnaces the hot product gas must be cooled down very quickly in order to prevent further reactions in the gas mixture. Without such cooling, ethylene yield is lower and waste product formation higher.

Fuel oil and the gasoline are separated. The water contained in the feed gas is condensed. Still further processing removes carbon dioxide and hydrogen sulfide, preparing the feed gas for cooling and separating the other key components. The remaining products go through what is called product distillation, which involves the final separation of the demethanized gas.

Emerging from this process is ethylene, the largest volume organic petrochemical made in the United States. Ethylene's strong growth rate results from its availability in large quantity and low price and its versatility as a chemical building block. The product's ability to combine with itself and a variety of other chemical reagents has resulted in large-volume commercial production of a wide variety of derivatives. About 60 percent of the ethylene produced in the United States is used to produce plastic products. These include polyethylene, polyvinyl chloride, and various styrene-based materials. Some significant products derived from ethylene include fibers, solvents, coatings, surfactants, and elastomers.

The value of byproducts in ethylene production is significant in determining what should be used as a feedstock, and possibly, whether or not olefins plants as a whole are profitable. If ethane is used as a feedstock, byproducts are only a small percentage of the total production. In a small olefins plant—one that produces 200 million pounds per year or less—byproducts may be valued only as fuel. In a larger plant, such as the size being built today (one billion pounds per year), byproducts are primarily propylene and butadiene. These are generally produced in large enough quantities to be sold advantageously.

When prices go higher for propylene and butadiene there will be a greater probability that either propane or naphtha will be used as feedstock. As with ethane, the importance of the byproducts increases when plant size increases, as more of these byproducts can be valued as products rather than fuel, because larger quantities are produced. Economies of scale result in a lower total ethylene manufacturing cost as plant size increases.

The concept of a West Coast olefins plant had become feasible from the marketing viewpoint within the last five years. One of the major reasons for this change was the recent and rapid growth of the West Coast petrochemical market. Because an olefins plant had to produce about one billion pounds per year to run economically, a market of sufficient scale had to develop before such a plant could be considered. In the early 1970s surveys indicated that the market might support a plant of optimal size. At that time ARCO Chemical

began to evaluate how much of a market there would be for the plants.

One problem that the company faced was the great amount of byproducts produced in addition to ethylene. This meant that the market researchers had to assess the market for each of the many byproducts. Based on these studies ARCO Chemical determined the exact proportion of each product desired in the output of its plant. Such fine tuning of the production process could be done only over a limited range and had to be fixed before the plans for the plant could be drawn.

ARCO Chemical sought customers who would build satellite plants near the site of the olefins plant. This would be the most profitable design for such an operation, as it was much cheaper and simpler to limit the transportation of the raw materials than the finished products.

One resulting problem was the need to have commitments from prospective customers. So market researchers also evaluated how successful they might be in convincing users of petrochemicals in other areas to build new plants near ARCO's proposed West Coast installation. Clients, however, did not want to become obligated before seeing the final plans for financing and construction. ARCO engineers, in turn, had difficulty in developing a final plan until they knew what proportions of each product customers would purchase. Someone had to take an initial step in order to avoid a stalemate.

The Alaskan Pipeline

In addition to more accessible raw materials, a West Coast olefins plant would have other benefits to offer. One would be stability in the supply of raw materials. Part of this stability would be a result of Atlantic Richfield's share in the Alaskan pipeline. The pipeline could guarantee a steady flow of feedstock to the West Coast and therefore assure customers of a dependable flow of petrochemical products to their plants. Without a local source, these customers were at the mercy of the national petrochemical market. In times of shortages supplies to the West Coast were the first cut off. As transportation costs were generally absorbed by the petrochemical producers and not the users, it was less profitable for Gulf Coast producers to ship to the West than to closer markets.

Atlantic Richfield's share in the Alaskan pipeline might also benefit its customers by providing them a more stable price for their raw materials. The Alaskan supply would give Atlantic Richfield complete control over its product from the time it left the ground as crude oil in Alaska to the time it entered its customer's plants. The firm would control the drilling operations, the transportation facilities to the West Coast, the refineries, the olefins plant, and finally the pipelines connecting the olefins plant to its customers. As a result of vertical integration it would be able to control and maintain a more stable price for its products than if it were forced to rely on outside sources. Given price stability, customers would have fewer reservations about contracts for the supply of petrochemicals. As ARCO Chemical's commercial development department found new customers, it worked out the terms of the contracts with the petrochemical marketing and production staffs to be sure they would not be committed to anything the plant could not economically or physically handle.

Although several advantages were offered by the West Coast olefins plant, there were several disadvantages that potential customers would have to consider. If ARCO Chemical's plant were shut down for any reason, this would force the eventual closing of the satellite plants, unless some economical way could be found to import raw materials from other areas, such as the Gulf Coast. For consumers located in the Gulf Coast area, this risk could be hedged by having all satellite plants connected to a main pipeline. From this pipeline they could draw from any of a number of suppliers.

To minimize the risk to its customers, ARCO Chemical had several options. One was to build two smaller plants instead of one large one. This presented a trade-off between the economies of scale of the larger plant and the risks involved. Such a strategy would greatly decrease the threat of a total shutdown due to mechanical problems. An alternative for limiting risk would be to arrange for ARCO Chemical's customers to be able to draw supplies from Dow's proposed plant. This plan would not be foolproof, because Dow might be working at or near full capacity. Another way to reduce customer exposure would be to build huge storage facilities. These would enable customers to continue operating for a reasonable period if their normal supply were temporarily cut off.

Another problem to be considered with a West Coast plant had to be the higher cost of construction for customers' satellite plants, further magnified by inflation. General operating costs would also be a problem because of higher costs for labor, material, and overhead on the West Coast. These would be important for any firm locating in ARCO Chemical's complex. The task of ARCO Chemical's commercial development people was to convince prospective customers that the cost disadvantages would be more than offset by the increased stability and revenue to be gained by increasing market share on the West Coast.

FINANCIAL CONSIDERATIONS

Many financial factors must be analyzed for an investment the size of a petrochemical plant. The responsibility of the Chemical Division was to conceive a project, gather relevant data, and then present their conclusions to Atlantic Richfield's executive committee and board of directors.

In gathering financial data the division looked to various sources and financial theories. Initially an outside consultant might be hired to help explore the feasibility of the proposed venture. For the West Coast olefins project the past trends of the West Coast chemical industry were studied, using regression analysis techniques and projecting data into the future.

An ethylene econometric model was derived with the help of an outside consultant's computer programs. From this data ARCO Chemical could anticipate any major changes in supply and demand for ethylene and related petrochemicals due to any changes in the usage of basic chemicals throughout a broad range of industries.

In addition to forecasting demand conditions for its product, the firm examined potential supply of feedstocks and raw materials. In the past few years there had been a noteworthy decrease in natural gas supplies, a condition certain to continue into the future. This meant ethylene would have to be produced from sources of crude that had been refined and then broken into basic petrochemical compounds. Only the largest plants could be expected to prove profitable, as economies of scale were crucial.

In planning for this project certain aspects of data were relatively easy to collect. One such study was the current West Coast supply and demand statistics for ethylene and its related petrochemical byproducts. ARCO Chemical was supplying such products to the area from its Gulf Coast plants, so an accurate estimate could be made of market factors for the area. This project then led to lining up the additional clients necessary for economies of scale.

In formulating its economic study, ARCO had to predict whether the new West Coast price would be high enough to justify the plant. On the other hand, if prices rose too much, they might depress demand, making it unprofitable to build the plant. To predict the future price and demand schedules accurately, customers had to be solicited and signed up ahead of time. Based on past experience, credibility rating factors were assigned to different responses and a profitability estimate was made.

In addition to the various studies just outlined ARCO followed several basic financial guidelines to determine the value of the investment. One method was the net value of the proposal. The petrochemical industry was dependent on the most modern technology possible. Should technological advances make a plant obsolete, returns from the large investment might be less than anticipated. Because the probability of obsolescence increases with the passage of time, a high discount rate was applied to place less emphasis on future revenues.

Internal rate of return was also used to evaluate investments. ARCO Chemical's standard for acceptable investment proposals was an internal rate of return of 12 to 15 percent after taxes. This was consistent with ARCO's need for immediate earnings.

Should this investment be approved by the senior management of Atlantic Richfield, it might be financed in several different ways. Probably the most logical option would be to finance the project internally with funds provided from Atlantic Richfield equity. Another possibility would be to set up a wholly-owned subsidiary whose only purpose would be to provide leasing for the olefins plant. The method of financing would depend on the cost of each alternative and the potential effect on Atlantic Richfield's bond rating.

For accounting purposes, a plant life of fifteen years was to be planned. In reality, the plant could still be in operation after thirty or forty years. Once a plant is fully depreciated, it runs as long as the technology proves profitable.

The vice president in charge of financial controls at ARCO Chemical believed that the West Coast olefins plant was a relatively low-risk project. The technology to be employed had already proved successful at the Gulf Coast installations. This could be ARCO Chemical's largest undertaking to date.

The latest development in the program had been the proposal of a $500 million West Coast plant. Options with regard to this project were:

1. Build the plant as proposed.
2. Build two smaller plants to lessen the risk of interruption of service to clients.
3. Build one plant slightly smaller than originally planned. This strategy might be implemented if a competitive plant were constructed by a rival company first.

EXHIBIT 1

ATLANTIC RICHFIELD COMPANY
Financial Summary
Figures Based on Gross Revenues
($ billions)

	Investment	Operating Revenues	Contribution to Earnings
Petroleum operations			
U.S.	3.275 (1974)	5.6	.477
	2.784 (1973)	3.7	.361
Foreign	.313 (1974)	2.0	.129
	.327 (1973)	.8	.83
Chemical operations	.361 (1974)	.547	.123
	.242 (1973)	.303	.028
Corporate	.183 (1974)		.013
	.219 (1973)		.015
Inter-group revenue eliminations		− .987 (1974)	
		− .305 (1973)	
Totals	4.131 (1974)	7.2	.743
	3.571 (1973)	4.5	.486
Net income	.475 (1974)	.270 (1973)	

EXHIBIT 2

ATLANTIC RICHFIELD MANAGEMENT

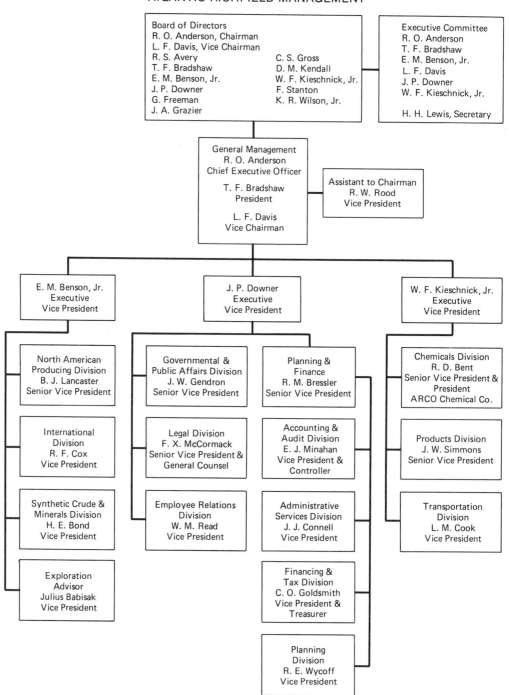

Board of Directors
R. O. Anderson, Chairman
L. F. Davis, Vice Chairman
R. S. Avery
T. F. Bradshaw
E. M. Benson, Jr.
J. P. Downer
G. Freeman
J. A. Grazier
C. S. Gross
D. M. Kendall
W. F. Kieschnick, Jr.
F. Stanton
K. R. Wilson, Jr.

Executive Committee
R. O. Anderson
T. F. Bradshaw
E. M. Benson, Jr.
L. F. Davis
J. P. Downer
W. F. Kieschnick, Jr.

H. H. Lewis, Secretary

General Management
R. O. Anderson
Chief Executive Officer

T. F. Bradshaw
President

L. F. Davis
Vice Chairman

Assistant to Chairman
R. W. Rood
Vice President

E. M. Benson, Jr.
Executive
Vice President

J. P. Downer
Executive
Vice President

W. F. Kieschnick, Jr.
Executive
Vice President

North American
Producing Division
B. J. Lancaster
Senior Vice President

International
Division
R. F. Cox
Vice President

Synthetic Crude &
Minerals Division
H. E. Bond
Vice President

Exploration
Advisor
Julius Babisak
Vice President

Governmental &
Public Affairs Division
J. W. Gendron
Senior Vice President

Legal Division
F. X. McCormack
Senior Vice President &
General Counsel

Employee Relations
Division
W. M. Read
Vice President

Planning &
Finance
R. M. Bressler
Senior Vice President

Accounting &
Audit Division
E. J. Minahan
Vice President &
Controller

Administrative
Services Division
J. J. Connell
Vice President

Financing &
Tax Division
C. O. Goldsmith
Vice President &
Treasurer

Planning
Division
R. E. Wycoff
Vice President

Chemicals Division
R. D. Bent
Senior Vice President &
President
ARCO Chemical Co.

Products Division
J. W. Simmons
Senior Vice President

Transportation
Division
L. M. Cook
Vice President

EXHIBIT 3

ATLANTIC RICHFIELD COMPANY
ARCO/Chemical Company

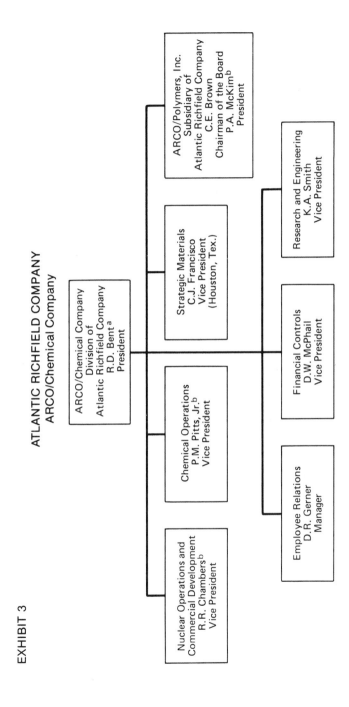

[a] Mr. Bent is also a Senior Vice President of Atlantic Richfield Company.
[b] Drs. Chambers, McKim, and Pitts are also Vice Presidents of Atlantic Richfield Company.

EXHIBIT 4

ARCO/CHEMICAL COMPANY
Division of Atlantic Richfield Company
Nuclear Operations and Commercial Development

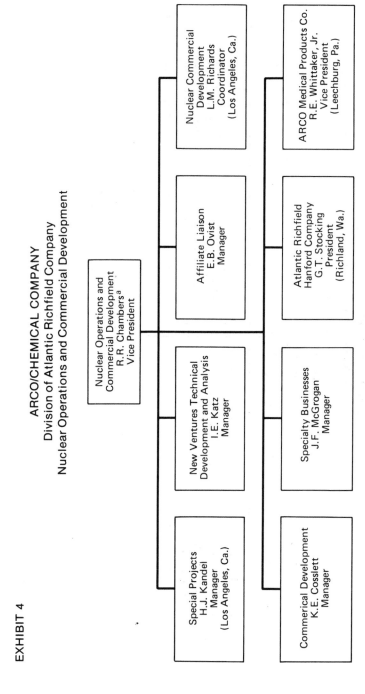

Nuclear Operations and Commercial Development
R.R. Chambers[a]
Vice President

Special Projects
H.J. Kandel
Manager
(Los Angeles, Ca.)

New Ventures Technical Development and Analysis
I.E. Katz
Manager

Affiliate Liaison
E.B. Ovist
Manager

Nuclear Commercial Development
L.M. Richards
Coordinator
(Los Angeles, Ca.)

Commerical Development
K.E. Cosslett
Manager

Specialty Businesses
J.F. McGrogan
Manager

Atlantic Richfield Hanford Company
G.T. Stocking
President
(Richland, Wa.)

ARCO Medical Products Co.
R.E. Whittaker, Jr.
Vice President
(Leechburg, Pa.)

[a]Dr. Chambers is also a Vice President of Atlantic Richfield Company.

213

EXHIBIT 5

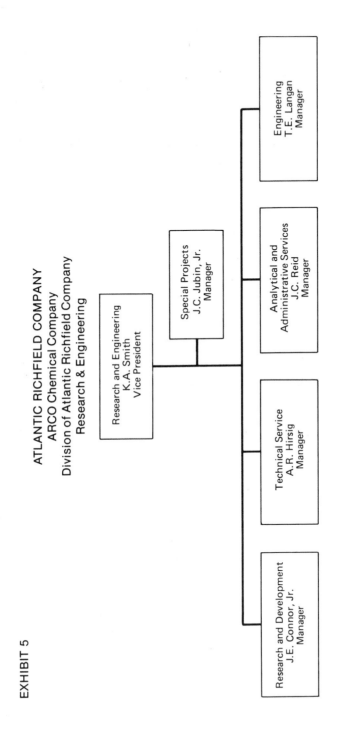

ATLANTIC RICHFIELD COMPANY
ARCO Chemical Company
Division of Atlantic Richfield Company
Research & Engineering

Research and Engineering
K.A. Smith
Vice President

Special Projects
J.C. Jubin, Jr.
Manager

Research and Development
J.E. Connor, Jr.
Manager

Technical Service
A.R. Hirsig
Manager

Analytical and
Administrative Services
J.C. Reid
Manager

Engineering
T.E. Langan
Manager

EXHIBIT 6

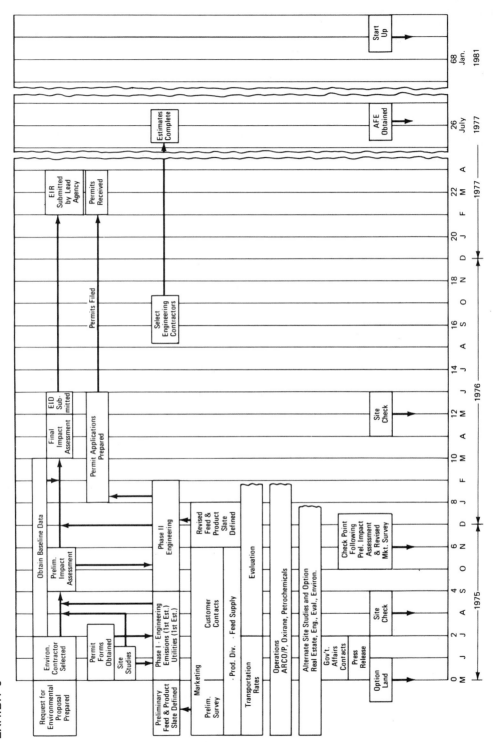

214

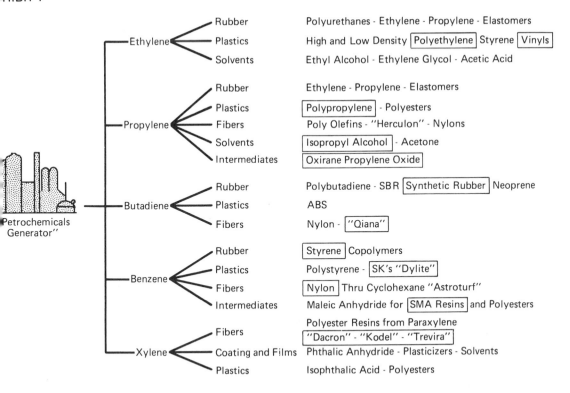

Ethylene
- Rubber — Polyurethanes - Ethylene - Propylene - Elastomers
- Plastics — High and Low Density Polyethylene Styrene Vinyls
- Solvents — Ethyl Alcohol - Ethylene Glycol - Acetic Acid

Propylene
- Rubber — Ethylene - Propylene - Elastomers
- Plastics — Polypropylene - Polyesters
- Fibers — Poly Olefins - "Herculon" - Nylons
- Solvents — Isopropyl Alcohol - Acetone
- Intermediates — Oxirane Propylene Oxide

Butadiene
- Rubber — Polybutadiene - SBR Synthetic Rubber Neoprene
- Plastics — ABS
- Fibers — Nylon - "Qiana"

Benzene
- Rubber — Styrene Copolymers
- Plastics — Polystyrene - SK's "Dylite"
- Fibers — Nylon Thru Cyclohexane "Astroturf"
- Intermediates — Maleic Anhydride for SMA Resins and Polyesters

Xylene
- Fibers — Polyester Resins from Paraxylene "Dacron" - "Kodel" - "Trevira"
- Coating and Films — Phthalic Anhydride - Plasticizers - Solvents
- Plastics — Isophthalic Acid - Polyesters

"Petrochemicals Generator"

EXHIBIT 8
GROWTH IN DEMAND CURVES
FOR U.S. ETHYLENE AND BENZENE,
EFFECT OF RECENT DEVELOPMENTS

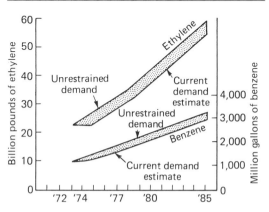

Source: ARCO Chemical Company, Division of Atlantic
Richfield Company. Presentation to Financial Analysts,
New York, N.Y., October 16, 1974, p. 11.

LAVENTHOL, KREKSTEIN, HORWATH & HORWATH*

In the spring of 1972 George L. Bernstein was named national managing partner of Laventhol, Krekstein, Horwath & Horwath's management advisory services. In this position Mr. Bernstein's responsibilities were, in the most general terms, to direct the development of LKH&H's management consulting practices. LKH&H had grown during the previous fifteen years, from a regional CPA firm, headquartered in Philadelphia, to international stature. This growth had been accomplished through a series of mergers, the largest of which occurred in 1967 combining Laventhol, Krekstein and Griffith with Horwath & Horwath. By 1972, LKH&H was among the ten largest CPA firms. Mr. Bernstein viewed his primary task as the development of a national consulting practice, tying the consulting activities of LKH&H's thirty-four domestic offices into a coherent whole.

THE ACCOUNTING PROFESSION

In the period since World War II, the public accounting profession had undergone profound changes in both structure and activities. Accounting firms ranged in size from the sole practitioner, servicing small businesses, to international firms with thousands of staff members and several hundred partners. In

*In the time since the situation described in this case occurred, the firm's name has been changed to Laventhol & Horwath.

This case was prepared by Randall Abrams, Barbara Emmett, Andrew Langdon, and Daniel Levy under the supervision of Professor Jules J. Schwartz as the basis for class discussion rather than to illustrate either effective or ineffective handling of an administrative action.

1972 well over 75 percent of the corporations listed on the New York Stock Exchange were serviced by the eight largest CPA firms. The need for credibility and the large staffs necessary to audit a major corporation have been the primary factors in the development of a high degree of concentration in the profession.

The primary functions of the CPA had been to attest to the fairness of financial statements and to ensure compliance with generally accepted accounting principles. This had been done through the annual audit, in which financial transactions were tested and accounts verified to determine the fairness of presentation of financial statements. The need for an independent auditor was clear in the cases of publicly-held corporations. Many privately-held and nonprofit organizations also engaged CPAs to attest to their statements, usually because they were seeking outside financing or ensuring control by their boards of directors.

Since 1950 CPA firms had begun to offer a broader range of services to their clients. The major growth of the national CPA firms had principally been in tax and management advisory services. Tax services offered included: planning and counseling on tax problems, obtaining rulings from the Internal Revenue Service, representing clients in tax examinations, and preparing and reviewing tax returns. National CPA firms offered management consulting services with broad ranges of expertise, but concentrated heavily in financial control systems and data processing and information systems. A few national CPA firms limited their consulting activities to these two areas, while others accepted consulting engagements ranging from public policy studies for the federal government to executive compensation and recruiting. In addition to functional specialization in consulting services, CPA firms had also developed distinct industry specializations.

One of the major questions posed by the growth of consulting and tax services has been that of independence. A primary attribute necessary for the performance of the attest function is that the auditor be independent of the client. In providing tax and management services a CPA firm acts as client advocate or client advisor. This raises questions as to whether a CPA firm can remain independent while playing one of these roles. However, the growth of tax and consulting services has occurred primarily because a CPA firm is in a unique position to provide these services to an audit client. The familiarity with client personnel and operations that is developed through a continuing audit relationship enables a CPA firm to recognize and develop consulting opportunities that may not be available to a specialized management consulting firm.

COMPANY HISTORY

LKH&H acquired its national character through a series of mergers during the 1960s. Early in that decade Laventhol, Krekstein & Griffith was a northeastern regional firm with five offices. Its practice was concentrated in Philadelphia, it's home office. Early growth strategy concentrated on the development of a mid-Atlantic practice and associations with firms in the mid- and far-west. By 1967 the firm had offices throughout the mid-Atlantic region and in southern California. In that year the largest of the mergers, with Horwath & Horwath, about doubled the size of the firm and clearly marked the transition from regional to national status.

Horwath & Horwath's attractiveness was based on its outstanding client base in the hotel and restaurant industries (leisure time industries) and its experience with health care organizations. This specialization, combined with Laventhol, Krekstein & Griffith's broader base of industrial and financial clients provided both the breadth of functional expertise and the industry specializations necessary for a national CPA firm.

Because of the differing client bases the management advisory services offered by the two firms were organized along different lines. LK&G had fewer, although larger, offices and its staff members tended to have functional strengths, such as electronic data processing. Horwath & Horwath had a larger number of small offices, staffed by individuals who were oriented toward its industry specialties.

During the five years following the merger with Horwath & Horwath, the question of management advisory services practice and policies was somewhat overshadowed by the more critical problem of integrating the audit services. This included the implementation of uniform audit standards and procedures, reassignment and, in some cases, termination of personnel, and development of a regional organization. Because of the attention given to integrating the audit staffs, local consulting practices enjoyed a high degree of autonomy, and each practice office pursued consulting opportunities as it saw fit. There was a substantial degree of local specialization. Many offices had only a few or even a single consultant, and hired temporary consulting staff to perform work related to their specific client needs. Problems became apparent in quality and consistency of service and in career opportunities for the consulting staff.

The economic downturn of 1970 to 1971 brought the problems in the consulting practice to the surface and accelerated the need to deal with them. Because approximately 60 percent of consulting activities were oriented toward the leisure time industries, which were particularly sensitive to the economic climate, the impact of the recession was severe. Substantial staff reductions were made in some offices. Although the pruning was necessary and in some cases beneficial, morale on the management advisory services staff suffered.

By 1972 the need to tie consulting into a national organization was recognized. The economic events only hastened, but did not in themselves create, the need for a national approach to management services. The major areas in which problems were recognized were:

1. *Quality control.* The lack of a national organization in consulting made it difficult to marshall all the firm's resources to deal with a client's problem. There was insufficient exchange of specialists among offices, and the smaller offices simply lacked sufficient depth for adequate review and control.
2. *Stability and growth of practice.* Although the leisure time industries practice represented the major portion of consulting work and promised high growth, it depended upon a highly cyclical industry. Diversification was necessary in order to provide a more stable practice. However, more than stability was necessary; LKH&H needed growth in order to attract and retain high caliber staff.
3. *Personnel development.* Although the turnover in the consulting profession was relatively high, LKH&H had particular problems because of the lack of advancement opportunities available in the smaller offices.
4. *Staffing.* There was a need for consultants with broad business and educational backgrounds. Too many members of the consulting staff were relatively narrow specialists and had difficulty working on engagements outside of their specialties. Conspicuously lacking in many management advisory service (MAS) offices were consultants capable of dealing with and winning the trust of client top management.

These questions were closely interrelated. The central issues were the organization and scope of the management consulting practice: What services should LKH&H develop the ability to or continue to provide? How should the consulting staff be organized to best offer these services? These issues had not been addressed at a national level; consequently, the consulting practice just ran itself.

ORGANIZATION

Laventhol, Krekstein, Horwath & Horwath was organized as a partnership, as were all national CPA firms. The partnership form, along with the relatively flat nature of a professional organization, combined to create an organizational structure that could not accurately be depicted with a typical organization chart. In the most general terms the partnership could have been described as a three dimensional matrix where the dimensions were functional specialization (for example, audit, tax, management services), industry specialization (for example, health care, leisure time industries), and geographic location (by geographic region and office within the region).

Clearly a partnership with over 275 partners could not be managed on an entirely decentralized basis. The partnership elected a national council, which in turn selected an executive partner. The national council and executive partner were analogous to the board of directors and chief executive officer in a corporate form of organization. Reporting directly to the executive partner were the six regional managing partners (who were line executives), two independent offices not associated with a region, and seven national partners with firmwide resonsibilities for management advisory services, personnel, accounting and auditing standards, administration, health care, tax services, and practice development. The national and regional organization is depicted in Exhibit 1.

Each practice office was directed by the local partner-in-charge (PIC) who had profit and loss responsibility for that office. Reporting to the PIC were the partners or managers in charge of the three functional areas (audit, tax, and management services). In the smaller offices, the PIC also functioned as the direct supervisor to the audit staff. Depending on the size of the tax or management service practices in a given office, these functional areas were headed up by a partner or by a manager. The reporting relationships in a larger office are illustrated in Exhibit 2. Though the PIC had direct line authority over the partners managing each functional area, there was also a "dotted line" reporting relationship to the national partner of the functional area.

At the time of the merger with Horwath & Horwath there were only eight offices offering consulting services. By early 1972 this number had increased to fifteen. The MAS staff in many offices consisted of only a single consultant, primarily with leisure-time industry expertise. The national partner, while without direct line authority, functioned primarily as a coordinator of MAS activities in different offices. In the areas of personnel utilization among offices or review of MAS work for technical adequacy, the national partner's responsibilities were clear. However, a natural tension had developed between the national partner and the PIC of the local office who, with ultimate profit and loss responsibility for his office, had been reluctant to allow the national office much control over his practice.

In 1971 management advisory services accounted for approximately 6 percent of the total revenue of the firm. In individual offices this percentage varied from 0 to 20 percent, with the larger offices of the firm generally having higher shares of revenue generated by MAS than the smaller ones. In those offices where MAS revenue had been a relatively small portion of the total, there was a natural tendency for the PIC to pay little attention to the profitability of the MAS practice so long as direct costs were covered. At times this had been necessary to develop a consulting practice in a particular geographic area, but mere coverage of direct costs did little to improve MAS contributions to overall firm profitability.

One of the major determinants of profitability had been the maintenance of a high degree of staff utilization, which was dependent upon the appropriate balancing of personnel from office to office. A temporarily overworked office could receive help from one that had a degree of slack in its work load.

Balancing of personnel was a more significant problem in MAS, where assignments were of generally short (two to eight weeks) duration and could not be predicted well in advance, than it was in the audit or tax practices where manpower requirements were more predictable. The local office PICs viewed a backlog of work as a guarantee of high utilization in the coming months and were somewhat reluctant to request help from other offices. The allocation of revenues among offices when personnel were shared did little to encourage a PIC to use personnel from other offices to reduce an excessive backlog. The regional managing partners, who had profit and loss responsibility for the several offices within their region, were more receptive to balancing personnel within their regions and often coordinated temporary reassignments of consulting staff.

Ultimately the PIC of an office was responsible for all the activities of his office, including profitability, review, quality control, and staffing. As LKH&H was a professional organization, relationships among partners were generally conducted on a collegial basis rather than through the exercise of authority. This often resulted in a bargaining situation; a PIC with higher than average profitability was usually in a better position to retain his office's autonomy.

STAFFING

The staffing policies pursued by a consulting organization are among the most crucial decisions it can make. Because the revenue of the firm is directly related to billable staff time, the staff's ability to execute engagements within the predicted budget and at the firm's standards of quality is one of the major factors affecting the profitability of the practice. There were four staff grades within LKH&H's management advisory services:

1. *Consultant.* Normally an entry level position for staff members with only a few years of work experience or for transfers from the audit staff.
2. *Senior Consultant.* An entry level position for

more experienced personnel. A senior consultant was expected to work independently, to supervise the work of consultants, and to deal directly on a one-on-one basis with client personnel.

3. *Supervisor.* A nonentry level position. Supervisory responsibilities included the budgeting and management of an entire engagement and often included client billing. Supervisors were expected to be able to work effectively with top client management and to develop and sell consulting engagements.

4. *Manager.* A manager was conceived of as a partner-in-training. In addition to being able to plan and manage several engagements simultaneously, a manager was expected to generate sufficient consulting revenue to support several less senior staff members.

Staffing policy was dictated by an "up or out" philosophy, with promotions based on a demonstrated ability to perform the functions of the next higher staff grade. Early in a staff member's career the primary criterion for evaluation was technical execution of engagements. At senior and supervisory levels management of one's own and of others' time was a required skill. A manager was required to demonstrate the ability to develop consulting engagements in order to be considered for a partnership. Thus a partner was expected to possess the full complement of skills necessary for the management of a consulting practice: technical competence, managerial skills, and the ability to develop the practice. Promotions up to the grade of supervisor were made by the PIC of the office. Promotions of supervisors to managers, while nominally a national office function, were almost always decided by the regional managing partner; admission to the partnership required approval of the national council. Managers not possessing the CPA certificate could be given partner status by being designated a principal.

In a large office the appropriate mix of staff was approximately 30 percent managerial (partners and/or managers), 40 percent senior (supervisors or senior consultants), and 30 percent junior (consultants). Although this was a target staff mix, the smaller offices usually had a higher percentage of managerial and senior personnel. Even in large offices significant departures from the target existed. When there was a need for detail work that could not be economically performed by a manager or partner because of their high billing rate, and junior level consultants were unavailable, personnel were borrowed from the audit staff on a temporary basis.

Salary ranges in each staff grade were quite broad and often overlapped substantially. Entry level consultants were paid approximately $12,000 per year; managers could earn as much as three times that amount. Partners' compensation consisted of a salary, known as a draw, and a share of the firm's profits. The degree to which a partner was allocated a share of profits was determined largely by the profitability of the segment of the practice for which he was responsible.

RECRUITING

LKH&H recruited staff members from two areas: experienced managers from industry and transfers from the audit staff. The leisure time industries practice was primarily staffed with experienced managers from the hospitality industries. Generally these recruits brought with them five to ten years experience in managing hotels, restaurants, or resorts, but did not necessarily have a business education. The systems consulting group hired approximately equal numbers of experienced managers, usually with data processing expertise, and intermediate-level audit staff members who had specialties in financial systems and accounting.

Some questions had been raised about the value of these recruiting practices. The transfers from the audit staff, while technically proficient in their specialties, often lacked the broad outlook required of a consultant. In addition, audit work gave a staff member little exposure, at least in the early years, to business development, a function that is far more important in the consulting practice. Hiring more experienced staff clearly brought valuable expertise to the firm; however, it had drawbacks in that promotion opportunities were often blocked and the career path for an older hire did not necessarily lead to the partnership.

An alternative recruiting policy would focus on hiring younger members directly from MBA programs or from the nation's leading hotel management schools. This approach would require substantially more staff training, and inexperienced staff might not be profitably utilized for several months.

As in most other matters staffing decisions were made at the local office, and the PIC was often reluctant to make the investment in developing a good consultant from a recent graduate. A PIC was usually more willing to hire an experienced staff member from industry because this approach yielded a more immediate improvement in his profitability. If the firm's recruiting approach was to be changed, a change in recruiting responsibilities would be necessary.

ECONOMICS OF CONSULTING

The central factor determining the profitability of a professional service practice was the achievement of a high level of staff utilization that was fully chargeable to a client. This implied both generation of sufficient consulting engagements to allow full utilization and budgetary control over the execution of these engagements. LKH&H used two forms of reporting to measure these factors: staff member and department utilization indices and a standard cost and variance reporting system at the project level.

The hourly rate at which a consultant was billed to clients was determined by multiplying his annual salary by three and dividing the total by the number of hours he was expected to bill to clients during the year.

$$\text{Hourly billing rate} = \frac{\text{Annual salary} \times 3}{\text{Expected number of chargeable hours}}$$

On a biweekly basis a utilization index was computed for each staff member and department as follows:

$$\text{Utilization index} = \frac{\text{Actual chargeable hours} \times \text{Billing rate}}{\text{Salary}}$$

As a general rule of thumb a utilization index of between 2.5 and 3.0 was required to maintain a profitable practice. The direct (salary) cost of a professional was one-third of the billing rate. Indirect costs (employee benefits, office space, administrative, and clerical support) were approximately equal to the direct costs. Thus a utilization index of greater than 1.0 indicated that direct cost recovery was achieved; 2.0 represented the breakeven point for all cost recovery.

The profit margin on consulting services was measured by the billable staff utilization in excess of 2.0. As the full utilization goal was reflected in an index of 3.0, profit, overhead, and direct costs each represented one-third of a staff member's billing rate. Billing rates for consulting staff varied from $25/hour for entry level consultants to almost $100/hour for the most senior partners and principals. Because a partner or principal had significant practice development responsibilities, their expected chargeable hours were lower than those for junior staff members. In general, as a consultant's career progressed, he was expected to spend a greater proportion of his time on engagement development, proposal writing, and other nonbillable, business generating activities.

The full utilization of professional resources also depended on the ability to estimate accurately the number of yearly chargeable hours per staff member and to generate sufficient engagements to occupy the projected chargeable hours. Chargeable hours were less predictable in MAS than in audit, where regular audit cycles permitted the January scheduling of 85 percent of the yearly workload. Flexibility in redirecting resources was a key factor enabling MAS to approach full personnel utilization, as accurate workload forecasting was not possible. Although utilization was one factor considered in staff evaluations, it was recognized that a more junior staff member did not have full control over his own utilization. However, persistently low utilization indices raised questions about an individual's value to the firm.

Consulting services were generally priced on a direct-time basis. An integral part of the fee estimation was the development of a work plan including estimated times and staff levels required. Engagements were then priced by multiplying the hourly billing rates by the estimated hours required for execution. Bids on government engagements were usually fixed fee, while on most other engagements the fee was dependent upon the number of hours actually worked. Fee estimates were submitted to the client in an engagement letter that specified exactly what service LKH&H would perform and clearly delineated the responsibilities of the firm and of the client. When an approved copy of the engagement letter was returned by the client, work could begin. The fee quoted in the engagement letter was an estimate of the maximum cost of the work; if an engagement took less time to complete than originally estimated, the saving was usually passed back to the client.

Some fee negotiation occurred in public sector engagements, but in general LKH&H believed that a willingness to negotiate indicated that the firm did not plan to render a quality service. Engagements that offered high visibility or were likely to generate additional business were often priced at less than full rate. Similarly premiums were charged for engagements with short lead times or other special client requirements.

Once an engagement was underway, cost control was maintained through the use of a standard cost reporting system. Biweekly reports, showing actual versus budgeted engagement costs enabled the partner in charge of an engagement to review its progress. At completion of the project a variance from budgeted costs was computed and attributed to the part-

ner managing the engagement. A partner's profitability and compensation were directly affected by his ability to bring projects to completion without negative variances.

Occasionally, planned variances occurred. If an engagement was undertaken at less than the standard billing rate or if managerial personnel had to be used to perform work that should have been done by junior staff members, the variance was reported but did not necessarily reflect unfavorably on the engagement manager.

One of the central responsibilities of a partner was to balance the need for high personnel utilization against the need to control variances. Clearly, high utilization could be achieved by allowing staff members to spend excessive time on engagements; however, if this occurred, negative variances would result. Similarly, negative variances could be avoided entirely by overpricing engagements, but then fewer would be accepted by clients, and staff utilization would suffer. As a partner's share of the firm's profits was dependent on his contribution to those profits, a partner was allowed substantial autonomy in pricing and controlling engagements and was fully responsible for balancing the utilization of his staff against variances on his engagements.

PRACTICE DEVELOPMENT—PRIVATE SECTOR

A CPA firm was in a somewhat different position to provide consulting services to clients than was a management consulting firm. There was a built-in client base consisting of those clients with which the firm had a continuing audit relationship. Audit partners were generally quite familiar with client operations and developed good personal rapport with client executives. The audit staff was therefore an ideal conduit to provide consulting leads and to make engagement recommendations to executives in the client organization.

However, because of the continuing nature of the audit service, as compared to the intermittent consulting services provided to a given client, audit partners had been reluctant to introduce MAS staff to a client unless they were convinced that the consultants would be effective. Thus, in selling their services, the MAS staff had had to sell themselves to both the client executive and to the audit partner with responsibility for that client. Because audits were conducted on a yearly basis, potential losses from a poorly executed consulting engagement were far greater than those faced by a management consulting firm.

The two major areas of consulting, systems and leisure-time industries, approached practice development somewhat differently. The systems practice provided expertise in data processing, cost accounting, and financial systems, and in these areas the audit staff was in a unique position to provide consulting references to the systems practice. The LTI practice performed substantially more work for nonaudit clients than did the systems practice. The Horwath & Horwath reputation was unsurpassed in LTI consulting and was invaluable in developing engagements. This reputation was primarily in the areas of hotel accounting systems, financial feasibility studies and operational studies. If the practice were to move into other closely related areas, such as real estate financial studies, a broadening of the reputation would be necessary.

Financial difficulties in hospitality industries due to the effects of the 1970 to 1971 recession had caused a drop off in LTI consulting. Several major hotel chains had recently been acquired by larger companies, particularly by airlines. When such a merger occurred, the audit of the consolidated company was generally performed by the auditors of the parent. These acquisitions meant the loss of several major LTI clients, and thus hampered the practice development effort.

Because LKH&H was prohibited by the ethics of the accounting profession from advertising or soliciting clients, an important part of developing a consulting practice was the achievement of a high degree of public awareness of its skills. Efforts to promote the firm's visibility were a substantial part of the responsibilities of partners and managers, and were accomplished through diverse activities, such as speaking at industry conferences, publishing articles in trade journals, becoming active in professional associations and working for local charities or civic organizations.

QUALITY CONTROL

Because a significant number of consulting engagements were developed as a result of referrals, the execution of quality work was crucial to the development of the consulting practice. A single poorly executed consulting engagement could destroy the firm's credibility.

One of Bernstein's concerns was simply the consistency of format of MAS work; financial feasibility studies performed by different offices bore little resemblance to each other. Of greater concern was the procedure for review of work content. Although the national MAS partner officially had authority for technical review of all MAS engagements, in practice, review was concentrated at the office level. Thus an MAS partner was essentially responsible for reviewing his own engagements. The office PIC whose training was on the audit staff often did not have sufficient technical competence in the consulting disciplines to effectively review and control MAS work quality.

PRACTICE DEVELOPMENT—PUBLIC SECTOR

Public sector consulting was an area of great potential growth. CPA professional ethics posed less of a constraint in developing public than private sector work. For example, the firm could develop a proposal for a public sector consulting engagement simply by responding to a request for proposal (RFP) issued by a government agency. However, LKH&H had not been particularly successful in pursuing public sector consulting. Much time was spent on the preparation of proposals for which the acceptance rate was poor.

Public sector work was composed of three significantly different markets. Federal government contracts, generally policy or organizational studies for a federal agency, attracted fierce competition from the largest consulting and CPA firms. These studies demanded large staffs and significant expertise in the subject area. Further, federal government work was not particularly profitable; a proposal bid at more than 75 percent of the standard billing rate stood almost no chance of acceptance. State government RFP's tended to attract fewer bids and were generally smaller than federal government jobs. Though ability and reputation were important factors in successfully bidding on state jobs, political factors often influenced the selection process. Local government assignments were usually smaller than state contracts; they required less specific expertise and even better political contacts. State and local work were more profitable then federal contracts, but it was still unusual to win such bids at the standard billing rate.

A manager in the Philadelphia office believed that government work was a natural complement to other areas of the practice, despite its low profitability. It provided substantial public exposure, particularly at state and national levels. A large government contract could provide a guaranteed backlog of work against which new consultants could be hired and on which they could be trained. He did not feel that LKH&H could be competitive at other than the local level without a significant front-end investment in staff who had the ability, experience, and contacts to develop a public-sector practice.

SCOPE OF PRACTICE

A sound definition of the scope of a consulting practice was of considerable importance to a practice development effort. In defining a national consulting strategy Bernstein believed that it was crucial to identify what services LKH&H should offer to its clients. The two basic options facing the firm were to intensify consulting activities in areas where LKH&H had experience or to broaden the range of services offered. If the latter course

were chosen, a decision would have to be made as to what services the firm should offer.

The consulting practice varied from office to office, depending on the local client base. Bernstein felt that a greater effort should be made to develop and offer a full range of consulting services to clients in all geographic regions. Though this did not require every office to have a complete range of consulting expertise on its staff, this spectrum of skills had to be available on a regional basis. In 1972 LKH&H offered consulting services in the following areas:

1. Management information and cost accounting systems;
2. Cost control and profit improvement;
3. Financial feasibility studies for hotel construction;
4. Electronic data processing equipment and software selection; and
5. Organizational studies.

Possible areas for expansion of the operation included:

1. Real estate planning and financial feasibility studies;
2. Health care financial feasibility studies;
3. Health care operations and financial control;
4. Marketing studies;
5. Federal government policy evaluations (e.g., of housing or criminal justice policies);
6. State and local government services;
7. Facilities layout for lodging and hospitality industries;
8. Detailed software systems design; and
9. Executive search.

Most of these practice areas under consideration required either adding to or broadening the skills available in LKH&H's consulting staff. A partner in the Philadelphia LTI practice did not believe that this extension would pose a serious problem. He felt that the key ingredient in a successful engagement was the utilization of bright, broad-gauge consultants. As long as the engagement was not too far afield from the staff members' competence, the learning and broadening of skills resulting from such an engagement was of great value to the firm. For example, there seemed to be a natural extension of financial feasibility work in the LTI practice into real estate and health care.

SUMMARY

As national partner Bernstein faced the task of defining a strategy for MAS practice growth and coordination. Among the questions he considered were:

1. In what areas should LKH&H develop its practice and how should this practice be developed?
2. What quality control standards had to be developed and how should they be enforced?
3. How should the MAS practice be organized and what should be the relationship between audit and tax practices?
4. How could the desired strategy be implemented?

EXHIBIT 1

LAVENTHOL, KREKSTEIN, HORWATH & HORWATH
National Organization

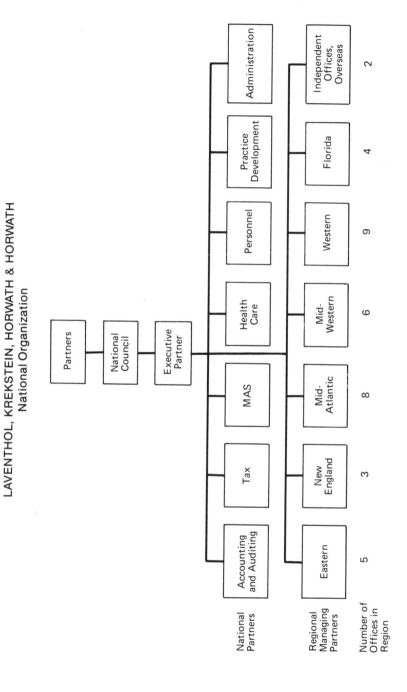

EXHIBIT 2
LAVENTHOL, KREKSTEIN, HORWATH & HORWATH
Local Office Reporting Responsibilities

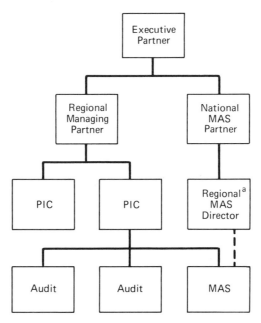

[a]The Regional MAS Director usually had practice responsibility for one of the larger offices in the region.

CHAPTER 4

Implementing Decisions

The mistake too many planners make is to plan what *ought* to be done, but not how to do it. This chapter will deal with the third task we've assigned to the general manager, implementing policy decisions. What follows is an examination of some of the tools that the executive has available to cause his organization to move on the course he has set for it and some hypotheses regarding the best way to get this job done.

DIRECT MANAGEMENT

Your earlier courses should have given you some of the current thinking on organizational behavior and the direct management of people. Whether you're a *Theory X* or *Theory Y* manager must depend on your own style and the specific environment in which you find yourself. In any event it is clear that a manager can give instructions to (or negotiate with) and then follow up on the activities of only a limited number of subordinates. This interchange deals with what, when, by whom, and, perhaps, how things are to be done. Such an assignment of responsibility usually leads to the question of whether there is commensurate authority. By now you should be convinced

that no mortal has sufficient authority to absolutely guarantee fulfillment of his responsibilities. This being the situation, in the cases that follow we shall only concern ourselves that an appropriate amount of authority has been delegated. A useful question to ask, before we grow too sympathetic regarding the dilemma any middle manager finds himself in, is: Has he exhausted all the logical means available to him to solve his problem? As a general manager he has profit responsibility, so the simple profit formula may serve as a checklist and a reminder of some of the factors he can influence to accomplish his job.

$$\text{Pre-tax profit} = \text{Volume} \times \\ (\text{Unit price} - \text{Unit variable cost}) - \\ \text{Fixed cost}$$

Has he considered all the tradeoffs available between the variables in the formula? The one most normally missed is a test of price elasticity. For example, will an increase in unit price result in a more or less than proportionate decrease in volume?

The other problem that usually arises in delegation is that of resolving conflicts between multiple goals, such as long- and short-run profit results. These will be discussed later.

SETTING CORPORATE CONTEXT

Beyond dealing with a limited group of subordinates, the general manager must seek to establish a context within his organization that will encourage things to happen the way he wants them to.

Foremost in his arsenal is the power to articulate strategy to his organization. Unless and until people in the firm understand what it is the company is trying to accomplish, it is unlikely they can make a direct contribution of effort or ideas.

Personal style is the next component of context. A willingness on the part of a general manager to participate in the firm's activities and to share ideas and risks greatly influences the working environment. As we concluded earlier when we looked at the decision process, competent translation and effective advocacy speed up essential decisions.

A general manager usually has the authority to organize his people so that they have specific, and sometimes, routine responsibility to do certain things. The dangers of too rigid a structure are obvious, particularly if new circumstances must be accommodated. Cannon[1] summarized the aims of organization:

1. To provide control over specialization;
2. To facilitate communication and authority flows;
3. To accelerate the development of personnel;
4. To facilitate making the key tradeoff decisions of business; and
5. To provide an environment and structure for dealing with uncertainty.

We saw earlier that specific proposals tend to arise among groups charged with accomplishing particular functions; that is, structure influences the development of strategic options. We see now that strategy also influences structure. A decision, for example, to diversify geographically into the Southwest might lead to the formation of a management team to supervise the effort in that area. But then,

[1] Cannon, J. T., *Business Strategy and Policy,* Harcourt Brace Jovanovich, 1968.

what kind of future proposals that might influence strategy would you expect from that team? Theoreticians are fond of discussing the issue of whether strategy follows structure or structure strategy. As practitioners you should be content to recognize their systematic relationship and know they affect each other.

In studies of Fortune 500 firms conducted at the Harvard Business School it was found that large companies were more likely to elect divisional than functional organizations. This is summarized in Table 4-1. Note the great increase in profit-center organizations between 1950 and 1969. This trend has been reversed somewhat in recent years. Several major integrated oil companies have decided to revert to functional forms, concluding that the proliferation of staffs at several levels increased overhead excessively.

TABLE 4-1
Proportion of Large Firms Electing Specific Organizational Forms

Organizational Form	1950	1969
Functional	75%	17%
Divisional	15%	80%
Holding company	10%	3%

The general manager also controls a number of organizational systems that can influence performance. These include the information, control, incentive, and resource allocation systems.

The formal information system can determine which people or groups in the organization get to know which things. The informal system also at work in all firms may actually be faster but it is seldom as authoritative or complete. Importantly, supplying information through a formal system enables management to exact accountability.

The control system establishes the set of performance criteria to be measured. What is measured is a signal to an employee of what his superiors regard as important. As most firms choose to measure many things, the subordinate must inevitably be faced with a tradeoff problem. For example, suppose we tell a plant manager he will be measured on (and rewarded for) his return on assets, but that we also expect a substantial reduction in lost-time accidents. There is probably some level of added investment in safety that will actually improve ROA, but beyond this point further expenditures will only improve the safety record at a cost to investment return. What is the appropriate safety effort to be? Almost every set of control criteria force such trades. The long- and short-run profit goal is the common example. Although business schools tend to emphasize long-term planning, don't forget to question whether the luxury of a long-run solution will be available to the manager who neglects the short run. The general manager must understand the implications of the control system and decide if he wishes the tradeoffs to occur at lower levels in his organization or if he wants to reserve them to himself. If he does, he may set more specific goals or put limits on the range any decision can take without consultation or approval.

Incentive systems try to systematize the rewards and punishments to be meted out to subordinates. Despite the best of intentions, they are rarely consistent with the control system. That is, people are not rewarded for doing what they are told will be measured. Beyond the evident problems involved in making measures of subjective contributions such as good ideas, there exist other questions about the form and timing of rewards. Different people value similar rewards differently. A salesman may opt for a cash bonus, but a scientist might prefer greater autonomy in his research efforts or a production supervisor might prefer a promotion to still greater responsibility. Rewards are signals that will be read differently within the organization.

Timing rewards is a problem because all efforts are not scheduled in the organization in the same time frame. Rewarding a 20 percent improvement in product rejects in the last fiscal quarter is fairly simple, but how do we encourage a pharmaceutical chemist who is half way, or so it seems, to a cancer cure?

Resource allocation is the final item of context we will deal with. The commitment of limited resources of money and personnel is a device management has for setting strategic priorities. The firm may try to systematize investment decisions by applying formulas like discounted cash flow or internal rate of return, but all these techniques can do is to compare relatively similar proposals. Where risks are different, it may still be possible to assign prior probabilities to various outcomes and go forward with the analysis. But finally, the quality of the input data must be assessed. Here the track records of the contributors are critical and the decision becomes "politicized."

MANAGEMENT RESERVE

It is a tested concept among military officers that a reserve is a leader's principal means for influencing the course of a battle. When he commits his reserve to exploit an opportunity or limit a threat, the leader's next concern is to set up a new reserve, using cooks and mechanics, if necessary.

There seems to be a similar argument for maintaining a reserve in business; that is, for not committing all available resources, scarce though they may be. By retaining some existing funds, or funds to be realized during the budget period, the general manager:

1. Retains his ability to influence projects;
2. Is able to reinforce good decisions;
3. Has flexibility to respond to unexpected opportunities or threats; and
4. Can react to the serial development of information on competitive response, research results, and other new developments.

As always, there is a tradeoff. Retaining funds in a reserve increases uncertainty for junior managers. If their work has been less than fully funded, can they count on getting necessary resources to complete the job?

You will discover that many of the risks faced by managers in the cases on implementation can be dimensioned in terms of time. For example, engineers will often bargain to deliver a given level of performance for a fixed budget. What is difficult to tie down is *when;* fixing the date for accomplishing a task makes the worker accountable. A reserve gives a manager a way to support work that is on-schedule and on-budget and to renegotiate projects that are not.

TESTS OF CONSISTENCY

Although every strategic decision requires a specific implementation plan, there are a few questions that you can ask to determine whether the plan is consistent with previous experience. These have to do with scheduling and budgeting and with what we have called context, as applied to both a specific product line and to the overall activity of the firm.

The operational question on schedules and budgets is whether they are feasible, given the tasks to be accomplished, whether the resources can be marshalled as needed and whether the result, if achieved, will be timely. One example is an addition to production capacity. Capacity additions often make the most sense if they're made before they're required. Given the time to plan, build, and make a new plant operational, a decision must be made long before the capacity is to come on stream. If the firm permits its capacity to become inadequate, it risks loss of market share. This may mean permanent loss of customers and certainly means that competitors can gain more production experience and bring their costs down. An essential test in such a case is whether a strategy that calls for maintaining or improving market share provides for timely opening of manufacturing lines.

R.V.L. Wright,[2] of Arthur D. Little, Inc., has suggested that management style, planning time frame, and financing, among others, should be tied to the life cycle of the product. These ideas on context for a particular product are summarized in Figure 4–1.

B.R. Scott and others have studied what they have termed "stages of corporate development." Scott concluded that, when companies grow from small, single-product businesses, into larger, more fully integrated activities, and perhaps later into diversified operations, they face a different set of strategic choices. The corporate context they choose to implement their new strategies changes rather predictably. These conclusions are summed up in Figure 4–2.

Your task, then, is to decide if the way a strategy is to be implemented makes sense, if the context is internally consistent and if it relates appropriately to the strategy, product life cycle, and stage of development of the firm.

CONCLUSION

Again, there are no simple prescriptions. But, by now you should be convinced that, while science has many rules, a general manager practices an art that has few. The best he can do is to narrow down his options by using his *science* to eliminate the obviously bad and patently illegal proposals. Beyond this he must apply his art to understanding the uncertainties that remain and the positions of the interested constituencies and then assert his own preference. The rewards and promotions will usually go to the person who is willing to decide and is lucky enough to be right.

[2] *Strategy Centers, A Contemporary Managing System.*

Category	Characteristics			
	Entrepreneur	Sophisticated Manager	Critical Administrator	Opportunistic Milker
Managerial Style				
Planning Time Frame	Long Enough to Draw Tentative Life Cycle (10)	Long-Range Investment Payout (7)	Intermediate (3)	Short Range (1)
Structure Organization	Free Form or Task Force	Semi Permanent Task Force, Product or Market Division	Business Division Plus Task Force for Renewal	Pared Down Division
Compensation System	High Variable/Low Fixed Fluctuating with Performance	Balanced Variable and Fixed Individual and Group Rewards	Low Variable-High Fixed Group Awards	Fixed Only
Communication System	Informal/Tailor-Made	Formal/Tailor-Made	Formal/Uniform	Little or None, Command System
Measuring and Reporting (Control)	Qualitative, Marketing Unwritten	Qualitative and Quantitative Early Warning System, All Functions	Quantitative Written Production Oriented	Numerical Written Balance Sheet Oriented
Functional Strategies to be Stressed	Market Research New Product Development	Operations Research Organization Development	Value Analysis Date Processing Taxes and Insurance	Purchasing
Market Situation	High Growth/Low Share	High Growth/High Share	Low Growth/High Share	Low Growth/Low Share
Financial Situation	Cash Hungry Low Reported Earnings Good P/E High Debt Level	Self-Financing Cash Hungry, Good to Low Reported Earnings High P/E, Low-Moderate Debt Level	Cash Rich High Earnings Fair P/E No Debt-High Debt Capacity	Fair Cash Low Earnings Low P/E Low Debt Capacity

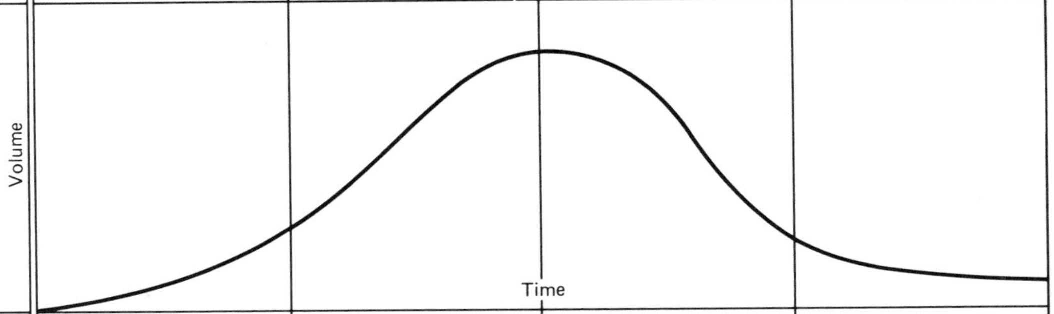

Volume

Time

FIGURE 4-1 Implementing a Product Strategy—Context and the Life Cycle

233

Stage Company Characteristics	I (Small)	II (Integrated)	III (Diversified)
1. Product line	1. Single product or single line	1. Single product line	1. Multiple product lines
2. Distribution	2. One channel or set of channels	2. One set of channels	2. Multiple channels
3. Organization structure	3. Little or no formal structure—"one man show."	3. Specialization based on function	3. Specialization based on product-market relationships
4. Product-service transactions	4. N/A	4. Integrated pattern of transactions 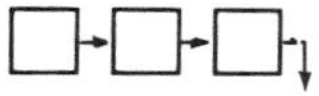 Market	4. Not integrated 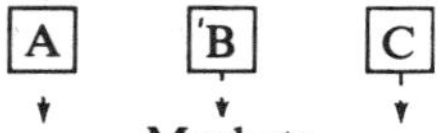 Markets
5. R & D	5. Not institutionalized—oriented by owner-mgr.	5. Increasingly institutionalized search for product or process improvements	5. Institutionalized search for *new* products as well as for improvements
6. Performance measurement	6. By personal contact and subjective criteria	6. Increasingly impersonal using technical and/or cost criteria	6. Increasingly impersonal using *market* criteria (return on investment and market share)
7. Rewards	7. Unsystematic and often paternalistic	7. Increasingly systematic with emphasis on stability and service	7. Increasingly systematic with variability related to performance
8. Control system	8. Personal control of both strategic and operating decisions	8. Personal control of strategic decisions, with increasing delegation of operating decisions based on control by decision rules (policies)	8. Delegation of product-market decisions within existing businesses, with indirect control based on analysis of "results"
9. Strategic choices	9. Needs of owner *vs.* needs of firm	9. —Degree of integration —Market share objective —Breadth of product line	9. —Entry and exit from industries —Allocation of resources by industry —Rate of growth

FIGURE 4-2 Three Stages of Organizational Development

STRATEGY AND
FINANCIAL STATEMENTS

Financial statements should reflect the strategic decisions of a firm. They record the results achieved, how the corporation has positioned its assets and how those assets were financed. An understanding of the strategy of a company should lead one to take certain expectations to an analysis of these financials. This case was developed to test this premise.

Following are ten billion-dollar corporations: (1) American Telephone and Telegraph, (2) Citibank, (3) Exxon, (4) Firestone Tire and Rubber, (5) International Business Machines, (6) International Paper Company, (7) Iowa Beef Packers, (8) Joseph Seagram and Sons (liquors), (9) United Air Line, and (10) Wal-

greens (retail drug chain). In Exhibits 1 and 2 are balance sheet data and other information selected from their annual reports. Your task is to identify which set of data refers to each of these firms, using only your understanding of how each does business. To help you, a worksheet that suggests several strategic variables that might help to discriminate between the companies has been provided. We suggest you devise a measure of each variable and decide where each firm would stand compared to the other nine on each measure. Would it be high, low, or average? For example, capital intensiveness might be measured by the proportion of total assets invested in plant and equipment. Which of the ten firms are the most and least capital intense? A series of such comparisons should enable you to identify the reports.

This case was prepared by Richard C. Oppelt under the supervision of Professor Jules J. Schwartz as a basis for discussion rather than to illustrate either effective or ineffective handling of an administrative action.

Worksheet

Firm	Strategic Variable								
	Capital Intensity	Sales Margin	Return on Investment	Debt Policy	Inventory Investment	Credit Policy	Labor Productivity	Liquidity	Other
1. AT&T									
2. Citibank									
3. Exxon									
4. Firestone									
5. IBM									
6. Int'l Paper									
7. Iowa Beef									
8. Seagrams									
9. United AL									
10. Walgreens									
Your measure									

EXHIBIT 1

BALANCE SHEET ITEMS
(Percent of Total Assets)

ANNUAL REPORT

	A	B	C	D	E	F	G	H	I	J
1. Cash and marketable securities	2.6	1.5	2.2	7.6	28.3	12.1	15.2	9.7	5.8	27.0
2. Accounts receivable	22.0	4.2	22.7	37.7	0.1	12.2	16.9	10.4	7.3	15.0
3. Inventories	27.4	0.6	37.2	11.5	—	11.9	13.4	3.9	52.9	4.2
4. Other current assets	—	0.2	1.0	0.3	1.1	1.0	1.9	0.8	1.3	1.2
5. Net plant and equipment	44.9	87.8	32.5	40.5	0.7	52.6	47.4	71.6	30.3	46.4
6. Other assets	3.1	5.7	4.4	2.4	69.8	10.2	5.2	3.6	2.4	6.2
Total assets	100.0	100.0	100.0	100.0	100.0	100.0	100.0	100.0	100.0	100.0
7. Notes payable	5.6	3.7	8.8	5.9	13.4	3.1	5.5	0.8	0.2	1.7
8. Accounts payable	7.7	2.6	12.1	8.7	—	4.5	18.8	13.9	18.7	11.8
9. Accrued taxes	4.2	1.1	1.4	2.2	2.3	5.2	6.1	—	1.4	7.2
10. Other current liabilities	8.3	2.3	5.0	3.7	78.6	4.6	—	3.3	11.0	—
11. Long-term debt	21.1	39.9	20.4	34.4	1.6	26.7	9.7	40.1	22.8	5.3
12. Other liabilities	4.6	7.5	7.2	4.1	0.5	5.8	9.7	12.4	4.1	2.2
13. Preferred stock	—	4.1	0.8	—	—	0.2	—	1.2	—	—
14. Capital stock and surplus	8.4	20.2	6.2	9.7	2.1	21.1	8.2	18.4	9.7	26.8
15. Retained earnings	40.1	18.6	38.1	31.3	1.5	28.8	42.0	9.9	32.1	45.0
Total liabilities and equity	100.0	100.0	100.0	100.0	100.0	100.0	100.0	100.0	100.0	100.0

EXHIBIT 2

SELECTED FINANCIAL RATIOS
ANNUAL REPORT

	A	B	C	D	E	F	G	H	I	J
1. Current ratio	2.02	0.68	2.31	2.79	0.31	2.14	1.56	1.38	2.15	2.28
2. Quick ratio	0.95	0.59	0.91	2.21	0.30	1.40	1.05	1.12	0.42	2.02
3. Total debt/total assets	0.52	0.57	0.55	0.59	0.96	0.50	0.50	0.70	0.58	0.28
4. Net sales/total assets	1.24	0.35	1.04	8.12	0.09	1.13	1.46	0.85	3.69	0.89
5. Net profits/total assets	0.05	0.04	0.02	0.09	0.01	0.10	0.10	0.02	0.03	0.13
6. Net profits/net worth	0.11	0.10	0.04	0.21	0.15	0.19	0.20	0.07	0.08	0.18
7. Net profits/net sales	0.04	0.12	0.02	0.01	0.06	0.08	0.07	0.02	0.01	0.14
8. Days inventory	83	7	131	5	0	42	35	17	52	20
9. Days receivables	64	43	78	17	5	39	42	44	7	60
10. Net sales/employee ($000)	31	26	116	25	111	60	344	37	37	40

CORNELL BUILDING SERVICES, INC.

Sales of Cornell Building Services, Inc., grew from $1 million in 1968 to $4.6 million in 1975. (See Exhibit 1.) William Baker, president, was aiming for a sales growth rate of 32 percent per year, bringing annual revenues to $20 million by 1980. Past revenue increases for Cornell had come primarily from building maintenance and related service contracts. Then a combination of more firms in the local market plus a decline in new construction had reduced the growth that could be expected from these activities. After considering the market and the firm's strengths, Baker and other officers decided in late 1973 to expand the business to include security services.

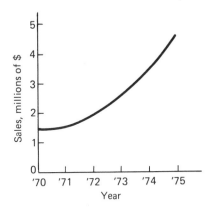

THE INDUSTRY

The building service contracting industry had grown substantially over the last twenty-five years. Contract maintenance revenues

had jumped from $81 million in 1948 to more than $1.5 billion in 1973; industry experts forecasted a continued growth rate of 15 percent.[1] The industry's growth paralleled that of the overall service sector of the economy, influenced also by an increasing tendency for building owners to contract out maintenance work.

Building maintenance firms provided janitorial services to businesses and homes. Common services included cleaning floors, restrooms, and walls and washing windows. Many firms expanded their services to "total maintenance," providing heating and air conditioning maintenance, elevator operators, and guard service.

The 1972 Census of Business reported 14,575 such firms with gross receipts of approximately $1.8 billion. It is estimated that over half of all building maintenance firms are unaccounted for in these statistics because they report no payroll in census data. The structure of the industry is reported in the breakdown by size of receipts of all the firms that reported in 1972 on p. 240.

The annual sales of a typical building service contracting firm working in a single metropolitan area were between $100,000 and $500,000.[2] Most firms were located in urban areas where there were concentrations of business, commercial and industrial buildings, as well as other large clients like airports and railroad stations.

There were few barriers for an entrepreneur who wanted to enter contract cleaning.

This case was prepared by Rita Kollar under the supervision of Professor Jules J. Schwartz as the basis for class discussion rather than to illustrate either effective or ineffective handling of an administrative action.

[1] Small Business Reporter, "Building Maintenance Services," 1974.

[2] Building Service Contractors Association, 1974 Industry Management Survey.

OTHER CLEANING AND MAINTENANCE SERVICES (SIC 7439)

Receipts Size of Firm	Firms (No.)	Establishment (No.)	Receipts ($000)	Payroll ($000)
All Firms, Total	14,575	15,492	1,721,796	1,049,133
Firms with Annual Receipts of				
$50,000,00 or more	4	144	260,098	176,210
$20,000,000 to $49,999,999	3	199	85,214	51,727
$10,000,000 to $19,999,000	6	42	86,282	60,059
$5,000,000 to $9,999,000	14	196	104,820	71,338
$1,000,000 to $4,999,000	167	322	313,111	210,446
$500,000 to $999,000	248	326	172,378	109,867
$250,000 to $499,000	483	544	170,425	104,457
$100,000 to $249,000	1,263	1,311	202,373	115,321
$50,000 to $99,000	1,689	1,697	125,417	63,664
$25,000 to $49,000	2,822	2,836	106,929	46,231
$10,000 to $24,000	4,161	4,167	73,943	29,851
Less than $10,000	3,715	3,716	20,806	9,962

Capital requirements were small; there were no special licensing requirements; and office or storage space was unnecessary for a small operation.

A building owner generally found it more economical to contract out janitorial and building maintenance functions. The building maintenance firm could afford to use more advanced equipment and could rely more heavily on specialization of labor. A building owner would generally compute the cost of building maintenance when estimating the overall cost of a building. On average if a commercial office building rented space annually at $6.50 per square foot, predicted maintenance costs were $.50 per square foot.[3]

There were definite economies of scale accruing to the building service contractor, usually beginning when an annual gross income over $500,000 was reached. These included savings on supplies that could be purchased from manufacturers rather than from distributors. There were also savings on machines because fewer needed to be purchased for each additional $100,000 of revenues.

[3] U.S. Economic Development Administration, "Building Service Contracting," April 1972, Urban Business Profiles, p. 7.

Maintenance work was a labor intensive business. Employees were for the most part unskilled. High turnover rate among employees was always a major problem for contractors. Industry sources indicated that most employees remained with a company for only two to six months.

CORNELL'S EARLY HISTORY

Cornell Buildings Services was founded by William Baker's grandfather in 1913 as a window cleaning business. Operations were expanded after World War II to include general cleaning. William Baker and his brother were brought up in the business, spending school vacations learning cleaning techniques and working on a variety of cleaning jobs, from washing windows to scrubbing floors. During the summers they were given their own routes and worked their way up. William Baker joined the firm full-time in 1962 as a supervisor and his brother, Gordon, joined about three years later in the sales department.

Sales reached $1 million by 1967, making Cornell the largest local cleaning contractor in its home county. The informal structure of a family-owned business could no longer support the volume of business. Responsibilities overlapped and some operations received too much attention while others were neglected. The Bakers decided to organize the company along functional lines. (See Exhibit 2.)

Then services available from Cornell were expanded to include heating, ventilation and air conditioning, as well as janitorial services. Exhibit 3 provides a complete listing of these services. Janitorial services were by far the largest part of the business, accounting for about 90 percent of total revenues. Mechanical services and window cleaning made up the balance.

Commercial and industrial clients purchased these services on a contract basis, with an average contract term of one year. All contracts had a thirty-day cancellation clause. Each spelled out in detail what services would be performed and how often. A contract might state, for example, that the floors were to be swept and buffed, and ashtrays emptied five nights per week; floors stripped and waxed once a month, and the windows cleaned every two months. As "clean" could be defined in many ways, each customer's requirements had to be established through individual consultation. Customers were questioned at length on how each room was used and how it should look. A receiving area, for example, would not require the same attention as a boardroom.

Cornell's customers included commercial and industrial buildings, apartment complexes, warehouses, and institutions such as schools. The company did not service residences or restaurants, and government contracts were limited to under 10 percent of the total billings. As a rule of thumb, the firm looked for contracts worth $30,000 per year or $2,500 a month minimum. Exhibit 4 gives a breakdown of the customers by billing size.

CORNELL'S STRATEGY

Cornell management had directed its sales efforts specifically toward corporate customers for several reasons. Most corporations had about the same cleaning standards, reducing the variation in client demands. Most wanted their offices to look "crisp and their floor to have high lustre." This kind of appearance required more cleaning, but corporations were generally willing to pay for it. This usually made for more loyal customers.

For a building like a warehouse, the client could contract primarily on the basis of price, because the cleaning standards were not likely to be high. As soon as someone who will do the job for less is found, the contract is lost. Baker noted that there is always someone who will do the job more cheaply in this highly fragmented business.

Building service contractors had traditionally confined their business to a narrow geographic area. It was generally too difficult to control the quality of the work when operations were widespread. Approximately 65 percent of Cornell's business was in New York State, 25 percent in New Jersey, and 10 percent in Connecticut.

Maintenance workers for each building were hired from the area in which the building was located. The majority—some 90 percent—of Cornell's maintenance people were part-time, and worked four hours daily. They reported directly to their assigned building each night. A worker performed the same task in the same area of a building each night.

The director of marketing explained that there were two reasons for this pattern: accountability and completeness. If problems arose after a job was completed, the person responsible for the area was always identifiable. In addition, working always in one area familiarized a person with it and made it less likely that any part of the job would remain undone. Equipment and supplies were usually stored on site. Some of the larger buildings held extra supplies for nearby smaller structures that lacked storage space.

Ability to provide quality services and a reputation for quality were key determinants of a maintenance contractor's ability to survive and grow. Cornell had instituted a system of checks within the framework of both its Marketing and Operations Departments to insure that the contracted work was performed in an acceptable manner. In all buildings requiring three or more workers a field supervisor checked every area at the end of each night's work. District managers responsible for several buildings rechecked their supervisors, visiting different buildings each night. Account executives, who are responsible for sales and the customer relations aspect of an account, also checked on a regular basis.

The building service industry had traditionally suffered from exceptionally high employee turnover. The director of marketing noted that Cornell "overpaid" its supervisory personnel in order to attract people who were willing to take on authority and responsibility. The supervisor in each building was responsible for hiring and firing his own workers, as well as training new employees.

In addition to performance Baker maintained that service was also an important factor in the operation. "Personal service is the key to our becoming the largest contractor in the area." Management placed a premium on total involvement with the customer. This extended from frequent and friendly contact with clients, to theater tickets and lunches. A customer, Baker stated, will cancel a contract; a friend will not. Ninety-five percent of the firm's accounts were retained year after year, and Baker estimated that the average time an account was held was over seven years.

Cornell also established what is called full-disclosure bidding. Cleaning is an intangible product so it is difficult for the customer to see the basis on which a bid is made. Each bid submitted by Cornell Services stated how many people would be in the building, their job level and equipment and overhead. This disclosure policy was said to be uncommon in the business.

CORNELL'S RECENT YEARS

Between 1968 and 1974 sales increased at an average rate of 26 percent and profits at an average rate of 30 percent per year. Cornell management attributed this rapid growth to the quality of the firm's work and the personal attention they provided to customers. This attention differentiated Cornell from the majority of area contractors at the time so that it was able to command a premium price for its services.

Several factors convinced Baker that he could not depend as heavily on maintenance contracts for future growth. Ease of entry continued to attract many new firms into the building service field and the local market was becoming increasingly competitive. Some of the newer entrants were willing to sign contracts at or below cost just to build up a client base. Competing firms had frequently been forced to lower their prices also.

This competitive situation was intensified during an economic recession. Moreover, a severe downturn might lead to cutbacks in the variety of services purchased, or even cancellation of contracts. The director of marketing estimated that there were some thirty-two cleaning contractors operating in Cornell's area; of these, nine could be considered major competitors. He noted that the landlord of a new building did not need to call cleaning contractors for bids—seventeen to eighteen firms would automatically submit bids. Finally, new construction, the primary source of new business for the company, was down.

Safeguard Security Systems

Baker weighed these external conditions, as well as the company's strengths when he considered what future growth avenues were available. In late 1973 the decision was made to expand Cornell's operations to include security services. Safeguard Security Systems began operations the next year.

The market for security services had been growing rapidly. Pressure from insurance companies, stricter building codes and tenant demands had led building managers to seek increased security services. For Cornell it was a natural expansion. The services could be offered to the existing customer base, and would enable the firm to present prospective customers with a total maintenance package. Operationally the people required for security jobs were very similar to those needed for maintenance—primarily part-time and unskilled.

Safeguard services included basic guard service, special assignments for highly trained officers, investigative services and security consulting. Safeguard was organized as a separate department with a general manager supervising all sales, operational and administrative functions. The service operated at a loss in 1974, but became profitable in the first quarter of 1975.

Cornell's billings for security services during the early part of 1975 were better than anticipated. Management concluded that its organization could not adequately support future growth. In particular better administrative and costing procedures and a training program for guards were needed immediately. Any change, however, had to be considered with respect to its effect on cleaning services.

Reorganization

In October 1975 a decision was made to reorganize the company. The new organization was based on service offered rather than on functional lines. (See Exhibit 5.) Cleaning Services and Safeguard Security Systems were organized as major divisions, with central services providing administrative support to both. Each division was made responsible for its own operations and marketing. The former director of operations took over as general manager of Safeguard Security Systems. His immediate tasks were development of a customer base and institution of administrative costing and training procedures. Gordon Baker, formerly director of marketing for cleaning services, now directed all aspects of that part of the business.

The cleaning services division was further reorganized so that a team composed of an account executive and a district manager serviced each of the sales territories: Southern New York, Northern New York and Connecticut; New Jersey; and the fourth "territory," for day operations, made up of maintenance workers who provided cleaning services during the working day. The account executive and the district manager were to be exclusively responsible for sales and public relations, and cleaning operations for each account in their territory. Baker expected the team approach to provide better service to the customer, as well as make each team's work more efficient and profitable.

Under the previous system accountability for each customer was quite loose. Accounts were sometimes lost because of the confusion over who was handling which customer. This problem would be eliminated under the new system; team members would meet on a regular basis to go over the accounts and work out the problems of their customers. Reward and compensation policy, though not yet fully formulated, would be structured to provide incentives for everyone to work as a team.

When asked about growth over the next five years William Baker expressed confidence that a 32 percent growth rate would be achieved. He considered the best growth prospects to be acquisition of a contract cleaning business and expansion into nearby geographic areas. He expected that increasing demand for security services would be a source of rapid expansion for Safeguard. Baker asserted that the contract cleaning industry was maturing rapidly. It would become increasingly difficult for small, inefficient firms to survive; future volume should be concentrated in a few large companies. The ability of any company to become larger would depend on its ability to manage its people and resources.

EXHIBIT 1

CORNELL BUILDING SERVICES, INC.
Statement of Income for the Fiscal Years Ended June 30
($ thousands)

	1970	1971	1972	1973	1974	1975
Service income	1433	1682	1951	2729	3562	4640
Cost of services	1139	1304	1635	2208	2839	3792
Gross profit	294	378	316	521	723	848
Selling, general, and administrative expenses	286	354	288	400	599	706
Operating profit	8	24	28	121	124	142
Other income (deductions) net	4	1	(8)	32	(6)	15
Income before taxes	12	25	20	153	118	157

EXHIBIT 2

CORNELL BUILDING SERVICES, INC.
Organizational Structure, 1967

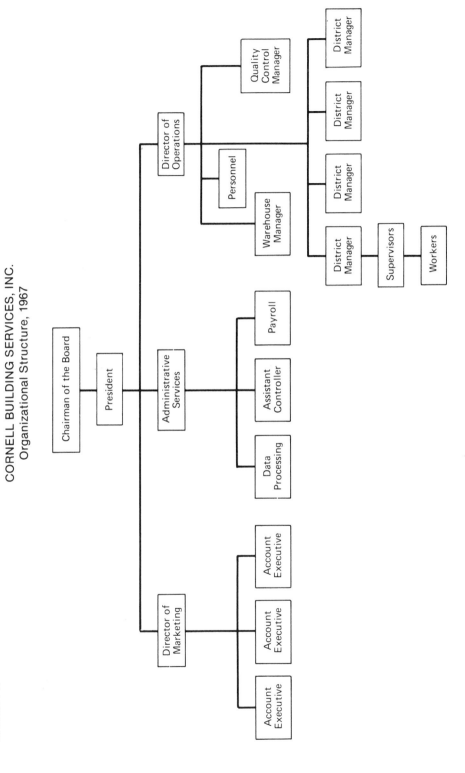

EXHIBIT 3

Janitorial Services
Nightly porter service
Daily porter and matron service
Floor care
Carpet care
Light maintenance
Window cleaning
Exterminating services
Heating/Ventilation/Air Conditioning
On-site engineer services
Preventive maintenance
Water treatment services
Filter replacement and cleaning

EXHIBIT 4

CORNELL CUSTOMERS BY MONTHLY BILLING
(October 1975)

Range ($)	No. of Jobs	Total Amount ($)	% of Sales
0–500	417	57,055	14
501–1500	70	59,994	14
1501–3000	19	40,991	10
3001–5000	25	92,505	22
5001–8000	8	51,873	12
8001–13000	3	31,205	8
13001–20000	2	30,428	7
20001–over	2	54,657	13
Total	546	418,711	100

EXHIBIT 5
CORNELL BUILDING SERVICES, INC.
Reorganization Chart, 1976

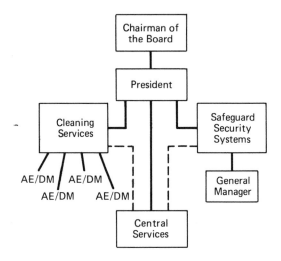

THE TASTY BAKING COMPANY

Early in 1975, Paul R. Kaiser was reviewing the history of the Tasty Baking Company. As chairman of the board and chief executive officer, it was his responsibility to coordinate plans to continue the company's sixty-one-year growth record.

COMPANY HISTORY

On Monday morning, April 27, 1914, Herbert C. Morris pulled his royal-blue, horse-drawn wagon, loaded with wicker baskets of individually wrapped cakes and pies, out into the Germantown section of Philadelphia. He returned with sales receipts of $28.32. It was a meager first day, considering Morris and his partner, Philip J. Baur, had borrowed $50,000 to start their business, primarily for the giant brick ovens they bought to bake their cakes. By the end of the year, however, Baur and Morris had sold $300,000 worth of their new product, Tastykake.

In its first year the Tasty Baking Company turned a profit, an accomplishment achieved every year through 1975. The firm succeeded through a series of unique approaches to the marketplace. In 1914 the American housewife either baked her own cake or purchased a piece from a grocer's big cake loaf. Sanitary conditions being what they were, most women baked their own. As a baker in a family-operated business in Pittsburgh, Philip Baur was aware of this. His partner, Mr. Morris, was a sales representative for a Boston firm that supplied dried eggs to the baking industry.

This case was prepared by Frank Burd under the supervision of Professor Jules J. Schwartz as the basis for class discussion rather than to illustrate either effective or ineffective handling of an administrative action.

(Interestingly Tastykake, to this day, did not use dried eggs. The firm used only fresh eggs bought as separated yolks and whites.)

Baur and Morris entered the baking market with a small, individually wrapped cake, and a slogan, "the cake that made mother stop baking." Sales hit $500,000 by 1916, with no more advertising than the word "Tastykake" on the side of the horse-drawn delivery trucks. That year, Tasty Baking began advertising on billboards, in trolleys, and between reels at theaters.

Shortages during and following World War I led to a situation where grocery shelves were often empty. Storekeepers were unable to accumulate an inventory and Tastykakes often reached the consumers' homes the day after they were baked. Morris and Baur decided to adopt this as a strategy during times of plenty to guarantee freshness. They resolved to control distribution, to be sure that there would be no stale Tastykakes on the shelves. This, they felt, would further enhance the quality image they wished to develop for their products. Storekeepers and Tasty's own salesmen criticized this revolutionary approach; but the company was guaranteeing a fresh product—a marketing strategy it saw as more important in the long run than permitting stores to buy more, stockpile inventories, and sell an older product.

Tasty called its strategy "controlled selling." The objective was for the salesperson to arrive with fresh cakes just as the customer purchased the last one on the shelf from the previous day's batch. Whenever he delivered cakes he recorded the number of items on a computer sheet. The firm attempted to predict patterns of consumption. Based on a store's history, the salesperson knew how many cakes to give the store, with no extras. Spats sometimes occurred between salespersons and storekeepers who wanted more cakes. However, the salesperson generally refused to leave additional cakes; any unsold items on the shelves after eight days were removed and charged to his account. Part of this active marketing effort included charting seasonal demand. In very cold weather people tended to consume products that were high in carbohydrates, while in warm weather, they stayed away from sticky products such as pies and cakes.

Tasty was one of the first companies to use open-coding on its boxes, long before this was a legal requirement. A Tastykake customer could read the date of expiration on an item in the years when other firms were still using private codes. A Tastykake was unconditionally guaranteed. A customer from anywhere in the country who wrote to the firm complaining of a stale or underweight product was sent a letter of apology from the director of public relations and a coupon for replacement cakes at the nearest store.

Tastykake executives would probably identify their most important asset as confidence —confidence in the sales force, in the freshness of the product as well as in its quality and its price. Salespeople were well liked and trusted by customers. They were carefully recruited. There were fifty salespersons in the Philadelphia area and 300 others in surrounding Middle Atlantic states. There were over 5000 applications on file for their jobs. Salespeople had typically waited six months for an interview and two years for their jobs.

It helped to have a relative working for the company; Tasty was very family-oriented and preferred to hire the relatives of present employees. The entire sales force was composed of males who were paid very well, typically earning $20,000 to $30,000 a year. They received a small salary plus commission. The average salesperson grossed $300,000 per year in sales from his small truck. Though few had college degrees, many applications had been received from college graduates with degrees in business administration, accounting, and marketing. After being hired each person was trained on a delivery route by a supervisor who would follow his performance throughout his career with the company. Evaluations were based on sales and customer relations. If a man's sales figures were not up to a computer-chartered level after a few weeks, he was fired.

GROWTH STRATEGIES

In 1922 the bakery moved to its present location. A series of four expansions occurred, the last in 1930, which provided the company with 350,000 square feet of floor space. A visit to the North Philadelphia bakery to watch Tasty's 1700 workers was like observing a chess match with someone constantly looking over someone else's shoulder. The "quality assurance" department was constantly pulling items off production lines at various stages of baking. The products were checked by the "finished product evaluator," a taster who judged cakes on appearance, aroma, and taste. The company was very proud of its traditionally fresh product. Only fresh raw materials were used, including fresh milk, eggs, shortening, fruits, and flavors. No artificial ingredients were used to insure shelf life.

Sales were off during the depression, but due to further marketing innovations, not very seriously. In 1931 the first commercial nonround pie was introduced. Originally a square the pie soon took on a rectangular shape, easy to hold and easy to include in a lunch pail. In 1932 the TandyTake, a mild chocolate item was introduced, and it became one of Tasty's most popular sellers. In 1933 a third cup cake was added to the nickel pack, instead of reducing the unit price. No one was laid off. Tastykake spread the work among its people and proudly boasted that it was paying higher wages than were called for under the baker's code of the National Recovery Act. Employee benefits had always been very generous, making unionization almost impossible. Throughout the years the firm never missed a single dividend.

The company continued to grow as Baur worked constantly at improving and expanding the product line while Morris pushed the limits of the Philadelphia market outward. By 1951 sales were over $16,000,000. But in that year, Tasty Baking faced a severe crisis. Returning from a European vacation Mr. Baur suffered a stroke and died. Following his death sales leveled off, earnings started to fall, and rumors began to circulate that the business was to be sold. The two families looked inside their ranks and turned to Paul R. Kaiser, the husband of Philip Baur's third daughter. Kaiser, who was thirty-six years old at the time, was an insurance executive, billing over $1,000,000 annually after only five years in the insurance business. He joined Tasty Baking in 1952 and was named president the next year. Morris, the surviving partner, became chairman of the board until his death in 1960. Meanwhile the age of the supermarket was dawning and the firm had to make a decision about its future.

In the next decade Tasty began a long-term capital investment program to mechanize production facilities and cut costs. As a result, the manufacturing process moved from man to machine and the production process was cut from twelve hours to forty-five minutes. The program cost $8 million; every cent of it was generated internally. Sales rose more than 60 percent during the period while profits doubled. As a result there were no layoffs due to mechanization.

Tasty also improved its marketing effort. With a color film strip, "Profit by the Foot," the salesperson demonstrated to buyers that giving Tasty's product more shelf space could generate much higher profits per shelf foot than other foods their store currently displayed because of the product's amazingly high turnover; average shelf time was less than two days. The advertising budget was tripled. Advertising had previously been chiefly on billboards. Tastykake now moved into all forms of media. Joe E. Brown, Shari Lewis, and Dick Clark were among the TV personalities endorsing Tastykake. In addition the company sponsored broadcasts of the games of the Philadelphia Phillies, a major-league baseball club.

The advertising budget grew every year, regardless of business conditions. There were three prime targets—mothers between twenty-nine and forty-four years of age (lunchbox items), children themselves, and sports enthusiasts. Tastykake tried to reach these groups with spots on television. The firm also sponsored broadcasts of the Phillies and the Baltimore Orioles in baseball, the Washington Redskins in football, and the Philadelphia Flyers in hockey. It later moved toward cents-off promotions aimed at both the trade and the customer.

During the fifties Tasty specifically allotted money for the first time for research and development. Recordkeeping was mechanized to keep closer, more regular controls. The company also sought to look after its workers; it set up a generous pension plan and continued to pay wages well above industry standards.

In the early seventies Tastykake also expanded its market through two supermarket chains. The company had a firm in downtown Philadelphia freeze its cakes with a new process. These were carried by the Seven-Eleven chain into many states not previously reached. Tasty had also just moved to the West Coast, selling its product through Alpha Beta stores. Every week two trucks left Philadelphia for California, filled with frozen products that were not thawed until they actually reached the shelf. Instead of the usual eight days before recall, the company placed a six-day limit on store shelf life to insure freshness. Naturally the farther the product was shipped from Philadelphia, the less control there could be over freshness.

The company tried New York City, but found the "deals" made there unacceptable to its selling style and was forced to retreat. The products were sold under a private label in New England. The firm had thus been very careful in expansion efforts. It had routes in Pennsylvania, New Jersey, Delaware, Maryland, Virginia, Washington, D.C., West Virginia, and Southwest New York. Tasty refused to sell retail as it did not wish to lose the goodwill of the stores it served. The company was fanatically devoted to the small Mom and Pop store. Some of these small establishments sold less than $10 worth of cakes a day, yet others sold $1,000 worth every week.

Pricing

Pricing was a major concern. Rising costs in 1974 led to nine price changes in the product. Tastykake had to develop the capacity for printing the price on the package. Previously, the entire package was made elsewhere. At one point package prices could not be changed fast enough and the company charged the new prices while using the old boxes, marked with a lower price. The cakes were accompanied by an explanation about the wasted paper that would have occurred in a period of shortages if Tastykake simply had gone ahead with dumping the old wrappers. There were no adverse reactions.

The danger of reaching the thirty-cent price level concerned the company. The firm felt that if the product cost were to go that high, sales would drop dramatically. As a result it was constantly examining ways to keep the cost down. It had been suggested that the plant was at full capacity five years earlier; yet, recently, the research and development department changed the number of cakes on the conveyor entering the oven from twelve to eighteen across. Baking was carried on twenty-four hours a day, six days a week.

Another major problem was culls, imperfects, often resulting from mispackaging or a color not quite consistent with the standard, totaling some 30,000 packages a day. Tastykake was trying to sell culls through thrift stores in New York, as it did not wish to sell them in Philadelphia.

The cost of commodities used by a food processing company represents its major production expense. In periods of rising commodity prices the consumer-oriented firm lacks the needed flexibility in adjusting its product prices to reflect changing commodity costs. Thus rising costs tend to cut into the company's profit margin.

During 1973 the prices of wheat, corn, and soybeans all hit record highs. Bakery-products industry profits dropped from $278 million in 1972 to $200 million in 1973, despite the more than 30 percent increase in sales. The squeeze continued in 1974 with the drastic rise in the cost of sugar.

In 1975 Philip Baur, Jr., son of the founder, was president. He was named to the job three years earlier, presumably to be groomed for the top position. As head of Tastykake he had already had some notable successes. For example, his purchasing agent, Chairman Kaiser's brother, wisely hedged sugar prices back in 1973, effecting great savings when sugar went soaring out of sight in 1974. Tastykake also tried, when possible, to replace sugar with other sweeteners to reduce cost without compromising quality.

A combination of this severe profit squeeze and continuing encroachment of supermarkets into the bakery area had resulted in the gradual demise of local family-run bakeries. Through automation and a careful acquisitions program, Tasty had managed to maintain its strong position. Tastykake was the eighth largest firm in Philadelphia. Bakery industry surveys showed that the geographical regions of the United States that consumed the most cake per capita corresponded exactly with Tasty's availability. More cake was eaten in Philadelphia than in any other American city. Over one billion cakes per year were sold in the area. Tastykake maintained an 80 percent share of the metropolitan area's snack cake market. Exhibit 1 gives some detailed comparisons of Tasty Baking's industry position.

Relocation

In 1968 Tasty looked around the neighborhood where its plant was located and was appalled at the deterioration. Small businesses were closing everywhere. Population was shifting from blue-collar white to blue-collar black. Real estate was declining and management worried about the value of its giant bakery. It was estimated that a move to the suburbs would cost about $16 million, just for the physical plant. It would probably cost Philadelphia 1800 jobs. These jobs were held by people with many years of service; 30 percent of Tasty's employees had been with the company over fifteen years. Personnel turnover was low. The company had never liked borrowing, and relocating would have necessitated financing a new facility. A decision was made not only to stay, but to try to revitalize the area.

Through the State Neighborhood Assistance Act, the company was allowed to deduct seventy-eight cents from taxes for every dollar spent on community projects. The Allegheny West Foundation was founded with $40,000 contributed by Tastykake. Twelve other businesses and the Chamber of Commerce assisted in rehabilitating fifty homes, which were sold to community people with low-interest mortgages. The community became more trusting of the business people over the years. In 1975 Tastykake's contribution to the foundation was over $250,000.

DIVERSIFICATION

In 1961 Tasty became a publicly-held company and its stock was traded on the over-the-counter market. In 1965, share trading began on the American and PBW Exchanges.

The firm began to look to new fields in the hope of accelerating growth. It moved to diversify when, in 1965, it acquired Philips and Jacobs, a regional graphics art distributor with 100 years in the business. Some worried, "Why graphic arts? Cupcakes and printing ink don't mix." The company response was that it sought compatibility—solid firms whose business philosophies were similar to Tasty's.

Tasty used three criteria as it looked at companies for its expansion program:

1. Find firms with top flight management who have already instituted personnel and industrial relations policies that most nearly match Tasty's liberal benefits;
2. Seek companies that have proven they can earn the same return on investment as Tasty (about 10 percent); and
3. Avoid any dilution of shareholder's holdings.

The following year the company acquired Bowden Graphic Arts and Supply of Baltimore, then Dixieplate Company in Atlanta (1967), and B&T Grinding and Supply in Dallas (1973). All were consolidated into Tasty's Graphic Arts Group. This group supplied fifteen states from New Jersey to Florida in the printing and allied trades. By 1974 the new group had annual sales of more than $30 million. This was well over the $27 million in sales generated by the Tasty Baking Company only two years before the expansion had begun.

In 1966 Tasty bought several Ohio cookie distributors, consolidating them in Buckeye Biscuit. In 1970 it acquired the Larami Corporation, a toy company with offices in Philadelphia and Hong Kong, which manufactured, imported, packaged and distributed dolls and rack and box toys for counter displays in supermarket and discount stores.

In the 1970s when bakery profits were being squeezed by sugar and wheat price increases, the nonbaking divisions showed solid profits. They constituted nearly half the corporation's total sales and profits. The company attributed this to its successful choice of acquisitions.

Only one acquisition error had been made so far. In 1967 the firm bought a pretzel and potato chip concern in Baltimore. But the Tasty people claim they didn't know that business. They didn't have expertise to assist the new management as they did in other acquisitions, and the venture was not especially successful.

The big modernization program in the fifties and sixties was done with internally-generated funds. Similarly no borrowing had been undertaken to finance the acquisitions of the last two decades. Since then funds generated from the acquisitions were used to add capital to the bakery. Tasty Baking Company borrowed for the first time in 1974. Management cited the reason as a cash flow problem. Accounts receivable were up and Tasty found itself short on operating funds. Tasty could call on a line of credit up to $12 million from local banks if necessary. (See Exhibits 2 to 6 for more financial data.)

ORGANIZATION (See Exhibit 7)

As chairman of the board and chief executive officer, Paul R. Kaiser headed the four divisions that made up Tasty Baking Company in 1975. In 1974 Tastykake, Inc., was formed into a fourth autonomous division, along with three acquired divisions (toys, cookies, and graphics). Each division had its own president, and its own research and development, marketing, engineering, and purchasing departments. Finance and personnel were responsible directly to the parent company. The family owned 31 percent of the company, which had some 4200 shareholders. As there were two classes of stock, the families actually controlled 42 percent of the vote.

EXHIBIT 1

INDUSTRY DATA
Comparative Company Analysis

CAPITAL EXPENDITURES
(in millions of dollars)

	Nabisco	Tasty Baking	Ward Foods
1973	92.1	3.90	5.3
1972	60.2	2.54	6.4
1971	34.4	1.79	10.0
1970	24.1	1.68	17.6
1969	31.9	1.93	21.5
1968	38.2	2.37	9.1
1967	37.5	3.25	6.5
1966	25.6	2.64	4.8
1965	23.1	1.71	3.1
1964	14.7	1.94	2.9
Yr. End:	Dec.	Dec.	Dec.

CAPITAL EXPENDITURES
(as a percentage of gross plant)

	Nabisco	Tasty Baking	Ward Foods
1973	14.0	13.6	5.3
1972	10.3	9.8	4.8
1971	7.0	14.5	7.5
1970	5.2	13.8	12.8
1969	7.6	15.4	18.0
1968	9.6	19.1	10.1
1967	8.3	28.0	9.5
1966	7.4	25.0	7.9
1965	6.6	21.0	6.3
1964	5.3	25.4	6.0

Definition: Capital expenditures during the fiscal year divided by gross property at the end of the fiscal year.

DIVIDENDS
(as a percentage of earnings)

	Nabisco	Tasty Baking	Ward Foods
1973	83.6	56.3	Nil
1972	60.1	57.7	Nil
1971	66.5	62.4	Nil
1970	76.1	76.5	Nil
1969	96.0	67.7	...[a]
1968	67.7	67.2	...
1967	63.7	51.9	...
1966	62.9	51.1	Nil
1965	63.6	52.7	Nil
1964	63.2	50.4	Nil

Definition: Fiscal year dividends paid per share, dividend by net earnings per share of common stocks.
[a] 3% in stock plus warrant in 1969.

EXHIBIT 1 (cont.)

INDUSTRY DATA
Comparative Company Analysis

PRICE-EARNINGS RATIOS

	Nabisco		Tasty Baking		Ward Foods	
	High	Low	High	Low	High	Low
1973	22	13	11	6	def.[b]	def.
1972	18	15	13	9	def.	def.
1971	17	15	13	10	31	17
1970	19	13	14	10	...[c]	21
1969	24	21	18	11	28	13
1968	17	14	19	15	31	18
1967	17	14	15	9	27	7
1966	18	13	11	10	17	6
1965	24	18	13	11	39	14
1964	17	12	13	11	def.	def.

[b]def. = Deficit
[c]Ratios over 50 not calculated

NET INCOME (1967 = 100)

	Nabisco	Tasty Baking	Ward Foods
1973	104	136	def.[d]
1972	138	128	def.*
1971	118	112	32
1970	103	88	26
1969	73	94	114
1968	99	83	105
1967	100	100	100
1966	97	91	78
1965	91	76	21
1964	86	69	def.
Net Income in 1967 Base period, in ~millions of dollars:	42.18	2.78	4.92

[d]def. = Deficit.

⟶ NET INCOME
(as a percentage of sales)

	Nabisco	Tasty Baking	Ward Foods
1973	3.0	↘ 3.3	def.[e]
1972	4.6	3.6	def.
1971	4.7	3.4	4.0
1970	4.6	2.8	.3
1969	4.2	3.1	1.4
1968	5.4	3.1	1.6
1967	5.5	4.1	1.6
1966	5.7	4.5	1.4
1965	6.1	4.6	.6
1964	6.0	4.8	def.

[e]def. = Deficit.

EXHIBIT 1 (cont.)

INDUSTRY DATA
Comparative Company Analysis

SALES RECORD (1967 = 100)

	Nabisco	Tasty Baking	Ward Food
1973	190	170	119
1972	168	148	119
1971	140	135	134
1970	124	129	132
1969	95	123	131
1968	101	111	104
1967	100	100	100
1966	94	82	92
1965	89	67	57
1964	80	60	54
Sales in 1967 base period, in millions of dollars:	763.6	67.4	301.0

PROFIT MARGINS (%)[f]

	Nabisco	Tasty Baking	Ward Foods
1973	8.7	8.3	2.5
1972	11.9	9.4	.5
1971	12.5	9.1	3.8
1970	12.4	8.0	3.6
1969	12.1	8.8	4.4
1968	14.3	8.1	4.2
1967	13.3	9.3	5.1
1966	13.4	10.2	3.9
1965	13.6	10.5	2.2
1964	14.6	10.4	1.1

[f] Profit margins are derived by dividing operating income by sales.

YIELDS (%)

	Nabisco		Tasty Baking		Ward Foods	
	High	Low	High	Low	High	Low
1973	6.5	3.8	8.9	5.3	Nil	Nil
1972	4.2	3.4	6.2	4.4	Nil	Nil
1971	4.6	3.8	6.4	4.8	Nil	Nil
1970	5.8	4.0	7.3	5.3	Nil	Nil
1969	4.6	4.0	6.2	3.8	1	1
1968	4.8	3.9	4.5	3.6	1..	1..
1967	4.7	3.8	5.5	3.4	1..	1..
1966	4.8	3.4	5.1	4.5	Nil	Nil
1965	3.5	2.7	4.7	3.9	Nil	Nil
1964	3.0	2.6	4.5	3.8	Nil	Nil

EXHIBIT 1 (cont.)

INDUSTRY DATA
Comparative Company Analysis

TASTY BAKING COMPANY

	Net Sales	Oper. Inc.	Net Bef. Taxes	Net Income	Earns.	Divs.	Common $ Per Share Price Range (calendar yrs.)	Book Value	Net Wkg. Cap. (mil $)	Curr. Ratio Assets to Liabs.
		(million $)								
1973	114.76	9.55	7.65	3.78	[1]1.60	0.900	17–10	[2]10.79	9.60	1.5–1
[4]1972	99.42	9.32	7.34	3.55	1.53	0.565	19–14	10.17	9.24	2.0–1
1971	91.24	8.34	6.68	3.12	1.36	0.329	17–13	9.77	8.97	2.2–1
1970	86.91	6.97	5.17	2.44	[2]1.03	0.813	15–11	9.35	8.05	2.0–1
1969	83.25	7.35	5.74	2.62	[3]1.19	0.315	21–12	9.23	6.46	1.7–1
1968	75.13	6.07	4.70	[3]2.31	[2]1.18	0.799	22–17	8.65	5.15	1.7–1
1967	67.44	6.28	5.12	2.78	1.42	0.734	22–14	3.13	4.11	1.6–1
1966	55.45	5.68	4.76	2.52	1.29	0.709	15–13	7.54	4.33	1.8–1
1965	45.51	4.76	3.81	2.11	1.16	0.636	15–13	7.30	3.80	2.1–1
1964	40.29	4.20	3.32	1.93	1.07	0.591	15–13	6.47	2.57	1.9–1

Funded Debt: $304,421; Cl. A Com., 2,248,420 Shs., $0.50 Par. Cl. B 119.325 Shs., $0.50 Par. Baur family owns 31% of Cl. A & 60½ of Cl. B Shs.

[1] On Comb. A & B shs. in all yrs. [2] On Cl. A shs. in all yrs. [3] Bef. spec. chge. of $0.05 in 1970; bef. spec. cr. of $0.13 in 1968. [4] 53 wks.
Note—Per sh. data adj. for 2% slk. divs. in 1965 thru 1974.

NABISCO, INC.[a]

	Net Sales	Oper. Inc.	Net Bef. Taxes	Net Income	Earns.	Divs.	Price Range	Book Value	Net Wkg. Cap. (mil $)	Curr. Ratio Assets to Liabs.
1973	1,454.6	126.10	89.03	43.97	2.75	2.30	61–35	19.36	215.1	2.0–1
1972	1,281.2	151.90	116.63	58.50	3.66	2.20	64–53	18.84	173.3	2.0–1
1971	1,070.4	134.00	105.20	49.89	3.31	2.20	57–48	17.71	172.9	2.3–1
1970	944.1	117.10	91.02	43.40	2.89	2.20	55–37	17.35	122.6	2.0–1
1969	726.2	88.14	67.99	30.84	2.27	2.17½	55–47	17.81	119.8	2.1–1
1968	770.1	110.47	90.03	41.76	3.07	2.07½	53–43	17.79	134.1	2.4–1
1967	763.6	101.81	83.96	42.28	3.11	1.97½	51–42	16.83	99.2	2.1–1
1966	719.6	96.23	78.05	40.82	2.99	1.87½	54–39	15.80	98.1	2.2–1
1965	675.6	91.99	74.62	38.40	2.80	1.77½	66–50	14.91	98.1	2.2–1
1964	607.5	88.72	74.04	36.47	2.66	1.67½	65–56	15.17	96.8	2.4–1

Funded Debt: $241,531,000. Min. Int., $7,556,000. Com. 15,959,600 Shs. $5 Par.

[a] Inc. Associated Products aft. 1971. J. B. Williams all 1969 & foreign subs. aft. 1964.

YEARS TO DEC. 31

EXHIBIT 1 (cont.)

INDUSTRY DATA
Comparative Company Analysis

WARD FOODS, INC.[b]

	Net Sales	Oper. Inc.[b]	Net Bef. Taxes	Net Income	Earns.	Divs.	Price Range (calendar yrs.)	Book Value	Net Wkg. Cap. (mil $)	Curr. Ratio Assets to Liabs.
		(million $)			Common $ Per Share				YEARS TO DEC. 31	
1973	355.1	9.00	0.03	(9.67)	(2.82)	Nil	12– 3	3.27	21.94	1.4–1
1972	357.0	1.91	(7.00)	(15.97)	(4.76)	Nil	14– 8	6.17	37.43	1.6–1
1971	402.3	15.31	1.60	1.58	[3]0.49	Nil	16– 8	13.04	50.14	1.9–1
1970	396.1	14.27	2.16	1.27	[3]0.40	Nil	28– 8	14.64	42.89	1.6–1
1969	395.7	17.34	9.23	5.60	[3]1.84	[2]...	51–24	15.77	45.90	1.8–1
1968	313.9	13.33	8.66	5.17	[3]1.75	[2]...	53–31	13.25	41.57	1.8–1
1967	301.0	15.22	9.23	4.92	1.73	[2]...	46–12	11.41	31.14	1.8–1
1966	276.3	10.76	5.11	3.84	1.59	Nil	27– 8	9.50	27.27	1.8–1
1965	171.7	3.77	1.17	1.04	0.40	Nil	15– 5	8.53	5.86	1.4–1
1964	163.2	1.75	(1.30)	(1.46)	(0.96)	Nil	7– 5	8.53	4.87	1.3–1

Funded Debt: $77,720,000; Com., 3,600,758 Shs., $1 Par. (26% owned by L. Yaeber). Warrants: 563,480 Shs. at $60 to 1/2/79.

[b]Consol. to incl. all significant dom. & fgn. subs.: Inc. Acct. restated in 1972, 1971 & 1970 to excl. (except in earns.) opers. discontinued in subseq. yr. [2]3% stk. in 1967, 1968 & 1969. [3]Fully diluted earns. were $0.46 in 1971, $0.35 in 1970, $1.70 in 1969 & 1.66 in 1968. Note—Earns. per sh. are bef. spec. crs. of $0.15 a sh. in 1971, $0.43 in 1963 & $0.59 in 1967; bef. spec. chgs. of $1.29 a sh. in 1972, $1.34 in 1970, $2.43 in 1969 & $0.39 in 1966. Per sh. data adj. for stk. divs. of 3% ea. in 1962–69.

257

EXHIBIT 2

FIFTEEN YEAR PATTERN OF GROWTH

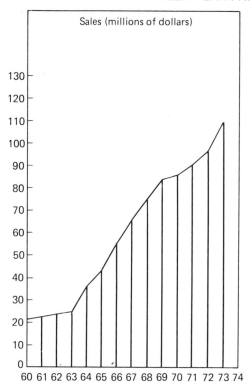

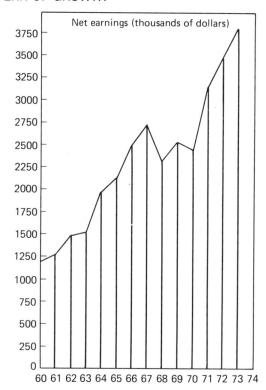

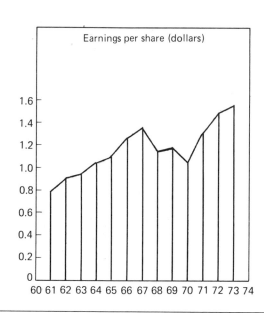

Restated to include subsidiaries acquired on a pooling of interests basis in the year of acquisition and the preceding year.

The Tasty Baking Company

EXHIBIT 2 (cont.)

FINANCIAL HIGHLIGHTS

	1974	1973
Net sales	$132,118,445	$114,758,752
Net earnings	$ 3,523,485	$ 3,778,112
Earnings per dollar of sales	$ .027	$ .033
Average number of common shares outstanding	2,413,835	2,401,312[a]
Earnings per share of common stock	$ 1.46	$ 1.57[a]
Cash dividend	$ .90	$ .92
Stock dividend	2%	2%
Working capital	$ 10,014,653	$ 9,572,574
Current ratio	1.70 to 1	1.82 to 1
Stockholders' equity	$ 28,195,620	$ 26,788,248
Equity per share of common stock	$ 11.65	$ 11.31

[a]Adjusted to reflect 2% stock dividend declared in 1974.

EXHIBIT 3

CONSOLIDATED STATEMENTS OF INCOME

	52 Weeks Ended Dec. 28, 1974	52 Weeks Ended Dec. 29, 1973
Net sales	$132,118,445	$114,758,752
Costs and expenses		
Cost of sales	92,965,569	76,939,197
Depreciation	2,003,481	1,825,155
Selling, general and administrative	29,641,629	28,271,013
Other expenses, net	477,168	76,544
	125,087,847	107,111,909
Income before provision for taxes on income	7,030,598	7,646,843
Provision for taxes on income		
Current	3,593,870	3,844,242
Deferred	(86,757)	24,489
	3,507,113	3,868,731
Net income	$ 3,523,485	$ 3,778,112
Earnings per common share	$1.46	$1.57[a]

[a]Adjusted to reflect 2% stock dividend declared in 1974.

EXHIBIT 4

TASTY BAKING COMPANY AND SUBSIDIARIES
Consolidated Balance Sheets
($000)

ASSETS	Dec. 28, 1974	Dec. 29, 1973
Current assets		
Cash	$ 945	$ 1,418
Marketable securities (market quotations, $544,448 and $700,839, respectively)	834	943
Receivables, less allowance of $198,008 and $214,434, respectively	12,423	10,259
Inventories	9,599	8,022
Prepayments and other	448	552
Total current assets	24,252	21,197
Property, plant and equipment		
Land	387	367
Buildings and improvements	2,954	2,228
Machinery and equipment	27,860	26,054
	31,202	28,650
Less accumulated depreciation	15,450	13,654
	15,752	14,996
Excess of cost of investment in subsidiaries over equity in net assets at acquisition	1,218	1,229
Other assets		
Spare parts inventory	852	716
Officers and employees stock loans receivable	297	367
Unamortized pension costs	1,749	1,922
Unamortized deferred compensation	455	469
Miscellaneous	774	797
	4,129	4,273
	$45,352	$41,696

EXHIBIT 4 (cont.)

261

TASTY BAKING COMPANY AND SUBSIDIARIES
Consolidated Balance Sheets
($000)

	Dec. 28, 1974	Dec. 29, 1973
LIABILITIES		
Current liabilities		
Current portion of long-term debt	$ 376	$ 375
Notes payable, banks	4,910	3,013
Accounts payable	4,252	4,227
Accrued payrolls	2,248	1,973
Accrued pensions	833	859
Accrued income taxes	1,105	824
Other	509	350
Total current liabilities	14,237	11,624
Long-term debt, less current portion	114	489
Deferred income taxes	2,427	2,514
Other liabilities	377	279
STOCKHOLDERS' EQUITY		
Class A common stock, par value $.50 per share, and entitled to one-tenth of a vote per share		
Authorized 3,000,000 shares, issued 2,318,368½ and 2,261,378, respectively	1,159	1,130
Class B common stock, par value $.50 per share, and entitled to one vote per share		
Authorized 150,000 shares, issued 130,800 shares	65	65
Capital in excess of par value of stock	11,762	11,265
Retained earnings	15,668	14,714
	28,655	27,175
Less treasury stock, at cost		
Class A, 16,365 shares and 11,778 shares, respectively	238	175
Class B, 859½ shares and 11,050 shares, respectively	221	211
	28,195	26,788
	$45,352	$41,696

EXHIBIT 5

LINES OF BUSINESS

The company considers its operations to be conducted in two major groups: consumer products and industrial products. The relative contributions to total sales and earnings before taxes by the two groups are:

	1974	1973	1972	1971	1970
			(in thousands)		
Sales					
Consumer Products	$ 99,806	$ 84,933	$75,765	$67,276	$63,517
%	76	74	76	74	73
Industrial Products	32,312	29,826	23,653	23,967	23,398
%	24	26	24	26	27
Total Sales	$132,118	$114,759	$99,418	$91,243	$86,915
Earnings					
Consumer Products	$ 5,959	$ 6,325	$ 6,272	$ 5,727	$ 4,449
%	85	83	85	86	86
Industrial Products	1,072	1,322	1,064	960	710
%	15	17	15	14	14
Total Earnings	$ 7,031	$ 7,647	$ 7,336	$ 6,687	$ 5,159

EXHIBIT 6

TEN YEAR FINANCIAL REVIEW[a]

	1974	1973	1972	1971	1970[d]
Operating Results[b]					
Net sales	$132,118	$114,759	$99,418	$91,243	$86,915
Earnings before income taxes	$ 7,031	$ 7,647	$ 7,336	$ 6,687	$ 5,159
Net earnings	$ 3,523	$ 3,778	$ 3,547	$ 3,124	$ 2,435
Per Share Statistics					
Earnings[c]	$ 1.46	$ 1.57	$ 1.50	$ 1.33	$ 1.07
Dividends—cash	$ .90	$ .92	$ .90	$ .88	$ .88
stock	2%	2%	2%	2%	2%
Stockholders' equity	$ 11.65	$ 11.31	$ 10.73	$ 10.53	$ 10.31
Financial Position[b]					
Working capital	$ 10,015	$ 9,573	$ 9,242	$ 8,971	$ 8,054
Total assets	$ 45,353	$ 41,697	$37,192	$34,456	$34,074
Stockholders' equity	$ 28,196	$ 26,788	$24,362	$22,845	$21,380
Shares of common stock outstanding	2,421	2,369	2,271	2,169	2,074
Statistical Information[b]					
Capital expenditures, net	$ 2,764	$ 3,672	$ 2,540	$ 1,791	$ 1,682
Depreciation charges	$ 2,003	$ 1,825	$ 1,739	$ 1,582	$ 1,581
% Earned on sales	2.7%	3.3%	3.6%	3.4%	2.8%
% Earned on net worth (before income taxes)	25.0%	28.5%	30.1%	29.3%	24.1%

	1969	1968[e]	1967	1966	1965
Operating Results[b]					
Net sales	$ 83,248	$ 75,134	$67,438	$55,450	$45,507
Earnings before income taxes	$ 5,736	$ 4,702	$ 5,113	$ 4,754	$ 4,006
Net earnings	$ 2,619	$ 2,311	$ 2,776	$ 2,517	$ 2,107
Per Share Statistics					
Earnings[c]	$ 1.20	$ 1.15	$ 1.39	$ 1.29	$ 1.13
Dividends—cash	$ .90	$ .90	$ .90	$ .83	$ .76
stock	2%	2%	2%	2%	2%
Stockholders' equity	$ 10.23	$ 10.03	$ 9.61	$ 9.04	$ 8.52
Financial Position[b]					
Working capital	$ 6,464	$ 5,150	$ 4,111	$ 4,331	$ 3,805
Total assets	$ 33,406	$ 28,963	$26,417	$23,606	$17,863
Stockholders' equity	$ 20,716	$ 17,966	$16,739	$15,410	$13,375
Shares of common stock outstanding	2,025	1,792	1,741	1,704	1,569
Statistical Information[b]					
Capital expenditures, net	$ 1,927	$ 2,368	$ 3,253	$ 2,644	$ 1,706
Depreciation charges	$ 1,513	$ 1,344	$ 1,179	$ 982	$ 870
% Earned on sales	3.1%	3.1%	4.1%	4.5%	4.6%
% Earned on net worth (before income taxes)	27.7%	26.2%	30.5%	30.9%	30.0%

[a] Restated to include subsidiaries acquired on a pooling of interests basis in the year of acquisition in the preceding year.
[b] 000 omitted.
[c] Based on average number of shares outstanding adjusted for stock dividends.
[d] Net earnings in 1970 excludes an extraordinary charge of $106,711 or $.05 per share from the loss on discontinuance of snack operations.
[e] Net earnings in 1968 excludes an extraordinary credit of $262,040 or $.13 per share from life insurance proceeds.

EXHIBIT 7

TASTYKAKE, INC.
Organizational Chart

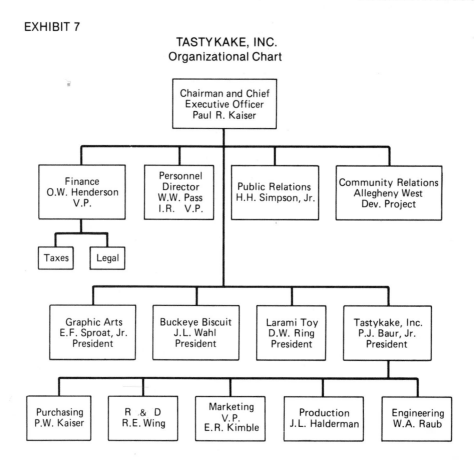

CLEVEPAK CORPORATION

Clevepak Corporation was organized in 1962 to acquire an Ohio company that operated nine paper converting plants across the United States and employed 500 people. Sales in 1963 were $9.7 million and income $118,000. When Clevepak went public in 1968, sales were $32.7 million and income $1.8 million, and by 1974 reached $74 million and $4.4 million respectively. (See Exhibit 1.)

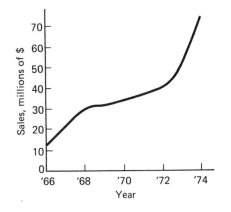

In twelve years Clevepak had expanded from a producer of composite paper containers and cores into a totally integrated manufacturer of paperboard[1] and packaging products made from paperboard. Clevepak now collected wastepaper that was recycled through its own mills and then used at its converting plants, where solid fiber and corrugated partitions, composite containers and folding cartons were manufactured. The

[1] Paper having a thickness of .009 inches or more.

This case was prepared by Rita Kollar under the supervision of Professor Jules J. Schwartz as the basis for class discussion rather than to illustrate either effective or ineffective handling of an administrative action.

firm's product line had been extended to include nonpaper items: elastic and nonelastic cords, flexible tubing, abrasive products packaging machines, and other industrial products.

Rapid growth had exposed some planning and personnel needs in the organization that were not being met adequately. During the last few years the company has devoted much effort to the development of control systems to accommodate the increasing size and diversity of Clevepak's operations.

THE INDUSTRY

Clevepak had carved its own niche in the $30 billion paper industry. Industry output was generally classified as either paper or paperboard. Paperboard products accounted for the largest portion of total industry production, representing approximately 52 percent of output. Paper is most commonly produced from woodpulp but can also be manufactured from the pulps of cotton, bamboo, straw, and grasses, as well as from recycled wastepaper. Clevepak manufactured its paperboard exclusively from wastepaper. The firm's competitive situation had to be viewed in the context of the paper industry as a whole, and also its specialized position as a recycling operation.

The paper industry was competitive, with a large number of producers. The largest company in the industry, International Paper, accounted for less than 10 percent of the domestic paper goods produced in 1973, and it was twice as large as the next largest firm. The industry was inherently cyclical, with demand tied directly to overall economic activity. During recessionary periods the industry operated at only partial capacity, bearing the fixed cost of its enormous investment in plant. Demand for paper and paperboard is relatively price inelastic, as it is derived and substitute materials are not available at competitive prices. In general paper and board are raw materials used in the manufacture of other products and represent only a small percentage of the value of the finished goods. Therefore price cutting will do little to alleviate overcapacity—consumption will not respond to price changes.

Demand for paper products was expected to grow at an annual rate of approximately 4 percent, but producers were cautious about adding new capacity. They were influenced by three considerations: capital costs, pollution control, and energy costs. It was estimated that it took a $2 investment to generate $1 of annual sales, compared to a 1 to 1 ratio fifteen years ago. This was largely attributable to higher construction costs. A senior vice president of a major firm estimated that in 1975 a minimum-sized, 600-ton-per-day kraft pulp mill would cost about $120 million and would return approximately 3 percent on investment after taxes. Projected long-term additions to capacity were expected to average only 2 percent per year. Higher capital costs have also resulted from the high rate of investment into nonproductive pollution abatement equipment. Nearly half the industry's capital expenditures in the last few years had been for such equipment; more than $1.7 billion was spent on pollution control during the years 1972 through 1974. Some experts contended that expenditures for pollution abatement purposes would account for 10 to 15 percent of the capital outlays for all new primary production units in the future.

Pollution Control and Energy Costs

The pulp and paper industry was the third largest water consumer among manufacturing industries and was directly affected by national water quality improvement programs. The 1972 amendments to the Federal Water Pollution Control Act required the paper industry to meet two progressively more stringent standards. The first, to be implemented by July 1977 and enforced by 1983, required the use of the "best practicable control technology currently available." The second standard, zero discharge goal, was to be met by all manufacturing facilities by 1985. Zero discharge was defined as removal of all heat and chemicals from the facility's waste prior to discharge. The industry was also the fourth largest consumer of fuel and energy among manufacturing industries.

The Wastepaper Market

Wastepaper consumption and price had historically fluctuated in response to short-term changes in the economy, both domestic and foreign. When pulp was in short supply, with relatively higher prices worldwide, demand for wastepaper went up, with a resulting improvement in prices. When there was an oversupply in the pulp market, the demand for wastepaper fell, with a consequent reduction in price. One commentator on the paper industry called wastepaper the "minority fiber input—last to be tried, first to be abandoned."

Wood pulp was still plentiful, but its high cost threatened to make wastepaper the primary raw material for a wider range of paper and board products. The skyrocketing cost of constructing new pulp mills, as well as the required investment in supporting timber resources, made the addition of new woodpulp capacity prohibitive. In late 1974 the cost of market pulp topped $340 per ton, while cities were getting an average of $20 per ton for wastepaper. Another factor that has worked in favor of wastepaper has been the improvement in the equipment for pulping, screening, washing, and cleaning wastepaper pulp.

A problem associated with wastepaper use, however, was the cost of labor involved in sorting and bailing collected paper. These operations could add as much as $15 a ton to the cost of wastepaper. Clevepak had eliminated this cost in its New York plant by installing a suction system that would carry loose paper from the drop point directly into a hydropulper, a machine that processed wastepaper by mixing it with water and breaking it down into pulp.

An essential condition for recycling was proximity to a developed area that could provide a continuous supply of wastepaper. Wastepaper's bulk and low unit value made it uneconomical to transport over long distances. Despite these factors, however, economic and environmental considerations were expected to shift the balance in favor of increased wastepaper usage in the future, assuring its importance as a major fiber source.

CLEVEPAK'S PRODUCT LINE

Clevepak's product line was divided into paperboard and packaging products and industrial products. (See Exhibit 2.)

Paperboard and Packaging Products

The Mill Division manufactured paperboard.

The Partition Division was the largest converting division, with eight manufacturing plants across the country. It produced solid fiber shipping case partitions. Virtually all the paperboard requirements of this division were supplied internally. (See Exhibit 3.)

The Composite Container Division manufactured fiber cans used in packaging chemicals, garden products, and foods such as grated cheese and refrigerated biscuits, and paperboard cores used for such products as gift wrap and aluminum foil. Only a small proportion of the paperboard requirements of this division were supplied internally.

The Folding Carton Division manufactured printed folding paperboard cartons for the grocery, drug, housewares, and fast food industries. A substantial portion of this division's paperboard was produced at company mills.

The Equality Specialties Division manufactured braided elastic and nonelastic ties, cords, and bonds used in the packaging of jewelry, cosmetics, toys, and clothing. These products were produced on highspeed automated production lines, designed and constructed by Clevepak.

The paperboard and packaging category encompassed every stage of production, from collection of wastepaper to manufacture of the finished packaging product. Clevepak obtained 65 percent of its wastepaper needs through its own paper collection centers at each of its three mills, in neighboring communities and at a number of its converting plants. The collection centers were supplied by large producers of wastepaper such as municipalities, supermarkets, army bases, or factories with which the company contracted, and by individuals and groups who were paid by the ton at current market prices. Principal outside suppliers of wastepaper were dealers who acted as middlemen between wastepaper producers such as municipalities or businesses.

Paper that was received loose had to be sorted and baled into three basic categories: newsprint, corrugated, and mixed. The proportion of different types of paper determined the type of paper produced. Clevepak's primary product was chipboard, manufactured principally from low-grade mixed wastepaper. The finished paperboard was shipped to the Partition, Composite Container, or Folding Carton Division, or sold to outside customers. In 1975, 70 percent of the company's output was used internally.

Industrial Products

Five other divisions were classified under the industrial products line. The Clevaflex Division manufactured flexible tubing used principally as ductwork for heating and air conditioning systems; the Rex-Cut Division manufactured abrasive products used mainly in metalworking operations; the Amattco Division developed and manufactured control and efficiency devices for the garment industry; the Pollution Control Division produced vacuum devices for the movement of materials, liquids and gases, and water pollution treatment equipment; the Systems Engineering Division manufactured a variety of machinery used principally in the manufacture and assembly of shipping case partitions.

Clevepak also operated three research and product development facilities; one served the Composite Container and Folding Carton Divisions, another the paper mills, and a third the Partition Division.

CLEVEPAK'S GROWTH STRATEGY

The managers of Clevepak had always held that their company's strength was based on proprietary products and on products manufactured on proprietary equipment. The goal was to become a strong converter of paper products, rather than just a fringe producer. Over the years they had followed a strategy designed to strengthen the primary business in paperboard converting, while diversifying into related, but nonpaper businesses, chosen to offset the cyclicality of the paper business and to make a strong contribution to the firm's growth rate. Control of raw material sources was secured as soon as it was warranted by internal demand. Cost-effectiveness in the company's major product categories was stressed, and unprofitable operations divested.

Clevepak began to integrate its operation in the late 1960s. Management concluded that the company's major weakness was a dependence on outside suppliers for raw materials. Acquisition of a solid-fiber partition manufacturing company broadened the company's product base and increased usage of paperboard enough to justify internal manufacture of paper. The following year the company integrated further backward by purchasing its first paper recycling mill. Philip Green, vice president of planning, commented on the company's decision to begin paper production:

Raw material constitutes not only the largest, but the most volatile cost factor in paper production. If the market swings, there is likely to be much more fluctuation in the price of raw materials than say, packaging. The company can be hamstrung, because cost increases can not always be passed through. Very simply the company desired strength where it was most vulnerable. Two other factors worked in favor of

owning our own paperboard production capacity. Most of Clevepak's products require paperboard of a similar grade; secondly, recycling mills are less capital intensive than virgin pulp mills. Recycling requires fewer chemicals, less energy, and less water than production of pulp from virgin fiber. The absence of the heavy pulping chemicals used in virgin mills reduces the expense of pollution control.

About this time the company also received overtures from some major manufacturing companies. Merger presented interesting possibilities: under the wing of a large, well-funded company, Clevepak could expect more stable growth. The principal shareholders, who controlled more than half of the outstanding equity, could look forward to substantial financial gain. On the other hand Clevepak's growth potential looked promising as it was; it had the strong support of a major New York bank and an experienced administrative and financial staff. Higher risk was associated with remaining independent, but the personal and financial rewards were also greater.

Clevepak aggressively pursued acquisitions and internal expansion during the next few years. The following table summarizes the results:

Year	Acquisition or expansion
1967	A partition company; expanded product base to include solid fiber partitions.
1968	A paper recycling mill.
1969	Two partition plants.
	A company that produced molded abrasive products.
1970	A company that produced control equipment and other products used principally in the garment industry.
1972	The second paper recycling mill.
	A plant incorporating three partition manufacturing lines.
	A flexible tubing plant.
	Fifty percent ownership in a German manufacturer of solid fiber cases and partition.
1973	A paper products company including a paper recycling mill, three folding carton plants, and a wastepaper reclamation center.

Year	Acquisition or expansion
	A manufacturer of elastic and nonelastic cords, and metal and plastic attachments.
	A company engaged in the development and manufacture of equipment for producing elastic and nonelastic cords.
1974	A wastepaper processing operation.
1975	A wastepaper processing operation.

ORGANIZATIONAL DEVELOPMENTS

For the first eight years of its operation major decisionmaking at Clevepak was essentially in the hands of two people: William Green and Hugh McPherson. Green, one of the original investors, was responsible for administrative and marketing tasks. McPherson, a CPA, was hired shortly after the firm was founded to handle financial control and planning. As the record indicates this worked well for some time, although growth in volume and diversity of operations demanded development of a more extensive corporate staff, as well as formalized planning and control procedures. During the last five years several measures had been introduced, aimed at bringing more professional management to operations.

Raymond Cartledge, hired in 1971 as executive vice president and later promoted to president and chief executive officer, and Philip Green, as vice president for corporate planning, had major roles in instituting many of the new procedures. Discussing the differences between the Clevepak run by two people and the Clevepak managed by a corporate staff, Green noted: "More than anything else, professional management is planning; it is the reduction of the degree of risk or impulsive decisionmaking that takes place in a company."

Clevepak had grown primarily through acquisition; its divisions had been left to themselves to a great extent, operating as autonomous units. Two functional areas remained centralized in New York headquarters: financial and accounting procedures and computer information services. The last area had become a source of friction between divisional management and the corporate staff. The larger divisions argued that they should have their own computer facilities because the growth rate and volume of their sales had increased their needs for frequent and more detailed sales information. Corporate management maintained that control and cost efficiencies outweighed what advantages satellite computer capacity could provide, and had kept data processing a centralized activity. Recognizing at the same time the validity of divisional requests for more information, the firm created a new position of staff financial analyst, reporting to the vice president for finance. The analyst worked closely with divisional people to supply their needs for sales information in any form they required, by territory, representative, or product. Additionally outside consultants were hired to recommend changes to systems and help analyze the company's needs.

Operating Plan/Bonus System

Three years earlier, in 1972, a formal procedure for representation of operating goals had been established. The company had always strongly believed in management by objectives. It sought a way to introduce the concept in a very concrete form. A plan was established where most salaried employees, from salespersons to president, submitted their operating targets for the coming year. Each activity was weighted according to the importance of its accomplishment, with the total weight of all activities equalling 100. The targets were to be detailed, with quantitative descriptions of the goals and a list of other participants in each project. A salesperson, for example, could not just state that he would get five new accounts; he had to name each company and product, and establish a timetable.

The operating plan was submitted by every employee to his supervisor in early December. Supervisors rejected plans that were too easy or unattainable and sent them back for revision. An accepted plan was passed on to the next supervisory level until it reached division and finally corporate management where it was reviewed by Green and the president. The operating plan was introduced on a gradual basis. In the first year of its implementation it was required only of division managers and company officers in order to acquaint them with the concept and format. Green admitted that it was very difficult to get the scheme moving, that nobody believed in it, assuming that it was just another whim of corporate headquarters. The following year the production people were also asked to submit a plan. And, in the third, the sales force wrote their first plans, so that most salaried people were involved. Despite the skepticism with which they were greeted, operating plans became an integral part of the company administration, and were submitted regularly.

> The use of operating plans has enabled individuals in the company to get away from functioning by crisis or on a day-to-day level exclusively. The president keeps a copy of the company operating plan on his desk. Both the president and the board of directors feel much more attuned to what is developing throughout the company. With thirty plants this is a very difficult task; the operation plans set out in advance what goals each plant will be working toward.

Green noted some reasons why he thought this approach was appropriate to Clevepak: 1) the company is diverse; 2) it had expanded at a very rapid rate; and 3) it had added new professional management required to accommodate this diversity and growth. When asked if he used any quantitative indicators of the success of the program, Green replied that a measure like percentage completion for the company was meaningless, as it did not indicate profit or reflect external factors that might have influenced events during the year. "The ultimate test of an operating plan would be if a high degree of completion would exceed the corporate budget."

Percentage completion rate was used in another way by Clevepak. The individual operating plan, the divisional profit objective, and the corporate profit objectives were used to determine each employee's annual bonus, with each factor contributing one-third. Speaking about bonuses in general, Green noted that "it is hard to keep people just through salary. The bonus is based on what a person actually did

and reflects in a very real way his contribution to the corporation. It has the effect of motivating good people to stay and of applying pressure on those whose work is not up to par." A 75 percent completion rate was generally regarded as the minimum for each of the three factors. The use of three different incentives increased the opportunity to receive some bonus. For instance, if a person did not achieve a minimum completion rate on his individual operating plan, it would still be possible to receive a bonus based on divisional and corporate profitability. Adherence to the stated operating plan was considered very carefully in bonus calculation. It was considered more important to accomplish what one set out to do, than to take advantage of some unusual opportunity to the detriment of the original goals. A salesman, for example, might receive an unexpected opportunity to develop a new account. If he were to gain the account, but in the process neglect other accounts and planned tasks, the result of pursuing the unexpected account might be negative in the total context of the operating plan.

LONG-RANGE PLANNING

Clevepak had drawn up its first five-year plan two years earlier and was in the process of drawing up a new one. Green described long-range planning as

> a tool for evaluating the company's present position, and where it is headed two, three, and five years down the road. It sets out the general direction in which you plan to proceed in the future. The value of long-range planning is not in being close to any sales or income target you have established. The value is in looking at the plans in a year or two to see if the direction you set for yourself is the one you are on, and in your ability to evaluate if the direction is still the correct one for your company.

The original plan pinpointed personnel recruitment and development as areas that would require attention in the near future. Green explained some of the actions taken in order to plan more effectively in these areas.

Personnel Development

Responsibility for personnel and training was charged to the Industrial Relations Group (IRG). Two major developments had taken place at Clevepak in the past four years. The first was a method for developing the abilities and responding to the needs of people already in the organization. This procedure grew out of an evaluation that had been conducted twice yearly. The firm believed that employees should be evaluated for job satisfaction, as well as job performance. Employees were now asked to indicate to their supervisors if they would like to be considered as a candidate for another job within the company. A salesperson might want to be considered for plant supervisor, for example. This indication was then relayed to IRG, which also received information on openings from plant managers and others. The company felt that it was already making much more efficient use of knowledge within the system. Green noted that he had received very favorable responses from employees who welcomed the opportunity to move to other positions in the company. Even those who did not care to change jobs found it very flattering to be considered for a different position.

Management Development

A second problem that had recently concerned Clevepak was how to bring people into the system who could provide continuity in the event of illness or death of key members of divisional or corporate management. As Green put it,

> we were very aware of our weakness in this area—if something happened to any member, we would have no replacement. Our desire then was to get creative, bright people in a position to develop as the company develops. The question was how do you do this from a corporate standpoint? There was no question about the need for such a program. Getting more capable people into the system is a very critical part of a company's growth potential; it is a major determinant of the ease with which growth can occur.

In 1971 the first management trainee program had been established in one of the plants. In 1975 three divisions, Mill, Partition and Corporate, had such programs. A general timetable of eighteen months to two years was set up to train people out of college or MBA programs to a point where they could assume major operational responsibility. An employee in the plant manager training program was to be technically capable of running a plant within two years. Someone hired for corporate accounting and financial work might spend six months in headquarters then be sent to one of the larger paper mills as a comptroller. The goal was to immerse a person in what makes the company tick. Green stressed that it was difficult for a small company to get this sort of program off the ground and that it was still in its initial stages.

HEADQUARTERS MOVE

In 1975 the decision was made to move corporate headquarters to White Plains, New York. Some considered this the most important decision of the last five years; to others it was merely a nuisance. The new building would house the entire corporate headquarters: all corporate staff functions were to be located there, as well as the top divisional management teams. For division heads this would mean moving their families from all over the country. Green explained the reason behind the change:

> Rapid growth through acquisition has created a relatively autonomous division management structure. Some duplication of effort has resulted, as well as inefficient use of people, money, and time. For some division managers at distant locations too much time was spent on airplanes. The move is designed to improve the ability to respond quickly to events in a well-coordinated fashion. Furthermore, the talents of division people will be drawn into and used in other areas besides direct operational responsibility. For division people the corporate staff support will be far more accessible; the chairman and president, as well as financial, accounting and information services, will all be located together. This is an incredibly important move and will probably take a year to adjust to.

EXHIBIT 1

TEN YEAR FINANCIAL REVIEW
Consolidated Statement of Income

	Year Ended December 31		
	1974	1973	1972
Net Sales	$74,998,856	$53,595,776	$41,102,762
Cost of sales	58,838,625	42,733,168	31,682,141
	16,160,231	10,862,608	9,420,621
Selling and administrative expenses	6,069,045	5,262,913	4,195,696
Income from operations	10,091,186	5,599,695	5,224,925
Interest expense	1,625,186	444,795	75,925
Income before taxes on income	8,466,000	5,154,900	5,149,000
Provision for taxes on income	4,034,000	2,344,000	2,481,000
Net Income	$ 4,432,000	$ 2,810,900	$ 2,668,000
Per share data			
Average common shares outstanding[a]	1,620,000	1,620,000	1,619,085
Net income per share	$ 2.74	$ 1.74	$ 1.65
Dividends paid per share	$ .60	$ .45	—
Shareholder's equity per share	$16.50	$14.36	$13.08
Financial position			
Current assets	$18,575,631	$16,922,600	$ 9,262,632
Current liabilities	6,179,465	8,469,074	2,891,874
Working capital	12,396,216	8,453,526	6,370,758
Property plant and equipment	21,709,072	20,390,078	10,980,731
Other assets	7,805,443	7,249,142	5,673,133
Total	$41,990,731	$36,092,746	$23,024,622
Long-term debt	$13,391,528	$11,251,543	$ 528,319
Deferred taxes on income	1,875,500	1,577,500	1,314,500
Shareholder's equity	26,723,703	23,263,703	21,181,803
Total	$41,990,731	$36,092,746	$23,024,622
Additional data			
Net sales increase over preceding year	40%	30%	5%
Net income increase over preceding year	53%	5%	18%
Return on shareholders' average equity employed	18%	13%	13%
Depreciation and amortization	$ 2,467,113	$ 1,569,649	$ 1,338,441
Capital expenditures, net	$ 3,100,125	$ 2,671,735	$ 1,696,951
Percent of long-term debt to shareholder's equity	50%	48%	2%
Percent of long-term debt to total capitalization	33%	33%	2%

[a]After stock splits in 1966 and 1968.

			Year Ended December 31			
1971	1970	1969	1968	1967	1966	1965
$39,284,706	$35,351,171	$33,058,921	$32,678,924	$22,667,189	$13,183,590	$10,951,579
30,691,616	27,374,494	26,112,051	25,796,147	18,262,254	10,852,950	9,279,905
8,593,090	7,976,677	6,946,870	6,882,777	4,404,935	2,330,640	1,671,674
4,009,721	3,292,019	3,175,426	2,723,712	2,138,883	1,167,436	1,013,071
4,583,369	4,684,658	3,771,444	4,159,065	2,266,052	1,163,204	658,603
148,022	224,911	229,255	398,434	207,719	93,988	91,589
4,435,047	4,459,747	3,542,189	3,760,631	2,058,333	1,069,216	567,014
2,170,347	2,233,747	1,645,089	1,916,616	952,770	518,462	244,000
$ 2,265,000	$ 2,226,000	$ 1,897,100	$ 1,844,015	$ 1,105,563	$ 550,764	$ 323,014
1,619,000	1,577,462	1,552,462	1,282,173	1,103,700	1,000,000	1,000,000
$ 1.40	$ 1.41	$1.22	$1.44	$1.00	$ .55	$0.32
—	—	—	—	—	—	—
$11.42	$10.29	$8.45	$8.49	$3.11	$1.98	$1.43
$ 7,691,993	$ 7,146,981	$ 6,185,000	$ 8,277,973	$ 6,265,883	$ 3,016,058	$ 2,553,651
2,721,838	3,002,854	2,653,401	4,387,657	3,121,794	1,180,882	1,136,616
4,970,155	4,144,127	3,531,599	3,890,316	3,144,080	1,835,176	1,417,035
10,622,220	10,332,819	10,023,986	6,507,765	4,864,394	1,805,764	1,642,282
5,077,751	4,530,056	2,928,375	2,477,348	2,310,050	20,674	25,033
$20,670,126	$19,007,002	$16,483,960	$12,875,429	$10,318,533	$ 3,661,614	$ 3,087,350
$ 1,000,000	$ 1,815,876	$ 2,634,834	$ 1,578,793	$ 6,040,901	$ 1,577,500	$ 1,600,000
1,174,000	960,000	669,000	408,000	243,000	103,000	57,000
18,496,126	16,231,126	13,180,126	10,888,636	3,434,632	1,981,114	1,430,350
$20,670,126	$19,007,002	$16,483,960	$12,875,429	$10,318,533	$ 3,661,614	$ 3,087,350
11%	7%	1%	44%	72%	20%	8%
2%	17%	3%	67%	101%	71%	93%
13%	15%	16%	37%	41%	39%	29%
$ 1,129,260	$ 969,200	$ 723,487	$ 512,781	$ 333,511	$ 183,785	$ 159,721
$ 1,418,661	$ 1,278,033	$ 4,239,708	$ 2,156,118	$ 3,389,731	$ 344,268	$ 330,447
5%	11%	20%	14%	193%	80%	112%
5%	10%	17%	13%	66%	44%	53%

EXHIBIT 2

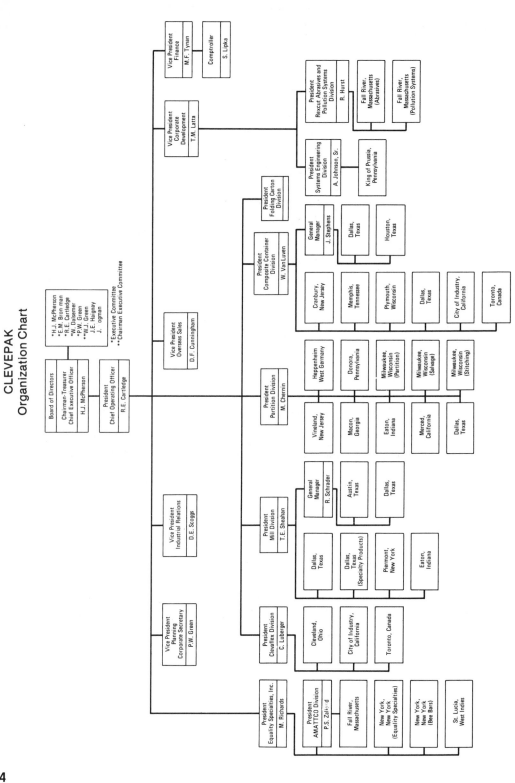

CLEVEPAK
Organization Chart

EXHIBIT 3

PARTITION DIVISION

Partitions are paperboard dividers used in shipping cases to provide protection for glass, plastic, and aerosol containers used by the beverage, food, and household product industries. Partitions can be of two types: corrugated or solid fiber. The corrugated partition is made by sandwiching a fluted layer of paperboard between two solid plies. The partitions are saw cut and the size cannot be matched exactly to the container. The fluting is designed to be flexible but may be crushed at some point during shipping and from then on offers greatly reduced protection against damage and breakage. The market for partitions is estimated to be $255 million, of which $165 million to $175 million is in corrugated; the rest is solid fiber. The solid fiber partitions are a relatively new product and represent several advantages over corrugated partitions. Die cutting permits production of a very exact size partition, is not easily crushed, and performs a superior job of protecting the containers. As they are less bulky, more containers can be packed in a given shipping case. They require 8 to 15 percent less paper than the three layered corrugated. Additional savings result from reduced warehouse space; solid fiber partitions require only about 20 to 25 percent of the total warehouse space

for the same number of corrugated partitions.

Despite its advantages, solid fiber accounts for only 20 to 30 percent of the partition market. This is explained by tradition and regulation. Solid fiber is relatively young and many partition users are simply reluctant to switch from tried and true corrugated. Part of the reluctance, particularly for glass containers, stems from ICC Regulation 41, which tightly controls rail and truck shipments. Until recently, the pertinent regulation specified that corrugated partitions must be used to qualify for insurance on certain products, such as liquor. This regulation was amended in 1975 and several new markets have now opened to solid fiber.

Many glass container manufacturers also produce their own partitions. Because they are equipped to produce corrugated and because they also are the major partition users, the switch to solid fiber is slow and generally accomplished when customers directly specify that they be used.

Nevertheless, the market for solid fiber partitions is estimated to be growing at twice the rate of the entire partitions market. Green estimated that Clevepak accounts for over 50 percent of solid fiber sales.

EXHIBIT 4

COMPOSITE CONTAINERS

The Composite Container Division manufactures composite can and paperboard cores in six plants in the United States and Canada. Composite cans are used in packaging a wide range of food, chemical, and other products including cocoa, grated cheese, and snack foods. Paperboard cores are used for such products as gift wrap, plastic films, and aluminum foil. The capabilities of the division include the combination of paperboard and metallic foils, or plastic films, using high speed

manufacturing techniques, on equipment largely developed by the company.

In addition to the raw materials of paperboard adhesives and liners and wrappers, several others are used in container and core products. Tinplate, aluminum, and plastics are used as ends for composite containers. The company fabricates substantially all of its metal ends but purchases its plastic ends externally, generally under contract from suppliers using Clevepak's molds.

JOHNSON CONTROL, INC.

By late September 1974 time had run out and Project Manager John Riley was faced with a critical decision concerning one of his division's major projects—the Eastern Electric contract. With a bachelor's degree in engineering, supplemented by additional academic and on-the-job managerial training and more than ten years' experience in the construction industry, Riley had negotiated many previous contracts as important as this one. However, the Eastern Electric contract was particularly critical because of the difficulties that the other divisions of the company had experienced during the year. Riley knew that senior management would be especially concerned if this contract were lost.

Riley was assigned to the Systems Engineering and Construction Division (SECD), which had been established in 1961 by Johnson Control to meet the needs of a new and growing field of instrumentation systems installation (ISI). Prior to this ISI-type work had been performed by the many varied specialty contractors throughout the United States. This new market opportunity developed as technological changes outmoded traditional methods of installing plant instrumentation. The company management recognized the need for a systems-oriented organization to serve this specialized field and SECD was their response. The chart below capsulizes Johnson Control's concept of SECD.

SECD organized, designed, installed and maintained sophisticated instrumentation systems. When dealing with a particular customer,

This case was prepared by George Pfender under the supervision of Professor Jules J. Schwartz as the basis for discussion rather than to illustrate either effective or ineffective handling of an administrative action.

The SECD Systems-Oriented Organization

With undivided responsibility for:

- Planning
- Installing
- Servicing

ISI *capabilities* include:

- Engineering
- Project management
- Fabrication of panels and racks
- Construction management
- Calibration/service/maintenance

it often served as integrator of the various other manufacturing and fabricating divisions.

ISI work consisted of pneumatic, electric/electronic, and speciality piping and wiring systems. The primary markets served were power generating plants (the majority of 1973 sales were to this market), process industries such as pulp and paper mills, chemical and petrochemical processing operations, water and waste treatment facilities, and aerospace and defense facilities.

The total estimated volume for ISI work done in 1973 was $94 million. This volume was distributed as shown in the table below. The

1973 Instrumentation Systems Market

Company	Market Share (%)
Johnson Control, Inc.	10–15
Honeywell	8–10
Mercury Piping (Div. of Fischbach & Moore)	5–7
Fischer & Porter	4–5
Others	73–63

SECD Eastern Division volume for 1973 was approximately $10 million.

COMPANY HISTORY

Johnson Control, Inc. began with the thermostat. In 1885 Professor Johnson invented it in his one-room shop, and opened the Johnson Electric Service Company. Since this humble beginning the thrust of Johnson Control, Inc. (name changed in 1902 and 1974) had been in controlling energy. The growth of the company had been comparable to the rate of growth in energy consumption in the United States economy, as well as the growth of increasingly sophisticated scientific technologies.

By 1974 Johnson Control had grown into nine basic divisions with twenty-one manufacturing facilities operating in the United States and abroad. A description of the nine operating divisions is presented in Exhibit 1. See Exhibit 2 for Johnson's "Fortune 500" rankings. A list of subsidiaries and offices is presented in Exhibit 3. A dynamic and aggressive company, Johnson Control had achieved record sales for twenty-seven consecutive years prior to 1973. A ten-year financial summary is shown in Exhibit 4.

In the 1973 Annual Report, Fred Brengel, president of Johnson Control, commented on the 1973 results of the company and the prospects for 1974:

> For the twenty-seventh consecutive year we are reporting a record sales volume. Earnings, however, are 10 percent below the record set in 1972. In the past we have mentioned the pressure on margins in the installed systems portion of our business. This situation, coupled with increasing costs of labor and material that could not be passed on, led to decreased profits. ... If the energy shortage causes an economic slowdown in 1974, this could affect a number of the markets in which our units operate. New commercial construction may slow down, which could affect the Johnson and Penn Divisions. On the other hand, Associated Piping, Kieley & Mueller, and our Industrial Contracting Division, with their involvement in the power generation and petrochemical field, should continue to enjoy strong markets.

INTERNAL ORGANIZATION

The division manager had direct responsibility for maintaining the efficiency of his operating units and for the overall financial results of the division. Because SECD's policy was to provide a systems-oriented package with unit responsibility to the client, it used a team approach with the project manager as the focal point. The SECD organization is shown in Exhibit 5. The basic operating unit within SECD was the division. The division was primarily a geographic unit. In mid-1974, there were three operating divisions in SECD.

The project manager had complete financial responsibility for one or more projects. His annual compensation was based upon the profitability of contracts under his responsibility. Because of the importance of his position, he was required to have broad experience in business disciplines, such as contract law, accounting and labor relations, and the additional areas of expertise noted in the diagram below.

Project Manager

Qualifications	Duties & Functions
Business disciplines	Initiator of actions (as required)
	Complete financial responsibility
	Estimating
	Planning
Proven capability	Forecasting costs
	Engineering
	Procurement
	Contract administration
Broad construction experience	Construction management

The project manager maintained control of project costs by weekly monitoring of field and office reports and accounting records. He was expected to control business spending to keep operating expenses at the lowest achievable level. In the event any problems occurred on a project, he was required to "... take immediate and decisive corrective action and to keep the division manager informed at all times of the project status. ..."

Before starting a project the project manager and project superintendent prepared a thorough analysis of the entire effort. All phases of the job were evaluated, labor and material requirements were estimated, itemized work schedules were developed, and a detailed cash-flow analysis was forecast for material, labor, and other direct project costs. From this detailed analysis a project planning and control systems schedule was developed. This schedule was programmed into a computer reporting system.

Thereafter during the course of the project weekly data from the field office, pertaining to man-hours used and units of the project completed, were reported to the computer and compared to the original project plan. These weekly reports depicted labor efficiency as man-hours used compared to man-hours originally estimated, and progress as a percentage of project completed. These reports were commonly referred to as "LEAP" reports (Labor Efficiency and Progress). Each manager received the report weekly. Exhibit 6 is a typical LEAP report. The overall project planning and control system and the information inputs are shown in Exhibit 7.

Because plant construction was so complex, it was not uncommon for an owner/builder to have several contractors working side by side on any given project. The project manager had to coordinate SECD's work with the owner/builder's in-house engineering effort and the other engineering being done by other contractors and consultants.

Complicated instrumentation systems required increasingly greater numbers of sophisticated components. The project manager had to assure the timely procurement of critical components required for projects under his supervision. He also supervised vendor evaluation and selection, requisitions, purchase orders, submittals, vendor inspection, and receiving of material and components.

The policy of SECD was to contract to do work on either a fixed-price or forced-account basis. The forced-account contract was often referred to as a cost-plus contract. On any

particular project, the type of contract and terms depended on factors that applied to the individual project, such as allocation of risk, completeness of design, schedule, field labor conditions, type of competition and the accuracy to which cost data could be estimated.

A number of methods were used to estimate costs for a particular contract. One of the more common ones, used by companies that had operating experience and good cost accounting records, was to aggregate both direct and indirect costs into a single hourly figure, which was then applied to the estimated man-hours required to complete the contract.

Once the type of contract was agreed upon and SECD was awarded the contract, it was the project manager's job to compare it for agreement with the bid documents. These documents provided the basis for establishing the overall cost of the project. The bid documents usually consisted of extensive blueprints, engineering drawings, and work timetables; but for some projects they might be only a group of sketches and drawings.

The project manager had to examine the "boiler plate" (fine print of the contract) to determine whether any questionable items required further negotiation. He had to decide whether any construction schedule incorporated in the contract was in accord with his prior estimating, planning, and scheduling procedures. He also had to evaluate the terms of payment to assure compatibility with the scheduled costs and to assure a positive cash flow throughout the project.

As the leader of the SECD team the project manager had to bring together the experience, methods, materials, and manpower to ensure that the project ran smoothly and on schedule. It was essential that he remain in contact with each project. To accomplish this, he visited each project field site periodically during the construction work to demonstrate his interest in both the work and the personnel. He also used these visits to evaluate the progress of the project and to become familiar with new construction practices. During these visits he set time aside for additional contacts with the client and his personnel to insure their satisfaction.

The project superintendent provided the on-site management for the SECD team. He was involved with the administration of the day-by-day site activities. He provided necessary information to the SECD management team and also served as the project manager's representative on the job site. His normal duties and functions are shown in the following diagram. Under unusual circumstances he might also perform certain functions usually done by the project manager.

Project Superintendent

Qualifications	Duties & Functions
Strong, dynamic leader	Planning
	Mobilizing
	Staffing
	Labor relations
Long construction experience	Material contracting
	Reporting
	Labor supervision
	For maximum productivity
	For quality workmanship
Specialist in instrumentation	

A NEW PROSPECT

In May 1973 Design Engineers & Construction, Inc., (D–E), one of America's top construction companies, specializing in the design, management, and construction of manufacturing process and utility plants, contacted SECD. D–E asked that SECD's Eastern Division office, which was based in Philadelphia, bid on a proposal to install a sulphur dioxide abatement system for an existing electrical generating unit owned by the Eastern Electric Company. The abatement project had an estimated contract value of approximately $70,000.

D–E was the prime contractor for the entire project, operating on a forced-account contract with Eastern Electric. The job consisted of building construction and installation of two new turbine-generator sets, as well as auxiliary equipment, with an estimated value in excess of $500 million. D–E called in SECD because it did not have the resources available at the time to perform the required specialized instrumentation systems work. SECD was on the preferred bidders list as a result of previous work it had done for D–E and because Johnson Control had a good reputation in the industry for quality work and on-time projects completion.

Anticipating the contract for the abatement system in July 1973, John Riley, the SECD project manager in charge, called on representatives of the local craft labor union office to discuss local labor availability. The response from the unions was favorable, even though the Eastern Electric project, along with several other major construction projects in process in the area, was causing a serious drain on manpower.

By mid-August a decision had still not been reached concerning the awarding of the sulfur dioxide abatement system contract. Riley visited the management of D–E to request at least an indication of when they would make the award. He was also interested in performing some of the installation work associated with the two new generating units and took advantage of the occasion to inquire about this work also. He received a negative response to both inquiries: D–E had not settled on a contractor for the additional abatement systems and it felt, because of the tight construction schedule, there would not be sufficient time for SECD to prepare a comprehensive proposal.

On September 3, 1973, Johnson Control received the order to start work on the abatement project. Within a week SECD had established a trailer office at the field site and had begun work. The project was scheduled to take six months.

By the first week of January 1974 the pace of the project had slowed perceptibly and the completion date had been extended. The delay was attributed in part to the impact of the energy crisis and to the resulting likelihood of a later completion date for the entire power plant. The SECD project superintendent who had directed the project was transferred at this time. Riley immediately assigned Ed Paulson, a capable and experienced young man, to this important position. Paulson began to institute several changes on the job.

D–E managed the total project, so it monitored SECD for compliance to contracted terms and quality of work performed. Because the D–E supervisor responsible for SECD's work seemed to have little appreciation for the scope of work performed by the SECD team and required detailed negotiation for each "extra work" item, Paulson requested that D–E assign someone new to the project.

Extra work items were those that SECD was asked to perform that had not been included in the original scope of the contract. Due to the difficulty of estimating and interpreting each detail of a job beforehand and because of the changing requirements of the prime contractor, it was not uncommon to encounter a number of extra work items. Payment for these items was generally provided for in the contract terms and conditions.

A new supervisor from D–E was appointed. Working closely with him, Paulson began to obtain positive results and feedback with respect to the productivity and quality of work done.

During the initial stages of SECD's work on the site a problem arose. The teamsters local union had not ratified its labor contract and to demonstrate their cause, the members decided to strike. Although the strike was not directed at SECD, it did prevent material deliveries to the job site. By the second week of the strike, SECD's stockpiles were dangerously low.

Fortunately, as a result of Ed Paulson's persuasive ability, the teamsters permitted minor material deliveries to SECD. These deliveries proved enough to keep SECD personnel productive until the strike was ended several weeks later.

In early February the abatement system area received an unannounced inspection by a group of five D–E supervisors and managers. Their tour was brief and they did not take time to discuss the project with any of the SECD personnel.

During the third week of April the D–E supervisor discreetly discussed local manpower availability with Paulson. He asked how fast personnel could be mobilized, should additional work be required. Paulson reported the conversation to Riley.

On Friday morning of the third week in April SECD received an urgent request for a proposal pertaining to the instrumentation systems work for Unit #1, the new boiler-turbine-generator set and its auxiliary equipment. Apparently a deadline had been established for completion and operation of the first unit.

Both Riley and Paulson were optimistic about the request. Estimating such a job, however, required a considerable effort by qualified people. Both men, as well as one SECD project engineer familiar with this particular project, started on the estimate immediately. Working nonstop through the weekend, they drafted a preliminary estimate.

The proposal called for an initial labor requirement in excess of 12,000 man-hours. It was submitted late Monday evening. A week later, although the entire scope of the project had still not been detailed, D–E authorized SECD to begin work on the project and provided $250,000 for the initial phases of the work. "Boil out" on the boiler section, which produces steam to drive the turbine-generator, was scheduled for July 31; "steam to turbine" was scheduled for August 30. SECD was to plan its workload to accommodate these critical schedules.

By the end of the second week the preliminary estimate was revised to include greater detail. The labor requirements were estimated to be in excess of 29,000 man-hours. A project planning control system analysis for this starting phase was drawn up to provide planning assistance. This chart is shown in Exhibit 6.

It was not until mid-June that all the paperwork related to estimating, bidding, and signing the final contract was completed. The final forced-account contract was valued in excess of $1.2 million, not including the work done on the abatement system. The SECD division manager in charge of the Philadelphia office was very pleased with the results obtained through the intensive efforts of Riley and Paulson, who were working under the pressure of time and adverse labor-market conditions.

The significance of this contract to SECD and to Johnson Control becomes apparent from a reading of the 1974 six-month interim report of the company. In the report Fred Brengel commented on the operating results of the company:

> Net earnings for the first six months of 1974 were $950,000 compared to $4,321,000 for 1973. Earnings per share were 22¢ for 1974 versus $1.00 for 1973. These earnings were based on sales of $105,298,000 in 1974 and $113,530,000 in 1973.[1]
>
> On a quarterly basis we had a loss for the second quarter of 1974 of $355,000 or 8¢ per share on sales of $51,907,000. For the same period of 1973 we had earnings of $2,155,000, earnings per share of 50¢ and sales of $60,217,000.
>
> The loss for the second quarter was primarily a result of a ten-week strike that was settled June 10 at our Georgetown, Kentucky, facility. ...
>
> Rapid inflation has put other pressures on our margins that we have taken steps to correct. In the installed systems contracting business, the majority of our backlog is fixed price contracts that do not include any escalation clause. We are attempting to mitigate the deleterious effect by reorganization and introducing new fiscal control systems. On new work, we are factoring projected increases for labor and material into our bidding process. Material cost increases in our noninstalled business have been offset by price increases that have been put into effect and should improve third quarter results of these units.
>
> Although the second quarter was an extremely difficult one for the company, we are encouraged by the fact that incoming business remains strong with new orders ahead of the same period last year by approximately 20 percent. The individual markets of our Systems Engineering Construction Division and our Power and Process Piping Division (Associated Piping & Engineering Corp.)

[1] Inventory accounting at Johnson Control is on a FIFO basis. In accounting for long-term construction contracts, the completed-contract method of accounting is used.

are exceptionally strong and are becoming an increasingly important segment of Johnson Control, Inc.

Manpower requirements on the Eastern Electric Unit #1 project peaked during July at eighty craft-labor workers plus five SECD personnel, including Paulson, two project engineers, a purchasing agent, and a timekeeper/accountant. By August the end of the project was in sight, and both Riley and Paulson became increasingly concerned over whether SECD would be retained as subcontractor for the instrumentation systems work on Unit #2.

Paulson started to discuss the upcoming work on Unit #2 with the D-E supervisors on the site. Riley also took each opportunity available to him to contact D-E management about the project. Their approaches received only vague and noncommittal responses. However, D-E did indicate that Eastern Electric was considering a fixed-cost contract on a competitive bid basis for the instrumentation systems work to be done on Unit #2. Riley was not pleased when he heard this.

During early September the project rapidly neared completion. Paulson demobilized both manpower and equipment to minimize unnecessary expenses. He tried to keep qualified workers, as they would be a critical asset if SECD were awarded the contract for the second unit. The D-E supervisors still would not tell him if further work would be awarded.

Paulson suggested to Riley that the SECD marketing manager call on Eastern Electric to discuss Unit #2 and impress upon the utility company the advantages in retaining SECD for this work. The marketing manager stressed past performance and on-time quality completions, familiarity with plant site and instrumentation requirements, manpower availability, offices already on site, and partial material inventory already on hand. Because of extended suppliers' schedules, Paulson had accumulated a partial inventory to provide for job continuity.

During the course of the call the marketing manager learned that Eastern Electric had applied to the Public Utilities Commission for a rate increase of $112 million. The hearings before the PUC were expected to last another four to six weeks. Although they were not sure, both Riley and Paulson felt Eastern Electric might be delaying the decision to continue with Unit #2 because of financial problems.

Unfortunately Eastern Electric was not the only company feeling increasing pressures on profit margins. Riley and Paulson, with the best job planning and scheduling possible, estimated they could remain on the site no later than October 4. Then all work would be completed and they would have to lay off their remaining workers and leave. Exhibit 8 shows

the job mobilization/demobilization schedule.

On Monday, September 23, Riley met with Paulson at the construction site to review the situation. There had been as yet no response from either Eastern Electric or D–E regarding Unit #2. A decision would have to be made soon. Both men realized that their division manager would be calling them for a status report by Friday. They had already told him that Unit #2 represented the opportunity for an additional $1.2 million or more in potential volume. As the meeting ended the only alternative Riley and Paulson could agree on was not to make a decision yet, but rather to wait just a few more days.

EXHIBIT 1

JOHNSON CONTROL, INC.
Operating Divisions

CONTROL VALUE DIVISION

Products manufactured by Kieley & Mueller, Inc., are diaphragm-operated control valves, displacement-level controllers, and pressure regulators.

ELECTRONIC SPECIALTIES

The Pioneer Electric & Research Corporation manufactures electronic communications and data processing systems primarily in support of the other company divisions. Additional products are produced for various electrical/electronic markets.

JOHNSON CONTROLS INTERNATIONAL

Australia
Belgium
England
France
Holland
Hong Kong/Singapore
Italy
Japan

JOHNSON CONTROLS INTERNATIONAL (cont.)

Mexico
Scotland
South Africa
South America
Switzerland
West Germany

JOHNSON CONTROLS LTD./LTEE

Canada

PENN DIVISION

Penn manufactures a complete line of automatic temperature, pressure and flow controls for air conditioning, refrigeration, commercial and residential heating, water pumping, and gas burning equipment. The division is dedicated to energy conservation. In 1974 it introduced a new line of solid state, electronic spark ignition systems that ignite the pilot in gas furnaces each time a demand is applied to the system, then automatically turns it off, thus eliminating fuel wastage.

EXHIBIT 1 (cont.)

JOHNSON CONTROL, INC.
Operating Divisions

JOHNSON CONTROLS INTERNATIONAL & JOHNSON CONTROLS LTD./LTEE. (CANADA)

These two divisions offer a selection of systems, programs, and services to assure efficient and economical operation of building environmental systems such as heating, ventilation, air conditioning, life safety, and security control. Johnson Controls is also dedicated to energy conservation. In 1974 it introduced two new products. One, an optimal start programmer that activates heating equipment in two stages (with and without fresh air) in direct response to outside conditions. Second, a controller that compares humidity and temperature of both internal and external air and decides what proportions of each should be used to facilitate the most economical cooling of a structure.

POWER & PROCESS PIPING

Associated Piping and Engineering Corporation and Western Piping manufacture piping and related hardware for fossil fuel and nuclear power plants.

PROTECTIVE SYSTEMS

Consisting of Central Station of Milwaukee, Southern Burglar Alarm, and Standard Electric Time, the division manufactures, sells, and supervises the installation of fire alarm systems and smoke detectors for schools and offices, as well as commercial and industrial buildings. These systems are often used in conjunction with the control system offered by the other divisions.

SYSTEMS & SERVICE

Systems and Services is the largest division of Johnson Controls, Inc. Staffed and equipped to design, specify, build, install, and then contract to maintain any building automation or instrumentation system anywhere, the division has been involved in the construction of more buildings than any other firm in the world. These buildings are equipped with an automation system that goes far beyond the ordinary heating, ventilating, air conditioning, fire safety, and security controls. All these systems are monitored and regulated from a central location for maximum utilization of energy and manpower.

EXHIBIT 2

JOHNSON CONTROL, INC.
1973 "Fortune 500" Rankings

Categories		Ranking
Sales	$231,434,000	462
Assets	$142,015,000	462
Net income	$ 10,194,000	369
Sales margin	4.4%	222
Return on equity	13.3%	130

EXHIBIT 3

JOHNSON CONTROL, INC.
Office & Subsidiaries

SUBSIDIARIES

JOHNSON CONTROLS
INTERNATIONAL, INC.
Milwaukee, Wisconsin

STANDARD ELECTRIC TIME CORP.
Springfield, Massachusetts

KIELEY & MUELLER, INC.
Middletown, New York

KIELEY & MUELLER LTD.
Montreal, Quebec, Canada

ASSOCIATED PIPING &
ENGINEERING CORP.
Compton, California

THE PIONEER ELECTRIC AND
RESEARCH CORP.
Forest Park, Illinois

JOHNSON CENTRAL SERVICE OF
ILLINOIS, INC.
Lincolnwood, Illinois

SOUTHERN BURGLAR ALARM OF
GEORGIA, INC.
Atlanta, Georgia

COMMERCIAL POLICE ALARM CO.,
INC.
Milwaukee, Wisconsin

REGIONAL OFFICES

Atlanta, Georgia
Chicago, Illinois
   (Lincolnwood)
Cleveland, Ohio
Dallas, Texas
   (Carrollton)
Denver, Colorado
Los Angeles, California
   (Compton)
Milwaukee, Wisconsin
   (Butler)
New York, New York
   (Long Island City)
Philadelphia, Pennsylvania
San Francisco, California
   (Burlingame)

U.S. SALES OFFICES

ALABAMA
Birmingham
Mobile

ALASKA
Anchorage

ARIZONA
Phoenix

ARKANSAS
Little Rock

CALIFORNIA
Fresno
Los Angeles
   (Compton)
Sacramento
San Diego
San Francisco

COLORADO
Denver

CONNECTICUT
Hartford
New Haven
   (Orange)

DISTRICT OF COLUMBIA
Washington
   (Arlington, Va.)

FLORIDA
Jacksonville
Miami
Orlando
Tampa

GEORGIA
Albany
Atlanta

HAWAII
Honolulu

ILLINOIS
Aurora
Chicago
   (Downers Grove)
   (Lincolnwood)
Chicago South
   (Lansing)
Moline
Peoria
Rockford

INDIANA
Fort Wayne
   (New Haven)
Goshen
Indianapolis
South Bend

IOWA
Cedar Rapids
Des Moines

KANSAS
Wichita

KENTUCKY
Louisville

LOUISIANA
Baton Rouge
New Orleans

MAINE
Portland
   (South Portland)

MARYLAND
Baltimore
   (Owings Mills)

MASSACHUSETTS
Boston
   (Woburn)
   (Brookfield)
Springfield
   (West Springfield)

MICHIGAN
Detroit
   (Ferndale)
Grand Rapids
Saginaw

MINNESOTA
Duluth
Minneapolis

MISSISSIPPI
Jackson

MISSOURI
Kansas City
Kansas City
   (Lee's Summit)
St. Louis

MONTANA
Great Falls

NEBRASKA
Omaha

NEW JERSEY
Cedar Grove
Union

NEW MEXICO
Albuquerque

NEW YORK
Albany
Binghamton
Buffalo
New York
   (Long Island City)
Rochester
Syracuse

NORTH CAROLINA
Charlotte
Greensboro
Raleigh
Wilmington

NORTH DAKOTA
Fargo

OHIO
Akron
Cincinnati
Cleveland
Cleveland
   (Brecksville)
Columbus
Dayton
   (Moraine City)
Toledo
Youngstown
   (Canfield)

OKLAHOMA
Oklahoma City
Tulsa

EXHIBIT 3 (cont.)

JOHNSON CONTROL, INC.
Office & Subsidiaries

OREGON
Portland

PENNSYLVANIA
Erie
Harrisburg
(Camp Hill)
Philadelphia
Pittsburgh
Wilkes-Barre

PUERTO RICO
San Juan
(Hato Rey)

RHODE ISLAND
Providence

SOUTH CAROLINA
Columbia
Greenville

SOUTH DAKOTA
Sioux Falls

TENNESSEE
Knoxville
Memphis
Nashville

TEXAS
Austin
Dallas
(Carrollton)
El Paso
Fort Worth
Houston
Lubbock
San Antonio

UTAH
Salt Lake City

VERMONT
Burlington

VIRGINIA
Fairfax
Norfolk
Richmond
Roanoke

WASHINGTON
Seattle
Spokane

WEST VIRGINIA
Charleston
(South Charleston)

WISCONSIN
Appleton
La Crosse
Madison
Milwaukee
Milwaukee
(Butler)

INTERNATIONAL OPERATIONS

JOHNSON CONTROLS INTERNATIONAL, INC.
Milwaukee, Wisconsin

ARGENTINA
Penn Controls Argentina S.A.I.C.
(Buenos Aires)

AUSTRALIA
SALES OFFICES
Adelaide
Melbourne
Perth
Sydney

BELGIUM
S.A. Johnson Control N.V.
Brussels
Voorschoten
(Holland)

CANADA
Johnson Controls Ltd./Ltee.
Main Office (Toronto, Ont.)
SALES OFFICES
Calgary, Alberta
Edmonton, Alberta
Halifax, Nova Scotia
(Dartmouth)
Hamilton, Ontario
(Burlington)
London, Ontario
Montreal, Quebec
Ottawa, Ontario
Quebec City, Quebec
Regina, Saskatchewan
Toronto, Ontario
Vancouver, British Columbia
Winnipeg, Manitoba
Penn Controls, Limited
Main Office (Scarborough, Ontario)
Unelco, Limited
Main Office (Pointe Claire, Quebec)

ENGLAND
Johnson Control Systems Ltd.
Main Office (Leatherhead, Surrey)
SALES OFFICES
Leatherhead, Surrey
London
Manchester
Glasgow

FRANCE
Johnson Control France S.A.R.L.
Main Office (Courbevoie)
SALES OFFICES
Courbevoie
La Garenne Colombes
Lille
Lyon
Paris
Toulouse

NEW ZEALAND
Penn Controls NZ Ltd.
(Christchurch)

WEST GERMANY
Johnson Controls A.G.
Main Office (Geneva, Switzerland)
Operational Headquarters
(Frankfurt, Germany)
SALES OFFICES
Cologne
Hamburg
Munich
Stuttgart

HOLLAND
Penn Controls Nederland, B.V.
(Leeuwarden)

HONG KONG

ITALY
Johnson Control S.p.A.
Technical Office (Milan)
SALES OFFICES
Milan
Rome

JAPAN
Saginomiya Johnson Controls Co. Ltd.
Main Office (Tokyo)
SALES OFFICES
Fukuoka
Hokkaido
Osaka
Tohoku
Tokyo
Saginomiya-Penn Controls (Japan) Ltd.
Main Office (Tokyo)

MEXICO
Controls Joseco S.A. de C.V.
Mexico, D.F.

SWITZERLAND
Johnson Controls S.A./A.G.
Headquarters European Operations
(Geneva)
SALES OFFICES
Geneva
Zurich

MANUFACTURING FACILITIES

BUENOS AIRES, ARGENTINA
CARROLLTON, TEXAS
CHRISTCHURCH, NEW ZEALAND
CLEARFIELD, UTAH
COMPTON, CALIFORNIA
FOREST PARK, ILLINOIS
GEORGETOWN, KENTUCKY
GOSHEN, INDIANA
HOUSTON, TEXAS
LEEUWARDEN, THE NETHERLANDS
LOMAGNA, ITALY
LOS ANGELES, CALIFORNIA
MIDDLETOWN, NEW YORK
MILWAUKEE, WISCONSIN
POINTE CLAIRE, QUEBEC, CANADA
POTEAU, OKLAHOMA
SCARBOROUGH, ONTARIO, CANADA
SPRINGFIELD, MASSACHUSETTS
TOKYO, JAPAN
TORONTO, ONTARIO, CANADA
WATERTOWN, WISCONSIN

EXHIBIT 4

JOHNSON CONTROL, INC.
Ten-Year Financial Summary

	1973	1972ᵃ	1971	1970	1969
Net Sales, Income, and Dividends					
Net sales	$251,187,000	$231,434,000	$209,500,000	$183,011,000	$173,388,000
Income before income taxes	17,601,000	20,116,000	18,812,000	17,664,000	17,116,000
Net income	9,077,000	10,194,000	9,720,000	8,955,000	7,902,000
Cash dividends paid on common	2,896,000	2,824,000	2,741,000	2,685,000	2,678,000
Financial Data—Year End					
Working capital	69,300,000	68,611,000	63,115,000	57,422,000	55,646,000
Plant and equipment—net	29,321,000	25,692,000	23,795,000	20,255,000	15,942,000
Capitalization					
Long-term liabilities	16,923,000	16,295,000	17,437,000	18,656,000	14,466,000
Shareholders' equity	81,798,000	76,712,000	69,660,000	63,439,000	58,011,000
Total	98,721,000	93,007,000	87,097,000	82,095,000	72,477,000
Common Stock Data					
Net income per common share	2.11	2.36	2.25	2.07	1.84
Cash dividends per share	.80	.80	.80	.80	.80
Book value per share	19.02	17.80	16.21	14.76	13.46
Shares outstanding	3,631,856	3,620,096	3,545,447	3,504,793	3,454,370

ᵃYears prior to 1972 have been restated to include companies acquired which have been accounted for by the pooling of interests method.

EXHIBIT 4 (cont.)

JOHNSON CONTROL, INC.
Ten-Year Financial Summary

	1968	1967	1966	1965	1964
Net Sales, Income, and Dividends					
Net sales	$158,702,000	$146,058,000	$141,474,000	$116,919,000	$107,601,000
Income before income taxes	15,144,000	13,018,000	14,533,000	11,214,000	10,093,000
Net income	6,966,000	6,581,000	7,043,000	5,727,000	4,843,000
Cash dividends paid on common	2,652,000	2,650,000	2,439,000	2,332,000	2,332,000
Financial Data—Year End					
Working capital	51,181,000	46,616,000	36,737,000	32,637,000	30,272,000
Plant and equipment—net	13,545,000	12,000,000	9,908,000	9,250,000	9,223,000
Capitalization					
Long-term liabilities	12,739,000	10,492,000	3,294,000	3,380,000	4,130,000
Shareholders' equity	53,228,000	49,475,000	45,558,000	41,414,000	38,042,000
Total	65,967,000	59,967,000	48,852,000	44,794,000	42,172,000
Common Stock Data					
Net income per common share	1.63	1.55	1.67	1.39	1.23
Cash dividends per share	.80	.80	.75	.73	.73
Book value per share	12.43	11.58	10.81	10.08	9.65
Shares outstanding	3,420,490	3,417,140	3,414,328	3,319,294	3,320,776

[a]Years prior to 1972 have been restated to include companies acquired which have been accounted for by the pooling of interests method.

EXHIBIT 4 (cont.)

JOHNSON CONTROL, INC.
Ten-Year Financial Summary

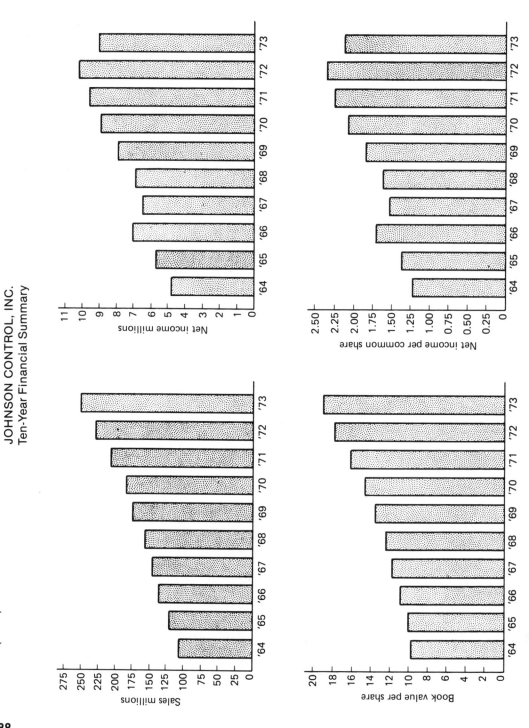

EXHIBIT 5

THE SECD ORGANIZATION

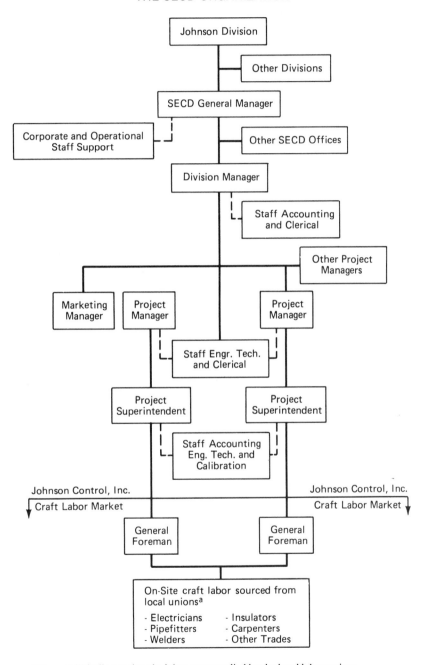

[a]"Sourced" indicates that the labor was supplied by the local labor unions.

EXHIBIT 6

LABOR EFFICIENCY AND PROGRESS REPORT
Estimated Completion Date, 9/75

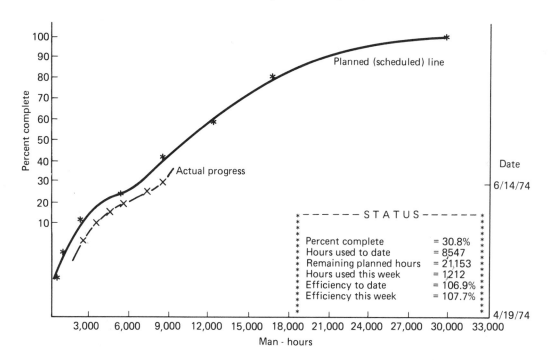

To meet or exceed the planned (scheduled) work the actual line must be on or above the planned line. An actual line that is below and diverging from the planned line signifies a problem and requires immediate action.

EXHIBIT 7

PROJECT PLANNING AND CONTROL SYSTEM

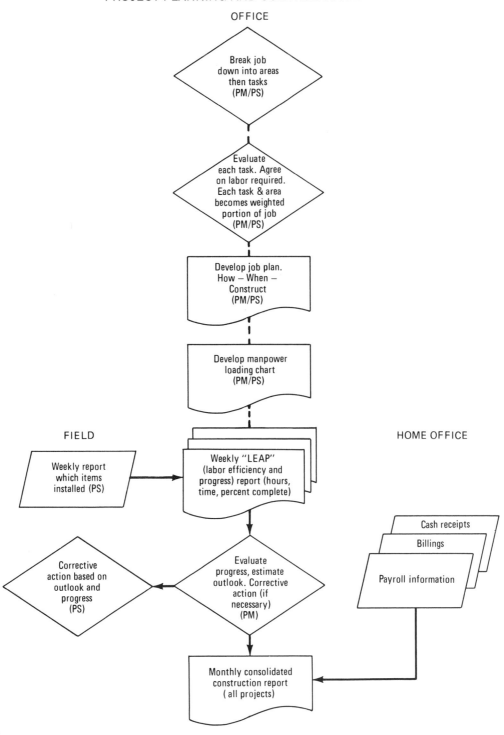

EXHIBIT 8

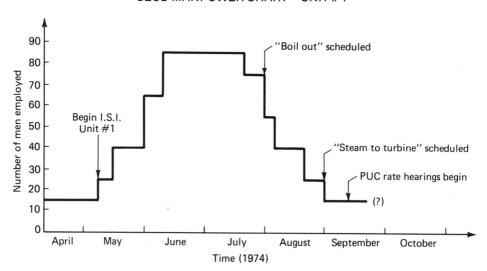

BURNS AND ROE, INC.

In mid-summer 1973 A. L. Hammett, assistant to the president of Burns and Roe, Inc., attended the annual meeting of the Atomic Industry Forum. He was contacted there by the Canadian marketing representative of Pechiney Ugine Kuhlmann who proposed a joint venture into the design and construction of uranium mills.

Both Pechiney Ugine Kuhlmann (PUK) and Burns and Roe, Inc. (B & R) had considerable expertise in the design, construction, and operation of nuclear energy processes.

Burns and Roe, Inc., was thus faced with the decision of whether to enter into an alliance with PUK. Competition, joint venture with another company, future demand for crucial energy, together with an analysis of their potential partner's motives had first to be examined. Hammett was assigned the task of evaluating the opportunity.

BACKGROUND

B & R was a medium-sized architectural engineering service company, specializing in engineering consulting, planning, feasibility studies, project design, and management.

It was one of fifteen affiliates controlled by a holding company, Roe Engineering Enterprises, whose chairman and president was Kenneth Roe. The parent was a family-held corporation, founded in 1935 by the father of the present president. Senior employees held minority interests. Among the affiliates were: Burns and Roe Construction Corporation (a

This case was prepared by Donagh McCarthy under the supervision of Professor Jules J. Schwartz as the basis for class discussion rather than to illustrate either effective or ineffective handling of a managerial problem.

contracting company), Roe Associates (an A/E firm), Burns and Roe International (an engineering firm oriented towards South America), and Burmot Ltd. (a joint consulting engineering firm in association with Motor Columbus Ind. of Switzerland).

BURNS AND ROE'S ORGANIZATION AND BUSINESS ENVIRONMENT

B & R headquarters was situated in Oradell, New Jersey. The firm employed approximately 2100 people, with a complement of 1500 engineering and technical staff. Nineteen hundred employees were located at headquarters and neighborhood offices, others in Los Angeles and overseas.

In 1973 B & R was ranked among the top ten American architectural engineering firms, with booked sales for its services exceeding $33 million and billings for 1972 surpassing $20 million. Traditionally the firm's major markets had been:

Market	Percentage
Utilities (particularly electrical power generation)	70–80%
Federal government	2–3
Transportation (projected to increase)	1
International	15
Industrial (domestic)	6–7

The types of projects in which B & R specialized and the scope of services it provided are broken down by market segment in Exhibit 1.

The organizational structure chosen by B & R was a form of matrix organization, highly adaptable to the ever changing needs of a project-management oriented company, exposed to frequent change, diversity, and varying size of contracts. The axis of the matrix divided functions by market type, technology, geographical location, and intrafirm services.

The organizational climate was friendly, informal and had project emphasis. This was generally the case for most consulting firms but was especially true in this instance. Top management's perspective had been domestically inclined, despite significant foreign bookings. However, according to Hammett, "there is an acceptance of change and the efforts necessary to cope with it ... objectivity and analysis are valued."

Corporate strategy was to keep B & R's technical capabilities ahead of industry's current requirements. The firm knew the advantages of being a leading entrant into a new market. To this end, the company had closely associated itself with research and development efforts in fields such as nuclear engineering, magnetohydrodynamics, and environmental control. The director of the Industrial Division, responsible for non-power related projects including the proposed new uranium milling area, saw the company "as a designer and constructor of the peripheral systems around the 'black boxes' or core processes, supplied by others." For example, in a nuclear power plant, B & R would design the building and all the systems except for the reactor. In recent years, however, B & R had come closer to being able to design the entire plant. Accordingly its research and development was done mainly by associating itself with sophisticated companies and research establishments. Exhibit 2 lists some of B & R's recent joint ventures with other companies in the nuclear field.

Hammett indicated that while the present character of the firm, a service-plus-operational management company, would in general be maintained, B & R was not averse to launching out into ventures in related fields. The firm would participate in production, not only as contracted operators as in the past, but as active financial partners, if such a venture could provide a substantial contribution to profits.

A plaque at corporate headquarters commemorating the founder, was inscribed with the following words: "We should not follow others, our firm should lead."

PECHINEY UGINE KUHLMANN

Pechiney Ugine Kuhlmann was among the world's largest firms. It was a major producer of metals and chemicals, with operations in thirty-five countries. (See Exhibit 3 for a financial summary of the years 1972 and 1973.) Through a subsidiary, it held 70 percent of the common stock of Howmet Corporation, an aluminum and gas turbine producer quoted on the New York and Pacific Stock Exchanges. It also owned Instel, Inc., a United States subsidiary of an international trading corporation. Instel's business involved the nuclear fuel cycle.

PUK's Nuclear and New Technologies Group was one of seven engineering divisions. The scope and location of involvement in the nuclear fuel cycle is shown in Exhibit 4. PUK had great experience in uranium ore extraction and proven intermediate-stage process technology. It had erected and commissioned several plants in France and abroad. The design of each uranium ore milling plant was unique, the process being highly dependent on the bedrock and ore characteristics. PUK's laboratories and design offices were equipped to handle every ore quality. This capability came about through the development and construction of its own pilot plant, giving the firm, said the director of international relations, "a definite lead in the uranium milling process."

THE NUCLEAR INDUSTRY[1]

The nuclear industry continued to grow from 1970 to 1973, as indicated by the large number of orders for nuclear plants during those years. During 1973 utilities placed orders for thirty-eight nuclear units totalling over 43,000 mwe (million kilowatts electrical) of capacity. This was the third successive year in which the capacity of new orders for nuclear steam generators exceeded that of orders placed by utilities for fossil-fueled, steam-generation units. As of December 31, 1973, there were 199 nuclear power plants operating, under construction, or contracted for, in the United States. The total generating capacity of these plants was about 188,000 mwe, representing an investment of approximately $74 billion. Of these, forty plants with a combined capacity of about 24,000 mwe were in operation. Atomic Energy Commission (AEC)[2] forecasts indicated that, by the end of 1980, nuclear electric generating capacity would amount to approximately 20 percent of the total electric power capacity in the United States. From these figures and because of growing environmental concerns, economic considerations, balance of payment problems, and shortages of oil and natural gas, coal and nuclear energy would undoubtedly be the major sources of energy for future base-load generation in the United States. Contrary to popular belief, uranium is not an exceedingly rare element; it is more abundant than such widely used metals as tin, mercury, bismuth, and cadmium.[3]

The AEC had initiated programs to encourage industry to build the uranium-enriching capacity that would be required in the early 1980s. In this regard it was making its classified enriching technology available to eight industrial organizations that had declared their intention to become suppliers of enriching services or equipment. According to a press release, the AEC was proposing a gradual reduction of existing restrictions on enrichment of uranium of foreign origin intended for use in domestic nuclear power plants, leading to total elimination of restrictions by 1984.

The AEC had also indicated that it would

be prepared to consider the participation of foreign entities in domestic enrichment projects, subject to provisions of the Atomic Energy Act. These firms would have no access to enrichment technology. The Atomic Energy Act established the framework for the licensing of nuclear reactors, research and development activities, and other programs involving nuclear materials.

THE NUCLEAR FUEL CYCLE

A flowchart indicating segments in the nuclear power generation industry is shown in Exhibit 5. The nuclear fuel cycle consisted of eight divisions, shown schematically, depicting the steps necessary for light water and high-temperature gaseous reactors.

The AEC, in cooperation with industry, was proceeding with the development of the liquid metal fast breeding reactor (LMFBR) on a priority basis to ensure an essentially unlimited low-cost energy supply, free from the problem of fuel resources and of the atmospheric contamination caused by combustion products and wasters. By taking full advantage of the fast breeder, available uranium reserves might be extended from decades to centuries, at the same time producing electric power economically. It was hoped that the LMFBR would be demonstrated successfully by the mid or late 1980s.

However, from B & R's perspective, future technological developments such as centrifugal enrichment, breeder reactors or plutonium cycle would not be commercially viable before 1990, well beyond the present planning horizon of the joint venture. In other words the economics of the fuel cycle were unlikely to undergo fundamental shifts or changes for a period of at least fifteen years.

Economics of the Nuclear Fuel Cycle

In ore-processing plants, uranium is recovered from the feed ore and concentrated into an intermediate semi-refined product, often referred to in the industry as "yellow-cake."

---

[1] U.S.-AEC, The Nuclear Industry 1973, Wash-1174-73

[2] Now the Nuclear Regulatory Commission.

[3] U.S.-AEC Grand Junction Office-090767: "Uranium Ore Processing"

This product is then reprocessed in separate facilities to obtain uranium fuel for commercial power plants. However, it was the mining and milling segments, eventually producing yellow-cake (U_3O_8) which were of interest to B & R and PUK.

In the United States yellow-cake prices were until recently lower than $8 per pound. As a result only relatively rich sandstone ore of greater than 0.25 percent U_3O_8 content was mined. However, in recent months U_3O_8 prices had climbed near the $15 per pound mark, well beyond the $8 figure used by AEC to project cutoff reserves. This ensured that inferior and "conglomerate" type ores in North America might be mined economically in the near future. The size of uranium ore reserves in the United States, and hence the future establishment of mills, is both a function of mining and milling costs per pound of yellow-cake and the fraction that these costs comprise in total nuclear light water reactor (LWR) generating costs. Exhibit 6 gives a breakdown of estimated 1981 fuel generation cost of LWR nuclear fuel. Cost components for a 1000 mwe power plant in 1981, adjusted for escalation, are also given.

From this exhibit it may be seen that at $10 per pound, U_3O_8 costs are only 3 percent of total generating costs. Even with a $1 increase in U_3O_8 prices generation costs shift only 0.04 mills/kwh.

Forecast of Uranium Demand

Demand projections for new uranium mills were primarily based on nuclear power generation forecasts made by the AEC and on demographic, industrial, and competitive fuel availability considerations. Exhibit 7 shows the projected electrical output that the nuclear industry is expected to generate up to the year 2000. It should be noted that the 1974 forecast is, in all cases, considerably lower than those made in the previous four years and reflects the current conservative approach towards energy consumption forecasting.

The analysis is complex and reflects four situations, A to D, based on varying assumptions, as given in Exhibit 7. These figures give rise to a table (Exhibit 8) for projected annual uranium demand under the four scenarios, together with varying assumptions of enrichment tails assay.[4] Current enrichment, according to AEC sources, is being operated at 0.27 to 0.29 percent tails assay. For B & R's purposes it is sufficient to consider case A and case C (each with 0.2 and 0.3 percent tails assay respectively) as encompassing the range of possibilities from conservative to optimistic. It should be noted that the spread is quite narrow, indicating, even under pessimistic assumptions, an inevitably rapid growth of nuclear power generation and the country's increasing dependence on this source.

Existing Milling Capacity

In April 1974 existing milling capacity was calculated by the AEC to be 16,000 tons of U_3O_8 output per year. (See Exhibit 9.) Two Susquehanna-Western, Inc., plants had closed down in 1973 but one additional plant was in the process of construction.

The immediate development plans of others in the field were not known. AEC sources felt that capacity might be somewhat understated because capacity is related to location and mining cut. This might then give rise to protracted adjustments in output.

It is also worth pointing out that there was no known instance of a mining company constructing a mill on its own. Milling companies, despite having sophisticated engineering staffs, usually brought in outside architectural engineering firms for design and construction.

U.S. and World Uranium Reserves

Exhibits 10 and 11 depict domestic and world uranium reserves in 1974. One of the most important factors in estimating reserves, price per pound of yellow-cake concentrate, had largely been ignored in previous analyses. A figure of $8 per pound had been used to date

[4] Tails assay refers to concentration of enriched ore, that is, 0.27 percent means enriched uranium is 99.73 percent pure; 0.29 percent is 99.71 percent pure.

by AEC. This was far lower than the following quoted prices:

$18 + per pound for 1978 deliveries;
$20 + per pound for 1980 and beyond; and
$27 + per pound beyond 1983 (estimated by the Nuclear Exchange Corporation)[5]

Exhibit 10 indicates that substantial reserves were available at prices greater than $15 per pound. It may also be assumed that further reserves would become available at higher price levels. Since yellow-cake at $10 per pound comprises only 3 percent of total generating costs and an increase of $1 increases the fuel component of total costs by only 1.6 percent (see Exhibit 6), a considerable upward shift of prices, even beyond $50, could easily be absorbed by the utilities and other users.

As stated previously pending legislation would be likely to permit importation of yellow-cake in gradually increasing fractions after 1977. These imports could impact on price levels and therefore domestic output, further impinging on the construction schedules for new domestic mills.

AEC sources within the Division of Production and Materials Management disagreed with this analysis. They asserted that United States prices tended to set international levels because the United States had approximately 40 percent of known world reserves and consumed just under 50 percent of world output.

Foreign requirements through 1985 were estimated to be 526,000 tons of U_3O_8. Although reserves abroad were slightly higher than in the United States, production capacity was projected to fall well behind requirements before 1985. It appeared therefore that imports of uranium would not pose a threat in the immediate future. In fact, foreign uranium supply and demand was developing along the same lines as in the United States. The world was going nuclear at a rate that would tax world supply unless large new discoveries were made in the near future. Thus the proposed legisla-

tion provided the opportunity to import. This did not imply that imports would actually occur. AEC sources indicated that, as a general rule, in the extractive-type industries in America, imports of raw materials had occurred only in cases where the demand for the resource exceeded the domestic economy's capability to meet supply fully. This eventuality was unlikely to occur in the case of uranium ores for decades, if ever.

Projection for the Construction of New Mills

The level of uranium ore processing was in the order of 12,500 tons/year of yellow-cake concentrate, as against a nominal capacity of 16,000 tons. This situation was not expected to last beyond mid-1975, when demand caused by the commissioning of new reactors was expected to exceed this capacity. Through 1977 and 1978, capacity shortfalls were expected to be met by increases in production at existing plants and by drawing down inventories. Current inventories were estimated at 19,000 tons of U_3O_8 concentrate. AEC stockpiles were not expected to be released in significant amounts.

Taking existing capacity to be 16,000 tons U_3O_8 per year and using conservative and optimistic forecasts new mill requirements could be computed:

CUMULATIVE CAPACITY SHORTFALL
(1000 Tons U_3O_8/Year)[a]

Year	1974	1976	1978	1980
0.2% tails assay (optimistic)	0	0	0	8
0.3% tails assay (pessimistic)	0	1	7	18

Year	1982	1984	1986
0.2% tails assay (optimistic)	19	31	42
0.3% tails assay (pessimistic)	32	51	73

[5] Testimony of George White before Congressional Committee on Atomic Energy, September 1974.

[a] Cumulative number mills required, with plant size assumed at 1000 tons/year capacity

As may be seen from Exhibit 9, the average mill size capacity per year was approximately 1000 tons/year U_3O_8 and was in accordance with past experience. Therefore the above cumulative capacity shortfall translates into the required number of mills needed to cater for future demand. It is worth mentioning that this data portrays general trends if all the old mills stay in production. In fact, many of the older mills may be shut down because of lack of ore at their location.

Exhibit 11 shows the AEC projection for U_3O_8 requirements (0.25% tails assay) for the next twelve years. AEC data indicated the mean mill size had an ore capacity of approximately 400,000 tons per year. This shows the required number of new mills assuming all present mills stay in production.

Even in the most pessimistic scenario, given the minimum normal three-year time lag between order point and start of production, the order point for the first mill had to be in 1975.

The preceding facts indicated a strong demand for mill construction starting immediately and lasting well into the next two decades. The forecasts used by the AEC recognized slippages in order positions for reactors and various other factors.

Size of Market

Multiplying the projected number of mills required by the capital cost of each, a dollar size for the market could be computed. Unfortunately virtually no capital cost data was available in terms of actual historic costs for mills previously constructed. Location and process methods used, depending on type of ore being milled, had a significant effect on costs and were difficult to predict at this stage.

However, a 1972 statistical survey[6] indicated costs ranging from $4,000 to $8,000 capital cost per ton-day ore input capacity, which for an average mill size of 1500 tons-per-day ore

[6] R. Kennedy, "Ore to Concentrates" AEC Meeting (Grenoble, France) September 1972.

intake (equivalent to 1000 tons per year U_3O_8 —average mill size), meant a capital investment of $12 million for a new mill, based on early 1970 costs. To translate this into current dollars necessitated the use of some economic index.

Scenario	Year	Cumulative Number of Mills Built	Required Capital Investment (millions 1975 $)
0.2% tails assay	1980	8	144
	1983	25	450
	1986	42	756
0.3% tails assay	1980	18	324
	1983	41	738
	1986	73	1314

If the November 1974 wholesale price index of 170 was used costs in 1975 could be estimated at $18 million per mill. On this basis, and using AEC "optimistic" and "pessimistic" projections for new mills, the total 1975 dollar size of the market could be computed.

This shows that under the worst AEC projections a cumulative market of $756 million would exist by 1986.

WHY A JOINT VENTURE

Even though B & R was approached by PUK in 1973, it did not become apparent that nuclear fuel would play a substantial role in future energy output in the United States until mid-1974, when more nuclear power plants than fossil-fueled were ordered for the third consecutive year.

B & R, having acquired a position and technological capability in nearly all facets of the nuclear fuel cycle, wanted to acquire expertise in the milling segment as well. PUK, the proposer of the joint venture, was capable of designing milling plants for a wide range of ore characteristics, especially where classical or poor ores called for a more efficient and rigorous design. It also had a laboratory and pilot plant, and had designed and constructed seven mills worldwide.

Hammett considered it impracticable for

B & R to enter the business of designing and constructing uranium mills on its own. The company had no previous experience in ore-milling process design. Thus, to achieve penetration into the uranium milling market, two courses of action were open to B & R: a joint venture with PUK or a joint venture with a domestic partner.

A joint venture with a domestic partner was not deemed feasible for two reasons:

1. The company did not have serious contacts with any potential partners in the United States and it would have taken considerable time to develop a relationship compatible with a joint venture. Any delay at this time would have postponed the company's entry into the market and would have created a competitive disadvantage.
2. More importantly, potential domestic partners in a joint venture possessed their own in-house design capability and were therefore more in the mold of competitors than potential partners.

PUK's Objectives for a Joint Venture

On the other hand, PUK's motives for initiating the joint venture were by no means clear. However, some inferences of the company's objectives were drawn from a meeting in New York in October 1974.

It could be construed that PUK's prime objective was to gain entry to, and acceptance in, the United States market, fronted by B & R. This would hopefully be achieved in the milling segment by selling its process, technology, and services, which it claimed were comparable to, or even better than, those available in the United States.

A joint venture would serve as a base for further expansion of PUK's services into other areas of the nuclear fuel cycle in America. Perhaps PUK could gain contracts with utilities and others while operating in the milling field. This firm might hope to gain access to B & R's acknowledged expertise in uranium enrichment. This might also open an avenue for potential investment in operations and facilities in the nuclear and other fields, such as metals, in which PUK was already engaged.

The Service Package

Once a prospective client had been booked, the services to be rendered could be broken down into three steps. This procedure was agreed upon at the October 1974 meeting in New York.

1. Preliminary: Most of this feasibility work would be done by PUK. This initial step would consist of an assay and evaluation of the ore from the client's site. This would involve laboratory analysis of the ore and determination of the best process, using PUK's pilot plant. Additional on-site work might be necessary to determine the amount and nature of the ore.
2. Design: After the preliminary work and receipt of the process flow chart from PUK, B & R would perform the engineering design of the mill.
3. Construction: B & R would supervise the construction and operation of the mill until commission. As B & R was new to the field, a great deal of technical advice would have to come from PUK initially.

PUK also had a worldwide purchasing network. It could aid in faster and cheaper acquisition of plant equipment and materials, making the joint venture more competitive.

The risk aspect was more difficult to agree upon. During the October meeting Philippe Courcier, PUK's International Director, stated that his company was reluctant to give any guarantee for its process and therefore was not prepared to accept any risk in the enterprise. Hammett stated that B & R felt that PUK should, in fact, shoulder the bulk of the risk for the entire venture.

Types of Association

If B & R was to embark on a joint venture, Hammett had to decide what type of association would be optimal. He conceived of three options:

1. A joint bidding consortium. B & R would bid jointly with PUK for the feasibility study, process and plant design, and construction. Each company's services would be independently contracted with the client. Individual responsibilities would be well defined and no turnkey arrangements would be possible.

2. A prime subcontract with PUK. B & R would accept prime responsibility for the project, not only including professional quality of its own services, but also for the process designed by PUK. B & R would also tender directly for the contract and would coordinate its own and PUK's plans and proposals. Basically there would be only one contract between the client and B & R, which would cover all services required for the execution of the contract. B & R would therefore offer the process subcontracted from PUK under its own auspices. Fixed cost, turnkey arrangements, though not presently envisaged due to restrictions of capital involvement and apprehension towards risk, would be possible.

3. A jointly-held subsidiary company. B & R, together with PUK, could form a small subsidiary, with respective shareholdings in proportion to services offered. Project management could be provided by the subsidiary, with other work subcontracted to both firms. An arrangement of this sort would serve to reduce liability and increase PUK's commitment.

MARKETING AND FINANCIAL ISSUES

In assigning the various marketing roles to both companies, Hammett in a letter to PUK dated June 26, 1974, stated:

> Each of our companies will underwrite its own cost in connection with this preliminary marketing effort. B & R will undertake the primary marketing role of selecting prospects, arranging for meetings, and providing follow-up contracts. PUK will provide basic marketing materials such as slides, firms, technical write-up material, and will also provide the technical support for the presentations. There is no exclusivity intended in

this initial working understanding between our two companies.

Marketing strategy would be governed to a large extent by the type of association formed between the two companies. Cost estimation might also prove somewhat of a problem, with neither company having prior milling experience in the United States. However, during the October 1974 meeting, Courcier finally informed Hammett that PUK had received a contract in mid-1974 from Amoco to design and construct a 1000 ton/year U_3O_8 plant in Saskatchewan, Canada, to be completed in 1977.

Financial arrangements and the consequences of entering the field of uranium ore milling with PUK had yet to be agreed upon. The pricing of the partner's services, the compensation for goodwill and technology, the financing of initial outlays for marketing and the assessment of fair amounts for hourly rates and overhead multipliers had yet to be determined. A decision as to whether services were to be sold on fixed-cost or cost-plus basis also had to be made.

Although it was probable that PUK's process could not be protected by patent legislation, it was foreseen that PUK would insist either on a license agreement with some form of front payment or an incomplete revelation of the process and technology to both B & R and the client, along with royalty payments.

THE FUTURE

Joint ventures are not and do not pretend to be everlasting relationships. It was therefore essential for Hammett to analyze the options and arrangements both from the present perspective and with regard to changing objectives before coming to a firm decision.

EXHIBIT 1

BURNS AND ROE, INC.
Projects

Types of Projects in Which Burns and Roe Specializes

1. Defense and aerospace facilities-Missile support; Electronic; Communication; Engine test; Wind tunnels; Laboratories; Hardened facilities; Airport facilities
   Nuclear facilities—Research and testing; Process
   Water-Sewage—Desalting; Water and waste treatment; Environmental
   Power-Nuclear, Fossil-fueled and Hydroelectric generating plants; Transmission and distribution; Environmental
   Industrial-Commercial Facilities; Environmental
   Master planning; Surveys and reports; Site development for all the above
   No order of precedence on above
2. Utilities; Air conditioning; Refrigeration; Ventilation; Heating plants
3. Acoustics; Sound suppression
4. Military standard design
5. Manuals
6. Chemical facilities
7. Petroleum facilities
8. Public buildings
9. Housing
10. Earthfill dam work
11. Highways
12. Harbor facilities
13. Irrigation or drainage
14. Bridges
15. Hospitals
16. Channel improvements

NOTE: Engineering, design, estimating, purchasing and construction services described in Item 14 are offered for all types of facilities or projects. Maintenance and operation services are offered for power, industrial, or experimental facilities and defense complexes.

EXHIBIT 1 (cont.)

BURNS AND ROE, INC.
Projects

Scope of Services Provided by Burns and Roe

All architectural, mechanical, electrical, civil, structural, sanitary, chemical, process and nuclear engineering, and all design, drafting, estimating, purchasing, quality assurance, construction and maintenance and operation services are provided with current staffing.

Consultation and Studies	Preliminary Engineering	Detailed Engineering and Design
Management advisory services	Site selection	Engineering analysis
Master planning	Criteria preparation	Specifications
Technical and economic feasibility	Conceptual design studies	Selection of bidders
Site and subsurface investigations	Cost estimates	Analysis of bids
Market surveys and appraisals	Logistics	Procurement of equipment
License applications	Scheduling-graphic and computer	Final drawings
Funding negotiations		Cost estimates
		Scheduling, expediting
		Quality control and assurance
		Progress reports
		Review of vendors' drawings

Construction Management Services	Maintenance and Operation
Planning and coordination	Technical manuals
Supervision of construction	Maintenance manuals
Resident engineering	Spare parts manuals
Expediting and inspection	Operating instructions
Progress and cost reporting	Operator training
Safety programs	Plant startup
Labor relations	Acceptance testing
Material control and warehousing	M & O reports
Construction	Operation and maintenance
As-built drawings	

EXHIBIT 2

B & R's ASSOCIATIONS WITH
OTHER COMPANIES
FOR DEVELOPMENTAL EFFORTS
IN THE NUCLEAR FIELD

1. *Electronucleonics/Hercules/Burns and Roe.* Development of the centrifugal process for nuclear fuel enrichment. In keeping with its current policy, B & R's participation is very small (details not divulged) and confined to the peripheral engineering and civil construction.
2. *Electronucleonics/Burns and Roe/T.V.A.* Feasibility study for T.V.A. for a reactor and enrichment plant.
3. *ARCO/Electronucleonics/Burns and Roe.* Proposal made to Texas Utilities to build and operate a uranium enrichment plant on turnkey basis and a management contract.
4. *A.E.C./Burns and Roe/Others.* Proposal to build an experimental 300 T centrifugal plant. This would be a demonstration unit, which would form the basis for an acceptance or rejection of the commercial viability of the centrifugal process of enrichment.

EXHIBIT 3

BURNS AND ROE, INC.,
Financial Summary

| | Year Ended December 31 (in millions of French francs or millions of dollars except for per share amounts) | | |
	1973		1972
Net sales	Fr. 16,027	$3,522[a]	Fr. 13,425
Income before extraordinary items	365	80	316
Net income	365	80	273
Dividends declared	205	45	201
Capital investments	1,656	364	1,364
Per common share			
Income before extraordinary items	14.5	3.19	12.6
Net income	14.5	3.19	10.9
Cash dividend[b]	8.4	1.85	8.0
At the year end			
Working capital	3,405	748	3,372
Shareholders' equity	6,275	1,379	6,115
Per common share	Fr. 249	$54.73	Fr. 243

[a] The conversion rate used is 4.55 francs to the dollar.

[b] Excludes a tax credit of 4.2 francs allowable under French fiscal regulations (4.0 francs in 1972).

Source: Press release June 12, 1974. P.U.K. Development, Inc.

303

EXHIBIT 4

PECHINEY UGINE KUHLMANN
Nuclear and New Technologies Group
Nuclear Engineering—References

Steps in Fuel Cycle	Process	Engineering							References	Capacity M.T.U./Year
		Studies	Pilot Engineering	Piloting	Plant Engineering	Plant Construction	Mining	Laboratories	Location	
Exploration	Geology	•						•	Uranium and various metals All countries and Australia Canada USA	
	Geophysic	•						•		
	Geochemistry	•								
	Drilling	•								
Mining	Open pit	•					•		France	400
	Open pit	•					•		Arlit · Niger	750/1500
	Open pit and underground	•					•		Mounana · Gabon	400/1000
	Leaching in situ	•		•						
Milling	Ores to concentrate (uranate of Mg, Na, ADU or oxydes)	•						•	Forez · France Ecarpiere · France Bassines · France Arlit · Niger Mounana · Gabon Urgeinica · Portugal	500 1000 750/1500 400/1000
	Ores to UF4 —electrolysis	•	•	•				•	Mol · Belgium	100
	—chemical route	•	•	•	•	•			Bessines · France	
Conversion	Concentrates/UF6 including F2 production —wet process	•	•	•	•	•		•	Pierrelatte · France	6000
	—dry process	•	•	•	•	•		•	Pierrelatte · France	400
	UNH/UF6	•						•	Pierrelatte · France	
Enrichment	Handling of UF6	•							CEA/Pierrelatte · France	
	Purification of UF6	•	•	•	•	•				
	Basic material and processes	•	•	•	•	•				
	Control and Miscellaneous				•	•				
	Purification and conversion of product	•			•	•				

EXHIBIT 4 (cont.)

PECHINEY UGINE KUHLMANN
Nuclear and New Technologies Group
Nuclear Engineering—References

Steps in Fuel Cycle	Process	Engineering						Laboratories	Location	References	Capacity M.T.U./Year
		Studies	Pilot Engineering	Piloting	Plant Engineering	Plant Construction	Mining				
Fuel Manufacture	Production of sinterable UO2										
	—wet process	•	•	•	•	•			Pierrelatte	France	400
	—dry process	•	•	•	•				CEA/Cadaracha	France	500
	Production of Uranium metal from UF6	•	•	•	•	•		•	Pierrelatte	France	500
	Graphite gas	•	•	•	•	•		•			1000
	Light water	•	•	•	•	•		•			200
	Pool reactor	•	•	•	•	•		•	Romans	France	20,000 plates
	High temperature				•	•		•			20
	Advanced technologies				•	•					30
Reprocessing	UNH by reprocessing to UF4										
	—wet process	•	•	•	•	•			Mol	Belgium	
	—dry process	•	•	•	•				CEA/Fontenay	France	
	UNH or UF4 ex reprocessing to UF6	•	•	•	•	•			Pierrelatte	France	400
Depleted Uranium	UF6 to metal	•	•	•	•	•			Pierrelatte	France	800
	Metal casting	•	•	•					Romans	France	
Waste Treatment	Fuel ponds purification	•	•	•	•				Levallois and Cadarache	France	
	Ruthenium removal			•					Levallois and Cadarache	France	
Transportation	Systems	•							France and various countries		
	Casks	•									
Miscellaneous	The Pechiney Ugine Kuhlmann Group manufactures also: titanium, zirconium, special steels and alloys, nuclear graphite, beryllium and sodium, and holds corresponding technologies.										

EXHIBIT 5

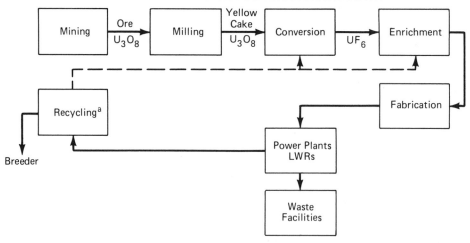

FLOWCHART INDICATING SEGMENTS
IN THE NUCLEAR POWER GENERATION INDUSTRY

[a]Contingent upon development in breeder technology and plutonium recycle, material will be reprocessed in the conversion and enrichment plants. These are crucial factors in energy demand beyond the 1980s.

EXHIBIT 6
ESTIMATED 1981 FUEL GENERATION COST
OF LWR NUCLEAR FUEL

Cost component	Cost (mills/kwh)
Mining/milling ($10/lb U_3O_8)	0.54
Conversion to UF_6 ($1.35/lb U)	0.07
Enrichment ($42/kg SWU)	0.76
Reconversion/fabrication ($70/kg U)	0.33
Spent fuel shipping ($5/kg U)	0.02
Reprocessing ($35/kg U)	0.14
Waste management	0.04
Plutonium credit	(0.22)
	1.68
Fuel Inventory Carrying Charge (12%)	0.82
	2.50

EXHIBIT 6 (cont.)
COMPARATIVE GENERATION COST
COMPONENTS FOR 1000 MWE LWR
POWER PLANT IN 1981
(INCLUDING ESCALATION) IN MILLS/KWH

Cost component	Coal	Oil	Nuclear
Capital	10.90	8.00	11.70
Fuel	5.50	24.60	2.50
O & M	1.60	0.80	1.00
	18.00	33.40	15.20

Sensitivity

At $10/lb U_3O_8 comprises 3% total generating costs. 0.04 mills/kwh cost increase for $1 increase in U_3O_8 prices, i.e., a 1.6% increase in fuel generation cost $(0.04/2.50 = 1.6\%)$

Source: A.E.C., Nuclear Industry 1973.

EXHIBIT 7

PROJECTED NUCLEAR GENERATING
CAPACITY
(Thousands of MW)
February 1974 Forecast

United States Case	1980	1985	1990	2000
A	85	231	410	850
B	102	260	500	1200
C	112	275	575	1400
D	102	250	475	1090

Assumptions:

Case A (lowest forecast): Slippages continue in order positions; construction time for plants continues to be 8 years or more; current decline in population growth rate continues; GNP growth rate below recent averages.

Case B (middle forecast): Improvement over current delays; higher industrial growth; construction time 6-8 years; shift to electrical energy use from fossil fuel use.

Case C (optimistic forecast): Current uncertainties of the nuclear program are removed and the nation embarks on a coordinated nuclear energy program; construction time no more than 6 years; considerable shift from fossil fuels to electrical energy; strong industrial growth and demand.

Case D (consumption restrictions): Assumes conservation measures for all energy forms, while having healthy growth in industrial and per capita income.

Source: Office of Planning & Analysis, "Nuclear Power Growth 1974-2000," February 1974, Reference AEC # Wash-1139 (74)

EXHIBIT 8

ANNUAL URANIUM DEMAND
(Thousands of STU₃O₈, 75% Capacity Factor, Pu Recycle)[a]

Calendar	ENRICHMENT PLANT TAILS ASSAY = 0.20%				ENRICHMENT PLANT TAILS ASSAY = 0.30%			
	United States Cases				United States Cases			
Year	A	B	C	D	A	B	C	D
1974	8.1	9.3	10.3	9.7	9.7	11.2	12.3	11.6
1975	9.8	11.3	11.6	11.7	11.8	13.6	14.0	14.1
1976	10.5	12.7	13.1	12.6	12.7	15.3	15.9	15.2
1977	12.8	15.4	16.6	16.0	15.5	18.7	20.1	19.4
1978	16.9	17.9	21.7	19.8	20.5	21.6	26.2	23.8
1979	21.9	24.2	26.3	25.2	26.3	29.1	31.6	30.4
1980	25.2	28.9	29.4	31.5	30.3	34.8	35.5	37.9
1981	28.4	30.9	34.2	35.0	34.2	37.3	41.3	42.2
1982	32.7	36.1	39.1	34.3	39.5	43.7	47.4	41.5
1983	36.2	41.1	43.1	34.1	43.9	49.7	52.3	41.9
1984	40.3	47.0	50.6	41.5	48.9	57.0	61.2	50.5
1985	45.5	52.9	58.5	49.8	55.2	64.2	70.9	60.4
1986	48.9	58.5	67.2	55.2	59.4	71.1	81.4	67.0

[a]Thousands of short tons of U_3O_8 (i.e., mill output) at normal operating efficiency of LWRs of 75% and assuming plutonium recycle initiated from 1978 onwards.

Source: "Nuclear Power Growth, 1974–2000," AEC # Wash–1139 (74) February 1974.

EXHIBIT 9

U.S. MILLS THAT PROCESSED URANIUM ORE IN 1973

Company and Location		Nominal Capacity (tons ore per day)
Anaconda Company	Grants, New Mexico	3,000
Atlas Corporation	Moab, Utah	1,500
Conoco & Pioneer Nuclear, Inc.	Falls City, Texas	1,750
Consolidated Edison (Cotter Corp.)	Canon City, Colorado	450
Dawn Mining Company	Ford, Washington	500
Exxon Company	Powder River Basin, Wyoming	2,000
Federal-American Partners	Gas Hills, Wyoming	950
Kerr-McGee Corporation	Grants, New Mexico	7,000
Petrotomics Company	Shirley Basin, Wyoming	1,500
Rio Algom Corporation	La Sal, Utah	500
Susquehanna-Western, Inc.	Falls City, Texas	1,000
Susquehanna-Western, Inc.	Ray Point, Texas	·1,000
Union Carbide Corporation	Uraven, Colorado	1,300
Union Carbide Corporation	Natrona County, Wyoming	1,000
United Nuclear-Homstake Ptns.	Grants, New Mexico	3,500
Utah International, Inc.	Gas Hills, Wyoming	1,200
Utah International, Inc.	Shirley Basin, Wyoming	1,200
Western Nuclear, Inc. (Philips Oil)	Jeffery City, Wyoming	1,200

Source: "Survey of United States Uranium Marketing Activity," USAEC, April 1974.

EXHIBIT 10

DOMESTIC URANIUM RESOURCES
As Reestimated January 1, 1974
(Tons U₃ O₈)ᵃ

Yellow-Cake Prices, Per Pound	Reasonably Assured Resources	Estimated Additional Resources	Totals
$ 8	277,000	450,000	727,000
$ 8–$10 increment	63,000	250,000	313,000
$10	340,000	700,000	1,040,000
$10–$15 increment	180,000	300,000	480,000
$15	520,000	1,000,000	1,520,000
$15–$30 increment	180,000	700,000	880,000
$30	700,000	1,700,000	2,400,000

URANIUM ORE RESERVES AS ESTIMATED
IN PREVIOUS YEARSᵇ

Year	Tons U₃O₈
1966	145,000
1967	141,000
1968	148,000
1969	161,000
1970	204,000
1971	246,000
1972	273,000
1973	273,000

Source: ᵃDivision of Production and Materials Management, AEC.
ᵇ"Nuclear Industry 1973," Table 3–3, AEC # Wash–1174 (73).

EXHIBIT 11

1974 ESTIMATED WORLD RESOURCES AT $10/LB. U_3O_8
(Tons U_3O_8)

Country	Reserves	Estimated Additional at $30/lb.	Total
Australia	140,000	48,000	188,000
Canada	241,000	247,000	488,000
France	47,000	31,000	78,000
Niger	52,000	26,000	78,000
Gabon	26,000	6,000	32,000
South and Southwest Africa	263,000	10,000	273,000
Others (noncommunist)	68,000	69,000	137,000
Total foreign	837,000	437,000	1,274,000
United States	340,000	700,000	1,040,000
Total (rounded)	1,180,000	1,140,000	2,300,000

Source: Statement by Frank P. Baranowski, Director, Production and Materials Management-Division AEC, before Joint Committee on Atomic Energy, September 1974.

EXHIBIT 12

DEMAND FOR NEW MILLS

Year	Requirements for U_3O_8 Concentrate 0.25% Tails Assay (tons/year)	Requirements for Uranium Ore (1000 tons/year)	Requirements for Incremental New Mill Capacity (1000 tons/year)	New Mills[a] Needed
1974	12,500	6,250	—	—
1975	16,500	8,250	—	—
1976	19,200	9,600	—	—
1977	21,700	10,850	1,562	3
1978	26,800	13,400	2,250	4
1979	31,200	15,600	2,750	4
1980	34,600	17,300	2,125	4
1981	39,900	19,950	3,312	6
1982	44,700	22,350	3,000	5
1983	50,400	25,200	3,562	6
1984	57,000	28,500	4,125	7
1985	64,500	32,250	4,680	8

[a]Mill size taken by AEC, 600,000 tons per year.
Source: AEC # Wash–1139 (74), February 1974.

BELMONT CHEMICAL COMPANY, INC.

During the late Spring of 1976 Peter Rogers, president of the Belmont Chemical Company, was considering the options open to him. His company was approaching a period of significant new growth. Founded in 1868 by his great-grandfather, the firm had grown steadily for more than a century as a marketer and distributor of industrial chemicals. Shortly after joining the firm in 1971 Rogers began an informal search for areas within the chemical industry where major growth was likely to occur.

COMPANY BACKGROUND

Located in Boston, Massachusetts, Belmont Chemical distributed most of its industrial chemicals on the East Coast. Rogers explained:

> We have a field sales force working for us that really does a fine job. We are fortunate in that we've managed to grow steadily in the past number of years with a relatively shallow management structure. (See Exhibit 1.) Our sales last year were about $10 million and our future looks very bright. (See Exhibit 2.)

As one of the country's oldest independent chemical distributors Belmont Chemical took pride in its record of maintaining a century-old tradition of fast, courteous service, backed by expert technical knowledge and experience. Besides warehousing a complete inventory of over 400 chemical products, Belmont had established a unique nationwide purchasing network to help customers find whatever specialty chemicals their operations required.

In 1973 and 1974 the energy crisis, price controls, and a surge in demand collectively generated a period of rapid inflation and severe shortages within the industry. Many basic chemical commodities, such as anhydrous ammonia, increased in price more than threefold and were in extremely short supply. (See Exhibit 3.) Sources of feedstocks and raw materials suddenly dried up and prices escalated sharply. Natural gas, for example, increased in some areas from $0.15/mfc (thousand cubic feet) to $2.75/mcf. Furthermore many major consumers of these chemical commodities suddenly learned that their sources of supply were not as reliable as they or their lawyers had expected.

In 1974 Rogers began a thorough investigation of the anhydrous ammonia market, gathering information on plant construction, alternative feedstocks (virtually all ammonia produced in the United States was made from natural gas), regional marketing practices, competition, normal contract terms, and production economics. Several major consumers who had been let down by their traditional suppliers were approached and offered a chance to enter into long-term contracts with Belmont Chemical, which planned to construct a new plant in a location favorable to these consumers. The only stumbling block was finding a reliable source of reasonably priced natural gas, in a location suitable for ammonia users.

At the same time Kenyon, a city of 500,000 in the Pacific Northwest, was seeking a solution to the growing problem of disposing of its mountains of trash.

This case was prepared by Grant G. Behrman under the supervision of Professor Jules J. Schwartz and Lecturer James Coyne as the basis for class discussion rather than to illustrate either effective or ineffective handling of an administrative action.

SOLID WASTE—AN EMERGING RESOURCE

Energy conservation and environmental concerns have no more appropriate application than in the field of municipal solid waste disposal. It had long been felt that solid waste, instead of being regarded as a nuisance, could somehow be recycled and turned into an energy resource. Energy and money are expended to bury this resource in landfills while more energy and money are devoted to the exploitation of natural resources elsewhere. Landscapes are marred by landfill operations and lakes and streams are subjected to leachate pollution.

Increased awareness of environmental needs and soaring costs for traditional energy resources led many to believe that energy values of solid waste should be tapped rather than unceremoniously dumped. Reliable industry sources indicated that a ton of municipal solid waste had more than 10 million BTUs of recoverable energy—a third as much as a ton of oil—and at $3 per million BTUs, that represented a $30 asset instead of a $15 liability.

Attempts to improve the recycling of trash in Kenyon began as early as 1970, but met with modest results. It was not until 1974 that a study initiated by Kenyon's mayor uncovered a viable economic answer to turn the city's solid waste liability into an asset.

This study considered a dozen schemes that had already proven successful in other cities. (See Exhibits 4 and 5.) The most attractive possibility was perhaps the most radical: build a plant to subject solid waste to pyrolysis and use the resulting gases to produce a chemical—either methanol, methane, or anhydrous ammonia. (See Exhibit 6.) This chemical conversion process is known as rechemistry.

The end product initially proposed was methanol, which was used in the manufacture of formaldehyde, dyestuffs, and as fuel in combustion engines and gas turbines. Prices of synthetic methanol had reached their highest since 1940 and production had been increasing steadily for many years. (See Exhibits 7 and 8.)

As the city weighed the possibility of building such a plant, however, a consultant suggested that ammonia should also be considered as the end product. About 90 percent of the ammonia produced in the United States, according to figures compiled by the Bureau of the Census, was used for fertilizer because of its nitrogen content. Industrial uses of ammonia included the production of paper, metals, explosives, and the manufacture of urea, which had value not only as a fertilizer, but also as a cattle feed supplement, in paper finishing, and even for coating pretzels. Ammonia is also familiar as an ingredient in household cleaning products. Annual ammonia production in this country was about 15 million tons in 1975.

Natural gas, by far the most common substance used in making ammonia, contains hydrogen, but practically no necessary nitrogen. Abundance and cheapness had been the advantages of natural gas; but these advantages were rapidly vanishing. Though regulation had prevented the price of natural gas from rising as much as those of petroleum-based fuels, producers were insisting that they must have higher prices as an incentive for exploration for new supplies. Current supplies were tight during periods of peak demand. The following chart shows natural gas usage by markets.

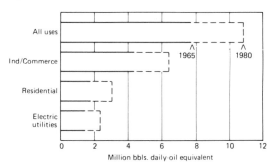

Source: Department of Commerce, *Outlook for Energy in the United States.*

The price of ammonia had soared in the past four years. In 1972, according to *Chemical and Engineering News,* it could be bought on the Gulf Coast for less than $30 a ton. By 1976 the price was about $180 to $190 a ton at the dealer level and approximately $325 a ton retail. Fluctuations occurred in part as a result of fertilizer demand conditions, which were affected by other variables such as weather, expected crop yields and prices, and the quantity of fertilizer applied in an earlier season.

Ammonia prices in the Pacific Northwest were much higher than in other parts of the country. This was because producers, using natural gas as a feedstock, tended to locate near natural gas wellheads, which were centered mainly around the Gulf Coast. As ammonia, a gas at standard temperature and pressure, must be shipped in either pressurized or refrigerated containers, the transportation costs to the Pacific Northwest were substantial. This explains why Gulf Coast ammonia prices were traditionally lower than prices in other parts of the United States.

Pyrolysis

The pyrolysis process concept can be charted as follows (see also Exhibit 9):

gas rises and permeates the solid waste providing heat for the conversion of cellulose (paper, wood, organics, and so on) into additional carbon monoxide plus hydrogen, carbon dioxide, and traces of methane. This mixture of gases and moisture from the waste is processed through a closed gas cleaning system in which the water is condensed and impurities are trapped (step 3).

The synthesis of ammonia from this pyrolysis gas is accomplished by catalytic processes now widely used by the petrochemical industry. Under heat and pressure and in the presence of a catalyst, nitrogen is combined with hydrogen to produce anhydrous ammonia (step 4).

THE PROPOSAL STAGE

With the new thought of ammonia in mind, Kenyon's government in early 1975 solicited proposals from private industry for participation in a project to make use of gases from the city's solid waste. From these proposals a decision was to be made as to:

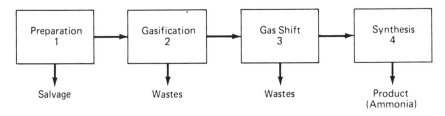

The solid waste/chemical process begins with shredding the solid waste to make it easy to handle and process (step 1). Following coarse shredding, ferrous materials are magnetically removed, and the remaining residues —paper, wood, glass, yard wastes, domestic wastes, organics, and plastics—are gasified by a heat process called "pyrolysis." Pyrolysis is accomplished by feeding the shredded solid waste into a closed vessel similar to a blast furnace. As the waste migrates downward, it is heated by rising carbon monoxide generated from the partial oxidation of carbon residues at the bottom of the vessel (step 2). This hot

1. Who would supply the waste preparation and gasification system;
2. Who would build and operate the end product conversion plant (pyrolysis gas into either methanol, methane or ammonia); and
3. Who would distribute the end product.

In April 1975 Belmont Chemical learned of Kenyon's solicitation and made a proposal outlining its interest and capabilities.

In May of that year the city received nine other proposals from private firms interested in the project. These proposals were evaluated from a technical, economic, and financial perspective, and, finally, reduced to the three possible options summarized below. Exhibit 10 compares net disposal cost of the three proposals to the present land fill approach. Net disposal cost was defined as the total cost of disposing of solid waste under any option, after deducting the revenues realized from the sale of gas products produced.

1. Methanol Proposal (Pritchard Chemicals, Inc.). Pritchard Chemicals, Inc., would rely on the city for construction and ownership of a methanol facility, but Pritchard would operate the facility under contract with Kenyon and provide technical assistance to the city during project development. Pritchard would enter into a long-term contract with the city for purchase of methanol at a price proportional to market price but with an assured floor price for the first five years only.

The floor price proposed would cover only city debt service. Kenyon would be required to ride market fluctuations with only partial downside protection.

City bond issue required	$110.9 million
City disposal cost	18.02[a]

[a]Based on methanol at 48¢/gallon in 1980.

2. Methane Proposal (State Natural Gas Company). State Natural Gas Company proposed the purchase of methane to be furnished by Kenyon from a methanation facility constructed, owned, and operated by the city. Methane price would be related to alternative sources of methane, with $2 per million BTU (1975) as a base value.

City bond issue required	$94.8 million
City disposal cost	27.18[b]

[b]Established by projecting methane prices to be at a level of $3/million BTU by 1980.

3. Ammonia Proposal (Belmont Chemical Company). Belmont Chemical Company would totally finance and operate an ammonia facility, selling ammonia by long-term contract to one or more Pacific Northwest users. Belmont would realize a marketing fee on product

sales and a management fee for the operation of the Belmont ammonia plant; all revenues beyond Belmont's fees and expenses would be split evenly with the city for pyrolysis gas service. All inflationary increases in Kenyon's variable costs associated with its disposal activities would be passed through to the ultimate ammonia purchaser by means of an escalation clause in the product buyer's contract. This proposal would provide a long-term fixed disposal cost to the city.

City bond issue required	$66.6 million
City disposal cost	12/ton[c]

[c]Fixed for project life.

In October 1975 the city of Kenyon selected the Belmont Chemical Company to build and operate the end product conversion plant. (See Exhibit 11.) The city chose the Union Carbide Corporation of New York to supply the waste preparation and gasification system.

Union Carbide would supply its PUROX Pyrolysis Process and operate the system for the life of the project. (See Exhibit 12.)

Some 550,000 tons of solid waste were generated in Kenyon each year. The proposed solid waste ammonia project would turn the discarded material into 140,000 tons of anhydrous ammonia. This conversion process had four major benefits:

1. Control of the cost and the negative environmental impact of solid waste disposal;
2. Energy recovery from a resource that would have been otherwise discarded;
3. Displacement of natural gas currently dedicated to ammonia production, allowing its use elsewhere; and
4. Production of ammonia for farm fertilizers.

State officials were looking for ways of garnering the support of area farmers who were faced with steadily increasing fertilizer costs not being met by corresponding increases in the prices of agricultural commodities.

A long laborious period of negotiation and market development continued throughout the autumn with the hope of finding one major ammonia consumer in the Northwest who would provide the contractual support that could underwrite the project. By February 1976 it was clear that the developmental nature of the project, the cautious, near-term perspective of major ammonia consumers, and the uncertainty surrounding the natural gas arena were all major hurdles that complicated the project's risk analysis in the eyes of counsel and financial advisors.

FINANCING THE KENYON PROJECT

The financing of the Kenyon project was of major concern to Belmont. The one factor that differentiated its proposal from all the others received by the city was that it was willing to finance *and* operate the ammonia plant.

Initially the company felt it had two possible options—financing could be arranged through traditional leasing or leverage leasing.

These options were particularly attractive to municipalities with limited debt capacity, as they eliminated the necessity for a city to raise the costly downpayment to purchase the facility. However, traditional leasing usually resulted in a correspondingly higher periodic payment than typical municipal bond flotation arrangements. A municipality could also reduce its obligation by allowing the private operator to run the plant and assume the responsibility of the lease payment. Here again the risk/return tradeoff was a factor, for the operator would take on the burden of making the lease payments in return for a share of the revenues from the sale of the plant's end products. The decreased risk factor, however, was often well worth the reduction in revenues that the municipal government might receive: The government is a nonprofit entity. In effect the operator's share of the revenues was his fee for assuming the operating risk.

Under traditional leasing arrangements, a third party lessor purchased the resource recovery plant and then leased it back to the operator. Leverage leasing, by contrast, is a rather complicated financial tool involving

three parties: 1) a long-term capital source; 2) a financial intermediary (lessor); and 3) an operator (lessee).

A financial intermediary (lessor) provided a portion (often about 20 percent) of the necessary capital for the construction of a plant, and borrowed the remainder in a conventional long-term loan, somewhat similar to a home mortgage, from a financial institution. The intermediary, who then had title to the plant, leased it to the operator for the life of his loan, which he paid back to the long-term capital source using the lease payments he received from the operator. The operation of the plant generated the revenues necessary for the operator to pay the lease payments. The benefits the intermediary received from this arrangement were the depreciation expense and the investment tax credit that came with ownership of the plant. The benefit to the operator was that his lease payments were relatively low—because the intermediary looked to the tax benefits rather than the lease payments as his main source of funds. Thus the operator obtained the equipment at a capital cost below the market rate.

At the end of the long-term lease, ownership of the plant was vested in the intermediary (lessor). However, the operator often had the option to buy the plant at a fair market price.

After long negotiation with various financial institutions Belmont decided to use leverage leasing as the major source of funds for the project.

Federal Support

In February and March 1976 the project team made several visits to Washington, with the hope of developing federal support for the project. Both the Environmental Protection Agency (EPA) and Energy Research and Development Administration (ERDA) were investing significant sums in solid waste disposal projects and in energy conservation systems. This project seemed to serve both objectives. Finally, with the support of the region's powerful Congressional delegation, a "price support program" was specifically designed

for the project and others like it. This legislation was included in the 1977 ERDA authorization bill and was introduced on the House
floor in September 1976. It was supported by
a wide range of political interests, from Ralph
Nader and the Sierra Club to conservative
Senators Goldwater and Buckley. Unfortunately the bill was delayed in passing and as
of this writing was still in Congressional committee.

The implications of this federal support
were profound. It would, of course, permit
Kenyon, Union Carbide, and Belmont Chemical to proceed with plant construction and
financing. Also, it would enable Belmont
Chemical to sell ammonia to a wider range of
customers under more favorable terms. A
triple-A customer with a fifteen-year contract
would no longer be needed to meet underwriting requirements. Such a contract had been
tentatively negotiated with a major oil company—but only with terms which included
major price concessions from normal wholesale levels. With a federal price support
"covering" the project against the long-term
risks, short-term and "spot market" contracts
could also be sought, enabling the project to
reap higher returns in these markets. This
also meant that lower project financing costs
could be achieved, further improving the
project's economics.

Rogers was confident that the Congressional bill would pass by March 1977. He
wanted to be ready, however, to capitalize on
the support it would lend to the project and,
therefore, began to consider the various
choices open to him for marketing the ammonia in the Northwest. His firm could:

1. Create directly an ammonia marketing force in
   the Northwest to move the 140,000 tons of annual production to retailers, independent and
   national distributors, cooperatives, and major
   industrial and agricultural consumers;
2. Develop medium and long-term contracts with
   ten to fifteen major consumers, renewing the
   contracts as required;
3. Develop an arrangement with a third-party
   ammonia marketing organization already active
   in the Northwest;

4. Develop import and "swap" markets to absorb
   a portion of the production; or
5. Seek one large consumer to take the entire production.

It was recognized that there were a number
of producers of anhydrous ammonia in the
Northwest United States and Western Canada,
who were essentially supplying the same
markets Belmont Chemical intended to penetrate. (See Exhibit 13.)

In June of 1976 Rogers hired a project
manager who had twenty-eight years of chemical business experience and charged him with
the responsibility of handling the Kenyon
project.

CONTINUED MARKET DEVELOPMENT

Rogers also pondered the timing and development of a marketing effort aimed at other
urban areas. Scores of cities were faced with
the same solid waste problems that plagued
Kenyon, though that city was months or years
ahead of most in recognizing the magnitude of
the problem and in marshalling its resources
to analyze the options. The chemical processes
that Belmont Chemical had researched and
developed were equally suited to the conversion of pyrolysis gas into methanol or
methane, although current market prices of
these end products were only marginally above
breakeven. Thus, Rogers faced several choices
as to what direction his marketing effort
should take.

Cities, towns, states, and countries that
were searching for solutions to the solid waste
problem would be spending significant
amounts of time and money in the future to
develop their own regional answer. Ammonia
and methanol would be needed in increasing
amounts in the years ahead, especially if the
effective use of fertilizer spread to the Third
World and if methanol fulfilled its promise of
becoming a replacement for or supplement to
petroleum-based gasoline.

In October 1976 Belmont Chemical Company submitted a feasibility study to the city
of Mount Vernon, New York, evaluating the
possibility of establishing a solid-waste-to-

methanol plant in that area. Clearly other similar studies would be forthcoming: the market potential for waste recovery systems seemed enormous in the United States and Rogers wondered how he would be able to capitalize on these opportunities.

Sitting in his office one Friday afternoon, Rogers began to turn over in his mind the risks inherent in his marketing activities and the unique position his company held in the rechemistry industry.

In addition to the obvious role played by the decisions of government authorities, the decisions of other firms in various areas of the resource recovery industry would have a profound effect on the success or failure of Rogers' efforts in marketing the concept of rechemistry of solid waste. One example would be the decisions made by companies in the pyrolysis industry. Without a workable pyrolysis unit, this rechemistry process would not be possible.

Furthermore whereas the conversion of pyrolysis gas into various end products had been successful on a pilot basis, it had not yet been proved either economically or technologically viable on a commercial basis.

In 1976 ERDA awarded Kenyon a grant of $500,000 to research the technological and economic aspects of pyrolysis gas-to-ammonia conversion. Belmont Chemical received half of this grant to design a gas conditioning and pilot plant system, to be tested before full-scale production in Kenyon would begin. The construction effort was subcontracted to Union Carbide.

Aware that growth only comes to a company whose management is willing to take risks, Rogers was reminded that his company had significant expertise in the marketing and distribution of chemicals but only limited experience in chemical manufacturing. He wondered whether the present organization could support his company's growth strategy.

EXHIBIT 1

BELMONT CHEMICAL COMPANY, INC.
Organizational Structure

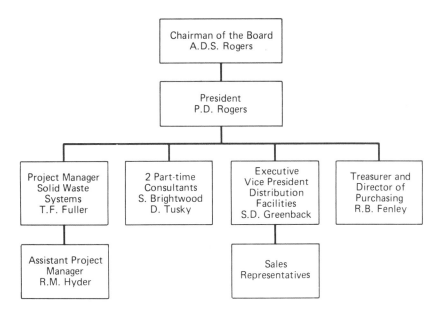

EXHIBIT 2

BELMONT CHEMICAL COMPANY
Balance Sheet 12/31/75
($000)

ASSETS			LIABILITIES AND NET WORTH		
Cash	$ 85		Current portion		
Accounts receivable	795		Long-term debt	$ 31	
Inventory	725		Accounts payable	831	
Prepaid expenses	110		Accrued expenses	185	
Total current assets		$1,715	Total current liabilities		$1,057
Land	168		Long-term debt	395	
Buildings	366		Capital stock	31	
Building improvements	175		Retained earnings	1,235	
Whs. office equipment	181				
Autos, trucks	274				
Other assets	55				
	1,219				
Less accum. depreciation	216				
Total fixed assets		1,003			
		$2,718			$2,718

EXHIBIT 3
U.S. AVERAGE AMMONIA PRICE
History and Projection ($/ton)

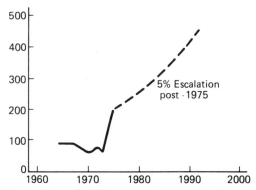

Source: Kenyon Solid Waste Ammonia Project, January 1976.

EXHIBIT 4

WASTE SYSTEMS AND UTILIZATION OPTIONS

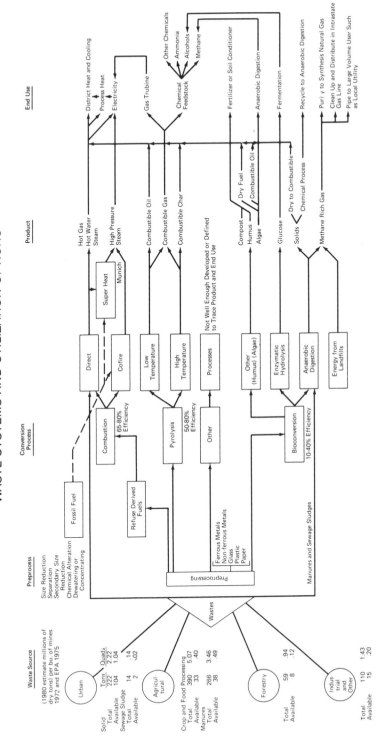

EXHIBIT 5

COMPARISON OF ENERGY RECOVERY PROCESSES (PLANT CAPACITY 1,000 TPD)

DOLLARS PER TON

	Wheelabrator-Frye Waterwall Incinerator	Combustion Power Incinerator Turbine	Horner & Shifrin Co-combustion of Shredded Refuse	Combustion Equipment Associates Eco-Fuel II	Black Clawson Wet Pulped Fibrous Fuel No. 2	Monsanto Environ-Chem Landgard System	Occidental Research "Flash Pyrolysis"	Carborundum Torrax System	Union Carbide Purox System	Dynatech R/D Anaerobic Digestion to Methane
Investment ($/daily ton)	30,800	22,500	10,400	17,700	13,500	21,500	21,900	16,500	22,900	19,600
Capital cost[a]	10.24	7.49	3.46	5.90	4.49	7.17	7.28	5.48	7.60	6.53
Operating cost										
Labor and supervision	3.40	3.10	2.59	3.10	2.59	3.10	3.94	3.10	3.40	3.10
Power	2.10	[b]	1.62	1.65	2.55	2.31	3.72	3.75	5.34	1.56
Other utilities and supplies	0.20	0.11	0.08	0.76	4.56	2.97	0.36	1.67	0.24	4.40
Maintenance	3.42	4.09	0.85	1.92	1.40	2.49	2.49	1.89	2.25	2.49
Miscellaneous	0.93	0.68	0.32	0.54	0.41	0.65	0.66	0.50	0.69	0.59
Disposal costs	1.08	1.50	0.90	0.72	0.60	0.48	1.14	—	—	6.28
Total operating cost	11.13	9.48	6.36	8.69	12.11	12.00	12.31	10.91	11.92	18.42
Total operating cost including amortization	21.37	16.97	9.82	14.59	16.60	19.17	19.59	16.39	19.52	24.95
Credits										
Energy	13.80	6.88	6.61	9.36	8.60	11.04	5.76	6.30	13.50	7.86
Materials	1.68	2.91	1.68	1.68	3.51	2.06	3.52	0.60	2.06	3.56
Total credits	15.48	9.79	8.29	11.04	12.11	13.10	9.28	6.90	15.56	11.42
Net disposal cost including amortization	5.89	7.18	1.53	3.55	4.49	6.07	10.31	9.49	3.96	13.53
Energy recovery efficiency	67%[c]	36%[d]	66%[e]	64%[e]	62%[e]	44%[c]	37%	45%	62%	25%

[a] 15-year amortization, 7% interest
[b] Self-generated
[c] Includes conversion to steam
[d] Overall conversion to electricity
[e] Reflects allowance for less efficient combustion as compared with oil/gas

EXHIBIT 6

PYROLYSIS

- Definition—Thermal decomposition in absence of oxygen
- Characteristics
    Produces a clean burning fuel gas
    Disposes of solid waste without polluting .
    Flexibility to handle differing wastes and high energy content input
    Compatible with resource recovery

EXHIBIT 7

SYNTHETIC METHANOL PRICES

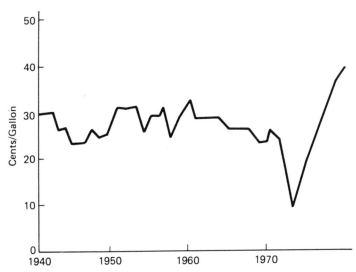

Source: Belmont Chemical Proposal to the city of Mount Vernon, New York, October 1976.

EXHIBIT 8

METHANOL PRODUCTION

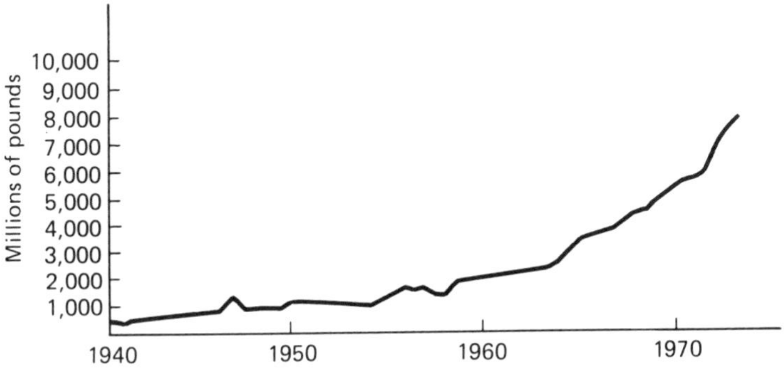

Source: Belmont Chemical Proposal to the city of Mount Vernon, New York, October 1976.

EXHIBIT 9

SOLID WASTE/AMMONIA SCHEMATIC

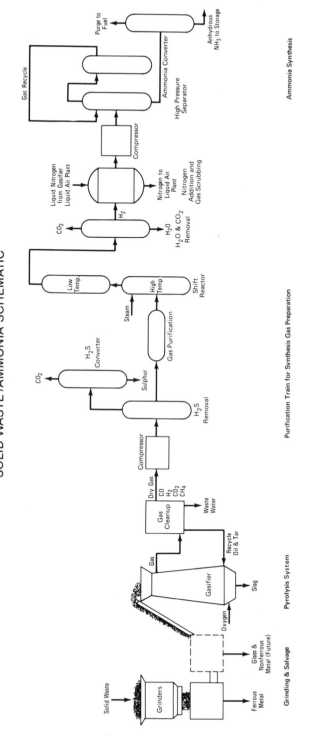

EXHIBIT 10
DISPOSAL COSTS: COMPARISON OF ALTERNATIVES

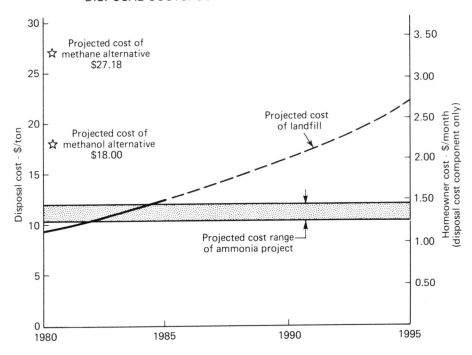

EXHIBIT 11
THE KENYON SOLID WASTE AMMONIA PROJECT

Estimated capital costs ($000)	
Waste preparation plant and gasification system	
Construction costs	$51,588
Financing costs	15,013
	$ 66,601
Ammonia plant	35,000
Total capital investment	$101,601

EXHIBIT 12
UNION CARBIDE PUROX SYSTEM

PROCESS DESCRIPTION

Pyrolysis in the PUROX System takes place in a vertical shaft furnace into which the shredded refuse is fed from the top. At the bottom of the shaft is a combustion zone where high-temperature (3000° F) oxidation of the carbon char generated from the ongoing pyrolysis reaction takes place. Pure oxygen is injected at this level to facilitate combustion. The heat from this combustion rises up through the waste and pyrolyzes the organic material in the middle portion of the shaft to form a gas, which leaves the furnace at the top. In the upper portion of the shaft the heat is not sufficient to pyrolyze the entering waste, but serves to dry it in preparation for pyrolysis in the middle portion. The noncombustible portion of the waste flows out of the combustion zone at the bottom of the shaft in molten form. Here it is quenched in water, forming a clear, gravel-like product.

In terms of energy requirements the PUROX System shows a favorable balance between operating requirements and energy output. About 20 percent of the total energy output is needed to meet internal requirements. The volume of the solid frit residue is about 2 to 3 percent of that of the untreated refuse. It is suitable for such uses as highway construction and general purpose fill.

EXHIBIT 13

325

ANHYDROUS AMMONIA
Estimated Plant Production Capacities (000 Net Tons)

NORTHWEST U.S.A. AND WESTERN CANADA

	Location	1976	1977	1978	1979	1980	1981	1982	1983	1984	1985
Northwest U.S.A.											
Beker Industries	Conda, Id.	100	100	100	100	100	100	100	100	100	100
Chevron (SOCAL)	Richmond, Cal.	130	130	130	130	130	130	130	130	130	130
Collier (Union Oil)	Kenai, Alaska	510	510	1,020	1,020	1,020	1,020	1,020	1,020	1,020	1,020
Hooker Chemical	Tacoma, Wash.	23	23	23	23	23	23	23	23	23	23
Pennwalt	Portland, Ore.	8	8	8	8	8	8	8	8	8	8
Phillips-Pac. Chem.	Finley, Wash.	155	155	155	155	155	155	155	155	155	155
Reichhold Chemical	St. Helens, Ore.	90	90	90	90	90	90	90	90	90	90
J.R. Simplot	Pocatello, Id.	108	108	108	108	108	108	108	108	108	108
Total Northwest U.S.A.		1,124	1,124	1,634	1,634	1,634	1,634	1,634	1,634	1,634	1,634
Western Canada											
Canadian Fert. Ltd.	Medicine Hat, Alb.	400	800	800	800	800	800	800	800	800	800
Cominco Ltd.	Calgary, Alb.	125	125	125	125	125	125	125	125	125	125
	Trail, B.C.	70	70	70	70	70	70	70	70	70	70
	Carseland, Alb.	—	400	400	400	400	400	400	400	400	400
Esso Chemicals	Redwater, Alb.	210	210	210	210	210	210	210	210	210	210
Sherritt Gordon Mines	Ft. Sask., Alb.	160	160	160	160	160	160	160	160	160	160
Western Coop Fert.	Calgary, Alb.	70	70	70	70	70	70	70	70	70	70
	Medicine Hat, Alb.	70	70	70	70	70	70	70	70	70	70
Total Western Canada		1,105	1,905	1,905	1,905	1,905	1,905	1,905	1,905	1,905	1,905
Grand Total		2,229	3,029	3,539	3,539	3,539	3,539	3,539	3,539	3,539	3,539

The major capacity is in the hands of three producers:

	Percent of Capacity	
	1977	1978 Forward
Collier % of USA	45	62
CFL % of Canada	41	41
Cominco % of Canada	31	31
	72	72

	Percent of Capacity	
	1977	1978 Forward
Collier % of Grand Total	16	28
CFL % of Grand Total	26	22
Cominco % of Grand Total	19	16
	61	66

Note: Sherritt Gordon had talked of a 495 expansion in 1981.

STAHL CORPORATION

Frank Silverman, the president of Stahl Corporation, examined the purchase contract for a Norris 4000-horsepower automobile shredder. He had recently obtained an option to buy this contract from another scrap metal company that had decided not to take delivery on the Norris it had ordered six months earlier. The total cost of the machine, including installation, would be $1.8 million, a significant investment for Stahl, whose sales in 1974 were $62.9 million on total assets of $39 million. (See Exhibits 1 and 2.) Silverman was not sure if any of Stahl's scrap yards really needed the installation or which yard could it use most.

THE INDUSTRY

The scrap metal industry had developed increasing importance in the national economy as the means of recycling over 110 million tons of scrap materials produced each year. It had also assumed a greater burden of risk in its position between the scrap metal producers and users.

Essentially, the scrap business involved buying material from the public and then selling it to mills, where it was reprocessed into new metal for reuse by the public. The scrap dealer's job was to buy the material and package it according to the steel mill's requirements. In 1973 over $8.7 billion worth of scrap was sold to mills in the United States.

In order to understand these requirements it is necessary to outline the needs of the scrap consumer. The first consideration was the type of product to be made and the particular

This case was prepared by Jeffrey D. Goldstein under the supervision of Professor Jules J. Schwartz as the basis for class discussion rather than to illustrate either effective or ineffective handling of an administrative action.

characteristics of that product. For example, sheet steel for automobile bodies had to be light and have the ability to be bent, shaped, or creased, and hold a painted finish. On the other hand reinforcing rods for construction and roadways had to be dense, hard, and very strong. Rods didn't have to be compatible with a painted finish because they would be buried in concrete. Each product, therefore, has different chemical requirements, depending on its intended application.

When steel products are made from virgin ore several different elements had to be combined to produce an alloy steel that had the desired characteristics. However, the mill could save money in two ways by using some scrap metal in the mixture. First, it was expensive to refine virgin ore because of the great amount of heat necessary to separate iron from rock. Ore contained less than 50 percent iron. Further, scrap, having already been refined, contained the mixing elements required for the product; the mill could save money by using scrap that already had quantities of the elements that would have to be added to the mixture anyway. Thus the mill required separation of scrap of different chemical composition depending on whether the product was to be cast, machined, creased, or whatever.

The mills had other needs regarding size and density of the scrap. Size was important because the material had to be in pieces small enough for the opening of the furnace charging box. Density was important because it contributed to more efficient use of heat in the melting process. Mills sought scrap with the highest possible density.

In addition to being sorted by chemical content, the scrap had also to be graded according to degree of contamination and weight.

Grading originated with the open hearth furnace, when it was found that melt loss was higher on light scrap than with heavy scrap. Thus, No. 1 scrap steel was defined as being at least ¼-inch thick and no greater than five feet in length; No. 2 steel scrap was at least ⅛-inch thick and no longer than three feet. For example, railroad rail is a high grade item as every piece of rail is made exactly of the same chemistry and contamination is very low. Rail also fit the weight requirements for No. 1 steel. On the other hand pieces from automobile bodies were a lower grade due to lighter weight and a high degree of contamination from copper, aluminum, and other foreign attached material. Thus higher grades warranted higher prices.

Since the advent of the baling press the grading had been determined mostly by the degree of contamination of the metal within the bale. Baling was developed as a means of getting higher density with light steel scrap. However, bales also contained much of the foreign material that had been attached to the steel before it was baled. Therefore, bales were graded No. 1 only if they contained clean steel, usually remnants from manufacturing plants with almost no contamination. Bales made primarily from automobile bodies were graded No. 2.

There was also subgrading of No. 2 bales. Much of the contamination in an automobile could be removed by burning the car before selling it to the scrap dealer. Thus No. 2 bales were graded as burnt or unburnt. The lower grade items were used in products that were so inexpensive that chemistry was unimportant. They could also be mixed with virgin ore as a diluter, usually on the basis of two tons of ore for each ton of scrap. The raw materials cost was thereby reduced and contamination was kept at a minimum by dilution.

The job of the scrap dealer was to satisfy the mills by 1) sorting the material according to chemistry and weight, 2) processing it to achieve the proper size and density, and 3) packaging the scrap in a form suitable for shipment. These functions were carried out in several ways that will be described later.

The previous discussion refers primarily to the open hearth furnace, which uses virgin ore as a primary input, generally using equal parts of ore and scrap. However, a recent development was the electric furnace, which uses nearly all scrap material as input. Scrap was less costly than ore and had a lower melt loss (only 2 to 3 percent) because there was no rock to separate. Greater efficiency in the use of heat was possible. As it did not add pure iron to raise the quality of the melt by dilution, the electric furnace mill was much more demanding and bought only the highest grades of scrap steel.

Essentially there were three major types of scrap produced. Most scrap, about 60 percent, was mill scrap that came from the production of ingots and other steel mill products. Mill scrap had never been used by the public and its return to the furnace was simply a matter of efficient operation. Industrial scrap, about 15 percent, was leftover steel from punch presses, metalworking equipment, and other machines used in such industries as automobiles and fabricating. The remaining 25 percent was obsolete scrap, discarded iron and steel products such as cars and appliances. Industrial and obsolete scrap were handled primarily by the scrap dealer.

Scrap was an inverted sort of industry. In most businesses dealers buy goods from a manufacturer, add a markup, and sell to the public. Scrap is the opposite, or recycling, portion of the materials cycle. Each mill would pay dealers a set price that depended on its particular scrap needs. Then the dealer subtracted his operating expenses and profit to determine the price he would pay the public for its scrap. Operating expenses included transportation, processing and packaging, merchandising, and warehousing of the material.

The dealer bought scrap principally from three sources, each having peculiar needs and problems. Industry needed someone to help dispose of its scrap. Its primary concern was to get a dealer who could efficiently keep the scrap out of the way. Generally the dealer picked up industrial waste in his own truck or left a lugger box at the supplier's plant. Double handling was avoided because the supplier could drop scrap directly into the empty box. When the box filled up the dealer's truck picked it up and left an empty one in its place. This type of truck system also offered the dealer better economies of transportation.

The obsolete scrap came from two sources, auto wreckers and other scrap dealers. The auto wrecker was the major channel for scrap from the 8 million cars junked each year. There was approximately 1900 pounds of steel in each car, or a total annual volume of 7.6 million tons. The wrecker usually stripped the car of all usable parts (lights, radiators, batteries, and tires) and sold the remaining hulk to the scrap dealer. Because an automobile hulk took up a lot of space relative to its weight, the auto wrecker had a problem in transportation. If he had an auto flattener to compress the bodies, he could get a full payload of twenty tons on a trailer. Without a flattener he could only carry two to four bodies, depending on the size of his truck. The possible payload determined the geographic size of an auto wrecker's market.

Some scrap came from other dealers. The size of a scrap operation ranged from one man with a truck to a multimillion dollar corporation with several yards. Regarding the relative sizes of scrap operations, one industry source suggested the following criteria:

Small. The small operation is usually a small yard with low volume and little inventory. This type of yard is often referred to as a "feeder" yard because it does little or no processing of material and has only a handful of employees. It is usually no more than a collection point to accumulate enough scrap to sell to a larger dealer. Often the business is run from a truck; the dealer picks up scrap, sells it immediately, and goes out to buy more. Small dealers can handle limited size lots while keeping good margins, as they have little inventory or overhead to finance.

Medium. The medium-size scrap dealer usually has a small hydraulic shear, a small baler, and four or five cranes. He carries on

material processing with small, relatively inefficient equipment. His volume, less than 5000 tons processed per month, does not justify the use of larger, more efficient equipment because the interest and depreciation costs would be too great.

Large. The large scrap yard processes at least 5000 to 10,000 tons each month. It has a minimum investment in land and equipment of $2 million or $3 million.

The small dealer had to sell to a larger one because steel mills preferred to buy through a few brokers who could guarantee delivery of several carload lots, rather than buying direct from a great number of small dealers.

The processing/packaging function was the major activity in a scrap yard. Material was sorted and then processed to the desired size and density. Depending on the material, one of the following processes (which are described further in later sections) was used.

Baling. The material, consisting of automobiles or other light scrap, was compressed into a bale or bundle measuring two by two by six feet.

Shearing. Heavy material, such as rail or plate, was sliced into smaller pieces by a guillotine shear. Automobiles were also sheared into slabs that were slightly smaller than bales.

Shredding. Automobile bodies or other light scrap items were literally ripped apart into small pieces in this process. The pieces were then passed over a magnetic separator that pulled the ferrous pieces away from the copper, glass, and other non-iron items.

Scrap had traditionally been an industry with high volume relative to fixed investment. Despite the modern emphasis on sophisticated processing equipment, small feeder-type operations, with low initial investment and healthy margins, were still attractive to entrepreneurs. Most scrap dealers, however, were family-owned operations of medium size. The owner, of necessity, had to be an expert manager, production superintendent, accountant, and salesperson, yet even with these skills he could never really achieve the efficiency of the large-volume dealer who could afford experts in all these fields. In recent years nearly a third of all medium-scale operations had failed. The medium-size dealer was vulnerable and was under pressure to grow larger and compete efficiently, or grow smaller and become a feeder or auto wrecker.

As mentioned earlier steel mills preferred to deal with a few suppliers. This situation gave rise to the other major aspect of the scrap industry: brokerage. Brokerage in scrap was not the same as brokerage in stocks or commodities. The stockbroker operated in an agency relationship between principals; the scrap broker bought and sold for his own account. He took ownership and assumed all risks arising out of such ownership.

There was no central exchange in which scrap brokers carried on public trading. Information was spread mostly by word of mouth. The broker kept in touch mainly by telephone, talking with consumers and suppliers, evaluating the demand for scrap and the prices at which it could be obtained.

Dealers generally sold to brokers who, in turn, sold to the steel mills. When a mill needed scrap it called three or four brokers. Each broker gave the mill an opinion of what the price should be. The mill evaluated the opinions in the light of its needs and decided on the price it was willing to pay. Orders were placed monthly and divided among several brokers. In this way the mill reduced the risk of running short of scrap or paying too much.

The broker subtracted his operating costs and profit from the mill's offer to determine how much he could pay the dealers who supplied the scrap. The dealers followed the same procedure to determine how much they would pay for material. In the absence of a better offer, if a dealer or broker refused to sell at his respective customer's prices, he had nothing on which to base his buying prices for that month, and also risked a reduction in volume through his plant.

The mill's final price decision generally had to be accepted by the industry. If buying was fairly easy, each party might lower his price further to see how suppliers reacted. If buying was difficult, they might have to raise their prices, perhaps taking a loss, in order to meet their contractual obligations to the mill. As the scrap sellers were very responsive to price changes, price became a control valve that adjusted the flow of scrap through the system. In 1974 the price of top-grade, heavy melting scrap varied between $50 and $125 per ton.

Brokerage involved continual risk taking. The broker did not receive a fixed commission on each transaction but rather made his money on his ability to buy low and sell high. The key to successful brokerage was the ability to predict accurately supply and demand in the scrap market, and to estimate as closely as possible how much could be bought and sold in a given market. If the broker felt prices would rise, he tried to buy long and if he thought they were about to drop, he sold short. As different areas had different markets, a broker was in the best position to make better predictions if he had information from several regions.

The broker generally paid his suppliers 75 percent of the purchase price when the order was shipped and the balance upon verification of the weights and quality received at the mill. He did not collect from the mill until the end of the month. As he held the title to goods while in transit, his major expense was financing this travel inventory. The broker had thirty days to effect shipment to the mill. If the order was late or failed to meet specifications, the mill had the right to cancel the order and reject the shipment. If prices rose during transit, the buyer usually accepted the shipment even if it was a few days late. However, if prices dropped significantly, the buyer might look for reasons to cancel.

COMPANY HISTORY

The Stahl Corporation was founded in 1918 as a small partnership in Davenport, Iowa. It purchased scrap from local industry and did any necessary processing by hand, often with no more than a sledge hammer. The mills paid premiums for scrap sold in large lots. Stahl found that it could purchase small lots from other local dealers at slightly below the mill small-lot price. The purchased material was added to Stahl's inventory to aggregate larger lots to ship to nearby consumers such as Keystone Steel and the John Deere Foundry.

At that time most scrap dealers were not involved in brokerage and most brokers were not directly involved in yard operations. Stahl was one of the first scrap dealers to combine these two functions. This arrangement worked well in both directions. If brokerage had difficulty acquiring enough material to meet a deadline, the yard could supplement from its inventory. On the other hand if sales from the yard were sagging, brokerage could give it a boost.

Stahl was still operating in its original mode. By taking a profit in both functions the company was able to generate cash for more rapid expansion at appropriate times. Stahl was the first scrap dealer west of Chicago to have a crane with a magnet (1930), a baler for automobile scrap (1934), and trucks with lugger boxes (1939). By the mid-1950s the company had expanded in this manner to create a market of 200-mile radius around Davenport. Throughout this time Stahl was building a solid reputation for fair dealing. This reputation was crucial because scrap prices changed so rapidly and all contracts were made verbally.

In 1956 the company moved its operations to a thirty-five-acre industrial site, the present location for the main offices and plant in Davenport. In the same year the market area was further expanded when the company started shipping its scrap to the mills by river barge. Freight rates by water had always been significantly lower than by rail. However, the 1956 barge rates still limited profitable transportation to the distance between Davenport and St. Louis.

In 1959 Stahl realized that, with slightly reduced barge rates, it could ship material profitably as far as the stronger Pittsburgh market. The company prevailed upon the barge lines to request a rate reduction in return for a guarantee of large volume going east. Scrap metal was a regulated commodity and common carrier rates were subject to the authority of the Interstate Commerce Commission (ICC). The reduction proposal was approved but the carriers then tried to have the reduction withdrawn. Their action was allegedly due to pressure from the St. Louis mills to block scrap movement from the Upper Mississippi River area to Pittsburgh. Fortunately, the carriers' attempt failed, but it was clear that future rate reductions would be unlikely. In 1960 Stahl bought its first towboat and four barges and became the first scrap company to haul a regulated commodity by private water carriage.

The firm began river operations by transporting scrap downriver under private carriage and then transferring to larger carriers for the rest of the trip. At first there was a problem in getting backhauls for the barges. Fortunately, a new coal-burning power plant was opening near Davenport. Stahl was able to convince the plant to contract for coal backhauls by offering a competitive price. Scrap shipments downriver were somewhat irregular, however, due to sales fluctuations and the time necessary to accumulate a bargeload of 1500 net tons.

During the 1960s a new demand for barge shipment arose. Huge crop surpluses in the Midwest sorely needed cheap transportation. Most of this grain was destined for export from New Orleans. Stahl was able to secure long-term contracts with grain shippers to fill unused barge capacity. The business provided both a reason and the funds to enlarge Stahl's barge and towboat fleet. By 1975 the company owned and operated seven large towboats and 175 barges.

Grain and other bulk commodities such as coal, phosphate, and salt, had the advantage of not being regulated by the ICC. The rates for unregulated carriage could be changed to meet the demand for transportation without going through the lengthy process of obtaining approval from the ICC. The result was that

Stahl's river carriage growth had for the most part been in bulk commodities rather than scrap. However, with this large river transportation network, the scrap marketing area had expanded to include the entire Mississippi River, the Ohio River, and inland canals along the Gulf of Mexico.

The company continued expansion in three areas: yard processing, scrap brokerage, and river transportation. Wherever possible, growth was designed to benefit all these operations. Initial penetration of a new scrap market was accomplished by brokerage. If the area appeared to have potential, Stahl opened a small yard operation to serve as a collection facility or feeder yard. Where feasible the material was shipped to the larger yards by water. Thus in 1961 a feeder operation was established in La Crosse, Wisconsin, on the Mississippi River. Later this yard also became a bulk storage facility for agricultural commodities.

Also in 1961 Stahl expanded into the Twin Cities area, and established a yard in St. Paul to serve as a major processing facility as well as a marine terminal and bulk storage location. In 1962 another major processing operation was opened in Council Bluffs, Iowa, to buy scrap in western Iowa and eastern Nebraska. Since then still another feeder operation was added in Des Moines, Iowa. Stahl had five scrap yards in the Midwest. The size of each is indicated by volume and investment in plant and equipment.

	Monthly Tonnage	Investment ($ millions)
Davenport, Iowa	10,000	3.0
Council Bluffs, Iowa	8,000	5.2
St. Paul, Minnesota	6,000	3.6
La Crosse, Wisconsin	1,000	0.2
Des Moines, Iowa	1,500	0.2
Total	26,500	12.2

Aware of the diseconomy of medium-size yards, Stahl operated only large processing and small feeder yards. The primary function of the feeder yards was to insure enough volume for the large yards to process at the lowest possible unit cost. The company also operated a fleet of trucks with on-off lugger boxers. The boxes were for scrap, coal, salt, grain, and other bulk commodities. The fleet included several semitrailers, which were used when barging was inappropriate for longer hauls.

Brokerage had always preceded yard operations into a new market area. As the yard grew it took over from brokerage the function of buying material in the area. Sales for all the yards were still handled at the main office. The yard could advise the sales staff of any potential customers in its area and, if necessary, personally contact a customer to lay groundwork for sales. While brokerage generally made one or two dollars per ton, the yard could make five to ten dollars per ton processed. After a yard took over its own buying the brokerage department could increase the radius of its activities. As always, brokerage and yard operations supplemented each other to maintain high volume. Throughout its expansion Stahl's emphasis had been on production. Yard operations had been developed with Davenport at the center. Brokerage grew in the same directions, somewhat ahead of, but still rather evenly paced with, production.

As different areas had different markets, the largest brokerage firms had offices across the country to collect information and make better predictions. Stahl's main strength was not market prediction, but it had a good idea of how much scrap was available, at least in its own area.

The firm's evenly paced development was also a major selling point. As the brokerage operations of larger companies were usually many times larger than their production capabilities, a broker did not have the assurance that his company's yard could back him up if he had difficulty buying brokerage material. Stahl had a much more secure position in this respect.

On the other hand Stahl might modify its brokerage expansion by setting up more remote offices. In this way it could take advantage of personal, instead of telephone, selling to bring about faster growth in brokerage. This, in turn, could contribute to faster yard growth.

ORGANIZATION

Until recently the company was organized on a cost center basis. Each yard, as a cost center, had a manager reporting directly to the president, Frank Silverman. Because the Davenport yard was close to the main office, Silverman managed it himself; but much of the direct supervision was handled by a strong plant superintendent. (See Exhibit 3.) It was felt that this type of organization was too functionally oriented, as the president was the only officer with a generalist outlook; further, there was no one to back up the president as general manager.

Several important changes were made in the organizational structure to create a system that could develop more generalists. First, each yard was changed from a cost center to a profit center, with a general manager having authority over production, inventory, buying prices, and other matters concerning his yard. Sales were still handled at the head office. Under the new system a salesperson phoned each manager to see how much that manager could commit to a sales order. In this way a yard manager had some control over how much he would sell from his yard, based on his perception of his market situation and inventory levels. The system also encouraged managers to work out their problems within and between yards. Top management intervened only when necessary in the interest of the company.

Second, profit responsibility for the Davenport yard was shifted to the marketing vice president, Charles Rogers, to give him more experience in production and provide still another generalist for top management. He was still backed up by the strong plant superintendent, with the intent that each would learn from the other. (See Exhibit 4.) Eventually Rogers was expected to become a general manager with authority over all scrap yards and all scrap marketing, and Davenport would have its own general manager. (See Exhibit 5.)

The long-term goal of Stahl was to solidify its position as the largest scrap company in the Midwest before further expanding its production operations. Each of the three large yards now processed all types of scrap metal. However, problems had arisen in processing a major scrap item—automobile bodies. These problems, if left unsolved, could pose a threat to the goal of dominance.

As described before No. 2 steel from car bodies could be processed by a baler. This process involves pressing the bodies into a No. 2 bundle measuring two by two by six feet. Baling had been desirable to the mills because of the density-efficiency relationship. Burnt No. 2 was preferred over unburnt No. 2 because it contained fewer contaminants and thus caused less smoke. It also provided more uniform chemistry in the melt. This led to higher prices for the auto wrecker who brought in burnt car bodies.

Environmental pollution laws had put an end to open-air burning of automobile bodies. The scrap dealer was forced to buy unburnt bodies. On the other hand the steel mills try not to overload the capacity of their new air pollution equipment. They seek to buy mostly low-contamination burnt No. 2 steel. Unless Stahl acquired the machinery to process car bodies without burning out the contaminants, the baler at Davenport would become almost obsolete. Even though light industrial scrap could still be baled, the volume was not nearly enough to keep the baler operating at efficient levels.

Stahl had attempted to solve this problem by installing a huge incinerator with air pollution equipment to treat the smoke. Thirty automobiles could be burned each hour in compliance with the new law. The project failed, however, because the insulation in the combustion chamber could not contain the heat adequately and the air pollution equipment did not clean the smoke satisfactorily.

In the early 1960s a new process called shredding was developed. The shredder literally ripped car bodies apart, forming small compressed pieces. The steel was almost completely torn away from contaminants such as copper, rubber, vinyl, and glass. The steel was then plucked away by magnetic separation. The end product was steel that had a contamination of only 2 to 3 percent with no burning involved. Even though the shredder's operating costs were higher than those of the baler, these costs were more than offset by the much higher prices paid for the cleaner, denser, shredded product.

The following table compares the relevant cost information for both processes. In this table the value of product is based on a representative market price. Cost of processing is based on 6,000 net tons processed per month and includes depreciation, interest, maintenance, and shredder loss due to weight shrink. Automobile bodies typically cost between $30 and $60, depending in part on how far the auto wrecker must ship his material.

Basic Costs and Revenues: Baler and Shredder
(dollars per net ton produced)

	Baler	Shredder
Value of product (price from customer)	$45	$78
Total cost of processing	3.5	20
Maximum price that can be paid for an automobile body	41.5	58
Amount of steel (percentage of product shipped)	78%	98%

The shredder consisted of a large drum, about 108 inches long and 104 inches in diameter. (See Exhibit 6.) The drum, weighing about 60 tons, spun inside its housing at speeds of nearly 70 miles per hour. There was a space of several inches between the drum and housing. The scrap auto body was fed into this space where it was shredded by the interaction of ring hammers on the spinning drum and liner plates on the inside of the housing. As the

pieces were discharged from the mill, magnetic separation facilitated sorting to conveyors that deposited materials in the proper containers. Special air suction and water spray attachments controlled dirt and dust.

As the entire facility sorted out the essentially nonsalvageable nonsteel pieces, there was an inherent weight reduction, or "shrink" in the processed steel compared to the weight of the automobile before shredding. This shrink factor was approximately 25 percent and represented the nonsteel items that were bought with the car body when it entered the scrap yard.

There were two variations of the shredder mill. One used an inner drum spinning on a vertical axis and the other, on a horizontal axis. The chief difference between the two was that the vertical mill produced smaller, more compressed pieces. This was because the metal had longer contact with the ring hammers as it fell through the mill. The horizontal mill had less contact between the metal and the hammers, as shown in the schematic diagram in Exhibit 6.

While both types of mills were still being perfected Stahl continued to produce unburnt No. 2 bundles and slabs for a diminishing market. Now there were only two steel mills buying limited quantities of unburnt No. 2 steel for dilution with higher grade scrap. These mills could not buy any larger quantity without overloading their pollution equipment and it was not known how much longer they would continue to buy.

The horizontal shredder was essentially perfected by 1973. There were still minor difficulties but, for the most part, the machine was now reliable. Back in 1969, however, Stahl felt the concept of the vertical shredder, introduced in the late 1960s, was more promising because of its higher quality product. At the time there were only a few vertical shredders on the market, none of which was performing satisfactorily. The problem seemed to be in the engineering of the machine, and Silverman felt that a manufacturer with a good staff could develop a suitable vertical shredder.

During the past decade Stahl had purchased several towboats and a large number of barges from the RJF Corporation. Even though RJF had no experience with scrap processing, both firms were confident that RJF had the engineering skills to design a vertical shredder that would work well. In 1970 Stahl entered into a purchase agreement with RJF for a vertical machine. The shredder was installed at the St. Paul yard and almost immediately encountered major problems. The machine developed so much stress in critical areas that certain key pieces failed. RJF tried to repair the shredder and made many design changes. The machine continued to tear itself apart. For every month it operated it was down a month for repairs. Finally in January 1975 Stahl ordered RJF to take the shredder out of St. Paul, as it obviously was not suitable for the intended application. Stahl was producing only bundles at Davenport and slabs at Council Bluffs.

The Council Bluffs yard opened in 1962 and had experienced steady growth. Its major piece of equipment was a hydraulic shear, which, like the baler in Davenport, was used for processing burnt automobile bodies. The shear produced No. 2 slabs that were slightly smaller than bundles and not packed so tightly. By 1973, however, the volume of material had become too great for the shear.

Management had two alternatives for the Council Bluffs yard. It could install a larger shear that could still produce No. 2 slabs, as well as cut heavy structural and plate scrap to size. The total cost of this shear would be $1 million. Or it could install a shredder at a higher cost. This would leave only the heavy scrap for the old shear to handle.

Though the horizontal shredder was supposedly perfected in 1973 Stahl believed it still had too many bugs. Further, the vertical shredder installed by RJF two years earlier still showed promise of success. There was a consensus among top management that even though shredders would eventually be needed in each of the major yards, competition from the horizontal shredder posed no immediate threat to operations. The company opted for the new shear at Council Bluffs.

While Stahl waited for RJF to perfect the St. Paul machine, other firms, including some steel mills, had installed their own horizontal shredders. These shredders were performing fairly well. The market for unburnt No. 2 scrap had dwindled and Stahl had found that the best markets for the Council Bluffs slabs were the Kansas City steel mills, which had their own shredders. In fact, the slabs got no better price than the auto wreckers in Council Bluffs who could flatten their car bodies and ship them to Kansas City by truck.

Shredders had thus started to pull some material away from the Council Bluffs operation. The Davenport baler had been getting enough volume from auto wreckers who could not afford to ship to St. Louis or Chicago. However the scrap supply for Council Bluffs had become endangered by the threat of direct competition in the Omaha area.

THE FUTURE

The Ace Metal Company was a Chicago based scrap firm. It was much larger than Stahl, with yards and brokerage offices in many different parts of the country. However, Ace was not as strong as Stahl in the Omaha-Council Bluffs area. In 1973 Ace made an offer to buy out Stahl. When the offer was refused, Ace offered to buy the Council Bluffs operation. Upon a second refusal Ace told Silverman that it would open its own yard in Omaha with a shredder that was already on order. The impact of a shredder on the Council Bluffs shear operation is indicated in the following comparison.

Basic Costs and Revenues: Shear and Shredder
(dollars per net ton produced)

	Shear	Shredder
Value of product (price from customer)	$40	$78
Total cost of processing	5	20
Maximum price that can be paid for an automobile body	35	58
Amount of steel (percentage of product shipped)	78%	98%

The value of No. 2 slabs was somewhat less than that of No. 2 bundles because, though both were identical in content and contamination, the slabs were not compressed as tightly as bundles. Given this price indication from consumers, the table indicates the maximum that can be paid for automobile bodies to be run through a shear operation. The shredder profit margin was again based on a representative market in the absence of competing shredders in the same area.

The amount of automobile scrap available in the area had been estimated at 72,000 tons annually. This volume would be ideal for one shredder to operate at top efficiency. There was also sufficient tonnage of the heavy No. 1 grade to keep the shear operating efficiently using nonautomobile scrap.

Stahl again had two alternatives. The first was to leave the Council Bluffs yard unchanged, use the shear for only No. 1 material, and pull out of the scrap auto business entirely. In this event the firm ran the risk of being forced out of Council Bluffs completely by long-run competition from Ace.

The other alternative was to install a shredder at Council Bluffs. The lead time for installation was about eighteen months. The Ace machine, already ordered, could be operating a year earlier. While investigating the shredder alternative, Silverman found another firm that already had a Norris 4000-horsepower shredder on order. That company was willing to sell its contract to Stahl because it had decided to buy a different shredder. If Stahl were to buy the contract, the facility could be operating within a year, or just six months after the Ace machine.

The total cost of the system was expected to be $1.8 million. Nearly half of this would go into a concrete foundation, electrical services, and other nonsalvagable items. The shredder itself could probably not be salvaged either, because it would cost too much to move.

There were many critical issues associated with the shredder installation at Stahl's yard. First, was the market share Stahl could achieve adequate in the presence of competition, given 6000 tons per month of total available scrap? Market share would be determined by how much each company would pay for car bodies. If the total volume were shared evenly, that is, 3000 tons for each shredder, Stahl could expect an annual return of 10 percent on its investment. This was the minimum Silverman would accept, but only with a promise of improvement in the near future.

The second issue was that there was no guarantee that 6000 tons would be available each month. Lower speed limits on the highway and higher prices for new cars could reduce the number of automobiles junked each year. If the volume decreased each manager would have to raise his buying prices to get more volume. The more difficult it became to buy enough cars, the higher the prices would rise. The result would be a price war. As the steel mills had already fixed their prices for the month, scrap margins would shrink at the shredder.

A third question involved customers. Several scrap consumers were planning new installations in western Iowa and eastern Nebraska. A shredder in Council Bluffs would be central to an area of new industrial growth; the demand for shredded scrap would insure high volume and healthy margins for one shredder. Most of these consumers had done business with Stahl in the past and would probably prefer to continue to do so. If two shredders were operating in the Council Bluffs area, Ace could attract Stahl accounts by offering a lower price. The question here was how loyal these consumers would be if Ace's price was significantly lower.

The final question involved the kind of competitor facing Stahl. As Ace was a much larger company, there was no way of knowing whether Ace would subsidize a losing shredder operation during a price war with funds provided from its other operations. On the other hand there was always the possibility that Ace would back out of Omaha altogether if Stahl announced plans to install its own shredder in Council Bluffs.

EXHIBIT 1

STAHL CORPORATION
Balance Sheet ($000)

ASSETS			LIABILITIES AND EQUITY		
	1974	1973		1974	1973
Cash			Notes	1,234	2,820
Accounts receivable	1,644	588	Maturities	2,331	875
Inventories	12,968	5,099	Accounts payable	9,557	3,401
Prepaid expenses	878	831	Taxes payable	588	100
Total current assets	18,604	9,066	Total current liabilities	13,710	7,196
Machinery	4,943	3,007	Long-term debt	19,294	3,647
Improvements	578	505	Deferred tax credits	690	357
Boats and barges	18,257	4,895			
Construction	2,357	1,823	Preferred stock	715	715
Gross P & E	26,135	10,230	Common stock	65	65
Less depreciation	5,693	4,306	Retained earnings	4,668	3,040
Net P & E	20,442	5,924	Total equity	5,448	3,820
Other assets	96	30			
Total assets	39,142	15,020	Total liabilities and equity	39,142	15,020

EXHIBIT 2

STAHL CORPORATION
Income Statement ($000)

	1974	1975
Net sales	62,920	49,205
Operating costs		
CGS	43,635	30,914
Production and direct	13,748	15,365
Sales and administration	2,391	1,556
	59,774	47,835
Operating income	3,146	1,370
Interest	975	564
Income before tax	2,171	806
Tax	543	202
Net income	1,628	604

EXHIBIT 3

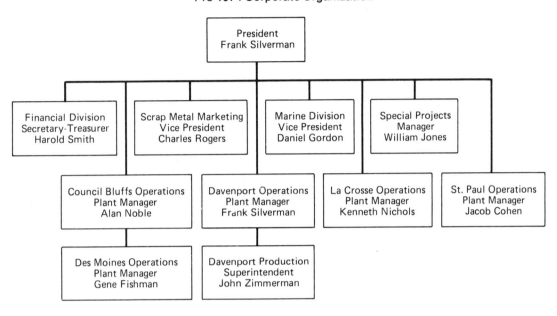

STAHL CORPORATION
Pre-1974 Corporate Organization

EXHIBIT 4

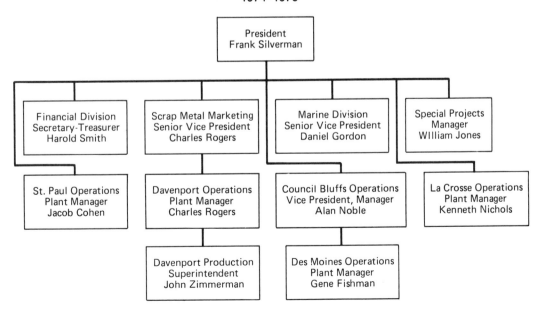

STAHL CORPORATION
Present Corporate Organization
1974–1976

EXHIBIT 5

STAHL CORPORATION
Projected 1977 Organization

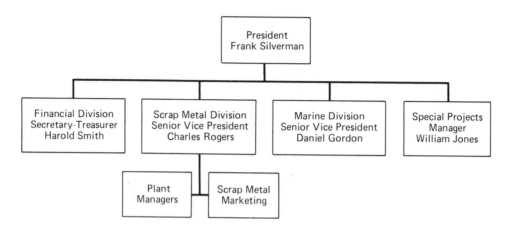

EXHIBIT 6

STAHL CORPORATION
Norris Shredder

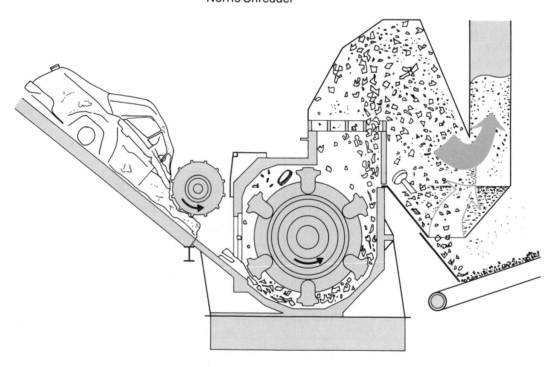

MUNICIPAL PUBLICATIONS, INC.

In early 1975 D. Herbert Lipson, the publisher and chief executive officer of Municipal Publications, Inc., noticed an item in the *Philadelphia Inquirer* that not only surprised him but started him thinking:

> A rumor has been tossed around that D. Herbert Lipson is in the process of starting a Center City oriented action weekly.

This relatively simple news item startled him because he had not actively been considering the establishment of such a newspaper. However, the possibility of such a publication excited him and he felt a favorable "gut" reaction concerning it.

The decision had to be made whether Municipal Publications should commit corporate funds and *Philadelphia Magazine's* reputation to the publication of a weekly newspaper. As he began to evaluate the proposal Mr. Lipson reflected upon the past history and operations of his firm.

HISTORY

Philadelphia Magazine was among the country's oldest existing magazines, tracing its descent directly from an official newspaper founded by the City's Board of Trade in 1908. The Chamber of Commerce later took over the publication and carried on its mission, which was to attract commerce and industry to the city.

This case was prepared by Richard D'Avino, Ann Finley, Edie R. Sonnenmark and Alan H. Tucker under the supervision of Professor Jules J. Schwartz as the basis for class discussion rather than to illustrate either effective or ineffective handling of an administrative action.

The forerunner of *Philadelphia Magazine* was primarily written for and distributed to businessmen in other cities. This practice continued until 1948 when a mounting deficit and poor product forced the Chamber of Commerce to sell the magazine to private interests. Municipal Publications purchased *Greater Philadelphia,* as the magazine was then named. The chief stockholder of the new corporation was Arthur Lipson, late father of the present publisher. Under Arthur Lipson's management the magazine began to show immediate financial improvement.

Herbert Lipson joined the magazine in 1952 as a twenty-two-year-old Lafayette College graduate and rose steadily to the position of chief executive. As chief executive he budgeted a great amount of money to the areas of research and writing, which contributed to the magazine's phenomenal growth rate. In an industry where 5 to 10 percent was considered normal, *Philadelphia Magazine* had grown at the rate of 25 percent a year.

CITY MAGAZINES

The city magazine phenomenon started at the beginning of this century as a booster or house organ for local Chambers of Commerce, and was distributed free of charge in places where a Chamber of Commerce thought it would have the greatest impact.

In recent years independent publishers, such as Municipal Publications, Inc., had started city magazines with editorial staffs dedicated to stimulating the "thinking populace" and improving their living and enjoyment. Editorial excellence was a trademark of the leading city magazines, as was the luxurious coated stock on which were spread their sophisticated graphics. As a result of the thought-provoking content and the leisure activity articles they featured, the city magazines attracted a select upper-class audience. To reach this audience, local retailers, restauranteurs, real estate and condominium developers, banks, stock brokers, and innkeepers endorsed the successful city magazine by placing a large amount of advertising.

The most important source of advertising, however, was national. City magazines often had difficulty attracting these revenues, as national advertisers leveled several complaints against them. First, the city magazine, by its very nature, had only regional appeal. Additionally, city magazines had no audience study figures, demography profiles, or product use figures to compare with other media. Thus the city magazine was placed in a situation similar to local newspapers. It had to produce its own local probability sample and measure its audience against the local coverage of national media. Finally, it was difficult to buy space in these publications. City magazines had to maintain representatives in cities where national advertising originated, most notably in New York, in order to insure advertiser convenience.

There were at least sixty city magazines nationwide, representing almost one for each of the country's seventy-five largest metropolitan areas. The only cities that seemed capable of supporting more than one magazine were New York and Chicago. (See Exhibit 1.)

ORGANIZATION

Municipal Publications, Inc., was organized along functional lines. When Publisher D. Herbert Lipson joined the company in 1952, his first task was to improve the circulation, which at the time was completely controlled, that is, mailed free of charge.

By the mid-fifties Lipson had assumed a greater share of responsibility for the magazine's business operations. He was searching for ways to increase circulation further and to bring in more advertising. He sensed that the problem was not one of distributing magazines but rather one of attracting readers. "I realized that no one really noticed the magazine," he said. "Even well written pieces went largely unread. To get their attention, we started doing things that were not done before. I evolved a little rule of thumb—that we had to have at least one bomb[1] per issue."

Lipson became a major shareholder of the corporation. He was responsible for all important business decisions as well as the overall profitability of the enterprise. The other two shareholders were silent and had no influence over the day-to-day operations of the company. Reporting directly to Lipson were Alan Halpern, the editor, and Frank DeLone, the director of advertising. (See Exhibit 2.)

Halpern was responsible for all editorial decisions. He was hired in 1951 to replace a departing editor, and was then the entire editorial staff. He recalled that the magazine was "dreadful" in those days. Halpern graduated from the University of Pennsylvania, where he majored in English. Following a year of postgraduate work he went to Paris looking for work as a writer. He obtained a job with *Now,* a picture magazine. *Now* quickly failed for lack of advertising but, while it lasted, it provided Halpern with invaluable experience gained as the assistant managing editor.

In 1949 Halpern was back in Philadelphia working as a freelance writer, contributing to trade journals and preparing educational programs for the now-defunct Meat Cutter's Institute of Chester, Pennsylvania. He was twenty-five years old when he joined *Greater Philadelphia* and, if his credentials did not quite fortell the editorial trailblazing he was to do, his promise matched that of the job.

Halpern gradually upgraded the editorial product. Faced with far more work than one

---

[1] A bomb is a sensational story that attracts peripheral readers.

editor could possibly handle and no budget for freelance writers or additional staff, he set an arbitrary goal for himself: to bring 15 percent of each issue up to professional standards. When he felt he had achieved that goal, he set a higher one. By 1975 he controlled an editorial staff of twelve and considered almost 70 percent of the magazine to be consistently excellent. He took no part in the financial activities of the firm. His only direct links to sales or advertising were attempts to increase newsstand sales, either by featuring popular subjects or by appealing to weak markets through special interest stories.

Frank DeLone was the man most directly responsible for the operations and profitability of *Philadelphia Magazine.* DeLone, another University of Pennsylvania alumnus, was hired as advertising director by Lipson in 1969. His primary challenge was to develop national business, a task for which his highly competitive nature eminently qualified him. He was employed in book publishing and in advertising before moving into magazine advertising sales management, first at *Women's Day* and later at the *Saturday Evening Post.* He had final say in production decisions (the size of the magazine and paper stock), scheduling, sales, and advertising. Another of DeLone's major areas of responsibility was budgeting and the control of operating expenses.

BUDGETING, COST CONTROL, AND EVALUATION

Each quarter DeLone and his sales force made a projection of sales. He tried to get a feel for the economy and adjust this projection accordingly. He also knew that the fall and spring quarters were the best of the year. For the year 1975 management had to revise its estimate downward due to the recession and the high level of attrition among potential advertisers.

DeLone emphasized that *Philadelphia Magazine* "ran a very tight ship." Extraneous expenses were kept at a minimum and no extra staff was hired. He tried to do most of the necessary extra tasks himself, but did recently hire a promotion director.

DeLone kept a track record of his ten sales people, who were evaluated on productivity and profitability of sales. They were also judged for client feedback, efficiency, and the quarterly presentations they made to him. The account executives were expected to produce sufficient volume to justify the expenses they incurred. Expenses of the sales staff for mileage and entertainment would be paid by the magazine only if DeLone, after reviewing the receipts submitted to him, decided they had been necessary. Thus he was able to control any unnecessary expenses. Besides being reimbursed for expenses, the account executives received a base salary plus a commission derived from the following formula:

Net billing =	
Gross revenue – Any agency commission	
Net billing	
Up to $100,000	7 percent commission
$100,000 to $150,000	9 percent commission
over $150,000	11 percent commission

Each account executive was held responsible for delinquent accounts. Billings on accounts that were delinquent for more than three months were deducted from the account executives' monthly commissions. For example, the salary statement for the January issue (prepared approximately February 10) would show a deduction for all accounts that were delinquent from October of the preceding year. When delinquent accounts were paid the commissions were then credited to the account executive and appeared on the statement.

Guidelines had been applied to accounts on which *Philadelphia Magazine* was obliged to issue credits because of legitimate complaints. If the complaint was not the fault of the magazine, the account executive received his full commission. If the complaint was a result of negligence on the part of the account executive, no commission was paid on the credit. A third guideline stated that if the complaint was clearly caused by an error in the production department, and the account executive had done his job satisfactorily, there would be no deduction from the sales commission.

It should be noted that the majority of complaints and adjustments arose from copy that came in late and had to be handled without sufficient time to submit proofs to the advertiser. In these cases it was the account executive's responsibility to clearly inform the client that he would not see a proof in time for correction and that he would have to trust management's judgement on minor editorial details such as type face, type size, and other elements that might not be clear in the advertiser's instructions. If there was any doubt in the account executive's mind about the magazine's ability to satisfy the advertiser, it was management's recommendation that the account executive suggest the advertiser wait until the next issue, rather than jeopardize the billing and the sales commission on the ad. (See Exhibit 3 for *Philadelphia Magazine* advertising rates.)

Seventy-five percent of *Philadelphia Magazine*'s account executives earned over $20,000 per year. The least an account executive earned was $12,000 a year. Half of them were women. All were college graduates and many had attended an industry-sponsored advertising school. DeLone personally handled most of the important accounts, such as large banks, department stores, and national advertisers.

CIRCULATION AND DISTRIBUTION

The circulation strategy of *Philadelphia Magazine* had three sales targets: people with incomes in excess of $15,000 per year, the college educated, and people having "better" jobs. Mr. DeLone felt that the editorial policy attracted these people. The magazine was very selective in buying mailing lists to use in direct mail promotional campaigns. Accordingly it purchased mailing lists solely for high-income zip code areas.

The size of the magazine's universe[2] was governed by four factors: editorial appeal, geography, demography of potential buyers, and demographics that were marketable to advertisers. The management had to study its readers to provide guidelines concerning the potential market for any additional circulation.

Statistics such as those shown in Exhibit 4 had been obtained from surveys sponsored by *Philadelphia Magazine* to illustrate the market being reached. The results were an integral part of the magazine's advertising campaign and were used as the standards of its audience profile.

Philadelphia Magazine was purchased by over 5 percent of all households in the Philadelphia Metropolitan Area. It should be noted that approximately 40 percent of these readers fell below the magazine's readership objectives in either income or education.

Philadelphia Magazine was not looking for large absolute circulation. The long-range goal was to maintain a market penetration of at least 20 percent of the households in the $15,000 and over income group. This figure was the main criterion used by advertising agencies in evaluating an audience profile. The maintenance of this penetration of the higher income cohort took a continuing effort because inflation and changes in the economy had brought about a rapid increase in the number of households in this category.

Management felt that editorial direction and execution[3] could probably do more to increase circulation than an equal amount of effort spent on promotion: It had been the editorial product that had stimulated the great circulation gains over the past few years.

A deliberate effort to feature stories about fringe areas of the market had been helpful in improving circulation where the magazine was doing poorly. The profitability of such stories

---

[2] An industry term for potential readership.
[3] Execution is an industry term for the way in which a magazine is put together.

was illustrated in the growth in newsstand sales in New Jersey, which resulted from articles about Pennsauken and Cherry Hill.

The circulation of newsstand copies showed dramatic increases. In the past six years it had more than doubled, rising from 15,000 copies in 1969 to 35,000 copies in late 1975. Newsstand sales represented about 30 percent of total paid circulation. This was one of the largest percentages of newsstand sales in the metropolitan area. There were, however, certain national publications that dwarfed this figure. *TV Guide* sold about 70 percent on the newsstand, *Playboy,* 75 percent and *Cosmopolitan* about 90 percent. There were other nationals, however, that sold only 5 percent on the newsstand. Newsstand sales were much riskier than subscriptions because the sale to the stand is on a consignment basis. Stimulation of these sales required a distinctively different, eye-catching cover each week. Price, distribution, and allotment (the number of copies distributed to each newsstand) also played important roles.

Philadelphia Magazine had very recently raised its price from $1.00 to $1.25. In making this decision the magazine consulted United News, its major distributor, and newsstand consultants, who decided the price rise would not severely hamper newsstand sales. The early feedback, according to Mr. DeLone, was that the sales were holding up very well.

In 1974 the magazine sold 81 percent of all copies distributed to newsstands. This was considered excellent, compared with *Time* and *Newsweek,* which sold only about 60 percent of their newsstand copies. Management hoped that it could improve on the 1974 result and gradually increased the number of copies it placed on newsstands.

The cover, which was selected by Halpern, was chosen to generate sales at the newsstands and to project the desired editorial image. One recent copy of the magazine featured a devastating fire at an oil refinery in which eight firemen were killed; another, the sexiest people in Philadelphia. Each of these graphically illustrated the different objectives of magazine

covers. (For information on circulation, see Exhibits 5 and 6.)

EDITORIAL STRATEGY

The quality of writing in *Philadelphia Magazine* had to be consistently high. To assure this, Halpern believed that he had to exert strong editorial control. His writers, however, saw him more as a fair leader than as the oligarch he sometimes professed to be. One writer said, "Alan trusts everybody. That's the key to the success of the operation. And that makes us really feel the pressure—we put it on ourselves. Alan can be thickheaded, just like anyone else, but he listens. You can get to him. If you're sure enough about it, you can convince him a story is worth following up." The atmosphere in the editorial department was participatory rather than authoritarian. "We decide together what we're going to do," Halpern said, adding, "my writers are such a diverse group that there are times when reaching a consensus seems impossible."

Halpern credited Lipson with providing and protecting an atmosphere of complete editorial freedom. Halpern estimated that his boss agreed with his editorials about 85 percent of the time. Final decisions about the editorials rested with Halpern.

The best city magazines exploited the natural advantage of reader interest by dealing with problems that affected the reader. *Philadelphia Magazine* fit into this category. It covered a wide range of subjects in greater depth than the newspapers it competed against for local attention. Sigma Delta Chi, the national journalism fraternity, had bestowed its coveted award for distinguished reporting on *Philadelphia Magazine* for two consecutive years. The only other magazine to match this accomplishment had been *Life.*

The magazine went after the tough stories. In 1967 it had exposed Harry Karafin, reporting that the newspaperman had traded on his position at the *Philadelphia Inquirer* to shake down public relation fees from businessmen whom he had threatened with bad publicity.

The story had uncovered a network of rackets and resulted in Karafin's conviction on over twenty counts of extortion. This exposé, among others, drew impressive journalistic comment in other publications.

URBAN SURVIVAL MANUALS

Philadelphia (circ. 122,000) has no peers among city magazines in investigative reporting. Among the imaginatively illustrated magazine's bigger muckraking scoops: the revelation that a Philadelphia *Inquirer* reporter was blackmailing banks and businesses by threatening to give them bad publicity (the reporter was suspended from the *Inquirer* and eventually convicted), and an exposé detailing how local politicians had fouled up Philadelphia's Bicentennial celebration by mismanaging funds (as a result, the city restored to the welfare fund $500,000 that it had earlier diverted to the Bicentennial). *Philadelphia's* success is due to the unwavering localism of Publisher Herbert Lipson, 46, who was a charter member of a booster organization, Action Philadelphia, before taking *Philadelphia* over from his father in 1961. "We wouldn't do a piece on Jerry Ford," he says, "unless it turned out he was born in Philadelphia."

Time, March 29, 1976

Halpern stated that editorially there had never been a game plan. But over the years *Philadelphia Magazine* had carried a lot of in-depth reporting. Additionally there were never any political endorsements in the magazine. As Lipson remarked, "Experience has taught us that there is no politician who performs so badly that his replacement couldn't do worse."

When Lipson was named publisher, his first official act was to make the editorial side a "legitimate operation." He did this by divorcing it completely from advertising to assure the independence and integrity of the editorial product. The magazine survived because of the gap left by the newspapers. Many stories that were ignored or glossed over by the daily press became the magazine's exclusive and valuable properties.

Halpern explained, "People complain our stories are too long; so does Herb. And they get longer and longer. The articles aren't predictable. We sometimes wind up with an entirely different article from what we thought we had when we started. It's easy to talk about following a story wherever it takes you, but exceedingly hard to do." It was this form of journalism, loosely labeled "investigative reporting," that had done the most to make *Philadelphia Magazine* famous. The magazine had been doing it for twelve years when the form finally spread from city magazines to national magazines. However, Halpern and his writers had managed to avoid becoming overspecialized or stereotyped.

Halpern wanted his readers to read the entire magazine. When a reader was interested enough to read cover to cover, the editor had done his job.

The letters to the editor had an effect on the content of the magazine. Halpern was not afraid to run critical letters. Controversial letters helped stir up interest. One reporter said that "the beauty of working at *Philadelphia Magazine* is that you never get the idea you have to write for a certain kind of audience."

ADVERTISING REVENUE

The major source of revenue was advertising. The magazine sought to attract ads from two sources: the local market, which consisted primarily of small advertisements placed by small or medium-sized businesses, and national advertising, which was usually placed by national agencies located in New York. *Philadelphia Magazine* serviced this demand with ten sales representatives in the Philadelphia area. These people tried to handle all aspects of the magazine-client relationship in the "bread and butter" areas of advertising, including real estate, boutiques and restaurants in the metropolitan area.

National accounts were handled by a two-person office located in New York. Such advertising consisted almost entirely of full-page ads placed on behalf of large national companies. The primary industries served were alcoholic beverages, airlines, automobile manufacturers, and fashion designers.

The local advertiser was usually an unsophisticated buyer who did not ask to be shown demographics or costs per thousand. He made advertising decisions based on his personal knowledge of the magazine and its regional impact. The marketing effort aimed at this client consisted largely of promotional material emphasizing the major stories *Philadelphia Magazine* had broken and the journalistic awards it had won. The local advertiser usually tried to keep his ad costs down; he was not constantly reminded by marketing people of the value of advertising. The results he obtained were largely intangible and not readily convertible into dollars and cents.

The sophisticated national advertisers, who realized the necessity of advertising, sought to minimize their cost per thousand and maximize their impact on groups who would be prime purchasers of their product. These clients were attracted by specialized surveys and by the lower costs to reach specialized groups of consumers. National advertisers who sold relatively expensive goods were attracted by *Philadelphia Magazine*'s readership.

The magazine's major competition in advertising came from two kinds of publications. The two local newspapers offered some competition, particularly in the areas of alcoholic beverages and investments. The other major sources of competition were the national news weeklies, many of which also published regional editions. These publications offered two-fold competition—first, in national advertising and, second, in their attempts to attract prominent regional advertisers such as banks and large department stores.

Given the excellence achieved by the editorial staff, the profitability of the magazine rested in the office of Frank DeLone. He determined that the advertising/editorial copy mix that resulted in the most profitable operation was 60 percent advertising and 40 percent editorial. It was this ratio that determined the

size of the magazine each month. After the quantity of advertising was set for the month, the editorial space and number of pages was easily determined.

Advertising provided the magazine with 70 percent of its operating revenue. Since 1970 the annual number of advertising pages had increased 30 percent, from 1211 pages to 1572 pages. In the same period advertising revenue increased almost 80 percent. (See Exhibit 7.) In 1975 these revenues were expected to be almost $2.2 million.

This growth had been achieved largely through the great emphasis placed on attracting national advertising. Lipson had a clear understanding of *Philadelphia Magazine*'s biggest problem, which, despite the magazine's strength relative to other city magazines, was advertising. It had been very successfully sold to local advertisers who recognized its impact in the community, but national advertisers, whose larger budgets represented important growth potential, contributed a disappointingly small percentage of the magazine's total billings. *Media Scope,* a trade publication edited for people who buy advertising space, and *Time Magazine* quoted Lipson on the subject:

> Our problem is uniqueness ... they don't know where to put us on their list. Spot television and radio, and the metropolitan advertising editions of national magazines are what national advertisers generally use when they want to blanket a market. When they think local, they think newspapers.

Six years before, *Philadelphia Magazine*'s advertising pages included only one percent national advertising—in 1974 national advertising represented between 25 and 30 percent of its total advertising volume.

To attract these advertisers, DeLone commissioned an outside research firm to do a detailed study of the magazine's audience. The results are shown, in part, in Exhibit 4. When he used this information to prove that the average household buying *Philadelphia Magazine* was affluent, advertisers became more interested.

BOSTON MAGAZINE

An additional factor likely to influence Municipal Publications' decision to start a newspaper was a previous acquisition, *Boston Magazine*. In early 1970 the firm was seeking new investments and a Boston Chamber of Commerce publication came to its attention. Lipson and his senior managers felt it would be much better to start operations in another city by buying an existing magazine than by creating a new one. This tactic provided an established name and distribution channels as well as reduced startup costs.

The magazine brought to Municipal Publications' attention was run by the local Chamber of Commerce, as had *Philadelphia Magazine*'s predecessor. Despite the fact that the publication had lost almost $250,000 during the first three quarters of 1970, it sounded like an ideal opportunity. The question arose—should it be tried?

Lipson's personal theory of the decision-making process was simple. "It's not the complex way people imagine ... you just get a 'twitch'." Upon hearing of *Boston Magazine*, he had the feeling that the city magazine would become profitable. But Municipal Publications did not purchase on this instinct alone. The staff of *Philadelphia Magazine* first did a feasibility study on the Boston market.

It appeared from the study that *Boston Magazine* could ultimately reach a circulation and advertising volume equal to three-fourths of that achieved by *Philadelphia Magazine*. The magazine would also have a strong attraction for national advertising, as it was in one of the country's ten most populated markets. The staff was convinced that, despite the fact that Philadelphia had a much larger population, Boston more than compensated in other statistical areas. Boston had a much larger white population as well as a larger income per household than Philadelphia. (See Exhibit 8.)

The feasibility study concluded that for *Boston Magazine* to be successful it would require a strong publisher and editor, and two aggressive local salespeople. The report cited the possibility of reducing *Boston Magazine*'s expenses by sharing functions such as national advertising, accounting, production, and sales with *Philadelphia Magazine*. The staff believed that if *Boston Magazine* were operated with the same caliber of management and editorial discretion as *Philadelphia Magazine*, it could be tremendously profitable.

The more important of the two factors was clearly Lipson's interest in the concept of another magazine in Boston. It presented a challenge—"an ego thing." He had been successful in Philadelphia, why not in Boston?

The decision to buy *Boston Magazine* was made in 1970, and Municipal Publications began to publish the magazine in early 1971. The magazine was purchased in partnership with a group of Boston investors who raised $300,000 in return for a 52 percent silent interest. The partners originally invested to shelter themselves from income tax, so an early profit was not an important consideration.

The management of Municipal Publications ran into significant problems at the outset of publication. The first problem dealt with management and personnel. There seemed to be a fundamental inconsistency in the fact that a strong chief officer was needed in Boston if the magazine was to be published and controlled from Municipal's Philadelphia offices. There was no one person at *Boston Magazine* who had profit responsibility and no one in Boston could make day-to-day decisions. The tight management organization that ran Philadelphia didn't exist in Boston. The only direct management came from Lipson's weekly or biweekly trips to Boston. His involvement was limited because Municipal's major publication was still *Philadelphia Magazine*.

Problems also arose in hiring of the magazine's staff. In its short history, the operation went through four advertising directors, because they didn't seem willing to respond to Lipson's and DeLone's direction. (Both the editor and the advertising director reported directly to Lipson and DeLone.) Lipson said that if he had been in Boston daily, he would have changed the cast a lot faster and more efficiently.

The other major problem that plagued the infant publication was the immediate surfacing of two competitors, both of whom had since failed. Although the magazine continued to operate at a loss, the prospects for a profit in 1976 appeared extremely favorable, perhaps beginning with the last quarter of 1975.

Lipson explained, "*Boston Magazine* has turned the corner, but the product is still weak; nice, but not exciting. The advertising was not under good management, but that has now been remedied. They must now get the editorial staff to catch up. The editorial portion still lacks quality, but this is the last major problem. Efficiency, skill, and ability are necessary to produce an exciting product."

THE NEW PAPER

In early 1975 Municipal Publications was not actively searching for additional investments. The results from *Boston Magazine* were not yet conclusive. The owners, however, were always receptive to new areas for investment. The idea of a weekly newspaper was not a new one. Similar publications had been successful in New York, Boston, and San Francisco. The major drawback to this type of publication was its tendency to have an illegitimate, underground appearance.

The idea of starting a newspaper had been in Lipson's mind for a few years. Nothing concrete had happened because all the necessary factors were never present at the same time. The article in the *Philadelphia Inquirer* reminded him of the issues involved.

According to Lipson, Municipal Publications' decision to consider starting *The New Paper* was mostly instinctive, involving very little research. He realized that sooner or later someone would start a "legitimate" weekly newspaper so, in his own words, "We should be our own competition."

Lipson believed there was a large potential market for *The New Paper* in terms of readership and advertising. Municipal Publications' other stockholders were not heavily involved in the decision. Lipson stressed the point that large dividends would not be paid; instead, most of any profits would be reinvested in the company. The newspaper's funding would come from internal sources. Despite the reliance on internal funding, Lipson felt that *Philadelphia Magazine* would not be hurt by the possible financial loss. DeLone reviewed the budgeting, personnel, and payroll with Lipson when the idea first arose. It was decided that a new staff with a separate office would have to be established.

The fact that *The New Paper* would necessarily be tied to *Philadelphia Magazine* caused Lipson to fear it might too closely resemble the magazine. *Philadelphia Magazine*'s reputation with advertisers would be one of the benefits of the association with the magazine. If *The New Paper* failed, however, the magazine's reputation might be severely tarnished.

The target copy ratio for *The New Paper* was the same as *Philadelphia Magazine*'s—60 percent advertising and 40 percent editorial. Lipson felt the bulk of advertisements would come from small and medium-sized retailers —pizza shops, barbers, beauty shops—and classified ads. Some national advertising might be attracted in areas such as liquor and cigarettes. The paper might also get national advertisers who were testing a market or a new product. For these companies saturation advertising and promotion were needed, and *The New Paper* could be the perfect medium. DeLone's preliminary studies foresaw problems in attracting the area's larger businesses until the newspaper permanently established itself as legitimate.

The New Paper would shoot for the masses in terms of readership. This might lower the paper's intellectual level but should help advertising. Lipson hoped that the paper would become the weekly bill for arts and leisure.

Secure in the knowledge that *Philadelphia Magazine* was the best editorial monthly city publication in the country, and the most profitable, Lipson faced the decision of whether or not to begin publishing a bright new weekly newspaper.

EXHIBIT 1

COMPARATIVE RATES AND CPMs[a]
Leading Metropolitan Magazines

Magazine	Open Rate B&W Page	Circulation	CPM
Chicago[b]	$1590	140,000	$11.36
PHILADELPHIA[b]	1390	115,000	12.09
Texas Monthly[b]	1615	125,000	12.92
New York[b]	4675	358,400	13.04
Phoenix	912	58,300	15.64
Washingtonian[b]	990	60,000	16.50
Los Angeles	1138	65,500	17.37
Cleveland[b]	705	40,000	17.63
Pittsburgh	565	28,200	20.04
BOSTON[b]	840	40,000	21.00
Palm Springs Life	1200	51,800	23.17
St. Louisan	485	18,000	26.94
Westchester	850	30,000	28.33
Honolulu	805	26,500	30.38
San Francisco	975	31,300	31.15
Atlanta[b]	865	27,400	31.57
D, The Magazine of Dallas	1050	32,000	32.81
San Diego[b]	725	22,000	34.86
Cincinnati	595	15,500	38.39
Gold Coast Pictorial	615	15,400	39.94
Houston	638	14,000	45.57
Baltimore	500	8,500	58.82

[a] Cost per thousand readers.
[b] Member, Audit Bureau of Circulations.
Source: Latest announced rates, July 1975.

EXHIBIT 2

MUNICIPAL PUBLICATIONS, INC.
Organization Chart

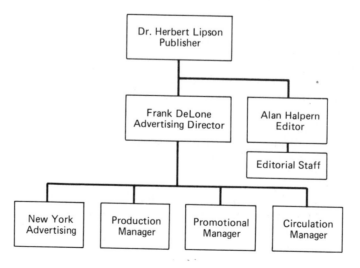

348

EXHIBIT 3

MUNICIPAL PUBLICATIONS, INC.
Advertising Rates
($/insertion)

	1 Month	6 Months	12 Months
Black/white rates			
1 page	1390	1290	1185
⅔ page	985	900	825
½ page	770	710	635
⅓ page	495	460	425
⅙ page	280	260	235
1 inch	85	80	75
Color rates (4 color process)			
1 page	2020	1925	1785
⅔ page	1650	1550	1465
½ page	1295	1235	1175
⅓ page	990	955	905
Covers			
2nd or 3rd cover	2325	2150	1995
4th cover	2585	2440	2235

EXHIBIT 4

OCCUPATION OF READERS

Occupation	Percentage	
Professional/managerial	32.0	
Clerical/sales	21.7	
Total white collar		53.7
Skilled workers	8.5	
Unskilled workers	15.0	
Total blue collar		23.5
Total not employed		22.8
Total		100.0

HOUSEHOLD INCOME

Income	Percentage	
Less than $5,000	3.3	
$5,000 to $9,999	25.5	
Less than $10,000		28.8
$10,000 to $14,999		24.6
$15,000 to $24,999	35.1	
$25,000 or more	11.5	
$15,000 or more		46.6
Total		100.0

AGE OF READERS

Age	Percentage
18–24	13.4
25–34	30.9
35–49	29.7
50–64	17.9
65 and over	8.1
Total	100.0

EDUCATION OF READERS

Education	Percentage	
Did not complete high school		21.7
High school graduate		28.8
Some college		19.2
No postgraduate	14.1	
Some postgraduate	16.2	
College graduate or more		30.3
Total		100.0

EXHIBIT 5

MUNICIPAL PUBLICATIONS, INC.
Detailed Circulation Data

ANALYSIS OF THE TOTAL NEW AND RENEWAL SUBSCRIPTIONS
Sold During 6 Months Period Ending June 30, 1975

5. Authorized Prices and total subscriptions sold:
   (a) Basic prices: Single copy $1.00
       Subscriptions: 1 yr. $9.00, 2 yrs. $14.50, 3 yrs. $21.00   26,119
   (b) Higher than basic prices: Outside United States, 1 yr. $11.00, 2 yrs. $16.50, 3 yrs. $23.00
   (c) Lower than basic prices: 18 mos. $12.00, 5 or more subscriptions 1 yr. $6.00, 6 mos.
       $3.00, 8 mos. $4.00, 10 mos. $5.00, 1 yr. $6.00, 1 yr. $4.00 for employees' gifts   21,922
   (d) Association subscription prices: none

       Total subscriptions sold in period   48,041
6. Duration of Subscriptions Sold
   (a) For five years or more   none
   (b) For three to five years   1,587
   (c) For one to three years   33,719
   (d) For less than one year   12,735

       Total subscriptions sold in period   48,041
7. Channels of Subscription Sales
   (a) Ordered by mail   34,143
   (b) Ordered through salesmen:
       1. Catalog agencies and individual agents   11,379
       2. Publisher's own and other publishers' salesmen   2,051
       3. Independent agencies' salesmen   2
       4. Newspaper agencies   none
       5. Members of schools, churches, fraternal and similar organizations   466
   (c) Association memberships   none
   (d) All other channels   none

       Total subscriptions sold in period   48,041
8. Use of Premiums
   (a) Ordered without premium   48,041
   (b) Ordered with material reprinted from this publication   none
   (c) Ordered with other premiums   none

       Total subscriptions sold in period   48,041

ADDITIONAL CIRCULATION INFORMATION

9. Arrears and Extensions: Average number included in PAID (Par. 1) which represents:
   (a) Average number of copies served on subscriptions carried in arrears not more than three
       months   3,987
10. Collection Stimulants   none
11. Basis on Which Copies Were Sold to Retail Outlets and Boys
   Fully returnable   100.00%
12. PAID CIRCULATION (Total of subscriptions and single copy sales) BY ISSUES:

Issue		Issue		Issue	
Jan.	99,493	Mar.	106,961	May	109,240
Feb.	103,491	Apr.	107,926	June	112,573

EXHIBIT 6

PHILADELPHIA MAGAZINE
Circulation Doubled in 7 Years

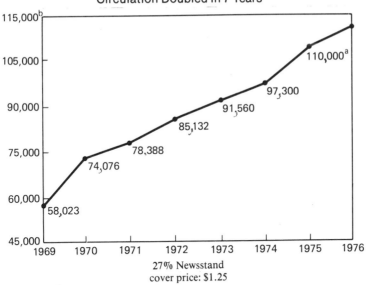

27% Newsstand
cover price: $1.25

[a] Estimated
[b] Circulation rate base eff. 9/1/75.
Source: Audit Bureau of Circulations.

EXHIBIT 7

PHILADELPHIA MAGAZINE

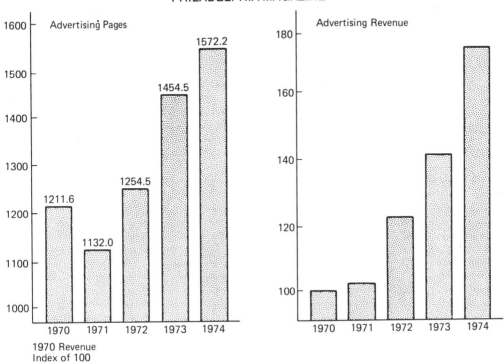

1970 Revenue
Index of 100

EXHIBIT 8

MUNICIPAL PUBLICATIONS, INC.

The following was excerpted from a memo summarizing the research study undertaken before the establishment of *Boston Magazine*.

Here are some comparisons between the Philadelphia and Boston markets:

	Metro Philadelphia	Metro Boston
Population (000)	4,843.5	3,255.7
Retail sales (000)	$7,757,540	$6,199,630
Income per household	$ 10,598	$ 11,419
% white population	84%	97%
National Rank		
Population	4	6
No. of households	4	7
Net effective buying income	4	6
Per household income	49	19

From these figures it appears that *Boston Magazine* could ultimately reach a circulation and advertising volume equal to about 70 percent to 80 percent of *Philadelphia Magazine.* It should also have a strong attraction for national business because Boston is one of the first ten markets.

The projected sales expenses will be lower percentagewise than *Philadelphia Magazine's* current ratio. We will be able to use our sales force in New York and Philadelphia and our representatives in Chicago, Miami, and California to sell both books, thereby lowering the cost of sales.

CHILTON COMPANY

When William A. Barbour became president and chief executive officer of Chilton Company in 1972 he and his new management team made a commitment to the company's share-holders to "clean house," expand the business, and improve profitability. These commitments later became formalized when the goals for 1980 were established at a 14 percent pretax profit margin, and a 12 percent aftertax return on equity. Barbour knew that attaining these goals would not be easy, but he had confidence in the ability of Chilton, a prominent force in the business periodicals publishing industry, to meet the challenge.

By April 1977 substantial progress had been made toward the 1980 goals. Sales had increased by 50 percent to $52 million, strong gains in profitability had been made since the 1974 to 1975 recession, and prospects for the future looked promising. Barbour recalled that during the five years since he had taken over as CEO, many of Chilton's publications had come under top management scrutiny. On his desk lay a copy of one of Chilton's most prestigious publications, *Iron Age,* which had just begun an aggressive editorial campaign outlining the major government obstacles hindering the free enterprise system. Barbour believed that the improvements made to publications like *Iron Age* had contributed greatly to the company's improved position in the business publications industry.

NOT TRUE

This case was prepared by Bruce Henderson, Charles Saddoris, Harvey Bertrand, Pat Cobb, and Pat Dillon under the supervision of Professor Jules J. Schwartz as the basis for class discussion rather than to illustrate either effective or ineffective handling of a managerial problem.

THE PUBLISHING INDUSTRY

Publishing accounted for half the revenues of the communications industry, which also includes broadcasting and printing. The largest sectors of the publishing industry were newspapers, books, and magazines, with books and magazines each comprising 20 percent of the printed media revenues. Financial statistics for a cross-section of companies in the book and magazine sector of the publishing industry are presented in Exhibit 1.

The Association of American Publishers estimated that 35 percent of all book sales occur in the textbook market. Other major categories of book publishing were trade books (hardbound books of general interest), professional books, mass market paperbacks, and religious books.

The magazine publishing market was segmented into publications that were oriented toward either professional, business, leisure, or general interest readers. *Newsweek* and *Business Week* were representative of general interest magazines, which were distinguished from the other categories most notably by their approach to circulation and advertising. Their publishers aimed for high-volume circulation through subscriptions and newsstand sales.

The relationship between price, circulation volume, and advertising in generating higher revenues was first investigated at the turn of the century. After the Civil War there had been a boom in magazine publishing. Initiated by the setting of very favorable postal rates in 1879, the boom was sustained by the general economic expansion brought about by the

353

industrialization of the 1880s. The industry was dichotomized sharply in price categories, with a significant gulf between the expensive, genteel publications, such as *Harper's* and *Scribner's* magazines, and the cheap weeklies. In 1893 *McClure's* magazine was introduced to fill this gap in the market. *McClure's* was brought to the marketplace at fifteen cents a copy, compared to the usual magazine price of twenty-five or thirty cents. Two popular monthly magazines—*Cosmopolitan* and *Munsey's*—reacted to the new entry by cutting their prices to twelve and ten cents, respectively.

Each of the three publishers was expecting an industry shake-out due to the price war. All were startled when the low prices quickly led to much larger circulation volumes for all three magazines. Although the magazines were each selling at a price below cost, the larger circulations attracted more advertisers. The increased ad revenues more than offset the production losses, and profits rose. Advertising, which in the nineteenth century had been spurned by magazine publishers in general, now became an essential factor in the economics of magazine publishing.

A corollary of this new large-circulation, high-ad-revenue profit strategy was that new magazines would require substantially larger front-end investments. As circulation gradually increased during the initial stage of low advertising rates, money had to be poured into operations in order to meet the climbing cost of producing more copies of each issue. This funds drain would continue until circulation became large enough to attract sufficient advertising revenues, and thus assure overall profits.

In contrast to general interest magazines, publishers of professional, business, and leisure magazines appeal to specialized groups of readers having relatively uniform readership interests. Typical of the way in which these publishers establish their marketing strategies is the approach used by publishers of business magazines. Their emphasis is placed upon complete coverage of a particular market,

rather than upon volume circulation. Business publications aim to reach a select group of top managers and decisionmakers who actually influence industrial buying patterns. Publishers carefully screen the qualifications of persons requesting to receive the magazine. By this process, publishers limit their distribution to a controlled (mailed free of charge) circulation, mostly nonsubscription. Advertisers can thus be assured that their messages are reaching a specific, identifiable audience of important readers.

One area of concern common to both business magazine publishers and mass market, general interest publishers is that of the continually increasing costs of paper, printing, and distribution, especially postal rates for magazines. Publishers have attempted to maintain profit margins by finding cheaper means of distribution and by raising advertising rates. However, costs can be trimmed only to a practical limit, and increasing advertising rates will inevitably meet with more and more resistance.

In 1976 there were approximately 2570 specialized business magazines published in the United States. This total number of publications did not vary by more than 10 percent over the years 1965 to 1976, dropping from a previous high of 2548 magazines in 1965 to a low of 2335 magazines in 1971. Total circulation also held steady, staying within plus or minus 6 percent of 61 million business publication issues. Exhibit 2 lists the various types included in the broad category of specialized business magazines and shows the allocation, by type, of total publications, advertising pages, advertising revenue volume, and percentage of total distribution.

CHILTON COMPANY

From its beginnings in the mid-nineteenth century as a printing company Chilton had evolved into a diverse organization whose primary business field was communications: the gathering and publishing of information for business and leisure readers in the United States and abroad. Headquartered in Radnor,

Pennsylvania, Chilton employed over 1500 people worldwide, with offices in thirteen major U.S. cities and eleven locations overseas. In addition to owning a printing plant in Philadelphia Chilton also had a 50 percent equity interest in Newton Falls Paper Mill, Inc., in New York. Financial reports for 1976, as well as a ten-year summary, are presented in Exhibits 3, 4, and 5.

Chilton's main product line was business periodicals; other product lines included special interest magazines, textbooks, technical books and catalogs, repair manuals, and novels. Support services included market research, data processing, direct mailing, printing, graphics, and translation. In addition to providing support for Chilton's publishing activities, each one of these services was organized and managed as a separate profit center.

CHILTON PERIODICALS

Business periodicals comprised approximately 60 percent of Chilton's total revenues. In 1976, 90 percent of sales growth came from business periodicals. These magazines, distributed entirely through the mail, accounted for 8 percent of total operating expenses. There were twenty-four company-owned magazines, plus nine "auxiliary" publications (newsletters, catalogs, reference indexes, marketing guides), which were published by several Chilton magazines for the particular markets those magazines served. These business periodicals were mostly industrial or merchandizing oriented. They carried articles on current events in the industry, management interviews, and market research updates, as well as editorial comment and, of course, advertising.

Iron Age was Chilton's largest and most prestigious publication. Established in 1855 it was the only weekly news magazine committed entirely to the metalworking industry.[1] *Food Engineering* focused entirely on production

and distribution in the food and beverage manufacturing industry. *Automotive Industries* served the automotive original equipment market, whereas *Motor Age* aimed at the automotive service and repair field. *Instruments & Control Systems* addressed engineers and engineering managers searching for techniques and equipment to optimize production processes. *Jewelers' Circular-Keystone* reached stores that accounted for over 90 percent of all retail jewelry business in the United States. *Hardware Age* was read by retailers, wholesalers, and industry executives. Exhibit 6 lists Chilton's many publications.

Chilton's newest publishing line was its leisure group. In the United States the two most active leisure sports, and the largest sports markets, were golf and tennis. Chilton published the official magazine for each of these sports—*Tennis USA,* endorsed by the United States Tennis Association, and *Golf Journal,* the official magazine of the United States Golf Association. Chilton's latest entry into the leisure market was *Going Places,* a magazine published for the travel industry.

CHILTON'S MAJOR SERVICE SUBSIDIARIES

The *Chilton Book Company,* started in 1955, contributed approximately 20 to 25 percent of Chilton Company's annual revenues. It was known as the world's largest publisher of automotive books, covering the entire spectrum of automotive expertise—from veteran automotive engineers to professional auto mechanics to do-it-yourselfers using the *Chilton Auto Repair Manuals.* The book company also published sports books and books for the arts and crafts field.

Chilton Research Services was one of the top ten market and opinion research firms in the United States. Originally an in-house group, it eventually expanded its market to include both government and industry. Chilton

---

[1] The metalworking industry includes firms that produce ferrous and nonferrous metals, use ferrous and nonferrous metals or machinery, or distribute metal products, machinery, or raw materials. The industry

encompasses nearly half of all industrial activity. It consumes almost half the dollars spent by industrial plants on materials, employs half of all industrial workers, and accounts for 40 percent of capital expenditures.

Research contributed approximately 10 percent of Chilton Company's gross revenues.

Chilton Printing Company handled all Chilton's periodical publications, as well as catalogs, advertising rate cards, and promotional pieces. Outside printing contracts included *Philadelphia Magazine* and New York's well-known entertainment journal, *Cue Magazine.*

The *Marketing/Communications Services* division included groups that were independent profit units, in addition to providing internal support services. *Ad-Chart* was a syndicated advertising readership service. Its purpose was to measure advertising effectiveness by surveying readers and reporting the percentage of those who noticed, started to read, and actually read half or more of the message. *Reader Inquiry* received, screened, and batched inquiry cards before mailing them along to the advertisers. *Market/Plant Data Bank* was used as a source of information for those planning new products or seeking new customers. It contained annually updated data on 70,000 industrial locations. Chilton's *Direct Mail Company* contacted potential buyers of products or services and was used mostly for new product announcements, fund raising, seminar announcements, and newsletters. *Chilton Translation Services* was involved in large-scale technical and engineering translations for companies with major industrial contracts abroad. *Naughton Studios* was Chilton's graphic arts department. In addition to selling its services outside, it also handled all graphic work for Chilton's publications.

ISSUES FACING MANAGEMENT

When the new management team took over in 1972 the firm was composed of about thirty profit centers, each with a separate manager responsible for profit and loss. Of the thirty profit centers, ten were highly profitable, ten were marginally profitable, and the remaining ten were money losers. In an effort to improve Chilton's earnings, the new management team decided to examine the profit-

ability and growth prospects of each profit center and, in the process, tighten up operations in Chilton's problem areas.

A number of these problem areas were in Chilton's business publications, the business area that provided the greatest share of the company's revenue. Each publication was staffed by "creative types," some of whom were too personally involved in their work to have perspective on the overall organization. It was very difficult to get these individuals and the organization as a whole to admit that a problem existed with a particular publication. To complicate the issue, each business publication was being run as an island unto itself with little accountability to top management for its performance.

Chilton had built its reputation on excellence in business publications. The creation of publications of this calibre required a tremendous amount of financial resources. A key issue that had to be addressed in this context was: "Do the markets and industries served justify top-quality publications?"

In 1972, in an effort to analyze this question, Chilton identified business publications that required immediate attention from top management. Each publication was examined in light of the market it served, the performance of competition, and the performance of the Chilton publication itself.

The analysis proposed to answer the question, "Is the publication adequately serving its market or industry? If not, why not?" All facets of the publications were scrutinized, including staffing, editorial content, and production. In addition, exogenous factors were examined to determine if the market for the publication had changed drastically.

Once these questions were answered the decision had to be made to either revitalize or terminate the publication. If revitalization was warranted, objectives would be established for return on sales and return on investment, along with marketing and editorial goals.

Chilton's top management did not want to dampen creativity in the publications by overcontrolling them, so it adopted a "management by exception'' principle to assist in monitoring the publication's activities. Certain key parameters for each publication, such as the goals for profitability and advertising market share, were fed into the company's accounting computers to be compared against actual results. If significant deviations from the plan occurred, the computer would automatically print out letters identifying the problem areas. These letters were sent to the appropriate profit and loss manager and to his immediate supervisors.

Boot and Shoe Recorder magazine is an example of a publication that succumbed under top management scrutiny. This magazine had been designed to serve shoe retailers when the independent "Mom and Pop" store predominated. *Boot and Shoe Recorder*'s advertising was directed to the owners of these stores in an attempt to influence their purchase decisions.

In recent years the publication had become unprofitable, primarily because of a drop in the number of advertising pages it carried. A market analysis by Chilton showed that the market had indeed changed drastically. Sixty percent of shoes sold in America were unbranded imports and the Mom and Pop stores were being replaced by factory brand name outlets (Nunn Bush, Florsheim, and so on). Because of these changes the footwear industry could no longer justify a top quality publication—and Chilton decided to get out of this market. It made similar decisions in eleven other cases.

IRON AGE

The publications that received top management's attention were not necessarily the biggest money losers. *Iron Age,* one of Chilton's most prized publications, and a big moneymaker, was also selected for analysis.

Iron Age had been effectively serving the metalworking industry since 1855. It was published weekly and employed twenty-three full-time editors who focused on all aspects of the metalworking industry, including business, finance, technical developments, and issues concerning labor, management, market prices, and new products. *Iron Age* was the seventh largest circulation business magazine and remained the leader in the metalworking field, with 3000 pages of advertising annually and controlled circulation of over 100,000 copies. In 1977 *Iron Age* reached 95 percent of all key people in the metalworking industry; weekly circulation plus pass-along readership was 512,000.

At the time the new management team took over at Chilton, *Iron Age's* premier position in the metalworking industry seemed in jeopardy. Although still profitable the magazine was experiencing a decline in the number of advertising pages it carried. As advertising was the lifeblood of the business periodicals industry, *Iron Age's* decline in advertising market share signaled problems on the horizon. The chief concern was the significant gains in advertising pages that were being made by the publication's competitors, *Industry Week, American Machinist, Business Week,* and other specialty business publications within the metalworking industry.

Barbour traced *Iron Age's* problems back to the period following a successful mid-1960s campaign to gain advertising market share from *Industry Week's* predecessor, *Steel Magazine.* During this effort a fierce competition developed between *Steel* and *Iron Age* to see who would be number one in the industry. The level of motivation and enthusiasm at *Iron Age* was exemplified by the "600" pins that *Iron Age* staff members wore: these pins represented the number of advertising pages by which *Iron Age* hoped to beat *Steel Magazine.* The final number was closer to 1300 pages. This vigorous and energetic campaign resulted in the ultimate demise of *Steel Magazine.*

In the years following the effort against *Steel* the editors and staff of *Iron Age* had grown somewhat complacent. There was a feeling that *Iron Age* could coast into perpetuity on its reputation alone and, as a result, the publication began to lose touch with the industry it served. Meanwhile, out of the ashes of *Steel,* Penton Publications built *Industry Week,* which emerged as a tough new competitor.

Through the early 1970s the competition, led by the fast-growing *Industry Week,* steadily chipped away at *Iron Age's* position as metalworking's leading publication. In early 1973 Chilton's management, realizing that it was facing another *Steel Magazine* situation, decided that the problem needed to be faced squarely. In preparation for deciding what strategic actions had to be taken against the competition Chilton Research Services conducted a thorough marketing study to reevaluate the competitive position of *Iron Age* in the metalworking industry market.

Chilton Research Services surveyed readers in an effort to determine how *Iron Age* was viewed relative to its competition. Readers evaluated *Iron Age's* strengths and weaknesses and suggested changes to the magazine. The survey considered the entire scope of the magazine—advertising, editorials, format, and content.

Although there were distinct differences in job functions and informational needs among the readership, the study discovered that:

1. *Iron Age* was equally strong across all job functions, scoring somewhat higher among production and purchasing personnel than in the corporate management, product design, and research ranks; and
2. *Industry Week* did not score strongly across all job functions. It appeared weakest among production people and strongest among product design/research and purchasing readers.

The readers who indicated *Iron Age* as their first choice stressed the following reasons:

1. *Iron Age* provided a broad spectrum of information specifically related to their job functions, such as raw material and product prices, business and industry forecasts, and information on new products, processes, and materials;

2. *Iron Age* was published frequently and had up-to-date information; and
3. *Iron Age* was short and concise.

Among the complaints voiced were that some readers felt that *Iron Age* was prounion, that it was designed for large businesses, and that it catered to advertisers.

Those readers who ranked *Industry Week* as their first choice stressed the following factors:

1. *Industry Week* was broadly educational, more so than *Iron Age;*
2. *Industry Week* was more relevant to decision-making concerning problems directly facing the readers;
3. *Industry Week* was more general than other industrial publications, providing information not easily found in other places;
4. *Industry Week* was simply written and easy to read; and,
5. *Industry Week* covered more matters of personal interest to managers, such as compensation, executive stress, and management philosophies and techniques.

The study also brought to light a more subtle marketing feature of *Industry Week*—the design and use of its cover and table of contents emphasized the "hot" articles in the issue.

As the management of Chilton read the results of the marketing study the findings seemed to highlight one particular decision area: Should Chilton continue to build upon the basic strength of *Iron Age,* that of bringing "hard" news and information to the metalworking industry? Or should it enter *Industry Week's* arena by softening up the format and content of *Iron Age* to more of a "soft news" article approach? This *Industry Week* approach would mean either less advertising per issue or larger editions in order to maintain the number of advertising pages. *Iron Age's* number of ad pages was already declining somewhat, yet larger issues (more pages) meant increased publication costs.

EXHIBIT 1

COMPOSITE INDUSTRY DATA
($ per share, except %'s)

Publishing[a]	1970	1971	1972	1973	1974	1975
Sales	245.27	239.54	247.91	246.06	281.08	327.74
Operating income	27.93	27.76	32.64	37.41	34.54	40.72
Earnings as a % of sales ?o⁴	4.35	4.45	5.26	5.92	4.67	5.06
Return on equity (%)	12.43	11.60	13.56	15.64	12.12	13.83
Capital expenditures	8.74	15.03	10.35	12.45	13.74	12.82

[a]The companies used for this series were Macmillan Inc., Harcourt Brace Jovanovich, McGraw-Hill, Meredith, Scott, Foresman, and Time, Inc.

EXHIBIT 2

BUSINESS PUBLICATIONS BY TYPE

Type	% of Total Number	% of Total Ad Pages	% of Total Ad $ Volume	% of Total Distribution
Industrials	47.9	51.9	55.6	44.8
Merchandising	18.8	20.7	17.0	16.1
Export, import, and international	2.8	2.6	2.1	2.1
Financial	5.8	5.4	4.1	4.5
Medical	16.0	15.0	16.4	19.5
Religious	0.5	0.2	0.2	0.5
Educational	5.7	2.8	3.2	9.9
Government	2.5	1.4	1.4	2.6
Total	100.0	100.0	100.0	100.0

EXHIBIT 3

CHILTON COMPANY AND SUBSIDIARIES
Consolidated Balance Sheet
December 31, 1976 and 1975

ASSETS	1976	1975
Current Assets		
Cash (Including certificates of deposit—		
1976–$150,000; 1975–$260,000)	**$ 1,870,417**	$ 1,365,619
Accounts and notes receivable—		
Net of allowance for doubtful accounts—		
1976–$168,307; 1975–$236,859	**10,610,145**	8,840,365
Inventories	**7,444,116**	7,926,869
Prepaid expenses	**2,267,975**	1,958,912
Real estate held for sale	**727,206**	775,206
	22,919,859	20,866,971
Notes Receivable, Advances, etc.	**3,320,901**	3,839,322
Investments in Associated Company	**3,311,346**	3,638,123
Property, Plant and Equipment—At Cost		
Net of accumulated depreciation and amortization—		
1976–$4,371,872; 1975–$4,078,961	**3,924,045**	3,748,621
Publications, Subscription Lists and Other Intangibles		
Substantially at cost	**7,226,329**	7,427,079
	$40,702,480	$39,520,116
LIABILITIES		
Current Liabilities		
Current portion of long-term debt	**$ 25,767**	
Notes payable—Banks	**1,800,000**	$ 5,150,000
Accounts payable	**4,345,974**	4,195,543
Accrued commissions, salaries, etc.	**1,600,870**	1,614,852
Accrued taxes	**1,182,647**	513,758
Advance payments from customers	**309,252**	379,142
Deferred income taxes	**343,436**	238,886
	9,607,946	12,092,181
Other Liabilities and Credits		
Long-term debt	**3,073,008**	
Unearned subscription income	**822,428**	802,073
Accrued pension and deferred compensation costs	**1,677,229**	1,674,059
Deferred income taxes	**296,914**	395,464
	5,869,579	2,871,596
Commitments		
SHAREHOLDERS' EQUITY		
Common Stock		
$10 par value		
Authorized—700,000 shares		
Issued—564,107 shares	**5,641,070**	5,641,070
Additional Paid-In Capital	**2,808,575**	2,809,516
Retained Earnings	**16,861,215**	16,208,064
	25,310,860	24,658,650
Less common stock held in Treasury—		
At cost—		
1976–5,584 shares; 1975–6,443 shares	**85,905**	102,311
	25,224,955	24,556,339
	$40,702,480	$39,520,116

EXHIBIT 4

CHILTON COMPANY AND SUBSIDIARIES
Consolidated Statement of Income and Retained Earnings
Years Ended December 31, 1976 and 1975

	1976	1975
Revenues	$52,303,856	$46,359,111
Costs and Expenses		
Operating costs	28,306,473	25,578,244
Selling, general and administrative expenses	21,107,040	18,911,114
Depreciation and amortization	573,031	525,151
	49,986,544	45,014,509
Operating Income	2,317,312	1,344,602
Other Income—Net	364,035	101,342
Income Before Income Taxes	2,681,347	1,445,944
Provision for income taxes	1,144,000	563,000
Income Before Equity in Loss of Associated Company	1,537,347	882,944
Equity in loss of associated company	(326,777)	(659,488)
Net Income	1,210,570	223,456
Retained Earnings—Beginning of Year	16,208,064	16,540,206
Cash dividends paid ($1 per share)	(557,419)	(555,598)
Retained Earnings—End of Year	$16,861,215	$16,208,064
Earnings Per Share of Common Stock	$2.17	$.40

EXHIBIT 5

CHILTON COMPANY AND SUBSIDIARIES
Summary of Operations
(000 omitted except for per share amounts, percentages and ratios)

	Years Ended December 31		
	1976[a]	1975	1974
Revenues	$52,304	$46,359	$43,867
Costs and Expenses	49,987	45,014	41,712
Operating Income	2,317	1,345	2,155
Interest Expense	(403)	(369)	(364)
Other Income and (Expense)—Net	767	470	205
Income before Income Taxes	2,681	1,446	1,996
Provision for Income Taxes	1,144	563	860
Income after Income Taxes	1,537	883	1,136
Equity in Earnings (losses) of Associated Company	(326)	(660)	793
Extraordinary Items—Net of Taxes	—	—	—
Net Income	1,211	223	1,929
Net Income per Share of Common Stock	2.17	.40	3.48
Average Common Shares Outstanding	558	556	554
Cash Dividends Paid	557	556	523
Per Share of Common Stock			
(as adjusted by the number of shares issued for stock dividends)	1.00	1.00	1.00
Stock Dividends	—	—	6%
Depreciation and Amortization	573	525	469
Current Assets	22,920	20,867	19,827
Current Liabilities	9,608	12,092	11,608
Working Capital	13,312	8,775	8,219
Current Ratio	2.39	1.73	1.71
Property, Plant and Equipment—Net of Accumulated Depreciation	3,924	3,749	3,862
Long-Term Debt (non-current)	3,073	—	—
Shareholders' Equity	25,225	24,556	24,870
Percent to Total Capitalization	89%	100%	100%

[a]All years restated, and reclassified to conform to 1976 classifications.

Stock Market Information		1976			1975		
The table on the right sets forth the low bid and high asked prices of the Company's common stock in the over-the-counter securities market (as reported in the National Association of Securities Dealers Monthly Stock Summary) and dividends paid, shown quarterly, during 1976 and 1975:				Dividend			Dividend
	Quarter	Low	High	Paid	Low	High	Paid
	First	$13½	$15	$.25	$14	$17½	$.25
	Second	12	16	.25	14	19	.25
	Third	16	18	.25	13½	19½	.25
	Fourth	14½	16½	.25	13	16	.25

			Years Ended December 31			
1973	1972	1971	1970	1969	1968	1967
$41,551	$39,278	$35,050	$34,285	$34,619	$31,759	$29,342
39,171	36,843	33,070	32,556	32,755	30,070	28,070
2,380	2,435	1,980	1,729	1,864	1,689	1,272
(113)	(114)	(67)	(156)	(110)	(170)	(164)
173	230	114	126	175	136	220
2,440	2,551	2,027	1,699	1,929	1,655	1,328
1,149	1,296	1,011	917	1,085	875	711
1,291	1,255	1,016	782	844	780	617
560	(114)	(293)	244	667	731	773
—	—	—	—	(175)	—	349
1,851	1,141	723	1,026	1,336	1,511	1,739
3.35	2.07	1.31	1.87	2.43	2.75	3.17
553	551	551	549	549	549	549
502	488	487	486	463	463	452
.94	.91	.88	.88	.88	.84	.84
4%	2½%	—	—	5%	—	2½%
407	365	341	334	337	310	297
16,558	14,281	12,903	10,864	10,392	8,907	8,007
9,919	7,774	7,383	4,719	5,415	4,802	3,521
6,639	6,507	5,520	6,145	4,977	4,105	4,486
1.67	1.84	1.75	2.30	1.92	1.85	2.27
4,091	3,786	3,982	4,479	4,259	3,842	3,449
5	—	—	150	133	1,020	2,010
23,437	22,059	21,380	21,145	20,545	19,684	18,636
100%	100%	100%	99%	99%	95%	90%

EXHIBIT 6

LIST OF CHILTON PUBLICATIONS

Business Magazines

Accent
Automotive Industries
Automotive Marketing
Commercial Car Journal
Distribution Worldwide
Electronic Component News
Food Engineering
Hardware Age
Instrument & Apparatus News
Instruments & Control Systems
Iron Age
Jewelers' Circular-Keystone
Motor Age
Optical Journal & Review of Optometry
Owner Operator
Product Design & Development
The Fleet Specialist

Special Interest Magazines

Going Places
Golf Journal
Tennis USA

International Magazines

Automotive Industries International
Food Engineering International
International Product Digest
Iron Age Metalworking International

Other Publications

Chilton's Oil & Gas Energy Newsletter
Control Equipment Master

Services

Ad-Chart Services
Automotive Datalog Division
Chilton Book Company
Chilton Direct Mail Company
Chilton International Company
Chilton Printing Company
Chilton Research Services
Chilton Translation Services
Data Processing Services
Information Services Division
Management Information Services
Naughton Studios

Affiliate

Newton Falls Paper Mill, Inc.

PRESQUE MAGNUM

At the fourth annual meeting of Presque Magnum (PM) on January 13, 1976, John Howe, PM's recently appointed chairman of the board, attributed the sharp rebound in profitability during 1975, after two disappointing years, to productivity increases and to further representation in areas of above-average growth. The path to yet increased profitability entailed, in his opinion, the recognition and greater acceptance of branch offices as profit centers managed by independent businessmen with good knowledge of the unique features of the local environment. In its efforts to become "a first-rate operation" he averred, "PM has fostered excessive regimentation. ... With Mayday[1] and its consequences, the time is ripe for us to let each branch office establish its own profit niche."

ECONOMICS OF THE BUSINESS

The brokerage and investment banking industry provided economic services to the financial community in three principal areas:

1. As an *underwriter,* the investment banker distributed new securities, such as corporate debt and equity, as well as municipals and federal issues, to many buyers, thus preventing accumulation in too few hands. The more fundamental economic aspect of this function was to underwrite any risk of a decline in market price until the securities were sold.

[1] In May 1975 the SEC had eliminated fixed commission rates for brokerage transactions and required competitive rate setting.

This case was prepared by Professor James E. Walter as the basis for class discussion rather than to illustrate either effective or ineffective handling of an administrative action.

2. As a *financial intermediary,* the investment banker, as a broker, brought together buyers and sellers of financial assets.
3. As a *dealer,* the investment banker provided liquidity and continuity to markets by taking positions where buyers and sellers were not active at precisely the same time.

The investment banking firm also provided important financial counsel to its clients to help determine the characteristics of new securities.

The business was unusual in that it was a high fixed cost, capital intensive, service industry. Service businesses traditionally had low fixed costs and were not generally capital intensive. The brokerage industry had high incremental, though low aggregate, profitability. Fixed and semifixed costs constituted approximately 64 percent of total operating expenses. Only 36 percent of costs varied with volume, making profits very dependent on incremental revenue. A low volume of stock transactions could potentially cause financial crisis within the industry. Examining industry profits during the 1966 to 1976 decade helps to illustrate this vulnerability. Pretax income of New York Stock Exchange member firms peaked at $1360 million in 1968. The decline that followed to a 1973 low of $13 million can be attributed to a few key developments. Rapid branch expansion and rises in Wall Street employment and wage rates in the 1960s added to fixed costs. Feverish speculative activity in 1967 and 1968 was followed by a decrease in public participation in the stock market. The short spurt in profitability experienced at the end of 1975 was chiefly due to abnormally high trading volume.

There were a large number of competitors

—approximately 425 member firms in January 1976. The economics of the industry were such that an individual firm could profitably cut prices if it could gain volume. This was much like the airlines where an increased load factor could produce much higher profits. By cutting prices a firm might be able to gain market share and take in more incremental revenue than the costs associated with its greater number of trades. In the past firms did not do this. For 180 years the New York Stock Exchange had fixed the minimum commissions that member firms could charge. In 1971 this rule was modified so that commissions on trades involving more than $500,000 would be negotiated between brokers and their customers. The cutoff was subsequently lowered to $300,000. Commissions were also negotiable on trades under $2,000, though virtually no price cutting occurred on these orders. Fixed commissions were entirely abandoned on May 1, 1975 (Mayday).

The industry sold service very much like a commodity product. On the retail side the service could be performed by all 425 firms and on the institutional side by about 150. Competitive pricing had occurred more within the institutional market than the retail market, as predicted by economists.

On the retail side a personal relationship was probably the most important factor in retaining a customer. A client tended to remain with one registered representative even if the RR moved to another firm. The institutional side was far more competitive. Commissions were based on a variety of services including research, execution, and trading efforts. Fully-negotiated commissions provided an additional way to compete for institutional customers. Though an institution might be satisfied with one brokerage firm it felt compelled to negotiate with others for the lowest possible rate, probably because of its legal and fiduciary responsibilities.

COMPANY BACKGROUND

Presque Magnum traced its history as an investment banking firm to 1926 when Merrill Presque and Packer Magnum, then recent business school graduates, opened an office in Philadelphia. PM established its New York office in 1935 and went national after World War II.

Early growth, largely confined to the eastern seaboard, involved careful capital management. Postwar expansion, however, relied heavily upon three major acquisitions. The first combination, in 1947, added underwriting strength; the second, in 1956, produced a national branch office network; and the third, in 1967, provided money management capability. Additional West Coast offices were purchased in early 1973.

PM was incorporated under the laws of Delaware in mid-1967 and on September 30, 1967, took over the business previously conducted by the partnership, Presque Magnum & Company. PM went public in November 1971 with an offering of 1.5 million common shares at $18 a share. Officers and relatives held about 65 percent of the outstanding shares.

BUSINESS AND OPERATIONS

Presque Magnum provided securities and commodities brokerage and investment banking services to individual, corporate, and institutional clients and made markets in over-the-counter securities by trading on its own account. Domestic business was conducted through four divisions (Northeastern, Southern, Midwestern, and Far Western) headquartered in New York, Miami, Chicago, and San Francisco. Each of the 100 branch offices reported to the divisional office in its geographic area. Each division was capable of dealing with all aspects of the investment banking business. International business was transacted primarily through offices in London and Geneva.

With minor exceptions PM was organized along typical lines. (See Exhibit 1.) The thirteen-member board of directors was composed wholly of insiders, although consideration was given to the feasibility of one or two outside directors at the time the firm went public. The four-man executive committee, comprising the board chairman, the chief operating officer, and two other officers, performed such duties as were assigned by the board from time to time. The finance committee, with five members, passed on all new commitments. The 1700 registered representatives were backed by approximately 1.15 operations personnel per stockbroker. Other staff members, numbering about 725, were divided among the various divisions identified in Exhibit 1.

Major revenue sources included commissions, market-making (principal transactions), interest, and investment banking.

Commission Business

As evidenced by Exhibit 2 almost half of total revenues were derived from brokerage transactions in listed securities. Consistent with the emphasis on branch operations, individual investors accounted for 70 to 75 percent of PM's revenues from securities transactions.

PM distributed mutual fund shares for eighty-six funds sponsored by twenty-five management companies. Revenue was derived from standard dealers' discounts ranging from .75 to 7.25 percent of the offering price. Through its 1967 acquisitions PM sponsored the Nero Capital Fund. This fund, offered at a maximum sales charge of 6.5 percent, emphasized "quality growth" stocks and discounted bonds, but was not a balanced fund.

Market-Making

In addition to executing orders in unlisted securities on an agency basis PM made markets in about 210 common stocks, preferred stocks, and warrants by offering to buy or sell these securities when other investors were not interested. Market-making activities remained appreciably above 1968 levels (forty stocks) but were well below the peak activity in 1972 (400 stocks). Officers of PM served on the boards of five companies in which PM made a market. The firm did not make markets in the securities of any broker–dealer. Net positions in equity securities ranged from $3 million to $11 million dollars.

PM also provided liquidity for its institutional customers by employing its capital to purchase or sell short securities as principal without full commitments from customers for their resale or repurchase.

Fixed Income Securities. To meet the increased client interest in government securities PM formed, in late 1971, its government securities unit, staffed with experienced professionals. By the end of 1972 net positions in United States government securities, including those held under repurchase agreements, reached $190 million, and PM was named to the select list of reporting government securities dealers. By mid-1973, however, PM had decided to stop trading government bills, bonds, and notes because those operations hadn't proved profitable. The decision was reached at a time when short-term interest rates had climbed progressively, raising operating costs and rendering it difficult for dealers to operate profitably.

The company continued to deal actively in municipal and corporate obligations and in federal agency issues. Positions averaged about $12 million in 1973. In mid-1975 PM inaugurated a retail bond department.

Interest Income

Interest on debit balances contributed substantially to the profitability of PM's retail business. The retail base provided customer credit balances against which aggregate customer debits could be "netted" on an interim basis.

Investment Banking

Over the past fifteen years PM had achieved a major position as an underwriter of corporate and municipal securities. In 1967 it broke into the top twenty in dollar volume of underwritten public offerings managed or co-managed and rose to eleventh by 1974.

In 1971 the company established PM International to exploit the internationalization of capital. By 1976 the firm had six overseas offices and had arranged two international banking partnerships, one in Hong Kong with a British merchant bank and the other in Rome. PM had five twenty-four hour a day lines from Europe to North America. According to one officer, "Today there is nothing we can't accomplish while just sitting behind our desks."

Risks. Despite its success in the investment banking end of the business and its efforts to diversify, PM remained heavily dependent on the volume of trading and the level of share prices for its profitability. Reduced trading volume and lower securities prices could result in lower commission revenues, reduced investment banking revenues, and losses in PM's inventory accounts and syndicate positions.

Share Volume

Presque Magnum's market share ranged between 1.5 and 2.0 percent of twice the total share volume on both the NYSE and AMEX. More specifically, PM had established that its average daily volume rose and fell with average exchange daily volume in the following manner:[1]

1. PM's NYSE volume = .0387 NYSE volume − 120.5
2. PM's AMEX volume = .0271 Amex volume + 26.7

These relationships could be expected to change as new branch offices were added.

That the volume of trading varied substantially is evident from Exhibit 3, which shows monthly trading volume (daily average) on the New York Stock Exchange for the thirty-six months ending December 1972.[2] Peak trading volume during this period was approximately double the minimum monthly level. The average price of shares traded on the NYSE, moreover, dropped from $43.20 for 1968 to $32.40 for 1970, rose to $36.20 for 1972, and fell to $26.20 for 1974.

Revenue per Ticket

PM's commission revenue per 100 shares transacted averaged $33.83 for 1969, $32.90 for 1970, $36.30 for 1971, and $33.53 for 1974.

[1] In thousands of shares, based upon monthly and quarterly averages.

[2] Average daily volume during 1973 and 1974 was respectively 16,084,000 and 13,904,000 shares.

The decline in revenues per ticket from 1969 to 1970 resulted from sharply dropping share prices. The loss in commission revenue on the average-priced, round-lot ticket was approximately $4 and was not fully compensated by the imposition of a $15 (or 50 percent minimum commission, whichever was lower) service charge as of April 6, 1970. The change between 1970 and 1971 reflected the moderate increase in average share prices and the continuation of the service charge over a full year period.

Revision in the minimum commission, effective March 24, 1972, incorporated the service charge into the rate structure. A further modification in the commission structure took effect as of September 26, 1973. The comparative rates on a round lot trade involving a $40 stock were:

Date	Commission
Before April 5, 1970	$39.00
April 6, 1970 to March 23, 1972	$39.00 + $15.00
March 24, 1972 to September 25, 1973	$58.00
After September 26, 1973	$63.80

Because of its emphasis upon individual investors, PM was less affected than institutionally oriented brokers by the Mayday negotiated commissions provision. "Nickel and diming" by institutional buyers forced negotiated commissions as low as $0.15 a share for a $50.00 stock taken into inventory. Previously, in late 1973, the fear that risk-taking houses might cease taking positions firmed negotiated commissions at about $0.27 per share for a $50.00 stock taken into inventory. Mayday had little initial impact upon retail commissions.

Fixed and Variable Expenses

The flow through of commission and other revenues to profits hinged on 1) the magnitude of variable expenses that were deducted from revenues to obtain revenues available to cover fixed expenses and 2) the level of fixed expenses. In PM's case, employee compensation —the main component of outlays that varied with commission revenues—had reached almost 60 percent of total revenues before being reduced appreciably in 1971. (The share of commissions going to registered representatives had averaged 30 percent of employee compensation.) Two comparatively fixed items, namely, communications and rental of space and equipment, consumed over 17 percent of total revenues in 1970, the company's poorest year in the decade prior to 1973.

Inventory Losses

In declining markets positions taken in stocks, either to facilitate block transactions or to support the market-making function, may be subject to loss. In periods of rising interest rates losses may also be sustained on positions taken in long-term bonds. High interest rates, in turn, add to the cost of carrying inventories and thereby increase the loss potential.

PLANNING FOR PROFIT AND STABILITY

In its 1972 Annual Report PM depicted itself as "*A Growth Company in a Growth Industry*" and announced to shareholders that its strategy for continued growth involved:

1. Further productivity increases among its present revenue producing units;
2. Further representation in above-average areas in a) growth and b) investment potential in which PM was not presently represented; and
3. Acquisition of companies that would a) further augment PM's offering of investment services, b) initiate the firm's representation in new market areas of above-average growth and investment potential, or c) supplement coverage of market areas in which PM was currently represented.

In 1974, as a means of facilitating diversification, Presque Magnum shareholders approved the formation of a new holding company; PM was to be its principal operating unit.

Implementation of the avowed strategy for continued growth under the post-Mayday environment required, in the opinion of senior management, concerted action by the home office, divisions, and branch offices. Specifically, the function of the home office was to offer products or services for sale by branch offices and to provide management services. The responsibility of each division was to evaluate branch office performance, recommend consolidation and termination of branch offices, and search for new office possibilities. The role of the branch office was to determine products and services to be offered for sale, price services, hire and fire, and recommend compensation. As a result of reorganization the branch office took on a new identity —it operated as an independent profit center, subject to minimal constraints.

Home Office Level

At the home office level substantial progress had been made in 1) reducing dependence on the "vagaries of New York Stock Exchange volume figures," 2) developing training programs designed to upgrade good producers, and 3) expanding services available for sale to retail clients. Commission revenue on listed securities, as a percent of 1975 total revenue, was down almost one-fourth from 1967.

Account executives were kept up on industry trends and innovations with graduate-level training courses in such areas as commodities, options, tax shelters, insurance, and portfolio management. As distinct from other courses that focused on content, the insurance program addressed itself to the education problems of teaching account executives to "appeal to fear" and not to "greed" as in the case of stocks. No course was compulsory; the branch manager recommended prospective participants.

In line with its policy of offering a full line of services, PM gave account executives access to institutional research as a selling point to retail clients. The firm also instituted a portfolio service for individual accounts of $30,000 to $300,000, marketed for a fee of 2.75 percent; the fee included all commissions for executions. Other retail-oriented proprietary services included syndications, municipal bonds, oil drilling programs, real estate, and miscellaneous financial packages.

Division Level

Presque Magnum's branch office system was constantly under review for profitability. Offices were closed when the long-term potential of an area did not warrant their continuation. Consolidations were arranged whenever economies could be affected without lessening overall marketing effectiveness. The company's policy of further concentrating its sales efforts had resulted in the rise in the average number of salespersons per office from approximately twelve in 1961 to sixteen in 1971 and to over seventeen in 1973. Eight offices had been closed in the past five years.

It had been, and continued to be, PM's policy to expand through the opening or acquisition of new offices in major marketing areas. At last count PM was represented in only fifty-four of the top one hundred geographical commission market areas in the United States.

With the modernization of the back office and the excess capacity it created, management argued that "We can add new offices without a substantial increase in costs." Acquisitions, which might contribute immediately to profit, were somewhat preferred over the creation of new offices. Presque Magnum had learned that a new branch office needed two years to become profitable under normal circumstances: Of the eleven offices that were presently unprofitable, seven had been opened within the past two years.

Branch Office Level

With the recent upgrading of branch office management PM felt confident that overall profitability would be enhanced by augmented branch office autonomy; each office would be able to adapt to the special skills of its personnel and to local competition. Consistent with the notion that the home office could wholesale products and services for retail distribution by independent, profit-oriented agencies, no branch office was compelled to sell unattractive merchandise. Each branch office was authorized to determine its own product mix, and pricing strategy as well as its staff composition, organization, and compensation schedule. A branch office could opt either to continue to offer tie-in (or package) sales of execution, research, and investment counseling or unbundle and price services individually. The alleged benefit of packaged sales was personalized contact, repeat business, and avoidance of cutthroat competition.

Organizationally speaking most branch offices treated the account executive as an individual entrepreneur. The bigger offices had added support staffs of specialists. A few offices had even adopted a team approach. "Often," said an experienced division chief, "one person is good at prospecting for new clients, but then can't really run the account. Wherever the team approach is followed, we have one person who sells, one who is trading oriented, and one who is interested in research. A good three-member team can do a million dollars a year, while each alone might do only $250,000."

The good producer was in the driver's seat. High commission payouts, direct wires to the most important accounts, private secretaries and offices, and fancy titles were just a few of the benefits. Others included up-front payouts and three- to six-month guarantees.

The name of the game was profits!

EXHIBIT 1

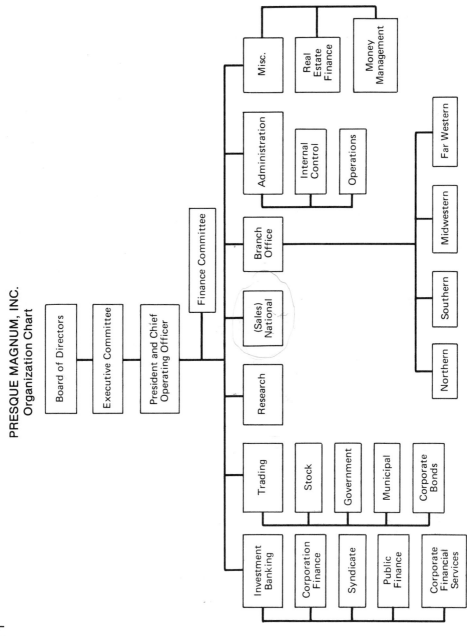

PRESQUE MAGNUM, INC.
Organization Chart

EXHIBIT 2

PRESQUE MAGNUM
Revenue Breakdown

Source	Fiscal Year Ended November 30							
	1967	1968	1969	1970	1971	1972	1973	1974
Commissions								
Listed securities	57.8%	54.7%	49.0%	48.9%	48.3%	49.0%	52.0%	44.1%
Over-the-counter	7.5	9.7	10.0	6.5	5.2	5.0	3.0	2.4
Mutual funds	5.8	5.8	6.5	4.0	1.9	1.4	1.0	0.2
Commodities	1.5	1.4	1.6	2.3	1.5	1.5	3.0	2.3
	72.6%	71.6%	67.1%	61.7%	56.9%	56.9%	59.0%	49.0%
Principal Transactions								
Corporate securities	0.9%	2.6%	2.3%	5.6%	8.0%	7.9%	7.9%	7.9%
Municipal and government	1.3	1.8	1.5	2.3	1.9	1.9	—	—
	2.2%	4.4%	3.8%	7.9%	9.9%	9.8%	7.9%	7.9%
Interest								
Margin balances	12.5%	11.7%	12.5%	13.7%	8.2%	10.9%	11.6%	10.9%
Securities and deposits	0.4	0.5	1.8	0.5	0.5	0.7	0.8	1.5
	12.9%	12.2%	14.3%	14.2%	8.7%	11.6%	12.4%	12.4%
Investment Banking								
Management fees	1.2%	1.6%	2.1%	2.0%	3.8%	4.5%	4.7%	4.7%
Selling concessions								
Corporate securities	8.5	7.1	9.5	9.5	15.2	11.6	10.1	12.1
Municipal securities	1.0	1.1	1.0	2.5	3.6	3.5	3.7	5.8
Private placement and other fees	0.8	1.5	1.9	1.5	1.3	1.4	1.5	3.6
	11.5%	11.3%	14.5%	15.5%	23.9%	21.0%	20.0%	26.2%
Other Revenue	0.8%	0.5%	0.3%	0.7%	0.6%	0.7%	0.7%	4.5%
Total Revenue	100.0%	100.0%	100.0%	100.0%	100.0%	100.0%	100.0%	100.0%
($ million)	$ 65.2	$ 83.3	$ 85.7	$ 79.3	$114.8	$122.6	$120.3	$125.1
Expenses								
Employee compensation								
Compensation	49.5%	53.3%	59.3%	58.6%	48.3%	51.4%	53.6%	49.9%
Bonuses	5.0	4.0	0.4	—	4.9	3.1	—	4.6
Business development	5.4	5.6	6.4	5.3	4.0	4.8	5.4	—
Communications	6.7	7.0	8.4	8.8	6.7	7.4	8.5	8.1
Office and equipment rental	4.2	4.6	4.9	8.4	6.4	6.4	8.4	8.2
Interest	5.5	3.1	2.3	4.6	4.5	6.9	8.6	10.8
Commissions and floor brokerage	3.3	3.6	2.6	2.7	3.1	3.7	4.0	3.3
Other operating	9.1	10.3	12.7	10.4	7.2	6.7	13.6	13.9
Total Expenses	88.7%	91.5%	97.0%	98.8%	85.1%	90.4%	102.1%	98.8%

EXHIBIT 3

PRESQUE MAGNUM, INC.
NYSE: Daily Average of Monthly Trading Volume
(1970–1972)

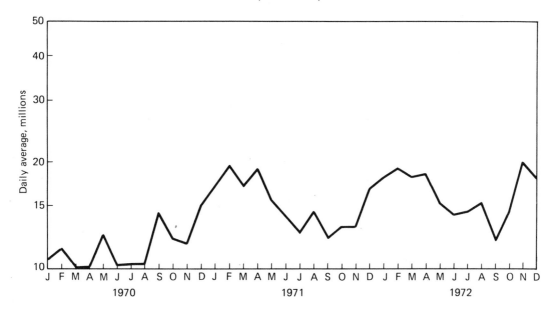

CHAPTER 5

The Integrative Role of Corporate Policy

The cases you have examined up to this point were designed to let you consider issues in formulating strategy and making and implementing strategic decisions. But as we discussed earlier, the general manager's problem is to do all of these. We separated these activities only for the convenience of the study. They are not truly separable. Strategic goals that lack a scheme for implementation are worthless; likewise, a strategic concept that cannot gain acceptance among management has little value.

Now is the time to put these ideas back together again. Analysis of the summary cases that follow requires the integrative tools of corporate policy. You are invited to apply yourself to the art.

LUCE LABORATORIES

In October 1973 Stephen Mahon, executive vice president of Luce Laboratories, faced the perplexing task of determining what strategy recommendations he should make to President Roger B. Dedham. In all his thirty-two years in the pharmaceutical business, Mahon could scarcely recall a more trying year than the one just passed. The outlook was bleak for his company's fastest growing new product, Slumberease, a sedative hypnotic prescription sleeping pill. The company had already spent an unusual amount of top management's time trying to solve the problem but success remained stubbornly elusive.

THE INDUSTRY

The prescription drug industry had to be considered among the fastest growing businesses in post-World War II America. Sales growth in drugs had far outstripped the all-manufacturing average between 1963 and 1970. Profit results were even more remarkable. (See Exhibit 1.) Of the three subcategories classified as drugs, the pharmaceuticals (that is, medication manufactured in dosage form) accounted for the lion's share of this growth. Pharmaceutical drugs were classified either as proprietary (promoted to the general public for over-the-counter sales) or ethical (usually sold by prescription only and promoted directly to members of the medical profession). The growth of ethical drugs had

This case was prepared by R. Mitchell Brown III under the supervision of Professor Jules J. Schwartz as the basis for class discussion rather than to illustrate either effective or ineffective handling of an administrative action.

been primarily responsible for the "high-flyer" status accorded to pharmaceutical companies during the 1960s. (See Exhibits 2 and 3.)

A drug was defined as a single chemical substance purported to have a positive therapeutic effect. Each drug was given a generic name. (There were about 8000 generic drugs in existence in 1973.) Generic drugs were used to make up a myriad of pharmaceutical products that differed in combination, strength, and dosage form. As each pharmaceutical could be made by numerous different manufacturers, a single product could be produced under a variety of brand names. However, relatively few pharmaceuticals were commercially successful. Joseph D. Cooper concluded in *The Economics of Drug Innovation* that only one out of every 6000 new compounds tested became a marketable product.

Firms competed by developing and introducing new drugs. For example, Smith Kline and French rose to market prominence through development of potent tranquilizers, and Searle was the first to market oral contraceptives, but such competition-free success was usually short-lived. Consequently, streamlined production techniques and improved quality control were also important.

Industry studies presented at the 1968 Nelson hearings in the United States Senate showed that, despite the high profitability enjoyed by the industry as a whole, pharmaceutical manufacturing emerged as the fourth riskiest industry out of fifty-nine studied over a fifteen-year period. Though pharmaceutical company stock maintained a high price-to-earnings ratio in the market, prospective investors had to consider the high risk of incurring losses when long-term research and development efforts failed to produce successful products or were negated by competition or government intervention.

COMPANY HISTORY

Luce Laboratories, Inc., became a wholly-owned subsidiary of Luce-Bekker, Inc., in 1968 when it merged with Bekker, Inc. Like many pharmaceutical companies, Luce started as a small business. The firm was founded in 1910 by Edward P. Luce and incorporated in 1927 when Edward's son, Henry, joined the family business. Another son, Robert E. Luce, entered the company in 1931 and, together the two brothers guided the business until Henry's death in 1962. Robert remained active in management until 1973, when he retired and became chairman of the board.

Roger B. Dedham joined Luce as executive vice president in late 1962, bringing experience gained from work in several other pharmaceutical companies. His vigorous, competent management style was quickly recognized and Dedham rose within Luce Laboratories to become president of Luce-Bekker when Robert Luce retired. It was Dedham who brought in Stephen R. Mahon as second in command at Luce Laboratories.

Luce had been a small, moderately successful firm until 1949 when it introduced Harmonine, a new ethical antacid with superior qualities. Harmonine caught on quickly and soon raised Luce to national importance. Primarily due to the introduction and expanded promotion of this new product, Luce's annual net sales rose from $850,000 in 1950 to over $47,100,000 in 1967; net income surged from $30,000 to $8,616,000 during the same years. Prior to the 1968 merger Harmonine, by then a comparatively old drug in the pharmaceutical industry, still held 45 percent of the market in its product class, contributing about 69 percent of the company's gross sales. Because it was the most widely prescribed and largest selling ethical antacid on the market, Harmonine had propelled Luce Laboratories to the rank of twenty-fifth largest United States producer of ethical pharmaceuticals in terms of sales.

Anxious to avoid a heavy dependence on one product, Luce management had begun stepping up its research and development budget in 1959 and was carefully but determinedly seeking ways to change its "one-product company" image. A number of new products had been introduced after Harmonine's advent, a few of which showed considerable promise. In 1968 Luce merged with Bekker Inc., an American-based specialty chemical manufacturer with several international subsidiaries. Luce's worldwide organization by this time was building a global distribution system for Harmonine and other products through Luce International, and the Bekker merger was planned to have a synergistic effect.

Luce had already acquired several smaller firms in the health care field. Following the Bekker merger, Luce continued to seek a broader product base through integration and diversification. Luce formed Briarwood Company in 1968 as an integrative step to secure a manufacturing source for Harmonine's chief ingredients. Burgoon Laboratories, a dermatological products manufacturer, joined the Luce family in 1971. By 1972 growth rate of most of the firm's new products exceeded that of Harmonine.

Worldwide sales of pharmaceuticals and other health care products continued their general trend, providing 57 percent of consolidated sales and 70 percent of net income to the parent in the record year of 1972. (See Exhibit 4 for a ten-year summary of financial data.) During that year the company had sought the public eye through a new cooperative advertising plan in an effort to capitalize on the largely untapped proprietary market for Harmonine and a related sister product. With Harmonine holding its own in an expanded market and with Luce's other products, notably Slumberease, growing at an increasing rate, the domestic outlook appeared bright for 1973.

MARKETING

Many other firms in the pharmaceutical industry could match Luce in manufacturing, quality control, and research and development capabilities, but Luce management believed its firm had distinctive competence in its marketing ability. Organized along functional lines, Luce sold primarily to wholesalers and retail outlets. The bulk of the Luce marketing budget went to salaries for regional and field sales managers and for a force of 375 detail-people. The detailers functioned as a missionary salesforce, explaining the benefits of Luce products to pharmacists, hospitals, and particularly to doctors. They performed an educational as well as a promotional function, providing the largest single source of new pharmaceutical information to doctors. Luce paid particular attention to its detailers, giving them extensive field support, audio-visual aids, and broad incentive plans. The firm also required that detailers be briefed by their managers every six weeks on the products they represented. Therefore Luce detailers generally were held in high regard by the customers and physicians they served, and this was reflected in the company's sales figures.

A NEW PRODUCT

In 1972 Luce's most promising new pharmaceutical was Slumberease (methaqualone), a sedative-hypnotic prescription sleeping tablet. Luce had purchased the technology to produce the drug from a French manufacturer in 1962 and had conducted an independent original clinical evaluation for three years while the product was under study by the FDA. Methaqualone was already in use worldwide and could be purchased over the counter in Japan. Luce first introduced its product to the American market in late November 1965. It was the company's first new pharmaceutical approved under the New Drug Application procedure since the Federal Drug Amendments Act was passed in 1962.

Although launched with considerable fan-fare in its initial 150 milligram dosage, Slumberease was slow to command significant market attention. Slumberease 300, a stronger dosage sleeping tablet, was introduced in 1967 and quickly found acceptance with physicians throughout the country. By 1970 Slumberease was the second largest selling domestic Luce product and its sales continued to accelerate through 1972.

Slumberease was a quality product with a significant advantage over competing drugs in its product class. In its recommended dosage form Slumberease had shown only remote possibilities of side effects or of physical or psychological dependence. Clinical studies indicated that it had a high order of efficacy even for chronic insomniacs where other hypnotics had failed. Slumberease usually induced sleep in ten to thirty minutes and patients usually awakened easily after six to eight hours of restful sleep without evidence of posthypnotic depression or "hangover." Clearly a drug that could produce such effective results with few or no aftereffects had a high potential in American markets.

By mid-1969 sales of Slumberease 300 had grown large enough to warrant committing investment funds to its promotion. An extensive advertising campaign was launched in 1970. Following general industry practice, this advertising appeared in trade journals and in direct mailings to physicians. During 1971 promotional mailings, distribution of free samples, and visits by detailers were intensified as sales responded to the promotional efforts. Sales figures rose from about $1 million in 1970 to $3 million in 1971 and $4.5 million in 1972. The 1970 five-year plan had conservatively aimed for $6 million to $7 million in sales by 1975. The product had thus far exhibited normal growth patterns.

A Drug Abuse Problem

In early 1972 the spectre of drug abuse was prominent in the media. Isolated reports of possible misuse of Slumberease began to filter in to Mahon's office. The pharmaceutical industry had traditionally tried to maintain a low profile, and family-name businesses were particularly sensitive to the possibility of adverse publicity. In addition the prospect of increasing government regulation in an already highly regulated industry acted as a positive check on responsible firms.

The implications about any alleged dereliction of corporate responsibility were most unpleasant for Mahon. Although policy decisions on such problems were made at Mahon's level and higher, he was the corporate officer who dealt with them on a day-to-day basis. When reports were confirmed, Mahon took swift action. He voluntarily stopped promotional mailing campaigns in April and implemented a strict sample accountability system. Orders were screened to detect possible overbuying by wholesalers or retailers. An outside consultant, who was the former head of the Bureau of Narcotics and Dangerous Drugs (BNDD, now the Drug Enforcement Agency, DEA), was hired to investigate the problem and conduct a study of the entire Slumberease operation at Luce.

The consultant's report covered twenty-five metropolitan areas. It indicated that the abuse was not national in scope, but was limited to a few urban centers and campuses in areas as diverse as Miami, Houston, New York, Philadelphia, and Boulder, Colorado. College students and reportedly some high school members of the so-called drug culture were using Slumberease as a "downer," to dull the senses and create a sense of euphoria. Although the inherent danger from overdosage of any drug should be obvious, this certainly did not dissuade the abusers. Reports of use in combinations with alcohol and other drugs ranged to the bizarre. Still the incidence of misuse appeared mainly in isolated, unrelated locations. As Slumberease was dispensed solely by prescription, the channel distribution system and plant security were scrutinized by management. Several small distributors were discovered to be mishandling the drug and were

prosecuted. Others, whose ordering trends were suspect, were cut back and closely monitored by the company.

Public hue and cry gathered steam when reports of abuse climbed. A twenty-minute segment of television's "60 Minutes" program was devoted to the problem of methaqualone abuse, detailing street prices of individual tablets, their misuse on campuses and in "juice bars," and showing students with Slumberease T-shirts. Although five other pharmaceutical companies also produced methaqualone, Luce, with approximately 60 percent of the market, was singled out for the brunt of the adverse publicity. During this time Mahon personally handled all telephone calls and details associated with the uproar, a task that effectively consumed most of his time.

In an effort to insure that the firm followed a properly responsible corporate role Luce instituted strict new plant security measures and installed a costly bank vault-type door on the Slumberease storage facility. In an October 1972 speech made before the National Association of Retail Druggists, the head of the Bureau of Narcotics and Dangerous Drugs quoted Mahon as saying, "We are in business to produce quality drugs for those who need them. But we are damned concerned about any misuse. If 100 tablets get diverted into misuse, that's 100 too many." The federal bureau chief added, "We in the BNDD feel the same way." Such statements and other clarifications of company policy were widely disseminated to Luce employees.

Next Luce wrote to the renamed Drug Enforcement Agency (DEA) expressing concern and requesting that Slumberease (methaqualone) be classified as a controlled substance in order to stem abuse. The significance of such a voluntary move should not be underestimated. The Controlled Substance Act mandated special handling of dangerous or potentially dangerous substances. Once a drug became a controlled substance its street sale became a felony rather than a misdemeanor. Placing a drug on the controlled list required that the DEA and the Food and Drug Administration (FDA) determine the appropriate schedule for handling the drug. (See Exhibit 5.) DEA supervised quotas, required use of special DEA order forms, and prohibited prescription refills when a drug was placed on Schedule II. Schedules III, IV, and V placed less severe restrictions on the drug.

The government followed up on the Luce letter with a request for a hearing. The management committee (see Exhibit 6) then had to decide what position to take. The issues they considered were: 1) company reputation; 2) moral responsibility to the public, physicians, and employees; and 3) financial impact of controls. Luce decided to cooperate fully with the government.

After President Dedham testified before a United States Senate Subcommittee in April 1973 drug industry critics in various states began to debate the schedule question. In the summer of 1973 Maryland placed Slumberease on Schedule IV and other states joined the issue. In Pennsylvania Luce worked closely with the Governor's Committee of Drug Abuse, cooperating in every conceivable way. A local university professor, arguing for strict control, presented three purported cases of drug dependency, but Luce effectively challenged the cases and was assured by the committee that Slumberease would receive a Schedule III or IV classification. When the Pennsylvania decision was handed down, however, it was for Schedule II control. New York and Michigan soon followed suit in placing Slumberease on Schedule II.

Dedham, Mahon, and Luce's director of research all testified at FDA hearings that summer, and Dedham was recalled to Washington to testify with the heads of other pharmaceutical manufacturers before a Senate Select Committee on Drug Abuse. Luce was urging classification on either Schedule III or IV, which would be compatible with controls on other pharmaceuticals in the same product class as Slumberease.

The final result of the joint FDA-DEA action was published in October 1973. The bulk of the report was generally supportive of Luce's position and at no time was it critical of the firm's actions. But the summary of the FDA findings was that Slumberease could cause "severe" psychological dependence and thus should be placed on Schedule II with reappraisal to begin one year later. No punitive action was proposed or implied. In fact the decision resulted in only slight changes in advertising and labeling letter size for the required warnings. But the entire mode of the Slumberease operation had to change.

Mahon and Dedham needed a clear perspective on their problem. What precisely were the implications of the hearing results? The issues they faced in light of the company's adherence to a moral corporate strategy were:

1. Should they continue aggressive promotion?
2. Should they detail, and was the return worth it?
3. What obligations did Luce have to its physicians and patients?
4. What criticisms were they likely to face?
5. What would be the effect on employee morale?
6. What backlash effect, if any, might there be on other Luce products?
7. What was the true cost of any strategy?
8. What lessons had been learned for the future?

In reflecting on the implications Schedule II held for future planning Mahon thought about the fact that none of his competitors' products were classified higher than Schedule III. Now Slumberease had to be manufactured under DEA-controlled quotas, and multicopied forms subject to monitored controls had to be used for every transaction in which any amount of Slumberease changed hands. Special inventory and distribution reports had to be submitted under the ARCOS system to enable the DEA's computers to identify problems. A separate and distinct set of records had to be kept for all transactions involving Schedule II drugs. All orders had to be edited in advance to identify excessive purchases by any account, and the patients could not obtain refills without getting a new written prescription.

Another major effect was that Luce's overseas source for methaqualone had to be discontinued. Mahon knew it might take the sole domestic supplier years to attain the quality Luce had enjoyed from the European manufacturer. Fortunately he had foreseen the problem and Luce had about a year's supply of ingredients in stock. The domestic source was bound to become reliable, but what would its price be at that point? In fact, what would be the cost of all these additional handling procedures on the manufacturing and marketing programs?

Thumbing through the file to begin the task at hand, Mahon came upon a recent copy of a popular acid-rock magazine in which Slumberease was featured on the front cover. He could not repress the feeling that the dregs of society had taken a hand in the management of a responsible company.

EXHIBIT 1

DRUG PROFITS
Range of Quarterly Post-tax Earnings
1957–1970

	Profit On Sales (%)	Profit On Stockholder's Investment (%)
All manufacturing	3.4– 5.9	6.8–14.7
Drugs	9.1–11.7	14.7–22.0

Source: U.S. Federal Trade Commission and U.S. Securities and Exchange Commission, *Quarterly Financial Reports for Manufacturing Corporations* (Washington, D.C.: U.S. Government Printing Office, 1958–1971), Tables 2 and 4.

EXHIBIT 2

COMPARATIVE GROWTH CHART
All-Industry Shipments of Pharmaceuticals by Type
($ million)

Type of Pharmaceutical		1963	1970	% Change
Domestic:	Ethical	$2,054.9	$3,781.3	+84.0%
	Proprietary	836.2	1,344.2	60.8
Export:	Unclassified	102.0	150.2	47.3
		$2,993.1	$5,275.7	76.2%

Source: U.S. Bureau of the Census, "Pharmaceutical Preparation, Except Biologicals," *Current Industrial Reports 1963, 1970* (Washington, D.C.: U.S. Government Printing Office, 1964 and 1971).

EXHIBIT 3

CONCENTRATION IN THE PHARMACEUTICAL INDUSTRY

Year	Number of Companies	Value of Company Shipments (Millions)	Percentage of Shipments Accounted for by			
			4 Largest Companies	8 Largest Companies	20 Largest Companies	50 Largest Companies
1954	1,128	$1,643	25%	44%	60%	(NA)
1958	1,064	2,533	27	45	73	87%
1963	944	3,314	22	38	72	89
1967	791	4,696	24	40	73	90
1970	(NA)	6,028	26	43	(NA)	(NA)

Source: U.S. Bureau of the Census, *Census of Manufacturers* (U.S. Government Printing Office, 1971).

EXHIBIT 4

LUCE-BEKKER, INC.
Ten-Year Summary

	1972	1971	1970	1969	1968
		Operations for the Year			
Net sales	$166,099,235	$149,901,815	$136,368,211	$118,184,043	$116,744,827
Income before income taxes	42,280,719	39,219,892	37,489,586	33,566,468	36,545,295
Income taxes	21,239,000	19,935,000	19,636,000	17,905,749	19,668,355
Net income	21,041,719	19,284,892	17,773,586	15,660,719	16,876,940
Per share	1.51	1.39	1.28	1.13	1.23
Dividends paid	10,401,743	9,952,579	9,463,279	9,396,609	7,194,191
Per share	.745	.72	.705	.70	.54
Depreciation	3,678,047	3,424,474	2,668,537	1,639,670	1,341,927
		Financial Status at Year End			
Working capital	$ 54,482,140	$ 49,595,023	$ 39,014,161	$ 37,999,343	$ 43,390,308
Property, plant and equipment, at cost	54,389,332	47,978,530	45,411,317	29,908,097	21,736,251
Total assets	139,218,311	117,497,938	101,851,501	93,273,748	80,721,123
Shareholders' equity	99,712,965	87,687,936	77,258,776	68,660,871	61,255,330

	1967	1966	1965	1964	1963
		Operations for the Year			
Net sales	$100,166,896	$87,031,996	$73,665,602	$60,466,578	$53,924,037
Income before income taxes	29,551,665	25,070,207	20,002,363	16,427,324	13,937,620
Income taxes	14,629,842	12,261,954	10,238,576	8,328,647	7,397,615
Net income	14,921,823	12,808,253	10,763,787	8,098,677	6,540,005
Per share	1.08	.93	.78	.59	.48
Dividends paid	5,840,625	5,146,752	3,892,811	2,895,001	2,290,599
Per share	.44	.39	.30	.22	.17
Depreciation	1,404,255	1,243,069	1,051,350	936,268	804,126
		Financial Status at Year End			
Working capital	$ 35,200,967	$27,606,069	$21,636,428	$19,078,281	$14,210,907
Property, plant and equipment, at cost	18,662,646	16,007,249	13,747,274	10,441,674	9,818,624
Total assets	67,729,898	58,930,979	47,759,358	38,412,207	31,312,522
Shareholders' equity	50,175,214	41,133,767	33,226,566	27,479,893	21,919,626

EXHIBIT 5

U.S. DRUG ENFORCEMENT AGENCY
Drug Schedules

Schedule	Criteria	Examples	Quotas	Order Forms	Prescription Refills
I	"Illegal" drugs No medical use	LSD Heroin Marihuana	Quotas (manufacturing and procurement)	Required	N/A
II	Medical use *with severe restriction; high* abuse potential; *severe* psychological or physical dependence	Raw opium Codeine Methadone Amphetamine	Quotas (manufacturing and procurement)	Required	No refills
III	Accepted medical use; *less* abuse potential than I or II; *moderate* or low physical dependence; *high* psychological dependence	Glutethimide Ascriptin® Codeine	No quotas	Not required	5 times; 6 months
IV	Accepted medical use; low abuse potential compared to III; limited psychological physical dependence	Phenobarbital (Chardonna®) Meprobamate Paraldehyde	No quotas	Not required	5 times; 6 months
V	Accepted medical use; abuse potential lower than IV; lower psychological physical dependence than IV	Parepectolin®	No quotas	Not required	18-year-olds; I.D.; 8 ounces per customer per 48 hours; bound record book

EXHIBIT 6
LUCE-BEKKER, INC.
Organization of Management Committee

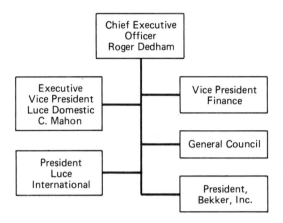

Capital Budget Approval Hierarchy

Under $10,000 — Subsidiary approval only
$10,000 - $100,000 — Dedham, Mahon, V.P. Finance
$100,000 - $250,000 — Management Committee
$250,000 and over — Board of Directors

EXHIBIT 7

ORGANIZATION OF LUCE-BEKKER, INC.

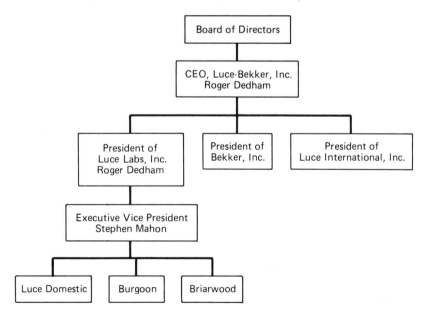

PHILADELPHIA ELECTRIC COMPANY

During 1974 Philadelphia Electric Company's (PECO) kilowatt-hour sales declined 2.8 percent and the peak load decreased 6 percent in response to cool summer weather, higher prices, and energy conservation. During the previous nine years, kilowatt-hour sales had increased at a compound rate of 5.9 percent annually. In fact, this was the first decline in both sales and net peak load since World War II.

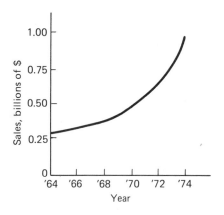

PECO had planned a $3.4 billion construction program for the 1974 to 1978 period to meet the growing needs of its customers. As 1974 progressed it became evident that an adjustment would have to be made. All costs were increasing, including the cost of capital. The growth picture, although presently slowed —declining in fact—did not seem to be an accurate forecast of the future. The market

This case was prepared by William J. Dawson, Jr., and L. George Henisee, Jr., under the supervision of Professor Jules J. Schwartz as the basis for class discussion rather than to illustrate either effective or ineffective handling of a managerial problem.

price of a common share of stock had fallen below $10, less than half of book value.

It was within the context of this environment that PECO management had to operate. In a speech on corporate strategy before the New York Society of Security Analysts, Robert F. Gilkeson, chairman of the board, stated:

> We will concentrate on a nuclear baseload capability—the economic fuel for us. We will also maintain our ability to burn coal to avoid undue concentration on a single fuel. We will maintain construction momentum on long lead-time generation projects to assure our ability to have adequate products to sell. We will maintain our financial viability as a private enterprise by curtailing expenditures on short leadtime projects during a period of economic recession, high capital costs, and low common stock prices. We will not seek government subsidies.

At the same forum, John H. Austin, Jr., vice president of finance and accounting said:

> We are committed to maintaining the good credit of Philadelphia Electric. This means maintaining a strong equity capital position. Yet, of course, selling any amount of new common stock below book value dilutes the present value and future earnings potential of our present shares.

He further stated, "short-term dilution to maintain minimum construction to insure the long-run health of the business is necessary."

THE INVESTOR-OWNED ELECTRIC UTILITY INDUSTRY

Regulated Monopoly

Much of the energy industry operated under controls, and the electric utility industry was no exception. Electric utilities were franchised monopolies. Generally only one electric utility was permitted to operate within a given geographic area. As the only such utility, it was obligated to serve all customers requesting service under the established tariffs, regardless of the economic feasibility of doing so. The utility was not allowed to discontinue service within its territory without prior regulatory approval. As a franchised monopoly the utility was subject to government regulation of prices and services.

A utility was permitted to operate as a monopoly in a given territory because economic theory held that it could operate at the lowest average cost when free from competition. Utilization of expensive capital equipment at close to full capacity minimized unit cost. If one only considers the distribution system, it is obvious that the duplication of this system by two competing companies—two lines of wire rather than one—would be unnecessary waste.

As given utilities were granted monopoly power by the government, it was expected that the government should be involved with their regulation. This was particularly true when the activities of the utility were essential to the public welfare. A formal rate structure governed both prices and services. The prices were based on the quantity of electricity consumed, the way in which it was delivered to the customer, and in some cases, the sustained (thirty-minute) peak demand during a given period. A formalized accounting structure was required to provide accurate and comparable cost and capitalization figures for rate adjustment.

The regulation process itself took place on federal, state, and local levels. The dominant agency in Pennsylvania was the state Public Utility Commission. Although there were significant variations from state to state, all the commissions were basically chartered to perform the same function. In Pennsylvania the five-member board was composed of people nominated by the governor to serve a ten-year term following confirmation by the state senate. The Pennsylvania board, with the assistance of its staff, reviewed each request by a utility—sometimes holding a public hearing—and then granted all, part, or none of the request.

Competition

Although the electric utility was free from the competition of other electric utilities in its service area, it faced other forms of competition. Natural gas, petroleum, and coal were substitute forms of energy that competed with electricity for use in home or industrial application. It also had to compete for the consumer's dollar with other suppliers of goods and services. It competed in the capital funds market with other users of capital. It hired employees in the competitive labor market.

Regulators had to evaluate the tradeoffs between the needs of the consumer and the needs of the utility to be competitive. The utility had to be permitted an adequate and fair return so that it could pay its employees, compensate its present owners and creditors, and attract new capital to support needed new construction for increases in service.

Capital Intensiveness

The electric utility industry was extremely capital intensive. At the end of 1974 the investor-owned electric utility industry had a gross investment in electric plant and equipment of approximately $150 billion (this was about 78 percent of the total value of the electric utility industry). The assets-to-revenue ratio for the industry was 4.18, as compared to the next most capital intensive industry, telephone, at 2.85, and an all-manufacturing ratio of 0.79. Capital outlays by the electric utility industry had been increasing. As a percentage of total United States industrial investment, outlays had also been increasing and were presently at 15.2 percent.

> For this reason, the cost of capital (i.e., interest charges, preferred dividends, common equity return and income tax) plays a very material part in determining the price the electric utility industry must charge its customers. Likewise the other "fixed charges" associated with

investments, i.e., depreciation, insurance and property taxes, weigh heavily in the total cost of delivered energy.[1]

An example of the heavy capital investment requirements is an economically sized nuclear generating station. Such a station, with a capacity of 1000 megawatts (mw) might cost upwards of one billion dollars before it would be operational in the early 1980s.

Generating Facilities

Several types of generating stations were used by the electric utility industry. Fossil-fuel burning stations burned coal, oil, or gas to generate steam. This steam was used to turn the turbines, which turned the electric generators. In the case of coal the plants might be located either in the service area or at the coal mine to save on transportation costs. Nuclear stations worked on the same principle as fossil-fuel stations except that nuclear reaction was used as the heat source to generate the steam. Hydroelectric generation was used where there was sufficient flow of water, usually over a dam, to provide the energy source. An extension of this was a pump storage facility. When there was excess generating capacity during off-peak periods this capacity could be used to pump water into a storage pond. During peak demand periods this water could be made to flow out, thus generating additional electricity. Another common type of generating facility was composed of several generating units driven by internal combustion engines or turbines. These were usually referred to as peaking units, because they could be brought into service rapidly to meet peak demand.

In a very general sense it may be said that the cost of fuel for a particular type of generating station was inversely related to the initial cost of the station. That is, hydroelectric and nuclear stations were the most expensive to build, but their energy source per kilowatt-hour was the least expensive. Peaking units were

[1] Section IIIB-6, Edison Electric Institute (EEI), *Economic Growth in the Future,* Pre-Publication Copy, EEI, New York, 1975.

the least expensive to build, but the fuel cost was the most expensive. Fossil fuel steam units were midway in both cost of construction and cost of fuel.

Growth and Planning

As utilities were required to provide service within their franchise area, they had to plan ahead to have capacity available when it was needed. Exhibit 1 shows the increasing demand for energy as it related to the change in GNP during the post-World War II period. The percentage change in total energy demand is approximately equal to the percentage change in GNP. However, when electrical energy is isolated from the total energy demand, it shows an average annual increase of almost 7.5 percent, twice as much as the increase in total energy demand.

When planning capacity a utility had to plan for a reserve (approximately 15 to 20 percent) above its expected peak demand in order to provide reliable service throughout the year in the face of maintenance needs, weather conditions, and unplanned outages. However, the average usage would only be in the range of 60 percent of peak demand, because customer use of electricity varied significantly during each twenty-four-hour period, as well as from day to day and from season to season. Under these conditions and with current technology, the need to minimize overall costs to consumers typically resulted in a mix of generating plants that combined plants with high capital costs and low fuel and operating costs for base and intermediate load use with plants with lower capital costs and higher fuel and operating costs for peaking use.

Complicating this need to meet future demand was the lengthy industry planning cycle. A nuclear station took ten years from initial planning to completion, a fossil-fuel station from five to eight. This time was partially the result of the extensive licensing procedure, particularly in the case of the nuclear station. Beside the Nuclear Regulatory Commission there were various environmental agencies to be dealt with—the Environmental Protection Agency, the Pennsylvania Department of Environmental Resources, and locally, the Delaware River Basin Commission, and Susquehanna River Basin Commission.

ECONOMICS AND INFLATION

Utility companies had a basic responsibility to continue to construct new facilities as necessary to meet the load requirements of their territories. Because of an established regulatory principle mandating that present customers may not be charged for services that will benefit only future customers, utilities were forced to invest large sums of capital without a return until the plants became operational. The long construction period for new facilities made this an especially important financial consideration for utility managements. The capital investment in new facilities did not become part of the "rate base" until those facilities were officially in service. The rate base was the measure used in the regulatory process to determine the utility's allowed cost of capital. This cost of capital was a significant part of the total cost of providing electrical service (typically 40 to 60 percent of the total), the remainder being the sum of various expenses such as labor and fuel.

The utility received partial relief in terms of an allowance for funds used during the construction period. By means of certain accounting transactions, the allowance for funds used during construction (the interest and dividend payments for the part of the utility's invested capital used to fund new construction projects) was extracted from the utility's current expense accounts and added instead to the cost of construction. Once a construction project was completed and the new facility placed in service, it was the responsibility of the regulatory authorities to permit the utility to earn a fair return on the new enlarged rate base. This split responsibility resulted in utility management being forced to invest capital and expand service without knowing whether it would be permitted to make an adequate return on its increased investment.

The uncertainty of this return was compounded by a regulatory lag. The lag, as illustrated in Exhibit 2, could be as long as twenty-seven months—and with the added effects of inflation it was conceivable that the utilities might never catch up to what they were entitled to earn.

Inflation significantly affected the capital intensive utility industry. It caused the depreciation funds, which accumulated as plant and equipment were used up, to be insufficient to cover costs of replacement.

In recent months industry fuel costs had increased greatly. Oil prices had quadrupled and the price of coal had increased 120 percent between 1967 and 1974. Natural gas prices had increased only 30 percent but its availability was down sharply, and the cost of nuclear fuel, which started at $8 per pound, was at $16 and was expected to reach $36 by the early 1980s.

CAPITAL STRUCTURE

Besides being capital intensive, it should be noted that the capital structure of the electric utility industry was a highly leveraged one. Long-term debt and preferred stock typically constituted 60 to 65 percent of a utility's total capitalization, with common stock equity accounting for the remaining 35 percent. Stable net income growth had permitted reliance on long-term debt and preferred stock, making possible a lower overall cost of capital. But this established structure was being threatened. Long-term interest rates and preferred dividends were increasing as a result of inflation. Regulatory agencies were reluctant to permit return on equity to rise. As a result equity could not be sold to investors without substantial dilution to present stockholders.

The industry was caught on a treadmill. Coverage ratios required that no new debt could be issued unless pretax earnings were at least twice total interest charges, including that on the new debt. With decreasing net income and increasing interest costs, this minimum allowable ratio of two was rapidly being approached by many companies. Issuing more long-term debt therefore had to be delayed. The decline in earnings, resulting from regulatory lag and inflation, had resulted in a decrease in the market price of common shares. In many cases the new share values were substantially below book. Raising funds in the equity market would thus result in more earnings dilution and erosion of present stockholders' positions.

Compounding this problem was the first major alteration of the historical growth pattern of the industry since World War II. Thus, while most industry spokesmen still called for an average growth rate over the next twenty-five years approaching 5.8 percent, the decline in demand in 1974 caused many to reconsider. Projected capital requirements for the energy industry are shown in Exhibit 3.

COMPANY HISTORY

Although electricity was first put in use in Philadelphia in 1881, it was not until 1899 that Philadelphia Electric Company came into being as a consolidation of two of the many small electric companies operating in the city. The early years were spent acquiring the remaining companies and consolidating them into an efficient system. This included the normal assimilation of organizational structures and the overcoming of the technical problems of integration. During the ensuing years the company grew in size as new customers were acquired and new uses were developed for electricity. Peak demand doubled approximately every decade except during the 1930s. At that time a merger with the Philadelphia Suburban-Counties Gas and Electric Company increased PECO's service territory to its present size.

PECO's history was marked by "first," "largest," and "best" in connection with its many operations and facilities. Over the years PECO's philosophy had evolved so that although it might no longer be first with technological improvements, it quickly adopted new developments when they had been proven.

PECO's labor history had been relatively smooth, resulting from good relations between management and the labor force. Early in its history PECO provided its employees with such things as an athletic association, an employee magazine, a company-financed service annuity program, and later, company athletic facilities, including a golf course. Over the years the wage rate paid the first-class lineman (an industry benchmark), had been among the highest in the industry, with an equivalent fringe benefits package.

In 1976 the employees of only one generating station were represented by a national labor union. However, many of the employees were members of the Independent Group Association, an organization that interacted with management on an unofficial basis in many labor related areas, including annual wage increases and fringe benefits.

CURRENT BUSINESS

The franchise area of PECO and its subsidiaries was 2475 square miles, including the City of Philadelphia and surrounding counties, and two counties in northeastern Maryland. The population of the area was approximately 3.9 million and was almost equally divided between Philadelphia proper and the remaining suburban areas. Electric service was supplied in an area of 2340 square miles to a total of 1.2 million customers. Natural gas was supplied to 274,000 customers in an area of 1475 square miles in the four counties surrounding Philadelphia. Steam services were provided to 710 customers in central Philadelphia.

Operating income (loss) before taxes from the three areas of operation for 1974 was: electric, $196.4 million; gas, $26.9 million; and steam, ($3.2 million). The operating loss from steam operations was due mainly to a delay in the recovery of increases in fuel costs.

Total operating revenues for 1974 were $1012 million with a net income of $129 million. Total assets were $3668 million with net utility plant of $3406 million, including nuclear fuel valued at $36.2 million. During 1974 the price of the common stock fluctuated from a high of $19½ to a low of $9⅜. Book value of the stock was $20.45. (For complete financial and operating records see Exhibits 4 and 5.)

Electric Operations

The net installed electric generating capacity of PECO on July 31, 1975, is shown in the following table:

Type of Capacity	Megawatts	% of Total
Service area, coal-fired	791	10.9%
Mine-mouth, coal-fired	705	9.8
Oil-fired	1,808	25.1
Internal combustion	1,632	22.6
Nuclear	886	12.3
Hydro (including pumped storage)	1,392	19.3
	7,214	100.0%

Much of the company's nuclear energy was generated by Peach Bottom Units 2 and 3, which were operated by PECO and owned jointly by PECO and other utilities in the middle Atlantic states. Peach Bottom Unit 2 had a capacity of 1051 mw, of which the company was entitled to 447 mw. Peach Bottom Unit 3 had a capacity of 1035 mw, of which PECO was entitled to 439 mw.

The Nuclear Regulatory Commission licensing board had imposed a requirement that a closed-cycle cooling system be installed at the Peach Bottom Station by July 1, 1977. However, the company reached agreement with Pennsylvania Department of Environmental Resources suspending this requirement until a determination could be made as to possible alternative thermal limitations. This agreement required the company to construct two additional cooling towers and, prior to their completion, to operate the station in accordance with interim thermal limitations. The closed-cycle cooling system would increase the construction costs of the station by an estimated $15 million and could lower the net capacity of the station by a maximum of 3.5 percent. This cost was included in the capital expenditures estimates given in Exhibit 6. (See also Exhibit 7.)

In December 1974 additional interim restrictions involving the emergency core cooling systems were placed on the operations of Peach Bottom Units 2 and 3. These restrictions could possibly result in some reductions in plant output for a limited period.

The maximum hourly demand on the PECO system as of August 1973 was 5.8 million kilowatts. The estimated average generating reserve margin for the five years, 1975 to 1979, based on normal weather and present construction plans, was approximately 18 percent.

PECO was a member of the Pennsylvania–New Jersey–Maryland Interconnection (PJM), which fully integrated the bulk power generation and transmission operations of the eleven utilities in the region. Installed reserves against peak demand were approximately 9.3 million kw for this system. Maximum demand, as of August 1973, was 31 million kw. The capacity available at any time for operation of the system might be less than installed capacity due to repairs, maintenance, inspections, or unforeseen circumstances. It was estimated that the capacity planned for the next five years would be sufficient to meet the required reserve margins set by the Mid-Atlantic Council. It was the function of the Council, which was made up of the eleven PJM companies and several municipal and cooperative electric systems operating within the PJM area, to coordinate planning and reliability within the region.

Gas Operations

Gas operations had suffered from shortages of gas supplies as well as from higher prices. The gas to which the company was entitled under its gas purchase contracts amounted to 79.1 billion cubic feet (bcf) in 1974. Actual deliveries fell 17.4 bcf (22 percent) short of the amount contracted for that year. This compared to a cutback of 10.1 bfc (12.8 percent) of the contracted amount for 1973. Estimated for 1975 were shortages of 21 bcf (27 percent) of the contracted amount.

It should be noted that a Pennsylvania Public Utility Commission (PUC) order then in effect stated that no public utility in its jurisdiction might accept any additional gas sales commitments unless it could show the commission that its present supplies were sufficient to meet the projected future needs of its existing customers. On the basis of this regulation, PECO's expectations included no commitments of additional gas to either present or new customers. PECO expected no improvement in the supply situation in the near future. Similarly, the company had no reason to believe that future supplies might not be curtailed further. The company was pursuing several options in its attempt to secure additional supplies of gas. These included the purchase of supplies of synthetic natural gas, an investment in a proposed synthetic gas plant using petroleum feedstocks, a joint venture to explore and drill for gas along the Gulf Coast, the exploration for gas in the Appalachian region, and support of a joint industry-government research and development program for the manufacture of gas from coal.

RATES

On January 31, 1974, PECO filed a request with the PUC for an increase in electric rates amounting to $136 million for all classes of customers, to become effective in three parts. The PUC permitted the first part to go into effect on April 1, 1974, resulting in a $24 million increase in annual revenues. However, this increase was subject to possible refund with interest. The remainder of the increase was suspended until January 1, 1975. This is indicative of the difficulties PECO had faced in its recent applications for rate relief as a result of consumer concern and political reality. The following chart summarizes PECO's recent rate increase history.

To alleviate the problems inherent in increasing fuel costs, the company had an electrical fuel adjustment clause: The average cost per kwh of electricity generated by fossil fuels was reflected in customer billing (after approximately a two-month lag). Litigation with the state concerning this clause was progressing through the courts. There would be a substantial adverse affect on the company if it should lose. Similar fuel adjustment clauses were applicable for gas rates. The company was entitled to compensation from its customers for the higher costs of natural gas and liquified natural gas, or alternative gas supplies converted from crude oil or naphtha or manufactured from coal.

Rate Increases

	Annual Revenue	Applied For (Date)	Approved Increase	Made Effective (Date)
Electric	$ 96,000,000	11/19/70	$42,000,000	2/18/71
			30,600,000	11/17/71
	48,000,000	7/14/72	16,000,000	10/ 5/72
			32,000,000	8/21/73
	136,000,000	1/31/74	24,000,000	4/ 1/74
			81,000,000	1/ 1/75
Gas	12,000,000	12/ 5/72	12,000,000	2/15/73
	14,000,000	4/ 3/75	6,400,000	6/ 2/75
Steam	1,100,000	11/19/70	1,100,000	1/18/71
	1,300,000	3/30/72	1,300,000	6/15/72
	1,750,000	4/ 3/73	1,550,000	8/31/73
	4,300,000	11/29/74	3,700,000	2/ 1/75
Electric Conowingo Power Co.	670,000	11/ 1/71	670,000	5/ 8/72
	1,900,000	12/ 5/73	1,900,000	4/16/74

FUEL

During 1974 PECO encountered substantial increases in the prices of all fuels and some curtailment of deliveries. As ordered by the Federal Energy Administration and Federal Power Commission, a reduction in output caused by unavailability of fuel oil would be equally shared intraregionally. PECO maintained its own storage facility for fuel, which contained about a twenty-three-day supply. Purchases were made in the spot markets when requirements were greater than contracted supply. Contracts through December 1975 had been made guaranteeing oil through that

Nuclear fuel orders had been contracted out to supply Peach Bottom Units 2 and 3, Limerick Units 2 and 3, and Fulton Units 1 and 2 through 1990. A supplier had indicated that it might not be able to meet 37 percent of the contracted deliveries. The company believed that this would not affect operations in these units until 1983. The Salem units had sufficient supplies until 1979; Summit Unit 1, until 1982; and Summit Unit 2, until 1984. These units were operated by other utilities and PECO was entitled to a portion of the output. The nuclear fuel supply cycle for the units operated by PECO was as shown below:

Unit	Uranium Concentrate	Conversion	Enrichment	Fabrication	Reprocess
Peach Bottom 2	1982	1982	1998	1980	1990
Peach Bottom 3	1981	1981	1998	1981	1990
Limerick 1	1981	1981	2001	1985	1990
Limerick 2	1981	1981	2001	1986	1990
Fulton 1	1983	1983	2009	1995	2000
Fulton 2	1985	1985	2011	1997	2002

date. It was expected that PECO would be able to renew or replace these contracts. This oil was in compliance with air pollution control standards of the Commonwealth of Pennsylvania.

Coal contracts had customarily been on a yearly, rather than a long-term contract basis, and one supplier had customarily supplied more than half of the company's needs over the past ten years. The average cost per ton of coal purchased was:

Year	Average Cost Per Ton
1970	$10.44
1971	12.67
1972	13.75
1973	14.46
1974	22.94

The company believed that sufficient coal inventories existed to handle up to a four-month delay in deliveries.

It was expected that the plutonium and uranium used in nuclear operations would be permitted to be recycled. If not, costs would have to be recovered through increases in customer charges.

FINANCIAL PROGRAM

Total capital requirements for 1975 were estimated at $505 million (Exhibit 6). Internal cash would provide about 37 percent of construction expenditures in 1975 (excluding bond refundings), and over 40 percent each year 1976 through 1979, as compared to only 16 percent in 1970. To help finance additional expenditures, $100 million in bonds would be offered in January 1975 and $80 million in bonds would be offered in August 1975 to refund a similar issue maturing at that time. This would be followed by a common stock rights offering in the fall and then another bond issue in the winter. Interim financing would be provided by short-term bank loans and commercial paper borrowing.

It should be noted that under PECO's mortgage, additional bonds could not be issued on the basis of property additions or cash deposits unless earnings before income taxes and interest were at least two times the pro forma annual interest on all such bonds outstanding and applied for. Earnings, for the purpose of this test, did not include the "allowance for funds used during construction" that it might not be able to meet 37 percent of cial statements in accordance with the prescribed system of accounts. The coverage under the earnings test of the mortgage for the twelve months ended August 31, 1975, was 2.35. Such coverage would permit issuance of approximately $175 million of additional mortgage bonds at an assumed interest rate of 11 percent, against property additions or cash deposits. PECO was also entitled to issue an additional $80 million of mortgage bonds, without regard to the earnings test, because it would repay $80 million of 8 percent bonds at maturity on August 15, 1975.

Under PECO's articles of incorporation the issuance of additional preferred stock required an affirmative vote of two-thirds of all preferred shares outstanding unless certain tests were met. Under the most restrictive requirement additional preferred stock could not be issued without such a vote unless earnings, after income taxes but before interest, were at least 1.5 times the aggregate of the pro forma annual interest and preferred dividend requirements of all indebtedness and preferred stock. The coverage for the twelve months ended August 31, 1975, was 1.56. Based on this earnings coverage, no significant amount of preferred stock could be issued at this time without a preferred shareholder vote.

If coverage under the earnings test described above remained at or below present levels, the result might be greater use of long-term and short-term unsecured debt or common stock in financing PECO's construction program. Another option would be to reschedule portions of the program if unsecured debt or

common stock were not marketable on acceptable terms. Management believed it would be able to issue sufficient amounts of bonds and stock to enable it to continue to meet its near-term capital requirements. However, PECO expected that its financing and construction programs for the foreseeable future would require further revisions unless PECO was able to obtain timely approval of its future rate increase applications and a more favorable market for its securities.

CONSTRUCTION PROGRAM

The perceived growth in customer demand dictated that PECO maintain an adequate continuous construction program. In July 1975 PECO estimated that its net utility plant had doubled in the past five years. Exhibits 6 and 7 show the breakdown of future estimated construction costs. The original program for the 1974 to 1978 period had been cut back $830 million and could be cut further depending on PECO's ability to finance construction. Estimated total construction costs for the five-year period 1975 to 1979 were $2.6 billion. It should be noted that construction expenditures for this period were lower in relative terms as well as in absolute dollars. Capital spending as a proportion of gross plant and investment had declined from 14 percent in 1970 to 11.6 percent in 1974. It was expected to reach 10 percent by 1979. If the effects of inflation were considered, the percentages would have been even lower.

The cuts in the construction budget were reflected in the postponement of a 600 mw oil-fired generating unit and in subsequent delays in the originally scheduled service dates of all the nuclear units included in the budget. The effect of these changes could result in some reduction in reserve capacity through 1986, but no substantial change in service reliability was expected.

Management summarized potential problems existing at the following units:

Salem—Potential delays exist in securing operating licenses.

Limerick—Environmental action in the courts has slowed progress and if the reservoir plans as drawn by the Delaware River Basin Commission are not followed, the company may require one or more reservoirs at a total cost of $35 million to $40 million. These costs are not included in the original estimates.

Fulton—The supplier for the nuclear steam supply systems has notified the company it is unwilling to continue work under present contract conditions. Therefore, work has been suspended and no estimate can be made as to the overall effect of this action.

In addition to normal construction requirements it was estimated that the company would spend approximately $71 million on existing plant and new construction for air and water pollution control. Further substantial expenditures might have to be made in these areas.

MANAGEMENT STRATEGY AND PERCEPTION OF THE PROBLEM

In his speech before the New York Society of Security Analysts, Board Chairman Gilkeson based his evaluation of the future of PECO as a profitable, privately-owned business enterprise on three fundamental assumptions:

1. There is a growing need and market for electric energy. Any long-run slackening of economic growth in a maturing economy will be offset by the need to shift energy uses from gas and oil to coal and uranium.
2. PECO has the proven scientific, engineering, construction, and operating capability to produce and distribute electric power reliably and economically, using the latest coal and nuclear technology.
3. Market and economic analyses show conclusively that if we can price our product close to any semblance of a free competitive market price (and we believe in the long run we can), we can produce and market our product at a sound profit margin.

On the basis of these assessments Mr. Gilkeson stated PECO's fundamental strategy:

1. We will concentrate on nuclear baseload capability—the economic fuel choice for us. We will also maintain our ability to burn coal to avoid undue concentration on a single fuel.
2. We will maintain construction momentum on long leadtime generation projects to assure our ability to have adequate products to sell.
3. We will maintain our financial viability as a private enterprise by curtailing expenditures on short leadtime projects during a period of economic recession, high capital costs, and low common stock prices. We will not seek government subsidies.
4. We will preserve the value of our present shareholders' investment, while assuring future earnings potential and our ability to raise capital in a free market.

It should be noted that while costs of a nuclear plant were nearly double that of an oil plant, nuclear fuel costs were only about one-tenth that of oil and total costs were 4.5 cents per kwh for oil as opposed to 2.7 cents per kwh for nuclear systems. Similar comparisons would exist between coal and nuclear systems. It was estimated that by 1986 total output would be approximately 75 percent nuclear. As for coal, the successful development and efficient use of new scrubber technology would enable the company to increase its use of coal and thus help avoid an overdependence on one type of fuel.

In keeping with the desire to maintain a viable financial position PECO entered 1975 with its financial house in order, 49 percent debt, 14 percent preferred, and 37 percent equity. (See Exhibits 8, 9, and 10.) Capital spending had been trimmed by over $800 million and other operating costs had been cut as far as performance standards would allow. With recent rate increases it was believed a more adequate product pricing structure would be found.

PECO was firmly committed to the maintenance of good credit and a strong equity position. This commitment presented PECO with the dilemma facing any company that needed substantial funds at a time when its stock was selling at substantially less than book value. If spending increased and an excessive number of new shares were sold, there would be an irreversible dilution of the value of shares presently outstanding. On the other hand PECO had to provide the necessary product to satisfy potential demand. Thus it had to walk the tightrope of dilution of shareholders' value and dilution in the quality and amount

of product and service it could supply. Based on its assessments of the future economy of the industry and demand in its operational area, PECO believed it had no other viable choice but to build nuclear plants and follow a middle-of-the-road financing program.

EXHIBIT 1

ENERGY USE AND REAL GNP ANNUAL GROWTH RATES (%)

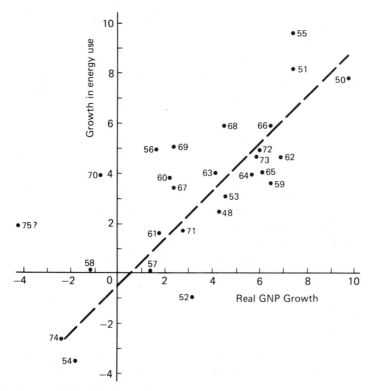

Source: Edison Electric Institute (EEI), *Economic Growth in the Future,* Pre-Publication Copy, EEI, New York, 1975.

EXHIBIT 2

REGULATORY LAG

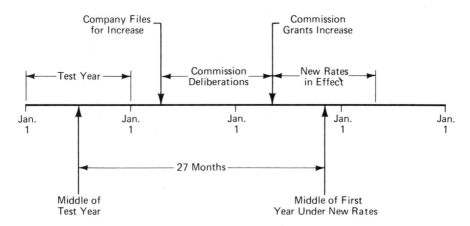

This example assumes three months are required for the company to ascertain final and accurate statistics for the test year and then to prepare the filing documents. It also assumes commission deliberations consume twelve months. Deliberation times vary from one company's filing to another's.

The middle of the test year and the middle of the first year under new rates are highlighted. This reflects the fact that, when costs are rising more or less continuously, the costs and revenues at each midyear point are reasonable approximations of the average costs and revenue for that year.

Source: Edison Electric Institute (EEI), *Economic Growth in the Future,* Pre-Publication Copy, EEI, New York, 1975.

EXHIBIT 3

ENERGY INDUSTRY CAPITAL NEEDS
(billions of current dollars)

Year	Electric Utility Industry	Petroleum Industry	Other	Total
1974	$ 17.5	$ 10.6	$ 6.5	$ 34.6
1975	17.3	12.3	7.1	36.7
1976	19.2	13.7	7.8	40.7
1977	22.8	15.3	8.7	46.8
1978	27.0	17.2	9.7	53.9
1979	31.0	19.2	10.8	61.0
1980	35.0	21.6	12.7	69.3
1981	39.5	23.7	13.6	76.8
1982	44.0	25.9	14.5	84.4
1983	47.0	28.5	15.5	91.0
1984	50.5	31.2	16.5	98.2
1985	54.0	34.3	17.4	105.7
1986	58.0	37.4	18.5	113.9
1987	64.0	40.9	19.6	124.5
1988	69.5	44.6	20.7	134.8
1989	75.0	48.7	22.0	145.7
1990	80.5	52.6	23.5	156.6
1974–85	$404.8	$253.5	$140.8	$ 799.1
1974–90	$751.8	$477.7	$245.1	$1,474.6

PROJECTION OF INSTALLED GENERATING CAPACITY FOR TOTAL UTILITY INDUSTRY IN THE UNITED STATES
(average for the year; capacities in million of kilowatts)

Energy Source	1975	1980	1985	2000
Coal	205	253	302	456
Oil and gas	172	200	229	254
Nuclear	45	100	236	820
Hydro and other	67	79	87	179
Total	489	632	854	1,709

Source: Edison Electric Institute (EEI), *Economic Growth in the Future,* Pre-Publication Copy, EEI, New York, 1975.

EXHIBIT 4

INCOME STATEMENT—ALL OPERATIONS

	1974	1973	1972	1971	1970
			(thousands of dollars)		
Operating Revenue	$1,011,726	$766,658	$685,038	$608,134	$504,371
Operating Expenses:					
Fuel and energy interchanged	439,231	260,294	211,971	189,818	137,302
Operation and maintenance	207,386	191,177	175,417	154,040	145,557
Provision for depreciation	77,802	64,271	60,515	55,937	53,947
Provision for Taxes:					
Federal income taxes	10,986	24,335	23,541	21,695	17,834
State and local income taxes	7,167	7,608	7,890	7,457	5,330
Investment tax credit adjustments—net	20,691	3,569	1,870	569	(836)
Deferred income taxes	28,313	9,601	7,306	3,947	(818)
Total income taxes	67,157	45,140	40,607	33,668	21,510
Taxes, other than income	67,143	57,353	52,980	47,109	38,410
Total Provision for Taxes	134,300	102,493	93,587	80,777	59,920
Total Operating Expenses	858,719	618,235	541,490	480,572	396,726
Operating Income	153,007	148,423	143,548	127,562	107,645
Other Income:					
Allowance for funds used during construction	70,841	58,743	42,450	31,691	18,513
Income tax credits net	25,441	3,374	(396)	(1,681)	180
Other net	271	2,643	157	3,197	35
Total Other Income	96,553	64,760	42,211	33,207	18,737
Income Before Interest Charges	249,560	213,183	185,759	160,769	126,382
Interest Charges:					
Long-term debt	106,298	84,837	73,383	60,854	50,336
Short-term debt	14,165	5,479	4,402	6,291	7,670
Total Interest Charges	120,463	90,316	77,785	67,145	58,006
Net income	129,097	122,867	107,974	93,624	68,376
Dividends on preferred stock	33,582	27,600	21,558	15,320	8,612
Earnings applicable to common stock	95,415	95,267	86,416	78,304	49,764
Dividends on common stock	86,458	78,350	67,735	60,689	53,683
Earnings retained	$ 8,957	$ 16,917	$ 18,681	$ 17,615	$ 6,081

Source: Annual Report, 1974.

EXHIBIT 4 (cont.)

INCOME STATEMENT—ALL OPERATIONS

	1969	1968	1967	1966	1965	1964
			(thousands of dollars)			
Operating Revenue	$440,494	$405,231	$376,528	$357,864	$340,881	$323,860
Operating Expenses:						
Fuel and energy interchanged	110,004	102,400	86,745	86,343	77,105	74,907
Operation and maintenance	126,092	115,571	108,984	101,068	100,422	93,787
Provision for depreciation	49,304	45,388	41,833	38,949	38,037	34,615
Provision for Taxes:						
Federal income taxes	28,671	29,841	28,578	33,591	32,598	32,099
State and local income taxes	7,664	4,270	4,739	4,173	4,069	3,953
Investment tax credit						
adjustments—net	(32)	506	5,063	1,199	1,256	1,803
Deferred income taxes	(818)	(818)	(818)	(818)	(818)	(818)
Total income taxes	35,485	33,799	37,562	38,145	37,105	37,037
Taxes, other than income	18,295	15,816	13,899	11,855	10,617	9,998
Total Provision for Taxes	53,780	49,615	51,461	50,000	47,722	47,035
Total Operating Expenses	339,180	312,974	289,023	276,360	263,286	250,344
Operating Income	101,314	92,257	87,505	81,504	77,595	73,510
Other Income:						
Allowance for funds used						
during construction	7,929	4,080	4,856	3,893	1,532	1,296
Income tax credits net	48	(617)	(372)	(270)	(501)	(352)
Other net	(14)	6,121	622	234	676	363
Total Other Income	7,963	9,584	5,106	3,857	1,707	1,307
Income Before Interest Charges	109,277	101,841	92,611	85,361	79,302	74,823
Interest Charges:						
Long-term debt	38,161	23,646	26,800	23,011	22,378	20,754
Short-term debt	6,819	2,557	2,607	1,459	421	1,211
Total Interest Charges	44,980	36,203	29,407	24,470	22,799	21,965
Net income	64,297	65,638	63,204	60,891	56,503	52,858
Dividends on preferred stock	5,931	3,696	3,696	3,696	3,696	3,696
Earnings applicable to common						
stock	48,366	61,942	59,508	57,195	52,807	49,162
Dividends on common stock	48,803	47,612	44,806	40,715	39,615	36,313
Earnings retained	$ 9,563	$ 14,330	$ 14,702	$ 16,480	$ 13,192	$ 12,849

EXHIBIT 5

CONSOLIDATED BALANCE SHEET
(thousands of dollars)

Assets	1974	1973	1972	1971	1970	1969	1968	1967	1966	1965	1964
Utility plant in service at original cost	$3,215,021	$2,582,819	$2,461,104	$2,301,959	$2,115,433	$1,954,846	$1,838,072	$1,731,752	$1,517,695	$1,475,725	$1,442,515
Construction work in progress (incl. nuclear fuel)	893,161	1,077,312	751,014	542,227	400,846	226,756	103,423	53,056	132,481	70,460	43,237
Plant held for future fuel	15,715	12,002	10,525	6,815	5,327	6,967	9,697	6,726	7,477	7,207	3,877
Total Utility Plant	4,123,897	3,672,133	3,222,643	2,851,001	2,521,606	2,188,569	1,951,192	1,791,534	1,657,653	1,553,392	1,489,629
Less: Accumulated provision for depreciation	717,808	665,425	624,244	585,670	549,548	514,218	491,373	459,855	428,943	402,506	379,242
Total utility plant less depreciation reserve	3,406,089	3,006,708	2,598,399	2,265,331	1,972,058	1,674,351	1,459,819	1,331,679	1,228,710	1,150,886	1,110,387
Nonutility property and other investments	12,701	11,474	9,463	6,021	3,895	5,026	4,019	6,328	8,155	9,736	11,832
Current Assets											
Cash	15,980	16,173	17,820	25,243	24,219	16,999	15,613	15,137	12,278	14,238	17,734
Pollution control funds held by trustee	21,655	12,239	38,002	—	—	—	—	—	—	—	—
Accounts receivable	111,888	75,629	72,103	62,909	50,839	44,134	41,253	46,966	34,220	31,802	32,682
Deferred fuel expense	72,497	—	—	—	—	—	—	—	—	—	—
Materials and supplies at average cost	21,174	40,218	38,845	34,219	33,564	29,086	25,990	23,834	22,406	21,406	20,285
Other current and accrued assets	—	3,764	2,753	1,931	1,831	1,629	1,724	3,048	2,573	3,408	1,613
Total Current Assets	243,200	148,023	169,523	124,302	110,453	91,848	84,580	88,985	71,477	70,854	72,314
Deferred debits	6,036	9,858	7,510	6,609	5,509	4,915	5,227	4,131	5,294	4,939	7,901
Total Assets	$3,668,026	$3,176,063	$2,784,895	$2,402,263	$2,091,915	$1,776,140	$1,553,645	$1,431,123	$1,313,636	$1,236,415	$1,202,434

EXHIBIT 5 (cont.)

CONSOLIDATED BALANCE SHEET
(thousands of dollars)

Liabilities	1974	1973	1972	1971	1970	1969	1968	1967	1966	1965	1964
Liabilities											
Capitalization											
Long-term debt	$1,597,690	$1,319,141	$1,287,264	$1,161,758	$1,019,803	$848,697	$778,746	$691,964	$651,302	$612,925	$590,173
Preferred stock	486,383	412,020	337,472	262,472	192,472	127,472	87,472	87,472	87,472	87,472	87,472
Common stock equity, incl. retained earnings	$1,077,969	1,059,239	894,686	784,165	665,602	601,704	526,920	512,599	460,519	440,046	426,854
Total Capitalization	3,162,042	2,790,400	2,519,422	2,208,395	1,877,877	1,577,873	1,393,138	1,292,035	1,199,293	1,140,443	1,104,499
Current Liabilities											
Bank loans	$ 115,000	$ 83,500	$ 41,100	$ 1,800	$ 14,625	$ 50,175	$ 26,100	$ 47,700	$ 32,275	$ 10,450	$ 19,550
Commercial paper	62,824	64,232	62,710	47,467	60,889	48,601	34,911	—	—	—	—
Accounts payable	66,125	55,961	36,699	32,288	36,840	28,770	23,413	19,243	17,842	18,208	15,471
Taxes:											
Accrued	16,512	18,126	18,429	22,305	9,423	8,324	7,163	6,786	13,684	18,989	16,032
Deferred—fuel	11,471	—	—	—	—	—	—	—	—	—	—
Interest accrued	30,462	21,870	18,066	17,545	14,829	10,903	8,664	6,703	6,041	5,373	5,061
Dividends declared	12,694	11,403	12,835	8,419	5,814	5,274	4,555	4,414	2,936	2,334	2,439
Current maturities of long-term debt	91,866	67,328	13,495	17,131	33,924	8,470	15,592	9,584	1,471	987	1,072
Other	3,859	5,476	5,422	3,167	3,602	1,924	3,045	2,690	2,682	2,573	2,404
Total Current Liabilities	410,913	327,896	208,756	150,122	179,946	162,441	123,443	97,120	76,931	58,914	62,029
Deferred Credits											
Accumulated deferred income taxes	56,533	39,692	30,091	22,785	13,075	13,892	14,710	15,528	16,346	17,164	17,981
Accumulated deferred investment tax credits	32,551	11,860	8,264	6,394	5,825	6,660	6,692	11,704	6,641	5,442	4,186
Other deferred credits	4,645	1,760	2,492	1,512	1,752	877	1,677	794	844	1,020	1,055
Total Deferred Credits	93,729	53,312	40,847	30,691	20,652	21,429	23,069	28,026	23,831	23,626	23,222
Operating reserves	1,342	4,455	3,237	1,071	1,754	2,973	2,937	3,056	3,020	3,230	2,961
Contributions in aid of construction	—	—	12,633	11,984	11,686	11,424	11,058	10,886	10,561	10,202	9,723
Total Liabilities	$3,668,026	$3,176,063	$2,784,895	$2,402,263	$2,091,915	$1,776,140	$1,553,645	$1,431,123	$1,313,636	$1,236,415	$1,202,434

Source: Annual Report, 1974.

EXHIBIT 6

PHILADELPHIA ELECTRIC COMPANY
Financial Analysts
Forecast Information[a]

	Actual	Budget Forecast					Compound Growth Rates 1974–1979
	1974	1975	1976	1977	1978	1979	
Sales and Load Data							
Electric:							
Sales (billion kwh)	25.6	27.3	28.7	30.7	32.7	34.5	6.1%
Peak Load—Net MW—Note 2	5,431	6,050	6,430	6,820	7,240	7,620	7.0
Generating Capability Net MW (at time of peak)—Note 5	6,968	7,373	7,829	8,293	8,293	8,767	4.7
Gas Sales (billion cubic feet):							
From distribution system	46.7	44.2	43.9	42.8	41.5	40.4	(2.9)
Direct from pipelines	15.4	12.9	10.4	8.9	7.2	5.6	(18.3)
	62.1	57.1	54.3	51.7	48.7	46.0	(5.8%)
Steam Sales (billions of pounds)	7.6	8.2	8.5	8.8	9.1	9.4	4.3%

							5 Years 1975–1979
Capital Requirements (millions of dollars)							
Construction Expenditures							
Electric	$451	$364	$429	$445	$502	$574	$2,314
Gas	12	13	13	14	17	19	76
Nuclear fuel	10	20	19	18	26	53	136
Other	4	13	8	4	5	28	58
Total Construction Expenditures	$477	$410	$469	$481	$550	$674	$2,584
Long-term debt and preferred stock retirements	69	95	64	41	32	135	367
Total Capital Requirements	$546	$505	$533	$522	$582	$809	$2,951

EXHIBIT 6 (cont.)

PHILADELPHIA ELECTRIC COMPANY
Financial Analysts
Forecast Information[a]

Sources of Capital (millions of dollars)

Internal Sources:							
Depreciation	$78	$98	$105	$120	$124	$133	$580
Other	(35)	52	100	82	109	153	496
Total Internal Sources	$43	$150	$205	$202	$233	$286	$1,076
Outside financing required	503	355	328	320	349	523	1,875
Total Sources of Capital	$546	$505	$533	$522	$582	$809	$2,951
Tentative Outside Financing:							
Long-term debt	$375	$290	$200	$180	$260	$320	$1,250
Industrial revenue bonds	12	—	—	—	—	—	—
Preferred stock	75	—	30	40	50	60	180
Common stock	11	140	102	104	118	148	612
Short-term debt—increase (decrease)	30	(75)	(4)	(4)	(79)	(5)	(167)
Total Tentative Outside Financing	$503	$355	$328	$320	$349	$523	$1,875

Significant Income Items
(millions of dollars)

Allowance for funds used during construction—Note 3	$71	$64	$77	$74	$98	$117
Income tax reductions allocated to construction—Note 3	$25	$28	$29	$31	$38	$45
Deferred tax reductions from liberalized depreciation	$19	$26	$34	$37	$33	$33
Investment tax credit—Note 4	$23	$14	$37	$15	$20	$28
Realized and deferred						
Amortization of prior deferments	(2)	(2)	(2)	(2)	(3)	(3)
Net Adjustment	$21	$12	$35	$13	$17	$25

[a]Note references are found in Exhibit 7.
Source: Annual Report, 1974

EXHIBIT 7

NOTES:

1. Forecast information has been set forth in anticipation that revenues in the forecast years will be sufficient to support the projected construction expenditures and financing. The financing indicated for 1975–1979 is subject to market conditions.

2. Peak load, which occurs during the summer months, is actual for 1974 and is estimated for 1975–1979 on the basis of the most severe temperature conditions that have a 50% probability of occurrence.

3. Allowance for funds used during construction is computed at a "net aftertax rate" of 8% in the 1975–1979 period, reduced by income tax credits arising from interest charges associated with debt used to finance construction, which are credited to other income.

4. Federal income tax reductions for investment tax credits are deferred and amortized by credits to income over the estimated useful life of the plant. The credit for the years 1975 and 1976 reflects the 10% investment tax credit rate for qualified plant permitted by the Tax Reduction Act of 1975. The years 1977 to 1979 assume a return to the 4% rate as provided under present tax laws.

5. Based on scheduled additions of an oil-fired generating unit at Eddystone in early 1976 (400 mw) and nuclear generating units at Salem in late 1976 (464 mw) and 1979 (474 mw), electric output by types of generation is forecast as follows:

ELECTRIC OUTPUT

Budget	1975		1976		1977		1978		1979	
	1,000 mwh	%	1,000 mwh	%	1,000 mwh	%	1,000 mwh	%	1,000 mwh	%
Nuclear	5,300	18.2	4,926	16.1	8,068	24.7	8,144	23.4	10,082	27.4
Coal (incl. mine mouth)	9,642	33.2	9,663	31.6	9,973	30.5	9,924	28.5	9,838	26.8
Oil (incl. internal combustion)	6,395	22.0	11,794	38.5	10,133	31.0	9,182	26.4	9,754	26.6
Other	7,721	26.6	4,241	13.8	4,495	13.8	7,551	21.7	7,062	19.2
Total	29,058	100.0	30,624	100.0	32,669	100.0	34,801	100.0	36,736	100.0

Source: Annual Report, 1974

EXHIBIT 8

CAPITALIZATION DATA

(thousands of dollars)

	1974	1973	1972	1971	1970	1969
Long-Term Debt:						
Mortgage bonds	$1,379,317	$1,223,859	$1,191,982	$1,105,161	$ 962,814	$ 790,938
Debentures	54,373	55,282	55,282	56,507	56,989	57,759
Pollution control notes	39,000	40,000	40,000	—	—	—
Other long-term debt	125,000	—	—	—	—	—
Total Long-Term Debt	1,597,690	1,319,141	1,287,264	1,161,758	1,019,803	848,697
Preferred Stock	486,383	412,020	337,472	262,472	192,472	127,472
Common Stock Equity:						
Common stock	782,916	771,765	622,501	528,217	424,921	365,042
Other paid-in capital	1,306	1,244	1,214	1,214	1,214	1,214
Retained earnings	293,747	186,230	270,971	254,734	239,467	235,448
Total Common Stock Equity	1,077,969	1,059,239	894,686	784,165	665,602	601,704
Total Capitalization	$3,162,042	$2,790,400	$2,519,422	$2,208,395	$1,877,877	$1,577,873

PLANT AND DEPRECIATION DATA

(thousands of dollars)

	1974	1973	1972	1971	1970	1969
Plant						
Plant in Service:						
Electric	$2,793,809	$2,167,903	$2,054,100	$1,971,111	$1,801,493	$1,657,655
Gas	265,696	261,700	256,403	226,749	213,748	202,310
Steam	42,255	41,998	39,850	38,807	36,484	35,133
Common	113,261	111,218	110,751	65,292	63,708	59,748
Total Plant in Service	3,215,021	2,582,819	2,461,104	2,301,959	2,115,433	1,954,846
Construction work in progress (incl. nuclear fuel)	893,161	1,077,312	751,014	542,227	400,846	226,756
Plant held for future use	15,715	12,002	10,525	6,815	5,327	6,967
Total Plant	$4,123,897	$3,672,133	$3,222,643	$2,851,001	$2,521,606	$2,188,569
Gross additions to plant	$ 476,696	$ 494,187	$ 399,676	$ 351,514	$ 351,554	$ 263,698
Plant in service per dollar of revenue	$3.18	$3.37	$3.59	$3.79	$4.19	$4.44
Electric plant in service per kw of net capability	$ 358	$ 326	$ 324	$ 310	$ 324	$ 324
Accumulated Provision for Depreciation						
Electric	$ 648,561	$ 599,604	$ 562,169	$ 525,157	$ 491,137	$ 458,931
Gas	34,811	34,173	32,460	31,657	29,714	28,973
Steam	15,862	14,852	13,802	12,956	12,745	11,832
Common	18,574	16,796	15,813	15,900	15,952	14,482
Total Accumulated Provision for Depreciation	$ 717,808	$ 665,425	$ 624,244	$ 585,670	$ 549,548	$ 514,218
% of Depreciable Plant	25.4	26.5	26.3	27.5	28.0	27.3

EXHIBIT 8 (cont.)
CAPITALIZATION DATA

	1968	1967	1966	1965	1964
	(thousands of dollars)				
Long-Term Debt:					
Mortgage bonds	$ 720,146	$ 632,564	$ 591,102	$ 551,925	$ 553,323
Debentures	58,600	59,400	60,200	61,000	36,800
Pollution control notes	—	—	—	—	—
Other long-term debt	—	—	—	—	—
Total Long-Term Debt	778,746	691,964	651,302	612,925	590,123
Preferred Stock	87,472	87,472	87,472	87,472	87,472
Common Stock Equity:					
Common stock	298,269	298,269	260,251	256,258	256,258
Other paid-in capital	1,214	1,214	1,214	1,214	1,214
Retained earnings	227,437	213,116	199,054	182,574	169,382
Total Common Stock Equity	526,920	512,509	460,599	440,046	426,854
Total Capitalization	$1,393,138	$1,292,035	$1,199,293	$1,140,443	$1,104,499

PLANT AND DEPRECIATION DATA

	(thousands of dollars)				
Plant					
Plant in Service:					
Electric	$1,561,577	$1,473,515	$1,274,934	$1,244,798	$1,216,924
Gas	191,007	179,932	170,395	159,849	155,892
Steam	31,975	30,101	28,776	27,311	27,003
Common	53,513	48,204	43,590	43,767	42,696
Total Plant in Service	1,838,072	1,731,752	1,517,695	1,475,725	1,442,515
Construction work in progress (incl. nuclear fuel)	103,423	53,056	132,481	70,480	43,237
Plant held for future use	9,697	6,726	7,477	7,207	3,877
Total Plant	$1,951,192	$1,791,534	$1,657,753	$1,553,392	$1,489,629
Gross additions to plant	$ 176,665	$ 145,594	$ 119,301	$ 79,710	$ 69,660
Plant in service per dollar of revenue	$4.54	$4.60	$4.24	$4.33	$4.45
Electric plant in service per kw of net capability	$ 306	$ 315	$ 348	$ 340	$ 332
Accumulated Provision for Depreciation					
Electric	$ 434,834	$ 405,941	$ 376,690	$ 341,792	$ 329,083
Gas	31,370	30,053	29,453	27,750	28,610
Steam	11,006	10,273	9,573	8,868	8,191
Common	14,163	13,588	13,227	14,096	13,358
Total Accumulated Provisions for Depreciation	$ 491,373	$ 459,855	$ 428,943	$ 402,506	$ 379,242
% of Depreciable Plant	27.8	27.6	29.4	28.4	27.5

EXHIBIT 9

ELECTRIC OPERATIONS DATA

ELECTRIC OPERATING STATEMENT

	1974	1973	1972	1971	1970	1969
			(thousands of dollars)			
Operating Revenue	$873,474	$646,758	$574,431	$506,670	$412,496	$355,292
Operating Expenses:						
Fuel and interchange	372,376	210,341	163,851	148,930	100,719	76,002
Operation	121,135	106,716	95,443	81,585	76,119	64,915
Maintenance	55,000	51,596	48,248	42,717	42,378	37,204
Total Operation and Maintenance	548,511	368,653	307,542	273,232	219,216	178,121
Depreciation	68,422	57,452	54,335	50,438	48,427	44,088
Taxes	121,080	90,329	84,760	70,959	51,354	45,829
Total Operating Expenses	738,013	516,434	446,637	394,629	318,997	268,038
Electric Operating Income	$135,461	$130,324	$127,794	$112,041	$ 93,499	$ 87,254

Electric Revenue
(thousands of dollars)

	1974	1973	1972	1971	1970	1969
Residential	$300,805	$246,325	$216,114	$193,284	$158,300	$132,818
House heating	13,629	8,050	6,602	5,030	3,466	2,162
Small commercial and industrial	121,951	97,507	88,094	78,573	66,289	58,866
Large commercial and industrial	388,072	257,505	228,615	198,235	158,370	138,160
Railways and railroads	31,005	13,597	12,891	11,714	9,974	9,152
Public authorities and highway lighting	16,832	13,521	12,549	11,425	9,674	8,524
Other electric cos. and interdepartmental	1,754	2,593	1,519	1,088	1,065	991
Misc. Elec. Rev.	9,426	7,660	8,047	7,321	5,358	4,619
Total Elec. Rev.	$873,474	$646,758	$574,431	$506,670	$412,496	$355,292

Electric Sales
(millions of kwh)

	1974	1973	1972	1971	1970	1969
Residential	6,689	7,119	6,525	6,378	6,165	5,668
House heating	470	374	330	271	216	144
Small comm. and ind.	2,558	2,663	2,504	2,428	2,365	2,292
Large comm. and ind.	14,622	14,953	14,011	13,296	12,970	12,663
RRs. and railways	756	716	727	714	742	759
Pub. auths. and hwy. lighting	289	289	283	286	270	268
Other elec. cos. and interdepartmental	172	187	126	85	85	79
Total Electric Sales	25,556	$ 26,301	$ 24,506	$ 23,458	$ 22,813	$ 21,873
Res.—Aver. Use per Customer (kwh)	6,460	6,829	6,317	6,187	5,990	5,557

Source: Annual Report, 1974

EXHIBIT 9 (cont.)

ELECTRIC OPERATIONS DATA

ELECTRIC OPERATING STATEMENT

	1968	1967	1966	1965	1964
	(thousands of dollars)				
Operating Revenue	$325,906	$300,938	$287,849	$274,116	$259,635
Operating Expenses:					
Fuel and interchange	71,260	58,707	58,305	51,011	47,847
Operation	61,565	57,895	57,093	56,092	53,664
Maintenance	32,740	29,790	25,200	25,610	23,936
Total Operation and Maintenance	165,565	146,392	140,598	132,713	125,447
Depreciation	40,787	37,493	34,853	34,100	31,093
Taxes	41,202	43,190	42,965	40,968	39,831
Total Operating Expenses	247,554	227,075	218,416	207,781	196,371
Electric Operating Income	$ 78,352	$ 73,863	$ 69,433	$ 66,335	$ 63,264

Electric Revenue
(thousands of dollars)

	1968	1967	1966	1965	1964
Residential	$120,137	$110,172	$104,309	$ 98,891	$ 92,540
House heating	1,125	568	296	203	136
Small commercial and industrial	56,490	43,964	52,941	51,692	49,571
Large commercial and industrial	126,180	115,476	109,989	103,531	98,030
Railways and railroads	8,975	9,243	9,359	9,202	9,191
Public authorities and highway lighting	7,938	7,466	7,075	6,945	6,668
Other electric cos. and interdepartmental	866	816	756	604	616
Misc. Elec. Rev.	4,195	3,233	3,124	3,048	2,883
Total Elec. Rev.	$325,906	$300,938	$287,849	$274,116	$259,635

Electric Sales
(millions of kwh)

	1968	1967	1966	1965	1964
Residential	5,253	4,725	4,440	4,158	3,840
House heating	76	38	16	10	7
Small comm. and ind.	2,256	2,125	2,087	2,003	1,912
Large comm. and ind.	11,961	10,724	10,267	9,470	8,749
RRs. and railways	746	780	823	831	826
Pub. auths. and hwy. lighting	260	246	231	219	210
Other elec. cos. and interdepartmental	70	65	60	47	51
Total Electric Sales	$ 20,622	$ 18,703	$ 17,924	$ 16,738	$ 15,595
Res.—Aver. Use per Customer (kwh)	5,187	4,699	4,477	4,263	4,002

EXHIBIT 10

ELECTRIC OPERATIONS

	1974	1973	1972	1971	1970	1969
Electric Customers						
Residential	1,088,894	1,085,112	1,077,342	1,068,669	1,061,700	1,053,919
House heating	24,142	18,051	13,579	10,916	8,612	6,457
Small comm. and ind.	117,237	118,009	118,522	119,203	120,034	120,997
Large comm. and ind.	5,724	5,663	5,645	5,517	5,465	5,359
All other	2,248	2,207	2,163	2,130	2,101	2,045
Total Elec. Cus.	1,238,245	1,229,042	1,217,251	1,206,435	1,197,912	1,188,777
Total Res. House Heating Units Connected	42,320	33,600	27,045	23,303	18,358	15,720
Electric Operating Information Output (millions of kwh)						
Nuclear	1,745	176	97	206	137	130
Coal-Phila. Stas.	4,811	5,771	5,310	4,811	5,611	8,463
Coal-Mine-Mouth	3,041	4,056	3,609	3,243	1,914	1,764
Oil incl. internal combustion	9,825	9,397	12,015	12,191	12,157	9,778
Hydraulic	1,938	2,132	2,242	1,738	1,877	1,342
Pumped storage output	1,075	1,318	1,430	1,639	1,829	1,733
Pumped storage input	(1,515)	(1,876)	(2,018)	(2,302)	(2,523)	(2,395)
Purchased and net interchange	5,300	7,094	3,472	2,889	2,886	2,293
Other	1,188[a]	27	194	630	553	361
Total Output	27,408	28,095	26,351	25,045	24,441	23,469
Net Capability (thousands of kw):						
Nuclear	926	40	40	40	40	40
Coal-Phila. Stas.	803	836	901	901	782	1,258
Coal-Mine-Mouth	696	696	696	696	514	344
Oil	2,301	2,199	2,033	2,051	2,210	1,734
Internal combustion	1,690	1,487	1,286	1,286	626	347
Hydraulic	512	512	512	512	512	512
Pumped-Storage	880	880	880	880	880	880
Total Net Capability— December 31	7,808	6,650	6,348	6,366	5,564	5,115
Net Peak Load (thousands of kw)						
Summer peak	5,431	5,760	5,313	4,922	4,712	4,592
Annual load factor	57.6%	55.7%	56.6%	58.1%	59.2%	58.3%
Net capability (thousands of kw) at time of peak (summer rate)	6,968	6,177	6,136	5,928	5,434	4,996
Res. capacity—percent at time of peak	22.1	6.8	13.4	17.0	13.3	8.1

[a]Includes 996 million kwh of pre-commercial nuclear generation.
Source: Annual Report, 1974.

EXHIBIT 10 (cont.)

ELECTRIC OPERATIONS

	1968	1967	1966	1965	1964
Electric Customers					
Residential	1,030,333	1,018,919	1,005,550	985,660	968,195
House heating	4,060	2,297	1,063	644	420
Small comm. and ind.	136,917	138,888	141,752	148,760	150,427
Large comm. and ind.	5,204	4,993	4,827	4,630	4,486
All other	2,009	2,021	1,926	1,909	1,899
Total Elec. Cus.	1,178,523	1,167,128	1,155,118	1,141,603	1,125,427
Total Res. House Heating					
Units Connected	10,424	6,239	3,437	2,691	1,726
Electric Operating Information					
Output (millions of kwh)					
Nuclear	124	144	—	—	—
Coal-Phila. Stas.	11,589	12,617	12,657	12,929	12,249
Coal-Mine-Mouth	1,260	351	—	—	—
Oil incl. internal combustion	4,892	4,082	3,369	2,207	1,725
Hydraulic	1,586	1,895	1,304	1,117	1,088
Pumped storage output	1,429	400	—	—	—
Pumped storage input	(1,971)	(555)	—	—	—
Purchased and net					
interchange	2,917	1,090	2,000	1,606	1,341
Other	283	146	—	3	292
Total Output	22,109	20,170	19,330	17,862	16,695
Net Capability					
(thousands of kw):					
Nuclear	40	40	—	—	—
Coal-Phila. Stas.	2,190	2,190	2,317	2,465	2,471
Coal-Mine-Mouth	378	189	—	—	—
Oil	913	913	786	638	639
Internal combustion	198	174	48	48	48
Hydraulic	512	512	512	512	512
Pumped-Storage	880	660	—	—	—
Total Net Capability—					
December 31	5,111	4,678	3,663	3,663	3,670
Net Peak Load (thousands					
of kw)					
Summer peak	4,375	3,727	3,673	3,366	3,285
Annual load factor	57.5%	61.7%	60.1%	60.6%	57.9%
Net capability (thousands					
of kw) at time of peak					
(summer rate)	4,749	4,111	3,572	3,571	3,817
Res. capacity—percent at					
time of peak	7.9	9.3	(2.8)	5.7	13.9

FEDERAL EXPRESS CORPORATION

From the start of its operations in July 1972 Federal Express Corporation had pioneered the development of a wholly new approach to a narrowly specialized, all-cargo air transportation service—the rapid and reliable movement of priority small package shipments on an overnight delivery basis. With the extraordinary shipper response to Federal Express' unique service, the company's sales were expected to reach $80 million in 1975, surpassing 250 competitors to become the fifth largest company in the air freight business. Such growth was not without its problems. As Arthur Bass, president of the firm put it, "Federal Express has completed Phase 1. We are now in a period of transition." Efficient handling of this explosive growth was critical.

THE INDUSTRY

Intercity priority transportation of small shipments was an industry where speed is of primary importance. Though airplanes were, of course, the most common vehicles of transportation, trucks, trains, and buses were also used to some degree, particularly over short route segments.

Economical transport of goods generally required the consolidation and distribution of shipments at both ends of the long-distance, line-haul portion of the movement. This pick-up and delivery function was usually accomplished by truck, supplementing the primary long haul by plane, train or truck. Often the line-haul portion was interrupted by interline transfers or regional sorting operations. The

This case was prepared by Wayne R. Duignan, James W. Soroka, Mark E. Brooks, Joanna Y. Dee, J. William Weinberg, and Barry D. Strasnick under the supervision of Professor Jules J. Schwartz as the basis for class discussion rather than to illustrate either effective or ineffective handling of an administrative action.

handling, consolidating, routing or sorting of shipments could create delays and bottlenecks, making the effective speed of the primary mode of transportation less than the actual speed of the vehicle used.

The industry also made widespread use of consolidators or forwarders who provided pick-up and assembly or consolidation services at the origin, and also broke down, distributed and delivered shipments at the destination. These forwarders provided the line-haul carriers with bulk freight by selling and consolidating smaller shipments.

The priority small shipments business was dominated by air freight forwarders. The forwarders, however, were in competition with the airlines themselves as well as with other modes of transportation. Further there were several other operators in the small package air shipment industry including United Parcel Service (Blue Label), Air Parcel Post, special courier services, and expeditors. However, in the expensive, high priority segment of the industry, the air freight forwarders had most of the business.

There were more than 250 air freight forwarders competing in the domestic market. The industry's largest twenty-five air freight forwarders accounted for over 90 percent of revenues; the top five forwarders had over 60 percent of the market. Emery Air Freight was the largest forwarder, followed by Airborne, UPS, WTC, and Shulman. Only the larger forwarders had been consistently profitable in the face of rather rapid proliferation of new entries and the general lack of any competitive advantage in the business. The air freight forwarders were almost completely dependent on the passenger airlines for line-haul capacity. The trend in the airline industry away from all-cargo operations and toward the efficiency of the "wide-body" aircraft had resulted in fewer flights and an emphasis on mass passenger markets. The result had been a decrease in schedule frequency in all but the larger markets and an extreme scarcity of night flights. A few of the larger forwarders had contracted for charter cargo flights or had made arrangements with air taxis to supplement this lost lift. The vast majority of the smaller forwarders simply concentrated on the major markets and ignored the second and third volume markets where airline lift was at its worst. In 1972 industry sources estimated the size of the intercity small shipment business to be some 1.7 billion shipments. The vast majority of these shipments were moved by truck via motor carriers, United Parcel Service, and the United States Post Office.

The priority intercity small shipment industry had shown remarkable growth. In the ten years from 1963 to 1972 air freight forwarder revenues increased at an annual compound growth rate of almost 23 percent. UPS Blue Label air service had grown from 5 million shipments in 1970 to 25 million shipments in 1973, a five-fold increase in four years.

The domestic revenue growth rates of the top five air freight forwarders from 1967 to 1974 were as follows:

	($ millions)							
	1967	1968	1969	1970	1971	1972	1973	1974
Emery	47.1	61.1	73.1	82.6	86.7	108.3	126.9	139.9
Airborne	35.9	41.6	49.3	61.8	63.4	69.8	75.3	81.6
UPS	9.6	9.6	12.5	15.5	32.1	53.4	71.1	79.8
WTC	14.1	17.1	21.4	24.8	29.5	33.8	37.4	44.2
Schulman	8.5	12.4	18.9	24.7	24.2	29.1	31.9	40.2

Note: These five forwarders accounted for approximately 62 percent of all forwarder revenues.

Only the air freight forwarders and airline direct service covered purely priority segments, although some portions of bus express, air parcel post, and UPS Blue Label could be considered of a priority nature. In 1974 Federal Express estimated the size of the priority intercity small shipment market as follows:

Carrier	Number of Annual Shipments (in millions)
Air freight forwarders	12.47
Airline direct	3.
Other[a]	2.
Federal Express	2.
Total	19.47

[a]Including expeditors, couriers, and a small component of UPS Blue Label, air parcel post and bus express.

The market took a downturn during the second half of 1974. This industry decline was attributable to the combined effects of a recession and a glut of manufacturing inventories caused by increased purchases as a hedge against inflation and raw material shortages.

COMPANY BACKGROUND

The concept of Federal Express and its service was developed by a thirty-year-old, Frederick W. Smith, who had decided upon the small package airline idea as the last minute choice for the subject of a master's degree thesis at Yale in the mid-1960s.

Smith, son of a founder of a Memphis-based bus company, grew up enamored with transportation. Crippled by a childhood bone disease, he nevertheless recovered and learned to fly at the age of fifteen. As a marine in Vietnam, he flew 250 combat missions and was awarded the silver and bronze stars, in addition to two purple hearts.

Outlining his simple premise, Smith explained,

We pick up a package at 3 P.M. in Boston, load it onto an airplane, haul it to a central sorting location, and put it on another airplane, which arrives in the destination city before daylight. We put that package on a truck and deliver it before noon. The secret of the concept's success is also its nemesis—you're successful because you can serve all the places nobody else does—but you've got to start up overnight. It has to be almost a turnkey operation. We had to have a massive capital investment to start with. That's the reason we've spent so much time at the front end, proving the concept.

To implement his plan, Smith first purchased two Dassault/Breguet Falcons and converted them into all-cargo planes. After obtaining five mail routes to establish cash flow and a base for additional operations, he bought ten more Falcons, financed by a division of Commercial Credit Corporation. By 1975 a fleet of thirty-three Falcons connected 5000 city pairs via seventy airports and a central sorting and routing center in Memphis.

THE FEDERAL EXPRESS CONCEPT

Four primary features made the Federal Express service concept unique:

1. *The system was operated solely on a "hub-and-spokes" pattern, with Memphis, Tennessee, as the hub for all package sorting, aircraft maintenance, training, and administrative functions.* As shown in Exhibit 1, in 1975 Federal Express served seventy-one airport cities—each linked with every other one by the common terminal at Memphis.

Each Federal Express city, regardless of size, received service of a quality identical to every other city;

The system attained substantial economies and high reliability by reducing package handling to a minimum;

There was significantly improved package flow control and tracing capability;

There was little duplication of heavy capital and operating expenses for adequate sorting, security storage, and related facilities;

The operation of a nonlinear service permitted service to more points with fewer aircraft and to

small points without a serious segment load factor penalty.

2. *Primary Federal Express flight operations were conducted at night.* The bulk of outbound "delivery" departures were tightly scheduled between 3:30 A.M. and 5:00 A.M. each morning, to reach the most distant delivery cities between 7:30 A.M. and 9:30 A.M. All package offloading, sorting and reloading, as well as normal line maintenance, for the primary cycle, was performed during the short interval between midnight and 3:00 A.M. A second cycle was operated during the daylight hours in certain of Federal Express' operating lanes to service traffic not requiring overnight delivery.

A combination of the nighttime cycle, the geographical location of Memphis, and the speed and range of its jet aircraft fleet, resulted in Federal Express' being able to provide a highly reliable "overnight" service to its customers, with late afternoon pickup and morning delivery, between any two points on its nationwide system. Federal Express operated a full daily cycle of flights, beginning its inbound or "pickup" run during the early evening and arriving in Memphis between 9:00 P.M. and 1:00 A.M. The principal advantages of the radial method of operation were that no city, or city pair, was "discriminated" against by reason of its relative traffic significance, and each point, and pair of points, received next-morning service.

At Philadelphia, a typical Federal Express station, the day started at 7:39 A.M. with the morning incoming flight. The aircraft carried parcels for the Philadelphia area. The packages were separated by zip codes for delivery. All top priority packages were delivered before noon. All other deliveries were usually finished by 1:00 P.M.

The drivers, using leased trucks, then began the pickups. The trucks were radio-dispatched to accommodate customers. Stops included daily customers as well as special pickups from occasional phone customers.

All pickups were brought back to the station by 6:00 to 6:30 P.M. The same plane that arrived that morning was loaded with all the packages destined for Memphis and the West. It left at 6:45 P.M. sharp, picked up packages at Baltimore, and arrived in Memphis at about midnight.

Another southbound plane stopped in Philadelphia at 9 P.M. to pick up any leftover parcels. As traffic increased Federal Express leased Lear jets and began to operate round the clock. Packages originating and remaining in the Northeast were circulated by these Lear jets in the early morning. Jets stopped at Philadelphia at 2:00 A.M. and again at 3:00 A.M. to pick up and deliver parcels. In the morning the cycle began again.

The stations were equipped with only the bare necessities to maintain operations—equipment for dispatching trucks, a computer terminal, and phone system. The staff was relatively young, and nonunion. The company's fringe benefits were considered good.

All accounting was handled in Memphis. Billing and receiving were handled out of Memphis also. Every day each station used one of the planes to send its delivery slips to Memphis for settlement.

3. *Federal Express provided its own pickup and delivery service at nearly every point on its system.* By retaining direct responsibility for the proper performance of each step of the door-to-door transportation function, Federal Express was able to minimize the shipper inconvenience and the shipment control problems common in the majority of alternative package express services. The shipper did not need to arrange separately for the movement of his packages to a distant airport; similarly his cosignee did not need to arrange the reverse task. The risk of loss or delay on route was virtually eliminated and the means of tracing an occasional misrouted package was greatly facilitated. Finally, Federal Express' own courier employees were a point of contact with each shipper and cosignee. They were trained to deal with any questions, problems, or unique situations that might arise, playing a valuable role for both Federal Express and its customers.

4. *Tightly controlled flight operations and a maintenance system geared for a rapid response and immediate aircraft turnaround were major factors in Federal Express' ability to provide overnight package service among 5000 American city pairs.* To offer overnight package delivery service among the 70 areas it served, the Federal Express fleet had to fly when offices of the shippers and cosignees were closed. This meant that the entire fleet of Falcons—except one in rotation through major scheduled maintenance at all times and another on standby—was in the air at night and on the ground by day, scattered around the route system.

Flights were not only at night, when larger fixed-base operations had only fueling crews on duty, but many planes flew into airports that had no capability to make emergency repairs to turbine aircraft, day or night. Without a maintenance team and facility in every city served, which would have been financially prohibitive, Federal Express had no alternative but to gear its 104-mechanic maintenance operation in Memphis to correct discrepancies immediately and to return the aircraft to flight status.

With Memphis as the sorting point for package operation, each of the aircraft—except for five assigned to mail routes in the upper Midwest—passed through Memphis at least once, sometimes twice, in every twenty-four hour period.

Most aircraft were at the sorting terminal no longer than two hours and fifty minutes, sometime between midnight and 3:30 A.M., during the five and one-half day week. It was during this interval—while the Falcons were being unloaded and loaded—that maintenance personnel had to do all the line work and rectify any problems that might have arisen during the previous day's outbound flight or the inbound flight that evening.

"This requires constant knowledge of what has gone wrong with the aircraft. The line crews must quickly diagnose the problem, get parts to the aircraft and repair it," explained James Riedmeyer, senior vice president of maintenance and engineering.

GOVERNMENT REGULATIONS

The air transportation industry operated under a myriad of government regulations, ranging from route authority to the establishment of fare structures. Many of these regulations were very restrictive in nature and virtually dictated to management conditions under which the airlines might operate.

Federal Express was in a unique position relative to these restrictions. Under the Federal Aviation Act of 1958, Federal Express qualified as a Part 298 carrier. Such carriers, commonly known as air taxis, were exempted from many of these federal regulations. They were free to take on new routes and could set up their own fare structure without seeking government approval. To qualify as an air taxi the carrier had to operate aircraft with a specified maximum payload capacity. If it exceeded this limit by using larger aircraft, it became subject to the same regulations as other carriers. Federal Express was seeking an exemption from this single restriction on maximum payload capacity. The company had reached the point of exhausting all available capacity in specific markets at certain critical times of the day.

FINANCING

To carry out Smith's original plan, it had been essential to set up an entire system almost immediately instead of gradually building up operations. Federal bought thirty-three jet aircraft to haul freight and a fleet of delivery vans for pickup and delivery of packages. It had leased expensive space at the airports it serviced. In addition Smith remodeled a hangar at Memphis International Airport for aircraft service and an elaborate corporate headquarters. Operations in Memphis needed space roughly the size of two football fields in order to allow for expansion during the next ten years.

It had taken nineteen months for Smith to work out his financial arrangements. His ideas and plans seemed sound, yet investors generally felt that such a startup in the transportation industry was highly risky. Venture capital

organizations were very hesitant. General Dynamics, which put up $5 million in cash, declined to buy control of the airline in July 1973, partly because of prohibiting CAB regulations. Moreover, investors, watching the problems of American and Eastern Airlines, were shying away from airlines in general.

Smith still managed to obtain the financial backing he needed. By 1975 there was over $80 million in loans and equity outstanding. (See Exhibit 2.) Among the major contributors were Prudential Insurance Co., Allstate Insurance Co., Chase Manhattan Bank, First National Bank of Chicago, New Court Securities, and White, Weld and Co. The three largest stockholders were Prudential, New Court, and Smith and his family.

During May and June 1975 Federal Express made its first interest and principal payments on the more than $40 million of senior debt. Its debt situation was relatively good in the opinion of one company executive, considering that the company had kept all its planes in operation and had continued to find the necessary financing.

When Peter S. Willmott became financial vice president in June 1973 he discovered that customer payments were received as late as sixty days after service. One of his first tasks was to improve this situation. Another problem was budgeting expenses. Costs ran well above budgeted expenses. The accounting and financial procedures of the company had to be carefully reviewed to correct these discrepancies.

It was not until October 1974 that the fledgling company moved into the black, posting an operating profit in excess of $100,000. (See Exhibits 3, 4, and 5.) "We have survived the first eighteen months of operations and can now look forward to substantial earnings growth," said one company executive in reporting the October 1974 profit.

THE CURRENT MARKET

In 1975, it was estimated that Federal Express had achieved an overall market share of 12 percent, based on some 20 million potential shipments per year. The most significant aspect of Federal's penetration of any market was that its share varied inversely with the size of that market. The larger the market, the smaller the firm's share. Despite this, however, in the top five American markets, which accounted for 52 percent of the air freight forwarder business, Federal Express did 37 percent of its volume.

As in the case of many markets the customers for priority air freight could be classified as "heavy users" and "occasional users." For example, 20 percent of the airline travelers buy 80 percent of the airline tickets sold. The heavy user could be categorized as a large, customer-oriented, commercial entity that sold time-sensitive, high-value, low-weight products to industrial markets.

Typical of this group were large electronic firms, manufacturers of light-weight machines or office products, producers of life-supporting devices, medicines or diagnostics, printers and suppliers in the graphic arts industry, producers and distributors of film and tape for the entertainment or advertising field, producers or distributors of time-sensitive financial materials, and any manufacturer of parts and components that supported expensive machinery or production lines. Excluded from this group were bulk air freight shippers such as agricultural producers, apparel manufacturers, and producers of leather goods, shoes, and home appliances. The key elements in defining the heavy user were industry, size (employees, sales volume), and type and location of customers.

The occasional user group would include anyone who sometimes needed expedited parcel service. This market consisted of more than 100,000 private, commercial, and government entities. A specific definition of this market was virtually impossible to formulate. Occasional users might be attorneys, doctors, engineers, and small businesses, such as advertising agencies, accountants, retailers and manufacturers. Generally this market consisted of small firms or individuals but could include larger firms that rarely used air freight,

such as firms in the lumber, steel, or coal industry.

The market for small shipments tended to follow population concentration. Of the sixty-five top originating markets, Federal Express served all but fourteen. The top three cities in the United States—New York/Newark, Los Angeles, and Chicago—accounted for nearly 50 percent of all originating tonnage. The top twenty locations accounted for 85 percent.

SALES STRATEGY

Federal Express began its first aggressive advertising campaign in December 1974 in attempt to build wide-scale awareness of the company's concept and its competitive advantages as quickly as possible. This campaign ran in twenty-eight cities serviced by Federal Express, representing some 31 percent of Federal Express' total volume. Plans for 1976 included the allocation of advertising dollars across the country with emphasis on the top ten markets, which accounted for 57.4 percent of the United States potential. These high potential markets were the areas where Federal Express' current penetration was at its lowest and where the firm had the greatest opportunity for growth.

Federal Express' rate structure, which included pickup and delivery service charges, was based on weight, distance, and service level. In general the rate structure was competitive with or below the rates charged for comparable weights and distances by the major air freight forwarders and certain airline airport-to-airport, small-shipment charges. It appeared certain that air freight rates would be increased in the near future as a result of a preliminary CAB ruling that United States air freight was priced "unlawfully" low. A CAB judge had recommended a total rate increase of 36 percent, in 12 percent annual increases. These increases were necessary because, in effect, current freight rates were being subsidized by passenger tariffs. Federal was immune to these rate increases, as it was totally independent of domestic airlines.

The 1975 sales strategy called for intense direct sales efforts to be targeted at the country's top 1000 potential shippers. To accomplish this, approximately twenty-five senior account managers were to be deployed throughout the country in areas of greatest potential. Each manager would be responsible for forty to fifty prospects.

FACING THE FUTURE

A critical factor in the success of Federal Express was the recognition that an operations-oriented management was needed. Largely at the insistence of its investors Federal Express hired as its chief executive, General Howell M. Ester, former president of World Airways, a large supplemental airline. One member of a venture capital organization with a sizeable investment in Federal Express said: "Federal Express really needed some nuts-and-bolts guy running the show." Explaining why Smith had to be replaced, he added: "They had a group of marketing people who assembled and sold a good concept, but there is not one in Memphis who really knew anything about running an airline." Officials at Federal Express conceded as much. Arthur Bass, then senior vice president, commented: "Smith just could not play the investor game and run the airline at the same time. It was something we began to recognize and finally had to move on."

Federal Express faced a number of problems at this stage of its growth. Efficient handling of operations, financial management, and marketing problems were critical. The firm's management philosophy was that such problems should be solved with new ideas rather than historical solutions. As President Bass put it, "We're doing things that have never been done and we have to face the problems in a new way."

One problem over which Federal Express had little control was the movement to larger aircraft. The present fleet was incapable of handling the increasing volume of packages. The capacity limitations of its present fleet in terms of both weight and volume had begun to present serious barriers to the continued growth of revenues. The company had asked for government approval to use McDonnel-Douglas DC-9s over selected routes. These aircraft would provide the needed additional lift. If permission to use such equipment was refused, the situation would become critical. Federal Express would stagnate. Management seemed confident that they would get approval and were gearing their operations accordingly.

EXHIBIT 1

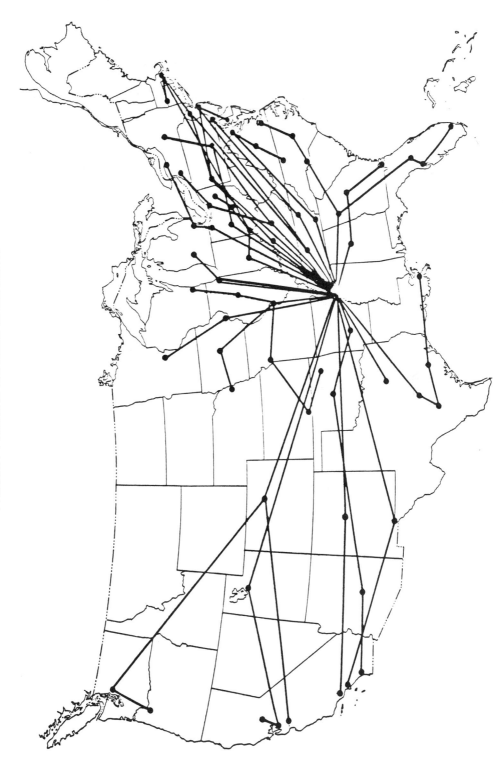

EXHIBIT 2

FEDERAL EXPRESS CORPORATION
Comparative Balance Sheet
Actual for the Month of October, FY 1976
Compared with FY 1976 Profit Plan and FY 1975 Actual
($000)

	FY 1976 Actual	FY 1976 Profit Plan	FY 1975 Actual
Current Assets			
Cash	$ 4,421	$ 1,000	$ 3,720
Accounts receivable	6,113	5,960	4,766
Inventory	2,860	2,637	982
Prepaid expenses and other	851	1,350	662
Total Current Assets	14,245	10,947	10,130
Property and equipment	64,596	67,485	64,500
Accumulated depreciation	(9,753)	(10,046)	(5,243)
Net	54,843	57,439	59,257
Other assets	1,241	1,221	4,821
Total Assets	$ 70,329	$ 69,607	$74,208
Current Liabilities			
Current notes	$ 6,760	$ 8,115	$ 2,012
Accounts payable	2,042	2,408	2,889
Accrued interest and expense	2,947	2,942	4,520
Total Current Liabilities	11,749	13,465	9,421
Long-term debt			
Senior debt	43,198	40,554	45,198
Subordinated debt	15,790	15,789	15,107
Other	12		
Total Long-Term Debt	59,000	56,343	60,305
Financing Needed		1,211	
Equity			
Stock and paid-in capital	27,827	27,827	27,827
Retained earnings/(deficit)	(28,247)	(29,239)	(23,345)
Net Equity	(420)	(1,412)	4,482
Total Liabilities and Equity	$ 70,329	$ 69,607	$ 74,208

EXHIBIT 3

FEDERAL EXPRESS CORPORATION
Semiannual Statement of Operations
October 1975 Compared with October 1974
($000)

	FY 1976		FY 1975	
	Monthly	Year to Date	Monthly	Year to Date
Revenue:				
Small package	$ 6,327	$ 23,717	$ 3,885	$ 13,636
Postal	613	2,462	282	1,258
Training	33	220	68	377
Charter	9	28	—	40
Service center	24	282	134	450
Insurance	87	348	59	213
Other	9	30	3	3
Total Revenue	$ 7,102	$ 27,087	$ 4,431	$ 15,977
Cost:				
Operations	$ 2,964	$ 12,420	$ 2,334	$ 10,381
Field sales and marketing	2,005	8,383	1,402	5,548
General and administrative	447	2,005	399	1,828
Total	5,416	22,808	4,135	17,757
Supplemental Operations	103	567	188	595
Total Operating Expense	$ 5,519	$ 23,375	$ 4,323	$ 18,352
Operating Income (Loss)	$ 1,583	$ 3,712	$ 108	$(2,375)
Other (Expense) Income				
Interest	$(638)	$(2,617)	$(656)	$(3,145)
Other	(94)	(2)	(15)	(215)
Total Other	$(732)	$(2,615)	$(671)	$(3,360)
Net Pretax Income (Loss)	$ 851	$ 1,097	$(563)	$(5,735)

EXHIBIT 4

FEDERAL EXPRESS CORPORATION
Source and Application of Funds Statement for Month of
October 1975 and Year-to-Date
Compared to Profit Plan
($000)

	Month		Year to Date	
	Actual	Profit Plan	Actual	Profit Plan
Sources				
Income (loss)	$ 851	$ 821	$ 1,097	$ 206
Depreciation and imputed interest	451	484	2,286	2,377
(Gain) loss on retirement of fixed assets	47		68	
Total Operating Sources	1,349	1,305	3,451	2,583
Other				
Proceeds from insurance claim (wrecked aircraft)	2,100		2,100	
Sale of equipment—customer services			20	
Sale of training aircraft			5	
Sale of simulator			1,080	1,080
Deferred gain on settlement (wrecked aircraft)	(484)		(484)	
Total Sources	$ 2,965	$ 1,305	$ 6,172·	$ 3,663
Applications				
Working capital (excluding cash)	$(14)	$ 1,262	$ 1,296	$ 1,158
Capital expenditures	316	219	955	1,877
Principal payments	604	11	2,025	3,342
Other liabilities	(22)	—	(22)	—
Total Applications	$ 884	$ 1,492	$ 4,254	$ 6,377
Increase (Decrease) in Cash	$ 2,081	$(197)	$ 1,918	$(2,714)

EXHIBIT 5

FEDERAL EXPRESS CORPORATION
Operating Cost as Percent of Revenue

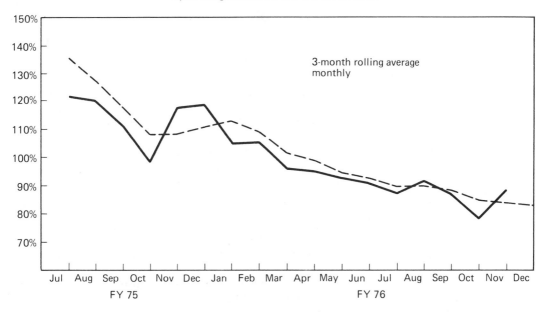

	% of Revenue			% of Revenue	
FY 1975	Month	3-Month Rolling	FY 1976	Month	3-Month Rolling
June	139.4	144.0	Feb.	104.5	108.6
July	122.0	135.8	Mar.	96.0	101.6
Aug.	120.5	126.8	Apr.	95.5	98.3
Sept.	111.7	117.9	May	91.1	94.3
Oct.	98.0	108.3	June	91.5	92.9
Nov.	118.2	108.3	July	87.3	89.7
Dec.	118.6	110.4	Aug.	91.1	89.9
Jan.	104.3	112.9	Sept.	87.9	88.7
			Oct.	78.2	84.9
			Nov. 9	88.2	84.7

REINHARDT'S BAKERY

Reinhardt's Bakery was a relatively small independent manufacturer of bread and related products located in Lawrence, Pennsylvania. It had an annual sales volume of approximately $11 million in 1974 and distributed its several lines of breads, rolls, and cakes primarily within a 100-mile radius of Lawrence. In June 1975 the president of the company relinquished his position to his twenty-six-year-old son, Arthur Reinhardt. With less than a year's experience in his inherited job, Arthur Reinhardt faced a number of significant decisions with respect to the future of the bakery.

The firm was founded in 1908 by Arthur Reinhardt's grandfather who began by selling doughnuts door to door. His business expanded rapidly in both volume and variety of products, leading to the purchase of the current plant site in 1931. By that time the company's name was well established.

Under the leadership of William F. Reinhardt, who had assumed control of the bakery from his father in 1935, the company continued to grow within the Lawrence area. With a secure source of sales in this market, William Reinhardt concentrated on making the bakery a well-run business enterprise. The bakery and its equipment were maintained in top condition and Reinhardt employees were among the best paid in the area.

Profits beyond those necessary to run the company were generally withdrawn from the business to support William Reinhardt's many

This case was prepared by Patricia H. Canfield, H. Scott Miller, Sharon B. Mosse, Edward Murphy, and John L. Sullivan under the supervision of Professor Jules J. Schwartz as the basis for class discussion rather than to illustrate either effective or ineffective handling of an administrative action.

charitable interests. Following the lead of his father, whose many gifts to his community included land for a school and park, Reinhardt donated an organ to his college and was a leading participant in a number of fund raising efforts. He was also generous with his time, serving on a number of public service committees.

This strong involvement in the community was clearly a factor in the strength of the Reinhardt name in its Lawrence market. Together with a quality product, this reputation enabled the company to maintain a 50 percent market share despite strong competition from rival firms.

In 1959 Reinhardt's began expanding beyond the Lawrence market by competing directly for market share with Freedholter's, a failing bakery, in the Grantville area. When that company went out of business in 1971 Reinhardt's took over some of its routes; that is, it hired several Freedholter routemen who had been servicing the area for years. In 1966, when Schweinler's Bakery closed its business in Nelson City, Reinhardt's acquired eight additional routes, with the routemen and their trucks, for $75,000 cash. (See Exhibit 1.)

Most recently, in 1974, Reinhardt's acquired the bankrupt Stern's Bakery in Bellminster at the request of dissatisfied creditors. This gave the company access to markets in Pearlton and Harburg. In this case, however, Reinhardt's took over the plant and equipment as well as the routes. By maintaining the sales force and decreasing the number of production shifts, the bakery was turned into a breakeven operation.

The turnaround for Stern's was Arthur Reinhardt's first substantial managerial responsibility after he joined the bakery in 1971 upon graduating from college. Before he took charge of Stern's in 1974 he had served in a number of staff positions that built on experiences gained working after school and during vacations from junior high school through college. After he attended the American Institute of Baking he was promoted to manufacturing vice president in July 1973. When his father retired in June 1975, he became president of the company.

THE INDUSTRY

The bread and bread products industry was characterized mostly by independent bakers competing in regional markets. Each firm generally supplied restaurant and institutional markets as well as the retail market. Price, service, quality, and relations between store managers and routemen were all significant factors in the marketplace. Exhibit 2 presents some selected statistics of the bakery industry according to product class.

In recent years, many problems had caused the baking industry to suffer from below-average profitability. Much of the difficulty was a direct result of soaring costs of raw materials coupled with government price controls. A loaf of bread basically consisted of 50 percent flour, 38 percent water, and 12 percent other ingredients including sugar, shortening, salt, and fermentation products. Wheat prices were a more significant factor than this formula indicates because it takes 160 pounds of wheat to produce 100 pounds of flour. Labor costs had also risen much more steeply in recent years. These problems were compounded because bakeries were generally unable to raise prices fast enough to meet rising costs.

Some of this pressure had abated in 1975. Price controls were off and costs of flour, shortening, sugar, and other raw materials had declined. (See Exhibit 3.) Bakers expected a much more profitable year for 1975.

The average firm in the industry had annual sales of about $8.5 million. The business operated on a low sales margin, typically up to only 1.5 percent profit after tax. The bread

was usually produced in a local bakery and moved from store to store in small trucks on a daily basis.

Most of the large retail grocery store chains had their own bakeries. Typically these in-house bread products had cost and shelf-space advantages over independent labels.

In Pennsylvania the bread and bread products industry had an unusually large percentage of small independent firms. This situation made the industry there more competitive, but as Arthur Reinhardt commented, it also made it more difficult for a large firm to come in and take over the market. Each small firm was well established in its local region. Most were large enough to achieve production and service economies, but would have had difficulty competing with the advertising a large firm could buy.

REINHARDT'S COMPETITION

Reinhardt's Bakery faced its stiffest competition from another family bakery, Armstrong's, located in Burnside approximately 107 miles northwest of Lawrence. Although established at about the same time as Reinhardt's, Armstrong's had pursued an aggressive acquisition and expansion program since the 1920s. It had two additional plants located in Burton, thirty miles southeast of Lawrence, and in Whitesburg, forty-two miles south of Lawrence. Armstrong's earnings had always been plowed back into the company. As a result it was much larger than Reinhardt's, with about $100 million in annual sales.

A number of other smaller firms also competed in Reinhardt's market. These brands included Meiger's, Heavenly, and Nebel's. None of the other bakeries was as large or aggressive as Armstrong's. Most approximated the industry average, though some were as large as Reinhardt's.

Reinhardt's and Armstrong's belonged to a nationwide cooperative, Quality Bakers of America (QBA). As a member, each was given a franchise to sell bread in designated areas under the Sunbeam label. Sales of QBA members in the region were $800 million in 1974 with companies averaging about $10 million each.

QBA did some national advertising for the Sunbeam brand name and also provided industry information and purchasing, consulting, and executive-search services. QBA also strictly monitored the quality of bread produced by its members through periodic testing and plant tours.

A QBA franchise to sell Sunbeam label bread in a particular region gave its owner a competitive advantage because advertising made the Sunbeam label relatively better known. In Lawrence, the Sunbeam franchise was held by Reinhardt's, and there Armstrong's competed under its own label. The reverse held in those markets where Armstrong's had the Sunbeam franchise.

The bread sold was distinguished only by its wrapper, which read either Reinhardt's Sunbeam, Armstrong's Sunbeam, Reinhardt's, or Armstrong's. Reinhardt's also produced bread under several private labels, but these represented less than 10 percent of total sales. Armstrong's Sunbeam was sold primarily in the areas west and north of the area.

COMPANY ORGANIZATION

All of the top management positions in the firm were held by members of the Reinhardt family: William Reinhardt was chairman of the board, Arthur was president, and Robert Tanner, Arthur's brother-in-law, was the executive vice president and treasurer. These three did all the planning and strategic decisionmaking.

Reinhardt's Bakery had three primary divisions: manufacturing, administration, and marketing. (See Exhibit 4.) The manufacturing division consisted of those operations that involved the actual production of bread. The division was headed by Ralph Diffenderfer, a dedicated, hard-working employee who had worked his way up through the organization. He had recently been appointed vice president of manufacturing over a distant member of the family.

Diffenderfer had four major areas of responsibility: production, shipping, sanitation, and plant maintenance. The production manager, under Diffenderfer, was responsible for line operations in the production of bread and rolls. The shipping manager was responsible for the movement of all products from the production area to the point of final distribution by sales. The plant maintenance manager supervised upkeep of the plant equipment and building. The sanitation manager was responsible for meeting health standards.

In addition to his role as executive vice president and treasurer, Robert Tanner served as the vice president of administration. In this capacity he supervised the areas of office operations, personnel, and purchasing. Of these functions, purchasing was by far the most important. Former sanitation manager Donald Volz had recently been promoted to purchasing manager to take over this position. The volatility of raw materials prices and their importance to the profit margin subjected this area to close monitoring by top management.

The third major division in the company was marketing. Edward Stegall, vice president of marketing, had held this position with Reinhardt's Bakery for most of his forty years with the company. Stegall and the sales manager exerted very close control over the route supervisors and the seventy routemen.

The routemen were the key to the sales organization. They drove the trucks and delivered bread and rolls to twenty to thirty accounts on each route. Their relationship with the store managers in each store was an important determinant of such crucial factors as shelf space and shelf location. Routemen each sold $2,000 to $4,000 of product each week. They were paid a base of $90.00 per week plus a 10 percent commission on all sales.

The two major issues currently facing the organization were related. First, a number of key personnel were approaching retirement age. The marketing vice president, the shipping manager, and the plant maintenance manager were all over sixty. Replacements would have to be found for them. It was company policy to promote from within the organization, but the number of employees available for promotion was limited. Second, it was difficult to develop quality management. Reinhardt's Bakery did not have the funds to provide a training program for developing new managerial talent from within the company. Additionally, it had had difficulty in attracting new managers from outside the Lawrence area, because of its location in a small town and its lower salaries. Thus, the company had to rely on a small local pool of labor and hope to develop successful managers from that source.

PRODUCTION

The majority of the company's production was done in the 50,000 square foot facility located in Lawrence. The plant layout was such that the breadmaking operations were physically separated from the rollmaking operations. The company employed 110 production personnel who produced approximately 700,000 pounds of product each week.

On Mondays, Wednesdays, Thursdays, Fridays, and Sundays the bakery operated three shifts. This manufacturing schedule was typical of the industry, reflecting high consumer demand for bread products on Monday and at the end of the week.

Firms in the industry, including Reinhardt's, had to pay a premium to their workers on Sunday, but efforts to change the consumer buying cycle had been unsuccessful.

Reinhardt's Bakery bought its flour in lots from arrival to processing was roughly two weeks. The only other major material purchased and stored was preprinted plastic bags shipped by rail to Lawrence. Each day a tank truck was sent from the bakery to the railyard to pick up a load of flour. Other raw materials such as sugar, yeast, and salt were purchased from wholesalers. Turnover of ingredients from arrival to processing was roughly two weeks. The only other major material purchased and stored was preprinted plastic bags for packaging the bread, which

were in volume sufficient for a twelve-week supply to take advantage of quantity discounts.

The bakery currently used two production techniques in its breadmaking operations. Approximately 60 percent of its bread was produced by the traditional "batch" method; the remaining 40 percent was produced using the more modern "continuous mix" method.

In the batch method a fermentation broth was prepared and stored, if necessary, prior to mixing it with the final ingredients. The fermentation step was the critical one. Temperature and acidity had to be monitored and controlled to obtain the desired texture and flavor characteristics. A measured amount of each broth prepared was pumped in fluid state into a mixer where it was combined with proportionate amounts of other ingredients to constitute a batch.

After being kneaded by the mixer the dough was transferred to troughs where it rose for fifteen to forty-five minutes. Rising time varied with the batch and was monitored by the bakery workers. When the dough was ready, it was physically transferred by bakery workers to a cutting and molding machine, which also transferred the dough to pans. These pans went through the steam "proofer" for a final rising and then on to the oven for baking.

In the continuous mix method the ingredients were continuously mixed after fermentation. The intermediate rising step was eliminated, as the dough was transferred directly from the developing mixer to the loaf pans.

The pans then followed the same path through the final proofer and oven. Continuous mixing was a cleaner, simpler process than the batch method and offered time, space, and handling advantages. Direct labor costs were also minimized because there was greater automation with this method. The drawback was that there were limitations to flavor development.

When the continuous process was first introduced a major portion of the industry switched over to it for its cost advantages. In recent years the superior taste of the batch process had generated increased demand for batch-processed bread. (Armstrong's Bakery used the batch process exclusively—in fact it used a sponge fermentation process that developed flavor and texture characteristics that differed from continuous-mix processing.)

The bakery's secondary manufacturing operations for rolls and cakes ran at less than capacity on a daily basis. During the summer and prior to holidays considerable demand for rolls and cakes went unmet, however. Currently Reinhardt's had a contract with Burger King to supply hamburger buns daily to several of its restaurants.

The major bottleneck in production was the bread proofer. It could handle only sixty loaves of bread per minute. The baking oven, however, had capacity for seventy-five loaves per minute. Compounding the problem was the trend toward shorter baking times. Loaves were at one time baked for thirty minutes, but now the baking required only seventeen minutes, increasing the capacity of the baking oven. Thus, a new proofer had the potential to increase capacity 25 percent.

A new proofer, however, would require an expenditure of $200,000 and a six-week shutdown for installation. The new machine would also occupy scarce space. Reinhardt commented that "the question becomes whether you should devote that much time, effort, and money to a 25 percent improvement or whether you should devote your time to finding the money and building a new plant that will double capacity."

FINANCES

The bakery was a closely-held corporation owned by three shareholders. William Reinhardt retained an 80 percent interest while Arthur and his sister shared the remainder of the stock. The other source of capital was long-term debt (see Exhibits 5 to 8), which was mainly used to pay for manufacturing equipment. The firm had also borrowed to buy the extensive truck fleet that it maintained. The equipment would be paid for over eight years, the vehicles over three.

Reinhardt had looked into the possibility of leasing to obtain his truck fleet; however, it had always appeared more expensive, chiefly because the bakery already had its own maintenance shop for its capital equipment. Part of the shop's duties consisted of servicing the company's vehicles, which it did well.

Reinhardt's had always been able to borrow at a favorable rate from the local bank. The company had an excellent reputation in the area and William Reinhardt was well known personally. He sat on the board of directors of the bank.

Currently the company was liquid enough so that it did not need to borrow short term from the bank. Its short-term debt was just trade credit, which was paid promptly to take advantage of any discounts. Overall the total debt of the firm amounted to 45 percent of the firm's assets and was roughly $1.1 million.

The company needed to perform building repairs during the next two to three years at a rate of $50,000 per year. Internal funds could finance these repairs and purchase small assets such as new bread loaf pans, which cost $8,000. However, large purchases such as a new bread proofer would require long-term financing. On a larger scale, a new one-line bread plant would cost about $3 million and would require financing beyond the capabilities of the local bank, probably necessitating involvement with an insurance company.

Fortunately the recently acquired Stern's Bakery had been running profitably. It had been able to pay off its creditors satisfactorily from its operations and had not been a drain on Reinhardt's financial resources.

MARKETING

Reinhardt's Bakery marketed three major product lines—breads (75 percent of production), rolls (22 percent), and cakes (3 percent). The firm was unable to and did not want to produce the full line of bakery products now purchased from other bakeries to fill out the product line.

Total sales were divided approximately equally between retail and institutional markets. Marketing was of particular concern for Arthur Reinhardt, not merely because this function was vital to the profitability of the company, but also because of sensitive points of disagreement between the marketing division and other divisions in top management. As the organization chart (Exhibit 4) indicates, the vice president of marketing, Edward Stegall, and his sales manager supervised the sales efforts of seventy routemen. Based on his forty years of experience, Stegall was convinced that the company's success had been due largely to the performance of his sales force. It was recognized that personal selling to retail grocers and the goodwill created by dedicated and enthusiastic routemen had given Reinhardt's an important competitive advantage over Armstrong's. Still Reinhardt's was concerned that the current operation of the sales force and its marketing effort might be less than optimal.

Disagreement over Reinhardt's product line was one manifestation of the differences between marketing and top management. The goal of marketing was to increase sales, particularly because the routemen were paid a commission based on total sales. Top management was interested in achieving as profitable a mix as possible. Routemen had traditionally gained access to institutional and retail outlets on the condition that they provide specialty items, such as doughnuts, pies and pastries, to supplement the standard Reinhardt's bread line. Stegall used his position of power and experience to defend the ordering of additions to the product line.

The firm's current market research study, conducted by QBA in 1971, revealed that the profitability of those items purchased by Reinhardt's to fill out the product line was "questionable." Reinhardt began to suspect that these specialty items were merely crutches that had little profit value and did not add significantly to the purchases of the firm's other products. Yet commissions for homemade and purchased items were identical, so the routemen had no incentive to emphasize Reinhardt's products when bargaining with retailers. Reinhardt had no concrete evidence

of marketing inefficiency and did not want to make a policy decision based on executive prerogative alone because this might alienate Stegall and the routemen.

PRICING

Pricing policy was also debated on a sales-versus-profit basis. Marketing argued that low prices yielded high sales. The general managers had to allow for rising input costs as well as profitability and saw no alternative but to raise prices. The price competition from other bakeries and the pressure from the marketing staff to keep prices low forced the bakery to seek greater production efficiency as its only way to increase the profit margin.

White enriched bread prices varied by only a few pennies within various regions. The average retail price was fifty-five cents for the standard loaf of white bread. Different markets forced price ranges from fifty-three cents to fifty-nine cents. Reinhardt's sold its bread to the retailer at forty-four cents per loaf. The resulting profit margin to the bakery ranged from one-quarter cent to two cents per loaf.

This highly competitive price situation was demonstrated in 1974 when Armstrong's sold a twenty-two ounce loaf at the same price at which Reinhardt's was selling its twenty-ounce bread. Within a short time Reinhardt's Bakery began to lose 80,000 units in sales per four week period. It was forced to recapture lost sales by increasing the size of its loaves. This required the purchase of larger oven pans at a cost of $10,000.

Advertising played a limited role in the company's marketing strategy. No in-house advertising capability existed nor was it deemed necessary. The advertising budget was limited to 1 to 2 percent of sales. All ads, billboards, and promotional material were developed and distributed through QBA to advertise Reinhardt's Sunbeam label.

LABOR

The labor situation placed a considerable constraint on the profitability of the bakery. Wages and benefits totaled 20 percent of sales.

Reinhardt viewed these costs as a fixed, perhaps increasing, percentage of sales because the unions were strong and the industry was so competitive. The production personnel in the bakery were members of the Bakers and Confectioners Union, a part of the AFL-CIO. The routemen were members of the Teamsters Union.

It was difficult to deal with the Bakers and Confectioners Union because its pattern of wage demands was determined for the industry by the regional union organization through a very close evaluation of operating costs and profitability in the industry. The result was that each time the bakery had a good year or achieved new efficiencies in production, wage demands reduced the higher margins. Fortunately, new labor contract talks with the Teamsters were not scheduled until 1978. Talks with the Bakers Workers were scheduled for 1977.

Because of the strength of the unions, the effect of a strike in the baking industry is particularly disastrous. People buy bread each week. In the absence of their normal brand, they will substitute. A strike can cause an irretrievable loss in sales for the period of the strike and an erosion of brand loyalty that is very difficult to rebuild.

Only one area of Reinhardt's was not unionized. This was the contract with Burger King. The operation was highly profitable because the restaurants lie outside normal routes and the Teamsters allowed deliveries to be made from trailer trucks driven by independent drivers.

One of the interesting factors in the competitive situation was the fact that Armstrong's Bakery had only recently been unionized. Previously the hourly wage rate for Armstrong's production personnel had been $0.60 per hour less than Reinhardt's. With Armstrong's wage rates in 1974, Reinhardt's would have reduced wage costs $180,000. Reinhardt did not understand how Armstrong's managed to operate so long without being unionized—or how now that firm was unionized it was still able to settle for less than the pattern.

THE FUTURE

As president of his family's bakery Reinhardt faced several operational difficulties that were limiting the efficiency of the company. There were problems of one sort or another in production, finance, marketing, labor, and in the organizational management.

But at age twenty-six, Arthur Reinhardt had his eye on the future. Despite his limited business background and relative inexperience in management decisionmaking, he was now charged with the responsibility of guiding the future of the company. Armstrong's Bakery was marketing its bread on three sides of Reinhardt's franchise territory. Could he follow in the spirit of his grandfather and father and continue to operate as a small independent bakery? Should and/or would he marshal capital, equipment, and personnel to launch a full scale reorganization and expansion of the company?

EXHIBIT 1

SUNBEAM'S TERRITORIAL MAP
Reinhardt's Bakery
Lawrence, Pennsylvania

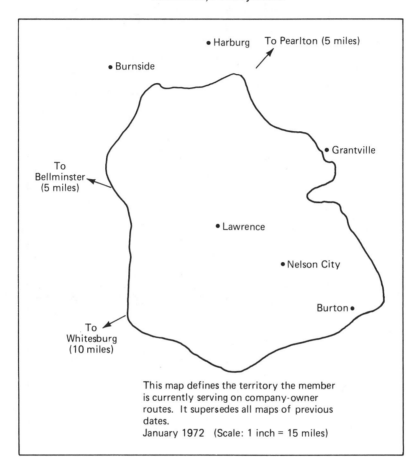

• Harburg   To Pearlton (5 miles)

• Burnside

• Grantville

To
Bellminster
(5 miles)

• Lawrence

• Nelson City

Burton •

To
Whitesburg
(10 miles)

This map defines the territory the member
is currently serving on company-owner
routes. It supersedes all maps of previous
dates.
January 1972   (Scale: 1 inch = 15 miles)

EXHIBIT 2

BAKERY INDUSTRY DATA

Industry or Product Class by Percentage of Specialization	Establishments (number)	All Employees		Production Workers			Value Added by Manufacture ($ million)	Cost of Materials ($ million)	Value of Shipments ($ million)
		Number (1,000)	Payroll ($ million)	Number (1,000)	Man-Hours (millions)	Wages ($ million)			
Bread, Cake, and Related Products									
Entire industry	3,323	194.4	1,700.6	110.0	220.2	879.8	3,530.0	2,625.6	6,152.6
Establishments with 75% or more specialization	3,290	190.9	1,673.3	107.4	215.5	860.6	3,477.1	2,573.7	6,049.9
White, wheat, and rye bread (Primary product class of establishment)	346	123.7	1,131.2	65.1	130.8	550.1	2,337.7	1,724.2	4,061.2
Establishments with 75% or more specialization	418	51.7	432.5	24.7	49.3	206.9	1,028.6	734.5	1,760.5
Rolls, bread-type, stuffing, crumbs, etc. (Primary product class of establishment)	167	14.5	122.9	9.3	18.9	71.4	248.9	198.4	447.3
Establishments with 75% or more specialization	89	4.9	36.7	3.1	6.3	20.5	79.5	67.1	146.6

EXHIBIT 3
WHOLESALE WHEAT AND FLOUR PRICES

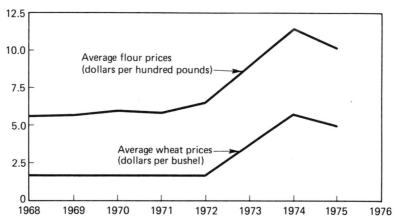

Source: 1972 Census of Manufacturers Bakery Produces 20E–13, U.S. Department of Commerce.

EXHIBIT 4

REINHARDT'S BAKERY
Organization Chart[a]

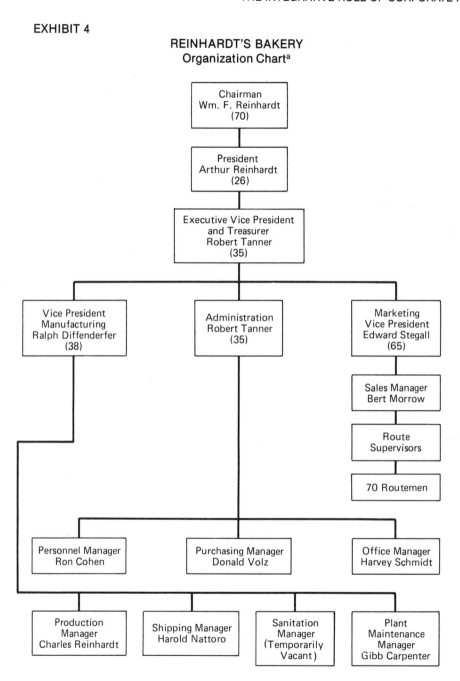

[a]Ages of executives given in parentheses.

EXHIBIT 5

BALANCE SHEET—NOT CONSOLIDATED
November 2, 1974 and November 3, 1973

	1974	1973
	($000)	
ASSETS		
Current Assets		
Cash	$ 45	$ 157
Receivables		
Trade		
Quality Bakers of America Cooperative, Inc.	694	527
Others	7	6
Inventories (at lower of first-in, first-out cost or market)	3	5
Finished goods		
Ingredients	18	14
Wrapping supplies	223	124
Bread tubes	131	76
Prepaid expenses		2
Insurance		23
Licenses and real estate taxes	30	9
Supplies	10	17
Pension	23	11
Total current assets	$1,184	$ 971
Investments		
Securities (at cost)	25	14
Cash surrender value, officers life insurance (face amount, $150,000)	27	26
Real estate (net of depreciation of $7,717 and $7,173 in 1974 and 1973)	4	5
Property, Plant, and Equipment (at cost)		
Land	31	81
Buildings	944	836
Machinery and equipment	1,774	1,625
Ovens	458	458
Office furniture and equipment	111	109
Automobiles and trucks	555	508
Pans and trays	241	223
Construction in progress	50	100
	$4,164	$3,940
Less: accumulated depreciation	$2,929	$2,797
	$1,235	$1,143
Other Assets		
Unamortized mortgage costs	—	—
	$2,475	$2,159

EXHIBIT 6

LIABILITIES AND STOCKHOLDERS' EQUITY

	1974	1973
Current Liabilities		
Notes payable (bank, demand)		
Secured by automobiles, trucks, and office equipment	$ —	$ 66
Unsecured	—	50
Current portion of long-term debt	149	52
Accounts payable		
Trade	431	295
Pension	25	—
Employees' payroll deductions	27	24
Accrued expenses		
Interest	2	2
Payroll	72	74
Payroll taxes	1	—
Pennsylvania corporate taxes	—	1
Salesmen's bonds	8	7
Estimated liability for income taxes	46	92
Total current liabilities	$ 761	$ 663
Long-Term Debt	$ 379	$ 305
Stockholders' Equity		
First preferred stock (5% cumulative—par value $50 per share)		
Authorized—4,000 shares		
Issued—3,922.9 shares	$ 196	196
Second preferred stock (5% cumulative—par value $50 per share)		
Authorized—2,000 shares		
Issued—1,358 shares	68	68
Common stock (par value $100 per share)		
Authorized and issued 2,000 shares	200	200
Donated capital	10	10
Retained earnings	1,019	871
	$1,493	1,345
Less stock held in treasury at cost		
First preferred—2475 shares	$ 1	1
Second preferred—97 shares and 96 shares	5	4
Common—483 shares and 476 shares	152	148
	$ 158	$ 154
Total Equity	1,335	$1,191
	2,475	$2,159

STATEMENT OF INCOME AND RETAINED EARNINGS—
NOT CONSOLIDATED
Years Ended November 2, 1974 and November 3, 1973
($000)

	1974	1973
Sales		
Bread	$ 8,169	$6,816
Cake	420	379
Purchased foods	2,549	2,093
Stale	216	134
	$11,354	$9,422
Less: sales discounts	1,158	1,034
	10,196	8,388
Plant Costs		
Raw materials used	$ 3,206	$2,260
Purchases for resale	1,729	1,424
Shop labor costs and expenses	2,192	2,068
Administrative expenses	606	493
	$ 7,733	$6,245
Earnings Before Selling Expenses	$ 2,463	$2,143
Selling Expenses	$ 2,253	$1,987
Operating Income	$ 210	$ 156
Other Income		
Miscellaneous	$ 19	$ 30
QBA patronage savings and refunds	21	15
Gain on sale of fixed assets	44	5
	$ 84	$ 50
Other Expenses		
Net expenses of leased properties	—	$ 1
Income Before Income Taxes	$ 294	$ 207
Provision for income taxes	134	$ 93
Net Income	160	$ 114
Retained Earnings (Beginning)	871	770
	$ 1,031	$ 884
Less dividends paid on preferred stock	$ 12	13
Retained Earnings (Ending)	$ 1,019	$ 871

H&R BLOCK, INC.

John D. Simmons, senior analyst of a major New York research firm, described H & R Block as a:

> ... highly profitable, strongly financed service enterprise that has a unique and valuable franchise in the "rent-a-brain" business. The company identified an important consumer need, pioneered and perfected a budget-priced service to meet this annually recurring need, and has developed a nationwide business to the point where the company has a proprietary niche in its chosen field.

In fiscal 1976 Block had achieved impressive gains in total number of returns prepared, profit margins, and per share earnings. (See Exhibits 1 to 3.) Though the company had grown in a planned and orderly manner from a small regional company to a nationwide service organization, Block's full potential remained to be exploited.

Although it made no acquisitions in 1976 Block continued to search for well-managed companies in growth situations that fit its diversification criteria.

COMPANY BACKGROUND

H & R Block was a Missouri-based corporation, founded in 1946 by the Bloch brothers as a family bookkeeping service that prepared tax returns free of charge as a courtesy for regular clients. In 1955 the Blochs decided to run an advertisement in a local paper to test the viability of an inexpensive tax service. The response was so overwhelming that the

This case was prepared by Barbara R. Birnbaum, Herbert Bogart, Gregg S. Davidson, Robert M. Wolk, and Clifford S. Yurman under the supervision of Professor Jules J. Schwartz as the basis for class discussion rather than to illustrate either effective or ineffective handling of an administrative action.

bookkeeping business was dropped; the brothers decided to specialize in income tax preparation.

The corporation operated and franchised a system of offices that prepared federal and any required state or local income tax returns for its customers. The offices featured a standard schedule of charges and quick service. By April 15, 1976, there were 7573 offices operating in all fifty states, the District of Columbia, Australia, Canada, England, Germany, Guam, Israel, Japan, New Zealand, Okinawa, Panama, South Korea, Taiwan, and the Virgin Islands.

The company had grown steadily to become the nation's leading income tax preparation firm. It prepared 10.5 percent of all 1976 federal individual returns filed with the Internal Revenue Service (IRS), compared with 9 percent in 1970 and 3.7 percent in 1967. (See Exhibit 4.) The quality of its service was perhaps best reflected in customer loyalty: In each of the last five years 75 percent of Block's clients had returned the next year.

The majority of Block customers had annual incomes between $8,000 and $18,000. In recent years the company had increased its percentage of higher-income taxpayers, who tended to itemize deductions. Block based its rates on the number of forms or schedules required rather than the income of the individual, so the firm also realized a higher per-return fee every year since 1972.

MANAGEMENT AND CORPORATE STRUCTURE

Henry Bloch majored in mathematics at the University of Michigan. His brother Richard worked his way through the University of Pennsylvania where he majored in economics. The two Bloch brothers served as the principal executive officers of the company and

438

inflation proof?

were actively involved in the daily management and long-range planning of the business.

It was an element of Block's marketing strategy to develop quickly a nationwide office network. As the company evolved from a local, to a regional, and then to a nationwide service organization, the Bloch brothers gradually decentralized operations under autonomous local management. With the rapid spread of the office network, this turned out to be a sound practice. Under this system the company-owned offices were managed on a decentralized, regional basis. (See Exhibit 5.)

Block's operations were organized geographically, with three division directors in the United States and some thirty-three subordinate regional directors supervising the activities of the city profit centers. City managers were responsible for five to fifteen local offices.

Block had established an operations council, consisting of selected city managers and regional directors who met once a year after the tax season for the purpose of giving first-hand appraisals of the year just ended and a general critique of operational policy and procedures.

To increase consumer confidence in the quality of commercially-prepared tax returns, the company had also formalized and stepped up its efforts to maintain a quality control system. Under this program the company sent out "undercover" taxpayers who had mock tax returns prepared. The quality and accuracy of the preparers' work was then analyzed, and local deficiencies in the standard of service and courtesy quickly corrected.

PERSONNEL

Recruitment began each year in the summer and fall. The employees included housewives, moonlighters, students, and retired accountants. Well over 30,000 preparers were employed during the peak season, of whom about three-fourths returned each year. Approximately 1100 full-time employees (well over 2000 in past years) staffed offices that were open year round for consultation, auditing, and handling of late returns.

Proper training of the worker who prepared the income tax return was the single most important task that faced field management during the off-season. In the fall of 1975 Block enrolled 57,130 tuition-paying students in its tax schools held in over 2000 locations throughout the United States and Canada. A majority of the graduates became Block tax preparers.

In addition to the basic eighty-one-hour course an advanced tax course was offered to returning employees. Returning consultants, as well as newly hired tax school graduates, received additional training prior to the tax filing season.

FINANCES

As Henry Bloch put it:

> We are pleased and satisfied to be engaged in what essentially is a cash business, without receivables or the extension of credit. ... We have freedom from any burden associated with inventories and periods of rapid changes in valuations.

Current operating requirements were met entirely from cash flow, and Block did not expect to resort again to the capital market. The company had virtually no long-term debt, and stockholder's equity continued to grow. In 1962 the firm had sold 75,000 shares of its common stock to the public at $4 a share. In October 1969 the shares were listed on the New York Stock Exchange. In 1976 there were over 11 million shares of common outstanding. Together, Richard and Henry Bloch held almost 3.5 million shares.

Aftertax margins ranged from 14 to 16 percent during the 1971 to 1976 period, with only one dip in 1972 to 11 percent. Earnings grew at an average annual compound rate of 19 percent. Revenues and earnings were mostly affected by an increase in the number of returns prepared and the growth of the average fee paid by the customers.

Returns on beginning equity had ranged from 33 to 38 percent in recent years. As a result of the continued growth in profits, dividends had been paid for the fifty-eight con-

return on equity 33-38%

secutive quarters. In September 1975 quarterly dividends were increased from $.10 to $.20 per share. In the following year the board of directors approved another increase of 25 percent. (See Exhibit 6.)

MARKETING

The company offered an essential service at a low cost. A tax return was prepared in the customer's presence, in most instances in less than an hour, on the basis of information furnished by him. After the return was drafted, the client was advised of the amount of tax or tax refund due. The return was retained for a careful review of mathematical accuracy and conformance to the tax code. Upon completion of this check, copies of the return were made and sent to the customer for signature and filing. Block offices guaranteed that they would pay any penalties and/or interest, but not additional taxes, resulting from errors made in the preparation of any return based on accurate information supplied by the customer.

Offices were of standard design and appearance. During the tax season, January 1 through April 15, most offices were open for business from 9 A.M. to 9 P.M. weekdays, and from 9 A.M. to 5 P.M. on Saturdays and Sundays. Offices were located in high traffic, densely populated areas such as storefronts in downtown business areas, in shopping centers, and in suburban business centers. Each Block location catered to local clientele, usually within a two-mile radius. Most offices were leased on an annual basis. Many locations were open only during the tax season, generally without benefit of offsetting revenues from subleasing during the rest of the year. At least one key office in each community remained open all year round and Block personnel could also be contacted through telephone listings. Should a customer's return be audited, a Block representative would accompany the client to the IRS at no cost and explain how the return was prepared.

Until 1971 Block had defined its principal market as taxpayers with annual incomes in the $5,000 to $15,000 range; in 1976 the range was $8,000 to $18,000. The customer mix had been changing over the years as a result of rising income, price inflation, and the upward mobility of wage earners. The $15,000 to $20,000 group had grown quickly and assumed greater importance in the overall customer mix. The lower income market had declined in relative importance due to increased unemployment, reduced discretionary purchasing power, and higher minimum income levels at which filing was required.

The average fee per return had increased almost every year, climbing from $9.10 in 1963 to $18.45 in 1976. The principal factors contributing to this rise had been selective price increases, the increasing complexity of the returns, the introduction of more state and local tax returns and greater patronage from higher-income taxpayers who filed supplementary schedules. The progression from FY 1972 to FY 1976 was as follows:

	Average Charge Per Client
FY1972	$12.02
FY1973	$13.33
FY1974	$15.13
FY1975	$17.18
FY1976	$18.45

Block's basic fee for the preparation of a tax return was a minimum charge of $6.00 throughout its own office system, but this amount might vary in franchised offices. The minimum fee covered the preparation of a federal and state tax return, where deductions were not itemized, and income was only from salaries. The total charge to the taxpayer depended not upon his income or tax liability, but upon the complexity of the tax return itself, as measured by the number and length of schedules involved.

COMPETITION

As the leading tax preparation service in the country with representation in every state and major urban area, Block dominated its industry. Competition had failed to erode Block's market position. The principal kinds of competition were:

1. Individuals who prepared their own tax returns;
2. Accountants, lawyers, and others who collected a fee for their services;
3. The Internal Revenue Service; and
4. Other commercial tax preparation companies.

These are discussed in turn.

Individuals

As stated in the company's Form 10K annual report to the SEC, "The Registrant considers its primary source of competition to be the individual who prepares his own tax return." The IRS estimated that 56 percent of the 79.9 million individual federal tax returns filed in 1976 were prepared and submitted by taxpayers themselves, including those who received assistance from friends, relatives, and the IRS. For various reasons each year more and more taxpayers sought outside assistance with their returns.

Accountants and Lawyers

Most professional tax preparations were the work of accountants and lawyers. For many professionals such tax returns were an unavoidable nuisance or a sideline service they sought to discourage in favor of more lucrative assignments. Yet few people who had had their returns prepared professionally would ever go back to doing them by themselves. Lawyers and accountants who did not wish to do taxes could opt to refer their clients to a specialist like Block. There were also other lawyers and accountants who sought tax return business. But to the extent that professional ethics prevented them from openly or aggressively soliciting new business, they were confined to servicing existing clients and relying upon referrals for new business. Practitioners generally catered to higher-income taxpayers and their fees were proportionately higher than Block's. All in all, though they still accounted for a significant portion of the tax

preparation business, their market share was likely to drop in the long run in the face of greater competition from Block, particularly from the firm's Executive Tax Service.

Internal Revenue Service

The Internal Revenue Service provided individual taxpayers with two forms of assistance in the preparation of their tax returns that could pose a threat to Block and other commercial tax preparation services. These were:

1. *Taxpayer assistance in completing his own return at a local IRS office.* Taxpayers traditionally used this free IRS service almost exclusively in the last week or so before the April 15 deadline. Fundamentally it consisted of either helping taxpayers to prepare their own returns properly or actually doing the chore for them in a very limited number of hardship cases. In practice, at the height of the tax-filing period, large numbers of anxious and confused taxpayers besieged their local IRS office and waited for a few overburdened employees to help them with their problems. They generally ended up unhappy, resolving not to repeat the experience the following year.

The IRS was not adequately staffed to cope with this kind of seasonal peak load, and frustration of this kind at IRS offices had probably convinced many taxpayers to use Block's services instead. Because of these deficiencies the IRS expanded its taxpayer assistance program but the program was still largely unorganized and inefficient. With development, however, the service could siphon off a portion of Block's clientele or attract taxpayers who might have become new customers.

2. *IRS computation of tax for taxpayers taking a standard deduction.* The IRS would compute the tax liability for any taxpayer whose only sources of income were wages, salary, and not more than $400 in dividends or interest if such taxpayer wanted to claim

only the standard deduction. In such cases the taxpayer inserted certain key data on specified lines of Form 1040A or Form 1040 and the IRS computed the tax and refunded any overpayment or billed for any tax owed.

In order to qualify for this service, the taxpayer had to read the instructions to determine his eligibility and make a rough calculation of his deductions to determine whether or not to take the standard deduction. Those who were discouraged by the preliminary analysis or confused by the regulations and the necessary preliminary calculations might decide against using the IRS service or might be induced to seek outside help from Block or others.

Commercial Tax Preparers

Entry into the tax return field was deceptively easy. The record showed that in the past various publicly-owned companies, as well as a considerable number of fly-by-night operators, had entered the business. Despite the competition, Block had prospered while others struggled. Block's success was primarily due to its repeat customers. Once the taxpayer sought assistance and was satisfied with the service provided, he tended to become dependent upon the service and would return each year.

Prominent among the would-be competitors were banks, department stores, personal loan companies, computer services, and some regional storefront preparers. The majority of these firms subsequently discovered that neither modern computers nor a duplication of the Block storefront approach was any guarantee of success. Among those who had dropped out of the race were G.A.C. Corporation, E.B.S. Tax Services, Inc., and several major banks.

There were three principal reasons for these failures:

1. It generally took about four years for a new office to make a meaningful profit, as volume was built primarily by repeat business and word-of-mouth advertising.
2. Many companies were deceived by the apparent ease of entry into the industry market and un-

derestimated the time and capital that would actually be needed to earn an adequate return on investment.
3. Computer-based services suffered from a major disadvantage—they offered the taxpayer only the bare minimum of personal service in the form of a conference between the client and the tax preparer; but as the people seeking professional assistance with their tax returns tended to feel somewhat intimidated or inadequate when faced with the 1040 tax form, they sorely missed the personal warmth and reassurance of a tax preparer when they were forced to deal with a computer.

Success of tax preparation services was not uniform geographically. In Kansas City and Denver, Block prepared at least 27 percent of all returns filed. However, in certain large key markets, including New York and Los Angeles, the company had only about a 5 percent share.

ADVERTISING

Block relied strongly upon advertising to communicate effectively the message that its service represented the solution to problems associated with income tax preparation. Traditionally, the company's advertising strategy had been:

1. To use its own "in-house" advertising agency for media placement and to hire an outside agency to handle the creative work for radio and TV advertising for company-owned offices;
2. To require each franchise office, with the exception of certain offices located in smaller communities, to pay for its own advertising and promotional expenses;
3. To tell the taxpaying public about the nature and availability of the firm's tax service;
4. To develop Block's "brand image" as the leader in its field, in order to presell the service to potential customers and develop a consumer franchise;
5. To "blanket" a city or regional market that had many office outlets with an intensive seasonal campaign using local advertising media; and
6. To adhere to the "two-mile" neighborhood concept, so that each neighborhood storefront office attracted maximum local traffic.

During the tax season, Block advertised heavily through local media. The amount budgeted for a particular city varied according to the size of the area, the number of offices and expected volume. Block noted in the 1976 Annual Report:

> As our years in tax preparation business increase, the demands we place on the role of advertising change because our communications' needs change. In the early years of the company, it was important to establish that we existed ... to build our identity. Today we have a strong equity in overall public awareness, and so our first objective is to be as specific as possible about the kind of help we offer and the quality of that help so that we can continue to attract new customers while maintaining our prior customers on the strength of our performance. Performance is all that we can ever expect to build upon. While advertising has its own part to play in helping to attract new customers and aiding and retaining our "priors," we are no longer what might be called an advertising intensive business.
>
> We continue to test advertising concepts and approaches through processes as scientific as we think possible and remain flexible to change approaches whenever findings dictate.

OFFICE NETWORK

The H & R Block office network consisted of four kinds of stores: company-owned, franchised, and franchised and company-owned satellites. The following table shows average revenues realized:

	FY1971	FY1972	FY1973
Average revenues per office ($)	17,429	14,289	17,867

	FY1974	FY1975	FY1976
Average revenues per office ($)	20,380	21,659	22,690

The company-owned offices were the backbone of the firm's operations and provided a stable source of revenues and earnings. In fiscal 1976 these offices accounted for 48 percent of the total number of offices in the Block system and contributed 76 percent to the total revenues. (See Exhibit 7.) The company-owned office system was comprised of conventional neighborhood storefronts, the Executive Tax Service, and department store and bank locations. Generally management had been very satisfied with the results of department store operations. People seemed to enjoy combining shopping and tax preparation in one easy trip to a familiar location.

In November 1972 the company reached an agreement with Sears, Roebuck & Company, whereby Block would operate tax preparation offices in over 100 Sears stores in eastern and southern states. Dual identification was to be used; the tax centers would be operated as concessions under the name of "Sears Income Tax Service by H & R Block". This venture had proven successful, and in 1976 Sears provided 713 of the 800 department store locations in which Block operated. As the table below shows, twenty-two more were anticipated for 1977.

Growth of Block Offices Operated in Sears Stores

	1973	1974	1975	1976	1977E
Offices	150	482	640	713	735

A typical Sears-licensed retail department was structured with a percentage of gross revenues paid to Sears for the right to operate the concession on its premises. Sears provided the traffic, the "endorsement by association," in-store advertising, fixtures and fittings, maintenance, utilities and janitorial service, preseason setup service, postseason cleanup, and the space to do business. Block had minimal front-end financial exposure and an incentive payout deal and it avoided the rental commitment associated with a company-owned office.

Management had perceived the need for a "customized" service to cater to a more sophisticated upper-income clientele. It created an Executive Tax Service. The client was offered scheduled appointments in a private office, usually in a major office building, for two separate interviews with an experienced senior tax preparer. The first interview, as in the regular service, developed the information necessary to prepare the return; the second interview, conducted about a week later, permitted a review and explanation of the completed return before payment of the fee. The number of Executive Tax Service offices had been expanded by 12 percent to 245 for the 1976 tax season. Both the number of returns prepared and dollar volume had grown at more than twice the rate of new office openings. Growth, of course, depended upon an expanding base of satisfied customers. As this service did not seem to lend itself to traditional forms of advertising and merchandising, management did not expect further dramatic growth for Executive Tax Service.

During 1974, in a deal similar to the one with Sears, Block had initiated on-premise service during regular banking hours in seventy-six Citibank branch offices. One year after the service was instituted four major regional banks also offered tax preparation service in forty-four branches under dual Block/bank identification. Canada Trust was scheduled to offer the service in at least fifty of its branches in the 1977 season.

Franchised Offices

Lacking working capital and trained personnel in its early years, Block had elected to establish a network of franchised offices. The franchisee contracted to pay Block a royalty based on a percentage of gross revenues earned by his offices. The royalty fee varied from 5 to 8 percent, based upon the age of the franchise and the location and character of the market. The franchisee operated under the H & R Block name, but, as an independent businessperson, selected and trained his own personnel. The company provided a Policy and Procedure Manual and other supervisory services. Block's regional directors were available to the franchisee to assist him in reviewing operations, setting expense budgets, and planning for

expansion. The company also sold furniture, signs, office equipment, tax forms, and office supplies to its franchisees. Data on the franchised office operation is presented in the following table:

Franchised Offices (excluding satellites)

Fiscal Year	Number of Offices	Royalty Fees (millions)	Average Fees Per Office
1976	988	$2.2	$2,211
1975	995	2.0	1,992
1974	962	1.7	1,730
1973	900	1.4	1,608
1972	896	1.4	1,514
1971	856	1.3	1,564
1970	828	1.3	1,604

Satellite Offices — mkt & geog pane

One of the firm's more successful marketing strategies was the H & R Block satellite program. "Satellite" was the name given to a franchised or company-owned Block office that was located in a community of less than 15,000 people and, normally, operated on a year-round basis. Block offered a satellite franchise to local businessmen who had established business offices and reputations. Real estate and insurance offices were typical locations for such satellites. The program had been a major source of growth for the company and provided residents of several thousand small communities with income tax services.

Rapid growth of the satellite franchise program had continued, as shown in the following table:

Growth in Satellite Offices

	1961	1962	1972	1973
Number of offices	5	10	2292	2381

	1974	1975	1976
Number of offices	2469	2715	2921

Under the terms of a satellite agreement, Block received 50 percent of the first $5,000 of gross revenues and 30 percent of any excess. The satellite program provided an excellent means for Block to increase its national market share in the United States and to serve effectively the highly dispersed population in the Canadian market.

Foreign Operations

Block operated a limited number of offices in several foreign markets and derived about 7 percent of its total volume from non-American operations. It was well established in Canada. The Canadian office network had grown impressively, from 179 offices in 1970 to 550 in 1976 and was Block's largest and most profitable foreign operation.

1972—"THE BAD YEAR"

The tax-paying public, in a year beset with unparalleled negative publicity for our industry, much of which was, in our judgment, ill-considered and certainly not applicable to this company, continued to make H & R Block the nation's largest tax service. More than 7,600,000 people entrusted us with the preparation of their tax returns, and significantly, our repeat customers increased from 73% to 76%.[1]

On the other hand 1972 had been marked by some difficulties. Almost all Block's revenues were earned in the four-month tax-filing period. Consequently revenues had to be estimated well in advance of the tax season in order to make commitments for additional offices, personnel, and supplies. For 1972 preseason expense commitments had been based upon overestimated preparation volume.

Several unexpected factors combined to produce a smaller increase in volume than expected. Block's estimate was based partially on the Internal Revenue Service's annual forecast of the number of individual tax returns to be filed. Though the IRS had predicted an increase, the actual number of returns remained about the same. In spite of this, the total number of returns prepared by Block increased by over 400,000.

Intensive, sustained national publicity, adverse to the income tax preparation industry,

[1] H & R Block Annual Report, 1972.

was prevalent during the 1972 filing season. This undoubtedly influenced the confidence of the public in all commercial tax preparation firms, regardless of quality. The assault started with the commissioner of the IRS announcing to over 75 million taxpayers, on the cover of Form 1040, that more than 30 million persons could prepare their own returns and that, if outside help were sought, the taxpayer should be wary of certain commercial preparers. A nationwide campaign called "You Can Do Your Own," publicized the IRS's assumption that most taxpayers were competent to prepare their own returns.

Finally, there was negative publicity from the Federal Trade Commission's allegations of wrongdoing by Block. The FTC charged that Block's advertising could mislead the public and that the company wrongfully used customer names and addresses. The FTC complaints against the company were the result of a year-long, industry-wide investigation of tax preparation concerns. All but one of the major companies involved agreed to consent orders in mid-1972. Block did not appear to have been singled out for action. The case against the company was not unique, except that, as the leading tax service, it was the most prominent target.

In fiscal 1973 the company quickly responded to the problems that had affected the previous year's earnings:

1. It closed nearly 400 offices, resulting in a $184,000 decrease in rent expense for the year.
2. It cut its advertising budget by $1.3 million.
3. It reduced the number of full-time employees by 20 percent, effecting a 12 percent decrease in payroll costs.
4. It sought to sublease vacant offices in the off-season and succeeded in generating a $300,000 increase in sublease revenues.

BLOCK AND THE LAW

Regulation

Consumers clearly needed protection from unscrupulous and incompetent tax preparers, so Block supported federal regulatory legislation for the industry. Abuses by a few shady operators had blemished the entire industry. In April 1972 company officials appeared before the House Subcommittee on Legal and Monetary Affairs in Washington to endorse a national registration system for income tax preparers. The company favored required registration for anyone who prepared more than ten income tax returns a year for a fee.

Several states had enacted legislation regulating commercial tax preparers. The United States House of Representatives had passed, and the Senate was currently considering, legislation (H.R. 10612) which, if enacted, would require tax preparers to: 1) file an annual information return; 2) set forth their names and identification numbers on the tax returns prepared; and 3) retain all records for three years. Tax preparers would also be subject to monetary penalties or injunctions for negligent or intentional disregard of rules and regulations in the preparation of returns.

Tax Reform

Tax reform and simplification proposals had continuously appeared in the headlines. The reintroduction of the 1040A short form in 1973, accompanied by widespread publicity encouraging taxpayers to prepare their form themselves, had hindered Block's growth. Over 26 million returns, equivalent to 34 percent of those filed in 1976, used this abbreviated form. In 1976 legislation was passed to reduce the number of tax tables. This had simplified the returns, but forced taxpayers, especially those in the lower- and middle-income group, to exercise mathematical skills beyond those needed in the past. Thus, changes in tax forms and instructions might well have resulted in further confusion. In December 1976 the *Wall Street Journal* noted:

> Perhaps the IRS should send us all a calculator for Christmas.
> More taxpayers than ever before will be doing more math than ever before to file 1976 returns. They can thank Congress, whose "simplification" efforts eliminated tables that millions had

used to figure their tax without having to compute deductions and adjusted gross income. House Ways and Means Chairman Al Ullman says Congress should correct the situation next year.

> And the Internal Revenue Service can help immediately, Ullman says, by issuing tables similar to ones Congress eliminated. But an IRS spokesman said there isn't any plan to do that. The IRS isn't sure it has the legal authority to issue them, he said. Jokers among congressional tax writers, who Ullman says are in part to blame for the tables' elimination, suggest that the IRS send every taxpayer a calculator. That would prove cheaper than unsnarling math mistakes, they say.

EXPANSION AND DIVERSIFICATION

The Group Tax Service (GTS) initiated during the 1972 tax season in two savings and loan association locations was still in its experimental stage. The service was provided at no charge to bank customers as a form of premium incentive and was designed to prepare income tax returns on premises for preferred depositors. Block believed that GTS could be a profitable addition to its tax services. The number of returns processed was growing slowly, but a major consideration from the company's viewpoint was that 65 percent of all taxpayers participating in this program had not previously been H & R Block clients. With a high repeat business factor, the company could probably expect to convert many of these first-timers into regular paying clients.

"Too much talk and not enough action ..." Stockholders and security analysts had voiced this criticism concerning Block's conservative diversification policies. In reply to this view, Henry Bloch commented:

> I'm not going to attempt to refute that criticism, but let me frankly tell you today that we refuse to yield to the pressures to diversify solely for the sake of accomplishing diversification. ... We would rather go cautiously than to make a serious mistake.

Management had indeed been highly selective in its requirements for acquisitions. Further diversification would be into other service-related businesses where there was a logical fit between operations and management. The published criteria for an acquisition were:

1. A proven history of profitability;
2. Earnings of at least $300,000 after taxes at the time of acquisition;
3. An annual growth potential of at least 15 percent for the service when properly marketed;
4. Low fixed labor costs;
5. High repeat customer business;
6. Industry peaks during tax preparation business off seasons;
7. A maximum cash investment in any single business of $20 million.

The acquisition of Consumer Communications Services Corporation (CCSC) and the rapid expansion of its operations provided evidence that management had seen possibilities for diversification. Purchased in January 1972, by 1976 this door-to-door distributor of advertising materials and local shopping news served nine midwestern cities. Block believed that this business had significant long-term growth potential and constituted a profitable avenue for investment of the company's substantial cash resources.

CCSC's 1976 pretax profit margin was estimated at 8 percent. Management planned to enter new metropolitan markets during the 1977 fiscal year, to serve a total of twelve cities. The following table charts CCSC revenues:

Sales Growth

Year Ended 4/30	Sales (000)	% Increase
1976	$5,747	(3%)
1975	5,902	9
1974	5,429	14
1973	4,783	113
1972	2,246	141
1971	931	146

H & R Block Insurance Co., Ltd., was an unconsolidated, wholly-owned, Bermuda-based subsidiary. Its underwriting operations were managed by an independent agency in Bermuda. In 1976 gross annual premiums exceeded $2.5 million compared to $1.5 million earned the year before. Underwriting profits were nominal in both years, reflecting the generally depressed condition of the property/casualty industry.

Block had found that it could choose either of two paths: Finding more niches, or expanding its present one. The need for its service was a sure one for as everyone knows: "There are only two things certain in life: Death and taxes."

EXHIBIT 1

SUMMARY OF EARNINGS[a]

	Year Ended April 30									
	1976	1975	1974	1973	1972	1971	1970	1969	1968	1967
Revenues										
To company-owned offices:										
Tax return preparation fees	$ 94,464	$ 87,251	$75,692	$61,901	$53,181	$50,996	$46,472	$32,482	$22,008	$14,368
Satellite franchise royalties[b]	13,756	11,986	9,962	8,305	6,427	5,314	3,851	2,207	—	—
Tax school tuition[c]	3,891	3,400	2,751	2,551	3,630	3,029	1,673	724	—	—
Franchise royalites[b]	2,184	1,982	1,696	1,447	1,356	1,339	1,328	1,084	1,980	1,187
Consumer Communication income	5,747	5,902	5,429	4,783	2,246	931	379	—	—	—
Other income	3,878	3,591	2,875	1,704	1,467	1,588	1,775	901	1,069	734
Total revenues	123,920	114,112	98,405	80,691	68,307	63,197	55,478	37,398	25,057	16,289
Operating expenses	84,531	79,140	69,309	58,127	54,715	46,765	42,155	29,121	20,035	13,073
Earnings before taxes on income	39,389	34,972	29,096	22,564	13,592	16,432	13,323	8,277	5,022	3,216
Taxes on income	19,561	17,437	14,477	11,039	6,114	7,436	6,819	4,660	2,713	1,497
Net earnings	$ 19,828	$ 17,535	$14,619	$11,525	$ 7,478	$ 8,996	$ 6,504	$ 3,617	$ 2,309	$ 1,719
Earnings per share[d]	$1.80	$1.58	$1.29	$1.01	$.66	$.80	$.59	$.33	$.21	$.16
Weighted average shares outstanding[d]	11,026	11,076	11,316	11,374	11,416	11,300	11,116	11,000	11,000	10,945

[a] All figures except earnings per share are shown in thousands. All figures have been adjusted retroactively, where appropriate, for acquisitions treated as poolings of interest.
[b] For the years 1968 and 1967, the satellite franchise royalties are included in franchise royalties.
[c] For the years 1968 and 1967, the tax school tuitions are included in tax return preparation fees.
[d] Based on the weighted average shares of common stock and common stock equivalents outstanding during each period retroactively adjusted for the stock splits in the form of stock distributions in prior periods, and for shares issued in connection with acquisitions treated as poolings of interest.

EXHIBIT 2

CONSOLIDATED BALANCE SHEET

	April 30	
	1976	1975
ASSETS		
Current Assets		
Cash (including certificates of deposit of $2,640,000 and $2,672,000)	$ 11,845,000	$ 7,689,000
Marketable securities	50,223,000	48,583,000
Receivables, less allowance for doubtful accounts of $394,000 and $387,000	2,966,000	2,433,000
Prepaid expenses	1,683,000	1,709,000
Total Current Assets	66,717,000	60,414,000
Investments and Other Assets:		
Investments in marketable securities	31,009,000	23,001,000
Investment in unconsolidated subsidiary	3,412,000	3,164,000
Excess of cost of operating offices and franchises over fair value of net tangible assets acquired, net of amortization	3,789,000	3,929,000
	38,210,000	30,094,000
Property and Equipment, at cost less accumulated depreciation and amortization	4,320,000	3,401,000
	$109,247,000	$93,909,000
LIABILITIES AND STOCKHOLDERS' EQUITY		
Current Liabilities		
Accounts payable, accrued expenses and deposits	$ 6,846,000	$ 6,961,000
Accrued salaries, wages and payroll taxes	8,164,000	8,666,000
Taxes on income	21,311,000	18,595,000
Current maturities on long-term debt	30,000	90,000
Total Current Liabilities	36,351,000	34,312,000
Long-Term Debt, 6½% note, less current maturities	—	30,000
Commitments and Contingencies		
Stockholders' Equity		
Common stock, no par, stated value $.01 a share; authorized, 15,000,000 shares	114,000	114,000
Additional paid-in capital	7,247,000	7,087,000
Net unrealized loss on noncurrent marketable equity securities	(735,000)	—
Retained earnings	68,994,000	56,834,000
	75,620,000	64,035,000
Less cost of 330,822 shares and 510,671 shares of common stock in treasury	2,724,000	4,468,000
	72,896,000	59,567,000
	$109,247,000	$93,909,000

EXHIBIT 3

TEN YEARS IN REVIEW

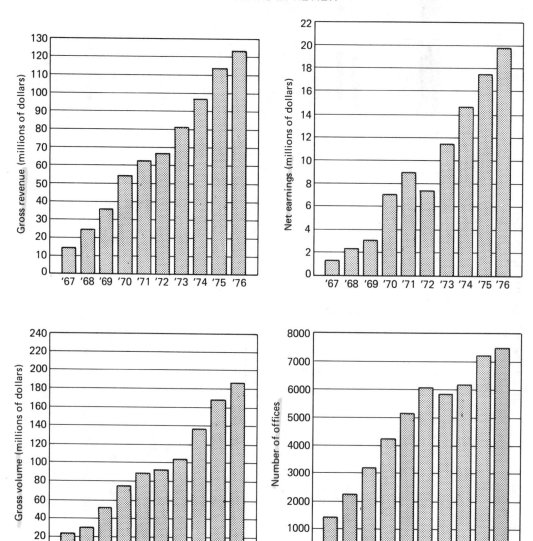

EXHIBIT 4

H&R BLOCK, INC.
Market Penetration
(For Fiscal Years Ended April 30)

Year	Individual U.S. Returns Prepared by H&R Block (millions)	Total U.S. Individual Returns Filed (millions)	H&R Block Share of Market	Average Fee per H&R Block Return
1976	8.400	79.953	10.5%	$18.45
1975	8.322	81.244	10.3	17.18
1974	8.168	78.627	10.5	15.13
1973	7.527	78.100	9.8	13.33
1972	7.284	74.600	9.6	12.02
1971	6.980	74.300	9.4	12.14
1970	6.800	75.800	9.0	11.75
1969	5.300	75.100	7.1	10.59
1968	3.650	72.800	5.0	10.50
1967	2.600	71.200	3.7	10.03
1966	2.150	70.150	3.1	9.35

Source: Company published information; William D. Witter, Inc., Computations

EXHIBIT 5

H & R BLOCK OPERATING STRUCTURE

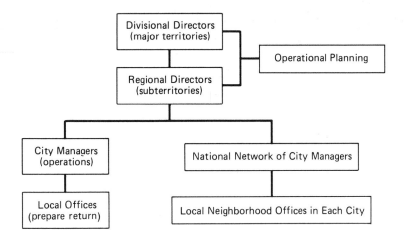

EXHIBIT 6

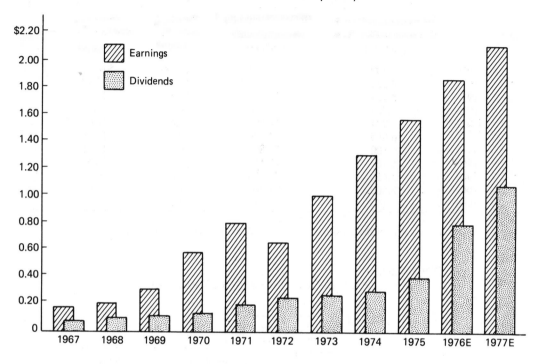

H&R BLOCK
Earnings & Dividends Per Share Growth
(For Fiscal Year Ended April 30)

EXHIBIT 7

H&R BLOCK
Breakdown of Offices in Operation

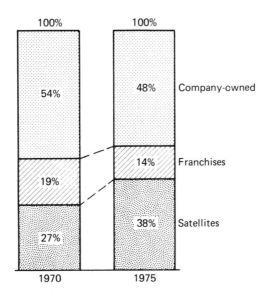

GROWTH OF OFFICES
(For Fiscal Year Ending April 30)

	1971	1972	1973	1974	1975	1976
Company-owned offices	2,683	3,298	2,795	3,097	3,502	3,664
Franchise offices	856	896	900	962	995	988
Satellites (of company)	1,425	1,939	2,038	2,062	2,263	2,448
Satellites (of franchises)	320	353	343	452	452	473
Total Offices	5,284	6,486	6,076	6,528	7,212	7,573

Index of Cases

A.H. Robins, Co., 191
Arcair, Inc., 177
ARCO Chemical Company, 202
Belmont Chemical Company, Inc., 311
Burns & Roe, Inc., 293
Chilton Company, 353
Clevepak Corporation, 265
The Colonial Beef Company, 17
The Colonial Pipeline Co., 73
Cornell Building Services, Inc., 239
Federal Express Corporation, 412
Flagstaff Corporation, 86
H&R Block, Inc., 438
Johnson Control, Inc., 276
Laventhol, Krekstein, Horwath & Horwath, 216
Luce Laboratories, 376
Minicomputer, Incorporated, 130
Municipal Publications, Inc., 339
Nelson Laboratories, 168
Philadelphia Electric Company, 386
Presque Magnum, 364
Reinhardt's Bakery, 424
Safeguard Industries, Inc., 43
Semiconductor Strategies, 96
Stahl Corporation, 326
Strategy and Financial Statements, 235
Sun Ventures, Inc., 156
The Tasty Baking Company, 247
Town Enterprises, Inc., 110
Woman's Medical College of Pennsylvania (A), 143
Woman's Medical College of Pennsylvania (B), 154
Zwickel Gymnastic Tailors, Inc., 30